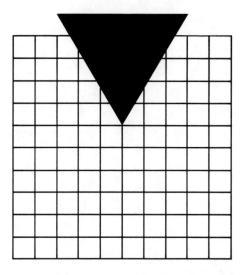

LABOUR MARKET

ECONOMICS

Theory, Evidence and Policy in Canada

Second Edition

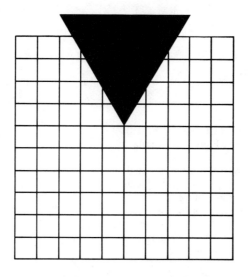

LABOUR MARKET

ECONOMICS

Theory, Evidence and Policy in Canada

Second Edition

Morley Gunderson
Professor of Economics
and Director of
Centre for Industrial Relations
University of Toronto

W. Craig Riddell
Professor of Economics
University of British Columbia

McGraw-Hill Ryerson Limited

Toronto   Montreal   New York   Auckland   Bogotá   Cairo   Caracas
Hamburg   Lisbon   London   Madrid   Mexico   Milan   New Delhi
Panama   Paris   San Juan   São Paulo   Singapore   Sydney   Tokyo

LABOUR MARKET ECONOMICS
Theory, Evidence and Policy in Canada
Second Edition
Copyright © McGraw-Hill Ryerson Limited, 1988.

ISBN 0-07-549079-X

2 3 4 5 6 7 8 9 0 JD 7 6 5 4 3 2 1 0 9 8

Printed and bound in Canada

Canadian Cataloguing in Publication Data
Gunderson, Morley
Labour market economics

2nd ed.
ISBN 0-07-549079-X

1. Labor supply – Canada.   2. Labor economics –
Canada.   3. Canada – Economic conditions –
1971–   .*   I. Riddell, Craig. II. Title.

HD5728.G85 1988   331.12′0971   C88-093192-2

To our parents,
Ann and Magnus Gunderson
and
Ethel and William Riddell

CONTENTS

PREFACE

This book is an expanded and revised version of *Labour Market Economics: Theory, Evidence and Policy in Canada* by Morley Gunderson. As the subtitle indicates, the emphasis of the book is on a *balance* between economic *theory*, empirical *evidence*, and policy relevance. Our purpose is to provide an integrated and modern treatment of labour market issues such as participation in the labour force, the determination of wages, and employment and unemployment. All too often courses in labour market analysis have relied too heavily on description and institutional detail and too little on economic theory or econometric analysis. At the same time, application of economic theory to labour market behaviour without an understanding of the institutional setting is naive and unwise. This book tries to bridge the gap between economic theory and labour market analysis by indicating that the field of labour economics is fertile ground for the application of economic theory and of econometric analysis to interesting and relevant policy issues. As a result, each chapter is organized around the following questions: Why are we interested in this phenomenon? What does economic theory imply about the issue? What is the empirical evidence; that is, what are the facts? What are the policy implications and trade-offs—specifically, what can we expect to happen from alternative policy scenarios?

As the title itself indicates, the emphasis of this book is on the *economic* aspects of the *market* for labour. For some persons, such an emphasis may appear misguided, given various peculiar characteristics of the labour market — a variety of factors with goals that often conflict; an abundance of sociological, legislative and institutional constraints; and a complex price (wage) structure with moral overtones because of the human element and because wages are often called upon both to allocate labour efficiently and to curb poverty. Because of these and other peculiarities, some have argued that the labour market is fundamentally different from other markets and that, therefore, economics is largely irrelevant — or at most can play only a minor role — in analysing labour market phenomena.

Although there are important differences between labour markets and many other markets — and they are what makes labour economics so interesting — a basic theme of this book is that these differences are ones of degree and not of kind. Rather than making economics irrelevant to the analysis of the labour market, these characteristics make economics even more relevant in understanding some of the basic underlying forces and in analysing the impact, and the reasons for the emergence, of a variety of sociological, legislative, and institutional constraints. In essence, the complexity of the labour market makes a basic theoretical framework even more necessary in order to understand the basic underlying forces, and not miss the forest for the trees.

The book is meant to provide a consistent theoretical framework that can be applied not only to current policy issues but also to new policy issues as they change and emerge over time. Policies that are relevant today may not be relevant tomorrow, but a good theoretical foundation will always be relevant in analysing changing issues.

Although the emphasis throughout the book is on Canadian data, examples, institutions, problems and policies, these are discussed within the context of a more general theoretical framework that is applicable to the labour problems of most developed countries. Because it is relevant to understanding labour market behaviour in Canada, empirical evidence is also cited pertaining to other countries, especially the United States where many of the empirical studies have been conducted.

The basic format of the text involves an analysis of the essential elements of a labour market — the various dimensions of labour supply and demand and their interaction in both union and non-union environments to determine wages, employment, and unemployment. Within this format many of the newer issues of labour economics are dealt with, including household production and family labour supply, pensions, retirement and deferred compensation, worksharing, male-female earnings differences, union behaviour, efficiency wages, and implicit contracts.

Many of the changes in this edition reflect recent theoretical and empirical developments in the subject. In addition we have expanded and improved our treatment of existing topics and have added a great deal more Canadian data and examples. Noteworthy changes in Part I on Labour Supply include new chapters, Household Production Functions and the New Home Economics (Chapter 3) and Additional Topics on Labour Supply (Chapter 8), and new sections on unemployment insurance — assisted worksharing and disability payments under workers' compensation in Chapter 4, Work Incentive Effects of Alternative Income Maintenance Schemes. In Part II we have expanded and improved the treatment of the basic theory of labour demand and added a new chapter, Labour Demand, Quasi-Fixed Costs and Worksharing. The treatment of labour market equilibrium has been significantly reorganized. Part III deals with wage and employment determination in non-union labour markets while Part IV discusses these issues in the unionized setting. Much of Part IV, Unions, is new to this edition, reflecting both the recent resurgence of interest in union behaviour by economists and our belief that knowledge of the impact of unions is essential to understanding labour market behaviour in Canada. Part V on Wage Structures has been reorganized, with a new introductory Chapter 17, which provides the basic theory of compensating wages with applications to fringe benefits and risk. The chapters on Human Capital Theory (Chapter 18), Public-Private-Sector Wage Differentials (Chapter 22), and Discrimination and Male-Female Earnings Differentials (Chapter 23) have been expanded and updated and are now included in Part V rather than elsewhere in the book. A new chapter on optimal compensation arrangements and mandatory retirement (Chapter 24) has been added, reflecting recent developments in this area. Part VI deals with unemployment and inflation — aspects of labour market behaviour that overlap with macroeconomics. Our treatment of unemployment has been substantially expanded, with separate chapters now devoted to the meaning and measurement (Chapter 25) and causes and consequences (Chapter 26) of unemployment. New material includes topics such as labour force dynamics and the duration and incidence of unemployment; search, implicit contracts and efficiency wage theories of unemployment, and the relationship between unemployment insurance and unemployment. The final chapter, Wage Changes, Price Inflation and Unemployment, has also been significantly expanded and updated.

The important issues of poverty and personal income distribution are raised throughout the text. Of particular relevance are Chapter 4 on the work incentive effects of alternative income maintenance schemes (e.g., negative income taxes, welfare, wage subsidies and unemployment insurance), Chapter 13 on the dual and radical critiques, Chapter 16 on the union impact on wage and non-wage outcomes, Chapter 18 on human capital theory, Chapter 19 on occupational wage structures, Chapter 23 on discrimination and male-female earnings differences, and Chapters 25 and 26 on unemployment.

By trying to integrate labour market analysis with the mainstream of economic theory, the text reflects the prevailing neoclassical paradigm with its emphasis on microeconomic foundations involving optimization subject to constraints. However, alternative perspectives and paradigms are discussed — some would say not enough, given their potential, and others would say too much, given their actual impact.

Each chapter ends with a series of questions designed to recapitulate some of the material of the chapter, to integrate material across chapters, to suggest possible criticisms of the analyses, and to extend the analyses to some issues that have not been dealt with specifically. In some instances, the questions are ones that currently have not been answered satisfactorily by labour economists, and it may even be that they are unanswerable, given our current state of knowledge.

In addition, each chapter ends with a set of references and further readings, mostly from the economics and labour journals that are listed in the key at the beginning of the text. The references are mainly Canadian and American but some are British. Obviously, these references will soon become dated; hence, there is no substitute for a judicious reading of the appropriate current journals to keep abreast of current developments in the field.

The text was written for students who have had an introductory course in economics and preferably — but not necessarily — a course in microeconomics. Formal mathematical analysis is sometimes utilized. To the greatest extent possible we have confined mathematical analysis to separate self-contained sections (marked by an asterisk) that can be omitted by those without the requisite training. The text is also suitable as a basis for graduate labour courses in business schools as well as economics departments.

Various people have aided in the preparation of this book. For helpful comments or discussion we thank John Ham, Noah Meltz, Sam Rea, and Frank Reid of the University of Toronto. We also wish to recognize the contributions of Glenn MacDonald, University of Western Ontario; Wayne Simpson, University of Manitoba; Felice Martinello and Douglas Smith, Carleton University; Paul Phillips, University College, University of Manitoba; Dennis Maki, Simon Fraser University; A. Frenzel, Wilfrid Laurier University; and John Vanderkamp, Guelph University . We particularly appreciate the helpful comments and suggestions of Chris Robinson, University of Western Ontario; Alan Harrison, McMaster University; Constance Briant, Ryerson Polytechnical Institute; and Michael Hinton, Concordia University. Our editors at McGraw-Hill Ryerson, Jackie Kaiser and David Scrimger, also contributed significantly. We especially wish to thank our wives, Melanie and Rosemarie, for their support and encouragement.

ACKNOWLEDGEMENTS

F. Weiskoff, "Women's Place in the Labor Market," *American Economic Review* 62 (May 1972), page 164, and H. Zellner, "Discrimination Against Women, Occupational Segregation, and the Relative Wage," *American Economic Review Proceedings* 62 (May 1972), page 157.

D. Brady, "Equal Pay for Women Workers," *Annals of the American Academy of Political and Social Science* (May 1947), pages 53 and 57.

J. Addison and J. Burton, "Wage Adjustment Processes: A Synthetic Treatment," *British Journal of Industrial Relations* 16 (July 1978), page 221.

To Butterworths for Institute for Research on Public Policy, for permission to reproduce material from Morley Gunderson, "Public-Private Wage and Non-Wage Differentials in Canada: Some Calculations From Published Tabulations," pages 128–66, and Richard M. Bird, "The Growth of the Public Service in Canada," pages 19–44, in David K. Foot, ed., *Public Employment and Compensation in Canada: Myths and Realities*, Toronto: Butterworths for Institute for Research on Public Policy, 1978.

P. Doeringer and M. Piore, *Internal Labour Markets and Manpower Analysis*, Lexington, Mass.: D.C. Heath, 1971, pages 85 and 165; D. Gordon, *Theories of Poverty and Underemployment*, Lexington, Mass.: D.C. Heath, 1972, pages 53 and 65.

To Journal of Economics and Business, for permission to reproduce material from C. Lin and J. Landon, "Market Structure, Nonpecuniary Factors and Professional Salaries: Registered Nurses," *Journal of Economics and Business* 28 (Winter 1976), page 151.

To Macmillan Company of Canada, for permission to use material from S. Ostry and M. Zaida, *Labour Economics in Canada* 3rd ed., Toronto: Macmillan of Canada, 1979, pages 17, 80, 81, 202–3.

T. Riblich, "Negative Income Taxes and Education," in T. Orr and others (eds.), *Income Maintenance*, Chicago: Markham, 1971, page 309.

To the Minister of Supply and Services Canada, for permission to reproduce material from D. Maki, *Search Behaviour in Canadian Job Markets*, Ottawa: Economic Council of Canada, 1971, page 24; N. Meltz and D. Stager, *The Occupational Structure of Earnings in Canada, 1931–1975*, Anti-Inflation Board Report, Ottawa: Supply and Services, 1979, page 4; B. Wilkinson, *Studies in the Economics of Education*, Economics and Research Branch, Ottawa: Canada Department of Labour, 1965, page 556; M. Gunderson, "Work Patterns," in *Opportunity for Choice: A Goal for Women in Canada*, edited by G. Cook, Ottawa: Statistics Canada, 1976, page 97. Reproduced by permission of the Minister of Supply and Services Canada.

To Queen's University Industrial Relations Centre, for permission to reproduce material from David Smith, *The Dual Labour Market Theory: A Canadian Perspective*, Kingston: Queen's University Industrial Relations Centre, 1976, page 3, and from P. Kumar, *Relative Wage Differentials in Canadian Industries*, Kingston: Queen's University Industrial Relations Centre, 1975, page 33.

xxii

H.G. Lewis, *Unionism and Relative Wages in the United States*, Chicago: University of Chicago Press, 1963, page 194.

To University of Toronto Press, for permission to use material from Morley Gunderson, "Earnings Differentials Between the Public and Private Sectors," *Canadian Journal of Economics*, XII, 2, University of Toronto Press, May 1979, pages 228–242.

L. Reynolds and C. Taft, *The Evolution of Wage Structure*, New Haven: Yale University Press, 1956, page 357.

KEY TO JOURNAL ABBREVIATIONS USED IN REFERENCES AND FURTHER READINGS

AER	American Economic Review
BJIR	British Journal of Industrial Relations
BPEA	Brookings Papers on Economic Activity
CJE	Canadian Journal of Economics
CPP	Canadian Public Policy
EI	Economic Inquiry (formerly Western Economic Journal)
EJ	Economic Journal
IER	International Economic Review
ILRR	Industrial and Labor Relations Review
ILR	International Labour Review
IR	Industrial Relations
IRJ	Industrial Relations Journal
IRRA	Industrial Relations Research Association Proceedings
JHR	Journal of Human Resources
JLR	Journal of Labor Research
JOLE	Journal of Labor Economics
JPE	Journal of Political Economy
MLR	Monthly Labor Review
QJE	Quarterly Journal of Economics
R.E. Stats.	Review of Economics and Statistics
R.E. Studies	Review of Economic Studies
RI/IR	Relations Industrielles/Industrial Relations
SEJ	Southern Economic Journal
WEJ	Western Economic Journal (now Economic Inquiry)

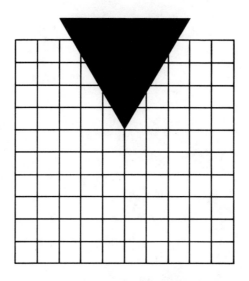

LABOUR MARKET
ECONOMICS

Theory, Evidence and Policy in Canada

Second Edition

Part

I

Labour Supply

CHAPTER

1 *Population, Fertility and Family Formation*

Labour supply has a dimension of quality, and of quantity. The *quality* of labour supply encompasses elements of human capital such as education, training, mobility, and health, and of human relations such as job enrichment, morale, and alienation. Although obviously important in the analysis of labour markets, the human relations aspects are more appropriately covered in texts on organization behaviour. The human capital elements are discussed in a subsequent chapter.

The *quantity* dimension of labour supply involves determining the size of various quantity elements, including our domestic population, that portion of our population that participates in labour force activity, and the hours of work of those who are in the labour force. The size of our domestic population in turn depends on fertility and deaths, as well as immigration and emigration. The dimensions of immigration and emigration are dealt with in the chapter on regional wage structures and geographic mobility. Fertility behaviour is the focus of this section.

The importance of understanding fertility behaviour is highlighted by the many problems that have arisen recently because, in part, of a basic failure to predict demographic changes in the size and composition of our population. Heavy demands were placed on our educational institutions and housing markets as the post-World War II baby-boom population passed through various phases of education and began to purchase housing. The massive entry of this generation into the labour market during the late 1960s created labour market adjustment problems, not the least of which was teenage unemployment. The decline in birth rates since the 1960s has resulted in a population that is both aging and growing more slowly — so that some have predicted labour shortages for the late 1980s and 1990s. When the post-World War II baby-boom population hits retirement age in the early 2000s, there could be a dependency problem if there are insufficient persons in the labour force at that time to sustain a large retired population.

An understanding of fertility behaviour and family formation would also be useful for other current policy issues such as the impact on family formation of income maintenance schemes, and the effect of child raising activities on related household decisions such as labour force participation and hours of work outside the home. Of crucial concern in a discussion of labour supply is our ability to predict future changes in our birth rate.

Until recent years, predicting fertility patterns was largely the purview of demographers, whose predictions were based largely on extrapolation from past trends. Such predictions usually assumed that the underlying structural relationships that determine fertility remain constant. Because of dramatic changes in these underlying factors, however, recent changes in fertility have departed from historical patterns. Lacking a theoretical explanation for the determinants of fertility, demographers were often at a loss to explain current patterns.

Partly out of dissatisfaction with predictions based on demographic extrapolation, economists have recently applied some of the basic concepts of economics to the question of fertility and family formation. Some have heralded the application as a bold and innovative step; others have treated it as simply another absurd encroachment of economics into questions that are perceived not to involve basic principles of economics. On balance, it would appear that the application of economics in this area has provided some new insights into fertility and family formation, even though the process of family formation is one in which non-economic factors play an extremely important role. These are insights into the determinants not only of family size, but also of the spacing and timing of children.

ECONOMIC THEORY OF FERTILITY

Consumer Demand Theory

The economic theory of fertility is basically an application of standard microeconomic consumer demand theory to household decision making. Consumer demand theory gives us the fundamental law of demand — the quantity purchased of a commodity is negatively related to its price; that is, as prices rise, the quantity demanded drops. This occurs because a price change has both income and substitution effects. The substitution effect of a price increase occurs as we substitute cheaper goods for the more expensive commodity, hence demanding less of the good whose price has risen. The income effect of a price increase occurs because the price increase is akin to a reduction in our real income, and consequently we have less to spend on all goods, including the commodity whose price has risen. Normal goods are defined as ones that we spend less on when our income declines, and inferior goods as ones that we spend more on when our income declines. For normal goods, the quantity demanded declines in response to a rise in the price because both the substitution and income effects work in the same direction. Inferior goods will also obey the law of demand providing the substitution effect is larger than the income effect.

Other factors, of course, can shift this demand curve relationship between prices and quantity demanded. Specifically, an increase in our income or wealth would shift the demand curve outwards (upwards and to the right) for all normal goods. An increase in the price of substitute commodities would similarly shift it outwards, while an increase in the price of complementary commodities would shift it inwards. Tastes and preferences — largely regarded by economists as exogenous or determined in some unknown fashion – could shift the demand curve either to the left or the right.

Largely based on the pioneering work of Becker (1960) and Mincer (1963), economists have applied the basic framework of consumer demand theory to the decision to have children. Montgomery and Trussell (1986) provide a current review of some of the economic literature and relate it to the demographic literature.

Although many find it obnoxious to think of children, even analogously, as if they are "consumer durables," few would deny that at least some families alter their child-bearing decisions because they cannot yet afford to have children (perhaps until they have at least saved for the down payment on a house or have finished paying for their education) or because it is too costly to have a child (perhaps because it would mean an interruption in a wife's career in the labour market). As long as these and other economic factors affect the decision to have children for some families, then economic factors will have some predictive power in explaining variations in birth rates.

Analogous to consumer demand theory, the basic variables affecting the fertility decision are income, the price or cost of a child, the price of related goods, and tastes and preferences. As we will see, however, noneconomic factors also play a strong role.

Variables Affecting Fertility

Income

Economic theory predicts that, *other things being equal*, there will be a positive relationship between income and the desired number of children, assuming children are analogous to "normal goods." This goes against casual empiricism, since we tend to think of poor families or poor countries as having more children per family. The problem, of course, is that in the real world other things are not equal. Specifically, factors such as contraceptive knowledge and the cost of having children tend to be related to the income variable, so that it becomes difficult to separate the pure effect of income alone. Poor families, for example, may have more children because they lack knowledge of family planning techniques. If we could hold these and other factors influencing the number of children constant, economic theory predicts a positive relationship between income and number of children.

As Easterlin (1971) points out, however, the relationship between income and number of children may not be as simple as that postulated by conventional economic theory. Specifically, new generations with higher incomes get exposed to whole new sets of wants that may serve as substitutes for the satisfaction previously obtained from raising a family. Some activities now affordable with a higher income — such as travel and entertainment outside the home — may actually conflict with raising a family. In other circumstances, the higher income may simply allow people to buy the new technology (contraceptive devices, abortion, family planning information) that enables them to have fewer children. In such circumstances, we may expect a negative relationship between income and family size, and this may offset the positive relationship predicted from conventional economic theory.

Price or Cost of Children
Although direct costs such as the additional food, clothing and housework associated with raising a child are an important aspect of the cost of children, the main element in the cost of having a child is the income forgone by the spouse (in our society this tends to be the wife) who takes time away from labour market activity to bear and raise the child. The forgone income of the wife tends to be positively related to such things as her education, training, labour market skills, and job opportunities. In addition to the immediate income forgone while not working, the effect can be longer run, involving the deterioration of work skills and the interruption of careers for women who take time out for child raising.

An increase in the potential earnings of wives can have both income and substitution effects on the decision to have children. The substitution effect says that wives with high potential earnings will have fewer children because the higher opportunity cost (forgone income) of having a child induces them to substitute away from the expensive alternative of having children and to engage in less expensive activities that do not impinge as much on their earnings capacity. The income effect, on the other hand, says that wives with a high earnings capacity can contribute more to family income and this will enable the family to spend more on all commodities, implying greater expenditures on children if children are "normal goods." Thus the income and substitution effects of a change in the wife's earnings capacity have opposing effects on desired family size.

Price of Related Goods
Having children entails the purchase of a variety of related commodities that are usually complementary to the raising of children. Medical expenses must be incurred as well as food, shelter, clothing, education, and daycare expenses. According to conventional economic theory, a rise in the price of such complementary goods would tend to reduce our desired number of children. Conversely, a fall in their price — perhaps from public subsidies to medical care, education or day care — could encourage larger family sizes. In most cases, the cost of any one of these related commodities is probably not large enough, nor does it vary sufficiently, to have any appreciable effect on family size. However, dramatic changes in the private cost of some of these items — such as free university tuition or universally free day care — could have an impact, as could any trend in the overall extent of state subsidies for medical care, education, or day care.

Tastes and Preferences

Economists tend to regard tastes and preferences as exogenously given from outside the economic system. In the area of family formation, our tastes and preferences have been dramatically changed, related to our ideas on religion, family planning, and the women's liberation movement in general. These factors have all changed over time in a fashion that would encourage smaller family sizes.

Some would argue that these changes were not really exogenous to the economic system, but rather were a result of some of the more fundamental economic changes. For example, such factors as improved job opportunities for females may have made women's liberation more necessary to ensure more equal employment opportunities. The dramatic increase in the number of women working outside the home may have changed attitudes towards women, their role in society and the nature of the family. Cause and effect works both ways: tastes and preferences both shape, and are shaped, by the economic system.

Education also has an important bearing on tastes and preferences. Not only does it raise the forgone income from raising children, but increased education may also widen our horizon for other goods (travel, entertainment outside the home), enable family planning, and encourage self-fulfilment through means other than having children.

Technology

The term technology is often used by economists as a general rubric to describe the general technological and environmental factors that influence our economic decisions. In the area of fertility and family formation, birth control knowledge and contraceptive devices — especially "the pill" — have had an important impact on the number of children, primarily by equilibrating the actual with the desired number of children. Medical advances with vasectomies and tubiligation can be expected to have a similar impact. The reduction in infant mortality that has occurred over time should also reduce the number of births since, in times of high infant mortality, it was often necessary to have large families simply to have a few children survive to adult age.

A medical advance that could have a dramatic impact on the number of children born would be the discovery of how to influence the sex of a child. If this were possible, then it would not be necessary for some couples to continue having children until they got at least one boy or girl, or whatever sex combination they desired in the family.

Most of the technological advances discussed so far are ones that would encourage or enable smaller families. Some, such as reduced danger and discomforts during pregnancy, and advances in fertility drugs and operations, could work in the opposite direction to encourage or enable more child bearing. Others, such as processed food and disposable diapers, have made care for children easier.

ADDITIONAL ASPECTS OF THE ECONOMICS OF FERTILITY

Before examining the data on fertility to see if the economic theory is empirically verified, it is first necessary to state some refinements of the theory. These additional aspects are especially important to help define the exact form of the variables used in the empirical work, and to interpret the results.

Investment Aspects

In the previous analysis, children were treated as though they were analogous to consumer durables, with expenditures being made on children because of the direct pleasures that they bring. In less-developed economies and perhaps in rural societies, children may also have an investment component. Not only are their services valued on the farm, but also they can serve as a form of pension in that, with the extended family, children can take care of parents upon their retirement. This could be important in societies where minimal care of the aged is not provided through public pensions, medical care or homes for the aged. To the extent that children have this additional investment component in less-developed economies and in rural societies, we may expect larger families in those circumstances. In addition, as Neher (1971) points out, alternative pension arrangements could serve as a population control device by reducing the investment need for children.

Quality vs. Quantity

In conventional consumer demand theory, we tend to think in terms of price and quantity — the way we label the axes on a demand curve diagram. It is possible, of course, that more of something can be purchased either through an increase in the quantity purchased, or an increase in its quality, or both. An increase in our income, for example, may enable us to buy a second car or a better first car. Similarly an increase in our income may enable us to afford to have more children, or it may be used for higher expenditures (education, travel) on the same number of children. This has obvious implications for empirical work since it is possible that high-income families may have fewer children rather than more because they incur higher expenditures per child — that is, they substitute quality for quantity.

Spacing and Timing of Children

Economic analysis not only has implications for the desired family size, but also for the spacing and timing of children. In fact, in response to a higher (opportunity) cost of having children, families may try to have their children closer together in time. Having two children born a year apart, for example, is less costly in terms of income forgone, career interruption, and deterioration of skills than having two children born three years apart, since the latter usually implies more time out of the labour market. For this reason, we would expect women who have high potential earnings not only to have fewer children but also to have them over a shorter time.

Desired vs. Actual

Household demand theory deals with factors influencing the desired family size. Obviously in this area of family formation, there may be a considerable gap between the desired and the actual family size. Unwanted pregnancies are a common phenomenon, as is the inability to have children and, possibly, even to adopt. The gap between desired and actual fertility is a natural result in an area where rational planning does not always prevail and where social mores are strong. In some instances, however, it results from time lags, imperfect information, and insufficient technology (especially medical technology). Many of these factors can be influenced by economic forces.

Short Run vs. Long Run

Family planning is obviously a long-run decision-making process. Consequently, the variables we examine should be cast in long-run terms. It is our anticipated lifetime or "permanent income," for example, that will influence our family size decisions. Short-run or temporary changes in that wealth would at best have a small impact, perhaps by interjecting an element of uncertainty into the decision-making process. Thus, for example, young couples who have a low temporary income because they are engaged in higher education may have (or plan to have) large families because their permanent income is high. A temporary bout of unemployment for a wife would probably reduce family size by only a small amount given that her long-run income could be high, although now perhaps subject to a greater degree of uncertainty.

Simultaneous Decision Process

The decision to have children is intricately related to a variety of other household decisions, such as the decision to get married, to participate in the labour force, to engage in geographic mobility, and even to become separated or divorced. From a theoretical point of view, this means that the simultaneous decision-making process should be considered in specifying the underlying determinants of fertility behaviour. From a policy point of view, the simultaneity implies that policies influencing any of these other factors will also influence the fertility decision.

EMPIRICAL RESULTS

The empirical evidence on fertility behaviour is confusing to interpret because of the difficulty of holding other factors constant when observing actual behaviour. For example, it is difficult to isolate the effect of family income, independent of the effect of the wife's education, because highly educated wives tend to marry husbands with high incomes. If we observe fewer children in high-income families, is this because of their high income, or is it because wives in such families tend to be highly educated and hence their forgone income or cost of having children is high?

Statistical techniques such as multiple regression analysis have been used by econometricians to isolate the effect of a single variable, while holding the impact of all other factors constant. This can also be achieved by cross-tabulations of the data or by restricting the analysis to families of the same characteristics except for the one characteristic whose impact is under examination. Figure 1.1 summarizes the general nature of the empirical results as found in such studies as Becker (1960), Mincer (1963), Cain and Weininger (1973), and Butz and Ward (1979).

As Figure 1.1(a) illustrates, there exists a negative gross relationship between number of children per family and the income of the family (i.e. when other things — such as the education of the wife – are *not* held constant). This observation has led to the conclusion that people in poverty (or poor countries) have larger families and this tends to exacerbate their poverty. While this conclusion may be true at face value, it tends to mask the real reason for the larger family size, that reason being the lower education of wives and hence lower forgone income or opportunity cost of children for poorer families. This is illustrated in Figures 1.1(b) and 1.1(c).

Figure 1.1(b) illustrates that when we hold other things equal — specifically such factors as the wife's education or income as well as contraceptive knowledge — then we do observe a positive relationship between the number of children and income. Other things equal, we have more children as our income or wealth increases: children are like "normal goods" rather than "inferior goods"! Cain and Weininger (1973), for example, estimate that a $100 increase in the income of husbands is associated with an increase of approximately 10 children per 1000 women in an area. Their estimated income elasticity of demand for children is approximately .20, indicating that a one percent increase in income is associated with a one-fifth of one percent increase in the demand for children.

Figure 1.1(c) illustrates this partial relationship between the number of children and their opportunity cost as represented by the wife's potential labour market earnings. Other things equal, families with wives who have high potential earnings have fewer children because the opportunity cost of having children is high. Cain and Weininger (1973), for example, estimate that a $100 increase in the wife's potential annual earnings is associated with a reduction of 20 children per 1000 women in an area. The wife's annual earnings have both an income and a substitution effect. Since the estimate of the income effect (from the husband's income) was an increase of 10 children per $100 of income, then we could subtract this income effect to get the pure or "compensated" substitution effect associated with an increase in the wife's earnings. That is, the income-compensated substitution effect would be $-20 - 10 = -30$ children per 1000 women for every $100 increase in the wife's earnings, holding constant the family income.

Clearly the cost of children, as represented by the forgone income of the wife, plays an important role in our desire to have children. In fact this substitution effect appears more important than the income effect, so that the gross relationship between the number of children and the potential

Figure 1.1 Gross and Partial Relationships Between Fertility and Incomes

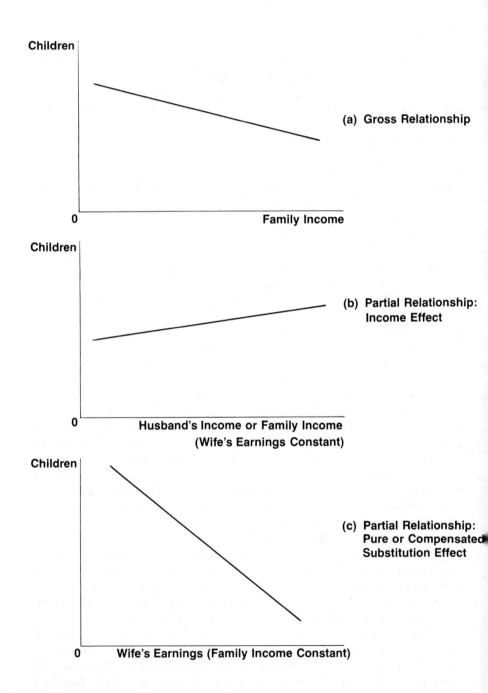

income of the wife is still negative. It is this fact that gives rise to the negative relationship between the number of children and family income as depicted in Figure 1.1(a). High-income families have fewer children because of their high opportunity cost (depicted in Figure 1.1(c)): because of the higher income itself they would have more children (depicted in Figure 1.1(b)). Conversely, low-income families have more children because of their low opportunity cost, not because of their low income *per se*.

POLICY IMPLICATIONS

Perhaps one of the most interesting policy implications to emerge from the economic analysis of fertility is that a viable population control policy, for less-developed economies especially, is to open up job opportunities for women to work. This will raise the (opportunity) cost of having children and, if the empirical estimates are applicable, this should outweigh any tendency to have more children from the additional income generated by their employment. Usually when we think of population control policies, we tend to focus attention on family planning and the dissemination of contraceptive technology. While these factors are obviously important, we should not omit consideration of the operation of economic forces as children become relatively more expensive to people with viable job opportunities.

The economics of family formation also suggests that more than Malthusian checks may be at work to prevent overpopulation. According to Malthus, the only checks on population growth would be starvation, malnutrition, and wars resulting from overpopulation (thus earning economics the title of "the dismal science"). The economics of fertility suggests that an alternative natural check on family size will occur because labour market alternatives simply make children an extremely expensive alternative. Thus improved opportunities can be as viable a natural check as starvation and malnutrition.

The economics of fertility also indicates that any transfer payment or subsidized service that is based on the number of children will have income and substitution effects that work in the same direction to encourage larger family sizes. Increases in the family allowance, for example, are predicted to encourage larger families because the additional income enables people to afford to have more children (the income effect) and because the cost of raising a child is reduced by the amount of the allowance (the substitution effect). These effects could also be at work for subsidies to day care and education as well as welfare payments and tax exemptions based on the number of dependents. While such payments would theoretically at least work in the direction of increasing family size, the magnitude of the effect would probably be very small since these transfers usually do not amount to much.

QUESTIONS

1. Based on your knowledge of the economic theory of fertility and family formation, indicate the expected impact on the birth rate of increases

in each of the following: women's wages, family allowances, the basic income tax exemption for each dependent, and the education of women.

2. Why has there been a long-run decline in fertility over time, even though income has risen?

3. What does the economic theory of fertility tell us about a viable population policy for less-developed economies experiencing a population explosion?

4. What does the economic theory of fertility tell us about the expected population problem in the year 2000?

5. What does the economics of fertility tell us about family size and urban versus rural location?

6. Cain (1971, p. 412) has stated that "there are a number of prices included in the overall price of a child, and each component price is potentially changeable by means of a wide variety of policy actions." Discuss this statement and indicate the policies that can have an impact on the decision to have children.

7. In the regression equation, $C = .10\ Y_H - .20\ E_W$, relating births per family, C, to the husband's income Y_H, and the wife's education E_W, evaluate the income elasticity of demand for children for the average family. Assume that the average husband's income is 9 when Y_H is measured in units of $1000, and that the average number of children per family is 3. Evaluate the income elasticity of demand for children for poorer families whose husband's average income is 5 when Y_H is measured in units of $1000 and whose average number of children is 2. From the information given in the regression equation, can you calculate the pure or compensated substitution effect for changes in the wife's income?

REFERENCES AND FURTHER READINGS

Anderson, K.H. The sensitivity of wage elasticities to selectivity bias and the assumption of normality: an example of fertility demand estimation. *JHR* 17 (Fall 1982) 594-605.

Bahr, S. *Economics and the Family*. Lexington: Lexington Books, 1980.

Becker, G. An economic analysis of fertility. *Demographic and Economic Change in Developed Countries*. Princeton: Princeton University Press, 1960, 209-231.

Becker, G. and H. Lewis. On the interaction between the quantity and quality of children. *JPE* 81 (March/April 1973) S279-S288.

Becker, G. and N. Tomes. Child endorsements and the quantity and quality of children. *JPE* 84 (August 1976) S143-S162.

Behrman, J. and B. Wolf. A more general approach to fertility determination in a developing country. *Economica* 51 (Aug. 1984) 319-340.

Ben-Porath, Y. Fertility responses to child mortality. *JPE* 84 (August 1976) S163-S178.

Ben-Porath, Y. and F. Welch. Do sex preferences really matter? *QJE* 90 (May 1976) 285-307.

Blandy, R. The welfare analysis of fertility reduction. *EJ* (March 1974) 109-129.

Bloom, D. What's happening to the age at first birth in the United States? A study of recent cohorts. *Demography* 19 (August 1982) 351-370.

Bloom, D. and J. Trusell. What are the determinants of delayed childbearing and permanent childlessness in the United States? *Demography* 21 (November 1984) 591-611.

Butz, W. and M. Ward. The emergence of countercyclical U.S. fertility. *AER* 69 (June 1979) 318-328.

Cain, G. Issues in the economics of a population policy for the United States. *AER* 61 (May 1971) 408-417.

Cain, G. The effect of income maintenance laws on fertility in the U.S. *Aspects of Population Growth Policy*, R. Parke and C. Westoff (eds.). Washington: Government Printing Office, 1973.

Cain, G. and M. Dooley. Estimation of a model of labor supply, fertility, and wages of married women. *JPE* 84 (August 1976) S179-S200.

Cain, G. and A. Weininger. Economic determinants of fertility: results from cross-sectional aggregate data. *Demography* 10 (May 1973) 205-223.

Carliner, G., C. Robinson and N. Tomes. Female labour supply and fertility in Canada. *CJE* 13 (February 1980) 46-64.

Coale, A. and S. Watkins, eds. *The Decline of Fertility in Europe*. Princeton: Princeton University Press, 1985.

Conger, D. and J. Campbell. Simultaneity in the birth rate equation: the effects of education, labour force participation, income and health. *Econometrica* 46 (May 1978) 631-641.

Dooley, M.D. Labour supply and fertility of married women: an analysis with grouped and individual data from the 1970 U.S. census. *JHR* 17 (Fall 1982) 499-532.

Easterlin, R. Economic-demographic interactions and long swings in economic growth. *AER* 56 (December 1966) 1063-1105.

Easterlin, R. Towards a socioeconomic theory of fertility: survey of recent research on economic factors in American fertility. *Fertility and Family Planning: a World View*, S. Behrman and others (eds.). Ann Arbor: University of Michigan Press, 1969, 127-156.

Eckstein, Z. and K. Wolpin. Endogenous fertility and optimal population size. *JPubEc* 27 (June 1985) 93-106.

Fleisher, B. and G. Rhodes. Fertility, women's wage rates, and labor supply. *AER* 69 (March 1979) 14-24.

Gregory, P. and J. Campbell. Fertility interaction and modernization turning points. *JPE* 84 (August 1976) 835-848.

Gregory, P., J. Campbell and B. Cheng. A cost-inclusive simultaneous equation model of birth rates. *Econometrica* 40 (July 1972) 41-47.

Gregory, P., J. Campbell and B. Cheng. A simultaneous equation model of birth rates in the United States. *R.E. Stats.* 54 (November 1972) 374-380.

Hashimoto, M. Economics of postwar fertility in Japan. *JPE* 82 Part 2 (March/April 1974) S170-S194.

Heckman, J., J. Hotz and J. Walker. New evidence on the timing and spacing of births. *AER* 75 (May 1985) 179-184.

Heckman, J. and R. Willis. Estimation of a stochastic model of reproduction. *Household Production and Consumption*. N. Terleckyj (ed.). New York: Columbia University Press, 1975.

Journal of Political Economy. New economic approaches to fertility. T. Paul Schutz (ed.) 81 Part 2 (March/April 1973).

Keeley, M. The economics of family formation. *Economic Enquiry* 15 (April 1977) 238-250.

Kramer, W. and K. Neusser. The emergence of countercyclical U.S. fertility: Note. *AER* 47 (March 1984) 201-202.

Leibenstein, H. An interpretation of the economic theory of fertility. *Journal of Economic Literature* 12 (June 1974) 457-479.

Leibenstein, H. An economic theory of fertility decline. *QJE* 89 (February 1975) 1-31. Comment by W. Cullison and reply 91 (May 1977) 345-350.

Leibowitz, A. Home investments in children. *JPE* 82 Part 2 (March/April 1974) S111-S131.

Lindert, P. *Fertility and Scarcity in America.* Princeton: Princeton University Press, 1977.

Meeker, E. Freedom, economic opportunity, and fertility: black Americans, 1860-1910. *EI* (July 1977) 397-412.

Mincer, J. Market prices, opportunity costs, and income effects. *Measurement in Economics.* Stanford University Press, 1963, 67-82.

Moffitt, R. The estimation of fertility equations on panel data. *JHR* 19 (Winter 1984) 22-34.

Moffitt, R. Optimal life-cycle profiles of fertility and labour supply. *Research in Population Economics* 5. T. Schultz and K. Wolpin eds. (1984) 29-50.

Montgomery, M. and J. Trussel. Models of marital status and child-bearing. *Handbook of Labor Economics*, Vol. I. O. Ashenfelter and R. Layard (eds.). New York: Elsevier Science Publishers, 1986.

Neher, P. Peasants, procreation and pensions. *AER* 61 (June 1971) 380-389. Comment by M. Ferber and reply 62 (June 1972) 451-452, and comment by W. Robinson and reply 62 (December 1972) 977-979.

Nerlove, M. Household and economy: toward a new theory of population and economic growth. *JPE* 82 (March/April 1974) S200-S218.

Nerlove, M., A. Razin and E. Sadka. Some welfare theoretic implications for endogenous fertility. *IER* 27 (February 1986) 3-32.

Newman, J. and C. McCulloch. A hazard rate approach to the timing of births. *Econometrica* 52 (July 1984) 939-961.

Olnek, M. and B. Wolf. A note on some evidence on the Easterlin hypothesis. *JPE* 86 (October 1978) 953-958.

Robinson, C. and N. Tomes. Family labour supply and fertility: a two-regime model. *CJE* 15 (November 1982) 706-734.

Rosenzweig, M. The demand for children in farm households. *JPE* 85 (February 1977) 123-146.

Rosenzweig, M. Birth spacing and sibling inequality: asymmetric information within the family. *IER* 27 (February 1986) 55-76.

Rosenzweig, M. and T. Schultz. Market opportunities, genetic endowments and intrafamily resource distribution: child survival in rural India. *AER* 72 (September 1982) 803-815.

Rosenzweig, M. and T. Schultz. Consumer demand and household production: the relationship between fertility and child mortality. *AER* 73 (May 1983) 38-42.

Rosenzweig, M. and T. Schultz. The demand for and supply of births. *AER* 75 (December 1985) 992-1015.

Rosenzweig, M. and D. Seiver. Education and contraceptive choice: a conditional demand framework. *IER* 23 (February 1982) 171-198.

Rosenzweig, M. and K. Wolpin. Life-cycle labour supply and fertility: causal inferences from household models. *JPE* 88 (April 1980) 328-348.

Schultz, T. An economic model of family planning and fertility. *JPE* 77 (March/April 1969) 153-180.

Schultz, T. The influence of fertility on labour supply of married women: simultaneous equation estimates. *Research in Labour Economics*, vol. 2, R. Ehrenberg (ed.). Greenwich, Conn.: JAI Press, 1978.

Schultz, T. Changing world prices, women's wages and the fertility transitions: Sweden, 1860-1910. *JPE* 93 (December 1985) 1126-1154.

Schultz, T. *The Economics of Population*. Reading, Mass.: Addison-Wesley, 1981.

Simon, J. *The Effects of Income on Fertility*. Chapel Hill: University of North Carolina Press, 1974.

Suits, D. et al. Birth control econometric simulation. *IER* 16 (February 1975) 92-111.

Tomes, N. A model of fertility and children's schooling. *EI* 19 (April 1981) 209-234.

Venieris, Y., F. Sebold and R. Harper. The impact of economic, technological and demographic factors on aggregate births. *R.E. Stats.* 55 (November 1973) 493-497.

Wachter, M. A time series fertility equation: the potential for a baby-boom in the 1980s. *IER* 16 (October 1975) 609-624.

Ward, M. and W. Butz. Completed fertility and its timing. *JPE* 88 (October 1980) 917-940.

Willis, R. A new approach to the economic theory of fertility behaviour. *JPE* 81: part 2 (March/April 1973) S14-S64.

Winegarden, C. Women's fertility, market work and marital status: a test of the new household economics with international data. *Economica* 51 (Nov. 1984) 447-456.

Wolpin, K. An estimable dynamic stochastic model of fertility and child mortality. *JPE* 92 (October 1984) 852-874.

2 Income-Leisure Choice Theory

Once the magnitude of the domestic population is determined, the next step is to analyse the various dimensions of labour supply for that population. Quantity dimensions of labour supply involve labour force participation and hours of work. Labour force participation involves the decisions of when to first enter the labour force, whether to remain in the labour force or interrupt one's working career, and when to retire. The quantity of labour supplied will also depend on the number of hours individuals in the labour force would prefer to work.

The basic theoretical framework underlying all of these dimensions of labour supply is the income- or work-leisure choice model. This chapter develops the work-leisure choice model and uses it to examine the effects of a wage change on labour force participation and preferred hours of work, and thus to derive the individual's supply curve of labour. A major extension of the basic model is discussed in the following chapter. In subsequent chapters the model is applied to analyse the work incentive effects of alternative income maintenance schemes, the labour force participation and retirement decisions, the various dimensions of hours of work, and the life-cycle allocation of time in a multi-period context that distinguishes between short-run and long-run changes.

BASIC INCOME-LEISURE MODEL

The income-leisure choice theory is simply an application of standard microeconomic theory (indifference curve analysis) to the household's choice between income and non-labour market activities including household work and education, as well as pure leisure activities. The phrase "leisure" is somewhat of a misnomer since it includes activities that obviously are not leisure activities. The term is used here, however, because it is the phraseology used by Robbins (1930) in his original work on the subject and it has been retained in the literature as a summary term for "non-labour market activities."

The individual is indifferent (has the same welfare) between the various combinations of income and leisure as given by the indifference curve U_o in Figure 2.1(a). The slope of the indifference curve exhibits a diminishing marginal rate of substitution between income and leisure. For example, at point A, the individual has an abundance of income and hence is willing to give up considerable income to obtain more leisure; hence the steeply sloped indifference curve at point A. At point B, the individual has an abundance of leisure and hence is willing to give up considerable leisure (i.e. work more) to obtain more labour income; hence, the relatively flat indifference curve at point B. At intermediate points such as C, income and leisure are more substitutable because the individual is not saturated with either. Higher indifference curves such as U_1 represent higher levels of utility or welfare since they involve more of both income and leisure.

The individual will try to reach the highest indifference curve possible, constrained by the potential income constraint as given in Figure 2.1(b). This is a "potential" income constraint because it indicates varying amounts of income that can be obtained by giving up leisure and working at the market wage rate. The actual amount of income will depend on the chosen amount of work in addition to the amount of income received from other sources, referred to as "non-labour income" and shown as the amount Y_N in Figure 2.1(b). Alternative phrases for the potential income constraint include wage, budget, wealth, income and full-income constraint.

The slope of the potential income constraint line depends on the individual's labour market wage rate. Persons with a high market wage rate, such as w_1 where $w_1 > w_0$, will be able to earn more income by giving up leisure and working more; hence the slope of w_1 is steeper than the slope of w_0. Note that work is measured from right to left; for analytical purposes it is regarded as the residual between the maximum amount of leisure available and the amount of leisure chosen.

Perhaps the simplest way to understand how wage changes (as well as other factors such as taxes and transfers which will be examined later) affect the potential income constraint is to first mark the end point on the leisure axis. This end point is the maximum amount of leisure available; depending on the units in which leisure is measured, it could be 24 hours per day, 7 days per week, 52 weeks per year, or some combination such as 8760 hours per year. The potential income constraint is then derived by plotting the income people receive as they give up leisure and work additional units; that is, as they move leftward from the maximum leisure end point. For a constant wage rate, this income constraint would be a straight line, since a unit of work would yield the same additional income throughout the range of work time. The end point on the income axis would be the maximum income the individual could attain by working all of the time; that is, by having zero leisure. For individuals with income from sources other than market work, the budget constraint begins vertically above the point T at which a maximum amount of leisure is attained, with the vertical distance (OY_N in Figure 2.1(b)) being the amount of non-labour income. This gives rise to a higher budget constraint, W_2, which involves the same high wage W_1 (hence W_1 and W_2 are parallel), albeit W_2 has the nonlabour income Y_N.

By putting the individual's potential income constraint and indifference curve together (Figure 2.1(c)), we can obtain the individual's optimal

Figure 2.1   Income-Leisure Indifference Curves, Wage Constraint, and Equilibrium

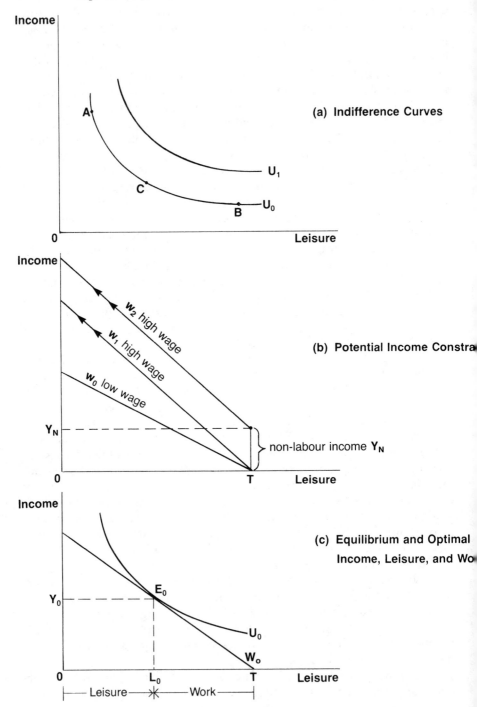

amount of income and leisure (and hence we can obtain the optimal work or labour supply). The utility maximizing individual will reach the highest indifference curve possible, constrained by the labour market earnings as given by the potential income constraint w_0. The highest feasible indifference curve in Figure 2.1(c) involves the point of tangency E_0 with optimal income Y_0, leisure L_0, and labour supply or work $T - L_0$. One can easily verify that E_0 is the utility-maximizing equilibrium by seeing what would happen if the individual were at any point other than E_0.

INCOME AND SUBSTITUTION EFFECTS OF A WAGE CHANGE

What will happen to the equilibrium amount of work effort if wages are increased? On the one hand, the individual may work more because the returns for work are greater; that is, the opportunity cost of leisure or the income forgone by not working is higher and hence the person may substitute away from leisure. This is termed the substitution effect and, in the case of a wage increase, it leads to increased work. On the other hand, the higher wage rate means that for each quantity of work the person now has more income from which to buy more of all goods including leisure. Alternatively stated, with the higher wage rate, individuals can reach their target level of income sooner and hence they can afford not to have to work as much. This is termed the income effect, and in the case of a wage increase it leads to reduced work, assuming that leisure is a normal good. In the case of a wage change, therefore, the income and substitution effects work in the opposite direction; hence, it is ultimately an empirical proposition as to whether a wage increase would increase or decrease the supply of work effort.

The income and substitution effects of a wage change are illustrated in Figure 2.2. After the wage increase from w_0 to w_1, the new equilibrium is E_2. Like all price changes, this increase in the price of leisure can be decomposed into an income effect and a substitution effect. The income effect can be illustrated by drawing a line parallel to the potential income constraint w_0 but tangent to the new indifference curve U_1. Since the lines are parallel, the relative price of leisure is the same at E_0 and E_1. Consequently the difference between E_0 and E_1 is purely a matter of having more potential income from which the individual can buy more of all goods including leisure. Hence if leisure is a normal good E_1 lies above and to the right of E_0 and consequently involves less work effort and more leisure. The difference between E_1 and E_2 is now a pure (or income-compensated) substitution effect, since household utility or satisfaction is held constant (as evidenced by E_1 and E_2 being on the same indifference curve U_1) and only the relative price of leisure is different. The relative price of leisure is higher on the steeper wage constraint w_1 as evidenced by the fact that giving up a unit of leisure (i.e. working more) yields more income. Consequently, the individual will substitute away from the more expensive leisure and work more: the pure (compensated) substitution effect of a wage increase will unambiguously increase work effort. In Figure 2.2, the substitution effect dominates the income effect; hence, in this illustration the wage increase resulted in a net increase in the amount of work. However, the income effect can dominate the substitution effect, in which case a wage increase will result in a decrease in the amount of work supplied.

DERIVING THE INDIVIDUAL
SUPPLY CURVE OF LABOUR

As the early writings of Robbins (1930) indicate, the income-leisure choice framework can be used to derive the individual's labour supply schedule, which indicates the amount of labour that will be offered at various wage rates. As Figure 2.2 indicates, we already have two points on that supply schedule: at wage rate w_0 the amount of labour supply (work) is $T - L_0$, and at wage rate w_1 the amount of labour supply is $T - L_2$. In this particular case, labour supply increased as wages increased because the substitution

Figure 2.2   Income and Substitution Effects of a Wage Increase

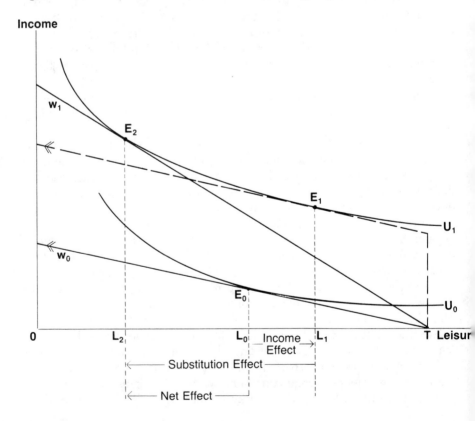

effect outweighed the income effect. By varying the wage rate, we can obtain a schedule of corresponding equilibrium amounts of work and hence trace out the individual's labour supply curve.

Derivation of an individual's labour supply schedule is further illustrated by the specific example of Figure 2.3 where leisure and work are measured in units of hours per day and wages in units of wages per hour. Income is the hourly wage multiplied by the hours of work. Figure 2.3(a) illustrates the equilibrium hours of work (measured from right to left) of 8 hours per day for a wage rate of $3/hr. The corresponding daily income is $24 per day. This gives us one point on the individual's labour supply schedule of Figure 2.3(c): at $3/hr the labour supply would be 8 hours. In Figure 2.3(b), wages are then raised to $5/hr and the individual is observed to increase work effort to 12 hours per day. This yields a second point on the labour supply schedule of Figure 2.3(c). In this particular case, the substitution effect of the wage increase outweighs the income effect so that hours of work have increased. In Figure 2.3(b), wages are next raised to $7/hr and the individual is observed to decrease work effort to 10 hours per day. This yields a third point on the labour supply schedule of Figure 2.3(c). At the higher wage rate, the income effect of the wage increase begins to dominate the substitution effect and the labour supply schedule becomes backward bending. In fact, this may be a reasonable approximation for many individuals: at low wage rates they have an abundance of unmet needs, so that higher wages will induce them to work more in order to fulfil these needs; at higher wages many of their needs are fulfilled, so that additional wage increases will be used to purchase leisure.

The fact that when leisure is a normal good the income and substitution effects of a price (wage) change act in *opposing* directions implies that consumer behaviour with respect to leisure time is fundamentally different from that with respect to other goods for which the income and substitution effects work in the *same* direction, when the good is normal. This difference arises because an increase in the price of leisure makes leisure time relatively more expensive but *raises* real income while an increase in the price of another commodity makes that good relatively more expensive and *lowers* real income.

CRITICISMS OF THE WORK-LEISURE FRAMEWORK

The work-leisure choice framework has been criticized in a variety of areas. Many of these criticisms, however, are not really criticisms of the basic framework. Rather they are extensions of the model and reminders of its limitations.

There is the belief that many individuals do not really have a choice between work and leisure. This may especially be the case for poor persons at a subsistence level of income, or people who are permanently attached to the labour force or who are required to work a fixed period of time if

Figure 2.3 Deriving the Individual Supply Curve of Labour

they are to work. These criticisms should not negate the viability of the work-leisure framework; in fact, they can easily be incorporated into the basic model. Poor persons existing at a subsistence income have a wage constraint close to the origin and an indifference curve between income and leisure that is flat to the right of the existing equilibrium — since they are at subsistence, they are unable to give up any income even for large increases in leisure. To the left of the existing equilibrium, their indifference curve could have a low slope indicating that they are willing to give up considerable leisure to attain the higher income and consumption patterns of middle class status.

People who are required to work a fixed period of time would not face a continuous wage constraint, but rather would be relegated to a specific point on that wage constraint, or to not working at all. This can be depicted in the work-leisure choice framework and, as we will see later, gives rise to interesting implications with respect to overtime and moonlighting. The point is simply that rather than negating the viability of the work-leisure model, these observations highlight its usefulness in analysing the impact of the different preferences and of the objective constraints facing individuals. In addition, the interpretation of the constraint need not involve the wage constraint of a single job. Workers may face a menu of wage-hours combinations across different jobs and firms.

The work-leisure choice framework has also been criticized on the grounds that leisure may not be a "normal" good. For low-income people, leisure may be an inferior good because they don't have the income to really enjoy the leisure. An increase in their income, other things being equal, may actually encourage work incentives since, for example, the more expensive vacation or the chance to send one of the children to a university now becomes a reality. Again, this does not negate the theory, since it does not deny the possibility that leisure is an inferior good. In fact, the basic theory of consumer demand merely states that an increase in income will lead to increased expenditure on all normal goods: this increased expenditure on leisure could well mean a lesser quantity of leisure and more quality leisure, in which case work incentives are increased.

QUESTIONS

1. In Figure 2.1(c), why is E_0 a stable equilibrium? In other words, why would the individual not move along the potential income constraint line W_0 to some other feasible combination of income and leisure? Why would he not move to a feasible point below the wage constraint line? Why would he not move to a point above the indifference curve U_0?
2. What would happen to an individual's labour supply schedule if leisure is an inferior good?
3. Use the basic work-leisure choice framework to analyse the possible labour supply response of various groups to changes in their wage rate.

The different groups could include the following: poor who are at minimum subsistence and who aspire to middle-class consumption patterns; wealthy who have acquired an abundance of material goods and who now aspire to be members of the idle rich; primary workers who have a fairly strong attachment to the labour force and who are reluctant to change their hours of work; secondary workers who have a weak attachment to the labour force and who have viable alternatives to labour market work; "workaholics" who have strong preferences for labour market work.

4. Illustrate the case where an individual responds differently to a wage increase and a wage decrease of the same magnitude. Specifically, have the person become "locked in" to a certain consumption pattern associated with the higher wage.

5. Depict the following situations in the basic work-leisure choice diagram: an individual works beyond his normal working hours, becomes less productive, and hence is paid less per hour; an individual works beyond his normal working hours, and an overtime premium is paid; the person takes a training program and increases his labour market productivity and wage; the government subsidizes the individual's wage by fifty percent; the government imposes a tax of twenty percent on labour market earnings; the government imposes a progressive income tax; the government gives everyone a basic demogrant of 1000 dollars per year.

6. Suppose an individual is on the backward-bending portion of his labour supply curve. Is there a sufficiently high wage such that his hours of work will go to zero?

REFERENCES AND FURTHER READINGS

Abbott, M. and O. Ashenfelter. Labor supply, commodity demand, and the allocation of time. *R.E. Studies* 42 (October 1977) 389-411.

Ashenfelter, O. and J. Heckman. The estimation of income and substitution effects in a model of family labor supply. *Econometrica* 42 (January 1974) 73-85.

Barzel, Y. The determination of daily hours and wages. *QJE* 87 (May 1973) 220-238.

Barzel, Y. and R. McDonald. Assets, subsistence and the supply curve for labor. *AER* 63 (September 1973) 621-633.

Berg, E. Backward sloping labor supply functions in dual economies — the African case. *QJE* 75 (August 1961).

Conlisk, J. Simple dynamic effects in work-leisure choice: a skeptical comment on the static theory. *JHR* 3 (Summer 1968) 324-326.

Darrough, M. A model of consumption and leisure in an intertemporal framework: a systematic treatment using Japanese data. *IER* 18 (October 1977) 677-696.

Deserpa, A. On the comparative statics of time allocation theory. *CJE* 8 (February 1975) 101-111.

Dowell, R. Risk preference and the work-leisure trade-off. *EI* 23 (October 1985) 691-702.

Feldstein, M. Estimating the supply curve of working hours. *Oxford Economic Papers* 20 (August 1968) 74-80.

Finegan, T. Hours of work in the United States: a cross-sectional analysis. *JPE* 70 (October 1962) 452-470.

Fishelson, G. Simple dynamic effects in work-leisure choice: a rejoinder to the skeptical comment on the static theory. *JHR* 6 (Spring 1971) 248-249.

Hanock, G. The backward-bending supply of labor. *JPE* 73 (December 1965) 636-642.

Heckman, J. Life cycle consumption and labor supply. *AER* 64 (March 1974) 188-194.

Heckman, J. Shadow prices, market wages and labor supply. *Econometrica* 42 (July 1974) 679-694.

Kagel, J., R. Battalio, R. Winkler and E. Fisher. Job choice and total labor supply: an experimental analysis. *SEJ* 44 (July 1977) 13-24.

Kaun, D. A comment on the work-leisure myth. *Review of Radical Political Economy* I (May 1969) 85-88.

Lampman, R. (ed.). Income redistribution and the labor supply: a symposium. *JHR* 3 (Summer 1968).

Lewis, H.G. Hours of work and hours of leisure. *IRRA* (December 1956) 196-206.

Lewis, H.G. Economics of time and labor supply. *AER* 65 (May 1975) 29-36.

Mabry, B. Income-leisure analysis and the salaried professional. *IR* 8 (February 1969) 162-173.

McCabe, P. Optimal leisure-effort choice with endogenously determined earnings. *JOLE* 1 (July 1983) 308-329.

Miracle, M. and B. Fetter. Backward-sloping labor-supply functions and African economic behavior. *Economic Development and Cultural Change* 18 (January 1970) 240-251.

Moses, L. Income, leisure and wage pressure. *EJ* 72 (June 1962) 320-334.

Murray, M. A reinterpretation of the traditional income-leisure model with application to in-kind subsidy programs. *JPubEc* 14 (August 1980) 69-82.

O'Connor, J. Smith and Marshall on the individual's supply of labor. *ILRR* 14 (January 1961) 273-276.

Owen, J. *The Price of Leisure*. Montreal: McGill-Queen's University Press, 1970.

Owen, J. The demand for leisure. *JPE* 79 (January/February 1971) 56-76.

Parsons, D. Health, family structure and labor supply. *AER* 67 (September 1977) 703-712.

Robbins, L. On the elasticity of demand for income in terms of effort. *Economica* (June 1930) 123-129.

Ryder, H., F. Stafford and P. Stephan. Labor, leisure and training over the life cycle. *IER* 17 (October 1976) 651-674.

Sharir, S. The income leisure model: a diagrammatic extension. *Economic Record* (March 1975) 93-98.

Sharir, S. and Y. Weiss. The role of absolute and relative wage differentials in the choice of work activity. *JPE* 82 (November/December 1974) 1269-1275.

Smith, J. Assets, savings and labor supply. *EI* (October 1977) 551-573.

Vatter, H. On the folklore of the backward sloping supply curve. *ILRR* 14 (July 1961) 578-586. Comment by T. Finegan and rejoinder (January 1962) 230-236.

Wales, T. Estimation of a labour supply curve for self-employed business proprietors. *IER* 14 (February 1973) 69-80.

Wales, T. and A. Woodland. Estimation of household utility functions and labor supply response. *IER* 17 (June 1976) 397-410.

Weiss, Y. On the optimal pattern of labor supply. *EJ* 82 (December 1972) 1293-1311.

Winston, G. Income and the aggregate allocation of effort. *AER* 55 (May 1965).

3 Household Production Functions and the New Home Economics

Perhaps the most substantial modification of the basic work-leisure model is that offered by exponents of the "household production" view, sometimes termed the "economics of the family" or the "new home economics," as evidenced in the writings of Gary Becker (1965, 1976). This perspective emphasizes that households are producers as well as consumers and hence it is important to analyse how the household allocates its scarce resources, especially time, to affect the economic well-being of the household. The view highlights the misnomer of the term "leisure" as it has historically been used in the income-leisure choice framework. Rather, the household time component can consist of pure leisure, household work, and the use of household time in other activities that may involve both a consumption and a production component.

The household's allocation of its scarce time resource, then, is the focus of the household production function approach. This approach focuses on technological considerations of production rather than relying on differences in "tastes" as determinants of certain elements of behaviour. It extends the explanatory power of consumer demand analysis by expanding the concept of "price" to include time costs, hence making it easier to explain certain patterns of behaviour that are hard to explain in the conventional framework.

BASIC FRAMEWORK

The basic notion behind the household production perspective is that the household combines inputs of market goods, X, and household time, T, to produce commodities, which ultimately yield satisfaction or utility, U, to the household. Such commodities (to use Becker's 1965 terminology), or characteristics (to use Lancaster's 1966 terminology) include eating, sleeping, or viewing a play, all of which require combinations of household time and market goods to produce and hence ultimately consume such commodities.

More formally stated, household utility is a function of the commodities it consumes; that is, $U = f(Z_1, Z_2 \ldots Z_n) = f(Z)$ where $Z = (Z_1 \ldots Z_n)$ is a vector of the various commodities consumed by the household. Each of these commodities in turn is also produced by the household via the household production function $Z = g(X,T)$, which involves various combinations of goods $X = (X_1, X_2 \ldots X_m)$ and time as inputs in the production function. Indirectly then, household utility is a function of market goods and household time as they are combined in the household production function; that is, $U = f(Z) = f(g(X,T)) = h(X,T)$.

UTILITY ISOQUANTS

Figure 3.1(a) depicts such a household utility isoquant (or indifference curve U_0) indicating how a given constant level of utility can be produced by varying combinations of market goods, X, and household time, T. The notation X can represent either an individual good X_i or a basket of market goods $X = (X_1, X_2 \ldots X_m)$. In the latter case the Hicksian aggregation conditions which allow us to treat a basket of goods like a single good are assumed to hold; that is, the relative prices of the goods in the basket are held constant. In this context, X is usually referred to as a "composite commodity."

The slope of the utility isoquant exhibits a diminishing marginal rate of substitution between the inputs. That is, in the upper left segment, where an abundance of market goods and little household time are used to produce commodities that yield utility, a large increase in the use of market goods is required to offset any further reduction in the use of household time, in order to maintain household production and hence utility at the same level. For example, if a household were trying to reduce its meal preparation time from one hour down to one-half hour per day, then it would take a larger increase in the use of market goods (e.g., more elaborate appliances, pre-packaged food) in order to maintain utility, than if the household were trying to cut its meal preparation time from four to three and one-half hours. The latter reduction could be acomplished with a substitution of simple market goods like basic appliances and equipment.

The slope of the utility isoquant can be thought of as the "home wage" or the household's implicit valuation of its time since it shows how many market goods and services, X, can be saved by using an additional unit of household time, T. (This will be important later in developing the notion of a reservation wage or the minimum market wage at which an individual will enter the labour market.) An exogenous event that would increase one's valuation of time or "home wage" in the household (e.g., having children or having a sick relative that needs family care) would rotate the isoquant to the right. This is depicted by the utility isoquant U_0' in Figure 3.1(b) with the "home wage" (slope of the utility isoquant) being higher for U_0' than for U_0. This is illustrated most clearly where the isoquants intersect since a small reduction in household time requires more inputs of goods and services to keep utility constant under U_0' than U_0.

The shape of the utility isoquant illustrates the substitutability between household time and market goods in the production of household utility. For example, Figure 3.1(c) illustrates the situation where neither market goods nor household time are good substitutes for each other below

Figure 3.1   Utility Isoquants and Household Production

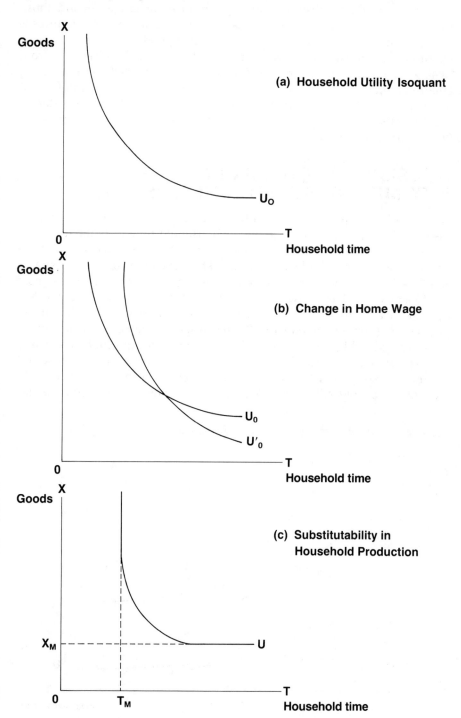

certain minimum threshold levels of goods, X_m, and time, T_m. However, they may be good substitutes in the intermediate range beyond those threshold levels. This could be the case if, for example, a minimum threshold amount of both household time and market goods is necessary to raise children (i.e., to attain a given amount of household satisfaction from raising a family). That is, it may be difficult to attain satisfaction from raising children if one cannot afford certain basic necessities or if one cannot afford to spend at least a certain amount of time with them. Alternatively stated, the threshold level, T_m, indicates that it is not always possible to completely "buy your way out" of raising children.

HOUSEHOLD EQUILIBRIUM AND INCOME AND SUBSTITUTION EFFECTS

Higher utility isoquants represent higher utility levels since more utility is associated with more market goods or household time or both. As under conventional consumer demand theory, households will try to maximize utility subject to their budget constraint. The slope of the budget constraint is determined by the market wage rate. A high labour *market* wage gives rise to a steep budget constraint, indicating that if the individual gives up household time for labour market work, more market goods, X, can be purchased. (Remember that the "home wage" is depicted in the utility isoquant with a high home wage giving rise to a steeper utility isoquant.)

Figure 3.2 indicates the equilibrium, E_0, amount of household time, T_0, and market goods and services, X_0, which yield the highest possible level of household satisfaction, U_0, given the individual's market wage,

Figure 3.2 Equilibrium and Optimal Time and Goods Inputs

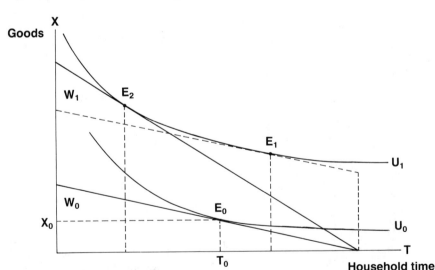

W_0, and home wage. (The home wage is depicted implicitly in the slope of the utility isoquant.) An increase in the market wage from W_0 to W_1 would rotate the budget constraint upwards yielding a new equilibrium E_2. As in conventional consumer demand theory, this price change can be decomposed into income and substitution effects. The income effect, from E_0 to E_1, implies that the household can afford to consume more of both goods- (X) and time- (T) intensive activities given the increased real income from the increased market wage. The pure or income-compensated substitution effect, from E_1 to E_2, implies that the household will utilize more goods-intensive and fewer time-intensive activities (i.e., substitute away from T and into X) to produce a given level of household satisfaction U_1.

As with the basic income-leisure choice model, the income and substitution effects work in the opposite direction for the household time input T; therefore, E_2 could be to the right or left of E_0 depending upon whether the income or substitution effect dominates. (In Figure 3.1 the substitution effect dominates so E_2 is to the left of E_0.) However, the use of goods and services, X, as an input into the household production function unambiguously increases (i.e., E_2 is above E_0) because the income and substitution effects work in the same direction towards the purchase of goods.

In this regard, there are two major differences between conventional consumer demand theory and the household production function approach. First, the household production approach emphasizes that commodities consumed require both goods and time input. This focuses attention on the extent to which particular commodities are goods-intensive or time-intensive, and how the choice between goods-intensive and time-intensive commodities responds to exogenous changes, in particular changes in the market wage rate or the opportunity cost of time.

This aspect of household behaviour is illustrated in Figure 3.3, which shows the choice between a commodity which is relatively goods-intensive and one which is relatively time-intensive. The initial equilibrium, based on the market wage W_0, is at E_0. (The choice of hours of work cannot be shown without extending the diagram to three dimensions; however, optimal hours of work are determined as shown in Figure 3.2 and these determine the position of the budget constraint marked W_0 in Figure 3.3.) An increase in the market wage to W_1 enables the household to consume more of both commodities (and may affect the choice of hours of market work, as shown in Figure 3.2), but also increases the relative price of the time-intensive commodity resulting in the steeper budget constraint denoted by W_1 in Figure 3.3. The movement to the new equilibrium can be decomposed into the income effect (E_0 to E_1) which results in increased consumption of both commodities providing both are "normal," and the substitition effect (E_1 to E_2) which results in increased consumption of the goods-intensive commodity and decreased consumption of the time-intensive commodity. Thus the income and substitution effects work in the same direction for the goods-intensive commodity but in opposite directions for the time-intensive commodity.

Figure 3.3   Household Choice Between Goods- and Time-Intensive Commodities

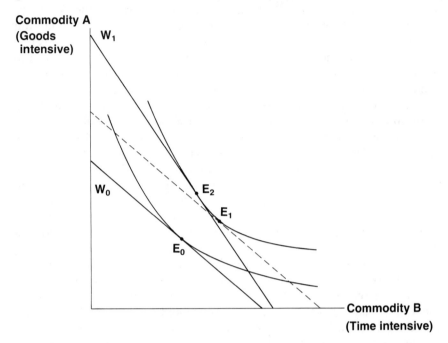

The second difference between conventional consumer demand theory and the household production function approach is that the substitution effect in the latter approach has two reinforcing components. The substitution in household *production* implies that for a given amount of every commodity consumed, the household will substitute away from more costly time inputs and toward relatively less costly goods inputs, following a wage increase that increases the opportunity cost of time. In addition, the substitution in household *consumption* implies that the household will substitute away from time-intensive commodities and toward goods-intensive commodities, again reducing the use of the more costly time input if the market wage increases. Basically, the household production function approach reminds us that price changes can yield substitution effects in production as well as in the consumption of the commodities that yield ultimate satisfaction.

APPLICATION TO THE NATURE OF MARKET GOODS AND SERVICES DEMANDED

The commodities that are the ultimate source of satisfaction generally require both time and goods in their production and consumption. This observation has significant implications. As real wages increase, the demand for goods-intensive commodities will increase at a relatively rapid rate due to the fact that the income and substitution effects reinforce each other. The consequences of this tendency are evident in many aspects of life: the growth of fast-food outlets and prepared foods; attempts to combine activities, sometimes with additional goods input (e.g. jogging with recorded music); even the choice of forms of exercise (popularity of jogging compared to walking). As real incomes rise in the future, households will be driven to more goods-intensive forms of consumption. Nonetheless, the tension between time available for market work and time available for household production and consumption may increase as the opportunity cost of time rises — a phenomenon captured nicely by the title of S.B. Linder's (1970) book *The Harried Leisure Class*. (Incidentally, the book is well worth reading — if you can find the time!)

APPLICATION TO DEMAND FOR CHILDREN AND LABOUR SUPPLY

As a further illustration, a wage increase can lead to an increased demand for children emanating from the income effect. It can also lead to a reduced demand for children because they are time-intensive and the opportunity cost of time has risen. This is the substitution effect involving a substitution in household consumption away from time-intensive activities and into goods-intensive activities.

However, there is also a substitution effect in household production. That is, given the higher opportunity cost of time, the household may substitute away from time-intensive and towards goods-intensive ways of raising children. The substitution effects in both consumption and production reinforce each other to reduce the use of the more costly time input. However, the substitution effect in production may mute some of the decline in demand for children emanating from the substitution in consumption. That is, a wage increase will not lead to as much of a reduction in the demand for time-intensive children if the household can easily substitute market goods and services (e.g., day care, disposable diapers) for household time. As these substitutes become more available over time, the demand for children may increase even if the market wages of women increase.

Alternatively stated, the declining family size that has gone on over time, as female labour market activity (and hence the income forgone by having children) has increased, could change if alternative market arrangements arise to facilitate the substitutability of market goods and services for household time in the household production function. The household production function approach illustrates explicitly how the demand for children may be affected, not only by the satisfaction they yield, but also by the availability of market goods and services that can be used as substitutes for household time in the raising of children.

The fact that a price increase can engender a substitution effect in production as well as consumption may also have implications for the labour supply behaviour of men and women. To the extent that women bear a disproportionate responsibility for the raising of children, then the substitution effect in production, emanating from a wage increase, would be stronger for women than for men. That is, a wage increase for women may induce them to substitute market goods and services for their now more expensive time. This in turn may facilitate their partaking in labour market activities and hence make their labour supply decision more responsive than men's to a wage change. (The differential responsiveness of the labour supply of men and women to a wage change will be expanded upon later in the discussion of labour force participation decisions.)

OTHER IMPLICATIONS

The household production function perspective has other implications that may not have been obvious from the conventional exposition of household commodity demand and labour supply behaviour. It reminds us, for example, that the consumption decisions of households depend not only upon their income and relative commodity prices, but also upon factor prices (especially the opportunity cost of their time) and factor productivity. Also, households with an efficient production function have a larger opportunity or choice set than those with less efficient production functions. That is, households are potentially better off (i.e., have a larger choice set) not only if they have high market wages or endowments of nonlabour income (the determinants of the budget constraint emphasized in the conventional income-leisure choice framework) but also if they are endowed with more efficient household production functions.

Emphasis on the household as a *producer* as well as a *consumer* also reminds us of the importance in household consumption and time allocation decisions of various laws of production. The principle of comparative advantage emphasizes that it may be economically efficient for different members of the household to specialize in their respective areas of comparative advantage. This may mean, for example, that it is economically efficient for one party to specialize in labour market tasks and the other to specialize in household tasks, depending upon their relative earning power in the labour market and productivity in household tasks. Such specialization may be artificially induced, however, if female market wages are reduced because of discrimination. This can lead to a vicious circle whereby females specialize in household tasks because their market wages are lower due to discrimination, and this household specialization prevents them from acquiring the labour market experience that would give them a potential comparative advantage to specialize in labour market tasks.

Economies of scale may also be an important law of production that has relevance to the concept of the household production function. For example, the average *per person* cost of preparing a meal may be high for a single person but not for a family of six; hence, inducing the single person to enter co-operative arrangements or to eat more often in restaurants.

Similarly, the extra cost of watching an additional child may be small once the fixed costs are incurred for watching one child; hence, the emergence of co-operative day care arrangements. Also, within the same family, the extra cost of raising a third child may be less than that of the second child which in turn is less than that of the first child; hence, the rationale for per capita poverty measures that do not simply divide family income by the number of family members.

The emphasis on the household as a producer also reminds us of the importance of the laws of derived demand in analysing how the demand for inputs of household time and market goods (as used in the household production function) would respond to changes in their prices. These laws of demand will be analysed in more detail in the subsequent chapter on the demand for labour. One implication that emerges is that the reallocation of time from household to labour market tasks in response to an increase in the market wage will be small if there are few good substitute inputs for household labour, if there are few substitute commodities for the sorts of things produced in the household, or if the time cost is a small proportion of the total cost of household production.

The household production function approach also emphasizes the importance of the family as a decision-making unit and hence the importance of joint decision making amongst family members with respect to various elements of behaviour. For example, the decisions to get married, participate in labour market activities, and have children are all intricately related for all family members. This also means, for example, that a change in the wage rate or price of time for one family member may affect not only their own allocation decisions, but also the decisions of other family members. Formally stated, cross-price effects can be important across family members.

The importance of allocating time over the life cycle is also highlighted in the household production function approach. For example, it may be economically rational to engage in time-intensive activities when the opportunity cost of time is low, perhaps because productivity is lower at certain stages in the life cycle. Thus, it may be efficient to work intensively and for long hours during the peak-earnings years of one's career and to engage in more leisure time when one's earnings are lower. For example, it may be efficient for students to take time off for time-intensive travel before they have established a career in the labour market, or for older workers to partake in early or partial retirement programs once they have passed the peak earnings years of their careers.

Lastly, from a methodological point of view, the household production function perspective emphasizes downplaying the importance of tastes and preferences in determining behaviour. Rather, the emphasis is on the objective constraints faced by households in their consumption and production decisions. Such constraints reflect a complicated array of income and prices including endowments of non-labour wealth, time, and the household production function, as well as the market wages and home wages of various family members and the prices of goods and services that can be purchased directly or used as inputs into the household production function.

For example, rather than treat declining family size as reflecting a change in tastes and preferences away from children, the household production function approach emphasizes the importance of the increasing price or opportunity cost of having children associated with the rising wages of women. Similarly, the differential labour market behaviour of men and women is viewed not so much as reflecting differential tastes for labour market or household work, as resulting from different constraints in terms of labour market versus home wages. Also, differences in behaviour among households may reflect differences in the ability of respective households to combine goods and time in the production of various commodities rather than pure differences in tastes. This emphasis on the array of constraints imposed by income, prices, and household technology, of course, gives more emphasis to economics as being able to explain a wider array of human behaviour, and this has been one of the purposes of the foray of economics into the economics of household behaviour.

QUESTIONS

1. Briefly outline the Becker-Lancaster approach to consumer demand theory ("household production function" approach: the "new micro-economics"; the new "home-economics") and its applicability to labour market economics. Specifically, indicate some labour market implications of this theory that we would not have been able to derive from conventional consumer demand theory.
2. Utilize your knowledge of household production theory to indicate
    (a) the expected effect of a wage increase on labour supply;
    (b) the expected effect, on the demand for children, of an increase in the wage of a wife;
    (c) why the income-compensated substitution effect on labour supply may be larger for women than men;
    (d) the effect, on an individual's "home wage," of the disability of a spouse who requires home and not institutional care;
    (e) the effect, on an individual's "home wage," if the government were to pay the family for the disability in (d).
3. In recent years economists have applied economic theory, especially the Becker-Lancaster "new consumer demand theory" or "household production function" approach to the decision to have children.
    (a) Briefly outline the relevance of this approach to the family formation decision.
    (b) Indicate the expected effect of an increase in the wages of women on the family formation decision, being careful to distinguish between substitution effects in production and consumption.
    (c) Discuss the implications of the theory for the spacing (i.e., how far

apart children are in age) and timing (i.e., when parents will have them in terms of the parents' life cycle) of children and on the gap between the desired and actual number of children.

(d) Comment on the expected impact on family formation of a policy to provide improved public pensions for the aged.

4. The household production function approach focuses on technological consideration of production rather than "tastes" to explain various aspects of behaviour. Discuss the virtues of this approach.

5. Utilize the household production function approach to illustrate the interrelatedness of the decisions: to get married, to acquire education and training, to participate in the labour force, and to have children.

REFERENCES AND FURTHER READINGS

Becker, G. A theory of the allocation of time. *EJ* 75 (Sept. 1965) 493-517.

Becker, G.S. *The Economic Approach to Human Behavior*. Chicago: University of Chicago Press, 1976.

Ben-Porath, Y. The production of human capital and the life cycle of earnings. *JPE* 75 (March 1986) 352-365.

Bovlier, B. and M. Rosenzweig. Schooling, search and spouse selection: testing economic theories of marriage and household behavior. *JPE* 92 (August 1984) 712-732.

Chiswick, C. The value of housewife's time. *JHR* 17 (Summer 1982) 413-425.

Corman, H. The demand for education for home production. *EI* 24 (April 1986) 213-230.

Dunn, L. Measurement of internal income-leisure tradeoffs. *QJE* 93 (August 1979) 373-393.

Graham, J. and C. Green. Estimating the parameters of a household production function with joint products. *R.E. Stats.* 66 (May 1984) 277-282.

Gronau, R. The effect of children on the housewife's value of time. *JPE* 81 part 2 (March/April 1973).

Gronau, R. The allocation of time of Israeli women. *JPE* 84 part 2 (August 1976) S201-S220.

Gronau, R. Leisure home production and work — the theory of the allocation of time revisited. *JPE* 85 (December 1977) 1099-1123.

Gronau, R. Home production — a forgotten industry, *R.E. Stats.* (May 1980) 408-415.

Gronau, R. Home production: a survey. *Handbook of Labor Economics*, Vol. 1. O. Ashenfelter and R. Layard (eds.). New York: Elsevier, 1986.

Grossbard-Shechtman, A. A theory of allocation of time in markets for labour and marriage. *EJ* 94 (Dec. 1984) 868-882.

Hawrylyshyn, O. The value of household services: a survey of empirical estimates. *Review of Income and Wealth* (March 1976) 101-131.

Hill, C. and F. Stafford. The allocation of time to pre-school children and educational opportunity. *JHR* 9 (Summer 1974) 323-341.

Hill, C. and F. Stafford. Parental care of children: time diary estimates of quantity predictability and variety. *JHR* 15 (Spring 1980) 219-239.

Juster, F. and F. Stafford, eds. *Time, Goods, and Well Being*. The University of Michigan, Survey Research Center, 1983.

Lancaster, K. A new approach to consumer theory. *JPE* 74 (January 1966) 132-157.

Leibowitz, A. Education and the allocation of women's time. *Education, Income and Human Behavior*. F. Juster (ed.). New York: McGraw Hill, 1974.

Linder, S. *The Harried Leisure Class*. New York: Columbia University Press, 1970.

Manser, M. and M. Brown. Marriage and household decision-making. *IER* 21 (February 1980) 31-44.

Michael, R. Education in nonmarket production. *JPE* 81 part 1 (March/April 1973) 306-327.

Michael, R. and G. Becker. On the new theory of consumer behavior. *Swedish Journal of Economics* 75 (1973) 378-396.

Mincer, J. Market prices, opportunity costs and income effects. *Measurement in Economics: Studies in Mathematical Economics and Econometrics in Memory of Yehuda Grunfeld*. C. Chris et al. (eds.). Stanford, Calif.: Stanford University Press, 1963.

Muth, R. Household production and consumer demand functions. *Econometrica* 34 (July 1966) 699-708.

Pollak, R. and M. Wachter. The relevance of the household production function and its implication for the allocation of time. *JPE* 83 (April 1975) 255-277.

Pollak, R. and T. Wales. Welfare comparisons and equivalence scales. *AER* 69 (May 1979) 216-221.

Ray, R. Measuring the costs of children: an alternative approach. *JPubEc* 22 (October 1983) 89-102.

Reid, M. *Economics of Household Production*. New York: Wiley, 1934.

Rosenzweig, M. and T. Schultz. Estimating the household production function: heterogeneity, the demand for health inputs, and their effect on birth weight. *JPE* 91 (October 1983) 723-746.

Williams, A. and N. Terleckyj. Household production and consumption. *JPE* 86 (February 1978) 168-170.

Work Incentive Effects of Alternative Income Maintenance Schemes

As a response to the problem of poverty, various income maintenance schemes have been proposed to raise the income of the poor and to supplement low wages. One concern with many of these proposals is that they may reduce work incentives — i.e., result in lower labour force participation or fewer hours worked among program participants — and hence exacerbate poverty in the long run. If an income maintenance program provides little incentive to work, this would raise the cost of the program to taxpayers and hence make the program politically less acceptable. In addition, it could prevent the poor from acquiring the on-the-job training and labour market experience that may raise their income in the long run. Clearly, it is important to understand the exact way in which income maintenance schemes could alter work incentives. The income maintenance programs examined here are demogrants, negative income taxes, welfare, wage subsidies, unemployment insurance, unemployment-insurance-assisted worksharing, and disability payments and workers' compensation.

STATIC PARTIAL EQUILIBRIUM EFFECTS IN THEORY

The basic income-leisure choice framework provides a convenient starting point to analyse the work incentive effects of alternative income maintenance schemes. At this point, the analysis is restricted to the static, partial-equilibrium effects of alternative income maintenance programs. Later, the analysis is extended to dynamic changes that can occur over time and to general equilibrium effects that can occur as the impact of the program works its way through the whole economic system.

Income support programs affect behaviour by altering the individual's opportunities (their potential income constraint). To analyse the effect of specific programs on the income constraint, ask first what is the effect on non-labour income, and second, what is the effect on the slope of the constraint — i.e., what happens as the individual gives up leisure and works more? Throughout this analysis, Y is defined as income after taxes and transfer payments, and E as labour market earnings, equal to wages times hours worked.

Demogrant

Perhaps the simplest income maintenance program to analyse is the demogrant. As the name implies, a demogrant means an income grant to a specific demographic group, such as female-headed families with children, or all persons aged 60 and over, or all family units irrespective of their wealth. Examples of demogrants in Canada include the Family Allowance program which provides monthly payments to families in respect of each child under the age of 18 and the Old Age Security program which provides monthly payments to individuals over the age of 65.

As illustrated by the dashed line in Figure 4.1(a), the demogrant would shift the potential income constraint vertically upwards by the amount of the grant. The slope of the new income constraint would be equal to the slope of the original constraint since the relative price of leisure has not changed. Thus there is no substitution effect involved with the demogrant; the new equilibrium, E_d, would be above and to the right of the original equilibrium; that is, work incentives would unambiguously be reduced. This occurs because the demogrant involves only a leisure-inducing pure income effect. The increase in actual take-home income is less than the amount of the demogrant because some of the demogrant was used to buy leisure, hence reducing earned income. This can readily be seen in Figure 4.1(a); if the individual did not alter working time, the outcome would be at the point E_1 vertically above the original equilibrium E_0.

Welfare

In Canada, welfare or social assistance programs are administered by the provinces but financed partly (approximately 50 percent) by the federal government under the Canada Assistance Plan. Benefits vary by province and according to other factors such as family type (single parent, couple) and employability. Welfare benefits also depend on the needs of the family and the family's assets and other sources of income.

For those who are eligible for welfare their new potential income constraint is given by the dashed line in Figure 4.1(b). If they do not work, they are given the welfare payment. Hence, at the point of maximum leisure (zero work), their income constraint shifts vertically upwards by the amount of the welfare payment. Under *many* welfare programs, as individuals work and receive labour market earnings they are required to forgo welfare payments by the exact amount of their labour market earnings. In this sense, there is a 100 percent tax on earnings. (See Fortin, 1985, for calculations of the implicit tax rates facing welfare recipients in Quebec and Ontario.) Their potential income constraint is thus horizontal at the amount of the welfare payment: as they work and earn income, they forgo a comparable amount in welfare and hence their income does not increase. Every dollar earned results in a dollar reduction in welfare. Of course, once they reach their original labour market wage constraint, then their take-home pay will be indicated by their original wage constraint: at this point their

Figure 4.1   Work Incentive Effects of Income Maintenance Plans

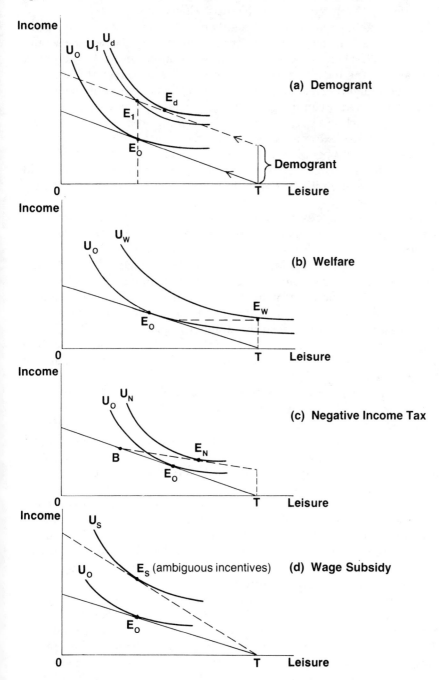

welfare payments have been reduced to zero so they cannot be "taxed" any further by being required to give up welfare.

If the welfare payment is sufficiently high, the individual would have a strong incentive to move to the corner solution at E_w where he would not work at all. There is no incentive to work more (move to the left of E_w), because of the 100 percent implicit tax on income from work that arises because the individual has to give up an equivalent amount of welfare for every dollar earned. Even though the person's take-home pay, Y, is lower at E_w than E_0, he chooses E_w because it involves considerably more leisure. Clearly welfare has extreme potential adverse effects on work incentives. Of course, for many people on welfare, work is not a viable alternative if they are perhaps disabled or unemployable. Yet for others, work would be a viable alternative if there would not be this 100 percent implicit tax on earned income.

This analysis suggests a variety of ways of reducing the number of people on welfare. Traditionally we think of making eligibility requirements more stringent or reducing the magnitude of welfare for those who are eligible. These changes would, of course, work. In Figure 4.1(b), for example, if the welfare payment were lowered to an amount lower than the height of U_0 at the point of maximum leisure, there would be no incentive to go on welfare since the individual would be maximizing utility at E_0. Although successful in reducing the number of people on welfare, these changes may have undesirable side effects, not the least of which are denying welfare to those in need and providing inadequate income support to those who are unemployable.

One alternative to these policies would be to increase the market wage rate of those on welfare and thereby encourage them to voluntarily leave welfare and earn income. In Figure 4.1(b), an increase in the market wage rate would pivot the wage constraint upwards from T. At some higher wage rate, the individual clearly would be induced to move to a higher indifference curve that would involve more work effort than under welfare (i.e. a new equilibrium to the left of E_w). The increased market wage could come about through training, job information, mobility, a government wage subsidy, or institutional pressures such as minimum wages or unionization. Obviously these policies may be costly, or in the case of minimum wages and unionization may involve a loss of jobs. However, they could have the benefit of voluntarily reducing the number of people on welfare and hence increasing work incentives.

Another way of improving work incentives would be to reduce the 100 percent implicit tax on welfare. In some welfare programs, this is accomplished by requiring welfare recipients to give up only a portion of their welfare if they earn income by working. For example, if recipients are required to give up 50 cents in welfare for every dollar earned in the labour market, they would have some incentive to work because the implicit tax rate would be 50 percent. In Figure 4.1(b), this could be shown by a wage constraint starting at E_w, with a negative slope of 50 percent of the slope of the labour market wage constraint, reflecting the fact that the recipient takes home 50 percent of every dollar earned by working. The negative income tax, discussed below, is a general scheme designed to ensure that individuals receiving income support face an implicit tax on income from work that is significantly less than 100 percent.

An alternative solution to reducing the number of welfare recipients would be to alter the preferences of welfare recipients away from being on welfare and towards labour market activity. In Figure 4.1(b), this would imply changing the shape of the indifference curves. If, for example, at all points to the right of E_0, the indifference curve U_0 were flat, then the individual would not have opted for the welfare equilibrium E_w. The flat indifference curve would indicate a reluctance to accept any cut in income even to get substantial increases in leisure. Traditionally, preferences have been altered by attaching a social stigma to being on welfare. Alternatively, preferences could be altered towards income-earning activities, perhaps by making potential recipients feel more a part of the non-welfare society or perhaps by attempting to break the inter-generational cycle of welfare.

Negative Income Tax

Negative-income-tax or guaranteed annual income plans involve an income guarantee, and an implicit tax rate of less than 100 percent applied to labour market earnings. Income after taxes and transfers would be $Y = G + (1 - t)E$, where G is the basic guarantee, t is the implicit tax rate, and Y and E as defined earlier are take-home pay and labour market earnings respectively. Most negative-income-tax plans differ in so far as they involve different values of the basic guarantee and the tax rate. The term *negative income tax* is used because recipients will receive more from the guarantee than they will pay out in taxes, even though they do face a positive implicit tax rate.

Although a comprehensive guaranteed annual income program has never been implemented in Canada, some programs which apply to particular groups — for example, the Child Tax Credit which supplements the income of families with children and the Guaranteed Income Supplement which supplements the income of individuals over 65 — have the negative income tax design. That is, there is a basic guarantee received by those with income below a certain level; those with higher income receive less income supplementation according to the program's implicit tax rate; and those whose income exceeds the program's breakeven point receive no benefits.

A negative-income-tax plan with a constant rate is illustrated by the dashed line in Figure 4.1(c). As with the demogrant, at the point of maximum leisure the basic income guarantee shifts the potential income constraint upwards by the amount of the guarantee: even if the individual does not work, he has positive income equal to the amount of the guarantee. Unlike welfare, as the individual works income assistance is not reduced by the full amount of labour market earnings. However, income support does decline as income from work increases; thus labour market earnings are subject to a positive implicit tax rate. Take-home pay does not rise as fast as labour market earnings; hence, the income constraint under the negative-income-tax plan is less steeply sloped than the original labour market income constraint. At the point B, often referred to as the break-even point, income received from the negative income tax program has declined to zero. Thus to the left of this point the original income constraint applies.

Assuming leisure is a normal good, the new equilibrium for recipients of the negative-income-tax plan will unambiguously lie to the right of the original equilibrium: work incentives are unambiguously reduced relative to a situation in which there is no other form of income support. This occurs because the income and substitution effects both work in the same direction to reduce work effort. The tax increase on earned income reduces the relative price of leisure, inducing a substitution into leisure and hence reducing work effort. The tax increase also has an income effect (working in the opposite direction); however, for *recipients* this is outweighed by the guarantee, so that on net their new potential income constraint is always above the original constraint — that is why they are defined as recipients. Because the potential income of recipients is increased, they will buy more of all normal goods including leisure. Thus the income effect works in the same direction as the substitution effect to reduce work effort.

The income-leisure choice framework predicts that work incentives will be unambiguously reduced as a result of a negative-income-tax plan. But this does not negate the viability of such a program. The adverse work incentive effects may be small, or the increased "leisure" may be used productively as in job search, mobility, education or increased household activities. In addition, the reduction in labour supply may have other desirable side effects, such as raising the wages of low-wage labour since it is now a relatively scarcer factor of production. Perhaps most important, the adverse incentive effects were predicted when a negative income tax was imposed in a world without other taxes and transfers. In most circumstances a negative-income-tax scheme is intended to replace some welfare programs which have even larger adverse incentive effects. In this sense work incentives may increase relative to incentives under welfare (as will be discussed in more detail in subsequent sections). While the basic conclusions from the work-leisure model should not be ignored, they must be kept in proper perspective. Empirical information is needed on the magnitude of any adverse work incentive effects and on the form in which "leisure" is taken. In addition, the effects on work incentives will depend on the programs that the negative income-tax scheme is intended to replace.

Wage Subsidy

Since one of the problems with the negative income tax and welfare is that the tax on earnings may discourage work effort, some have suggested that rather than tax additional earnings, the government should subsidize wages in an attempt to encourage work. Although there are a variety of forms of a wage subsidy — most often associated with the proposals of Kesselman (1969, 1971, 1973) — the simplest wage subsidy schemes have the common result that the recipient's per-hour wage rate is supplemented by a government subsidy. This could be accomplished, for example, by having the government guarantee a minimum wage w_G, and then applying a tax rate t_w to the market wage rate w, in which case the person's wage rate after the subsidy w_S would be $w_S = w_G + (1 - t_w)w$. If, for example, the government guaranteed a minimum wage of \$1.50 per hour, and applied a wage tax of 50 percent, then a person whose market wage is \$2.00 per hour would now receive a post-subsidy wage of $1.50 + (1 - .5)2 = \$2.50$, or a per-hour wage subsidy of \$.50. Alternatively, as Haveman (1973, p. 59) suggests, the subsidy could be an earnings subsidy which would involve a subsidy that is a given proportion of earnings, and hence wages, for low-income recipients. For example, the government could agree to subsidize low-income workers by supplementing their earnings by a fixed percentage, say 50 percent, of their earnings. Although this would change the potential income constraint the same as the wage subsidy, as we will see later it may involve different dynamic incentive effects because it doesn't involve a guaranteed wage or a tax on wages.

The static, partial equilibrium effect of the wage subsidy is illustrated by the dashed line in Figure 4.1(d). For the recipients, it is exactly like a wage increase, hence the potential income constraint rotates upwards from the point of maximum leisure T. If the person does not work (i.e. is at T), his income is still zero even though his wage is subsidized. However, as the person works more, his take-home pay rises more under the wage subsidy than would be the case if he were only receiving his market wage.

Just as an increase in wages has both an income and a substitution effect working in opposite directions in so far as they affect work incentives, so will the wage subsidy have an ambiguous effect on work incentives. The higher wage means higher potential income from which the individual will buy more of all normal goods, including leisure; hence, work incentives are reduced via the income effect. This income effect will be at work even though the individual has to work to receive the income: the increased leisure could come in the form of reduced hours or longer vacations or periodic withdrawals from the labour force or reduced work from another family member. The higher wage also means that the price (opportunity cost) of leisure has now increased; hence, work incentives are increased via this substitution effect. On net, theory does not indicate which effect dominates; hence the work incentive effects of a wage subsidy are ultimately an empirical proposition.

Although the work incentive effects of a wage subsidy are theoretically indeterminant, Kesselman (1969) and Garfinkel (1973) show that, other things equal (the recipients' welfare, their post-transfer income, or the size of the subsidy), the adverse work incentive effects of the wage subsidy are not as great as those of the negative income tax. This is illustrated in Figure 4.2 for the case where the recipients' welfare is held constant at U_0 so that they are indifferent between the two plans. The equilibrium E_S under the wage subsidy *must* lie to the left of the equilibrium E_N under the negative income tax. That is so because the potential income constraint under the wage subsidy is steeper than the negative income tax constraint since it involves a net subsidy to the wage of recipients. Since the wage subsidy constraint must be tangent to U_0 in order for the recipients to be indifferent between the two plans, this tangency must be to the left of E_N because only to the left of E_N is the indifference curve more steeply sloped than at E_N (when we have less leisure, more income is required to give up a unit of leisure and remain indifferent).

Figure 4.2   Work Incentive Effects of Wage Subsidy vs. Negative Income Tax

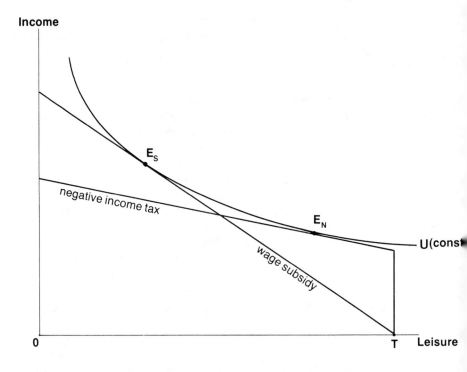

Although the work incentive effects are greater under a wage subsidy than a negative income tax, this does not necessarily make the wage subsidy a better plan. One distinct disadvantage of the wage subsidy is that it does nothing to maintain the income of those who are unable to work. Although it may help the working poor, it does nothing to help those who legitimately cannot work. For the latter group, a negative-income-tax plan would at least provide a guaranteed minimum income. Zeckhauser and Schuck (1970)

have suggested having both plans and allowing an individual to choose between them.

Because funds for income assistance are limited, an important aspect of an income maintenance scheme is the extent to which the program helps those most in need of assistance. Poverty and need are usually defined in terms of family income. For this reason, the negative income tax, which is based upon family income, is more likely to target payments to those in greatest need than a wage subsidy, which is based on individual wage rates. Many low-wage earners — especially youth and spouses of the primary income earner — are members of families with average or above-average income, resulting in a weak association between low individual wages and low family income. Simpson and Hum (1986) compare negative income tax and wage subsidy programs with equal budgets using microdata on Canadian families in 1981. They conclude that the negative income tax is clearly superior to wage subsidies in terms of its ability to divert payments to those families in greatest need of assistance.

Unemployment Insurance

In 1971 Canada's unemployment insurance legislation was changed to allow easier eligibility, extended coverage, larger benefits, and a longer duration of benefits. In part because of the high unemployment rate that prevailed during the 1970s, there has been considerable criticism of the changes. Specifically the concern was that the changes reduced the incentive to work and hence increased unemployment.

The income-leisure choice framework can be used to analyse the static, partial equilibrium effect that unemployment insurance will have on work incentives. Although the exact details of the Canadian legislation are extremely complicated, three key features are the minimum number of weeks of previous employment required to qualify for UI benefits, the maximum number of weeks of benefits that can be received, and the magnitude of UI benefits (usually expressed as a proportion of the individual's previous earnings). These characteristics of the Canadian UI program have changed over time and also vary across individuals according to such factors as the regional unemployment rate. The theoretical impact of these features of the UI system can be captured by a stylized example of an unemployment insurance scheme that gives recipients two-thirds of their weekly pay for a maximum period of one-half of a year (26 weeks) and that requires a minimum of 12 weeks of employment in order to qualify for benefits.

This hypothetical scheme is illustrated in Figure 4.3, using a one-year time horizon. The solid line AF is the potential income constraint in the absence of a UI program and the dashed line ABCDF is the constraint with unemployment insurance. If the individual works less than 12 weeks during the year, he does not qualify for UI benefits and his income constraint is the segment DF. If the individual works 12 weeks, he is eligible for benefits for an additional 26 weeks; thus his income equals 12 weeks of

Figure 4.3 Income Constraint for a Simplified Unemployment Insurance Scheme

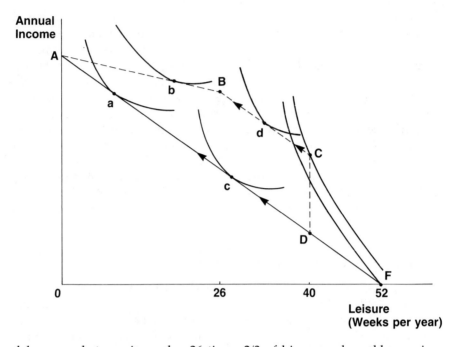

labour market earnings plus 26 times 2/3 of his normal weekly earnings; i.e. annual income Y = 12E + (2/3) 26E where E is weekly earnings. This gives the point C in Figure 4.3, the vertical distance CD equalling (2/3) 26E. As the person works additional weeks (moves from right to left from the point C), he can earn his weekly earnings as well as his unemployment insurance for a maximum period of 26 weeks. Thus his unemployment insurance constraint line is parallel to his original wage constraint between 40 and 26 weeks of leisure. If he works beyond 26 weeks in the year he takes home his weekly earnings, but forgoes the chance to collect the two-thirds of his weekly earnings through unemployment insurance. This occurs because he cannot legally work and collect unemployment insurance at the same time. Thus between 26 and 0 weeks of leisure, the unemployment insurance constraint has a slope of one-third, reflecting the fact that work beyond 26 weeks only increases potential income by one-third since one forgoes the unemployment insurance benefits of two-thirds of weekly earnings.

The nature of the work incentive effects of unemployment insurance depend on where the individual would be located in the absence of the UI system. Three different possibilities are shown in Figure 4.3. For individuals working more than 26 weeks (e.g. at the point a on AF), the income and substitution effects work in the same direction to *potentially* decrease weeks worked (moving to the point B on AB). For individuals such as those originally at the point c on AF, the unemployment insurance system constitutes a pure income effect, again *potentially* decreasing work incentives (moving to the point d on BC). These adverse work incentive effects are potential because the vast majority of people will not collect unemployment insurance. Many employees would not leave their job because they may not be able to return once they have exhausted unemployment insurance. However, for those with a guaranteed or reasonably certain job — be it seasonal, or with family friends, or in household activity, or perhaps one of many low-paid dead end jobs that can't attract other workers — there may be an incentive to collect unemployment insurance. In addition, the incentive would certainly be there for those who have lost their job, perhaps because of a recessionary phase in the business cycle, and hence who have no labour market alternatives.

The third possibility illustrated in Figure 4.3 applies to individuals who would be outside the labour force in the absence of a UI program. These individuals are originally located at the point F, reflecting the high value of their time devoted to non-market activities. Many such individuals would choose to remain outside the labour force and neither work nor collect unemployment insurance. Others, however, would enter the labour force and work a sufficient number of weeks in order to qualify for unemployment insurance benefits, locating at the point C in Figure 4.3. In this case the UI program has *increased* work incentives by making it attractive for these individuals to devote less time to non-market activities and to enter the labour force for relatively brief periods. Similar conclusions apply to those who would work fewer than 12 weeks in the absence of a UI system (i.e. those who would be located in the segment DF).

In summary, work incentives may be either increased or decreased by unemployment insurance. Some of those individuals who would, in the absence of a UI system, either be outside the labour force or work fewer weeks than are required to qualify for UI benefits will increase their weeks worked per year in order to receive unemployment insurance. In contrast, some of those individuals who would, in the absence of a UI system, work more than the minimum number of weeks required to qualify for UI will reduce their weeks worked per year and increase the number of weeks during which unemployment insurance benefits are received. Both these consequences of unemployment insurance may increase the unemployment rate, the former because it draws into the labour force individuals with marginal employment attachments who devote much of their time to non-market activities, and the latter because it reduces employment and increases unemployment of those with strong labour force attachment. The impact of the unemployment insurance system on unemployment is discussed further in the chapter on unemployment.

Unemployment-Insurance-Assisted Worksharing

One of the more recent innovative income maintenance schemes pertains to modifications to the unemployment insurance system to encourage worksharing. As defined in Meltz, Reid and Swartz (1981, p. 3), "Worksharing is an attempt to combat unemployment by reducing the number of hours each employee works rather than laying employees off when there is a reduction in the demand for labour." In the context of unemployment-insurance (UI)-assisted worksharing, the rationale was to encourage the sharing of unemployment amongst a broader work-force rather than having it concentrated in the hands of a few. As pointed out by Reid (1982, 1985) this could be not only more equitable but also more efficient if the larger work-force willingly accepted unemployment insurance payments for a small reduction in its workweek. Whether UI-assisted worksharing is a socially desirable method of combating unemployment depends on a number of factors such as whether the reduction in demand is temporary or permanent in nature, how the total UI costs associated with the reduction in labour demand are affected, and how the UI program is financed. These issues are discussed further in the chapter on unemployment. Rather than having the unemployment concentrated, for example, in 20 percent of the work-force who may be laid off (and receiving unemployment insurance), under UI-assisted worksharing the whole work-force of the firm may willingly accept a 20 percent (e.g., one day per week) reduction in their work in return for receiving unemployment insurance for the one day that they are each engaging in worksharing. This, of course, would require modification of the conventional unemployment insurance rules which are based on continuous unemployment, not on being "unemployed" for one day per week.

In 1977 on an experimental basis, and in 1982 on an economy-wide basis, Canada modified its unemployment insurance scheme to allow firms to apply for unemployment insurance for its work-force that willingly engaged in such worksharing. The scheme (discussed in Reid 1982, 1985) basically provides unemployment insurance benefits of two-thirds of each employee's lost wages for giving up an average of one day of work per week so that other workers in the firm would not have to be laid off.

Such an unemployment-insurance-assisted worksharing scheme is illustrated in Figure 4.4. The initial equilibrium at E_0 shows a hypothetical situation for a representative worker who works five days per week and takes home a weekly income of Y_0. An unemployment-insurance-assisted worksharing scheme that would allow each worker to choose any amount of work reduction would be illustrated by the dashed line budget constraint above the original budget constraint. For any work reduction (i.e., movement to the right of E_0) income would not fall by the loss of a day's pay for every day of work reduction, as would be depicted by the original budget constraint. Rather, it would fall by only one-third since two-thirds would be supported by the receipt of unemployment insurance. Figure 4.4 depicts the case where the parties agree to a one-day reduction in the workweek, and shows that this corresponds to the typical worker's preferred reduction (i.e., E_s is an equilibrium).

In reality, the negotiated reduction need not always correspond to

Figure 4.4   Unemployment-Insurance-Assisted Worksharing

the preferences of the work-force, in which case E_s need not be tangent to the new budget constraint; however, it is likely to involve a higher level of utility (i.e., $U_s > U_0$) because the worker gets an extra day of leisure by giving up only one-third of a day's pay, the remainder coming from unemployment insurance. Clearly, the unemployment-insurance-assisted worksharing can provide an incentive for workers to voluntarily reduce their working time and enter into worksharing arrangements.

Disability Payments and Worker's Compensation

Income maintenance programs for the disabled also exist in a variety of forms such as worker's compensation, disability pension entitlements from public and private pensions, long-term disability insurance (with premiums usually paid from joint contributions from employers and employees), and court awards for personal injury. In most cases, of course, the work incentive effects of such income maintenance programs are not of interest as payment is made precisely because the disability legitimately prevents a person from working and the person may have little discretion over how much to work. In some cases, however, there may be more discretion over whether to work and if so, how much to work. In such cases, the work incentive effects of disability income maintenance programs become a legitimate policy concern.

Prior to examining the impact of disability compensation, it is informative to examine the effect of the disability or injury itself.

Effect of Disability on Budget Constraint

Depending upon its nature, the injury may have a number of different effects on the individual's budget constraint (i.e., ability to earn income). A partially disabling injury could reduce the amount of time the individual can spend at the job, but not affect the person's performance and hence wage at the job. This is illustrated in Figure 4.5(a). Without any disabling injury, the worker's choice set is $Y\,H_f$, given the market wage rate as illustrated by the slope of the budget constraint. In this particular case the worker chooses E_0 with corresponding utility of U_0 and hours of work (measured right to left) of H_0. The partially disabling injury, for example, could reduce the amount of time the worker is able to work from H_0 to H_p. The worker's choice set is now limited to $E_p\,H_f$ with a corresponding drop in utility to U_p. If the injury were completely disabling so that the person could not work at all, then the person would be constrained to H_f, with no labour market income and utility reduced to U_f. This again highlights the misnomer associated with the phrase "leisure" — it is a catchall for all activities outside of the labour market, ranging from pure leisure to being unable to work because of disability.

In addition to affecting one's ability to earn income, a disabling injury may also require medical expenses. This affects the budget constraint, reducing income by the amount of medical expenses at each level of hours of work, analogous to a reduction in non-labour income. If the disabling injury led to such medical expenses but did not affect one's wage or ability to work in the labour market, then this would lead to a lower budget constraint like the dashed line $Y_m\,M$ in Figure 4.5(b). The individual's wage is not affected (i.e., $Y_m\,M$ is parallel to $Y\,H_f$), and the individual can work as much as before (i.e., $Y_m\,M$ is the full choice set); however, there are some fixed medical costs equal to $H_f\,M$ which also equals $Y\,Y_m$. If the individual does not work (i.e., the injury is a full disability so that the individual is compelled to move to H_f), then the medical costs are debts, as illustrated by the point M being below the axis (i.e., income is negative).

Because such fixed costs associated with medical expenses shift the budget constraint inwards without altering its slope, they will have a pure income effect, unambiguously reducing leisure and increasing hours of work, assuming leisure to be a normal commodity. The reduction in wealth associated with the injury cost means the household will buy less of all normal commodities, including leisure. Alternatively stated, the additional expenses mean that the individual would have to work more to prevent expenditure on goods from falling by the full amount of the medical ex-

Figure 4.5   Effect of Disability

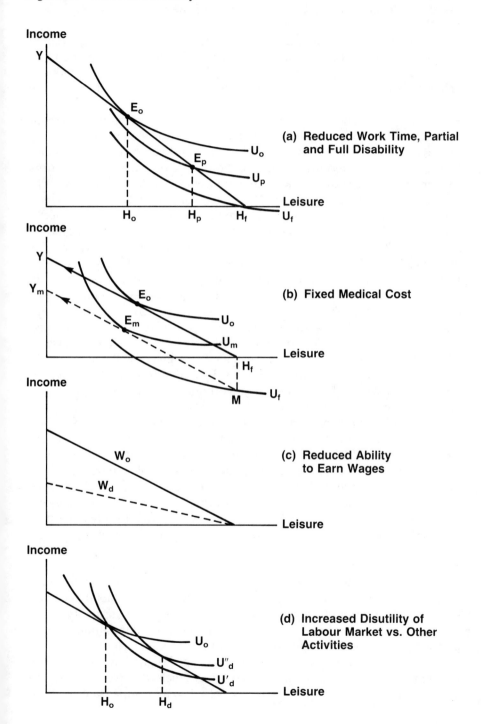

(a) Reduced Work Time, Partial and Full Disability

(b) Fixed Medical Cost

(c) Reduced Ability to Earn Wages

(d) Increased Disutility of Labour Market vs. Other Activities penses. This is illustrated in Figure 4.5(b) by the equilibrium E_m with its associated level of utility U_m, where E_m is to the left of E_0 and U_m is less than U_0.

If, in addition to these fixed medical costs, the injury also prevented the person from doing any labour market work, then the segment Y_m M of the budget constraint would not be available. In effect, the individual's "choice" set would be point M, with the corresponding reduced utility level U_f.

A disability that reduced one's ability to earn wages in the labour market would rotate the budget constraint downwards as in Figure 4.5(c). This would give rise to conventional income and substitution effects and hence have an indeterminate effect on hours of work. That is, the returns to work are reduced and hence one would work less (substitution effect). But one's wealth is also decreased, hence reducing one's ability to purchase commodities including leisure, thereby inducing more work (income effect).

A disability may also have a differential effect on the disutility associated with work or the ability to enjoy non-labour market activities. For example, if the disability gave rise to more pain and suffering associated with labour market activities than with household work, it would rotate the household utility isoquant as in Figure 4.5(d) so that the indifference curves U_d' and U_d'' are steeper in the disabled state, U_d, than in the non-disabled state, U_0. That is, to remain at the same level of utility, the disabled individual would require more income in return for a given increase in hours of work. For a given market wage rate (as given by the slope of the budget constraint) this would induce a substitution from labour market to non-labour market activities, reducing worktime from H_0 to H_d (work being measured from right to left on the diagram).

Obviously a disability may have a variety of the above effects. They were treated separately here only for expositional purposes. It is a relatively straightforward matter to portray them in various realistic combinations. For example, the disability may reduce the time one is able to work, reduce the wage, impose medical costs, and increase the disutility associated with labour market work as opposed to other activities. In such circumstances, the budget constraint and utility isoquants will change to reflect each of these effects and the incentive to work will be affected accordingly.

Effect of Compensation
To compensate for the previously discussed type of disability, various forms of compensation exist including worker's compensation, disability pension entitlements from public and private pensions, long-term disability insurance and court awards. The effect of such compensations upon welfare and work incentives depends upon the form of compensation.

Worker's compensation, for instance, is designed to support the recipient's income so it is not reduced by as much as it would be in the absence of the compensation. For example, it may compensate for two-thirds of the loss in one's former potential income, in which case the worker's compensation budget constraint appears as the dashed line $E_0 Y_d H_f$ in Figure 4.6(a). That is, as the worker is compelled to reduce work activity (move to the right of E_0), income does not fall by the full drop in take-home pay (as it would along $E_0 H_f$), but rather it falls by the proportion that it is not supported by worker's compensation. If worker's compensation were two-thirds of one's income loss then the fall in income would be one-third.

The policy challenge is to design a compensation scheme that compensates those who are legitimately disabled and hence in need of compensation and yet provides an incentive for them to return to work where feasible. The potential for an adverse work incentive effect for those who could legitimately return to work is exhibited by the fact that the worker's compensation budget constraint is like the previously discussed budget constraint under a negative income tax. That is, the additional income enables one to afford to work less (income effect); further, the reduced opportunity cost of leisure time that comes about because one forgoes disability payments as one increases hours of work (substitution effect) also discourages work activity. Obviously, for those who have no discretion over their ability to engage in more work activity, the incentive effects are not at issue. For some, however, they may discourage a return to work activity that they are capable of doing.

The availability of the full budget constraint $E_0 Y_d H_f$ presupposes that such compensation is available for any combination of partial disabilities that would reduce the person's work between H_0 and H_d. That is, depending upon preferences, workers could locate anywhere along the segment $E_0 Y_d$. If the compensation were available only if one could prove full disability, H_f, then the worker's options would be only the points Y_d and E_0. Assuming Y_d were above the indifference curve, U_0, as shown in Figure 4.6(a), then the worker would choose the point Y_d.

Figure 4.6(b) illustrates such a situation where the worker receives the worker's compensation for the full disability and has no incentive to return to work, assuming of course that such an option were feasible. The compensation ($E_c H_f$) is such that the worker is better off by not working and receiving the compensation (point E_c) than by returning to work (point E_0). That is, utility under compensation (U_c) is greater than utility under work (U_0). Even though income by working would be greater than income under compensation, it is not sufficient to offset the disutility associated with the additional work.

However, not providing any compensation runs the risk that individuals who legitimately cannot return to work have their utility level reduced to U_f. Clearly, lowering the compensation level so that U_c is below U_0 would induce a return to work activities from those who can legitimately engage in such work; however, it runs the risk of penalizing those who legitimately cannot return to work. Also, when one considers the consid-

Figure 4.6 Effect of Compensation

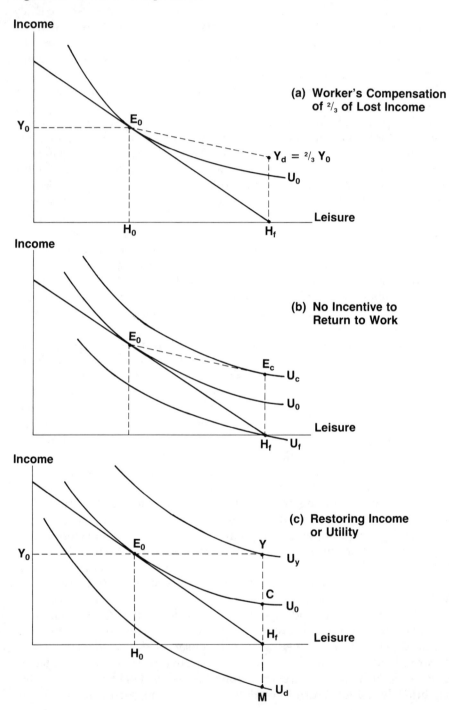

(a) Worker's Compensation of $2/3$ of Lost Income

(b) No Incentive to Return to Work

(c) Restoring Income or Utility

erable medical costs and pain and suffering that are often associated with disability, it becomes less likely that compensating someone for a portion of their lost earnings would make them better off.

Different amounts of compensation are also involved depending upon the position to which the recipient is to be returned. Figure 4.6(c) illustrates the situation where a permanently disabling injury prevents the individual from working at all (i.e., forces the individual to locate at H_f) and gives rise to medical costs of H_f M. These events reduce the individual's well-being from U_0 to U_d. A court award to compensate for the individual's loss of earnings, Y H_f, plus medical costs, H_f M, would lead to a total award of YM. This would clearly leave the individual better off than before ($U_y > U_0$) because the individual is not experiencing the disutility associated with working. If, however, the disability results in pain and suffering then the individual's ability to enjoy goods and leisure consumption may be reduced and the individual could be worse off than before, even with the compensation award of YM (and possibly even with some additional compensation for pain and suffering).

If the court wanted to restore an individual to their former level of well-being or utility, U_0, then an award of CM would be appropriate. The problem is to assess the value the individual may attach to not having to work. This is given in the diagram by YC, which is the income reduction the individual would have willingly accepted to reduce work activity from H_0 to H_f (equal to E_0 Y) and to remain indifferent to being at E_0 with utility U_0. The problem is that YC is not observed; all that is observed is the person's income Y H_f.

This clearly illustrates the dilemma any court or administrative tribunal would have in arriving at compensation to "restore the person in whole." Different amounts are involved if this is interpreted to be the previous level of income as opposed to welfare or well-being.

LONG-RUN DYNAMIC EFFECTS OF INCOME MAINTENANCE

The previous analysis dealt with the short-run, static effects of income maintenance programs on the incentive to work. It was found, not surprisingly, that most forms of income maintenance would probably reduce work incentives in the short run. Some, such as welfare, would reduce effort more than others. Others, such as a wage subsidy program, raised the possibility (but not necessity) of increasing work incentives.

In a dynamic context, over a longer period of time, other factors may be affected by the particular income maintenance program, and these in turn may affect work incentives. Some of these dynamic factors are discussed in Boskin (1967), Conlisk (1968), Garfinkel (1973), Kesselman (1969, 1974), Rea (1974), and Ribbich (1971). The most important factors that could change over time are motivation and human capital formation, the latter involving investments in education, training, health, mobility or job search.

Obviously, income maintenance programs could affect these factors, and they in turn could affect work incentives, leading to a modification of the original conclusions concerning the adverse incentive effects of most income maintenance schemes.

Conlisk (1968), for example, criticized the static, work-leisure model for ignoring the effect of income maintenance schemes on motivation to work. In a formal, dynamic model, he illustrated the common-sense conclusion that an income maintenance program that supplements low incomes may increase the motivation of low-income people to work and that, in the long run, this may offset the static, adverse incentive effects. Their increased motivation to work could occur as their increased income expands their aspirations and preferences for additional income as they "get hooked" on a new set of wants or incur debts and mortgages associated with middle income consumption patterns.

In his criticism of the work-leisure "myth," Kaun (1969) emphasizes that leisure may be an inferior good for low-income people, mainly because they do not have the income to enjoy the leisure. Rather than purchase an additional "quantity" of leisure with their supplemented income, they may choose to work more and purchase higher "quality" leisure, in the form of shorter but perhaps more expensive leisure.

Perhaps the most important long-run adjustments that result from income maintenance programs occur in the area of changes in the *quality* of labour. This process — termed human capital formation — involves incurring costs in the present to increase earnings capacity in the future. Economic theory predicts that human capital formation occurs until the extra benefits are no longer worth the extra costs. If income maintenance schemes increase the benefits from human capital formation, then human capital formation would increase; if income maintenance increases the costs (where costs include the forgone income or opportunity cost of not working), then human capital formation would decrease. Therefore, to analyse the effect of income maintenance on the quality of labour, we must know how it affects the benefits and costs of human capital formation via such processes as education, training, mobility, health or job search.

Since most of the income maintenance schemes result in a reduction of work incentives, then there would be a reduction in the benefit period from which to recoup the investment costs of human capital formation. In addition, if work incentives are reduced, experience and informal on-the-job training (learning by doing) are reduced and skill obsolescence becomes more likely. This is especially the case if the reduced work incentives involve leaving the labour force for an extended period of time. These factors would tend to reduce human capital formation. Since the wage subsidy involves the possibility (but not necessity) of increased work incentives, it has the potential of increasing human capital formation. On the other hand, a reduction in labour supply may provide the time necessary for productive activities like job search or education. An example may clarify these forces. Suppose an income supplement program encourages a family to reduce its labour supply by having one of its members withdraw from the labour force. This person would not only lose the experience and informal training associated with the labour market, but will have little incentive to acquire formal training or job search that would improve labour market productivity. On the other hand, the withdrawal from the labour force may enable this person to have time to engage in such activities as formal education or job search that could improve labour market productivity in the future.

Income maintenance programs may also affect human capital formation through their impact on the tax rate of recipients. If they involve a tax on labour earnings, as with the negative income tax and welfare, then there is less incentive to acquire human capital since the *benefits* in the form of higher earnings will be taxed. On the other hand, since after-tax earnings are reduced, the income forgone during the human capital formation period is reduced; hence the opportunity *cost* of human capital formation decreases and this may encourage improvements in labour quality. The net effect of the tax increase depends on the relative strength of the above two forces which, in turn, depends on the length of time of the human capital formation period and the degree of permanency of the income maintenance scheme. If the human capital formation takes a long time or if the income maintenance program is temporary, so that the opportunity cost is reduced during the human capital formation period but earnings are not reduced afterwards, then investment in human capital will increase. However, in the more usual case that would involve a short human capital formation period and a more permanent income maintenance program, then investment in labour quality would decrease.

The dynamic work incentive effects from the tax in a wage subsidy scheme are more complicated and depend on the particular form of the wage subsidy. If, as outlined earlier, the wage subsidy involves a guaranteed minimum wage and a tax on market wages, then there would be less incentive to engage in human capital formation to raise wages because of the tax on wages. And, if the guaranteed minimum wage were independent of the market wage, then there would be no incentive to raise one's market wage so as to get a higher guaranteed wage. On the other hand, if the subsidy were an earnings subsidy (e.g. Haveman, 1973, p. 59) that was a certain percentage of earnings and hence wages, then there would be an incentive to increase wages through human capital formation to get a larger subsidy. This is illustrated in Rea (1974, pp. 42-44).

Since income maintenance programs by definition increase the potential wealth of the recipients, this wealth effect may encourage human capital formation in a variety of ways. The extra income could be used to finance the investment, which for low-income families may be important, especially if they were previously unable to borrow to finance their investment in human capital. In addition, the increased wealth may alter preferences towards income-earnings activities, and hence encourage human capital formation that would improve future income. Finally, the increased wealth may encourage the consumption of such things as education and, to the extent that the consumption and investment components of such activities are inseparable, human capital formation would increase.

Income maintenance schemes may also increase human capital formation through what may be termed an eligibility effect. Individuals may engage in human capital investments in order to be eligible for income maintenance schemes, either because their income would be sufficiently reduced while in the human capital process, or because human capital formation may be a sufficient condition for receipt of the income support. This would lower the opportunity cost of human capital formation, since the loss of labour market earnings would be lessened by the income support. In the case of those eligible for a negative income tax, for example, the opportunity cost of human capital formation would be their potential earnings less the guarantee. Hence human capital formation would increase. This process is described in Ribich's (1971, p. 309) discussion of the effect of a negative income tax on the decision to acquire further education: "An individual who is currently spending a good part of his time earning income will find that if he chooses to spend some of that time in pursuit of education, the forgone earnings portion of his educational investment will be at least partially covered out of public funds. For some individuals the subsidy will of course not apply, since their incomes during an education program will not drop below the levels required for payment eligibility, but for many others the negative income tax will figure in decisions about undertaking full-time education or training."

Discussion of both the short- and long-run effects of income maintenance programs often proceeds by comparing the consequences of each policy to those that would occur without income maintenance. However, for most policy purposes the relevant issue is the form which income maintenance should take rather than whether or not to engage in income maintenance. As with the short-run effects, some forms of income maintenance may have more favourable long-run consequences than others. For example, an advantage of a negative income tax program over welfare is that the negative income tax scheme encourages some of those who would not work at all under welfare to engage in some work activity, thus gaining some experience and on-the-job training and potentially improving their future wage and employment prospects.

Clearly the long-run, dynamic incentive effects that income maintenance programs will have on human capital formation are extremely complicated. They differ depending upon the particular income maintenance scheme, and even for a given scheme the effects are often theoretically ambiguous. This highlights the importance of obtaining empirical evidence not only on the short-run work incentive effects on the *quantity* of labour supplied, but also on the long-run incentives on the *quality* of labour. Only with this evidence will we know whether the long-run effects exacerbate or mitigate the short-run effects which usually predict a reduction in work effort.

GENERAL EQUILIBRIUM EFFECTS OF INCOME MAINTENANCE

Income maintenance programs will also have general equilibrium effects as their initial impact is spread through the economy as a whole and has feedbacks on the behaviour of recipients. Of particular interest is the general equilibrium effect on the (before-tax) market wages of both recipients and taxpayers.

Browning (1973) discusses the general equilibrium effect for a negative income tax and a wage subsidy: the former will be illustrated here. Since a negative income tax unambiguously reduces work incentives relative to a situation in which there is no income maintenance, then the reduction in labour supply will raise the market wages of transfer recipients. This is illustrated in Figure 4.7 where S_0 is the supply of transfer recipient labour without the negative income tax and S_N represents a new reduced supply after the program. S_N lies to the left of S_0 by an amount equal to the sum of the labour supply reductions of all recipients. Clearly their wages after the negative income tax will rise to w_N. If the supply of labour is upward-sloping to the right, then this increase in their market wage will induce an increase in labour supply (along S_N), thereby offsetting some of the initial adverse work incentives. In the final equilibrium, the reduction in labour supply will be only $N_0 - N_G$, not $N_0 - N_N$.

Figure 4.7   General Equilibrium Effects of a Negative Income Tax

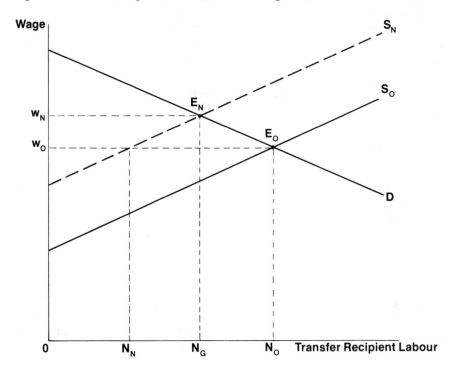

This has important policy implications since it suggests not only that the adverse work incentives will be partly offset, but also that the pre-transfer income of recipients is less likely to fall because, although their labour supply is reduced, their market wage increases. In addition, the increased market wage suggests that minimum wage legislation would be less necessary for recipients since market forces will serve to raise their market wage. This conclusion is in marked contrast to the suggestion that minimum wage laws would have to be more strictly enforced to prevent employers from cutting wages, knowing that the government will support the earnings of low-wage individuals. This latter conclusion is based on the tenuous assumption that firms pay wages on the basis of the economic needs of their employees and it ignores the basic economic forces that would be at work to raise wages of workers in reduced supply.

The general equilibrium effects of replacing existing welfare programs by a negative income tax scheme are more complex. The negative income tax increases labour supply of those individuals receiving welfare assistance, thus tending to reduce their wage (i.e. a rightward shift of the supply curve in Figure 4.7). However, the negative income tax also tends to reduce the labour supply of those individuals earning less than the break-even income (point B in Figure 4.1(c)) but not receiving welfare — the working poor. This reduction in labour supply increases the wages of low-wage workers, as illustrated in Figure 4.7. These effects offset each other; thus the net effect on the wages of transfer income recipients of replacing existing welfare programs by a negative income tax is theoretically ambiguous and depends on which of the two effects is larger.

A negative income tax will also have an effect on the wages, income and welfare of the rest of society — those who pay for the plan. If the negative income tax reduces labour supply, the real income of non-recipients as a group will fall because society's total output declines due to the decline in labour input and the real income of recipients rises due to income supplementation. It is possible that the income of *some* taxpayers will rise if they are good substitutes for the transfer recipient labour that is in reduced supply. Nevertheless, on net their income as a group must fall because their productivity is reduced as they work with fewer units of transfer recipient labour.

This has important policy implications since it suggests that the cost of the program to the rest of society is not only the transfer cost (the income supplement to the recipients), but also the lower income that taxpayers have because of the reduction in society's total output. This general equilibrium effect may lead to more resistance on the part of taxpayers to such a program.

EVIDENCE OF INCENTIVE EFFECTS

Evidence on incentive effects of income maintenance programs comes from both non-experimental and experimental sources. Non-experimental studies relate measures of labour supply to various parameters related to the income maintenance scheme, notably wages and non-labour income. In addition, results from experiments in the U.S. are available on the incentive effects of various negative income tax plans. These results are discussed in more detail in Watts and Rees (1973), Cain (1974), Peckman and Timpane (1975), Moffitt (1981), and Basilevsky and Hum (1984).

Results from the non-experimental literature are of dubious use in analysing the work incentive effects of low-income families, not only because of their wide variation in results, but also because they generally apply to middle- and high-income families. In spite of their wide variation in results, they generally confirm the static predictions of the work-leisure model. Other things being equal, an increase in non-labour income (such as would come about from a demogrant, a negative income tax guarantee, welfare, or unemployment insurance) reduces labour supply, confirming the existence of a pure income effect. Other things being equal (including family income), a decrease in wages (such as would come about from the tax rate in a negative income tax or welfare) also decreases labour supply, confirming the existence of a pure or compensated substitution effect. For most groups in the economy, the income effect appears to dominate the substitution effect, so that wage increases have been associated with a reduction in labour supply. For women, especially married women, most studies conclude that the substitution effect dominates the income effect, so that wage increases have been associated with an increase in labour supply. However, as discussed subsequently, some recent research has questioned this conclusion and has found that, for women who work full time, wage increases are associated with a decrease in labour supply.

This suggests that for most income maintenance programs, work incentives will be altered as predicted by the static theory. Demogrants involve only a pure income effect which would reduce incentives similar to increases in non-labour income. Negative income taxes, welfare, and unemployment insurance have income and pure substitution effects working in the same direction to reduce incentives. Wage subsidies with their income and substitution effects working in the opposite direction would probably reduce work incentives for most groups except perhaps females, especially married females and those who work part-time.

Because of the variety of results from these empirical studies, and because they were not obtained by observing the behaviour of low-income individuals, experiments have been conducted using low-income families. The available evidence comes mainly from four U.S. negative-income-tax experiments: New Jersey and Pennsylvania (1968-72); rural areas of North Carolina and Iowa (1970-72); Seattle and Denver (1970-78); and Gary, Indiana (1971-74). (A Canadian experiment was carried out in Manitoba during the period 1975-79; however, analysis of the results of this program has yet to be carried out.) Different families were given varying amounts of basic guaranteed income and their labour market earnings were subjected to various tax rates. Their work behaviour was then compared to that of a control group of similar families that were not under a negative-income-tax plan.

Moffitt (1981, p. 24) summarizes the effect on work incentives of the four experiments, based on an average tax rate of 0.50 and a guarantee level about equal to the poverty line. The conclusions are: (1) overall hours of work are unequivocally reduced by the presence of the negative income tax; (2) the disincentive effects vary considerably by demographic group with the reduction in hours of work ranging from 1 to 8 percent for husbands, 0 to 55 percent for wives, and 12 to 28 percent for female heads of families; (3) the work reduction for men occurred more in the form of reduced employment to zero hours of work for a small number of the men rather than marginal reductions in the hours of work of those who remained employed; (4) some marginal reductions in hours of work did occur through reduced overtime; (5) the reduced employment often occurred in the form of a lengthening of time spent between jobs for men and increased school attendance for youths; however, these responses did not appear to lead to subsequent wage gains; (6) for most groups, disincentive effects generally occurred in response to both the guarantee and the implicit tax rate, although the groups seemed more responsive to changes in the guarantee than the tax rate; (7) the longer the program the greater the disincentive effects, suggesting that the disincentive effects may be larger for a permanent as opposed to temporary program.

INCOME MAINTENANCE: CURRENT POLICY ISSUES

Recent proposals for changes to the Canadian income security system illustrate several of the issues raised in this chapter. In its 1985 Report, the Royal Commission on the Economic Union and Development Prospects for Canada (the Macdonald Commission) recommended fundamental reform of existing income maintenance programs. The centrepiece of its proposal was the Universal Income Security Program (UISP), a negative income tax program that would supplement the income of families with low incomes. Also recommended were substantial changes to the existing Unemployment Insurance (UI) system and the introduction of a Transitional Adjustment Assistance Program (TAAP) designed to assist individuals to adjust to changing economic circumstances through relocation and retraining. Subsequently, in its 1986 Report, the Commission of Inquiry on Unemployment Insurance (the Forget Commission) also recommended substantial changes to the unemployment insurance system and proposed a negative income tax scheme for supplementing low family incomes. Proposals similar to those of the Macdonald and Forget Commissions were also made by the Newfoundland Royal Commission on Employment and Unemployment (the Hause Commission) in its 1986 Report. Although the details of the proposals made in these Commission Reports differ in important ways, the general nature of the proposed reforms — in particular the adoption of a universal negative income tax scheme — are similar.

A common theme of these three Commission Reports is the need for substantial reform of existing income maintenance programs. Several factors contribute to the need for reform. The adverse incentives associated with the existing welfare or social assistance programs are an important consideration. As discussed previously, most welfare programs involve an implicit 100 percent tax on income from work, as welfare benefits are reduced dollar-for-dollar in response to any employment income. The tax can exceed 100 percent if those who earn income not only forgo their welfare benefits but also additional benefits such as subsidized housing or dental care. Relative to welfare, the negative income tax scheme provides stronger work incentives as individuals who are able to do some market work earn higher after-tax incomes. In the short run this employment income reduces the amount of income received from the state (although not dollar-for-dollar, so that the implicit tax rate is less than 100 percent) and thus reduces the burden on other taxpayers. In the long run the need for income assistance may be eliminated as individuals gain work experience and skills.

A second reason for reform is the existence of a significant number of the "working poor" — individuals who are employed but whose family incomes fall below the poverty line. In Canada these individuals receive little or no assistance from the state. A negative income tax scheme would supplement the income of these families, thus reducing the amount of poverty in Canada. Some reduction in the hours of work of these individuals may occur; as noted previously, relative to a situation of no income assistance, the negative income tax produces income and substitution effects which tend to reduce hours of work. The magnitude of these adverse work effects will depend on the program parameters — specifically, the income guarantee and the implicit tax rate.

The Macdonald Commission's proposed UISP would provide a low basic income guarantee (in 1984 dollars, $2750 per adult and $750 per child under 18, with an extra $2000 for single parents and an extra $1075 for the single elderly) and a low tax rate (20 percent). This combination of design parameters minimizes adverse work incentives for those who are able to work yet provides substantial additional income for the working poor. However, for those who are unable to work, the income guarantee (for example, $7000 per year for a family of four) is not sufficient to meet basic family needs. For this reason, the Macdonald Commission proposed a "two-tier" system, with unemployables receiving the basic income guarantee from the federal government and additional assistance from the relevant provincial government. Those able to work would not be eligible for these provincial "top-ups."

This type of two-tier negative income tax scheme, in which a distinction is made between employables and unemployables, has significant advantages over a single-tier scheme. In particular, it is extremely difficult to design a single-tier negative income tax system which (i) has a minimum income guarantee that is sufficient to meet the basic needs of those who are unable or not expected to work, (ii) has a low implicit tax rate so that incentives to work are maintained and (iii) is feasible in terms of total cost.

A third aspect of reform is the unemployment insurance program. Although the primary purpose of this program is to provide insurance against the risk of income loss associated with unemployment, UI has evolved into an income maintenance program in certain regions (especially the Maritimes and eastern Quebec) and industries (especially fishing, forestry and construction). However, UI is not well suited as an income maintenance program for several reasons. Income maintenance objectives focus on family income and need whereas UI benefits are based on the individual worker's income and are not related to assets or need. In addition, income support programs attempt to reconcile family income and need over periods of six months to one year whereas UI is based on a much shorter accounting period (weekly). Unemployment insurance could be altered further to achieve income distribution goals — for example, by basing UI benefits on family income and need (e.g. number of dependents) and testing for other income and assets — but such changes would reduce the program's insurance role. The proposals of the Macdonald and Forget Commissions are designed to focus UI strictly on the insurance objective and to leave income distribution objectives to programs explicitly designed for that purpose — such as the Macdonald Commission's UISP. In addition, the proposals are designed to reduce some of the adverse work incentive effects that have been found to be associated with the existing unemployment insurance program. (These are discussed further in the chapter on unemployment.)

In summary, recent analyses of Canada's income security programs have concluded that the work incentive effects of these programs — in particular, welfare and unemployment insurance — are a matter of policy concern. At the same time, significant gaps exist in these programs, especially with respect to the working poor. In order to remedy these deficiencies, public inquiries have recommended replacing existing income support programs (such as the Canada Assistance Plan, Child Tax Credit, Family Allowances, and Guaranteed Income Supplement) by a universal two-tier negative income tax scheme. Major revisions to the unemployment insurance program have also been proposed.

QUESTIONS

1. Use the work-leisure choice diagram to illustrate that, under normal circumstances, if an individual is given a demogrant, take-home pay will not increase by as much as the demogrant. Why is this so?

2. Illustrate the work incentive effects of a demogrant on a disabled person who is unable to work.

3. The negative income tax involves a positive guarantee which has a pure income effect reducing work effort. It also involves a tax increase on the earned income of recipients, and this has both an income and sub-

stitution effect working in the opposite direction in their effect on work incentives. Consequently, we are unable to predict unambiguously the static, partial-equilibrium effects that a negative-income-tax plan would have on work incentives. Indicate why this last statement is wrong.

4. Use the work-leisure choice diagram to illustrate the following cases where an individual is: unwilling to go on welfare because the welfare payment is too low; indifferent between welfare and work; induced to move off welfare because of an increase in his wage; induced to move off welfare because of a change in his preferences between income and leisure; induced to move off welfare by a reduction of the 100 percent implicit tax on earnings.

5. What is the break-even wage rate for the wage subsidy scheme outlined in the text? (The break-even wage is the wage rate at which the post-subsidy wage equals the market wage so that the subsidy is zero.)

6. Use the work-leisure framework to illustrate that if we hold the post-subsidy income of the recipients constant or the size of the subsidy constant, a negative income tax will involve more adverse work incentives than would a wage subsidy.

7. In an unemployment insurance diagram like Figure 4.3, depict the case where the individual must work eight weeks before becoming eligible to collect unemployment insurance.

8. Compare the effects that a wage subsidy and a negative income tax would have on the decision to acquire more education that is labour market oriented.

9. Indicate the general equilibrium effects of a wage subsidy on the market wages and work incentives of recipients, and on the income of the rest of society. Assume that the labour supply schedule of transfer recipient labour is upward sloping to the right.

REFERENCES AND FURTHER READINGS

Barr, N. and R. Hall. The probability of dependence on public assistance. *Economica* 48 (May 1981) 109-124.

Basilevsky, A. and D. Hum. *Experimental Social Programs and Analytical Methods: An Evaluation of the U.S. Income Maintenance Projects.* New York: Academic Press, 1984.

Berkowitz, M., W. Johnson and E. Murphy. *Public Policy Toward Disability.* New York: Praeger Publishers, 1976.

Betson, D. and J. Bishop. Reform of the tax system to stimulate labor supply: efficiency and distributional effects. *IRRA* (September 1980) 307-315.

Binmore, K., A. Shaked and J. Sutton. Race, recent entry and labor market participation, testing non-cooperative bargaining theory: a preliminary study. *AER* 75 (December 1985) 1178-1180.

Bishop, J. The general equilibrium impact of alternative antipoverty strategies. *ILRR* 32 (January 1979) 205-223.

Blau, D. and P. Robins. Labor supply response to welfare programs: a dynamic analysis. *JOLE* 4 (January 1986) 82-104.

Blomquist, N. The effect of income taxation on the labor supply of married men in Sweden. *JPubEc* 22 (November 1983) 169-198.

Boskin, M. The negative income tax and the supply of work effort. *National Tax Journal* 20 (December 1967) 355-357.

Browning, E. Alternative programs for income redistribution: the NIT and the NWT. *AER* 63 (March 1973) 38-49.

Burkhauser, R. and R. Haverman. *Disability and Work: The Economics of American Policy*. Baltimore: The Johns Hopkins Press, 1982.

Burtless, G. and D. Greenberg. Inferences concerning labor supply behavior based on limited-duration experiments. *AER* 72 (June 1982) 488-497.

Burtless, G. and D. Greenberg. Measuring the impact of NIT experiment on work effort. *ILRR* 36 (July 1983) 592-605.

Burtless, G. and J. Hausman. The effect of taxation on labor supply: evaluating the Gary negative income tax experiment. *JPE* 86 (December 1978) 1103-1130.

Cain, G. (ed.) Symposium articles — the graduated work incentive experiment. *JHR* 9 (Spring 1974).

Cain, G. and H. Watts. *Income Maintenance and Labor Supply*. Chicago: Rand McNally, 1973.

Cogan, J. Labor supply and negative income taxation: new evidence from the New Jersey-Pennsylvania experiment. *EI* 21 (October 1983) 465-484.

Conlisk, J. Simple dynamic effects in work-leisure choice: a skeptical comment on the static theory. *JHR* 3 (Summer 1968) 324-326.

Cowell, F. Taxation and labour supply with risky activities. *Economica* 48 (Nov. 1981) 365-380.

Cowell, F. Tax evasion with labour income. *JPubEc* 26 (February 1985) 19-34.

Daymont, T. and P. Andrisani. Some causes and consequences of disability benefit receipt. *IRRA* (December 1983) 177-188.

Fenn, P. Sickness duration, residual disability, and income replacement: an empirical analysis. *EJ* 91 (March 1981) 158-173.

Fortin, B. Income security in Canada. In *Income Distribution and Economic Security in Canada*. F. Vaillancourt (ed.). Toronto: University of Toronto Press, 1985, 153-86.

Garfinkel, I. A skeptical note on the optimality of wage subsidy programs. *AER* 63 (June 1973) 447-453.

Garfinkel, I. and S. Masters. *Estimating Labor Supply Effects of Income Maintenance Alternatives*. New York: Academic Press, 1978.

Green, C. Negative taxes and the monetary incentives to work: the static theory. *JHR* 3 (Summer 1968) 280-288.

Greenberg, D. and H. Halsey. Systematic misreporting and effects of income maintenance experiments on work effort: Evidence from the Seattle-Denver experiment. *JOLE* 1 (October 1983) 380-407.

Gwartney, J. and R. Stroup. Labor supply and tax rates: a correction of the record. *AER* 73 (June 1983) 446-451. Also, comments and replies 76 (March 1986) 277-285.

Hanoch, G. and M. Honig. The labor supply curve under income maintenance programs. *JPubEc* 9 (February 1978) 1-16.

Hansson, I. and C. Stuart. Taxation, government spending, and labor supply: a diagrammatic exposition. *EI* 21 (October 1983) 584-587.

Haveman, R. Work-conditioned subsidies as an income maintenance strategy. *Studies in Public Welfare*, Joint Economic Committee. Washington: U.S. Government Printing Office, 1973.

Haveman, R. and B. Wolfe. Disability transfers and early retirement: a causal relationship? *JPubEc* 24 (June 1984) 47-66.

Heckman, J. Effects of child-care programs on women's work effort. *JPE* 82 (March/April 1974) S136-S163.

Hemming, R. Income tax progressivity and labor supply. *JPubEc* 14 (August 1980) 95-100.

Hurd, M. and J. Pencavel. A utility-based analysis of the wage subsidy program. *JPubEc* 15 (April 1981) 185-202.

Ippolito, R. Income tax policy and lifetime labor supply. *JPubEc* 26 (April 1985) 327-348.

Johnson, T. and J. Pencavel. Forecasting the effects of a negative income tax program. *ILRR* 35 (January 1982) 221-234.

Johnson, W. The effect of a negative income tax on risk-taking in the labor market. *EI* 18 (July 1980) 395-407.

Kaun, D. A comment on the work-leisure myth. *Review of Radical Political Economy* 1 (May 1969) 85-88.

Keeley, M. *Labor Supply and Public Policy.* Toronto: Academic Press, 1981.

Keeley, M., P. Robbins, R. Spiegelman and R. West. The estimation of labor supply models using experimental data. *AER* 68 (December 1975) 873-887.

Keeley, M., P. Robbins, R. Spiegelman and R. West. The labor supply effects and costs of alternative income tax progams. *JHR* 13 (Winter 1978) 3-36.

Kesselman, J. Labour supply effects of income, income-work, and wage subsidies. *JHR* 4 (Summer 1969) 275-292.

Kesselman, J. Conditional subsidies in income maintenance. *WEJ* 9 (March 1971) 1-20.

Kesselman, J. A comprehensive approach to income maintenance: SWIFT. *JPubEc* 2 (February 1973) 59-88.

Kesselman, J. Egalitarianism of earnings and income taxes. *JPubEc* 5 (April/May 1976) 285-302.

Kesselman, J. Tax effects on job search, training and work effort. *JPubEc* 6 (October 1976) 255-272.

Kesselman, J. and I. Garfinkel. Professor Friedman meet Lady Rhys-Williams: NIT vs. CIT. *JPubEc* 10 (October 1978) 179-216.

Killingsworth, M. Must a negative income tax reduce labor supply? *JHR* 11 (Summer 1976) 354-365.

Leuthold, J. An empirical study of formula income transfers and the work decision of the poor. *JHR* 3 (Summer 1968) 312-323.

Leuthold, J. The effect of taxation on the hours worked by married women. *ILRR* 31 (July 1978) 520-526.

Levy, F. The labor supply of female household heads, or AFDC work incentives don't work too well. *JHR* 14 (Winter 1979) 76-97.

Lindbeck, A. Tax effects versus budget effects on labor supply. *EI* 20 (October 1982) 473-489.

Lurie, I. *Integrating Income Maintenance Programs.* New York: Academic Press, 1975.

Marvel, H. An economic analysis of the operation of social security disability insurance. *JHR* 17 (Summer 1982) 393-412.

Masters, S. and I. Garfinkel. *Estimating the Labor Supply Effects of Income-Maintenance Alternatives.* New York: Academic Press, 1978.

Meltz, N., F. Reid and G. Swartz. *Sharing the Work.* Toronto: University of Toronto Press, 1981.

Meyer, J. The impact of welfare benefit levels and tax rates on the labor supply of poor women. *R.E. Stats.* 17 (May 1975) 236-237.

Moffitt, R. The negative income tax: would it discourage work? *MLR* 104 (April 1981) 23-27.

Moffitt, R. and K. Kehrer. The effect of tax and transfer programs on labor supply: the evidence from the income maintenance experiments. In R. Ehrenberg (ed.) *Research in Labor Economics*. Greenwich, Conn.: JAI Press, 1981.

Nagi, S. and L. Hadley. Disability behavior, income change and motivation to work. *ILRR* 25 (January 1972) 223-235.

Parsons, D. The decline in male labor force participation. *JPE* 88 (Feb. 1980) 117-134. Also comments by R. Haveman and B. Wolf, and reply, 92 (June 1984) 532-549.

Parsons, D. The male labour force participation decision: health, reported health, and economic incentives. *Economica* 49 (Feb. 1982) 81-92.

Peckman, J. and P. Timpane (eds.). *Work Incentives and Income Guarantee: The New Jersey Negative Income Tax Experiment*. Washington: Brookings, 1975.

Prescott, D., R. Swidinsky and C. Wilton. Labour supply estimates for low-income female heads of households using M income data. *CJE* 19 (February 1986) 134-141.

Rea, S. Incentive effects of alternative negative income tax plans. *JPubEc* 3 (August 1974) 237-249.

Rea, S. Investment in human capital under a negative income tax. *CJE* 10 (November 1977) 607-620.

Reid, F. UI-assisted worksharing as an alternative to layoffs: the Canadian experience. *ILRR* 35 (April 1982) 319-329.

Reid, F. Reductions in worktime: an assessment of employment sharing to reduce unemployment. *Work and Pay*. W.C. Riddell, ed. Toronto: University of Toronto Press, 1985.

Ribich, T. Negative income taxes and education. *Income Maintenance*. L. Orr and others (eds.). Chicago: Markham, 1971, 308-324.

Rosen, H. Tax illusion and the labour supply of married women. *R..E. Stats.* 58 (May 1976) 167-172.

Rosen, H. Taxes in a labor supply model with joint wage-hours determination. *Econometrica* 44 (May 1976) 485-507.

Scheffler, R. and G. Iden. The effect of disability on labor supply. *ILRR* 28 (October 1974) 122-132.

Slade, F. Older men: disability insurance and the incentive to work. *IR* 23 (Spring 1984) 260-269.

Solon, G. Work incentive effects of taxing unemployment benefits. *Econometrica* 53 (March 1985) 295-306.

Stelcner, M. and J. Breslaw. Income taxes and the labor supply of married women in Quebec. *SEJ* 51 (April 1985) 1053-1072.

Swisher, I. The disabled and the decline in men's labor force participation. *MLR* 96 (November 1973) 53.

Walsh, W. A time series analysis of female labor force participation rates disaggregated by marital status. *RI/IR* 37 (1982) 367-382.

Watson, H. Tax evasion and labor markets. *JPubEc* 27 (July 1985) 231-246.

Watts, H. and A. Rees (eds.). *The New Jersey Graduated Work Incentive Experiments*, Vols. 1-3. Madison: University of Wisconsin Institute for Research on Poverty, 1973.

Watts, H. and A. Rees (eds.). *The New Jersey Income Maintenance Experiment*. New York: Academic Press, 1978.

Zeckhauser, R. and P. Schuck. An alternative to the Nixon income maintenance plan. *Public Interest* 19 (Spring 1970) 120-130.

5 Labour Force Participation

The labour force participation decision is basically a decision to participate in labour market activities as opposed to other activities such as household work, education or retirement. As such it influences the size and composition of our labour force and it has an impact on household activities, education and retirement programs.

The policy implications of these changes can be dramatic. Changes in the size and composition of our labour force affect our growth and unemployment rates, as well as the occupational and sex composition of the labour force. The latter in turn affect such factors as relative wages, demands for unionization, day care, and equal pay and equal employment opportunity legislation. Changes in household activities can involve family formation and mobility. Retirement programs can be affected in so far as new labour force participants will add contributions to pension funds, while those who retire (i.e. do not participate in the labour force) will be a drain on the funds.

Clearly, various public policy decisions are both affected by, and have an impact on, the labour force participation decision. Consequently, it is useful to be able to forecast changes in labour force participation and to predict the impact of policy changes on this decision. This requires an understanding of the determinants of the labour force participation decision. The basic theoretical framework for analysing this decision is the income-leisure choice model, developed formally in Chapter 2. The collection of international studies in Layard and Mincer (1985) illustrates the usefulness of this basic economic framework in understanding labour force participation patterns in a variety of countries with very different economic and other conditions. These studies also illustrate the interrelatedness of decisions on participation, education and family formation.

In this chapter, the income-leisure choice framework is applied to the labour force participation decision. Before presenting the theory and empirical evidence, however, it is necessary to discuss a variety of definitions associated with the labour force concept.

DEFINING THE LABOUR FORCE

The labour force (LF) basically consists of persons who are working or looking for work: it consists of the employed (E) plus unemployed (U).

Those who are not in the labour force (NLF) are usually students, retired people, housewives, female heads of families and some "discouraged workers" who simply give up searching for work (according to labour force surveys, the latter are usually not considered as unemployed because they are not actively seeking work). In Canada, estimates of these various groups are based on a monthly survey of the non-institutional, civilian population 15 years and over, excluding the Yukon, Northwest Territories and reservations: these constitute the universe or population (POP) from which the survey samples.

By way of definition, then, the overall labour force participation rate (LFPR) is simply that portion of the eligible population that participates in labour force activity, either employed or unemployed: that is, $LFPR \equiv LF/POP \equiv (E + U)/POP$. (The $\equiv$ rather than $=$ sign simply illustrates that this is purely a definitional relationship; it is not a behavioural relationship derived from any underlying theory of labour market behaviour.) The unemployment rate (UR) is simply that portion of the labour force that is unemployed, i.e., $UR \equiv U/LF \equiv U/(E + U)$. This does not include "discouraged workers" who have given up searching for work, since they are usually categorized as outside the labour force. Other definitions can be illustrated by algebraic manipulation; that is,

$$POP \equiv LF + NLF \equiv E + U + NLF \text{ and } U \equiv LF - E.$$

The Canadian Labour Force Survey conducted by Statistics Canada is currently based on a monthly sample of approximately 48,000 households and the results are published monthly in *The Labour Force* (Cat. No. 71-001). Between 1945 and 1952, the survey was quarterly, and in 1976 it was revised substantially: a comprehensive description of the old survey is given in D.B.S. *Canadian Labour Force Survey — Methodology* (Cat. No. 71-504), and the new survey is described in Macredie and Petrie (1976). The new survey is more comprehensive and detailed, giving more information on part-time workers and persons who are marginally in or out of the labour force (e.g. unemployed who are not really looking for work and discouraged workers who actually would look for work if they thought that some were available). In addition, the survey asks more questions on the reasons for not working, the methods of job search, and the activities of non-workers. The new survey also provides a larger sample so as to give a better provincial and regional breakdown.

While the Labour Force Survey provides the most often used estimates for our labour force, employment and unemployment figures, other sources are available. In particular, the Canadian Census is conducted every five years, the most recent being in 1986 referring to activity during 1985. The census is more comprehensive (not being based on a sample from a larger population), and consequently includes richer details on such factors as unemployment by industry and occupation. However, its use is limited because it is conducted only every five years and its reliability on labour force questions may be questioned because, unlike the Labour Force Survey, it does not focus only on labour force activity.

LABOUR FORCE PARTICIPATION THEORY

The income-leisure choice model provides the underlying theoretical framework for both the labour force participation decision and the hours-of-work decision of those who participate. The main difference between the two decisions is that the participation decision involves a discrete choice between two labour force states (in or out of the labour force) while the hours decision involves a choice over a continuous variable.

The labour force participation decision is illustrated in Figure 5.1. Panel (a) shows an individual who will not participate given the individual's preferences concerning income and leisure, the amount of non-labour income received per period (Y_0) and the market wage w_0 (which determines the slope of the potential income constraint). The highest possible utility is attained at the point on the budget constraint corresponding to maximum "leisure" (zero hours of market work). This outcome is referred to as a "corner solution" because the household equilibrium occurs at one of the two extreme points on the potential income constraint. Figure 5.1(b) shows an individual who will participate given the individual's preferences and constraints. In this case the household equilibrium occurs in between the two extreme points on the potential income constraint, and is referred to as an "interior solution." With an interior solution the household equilibrium is characterized by a tangency between the budget constraint and the highest attainable indifference curve. At a corner solution, the tangency condition usually does not hold; the slopes of the highest attainable indifference curve and budget constraint typically differ, the indifference curve being more steeply sloped than the budget constraint.

A useful way of viewing the participation decision is to compare the individual's marginal rate of substitution (MRS) between income and leisure at the point of maximum leisure (point a in Figures 5.1(a) and 5.1(b)) with the market wage. The former measures the individual's *willingness* to exchange non-market time for income beginning from an initial position in which all time is devoted to non-market activities, while the market wage measures the individual's *ability* to exchange leisure time for income. When the MRS at zero hours of work (slope of indifference curve at a) exceeds the wage rate (slope of budget constraint), as at point a in Figure 5.1(a), the individual's implicit value of non-market time is high relative to the explicit market value of that time and the individual will therefore not participate. When the MRS at zero hours of work is less than the wage rate, as at the point a in Figure 5.1(b), the individual's implicit value of leisure time is less than the explicit market value of that time and the individual will participate in the labour market. In this case the individual increases hours of work until the marginal rate of substitution between

Figure 5.1 The Labour Force Participation Decision

(a) Equilibrium of a Non-Participant

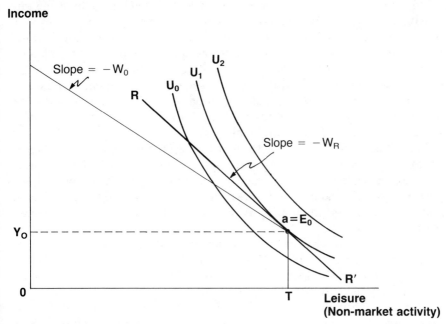

(b) Equilibrium of a Participant

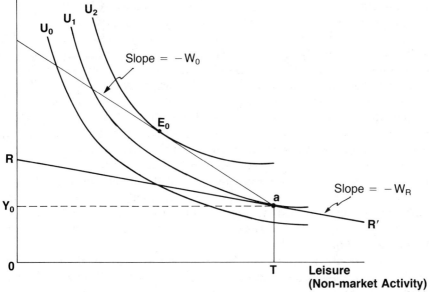

income and leisure equals the wage rate, thereby exhausting all "gains from trade" associated with exchanging non-market for market time.

In analysing labour force participation behaviour, economists often use the concept of a "reservation wage" which is defined as the wage rate at which an individual would be indifferent between participating and not participating in the labour force; i.e., the wage at which an individual would be indifferent between work in the labour market as opposed to non-labour market activities such as household work, retirement, or leisure activities, all of which require time. If the market wage rate were equal to the reservation wage w_R, the individual's potential income constraint would be given by the line RR' in Figures 5.1(a) and 5.1(b). That is, the reservation wage is the slope of the individual's indifference curve at zero hours of work. If the market wage is less than the reservation wage, as in Figure 5.1(a), the individual will not participate in the labour force; if the market wage exceeds the reservation wage, as in Figure 5.1(b), the individual will participate in the labour force since the return from engaging in labour market activity exceeds that individual's valuation of time in non-labour market activities.

The effects of changes in the wage rate and non-labour income on labour force participation are illustrated in Figure 5.2. For a participant an increase in the wage rate has both income and substitution effects; because these are opposite in sign, hours of work may either increase or decrease. However, even if the income effect dominates the substitution effect so that hours of work decline, an increase in the wage rate can never cause a participant to withdraw from the labour force. This prediction of income-leisure choice theory is illustrated in Figure 5.2(a). As the wage increases, the household can achieve higher levels of utility and would never choose to not participate in the labour force which yields the utility level U_0.

For a non-participant, an increase in the wage rate may result in the individual entering the labour force or may leave labour force participation unchanged, depending on whether the now higher market wage exceeds or is less than the individual's reservation wage. As illustrated in Figure 5.2(b), the increase in the wage from w_0 to w_1 leaves the individual's preferred outcome at E_0; i.e. out of the labour force. However, the further wage increase to w_2 results in the individual entering the labour force (point E_2). This prediction can be explained in terms of income and substitution effects. An increase in the wage rate raises the opportunity cost of leisure time and tends to cause the individual to substitute market work for non-market activities. However, because the individual works zero hours initially, the income effect of an increase in the wage rate is zero. Thus for non-participants a wage increase has only a substitution effect which tends to increase hours of work.

These predictions can also be expressed in terms of the reservation wage. An increase in the market wage will not alter the labour force status of participants because the market wage already exceeds their reservation

Figure 5.2(a) The Effect of a Wage Increase on a Participant

Figure 5.2(b) The Effect of a Wage Increase on a Non-Participant

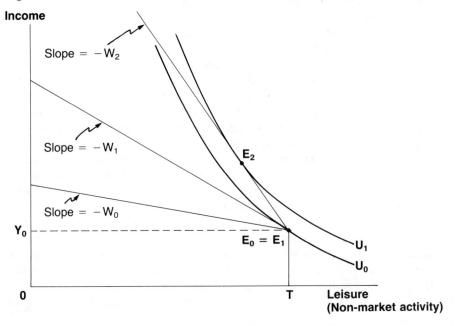

wage. However, an increase in the market wage may cause some non-participants to enter the labour force if the increase in the wage is sufficiently large that the now higher market wage exceeds the reservation wage.

Together these two predictions of the income-leisure choice model imply that an increase in the wage rate can never reduce and may increase labour force participation.

The effects of an increase in non-labour income on labour force participation are opposite to those of an increase in the wage rate. If leisure is a normal good, an increase in non-labour income will never cause a non-participant to enter the labour force and may cause some participants to withdraw from the labour force. These predictions follow from the fact that an increase in non-labour income has a pure income effect. Thus if leisure is a normal good, the amount of time devoted to non-market activities must either rise (if the individual was a labour force participant in the initial equilibrium) or not decline (if the individual was already at the maximum leisure point initially).

These predictions of the income-leisure choice model can alternatively be stated using the concept of a reservation wage. If leisure is a normal good, an increase in non-labour income will increase the individual's reservation wage. (Proof of this statement is left as an exercise; see question 1 at the end of this chapter.) Thus some participants will withdraw from the labour force, their reservation wage having risen above the market wage, while non-participants will remain out of the labour force, their reservation wage having been above the market wage even prior to the increase in non-labour income.

The determinants of an individual's labour force participation decision can be conveniently categorized as to whether the variable affects the individual's reservation wage, market wage or both. Other things equal, a variable that raises the individual's reservation wage would decrease the probability of participation in labour market activities. Such variables could be observable in the sense that data are often available on characteristics such as the presence of children, the availability of non-labour market income, and the added importance of household work as on a farm. Or the variables could be unobservable in the sense that data are not directly available on the characteristic, such as a preference for household work.

While some such variables may affect primarily an individual's reservation wage and hence have an unambiguous effect on their labour force participation decision, others may affect both their market wage and their reservation wage and hence have an indeterminate effect on their labour force participation decision. An increase in a person's age, for example, may be associated with a higher market wage which makes participation in labour market activities more likely. However, it may also raise their reservation wage if the disutility associated with work increases relative to leisure time, and this may induce them to retire from the labour force.

An alternative way to analyse the participation decision is in terms of the allocation of time between market work and non-market activities over the individual's lifetime. That is, the income-leisure choice model can be used to examine the individual's preferences and opportunities between lifetime income (measured in present value) and years devoted to market and non-market activities. The slope of the budget constraint is the annual wage and the non-labour wealth is the present value of the individual's lifetime non-labour income. In this framework, a non-participant (such as in Figure 5.1(a)) is someone who will not engage in market work throughout his or her lifetime. For an individual who will engage in some market work activity, as shown in Figure 5.1(b), the equilibrium E_0 shows the division of the individual's lifetime into non-market activity (out of the labour force) and market activity (in the labour force).

The effects of changes in the annual wage and non-labour market wealth on labour force participation can be analysed using this lifetime income-leisure choice framework. An increase in the annual wage will have both an income effect (which tends to reduce the number of years worked over the lifetime, assuming that leisure is a normal good) and a substitution effect (which tends to increase the number of years worked). Thus an increase in the wage may either increase or decrease the amount of labour force participation over the lifetime, depending on the magnitudes of the income and substitution effects. An increase in non-labour market wealth will have a pure income effect, thus reducing the amount of lifetime labour force participation (assuming leisure time is a normal good).

The lifetime income-leisure choice model shows how individuals allocate their lifetimes between market work and non-market activities. However, the model does not show which periods the individual will be in the labour force and which out of the labour force. The current period income-leisure choice model can be used to indicate how this choice is determined. During periods in which the value of time spent in non-labour market activities (and therefore the individual's reservation wage) is high relative to the current market wage, the individual will be out of the labour force. For most individuals these periods occur early and late in their lifetimes when the alternative non-market activities education and retirement have a high value. Reductions in the amount of labour force participation over the lifetime (resulting, for example, from an increase in the market wage) thus generally take the form of later entry into and/or earlier retirement from the labour force.

EMPIRICAL EVIDENCE, MARRIED FEMALES

The basic theory of labour force participation is often tested with data on married women since they have considerable flexibility to respond to the determinants of labour force participation. In addition, their responses have been dramatic in recent years, and this has policy implications for such things as sex discrimination, family formation, and the demand for day-care facilities.

Empirical evidence in both Canada and the United States tends to confirm the predictions based on the economic theory of labour force participation. For Canada, some illustrative figures are given in Table 5.1.

TABLE 5.1
LABOUR FORCE PARTICIPATION RATES OF MARRIED WOMEN
AGE 15–64, HUSBAND PRESENT, CANADA 1971

Education	
Incomplete high school	.36
Complete high school	.50
Complete university	.55
Family income less wife's own earnings	
$3,000 or less	.47
$3,000–5,999	.44
$6,000–8,999	.44
$9,000–11,999	.38
$12,000–14,999	.33
$15,000 or over	.27
Child Status	
No children	.57
Pre-school children only	.30
School children only	.42
Both pre-school and school children	.25

Source: Extracted from M. Gunderson, "Work Patterns," in *Opportunity for Choice: A Goal for Women in Canada* edited by G. Cook, Ottawa: Statistics Canada, 1976, p. 100, 101. (Based on special tabulations from the 1971 Canadian Census.) Reproduced with permission of the Minister of Supply and Services Canada.

Labour force participation rates are higher for married women with high education, reflecting their high opportunity cost of not working, as well as, perhaps, preferences for labour market as opposed to household work. The impact of the income effect is illustrated by the decline in their participation as family income increases. With higher family income, the household can afford to buy more of everything, including the opportunity to have some members not participate in labour market activities. Alternatively stated, low family income, or perhaps poverty, will compel many married women to engage in labour market activities. The presence of children, especially preschool age children, is a strong deterrent to the labour force participation of married women. In economic terms, the presence of children raises their reservation wage and hence encourages them to engage in household rather than labour market work.

These results are also confirmed when the determinants of the labour force participation of married women are analysed via multiple regression analysis, which enables one to estimate the separate, partial effect of one variable while holding other factors constant (e.g. Spencer (1973), Skoulas (1974), Gunderson (1976), Nakamura, Nakamura and Cullen (1979), Nakamura and Nakamura (1981, 1983), and Robinson and Tomes (1982, 1985).

Nakamura and Nakamura (1985) provide a survey of these and related studies. The probability that a woman will participate in the labour force is consistently found to be negatively related to the number of children (especially young children) and the husband's income and positively related to the woman's potential market wage and educational attainment.) For example, in Gunderson (1976, p. 7) the probability of participation was 23 percentage points higher for university graduates as opposed to those who did not complete high school; it was 35 percentage points lower for married women who had both preschool and school-aged children as opposed to those who had no children; and it was 24 percentage points lower for those who had family income of over 15,000 dollars as opposed to less than 3,000 dollars per year.

MAJOR LONG-RUN TRENDS

The basic theory of labour force participation also helps explain the major long-run trends that have been observed with respect to labour force participation in Canada. The trends, as shown in Table 5.2, include a fairly stable and high participation rate for middle-aged males, a drop in the participation rates of older persons, a drop in the participation rate of younger persons until the 1960s and an increase in the participation rate of females.

The high and fairly stable participation rate of middle-aged males indicates their continuous strong attachment to labour market activities. Until the 1960s, 98 to 99 percent of males 25-34 participated in labour market activities: the corresponding figure for men 35-64 was 95 to 97 percent. Only during the 1960s did a slight fall begin to occur, until by 1981 the participation rates were 95 percent for males 25-34 and 89 percent for males 35-64. Clearly, these are still high figures, yet they do indicate that in recent years labour force participation is not the sole activity for these persons. Continuing education and early retirement have extended even into the age groups that were once thought to be exclusively involved in labour market activity.

The continuous drop in the participation rate of older males over 65 — from 60 percent in 1921 to 17 percent in 1981 — indicates the increasing tendency to retire from labour market activities. To a large extent this may reflect a pure wealth or income effect; that is, as we become wealthier over time we buy more of everything, including leisure in the form of early retirement. It may also reflect increased social insurance benefits and the availability of private and public pension funds. The decrease in self-employment, where retirement comes later and where pensions have not always been arranged, may also have contributed to the growth of early retirement. The early retirement decision is particularly remarkable when one considers that health factors and life expectancy increases have enabled people to participate longer in labour force activities. The fact that they do not indicates the strength of the economic factors inducing retirement,

TABLE 5.2
LABOUR FORCE PARTICIPATION RATES BY AGE AND SEX, CANADA, CENSUS YEARS 1901–1981

Year	Sex	14–19[a]	20–24	25–34	35–64	65+	All Ages
1901	Male	n.a.	n.a.	n.a.	n.a.	n.a.	88
	Female	n.a.	n.a.	n.a.	n.a.	n.a.	16
1911	Male	n.a.	n.a.	n.a.	n.a.	n.a.	91
	Female	n.a.	n.a.	n.a.	n.a.	n.a.	19
1921	Male	68	94	98	97	60	90
	Female	30	40	20	12	7	20
1931	Male	57	94	99	97	57	87
	Female	27	47	24	13	6	22
1941	Male	55	93	99	96	48	86
	Female	27	47	28	15	6	23
1951	Male	54	94	98	95	40	84
	Female	34	49	25	20	5	24
1961	Male	41	94	98	95	31	81
	Female	32	51	29	30	6	29
1971	Male	47	87	93	89	24	76
	Female	37	63	45	42	8	40
1981	Male	49	91	95	89	17	78
	Female	45	77	66	53	6	52

Note: [a]For 1971 and 1981, the youngest age group is 15–19.

Source: M. Gunderson, "Work Patterns," in *Opportunity for Choice: A Goal for Women in Canada*, edited by G. Cook, Ottawa: Statistics Canada, 1976, p. 97. Reproduced by permission of the Minister of Supply and Services Canada. Figures for 1971 were computed from the 1971 Census of Canada, *Labour Force and Individual Income*, Cat. No. 94-704, Bulletin 3.1-4, October 1974, Table 9. Figures for 1981 were computed from the 1981 Census Cat. 92-915, Vol. 1, Table 1, pp. 1-1. Figures for the other years are from S. Ostry and F. Denton, *Historical Estimates of the Canadian Labour Force*, 1961 Census Monograph, Ottawa: Queen's Printer, 1967.

namely increased income and pension coverage. Because of their obvious importance, and the growing policy concern in this area of retirement, these factors are examined in more detail in Chapter 6.

The drop in the participation rates of younger persons 14-19, at least until the 1960s, reflects their increased educational activities, as institutionalized in the higher legal school leaving age, the increase in the length of the school year and the decline in the importance of farm work. Whether this resulted from an increased awareness of the value of education, or simply greater "consumption" of educational activities as society became wealthier, remains an open question: presumably both the investment and consumption aspects have contributed. The rural to urban shift that has gone on over time also would reduce participation, since in agricultural sectors younger persons tend to work on the farms.

The fact that the continuous drop in participation of younger males seems to have ceased during the 1960s is interesting. Since that time the participation rates of both male and female youth have risen modestly. Some of this change may be explained by the fact that the youngest age category in 1971 and 1981 is 15-19, not 14-19, and presumably even in earlier years many 14-year-olds would be in school and hence not participating in the labour force. In essence, the 15-19 age category is simply likely to have more participants than the 14-19 category, since 14-year-olds tend to be in school. However, examination of the data indicates that the modest rise in youth labour force participation since the 1960s cannot be explained by this change alone. Other factors — such as the rise in part-time employment which allows some to combine work and educational activities and possibly a decline in the perceived benefits of additional education — appear also to have played a role.

Perhaps the most dramatic change that has occurred is the increased labour force participation of females. The trend has been continuous — from 16 percent in 1901 to 52 percent in 1981. However, the most dramatic changes have occurred during the post-war period, especially the 1960s and 1970s. Although not shown in the data of Table 5.2, the increase has been most dramatic for married women, increasing, for example, from 10 percent in 1951 to 51 percent in 1981, almost equal that of unmarried women.

Thus the salient long-run trends include a moderate decline in male labour force participation and a substantial increase in the participation rate of females. Following Mincer (1962), economists have explained the contracting time series behaviour of male and female labour supply in terms of the magnitudes of the income and substitution effects of real wage increases for male and female workers. These important differences can perhaps best be explained using the lifetime income-leisure choice model. Most males have traditionally been in the labour force for much of their lives and work a substantial number of hours per year. Thus the income effect of an increase in the real wage is substantial and is expected to be larger than the substitution effect. Increases in real wages thus lead to a reduction in lifetime labour supply for males. This reduction is divided among hours worked per week, weeks worked per year and years worked over the lifetime according to the individual's preferences and opportunities. Females, in contrast, have traditionally been outside the labour force for much of their lives or, if employed, have worked fewer hours than men. Thus the income effect of an increase in the real wage is small, and is likely to be dominated by the substitution effect. As a result, increases in real wages lead to an increase in lifetime labour supply of females, some of which takes the form of increased labour force participation.

Nakamura and Nakamura (1985), survey a number of empirical studies of the labour supply behaviour of Canadian women. These studies confirm that increases in the market wage have induced women to enter the labour force. For married women, increases in the husband's earnings act like an income effect, increasing the wife's reservation wage and reducing labour force participation.

The dramatic increase in the labour force participation of women also reflects a variety of additional factors, many of them a result as much as a cause of their increased participation. Increased female education that is more labour market oriented makes the opportunity cost of not working much higher. Having fewer children, and having them spaced more closely together, reduces the reservation wage and enables labour force participation. Household work has become easier, due to technological changes and substitutes for household production in such things as child care, cleaning, food preparation, and even entertainment, although there still does not appear to be a sharing of household tasks between husband and wife when both engage in labour market activity (Gunderson (1976, p. 96)). The decline in the participation of other groups, namely the young and the old, has helped create a vacuum that the large influx of women has filled: in essence, their increased participation has tended to offset the decreased participation of other groups. The rapid growth of white-collar and part-time jobs has also been conducive to the growth of female employment, as has been the increased social acceptance of women working outside the home. The women's liberation movement itself has helped change these attitudes, both on the part of society at large, and on the part of women themselves. Legislative changes — especially equal pay and equal employment opportunity legislation, as well as unemployment insurance — may have helped make labour force participation more attractive for women although, as we will see in later chapters, their impact may be ambiguous.

Clearly these various factors have had an impact by encouraging the labour force participation of women, and this impact has been sufficiently strong to offset the tendency — observed in most other groups — to participate less as we become wealthier over time. What is particularly noticeable concerning several of these factors that have influenced the labour force participation of women is that they are both a cause and an effect of their increased participation. This also highlights the importance of the simultaneous and interrelated nature of many household decisions, such as the decision to marry, have children, and participate in the labour force, as well as the choice of occupation and region in which people work. The participation decision, like other labour market and household decisions, cannot be viewed in isolation.

ADDED AND DISCOURAGED WORKER EFFECTS

Labour force participation is also responsive to changes in unemployment in the economy. Specifically, in periods of high unemployment people may become discouraged from looking for work and drop out of the labour force returning to household activities or to school or perhaps even entering early retirement. This is termed the discouraged worker effect. On the other hand, in periods of high unemployment, some may enter the labour force to supplement family income that may have deteriorated during the period of high unemployment. This is termed the added worker effect.

Changes in unemployment are a proxy for transitory changes in expected wages and other income, and thus the discouraged and added worker effects can be interpreted as short-run substitution and income effects respectively. That is, if unemployment is high, then opportunities in the labour market are lowered temporarily: the price of leisure (opportunity cost or forgone income from not working) is reduced temporarily and hence people substitute leisure for labour market activities. On the other hand, the high unemployment means that it is more likely that family income is lowered temporarily, and additional members may have to participate in labour market activities so as to restore that income.

Since the added (income) and discouraged (substitution) worker effects operate in the opposite direction, it is necessary to appeal to the empirical evidence to see which dominates. Again, most of the empirical tests have been based on data of married women since they are more likely to respond to changes in unemployment.

In the U.S., the empirical evidence clearly indicates the dominance of the discouraged worker effect for most married women. That is, in periods of high unemployment, women become discouraged from entering the labour force to look for work, and this dominates any tendency to add themselves to the labour force to maintain their family income. In Canada, however, the empirical evidence is mixed. Studies based on time series data — Proulx (1969), Officer and Anderson (1969), Davis (1971), Swidinsky (1973), Donner and Lazar (1974), and Swan (1974) — often find the added worker effect to dominate, although the discouraged worker effect appears to be becoming more predominant over time. Cross-section studies comparing participation rates across census areas or participation probabilities for different married women tend to show mixed results. Based on data from the early 1960s, Ostry (1968) and Spencer and Featherstone (1970) cite evidence of an added worker effect, while Swidinsky (1973) finds evidence of a weak discouraged worker effect, and Skoulas (1974) finds no relationship between participation and unemployment. Based on more recent data, Spence (1973) and Skoulas (1974) find evidence of a weak discouraged worker effect and Gunderson (1977) finds no evidence of any substantial added worker effect, but possible evidence of a discouraged worker effect.

Clearly the Canadian evidence is by no means conclusive. At most, one may say that the discouraged worker effect appears to be becoming more predominant over time, but that it is not as strong as in the U.S.

HIDDEN UNEMPLOYMENT

The discouraged worker effect also gives rise to the problem of hidden unemployment — a topic that we will return to in a later chapter on unemployment. During a recession when the unemployment rate is high, there may also be a large number of discouraged workers who do not look for work because they believe that no work is available. They are considered as outside of the labour force because they are not working or actively looking for work. However, because they would look for work were it not for the high unemployment rate, they are often considered as the hidden unemployed; that is, people who the unemployment figures tend to miss because they are considered as outside of the labour force rather than as unemployed persons in the labour force.

In this sense, in times of high unemployment our unemployment figures may understate the true unemployment by missing those discouraged workers who constitute the hidden unemployed. Recent developments in our Labour Force Survey, in fact, have been designed to ascertain this hidden or disguised unemployment, and to find out why they are not looking for jobs.

The notion of the discouraged worker is especially important as groups like married women and teenagers become a larger portion of our potential labour force. Such persons often have a loose attachment to the labour force, moving in and out in response to changing economic conditions. They often, but not always, have other family income upon which to rely. For these reasons they are often labelled secondary or marginal workers — unfortunate misnomers if they are used to belittle their employment problems or the contribution to the family income of such workers. This is especially the case if they are contrasted with the terms primary workers or breadwinners, terms that are often used to describe the employment position of males.

However, because of their flexibility with respect to labour market activities, married women and teenagers do constitute a large portion of discouraged workers who would enter the labour force and look for work if employment prospects increased. Hence, the recent emphasis in labour force surveys to find out exactly what these people are doing, and why they are not looking for work.

Clearly the decision to include such persons either in the category of unemployed, or as outside of the labour force, is a difficult one. What is more important, however, than labelling them as either unemployed or outside of the labour force, is to know their approximate magnitude and the degree to which they seriously would look for work if employment prospects improved. Only then can we attach meaning to the phrase "hidden unemployed."

QUESTIONS

1. Using the income-leisure choice model, show that an increase in non-labour income will increase the individual's reservation wage if leisure is a normal good.

2. Given the basic determinants of labour force participation, do you feel that the main trends in labour force participation will continue into the future?

3. Indicate the expected impact on the labour force participation of married women of changes in each of the following factors, other things held constant:
   (a) an increase in the education of women;
   (b) a more equal sharing of household responsibilities between husband and wife;
   (c) a reduction in the average number of children;
   (d) an increased tendency to have children spaced more closely together;
   (e) an increase in the earnings of husbands;
   (f) day care paid out of general tax revenues;
   (g) allowing day care expenses to be tax deductible;
   (h) paying housewives a fixed sum out of general tax revenues for household work.

4. In U.S. studies, and in Canadian empirical studies based on cross-section data, evidence of a net discouraged worker effect tends to be found. However, Canadian studies based on time series data often find evidence of a net added worker effect. How might these differences be explained?

5. Assume that the following regression equation has been estimated where P_W is the labour force participation rate of married women (measured in percent with the average $\bar{P} = 35.0$), Y_H is husband's income (measured in thousands of dollars with average $\bar{Y}_H = 10$), Y_w is wife's expected income (measured in thousands of dollars with average $\bar{Y}_W = 6$) and u_H is the male unemployment rate (measured in percent with average $\bar{u}_H = 6.0$):

$$P_w = -7{\cdot}0Y_H + 18Y_W - {\cdot}5u_H$$

   (a) What is the expected effect of an increase of 1,000 dollars in the income of husbands on the participation rate of their wives?
   (b) What is the expected effect of an increase of 1,000 dollars in the income of the wives themselves?
   (c) Decompose the latter impact into its separate income and substitution effects.
   (d) Given the magnitude of the latter two effects, what would be the impact on female participation of an equal pay policy that increased the expected earnings of females by 1,000 dollars while at the same time decreasing the expected earnings of their husbands by 1,000 dollars?
   (e) Calculate the pure income and the gross or uncompensated wage elasticities of participation, evaluated at the means.
   (f) Does this equation shed any light on why the labour force participation of married women has increased over time, even though their non-labour income has also increased?

(g) What does the equation tell us about the relative importance of the added and discouraged worker effect?

(h) If the unemployment rate of males were to drop to a "full employ-ment" of 2 percent, what would have been the participation rate of married women?

(i) What does this tell us about hidden unemployment that may exist when the unemployment rate is above the full employment level?

REFERENCES AND FURTHER READINGS

Allingham, J. *The Demographic Background to Change in the Number and Composition of Female Wage Earners in Canada.* Special Labour Force Studies, Series B, No. 1. Ottawa: Dominion Bureau of Statistics, 1967.

Allingham, J. *Women Who Work: Part 1, The Relative Importance of Age, Education and Marital Status for Participation in the Labour Force.* Special Labour Force Studies No. 5. Ottawa: Dominion Bureau of Statistics, 1967.

Allingham, J. and B. Spencer. *Women Who Work: Part 2, Married Women in the Labour Force: The Influence of Age, Education, Child-bearing Status and Residence.* Special Labour Force Studies, Series B, No. 2. Ottawa: Dominion Bureau of Statistics, 1968.

Ben-Porath, Y. Labor-force participation rates and the supply of labor. *JPE* 81 (May/June 1973) 697-704.

Berg, S. and T. Dalton. Labor force participation in goods and services. *R.E. Stats.* 57 (November 1975) 518-522.

Blank, R. The impact of state economic differentials on household welfare and labor force behavior. *JPubEc* 28 (October 1985) 25-58.

Boothby, O. The continuity of married women's labour force participation in Canada. *CJE* 17 (August 1984) 471-480.

Bowen, W. and T. Finegan. *The Economics of Labor Force Participation.* Princeton, N.J.: Princeton University Press, 1969.

Breton, A. *Marriage, Population and the Labour Force Participation of Women.* Ottawa: Economic Council of Canada, 1984.

Cain, G. *Married Women in the Labor Force.* Chicago: University of Chicago Press, 1966.

Carliner, G. Female labour force participation rates for nine ethnic groups. *JHR* 16 (Spring 1981) 286-293.

Cave, G. Job rationing, unemployment and discouraged workers. *JOLE* 1 (July 1983) 286-307.

Clark, K. and L. Summers. Labour force participation: timing and persistence. *R.E. Studies* 49 (No. 5, 1982) 835-844.

Cohen, M., R. Lerman and S. Rea. Area employment conditions and labor-force participation: a microstudy. *JPE* 79 (September/October 1971) 1151-1157.

Cohen, M., S. Rea and R. Lerman. *A Micro Model of Labor Supply.* BLS Staff Paper. Washington: U.S. Government Printing Office, 1970.

Davis, N. *Some Methods of Analysing Cross-Classified Census Data: The Case of Labour Force Participation Rates.* Special Labour Force Studies, Series B, No. 3. Ottawa: Dominion Bureau of Statistics, 1969.

Davis, N. *Cycles and Trends in Labour Force Participation, 1953-1968.* Special Labour Force Studies, Series B, No. 5. Ottawa: Dominion Bureau of Statistics, 1971.

Denton, F. A simulation model of month-to-month labour force movement in Canada. *IER* 14 (June 1973) 293-311.

Denton, F. and S. Ostry. *Historical Estimates of the Canadian Labour Force.* 1961 Census Monograph. Ottawa: Dominion Bureau of Statistics, 1967.

Dernburg, T. and K. Strand. Hidden unemployment 1953-1962. *AER* 56 (March 1966) 71-95.

Donner, A. and F. Lazar. Employment expectations and labour force participation in Canada. *RI/IR* 29 (No. 2, 1974) 320-330.

Dooley, M. and P. Gottschalk. Earnings inequality among males in the United States: trends and the effect of labor force growth. *JPE* 92 (February 1984) 59-89.

Douglas, P. and E. Schoenberg. Studies in the supply curve of labour. *JPE* (February 1937) 45-79.

Fellegi, J., G. Gray and R. Platek. The new design of the Canadian labour force survey. *Journal of American Statistical Association* (May 1967) 465-481.

Finegan, T. Discouraged worker effect. *ILRR* 35 (October 1981) 88-102.

Fleisher, B. The economics of labor force participation: a review article. *JHR* 6 (Spring 1971) 139-148.

Fleisher, B. and G. Rhodes. Unemployment and the labor force participation of married women: a simultaneous model. *R.E. Stats.* 68 (November 1976) 398-406.

Flinn, C. and J. Heckman. Are unemployment and out of the labor force behaviorally distinct labor force states? *JOLE* 1 (January 1983) 28-42.

Gregory, P. Fertility and labor force participation in the Soviet Union and Eastern Europe. *R.E. Stats.* 64 (Feb. 1982) 18-31.

Gunderson, M. Work Patterns. *Opportunity for Choice: A Goal for Women in Canada,* G. Cook (ed.). Ottawa: Statistics Canada, 1976, 94-103.

Gunderson, M. Logit estimates of labour force participation based on census cross tabulations. *CJE* 10 (August 1977) 453-462.

Gunderson, M. Probit and Logit estimates of labor force participation. *IR* 19 (Spring 1980) 216-220.

Hartley, M. and N. Revanker. Labor supply under uncertainty and the rate of unemployment. *AER* 64 (March 1974) 170-175. Comments by D. Sjoquist 66 (May 1976) 929-930 and G. Yaniv 69 (March 1979) 203-205.

Heckman, J. Shadow prices, market wages and labor supply. *Econometrica* 42 (July 1974) 679-694.

Heckman, J. A partial survey of recent research on the labor supply of women. *AER Proceedings* 68 (May 1978) 200-207.

Heckman, J. Income, labor supply, and urban residence. *AER* 70 (September 1980) 805-811.

Heckman, J. and R. Willis. A beta-logistic model for the analysis of segmented labor force participation of married women. *JPE* 85 (February 1977) 27-58. Comment by J. Mincer and H. Ofek and reply 87 (February 1979) 197-211.

Hill, M. Female labor force participation in developing and developed countries. *R.E. Stats.* 65 (Aug. 1983) 459-468.

Hughes, B. Direct income and substitution effects in participation decision. *JPE* 80 (July/August 1972) 793-795.

Joshi, H. Secondary workers in the employment cycle. *Economica* 48 (Feb. 1981) 29-44.

King, A. Industrial structure, the flexibility of working hours, and women's labor force participation. *R.E. Stats.* 60 (August 1978) 399-407.

Kuch, P. and S. Sharir. Added and discouraged worker effects in Canada. *CJE* 11 (February 1978) 112-120.

Layard, R., M. Barton and A. Zabalza. Married women's participation and hours. *Economica* 47 (Feb. 1980) 51-72.

Layard, R., and J. Mincer (eds.) Trends in women's work, education and family building. *JOLE* 3, Part 2 (Jan. 1985).

Leuthold, J. Income-splitting and women's labor-force participation. *ILRR* 38 (October 1984) 98-105.

Levy, F. The labour supply of female household heads. *JHR* 14 (Winter 1979) 76-97.

Long, J. and E. Jones. Labor force entry and exit by married women. *R.E. Stats.* 62 (Feb. 1980) 1-6.

Lundberg, S. The added worker effect. *JOLE* 3 (January 1985) 11-37.

Macredie, I. and B. Petrie. *The Canadian Labour Force Survey.* Ottawa: Labour Force Survey Division, Statistics Canada, 1976.

McCaffery, S. Vacancies, discouraged workers and labor market dynamics. *SEJ* 47 (July 1980) 21-29.

Mincer, J. Labor force participation of married women. *Aspects of Labor Economics.* Princeton, N.J.: Princeton University Press, 1962.

Mincer, J. Labor force participation and unemployment. A review of recent evidence. *Prosperity and Unemployment.* R. and M. Gordon (eds.). New York: John Wiley and Sons, 1966.

Mincer, J. Labor force participation. *International Encyclopedia of Social Science,* Vol. 8. New York: Macmillan, 1968.

Mooney, J. Urban poverty and labor force participation. *AER* 57 (March 1967) 104-119. Comment by G. Cain and J. Mincer and reply 59 (March 1969) 85-96.

Morgenstern, R. and W. Hamovitch. Labour force supply of married women in part-time and full-time employment. *ILRR* 30 (October 1976) 59-67.

Nakamura, A. and M. Nakamura. A comparison of the labour force behaviour of married women in the United States and Canada, with special attention to the impact of income taxes. *Econometrica* 49 (March 1981) 451-489.

Nakamura, A. and M. Nakamura. Part-time and full-time work behaviour of married women: a model with a double truncated dependent variable. *CJE* 16 (May 1983) 229-257.

Nakamura, A. and M. Nakamura. A survey of research on the work behaviour of Canadian women. *Work and Pay: The Canadian Labour Market,* W.C. Riddell (ed.). Toronto: University of Toronto Press, 1985.

Nakamura, A., M. Nakamura and D. Cullen. Job opportunities, the offered wage, and the labor supply of married women. *AER* 69 (December 1979) 787-805.

Officer, L. and P. Anderson. Labour force participation in Canada. *CJE* 2 (May 1969) 278-287.

Ostry, S. *The Female Worker in Canada*. 1961 Census Monograph. Ottawa: Dominion Bureau of Statistics, 1968.

Parsons, D. The decline in male labour force participation. *JPE* 88 (February 1980) 117-134.

Proulx, Pierre-Paul. La variabilité cyclique des taux de participation à la main d'ouvre au Canada. *CJE* 2 (May 1969) 268-277. Comments by L. Officer and P. Anderson, and R. Swidinsky, 3 (February 1970) 145-151.

Quinlan, D. and J. Shackelford. Labour force participation rates of women and the rise of the two-earner family. *AER* 70 (May 1980) 209-212.

Rea, S. Unemployment and the supply of labor. *JHR* 9 (Spring 1974) 279-289.

Robinson, C. and N. Tomes. Family labour supply and fertility: a two-regime model. *CJE* 15 (November 1982) 706-34.

Robinson, C. and N. Tomes. More on the labour supply of Canadian women. *CJE* 18 (February 1985) 156-163.

Rosen, S. and F. Welch. Labor supply and income redistribution. *R.E. Stats.* 53 (August 1971) 278-282.

Rosenzweig, M. Neoclassical theory and the optimizing peasant: an econometric analysis of market family labour supply in a developing country. *QJE* 94 (February 1980) 31-55.

Ruggeri, G. Hidden unemployment by age and sex in Canada. *RI/IR* 30 (No. 2, 1975) 181-195.

Sandell, S. Attitudes towards market work and the effect of wage rates on the lifetime labor supply of married women. *JHR* 12 (Summer 1977) 379-386.

Sander, W. Women, work and divorce. *AER* 75 (June 1985) 519-523.

Sawers, L. Urban poverty and labor force participation. *AER* 62 (June 1972) 414-421.

Sjedule, T. and K. Newton. *Discouraged and Additional Workers Revisited*. Discussion Paper No. 141. Ottawa: Economic Council of Canada, 1980.

Sjedule, T., N. Skoulas, and K. Newton. *The Impact of Economy-Wide Changes on the Labour Force: An Econometric Analysis*. Ottawa: Economic Council of Canada, 1976.

Skoulas, N. *Determinants of the Participation Rate of Married Women in the Canadian Labour Force*. Ottawa: Information Canada, 1974.

Sloan, F. and S. Richupan. Short-run supply responses of professional nurses. *JHR* 10 (Spring 1975) 241-257.

Smith, J. (ed.) *Female Labor Supply*. Princeton: Princeton University Press, 1980.

Sobol, M. A dynamic analysis of labour force participation of married women of childbearing age. *JHR* (Fall 1973) 497-505.

Spencer, B. Determinants of the labour force participation of married women: a micro-study of Toronto households. *CJE* 6 (May 1973) 222-238.

Spencer, B. and D. Featherstone. *Married Female Labour Force Participation: A Micro Study*. Special Labour Force Studies, Series B, No. 4. Ottawa: Dominion Bureau of Statistics, 1970.

Strand, K. and T. Dernberg. Cyclical variation and labor force participation. *R.E. Stats.* 46 (November 1964) 378-391.

Strober, M. Wives' labor force behavior and family consumption patterns. *AER Proceedings* 67 (February 1977) 419-427.

Sum, A. Female labor force participation: why projections have been too low. *MLR* 100 (July 1977) 18-24.

Swan, N. The responses of labour supply to demand in Canadian regions. *CJE* 7 (August 1974) 418-433.

Swidinsky, R. Unemployment and labour force participation: the Canadian experience. *RI/IR* 28 (No. 1, 1973) 56-75.

Wachter, M. A labor supply model for secondary workers. *R.E. Stats.* 54 (May 1972) 141-151.

Wachter, M. Intermediate swings in labor-force participation. *BPEA* (No. 2, 1977) 545-576.

Wales, T. Estimation of a labor supply curve for self-employed business proprietors. *IER* 14 (February 1973) 69-80.

6 Retirement Decision and Pensions

The retirement decision is essentially a decision by older persons not to participate in the labour force. Hence it is amenable to analysis utilizing labour force participation theory, and its underlying income-leisure choice model. The retirement decision is treated separately simply because it is an area of increasing policy concern and, as the references indicate, it has developed its own empirical literature. This chapter applies the basic income-leisure framework to the retirement decision. Subsequently, Chapter 24 deals with the reasons for the existence of mandatory retirement rules that lead to a "bunching" of retirement dates, often around age 65.

The notion of retirement has many meanings, ranging from outright leaving of the labour force, to a reduction of hours worked, to simply moving into a less onerous job. The process itself may also be gradual, beginning with a reduction in time worked (perhaps associated with a job change) and ending in full retirement. Throughout this chapter, we will generally talk of retirement as leaving the labour force; however, the importance of various forms of quasi-retirement and the often gradual nature of the retirement process should be kept in mind.

The policy importance of the retirement decision stems from the fact that it can have an impact on so many elements of social policy. For the individuals themselves, and their families, the retirement decision has implications ranging from their financial status to their psychological state. For the economy as a whole, the retirement decision also has macroeconomic implications with respect to such factors as private savings, unemployment, and the size of the labour force, all of which have implications for the level of national income.

In addition, there is concern over the solvency of public pension funds if large numbers retire and few are in the labour force to pay into the fund. This problem may be especially acute around the turn of the century, when the post-World War II baby-boom population reaches potential retirement age and, depending on fertility factors and patterns of female labour force participation, when there may be few other participants in the labour force paying into the funds. The problem will be compounded if high unemployment and low productivity increases result in low labour market earnings and hence a smaller tax base for social insurance pensions.

The policy importance of the retirement decision is further heightened by the fact that it is an area where policy changes can affect the retirement decision. This is especially the case with respect to such "policy parameters" that are subject to policy change as the mandatory retirement age and the nature and availability of pension funds. However, to know the expected impact of changes in these factors, we must know the theoretical determinants of the retirement decision, and the empirical evidence on the retirement response.

THEORETICAL DETERMINANTS OF RETIREMENT

Mandatory Retirement Age

As indicated by Kittner (1977, p. 60), the term mandatory retirement provisions refers to both compulsory retirement provisions and automatic retirement provisions. Under automatic retirement, people *have* to retire at a specific age and cannot be retained by the company. Under compulsory retirement provisions, however, the company can compel the worker to retire at a specific age, but it can also retain the services of a worker, usually on a year-to-year basis.

The term mandatory retirement is somewhat of a misnomer, since there is no magic age embodied in *legislation* that says a person *must* retire by a specific age. The mandatory retirement age may be part of an employer's personnel policy, or it may be negotiated in a collective agreement. In addition, there is an age at which public pensions become available, although they do not *prevent* people from continuing to work. As well, aspects of labour legislation may not apply to workers beyond a specific age. Thus the so-called mandatory retirement age — of which age 65 appears to be the magic number in North America — is really a result of personnel policy and is influenced, but not determined, by government programs. It is neither fixed nor immutable.

This is illustrated by the fact that Europe and the United States appear to be moving in the opposite direction with respect to changes in the mandatory retirement age. Presumably to help alleviate problems of youth unemployment, in Europe the tendency is to encourage a lowering of the retirement age. In the U.S., on the other hand, the trend seems to be in the opposite direction. Recent legislation has removed any mandatory retirement age in the federal public service and has forbidden a mandatory retirement age below 70 in most other sectors. Certainly, workers can retire before age 70, and employers may try to induce them to do so. Nevertheless, they cannot be forced to retire against their wishes.

The fact that the mandatory retirement age is not immutable suggests that it can change in response to other basic forces that affect the retirement decision and that account for the existence of mandatory retirement itself. These factors are dealt with in Chapter 24, which looks at the rationale for mandatory retirement in the context of an optimal compensation system.

The remainder of this chapter deals with the basic forces that affect the retirement decision, either directly as people are induced to retire, or indirectly as pressure is exerted to change the mandatory retirement age or the age at which various retirement benefits become available.

Wealth and Earnings

Economic theory, in particular the income-leisure choice theory discussed earlier, indicates that the demand for leisure — as indicated, for example, by the decision to retire early — is positively related to one's wealth, and is related to expected earnings in an indeterminate fashion. The wealth effect is positive, reflecting a pure income effect: with more wealth we buy more of all normal goods, including leisure in the form of retirement. The impact of expected earnings is indeterminate, reflecting the opposing influences of income and substitution effects. An increase in expected earnings increases the income forgone if one retires and therefore raises the (opportunity) cost of retirement: this has a pure substitution effect reducing the demand for retirement leisure. On the other hand, an increase in expected earnings also means an increase in expected wealth and, just like wealth from non-labour sources, this would increase the demand for retirement leisure. Since the income and substitution effects work in opposite directions, then the impact on retirement of an increase in expected earnings is ultimately an empirical proposition. Thus the increase in our earnings that has gone on over time, and that presumably will continue, should have an indeterminate effect on the retirement decision.

Social Insurance Pension

By altering our wealth and net earnings position, social insurance schemes can also affect the retirement decision. Social insurance refers to public pension schemes that are financed by compulsory employer and employee payroll contributions, and that pay earnings-related pensions to those who qualify by virtue of their age and work experience. As the term "insurance" implies, receipts depend on contributions, and the fund is usually designed to be self-financing without support from general tax revenues. The Canada and Quebec Pension Plans are the primary social insurance pension schemes in Canada.

Other Pension Schemes

Other pensions often can be received at the same time as the social insurance pension. In particular, universal pensions are a flat rate paid out of general tax revenues to persons who reach a specified age. Receipt of the pension is not earnings-related in the sense that it does not depend on having worked, nor is receipt of the pension means-tested since it is a flat rate irrespective of income or need. The term demogrant is often applied to this type of program whereby a flat rate is given to a specific demographic group — in this case, all those over the specified age. Popular parlance often uses the term "old-age pension" because receipt is forthcoming at a specific age, or "government pension" because it comes from general tax revenues rather than payroll taxes. The Old Age Security program, which provides monthly payments to those over the age of 65, is the main such program in Canada. In addition, the Guaranteed Income Supplement provides payments to those over 65 depending on their income.

In addition to social insurance and universal pensions, private pensions may also exist. They can be arranged through employment — often termed "company pensions" — or through private financial institutions. They are really a form of private savings, earmarked for retirement. A fourth pension system — social assistance — may also be available to those who qualify through an age and means test, indicating financial need. Such social assistance is really a form of "welfare" payment out of general tax revenues, and is designed to supplement the income of the elderly who are in need.

All of the various pension schemes can have a potential impact on work incentives and hence the retirement decision. Social assistance pensions may have the same impact as welfare or a negative income tax, depending on their design, and universal pensions will have the same potential impact as a demogrant. (Each of these has been discussed in Chapter 4.) The retirement decision can also be affected by features of private pensions, for example the right to retire on a full company pension at the age of 55, or after 30 years of service.

Features of Social Insurance

Social insurance pensions have received particular attention in recent years because many of their features are ones that can induce early retirement. Social insurance usually involves payment of an earnings-related pension upon retirement; however, if the recipient continues to work and earn income, then the pension gets reduced. This pension reduction — often termed the *retirement test* or work-income test — is really an implicit tax on earnings. It is implicit in that it involves forgoing pension payments as one earns additional income. In addition, there is usually an explicit payroll tax on earnings used to finance the social insurance fund.

As Kirkpatrick (1974) indicates, the retirement test tends to be prevalent in the vast majority of countries with social insurance. Developing economies usually require complete withdrawal from the labour force in order to receive the pension (i.e., implicit 100 percent tax on earnings) mainly because such countries cannot afford to pay pensions to people who also work. In contrast, some countries with the longest history of social insurance schemes have no retirement test, allowing the person to retain full earnings and pension. The motivation for this may be different: in France it appears to be because pension benefits are low and earnings are needed to supplement income; in Germany it appears to be because of a desire to encourage the work ethic.

In the Canada Pension Plan the retirement test was eliminated in

1975. In the U.S., recipients who work are allowed to keep their full pension as long as their earnings do not exceed a specific amount; thereafter, pension benefits are reduced by $.50 for every $1.00 earned (50 percent implicit tax) up to another specified amount, and after this pensions are reduced by $1.00 for every $1.00 earned (100 percent implicit tax).

Effect on Retirement

These features of the Canadian and American social insurance schemes can have a substantial impact on the retirement decision. The pension itself, like all fixed benefit payments, has a pure income effect inducing retirement. In addition, for those who work, the implicit tax of the pension reduction associated with the retirement test, and the explicit payroll tax used to finance the scheme, both lower the returns to work and hence make retirement more financially attractive. That is, both taxes involve a substitution effect towards retirement because the opportunity cost of leisure in the form of retirement is lowered by the amount of tax on forgone earnings. To be sure, the tax on earnings also involves an income effect working in the opposite direction; that is, our reduced after-tax income means we can buy less of everything including leisure in the form of retirement. However, this income effect is outweighed by the income effect of the pension itself, since for all potential recipients their income is *at least* as high when social insurance is available. Thus, as with the negative-income-tax plans analysed in Chapter 4, both the substitution effect and the (net) income effect of the features of social insurance serve to unambiguously induce retirement.

Modelling Social Insurance in Income-Leisure Framework

These features of social insurance and their impact on retirement can be modelled somewhat more formally, along the lines of the income-leisure framework developed in Chapter 2. With Y defined as income after taxes and transfers, W the wage rate, T the maximum amount of leisure (L) available, B the pension received upon retiring, p the explicit payroll tax used to finance social insurance, and t the implicit tax involved in the pension reduction through the retirement test, the budget constraint with social insurance is:

$$Y = B + (1 - p - t) W(T - L)$$

This can be compared to the constraint without social insurance, which is:

$$Y = W(T - L)$$

The new budget constraint is illustrated in Figure 6.1 for various possible social insurance schemes. Figure 6.1(a) illustrates the case when there is no retirement test; that is, the recipient is given a pension and is allowed to work without forgoing retirement. (For simplicity, the payroll tax for financing the pension has been ignored. With the payroll tax as a fixed percentage of earnings, the budget constraint would have rotated downwards from the point B.) The new budget constraint is Y = B + W(T

Figure 6.1 Budget Constraints Under Social Insurance Pensions
(Assuming payroll tax p = 0)

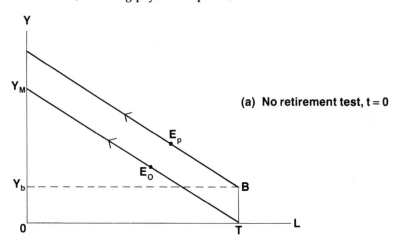

(a) **No retirement test, t = 0**

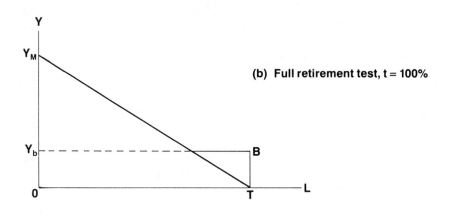

(b) **Full retirement test, t = 100%**

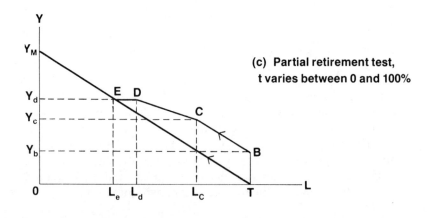

(c) **Partial retirement test,**
t varies between 0 and 100%

− L) when p = 0 and t = 0. Such a pension scheme simply has a pure income effect, encouraging potential recipients to retire. Although not shown in the diagram, the new indifference curve may be tangent to the new budget constraint, at a point such as E_p above and to the right of the original point E_0. The new equilibrium may also involve a corner solution at B, in which case the recipient retired completely, or it may be at a point like E_p, signifying partial retirement, or, if leisure is not a normal good, it may be at a point vertically above E_0, in which case the recipient continued to work the same as before and received the full pension.

Figure 6.1(b) illustrates the new budget constraint under a full retirement test whereby the pension recipient is required to give up $1.00 of pension for every $1.00 earned. This implicit 100 percent tax rate makes the budget constraint similar to the one for welfare discussed in Chapter 4, and the adverse work incentive effects are similar. In particular, there will be a strong incentive to retire completely (move to point B).

The typical case with a partial retirement test is illustrated in Figure 6.1(c). The first arm of the budget constraint, TB, indicates the pension benefits payable upon complete retirement. (Income is Y_b = TB when leisure is OT.) The second arm, BC, illustrates that up to a specific amount of labour market earnings, $Y_c − Y_b$, for working T − L_c, the recipient may keep the full pension benefits of Y_b (= TB), so that his total income with pension and labour market earnings could be up to Y_c. The new arm of the budget constraint is parallel to the original constraint of TY_m because the implicit tax is zero; that is, recipients who work keep their full labour market earnings.

The third arm, CD, illustrates the implicit tax that is involved when the recipient is required to give back a portion of the pension for the additional labour market earnings of $Y_d − Y_c$ that result from the additional work of $L_c − L_d$. An implicit tax of 50 percent results in the slope of CD being one-half of the slope of the original constraint TY_m; that is, for every dollar earned, the recipient forgoes $.50 in pension. When the recipient's labour earnings exceed $Y_d − Y_b$, then the pension is reduced by the same amount of the additional earnings and the fourth arm of the budget constraint is the horizontal portion DE, reflecting the 100 percent implicit tax rate for any additional work activity of L − L_e. At the point E, the person would no longer receive any pension and any additional work activity of $L_e − 0$ would result in additional income as shown by the fifth arm of the budget constraint EY_m.

The work incentive effects of the new budget constraint, $TBCDEY_m$, are such as to unambiguously induce retirement. Basically two things have happened. The budget constraint has shifted outward (upward to the right) from the original constraint of TY_m and this has a wealth or income effect encouraging the purchase of more leisure in the form of retirement. In addition, the slope of the new budget constraint is always equal to or less than the original constraint; that is, the opportunity cost of leisure is reduced and this would encourage the substitution of leisure for other commodities. Both the income and the substitution effect of the partial retirement test work in the same direction to encourage early retirement.

Obviously not all eligible people respond immediately to the incentive effects of the partial retirement test. The analysis is complicated by the existence of private pension plans, early retirement schemes, and by the fact that pension receipts are often a portion of previous earnings.[1] Nevertheless, the fact remains that social insurance pensions as they presently exist in North America theoretically will encourage early retirement on the part of some individuals.

Health and Other Determinants of Retirement

In addition to the mandatory retirement age, wealth and earnings, and the existence of social insurance and other pensions, the retirement decision can be affected by other factors. The changing nature of work towards more white-collar jobs and away from physical tasks may make it feasible for many to work longer. As well, the decline of the extended family may make retirement less attractive. On the other hand, individuals may be induced into early retirement to the extent that their jobs disappear due to economic change and dislocation.

Of prime importance in the retirement decision, however, is the potential impact of health. People approaching the usual retirement age obviously can be subject to health problems that could encourage them to retire. This may be the case, particularly if their accumulated wealth or pension income enables them to retire at a reasonable income. The various determinants of the retirement decision are obviously interrelated.

EMPIRICAL EVIDENCE

The empirical evidence on the determinants of the retirement decision is reviewed in Campbell and Campbell (1976), Boskin (1977) and Lazear (1986). Basically, there have been two techniques — survey interviews and labour force participation studies — that have been used to estimate the relative importance of the determinants of the retirement decision, and these two techniques tend to give conflicting answers with respect to the importance of health factors as opposed to social insurance.

Survey interviews asking people why they have retired, or would retire, usually find that ill health is the prime motivating factor — and that social insurance pensions have not induced early retirement. This is the conclusion reached in the study by Steiner and Dorfman (1959) and in numerous studies by the U.S. Social Security Administration as reviewed in Campbell and Campbell (1976, pp. 372-3). The interview technique may

---

[1] For the pre-retirement years, elements of a wage subsidy may be involved in pension plans whereby receipts are based on earnings, for example, in the last five years of work, or the five years of highest earnings. In such circumstances, the returns to an additional year of work may involve not only the additional earnings but also the additional future pension that results from the higher earnings.

yield biased results, however, in that respondents may feel that retiring for reasons of ill health is a more socially acceptable response than retiring because of social insurance pensions. In addition, in retrospective surveys taken after retirement, the respondent's health may have declined since retirement, and this may induce them to respond that ill health was a motivating factor.

In contrast to the interview surveys, econometric studies of the *actual* retirement decision generally find that retirement is strongly affected by the retirement-inducing features of social insurance pensions. This is the case in the studies by Feldstein (1974) based on international data, and by Boskin (1977), Quinn (1977), and Boskin and Hurd (1978) based on U.S. data. In addition, econometric studies of the *planned* retirement decision, based on prospective survey data, also find the economic features of pensions to be retirement-inducing. (Hall and Johnson (1978).)

Boskin (1977), for example, found that the income effect from expected social security pension benefits was seven times more powerful in inducing retirement than the income effect from other assets. This he attributed to a variety of factors: social security benefits are certain, since they are guaranteed for the remainder of one's life and often indexed against inflation; income from assets can be bequeathed, and therefore the elderly may not want to use up the income by retiring early; and people may be reluctant to borrow against the imputed income from assets like a house, because they may completely use up their assets. In contrast to the studies based on interview surveys, Boskin finds that ill health is not an important inducement to retire early.

Quinn (1977), on the other hand, finds that reporting a health limitation and being eligible for social security and other pensions were equally important factors in inducing retirement. He also found that persons reporting a health limitation were much more likely than those without a health limitation to retire if they were eligible for pensions. This suggests that eligibility for pensions is a strong factor *enabling* those with ill health to retire early, at the same time as the features of social security also *encourage* the early retirement of others.

Based on prospective survey data of the planned retirement decision, Hall and Johnson (1978) also find that both social insurance and ill health are retirement-inducing, and that government pensions provide much larger inducements to early retirement than private pensions.

In summary, the econometric studies[2] of the retirement decision are

[2] Evidence from econometric studies of labour force participation as discussed in Chapter 5 would also support the importance of economic factors in inducing retirement. Such studies generally found a positive income elasticity of demand for leisure and a negative (pure, compensated) wage elasticity of demand for leisure. However, one should be cautious in utilizing these results to infer retirement responses, even for those studies based on the labour force participation of the aged. Firstly, if non-labour income included pension income then this would be an endogenous, not exogenous, variable; that is, the retirement response would influence the amount of non-labour income rather than vice versa. Secondly, if Boskin's (1977) finding of a greater income elasticity for pension income as opposed to other non-labour income is correct, then the income elasticities based on participation equations for the elderly could not be used directly to infer retirement responses from pension income.

conclusive in finding the features of social security pensions to encourage retirement. The impact of *reported* health limitations is still open to debate, although pensions appear to be a strong factor enabling those with ill health to retire early.

The importance of the economic factors inducing retirement is also supported by statistical tabulations presented in Campbell and Campbell (1976). They cite the dramatic increase in retirement at age 65 when people become eligible for full social security benefits, the large increases in retirement just after amendments that extended the coverage and benefits of social security, the continuous trend towards early retirement at the same time as social security benefits increased over time, and the dramatic increase in early retirement when social security paid partial benefits for early retirement. To be sure, other factors have been at work at the same time to alter the retirement decision. Nevertheless, the evidence from basic statistical tabulations as well as econometric studies both tend to confirm that economic factors — especially the features of social insurance pension schemes — tend to encourage early retirement.

SOME POLICY ISSUES

The fact that social insurance pensions have a substantial impact on the retirement decision has important policy implications. This is especially the case since many features of pension schemes are policy parameters, subject to change by policy makers. This is the case with respect to such features as the retirement test (implicit tax on earnings as pensions are reduced if one continues to work), the explicit payroll tax used to finance social insurance, the replacement ratio (amount of social insurance benefits relative to pre-retirement earnings), coverage and eligibility for social insurance, pensions for early retirement, and the indexing of pensions for inflation. In addition, features of private pensions can be altered through their tax status, portability, and the mandatory retirement age.

As Kirkpatrick (1974, pp. 14-16) indicates, experience outside North America also suggests that features of social insurance can be altered selectively to achieve very specific human resource objectives. Communist countries have often reduced the retirement test for older workers willing to work in specific occupations, industries and geographic areas experiencing labour shortages. Many European countries and Japan have utilized social insurance to encourage early retirement in agriculture so as to promote efficiency by reducing the number of agricultural workers. Specifically, farmers may be required to sell their land or cease full-time farming in order to receive a pension.

Clearly, retirement policies can and do have a substantial impact on the retirement decision, and this in turn has implications for a variety of factors including the size, composition and deployment of our labour force, the extent of poverty, the magnitude of private savings, company personnel policies, and the solvency of social insurance funds. Because of this importance, the retirement decision merits careful analysis if it is to be altered by various policy instruments. Hopefully labour market analysis can contribute to this area of growing policy concern.

QUESTIONS

1. Outline the main areas of public policy that are affected by the retirement decision. Discuss the impact on these areas of public policy of a policy of making the mandatory retirement age illegal.
2. Outline the main features of pension schemes that can be considered as policy parameters, subject to change by policy makers.
3. Discuss the main factors that affect the solvency of the social insurance pension fund. Indicate how these factors are changing over time and what this implies about the solvency of the fund. What assurances do we have that future generations will accept increased payroll taxes if the solvency of the fund becomes in doubt?
4. Discuss the extent to which the mandatory retirement age is both an exogenous determinant of the retirement decision, and an endogenous result of the retirement decision.
5. Discuss the econometric problems involved with each of the following ways of estimating the retirement response and indicate what you would do to account for these problems:
    (a) estimating a labour force participation equation based on microdata where the unit of observation is the individual who either participates or does not participate in the labour force;
    (b) estimating an hours-of-work equation based on microdata where retired persons would be clustered at zero hours of work;
    (c) estimating a labour force participation equation based on microdata with the individual as the unit of observation and with a non-labour income variable that includes social insurance benefits.
6. Discuss the expected impact on the retirement decision of an increase in each of the following factors:
    (a) non-labour wealth;
    (b) labour market earnings;
    (c) earnings of spouse;
    (d) replacement ratio in social insurance pensions;
    (e) retirement test;
    (f) payroll tax to finance social insurance.
7. Based on Figure 6.1(a) draw the indifference curves, before and after the pension, for persons who:
    (a) retire completely;
    (b) retire partially;
    (c) work the same.
    Compare their income in each case.
8. Based on Figure 6.1(b), draw the indifference curves for a person who is indifferent between retiring completely and continuing to work. Why

would a person ever be indifferent between these two alternatives assuming that retirement is regarded positively? Based on the various factors given in the diagram, indicate how people may be induced to stay in the labour force rather than retire.

9. Based on Figure 6.1(c), draw the indifference curve for a person who:
   (a) retires completely;
   (b) works part time and only earns income up to the maximum amount before it becomes retirement tested;
   (c) works and earns income up to the maximum amount before it becomes retirement tested at a 100% implicit tax;
   (d) works and earns so much income that no pension is forthcoming.
   Compare the pension cost under each alternative.

10. Assume that an individual earned an average of $10,000 during his last 5 years prior to retirement. Depict the budget constraint for a social insurance pension with a replacement rate of 50%, and a retirement test allowing one to earn up to $2,000 without having to forgo any pension, but which requires a pension reduction of $.50 for every dollar for income between $2,000 and $4,000, and requires one to completely forgo pension income if earnings exceed $4,000.

11. Indicate why pensions may actually increase poverty as it is conventionally measured.

12. Discuss the advantage and disadvantage of the full retirement test versus no retirement test.

13. Do you think that the trend towards early retirement will continue into the future?

14. If the retirement test is an implicit tax on earnings and if a tax increase has an ambiguous effect on work incentives, why is it that the features of social insurance pensions can be said to unambiguously encourage retirement?

15. You have been asked to estimate the impact on retirement of a policy of raising the replacement rate from 40% to 60%, and of lowering the implicit tax of the retirement test from 50% to 30%. You have access to comprehensive microeconomic data where the individual is the unit of observation. Specify an appropriate regression equation for estimating the retirement response and indicate how you would simulate the impact of the change in the two policy parameters.

REFERENCES AND FURTHER READINGS

Anderson, K. and R. Burkhauser. The retirement health nexus: a new measure of an old puzzle. *JHR* 20 (Summer 1985) 315-330.

Barfield, R. and J. Morgan. *Early Retirement: The Decision and the Experience and a Second Look*. Ann Arbor, Michigan: University of Michigan Press, 1974.

Barfield, R. and J. Morgan. Trends in planned early retirement. *The Gerontologist* 18 (February 1978) 13-18.

Bazzoli, G. The early retirement decision: new empirical evidence on the influence of health. *JHR* 20 (Spring 1985) 214-234.

Blinder, A., R. Gordon and D. Wise. Reconsidering the disincentive effects of social security. *National Tax Journal* 33 (December 1980) 431-442.

Boskin, M. Social security and retirement decisions. *EI* 15 (January 1977) 1-25.

Boskin, M. and M. Hurd. Effect of social security on early retirement. *JPubEc* 10 (December 1978) 361-377.

Burbidge, J. and L. Robb. Pensions and retirement behaviour. *CJE* 13 (August 1980) 421-437.

Burkhauser, R. The pension acceptance decision of older workers. *JHR* 14 (Winter 1979) 63-75.

Burkhauser, R. The early acceptance of social security: an asset maximization approach. *ILRR* 33 (July 1980) 484-492.

Burkhauser, R. and J. Turner. A time series analysis of social security and its effects on the market work of men at younger ages. *JPE* 86 (August 1978) 701-716.

Burkhauser, R. and J. Turner. Labour market experience of the almost old and the implications for income support. *AER* 72 (May 1982) 304-308.

Burtless, G. and J. Hausman. "Double-dipping": the combined effects of Social Security and civil service pensions on employee retirement. *JPubEc* 18 (July 1982) 139-160.

Burtless, G. and R. Moffit. The joint choice of retirement age and postretirement hours of work. *JOLE* 3 (April 1985) 209-236.

Campbell, C. and R. Campbell. Conflicting views on the effect of old-age and survivors insurance on retirement. *EI* 14 (September 1976) 369-387. Comment by V. Reno, A. Fox and L. Mallan and reply 15 (October 1977) 619-623.

Crawford, V. and D. Lilien. Social security and the retirement system. *QJE* 96 (August 1981) 505-530.

Diamond, P. A framework for social security analysis. *JPE* 8 (December 1977) 275-298.

Dorsey, S. A model and empirical estimates of worker pension coverage in the U.S. *SEJ* 49 (October 1982) 506-520. Comment by D. Cymrot and reply by S. Dorsey 51 (April 1985) 1245-1248, 1249-1251.

Driffill, E. Life-cycles with terminal retirement. *IER* 21 (February 1980) 45-62.

Duggan, J. The labor-force participation of older workers. *ILRR* 37 (April 1984) 416-430.

Ehrenberg, R. Retirement policies, employment and unemployment. *AER Proceedings* 69 (May 1979) 131-136.

Ethier, M. Survey of pension issues. *Income Distribution and Economic Security in Canada*, F. Vaillancourt (ed.). Toronto: University of Toronto Press, 1985, 215-49.

Feldstein, M. Social security, induced retirement and aggregate capital accumulation. *JPE* 82 (September 1974) 905-926.

Fields, G. and O. Mitchell. The effects of pensions and earnings on retirement: a review essay. *Research in Labor Economics*, R. Ehrenberg (ed.). New Haven: JAI Pres, 1982.

Fields, G. and O. Mitchell. Economic determinants of the optimal retirement age: an empirical investigation. *JHR* 19 (Spring 1984) 245-262.

Fields, G. and O. Mitchell. The effects of Social Security reforms on retirement ages and retirement incomes. *JPubEc* 25 (November 1984) 143-159.

Gordon, R. and A. Blinder. Market wages, reservation wages, and retirement decisions. *JPubEc* 14 (October 1980) 277-308.

Gustman, A. and T. Steinmeier. Partial retirement and the analysis of retirement behavior. *ILRR* 37 (April 1984) 403-415.

Gustman, A. and T. Steinmeier. The 1983 Social Security reforms and labor supply adjustments of older individuals in the long run. *JOLE* 3 (April 1985) 237-253.

Hall, A. and T. Johnson. *Social security, health and retirement plans*. Menlo Park, California: SRI International, 1978.

Hall, A. and T. Johnson. The determinants of planned retirement age. *ILRR* 33 (January 1980) 241-254.

Hamermesh, D. Social insurance and consumption: an empirical inquiry. *AER* 72 (March 1982) 101-113.

Hamermesh, D. Life-cycle effects on consumption and retirement. *JOLE* 2 July 1984) 353-370.

Hanoch, G. and M. Honig. Retirement, wages, and labor supply of the elderly. *JLE* 1 (April 1983) 131-151.

Hartman, R. Retirement for federal civil servants: down from the incomparable. *IRRA* (September 1980) 82-89.

Hemming, R. The effect of state and private pensions on retirement behaviour and personal capital accumulation. *R.E. Studies* 44 (February 1977) 169-172.

Honig, M. and G. Hanoch. Partial retirement as a separate mode of retirement behavior. *JHR* 20 (Winter 1985) 21-46.

Hu, S.C. Social security, the supply of labor and capital accumulation. *AER* 69 (June 1979) 274-283.

Jackson, M. Early retirement: recent trends. *IRJ* 15 (Autumn 1984) 21-28.

Kirkpatrick, E. The retirement test: an international study. *Social Security Bulletin* (July 1974) 3-16.

Kittner, D. Forced retirement: how common is it? *MLR* (December 1977) 60-61.

Mitchell, O. and G. Fields. The economics of retirement behavior. *JOLE* 2 (January 1984) 84-105.

Pellechio, A. Social security financing and retirement behavior. *AER Proceedings* 69 (May 1979) 284-287.

Pesando, J. and S. Rea. *Public and Private Pensions in Canada*. Ontario Economic Council Study. Toronto: University of Toronto Press, 1977.

Quinn, J. Microeconomic determinants of early retirement: a cross section view of white married men. *JHR* 12 (Summer 1977) 329-346.

Quinn, J. Job characteristics and early retirement. *IR* 17 (October 1978) 315-328.

Reno, V. Why men stop working at or before age 65. *Social Security Bulletin* (June 1971).

Rones, P. Older men — the choice between work and retirement. *MLR* 101 (November 1978) 3-10.

Schiller, B. and R. Weiss. The impact of private pensions on firm attachment. *R.E. Stats.* 61 (Aug. 1979) 369-380.

Sheppard, H. The issue of mandatory retirement. *Annals of the American Academy of Political and Social Science* 438 (July 1978) 40-49.

Smith, J. On the labor supply effects of age-related income maintenance programs. *JHR* 10 (Winter 1975) 25-43.

Steiner, P. and R. Dorfman. *The Economic Status of the Aged*. Berkeley: University of California Press, 1959.

Warlick, J. Participation of the aged in SSI. *JHR* 17 (Spring 1982) 236-260.

Wolfe, J. Perceived longevity and early retirement. *R.E. Stats.* 65 (Nov. 1983) 544-551.

Wolfe, J. A model of declining health and retirement. *JPE* 93 (December 1985) 1258-1267.

Zabalza, A. and D. Piachaud. Social security and the elderly: a simulation of policy changes. *JPubEc* 16 (October 1981) 145-170.

Zabalza, A., C. Pissarides and M. Barton. Social security and the choice between full-time work, part-time work and retirement. *JPubEc* 14 (October 1980) 245-276.

7 Hours of Work

The hours-of-work aspect of labour supply has a variety of dimensions including hours-per-day, days-per-week and weeks-per-year. Changes in any or all of these dimensions can alter the hours-of-work aspect of the labour supply decision. Phenomena such as the eight-hour day, the shorter work week, and increased vacation time are institutional embodiments of a reduction in hours of work. Similarly, moonlighting and overtime are institutional arrangements that alter the typical pattern of hours of work.

In the short run, hours of work appear to be relatively fixed with little scope for individual variation. The eight-hour day, five-day work week and fixed vacation period are fairly standard for most wage and salary earners. However, as we will analyse later in this chapter, the increased importance of flexible working hours is altering these arrangements. In addition, occupational choice provides an element of flexibility as people choose jobs partly on the basis of the hours of work required.

Greater flexibility is possible in the long run when firms and workers have sufficient time to adjust to new preferences and constraints they may face. The adjustment process may be subtle, as for example when workers choose jobs partly on the basis of the hours of work required. Or it may be overt, as for example when workers bargain through their unions for longer vacations or a reduced work week or workday.

The policy importance of the hours-of-work decision is illustrated in a variety of ways. Changes in the hours-of-work decision can affect not only the quantity but also the quality of our overall labour supply (and hence national output), as well as absenteeism, turnover, employment opportunities, and the demand for related activities, notably those involving leisure time and flexible working hours. Changes in hours of work, in turn, can be affected by changes in the age and sex structure of the labour force, as well as government policies and laws and, of course, the basic economic determinants — wealth and expected earnings. Only by analysing these determinants can we forecast the future time pattern of hours of work and predict the impact of alternative policies and institutional arrangements.

The focus of this chapter is on the supply side of the market; that is, on the determinants of the hours of work that individuals decide to offer or supply to the labour market. The demand side, emphasizing the firm's hours-of-work decision, is discussed in Chapters 9 and 10.

THEORETICAL DETERMINANTS OF HOURS OF WORK

Institutional Factors

At first glance it appears that hours of work are largely influenced by institutional factors. Unions have fought long and successfully for reduced working hours in a variety of forms. Labour standards legislation has specified maximum hours that can be worked and has required overtime premiums in certain circumstances. In addition, as we will analyse later, legislation can affect the number of hours for which it is optimal to employ certain types of labour. The age and sex structure of the work-force can also affect hours worked because of the varying preferences for leisure and work activities amongst various elements of the work-force.

However, rather than exerting independent influences on the choice of hours of work, many of these factors can be thought of as being the institutional embodiments through which the preferences of the work-force are registered. Presumably unions have pushed for reduced hours because this is what the rank and file wanted, given their changing circumstances. Similarly, legislation governing hours of work would change in response to the pressures of the parties influencing the legislative process. What then are the basic forces that, in part at least, have worked through these institutional channels to alter the hours-of-work decision?

Economic Factors

As with the labour force participation decision, the basic economic determinants of the hours-of-work decision are one's non-labour income and hourly wage — the respective income and price variables of economic theory. The income-leisure choice framework predicts that an increase in our non-labour income will have a pure income effect increasing the demand for leisure and hence reducing the hours of work. An increase in the wage will have both an income and a substitution effect, each working in the opposite direction. On the one hand, the increased wage means that the price (opportunity cost, forgone income) of leisure has gone up, and hence the individual will "buy" less leisure and work more hours. On the other hand, the increased wage means that potential wealth is higher, and as with non-labour income, this means an increased demand for leisure and a reduction in hours of work. To ascertain the net impact of these respective substitution and income effects of a wage change, we must appeal to the empirical evidence.

EMPIRICAL EVIDENCE

Trend Data

The analysis of trends in the work week is complicated by the various measures of hours of work. As discussed in Hameed and Cullen (1975, p.

3), the most common measures used in Canada include standard hours, actual hours worked, and hours paid for. All measures, however, suggest the same trend: a pronounced and continuous decline over time in hours of work.

This is illustrated in Table 7.1, which traces the standard work week in Canadian manufacturing. Between 1901 and 1981 the standard work week declined from almost 60 hours to less than 40 hours. The decline slowed down in the depression years of the 1930s, and the war years of the 1940s, and it appears to be slower in the postwar period. However, as the last column illustrates, when vacations and holidays are considered the decline in average working hours is more noticeable. In essence, in recent years the work-force has reduced its working hours more in the form of increased vacations and holidays rather than a reduction in hours worked per week. The decline in net weekly hours in the postwar period and in standard hours prior to World War II give a long-run trend reduction of about two hours per decade.

TABLE 7.1
STANDARD WEEKLY HOURS IN MANUFACTURING, CANADA, 1901–1981

Year	Standard Weekly Hours[a]	Hours Net of Vacations & Holidays[b]
1901	58.6	n.a.
1911	56.5	n.a.
1921	50.3	n.a.
1931	49.6	n.a.
1941	49.0	n.a.
1951	42.6	40.7
1961	40.4	38.1
1971	39.8	36.7
1981	39.2	34.8

Note: [a]Standard hours are usually determined by collective agreements or company policies, and they are the hours beyond which overtime rates are paid. The data apply to non-office workers.
[b]Standard hours minus the average hours per week spent on holidays and vacations.

Source: Figures for 1901–1971 for standard weekly hours are from S. Ostry and M. Zaidi, *Labour Economics in Canada*, 3rd ed. Toronto: Macmillan, 1979 pp. 80,81. Figures for 1951–1971 for hours net of vacations and holidays are from Labour Canada (1974, p. 6). Both sources used as their primary data the Survey of Working Conditions conducted annually by the Canada Department of Labour and published as *Wage Rates, Salaries and Hours of Labour*. This survey is also the source for the 1981 figure.

This long-run decline in hours of work suggests the dominance of the income effect over the substitution effect with respect to the hours-of-work decision. That is, as real wages have increased over time, the resulting increased income has been used to buy more leisure in the form of reduced hours of work, and this has dominated any tendency to buy less leisure because it is more expensive as wages increase. The income effect of the wage increase appears to have dominated the substitution effect, with the result that hours of work have similarly decreased over time as wages have increased.

Econometric Studies

More precise estimates of these income and substitution effects can be gleaned from econometric studies of the determinants of hours of work. Finegan (1962) used multiple regression analysis to estimate an hours of work (per week) equation for males based on U.S. occupational data. The independent or explanatory variables included hourly wages (cents per hour), as well as a variety of control variables designed to control for other factors that influence hours of work, such as marital status, education, age and race. The estimated regression coefficient for the hourly wage variable was a statistically significant −.085, indicating that a one cent per hour increase in the wage rate is associated with a .085 reduction in hours worked per week. Alternatively stated, an 11.5 cent increase in the hourly wage is associated with approximately a one hour decrease in hours worked per week. Clearly, the income effect of the wage increase dominates its substitution effect, so that wage increases tend to be associated with reductions in hours worked. Thus the historical decline in hours of work would be expected from the increase in real wages that has gone on over time. If one were to add the income effect resulting from increases in non-labour income (e.g. income of spouse), the decline in hours worked is even more predictable.[1]

Econometric studies of the Canadian postwar experience with respect to hours of work have been carried out by Hameed (1975), Newton and Leckie (1979) and Aw (1982). These studies also conclude that the rise in real wages has been a major factor contributing to the decline in hours of work. Newton and Leckie (1979), who study the simultaneous determination of the demand for and supply of hours of work, find that child-rearing costs and recreational costs affect the supply of hours and that labour productivity and capacity utilization affect the demand for hours.

MOONLIGHTING, OVERTIME AND FLEXIBLE WORK HOURS

Any analysis of the hours-of-work decision must confront the following basic question: why is it that some people moonlight at a second job at a

[1]The elasticity of supply of hours with respect to wages (i.e. percentage change in hours that results from a one percent change in wages) is calculated as $\varepsilon_{HW} = (\partial H/\partial W)\,(W/H)$. Assuming an average wage W of 150 cents per hour and an average work week H of 40 hours per week in 1962, and based on the estimated regression coefficient, $\partial H/\partial W$, of −.085, the calculated elasticity is $\varepsilon_{HW} = -.085(150/40) = -.32$ approximately. Thus a one percent increase in wages is associated with approximately a one-third of one percent reduction in hours worked, according to Finegan's (1962) estimates.

wage less than their market wage on their first job, while others require an overtime premium to work more? This apparent anomaly occurs because people who moonlight are underemployed at the going wage on their main job while people who require an overtime premium are already over-employed at the going wage on their main job. Underemployment and overemployment, in turn, occur because different workers have different preferences and they tend to be confronted with an institutionally fixed work schedule. The fixed hours of work, in turn, can arise because of such factors as legislation, union pressure, or company personnel policy. The need for interaction among employees (or between employees and the firm's physical capital) may cause the employer to set standardized hours of work, rather than allowing each employee to work his or her preferred number of hours. Again, economic theory will enable us to analyse the labour market impact of these important institutional constraints.

The fixed hours-of-work phenomenon is illustrated in Figure 7.1(a). In this case, the worker is faced with two constraints. The first is the usual budget constraint L_tY_t as determined by the person's hourly wage. This restricts the worker's maximum choice set to the triangular area L_tY_tO. The second constraint of the fixed workday of L_tL_c hours (recall work is meas-ured from right to left) restricts the worker's maximum choice set to the area L_cCY_cO: the worker can take no more leisure than OL_c (work no more than L_tL_c), and no more income than OY_c even if he worked more than L_tL_c. In effect, this reduces the worker's realistic choice set to the point C since C will always be preferred to other points within L_cCY_cO.

Moonlighting and Underemployment

Some individuals, however, may have preferences such that they would prefer to work more hours at the going wage rate. Figure 7.1(b) illustrates the case for an individual whose preferences (indifference curve U_d) are such that he would prefer to be at D, working L_tL_d hours at the going wage and taking home an income of Y_d. However, because of the hours of work constraint, the worker must be at C, obviously being less well off since $U_c < U_d$. In fact, the difference between U_d and U_c is a measure of how much the worker would be willing to give up in order to have the fixed hours constraint relaxed.

A variety of implications follow from this analysis. The worker is *underemployed* because he would like to work more at the going wage rate. Because of the additional constraint of the fixed working hours, the worker is also less well off ($U_c < U_d$) and may be seeking a different job that would enable him to achieve his desired equilibrium at D. In addition, the worker may be willing to *moonlight* and do additional work at a wage rate that is lower than the wage rate of the first job.

This moonlighting equilibrium is illustrated in Figure 7.1(c) by the budget constraint CY_m. (To simplify the diagram the details of Figure 7.1(b) have been omitted). This new budget constraint rotates downward from

Figure 7.1 Fixed Hours Constraint, Underemployment, and Moonlighting

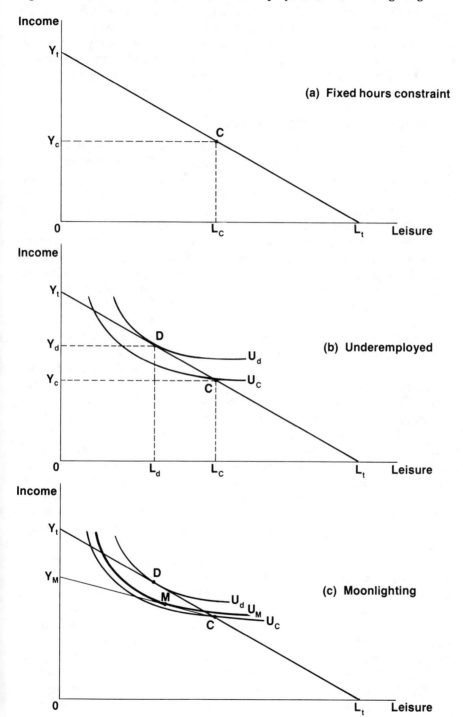

CY_t because the moonlighting wage, which is less than the regular wage as given by the slope of CY_t, applies only to hours of work beyond L_tL_c. In spite of the lower moonlighting wage, the worker is willing to work more hours (move from C to M) because of the greater utility associated with the move ($U_m > U_c$). That is, workers who are underemployed at the going wage rate would be willing to moonlight at a lower wage rate on their secondary job.

Overtime and Overemployment

Other individuals, however, may have preferences such that they would prefer to work fewer hours at the going wage rate. Figure 7.2(a) illustrates the situation where the worker would prefer (maximize utility) to be at D, working L_tL_d hours for an income of Y_d. However, because of the institutionally fixed work week, he is compelled to be at C, being less well off ($U_c < U_d$) even though he takes home more income ($Y_c > Y_d$).

Such a worker is *overemployed* at the going wage rate and consequently would support policies to reduce the institutionally fixed work week. In addition, he also may be seeking a different job that would enable him to work fewer hours at the going wage rate, and he may even exhibit absenteeism and tardiness as ways of moving towards his desired work week. Because such a worker is already overemployed at the going wage rate, he would not willingly work more hours at the wage rate; however, he may be induced to do so by an *overtime* premium.

This overtime premium is illustrated in Figure 7.2(b) by the budget constraint CY_o that rotates upwards from CY_t because the overtime premium, which is greater than the normal wage which determines the slope of L_tY_t, applies only to overtime hours of work beyond L_tL_c. If, for example, the overtime premium is time-and-one-half, then the overtime budget constraint has a fifty percent greater slope than the regular straight-time budget constraint. As long as the worker is willing to give up some leisure for additional income, then there is an overtime premium that will induce him to work more, for example, to move to point O on Figure 7.2(b) (on the indifference curve U_o). Because the worker is overemployed at the going wage rate, the overtime premium is necessary to get him to work more hours.

The person works longer hours even though he was overemployed at the going wage rate because the overtime premium results in a large substitution effect, by making the price (opportunity cost, income forgone) of leisure higher only for the overtime hours, and a small income effect. That is, the budget constraint rotates upward *only* for the overtime hours; consequently, it does not have an income effect for the normal straight-time hours. Recall that the substitution effect was illustrated by a changed *slope* in the budget constraint, while the income effect was illustrated by a *parallel shift* of the constraint. Since the overtime premium changes the slope for the overtime hours, it is primarily a work-inducing substitution effect, with little leisure-inducing income effect.

Figure 7.2 Overemployment and Overtime

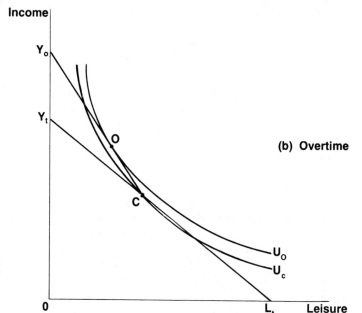

Overtime Premium Versus Straight-time Equivalent

The importance of the relative absence of the income effect in the overtime premium can be illustrated by a comparison of the overtime premium with the straight-time equivalent. One might logically ask the question: if workers are constantly working overtime, why not institutionalize that into a longer workday and pay them the straight-time equivalent of their normal wage plus their overtime wage?

This alternative is illustrated in Figure 7.3. The overtime situation is

Figure 7.3   Overtime Premium Versus Straight-time Equivalent

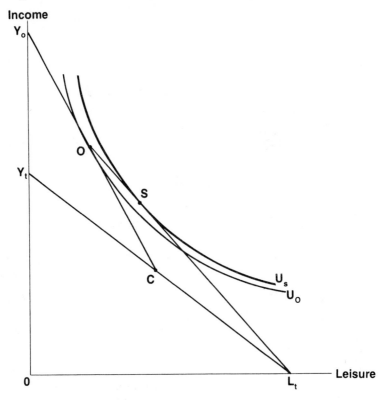

illustrated by the budget constraint L_tCY_o with L_tC being the normal wage paid during the regular work period and CY_o being the overtime premium paid for overtime hours. The regular work period would be L_tL_c hours and overtime hours would be L_cL_o. (To simplify the diagram, these points are not shown; however, as in Figure 7.2(a), they are simply the points on the horizontal leisure axis vertically below their corresponding equilibrium points.) The straight-time hourly equivalent for L_tL_o hours of work is given by the budget constraint L_tO, the slope of which is a weighted average of the slopes of the regular wage L_tC and the overtime premium CO. The straight-time hourly equivalent is derived by simply taking the earnings associated with the overtime plus regular time hours of work, L_tL_o, and determining the straight-time wage, L_tO, that would yield the same earnings.

A worker who is paid the straight-time equivalent, however, would not voluntarily remain at O, but rather would move to the point S which involves less work. This is so because the wage line L_tSO has a larger leisure-inducing income effect, whereas the overtime premium COY_o is dominated by the work-inducing substitution effect (rotation of the budget constraint). In essence, since the overtime premium is paid only for hours *beyond* the regular workday, the person has to work more to get the additional income.

Overtime premiums, therefore, may be a rational way for employers to get their existing work-force to voluntarily work more hours, even if they are overemployed at their regular workday. Employers, in turn, may want to work their existing work-force longer hours, rather than hiring additional workers, so as to spread their fixed hiring costs over longer hours. The importance of these fixed hiring costs will be analysed in more detail when labour demand is discussed.

Workers need not be overemployed at their going wage rate for the overtime premium to work. One can easily portray the situation for a worker in equilibrium at the regular wage rate who would unambiguously work more when offered an overtime wage premium, but who may work less if offered a straight-time hourly wage increase. Firms that want to work their existing work-force longer hours may prefer a wage package that involves a low regular wage and a high overtime premium, to a package that costs them the same but that involves a straight-time wage increase.

Again, what at first glance appear to be costly and irrational actions on the part of firms — in this case the coexistence of overtime and moonlighting rates and a preference for overtime premiums over straight-line equivalent earnings — may well be rational actions when viewed in the larger picture where the parties are optimizing with respect to legal-institutional constraints and when the varying preferences of individual workers are considered. Rather than rendering economic theory irrelevant in the force of such constraints, they highlight the usefulness of economics in analysing the impact of the constraints and in explaining why, in fact, they may arise as an endogenous institutional response to the peculiarities of the labour market.

Flexible Working Hours

The basic income-leisure choice framework is also useful in understanding the phenomenon of flexible working hours (often termed flexitime) that has increased dramatically in recent years. Specifically, economic theory indicates that there are gains to be had by following flexitime to meet the divergent tastes and preferences of different workers. Of course, these gains must be weighed against the additional costs that flexitime may impose. Such costs could include costs of monitoring, supervision, communication and coordination that are involved as workers have greater flexibility in choosing their working hours. Recent increases in the use of flexitime, however, suggest the benefits are outweighing the costs in many circumstances.

The benefits of flexitime are illustrated in Figure 7.4. The point C illustrates where workers are constrained to operate given the all-or-nothing choice of working L_tL_c hours (points on the leisure axis are not marked, to simplify the diagram) at the going wage (slope of L_tY_t). However, many

Figure 7.4 Gains From Flexitime

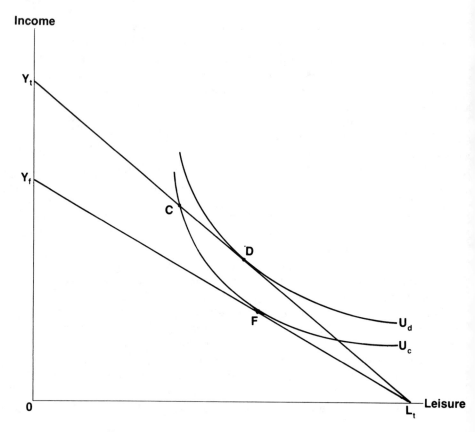

workers have different preferences. Some, for example, may prefer to be at point D. Because they are overemployed at the going wage rate, their discontent ($U_c < U_d$) may be exhibited in the form of costly absenteeism, high turnover, and perhaps reduced morale and productivity.

Obviously firms that allowed such workers to work their desired hours of work could save on these costs. Alternatively, such firms could lower their wage rates and still retain their work-force. This is illustrated by the wage line L_tY_f, which could be lowered until the point of tangency, F, with the original utility curve U_c. Workers are equally well off at C and F (same level of utility U_c) even though F implies a lower wage rate, simply because they are at an equilibrium with respect to their hours of work. In essence, they are willing to give up wages in return for a work schedule that meets their preferences.

Competition for such jobs would ensure that firms could offer lower wages in return for more flexible work schedules. In this sense, the gains from flexitime could be recouped by the firm to cover the other costs that may be associated with flexitime. Firms that offer more flexible hours need not lower wages, but may take the benefits in the form of reduced absenteeism, lower turnover and improved worker morale. Various combinations of reduced wages (downward rotated wage line) and improved worker morale (higher indifference curve), of course, are possible.

The realities of flexitime are such that, subject to certain limitations, firms usually allow workers to work a fixed number of hours, but to work them at times of their own choosing. Whatever the form of flexitime, the basic point remains: there are gains to be had by following flexitime to meet the divergent tastes and preferences of workers.

QUESTIONS

1. Indicate the various ways in which workers may alter their hours-of-work decision and discuss the factors that may influence why a particular way is chosen. Discuss, for example, why increased vacation time may be chosen over a shorter workday.
2. Indicate the ways in which some of the recent decline in average hours worked may be explained by changes in the age and sex structure of our work-force.
3. What factors may influence our decision to alter labour supply through changes in hours of work rather than labour force participation? Is it possible that some groups may choose to increase one dimension of labour supply while simultaneously decreasing another?
4. Utilize economic theory to suggest the relevant variables and their functional form that are appropriate for estimating the determinants of hours of work.
5. Discuss the econometric problems involved in estimating an hours-of-work equation based on microeconomic data where the individual is the unit of observation. If the full sample were to include those who worked and those who did not work, how might you construct a variable to reflect the expected wage for those who did not work?
6. Based on the diagrams of Figure 7.1, illustrate how an underemployed worker would respond to:
   (a) an offer to work as many more hours as the worker would like at the going wage;
   (b) payment of an overtime premium for hours of work beyond C;
   (c) an offer to work an additional fixed number of hours, as determined by the employee at the going wage.
7. Based on the diagrams of Figure 7.2, illustrate how an overemployed worker would respond to:
   (a) an offer to work as many more hours as the worker would like at the going wage;
   (b) payment of a moonlighting rate for hours of work beyond C.
8. Based on Figure 7.2(b), precisely illustrate the following overtime rates for hours worked beyond L_tL_c:
   (a) time-and-one-half,

(b) double-time,

(c) time-and-one-half for the first two hours of overtime, and double-time thereafter.

9. Why might a company constantly pay an overtime premium rather than pay the straight-time hourly equivalent? For example, if a company was paying its workers five dollars an hour for the first eight hours and 7.50 dollars for the next two hours (for a total of 55 dollars per 10-hour day), why might the company not be willing to offer its workers the straight-time hourly equivalent of 5.50 dollars per hour since that is in fact what they are earning?

10. Based on Figure 7.3, why wouldn't the company simply offer the all-or-nothing choice of working L_tO_t hours for the straight-time hourly equivalent wage of L_tSO? Why might unions bargain for the straight-time equivalent?

11. Utilize your knowledge of the income-leisure choice framework to illustrate formally the proposition that there are gains to be had by allowing flexitime to meet the divergent tastes and preferences of different workers. Who would ultimately receive these gains?

12. Specifically, what are some of the costs that might be involved in various forms of flexitime and how might these costs be minimized?

REFERENCES AND FURTHER READINGS

Aw, C.F. Standard Hours of Work: Determinants and Implications. Ottawa: Department of Labour, 1982.

Barzel, Y. The determination of daily hours and wages. *QJE* 87 (May 1973) 220-238.

Bernanke, B. Employment, hours and earnings in the depression: an analysis of eight manufacturing industries. *AER* 76 (March 1986) 82-109.

Best, F. Preferences in worklife scheduling and work-leisure tradeoffs. *MLR* 101 (June 1978) 31-37.

Borjas, G. The relationship between wages and weekly hours of work: the role of division bias. *JHR* 15 (Summer 1980) 409-423.

Bosworth, D., P. Dawkins, and A. Westaway. Explaining the incidence of shift-working in Great Britain. *EJ* 91 (March 1981) 145-157.

Doherty, N. National insurance and absence from work. *EJ* 89 (March 1979) 50-65.

Evans, A. *Hours of Work*. Geneva: International Labour Organization, 1975.

Fan, L. Leisure and time elements in consumer behavior. *SEJ* 38 (April 1972) 478-484.

Feldstein, M. Estimating the supply curve of working hours. *Oxford Economic Papers* 20 (August 1968).

Finegan, T. Hours of work in the United States: a cross-sectional analysis. *JPE* 70 (October 1962) 452-470.

Gilbert, F. and R. Pfouts. A theory of the responsiveness of hours of work to changes in money rates. *R.E. Stats.* (May 1958) 116-121.

Hall, R. Wages, income and hours of work in the U.S. labor force. *Income Maintenance and Labor Supply*, G. Cain and H. Watts (eds.). Chicago: Rand McNally, 1973.

Hameed, S.M.A. Economic and institutional determinants of the average work week in Canada. *Work and Leisure in Canada*, S.M.A. Hameed and D. Cullen (eds.). Edmonton: University of Alberta, 1975.

Hameed, S. and D. Cullen. *Work and Leisure in Canada*. Edmonton: University of Alberta, 1975.

Hameed, S. and G. Paul. *3 or 4 Days Work Week*. Edmonton: University of Alberta, 1974.

Hanock, G. The backward-bending supply of labor. *JPE* 73 (December 1965).

Hughs, J. The reduction in the working week: a critical look at Target 35. *BJIR* 18 (Nov. 1980) 287-296.

Jamal, M. and R.L. Crawford. Moonlighters: a product of deprivation or aspiration? *RI/IR* 36 (No. 2, 1981) 325-334.

Johnson, T. and J. Pencavel. Dynamic hours of work functions for husbands, wives and single females. *Econometrica* 52 (March 1984) 363-390.

Jones, E. State legislation and hours of work in manufacturing. *SEJ* 41 (April 1975) 602-612.

Jones, E. The full-time workweek in the United States, 1900-1970. Comment. *ILRR* 33 (April 1980) 379-384.

Kalachek, E., W. Mellow and F. Raines. The male labor supply function reconsidered. *ILRR* 31 (April 1978) 356-367.

Kniesner, T. The full-time workweek in the United States, 1900-1970. *ILRR* 30 (October 1976) 3-15.

Labour Canada. *Trends in Working Time*. Ottawa: Wages Research Division, Economics and Research Branch, 1974.

Larson, D.A. Labor supply adjustment over the business cycle. *ILRR* 34 (July 1981) 591-595.

Leon, G. and R. Bednarzik. A profile of women on part-time schedules. *MLR* 10 (October 1978) 3-12.

Lewis, H. Hours of work and hours of leisure. *IRRA* (December 1956) 196-206.

Link, C. and R. Settle. Wage incentives and married professional nurses: a case of backward-bending supply. *EI* 19 (January 1981) 132-143.

Long, J. and E. Jones. Part-week work by married women. *SEJ* 46 (January 1980) 716-725.

Mabry, B. Income-leisure analysis and the salaried professional. *IR* 8 (February 1969) 162-173.

Mauziri, A. Empirical evidence on labor supply: the case of dentists. *IRRA* (December 1966) 354-364.

Maynes, J. Alternative working hours: who needs them? *The Journal of Industrial Relations* 22 (December 1980) 480-483.

McCormick, B. Hours of work in British industry. *ILRR* 12 (April 1959) 423-433.

Meissner, M. The long arm of the job: a study of work and leisure. *IR* 10 (October 1971) 239-260.

Meltz, N. and F. Reid. Reducing the impact of unemployment through work-sharing: some industrial relations considerations. *The Journal of Industrial Relations* 25 (June 1983) 153-161.

Moffitt, R. The Tobit model, hours of work and institutional constraints. *R.E. Stats.* 64 (Aug. 1982) 510-515.

Newton, K., and N. Leckie. Determinants of weekly work hours in Canada. *RI/IR* 34 (No. 2, 1979) 257-271.

Northrup, H.R. and T.D. Greis. The decline in average annual hours worked in the United States, 1947-1979. *JHR* 4 (Spring, 1983) 95-114.

Olsen, E.O. The effort level, work time and profit maximization. *SEJ* 42 (April 1976) 644-652.

Owen, J. *The Price of Leisure*. Montreal: McGill-Queen's University Press, 1975.

Owen, J. Workweek and leisure: an analysis of trends, 1945-1975. *MLR* 99 (August 1976) 3-8.

Owen, J. Flexitime: some problems and solutions. *ILRR* 30 (January 1977) 152-160.

Owen, J. *Working Hours: An Economic Analysis*. Lexington, Mass.: Lexington Books, 1979.

Perlman, R. Observations on overtime and moonlighting. *SEJ* 33 (October 1966) 237-244.

Reid, F. Reductions in work time: an assessment of employment sharing to reduce unemployment. *Work and Pay: The Canadian Labour Market*, W.C. Riddell (ed.). Toronto: University of Toronto Press, 1985, 141-170.

Reza, A. Labour supply and demand, absenteeism, and union behaviour. *R.E. Studies* 42 (April 1975) 237-248.

Ross, D. A new view of leisure. *RI/IR* 27 (No. 4, 1972) 746-756.

Salkever, D. Effects of children's health on maternal hours of work: a preliminary analysis. *SEJ* 47 (July 1980) 156-166.

Sherman, R. and T. Witlet. Notes on overtime, moonlighting and the shorter work week. *SEJ* 35 (July 1968) 78-81.

Sloan, F. and S. Richupan. Short-run supply responses of professional nurses: a micro analysis. *JHR* 10 (Spring 1975) 241-257.

Sloan, P. Economic aspects of shift and night work. *ILR* 117 (March/April 1978) 129-142.

Sowell, T. The shorter work week controversy. *ILRR* 8 (January 1965).

Tandan, N. *Workers with Long Hours*. Special Labour Force Studies, Series A, No. 9. Ottawa: Information Canada, 1972.

Wallace, Joan (Commissions). *Part-time Work in Canada*. Ottawa: Labour Canada, 1983.

Weeks, W. Collective bargaining and part-time work in Ontario. *RI/IR* 33 (No. 1, 1978) 80-90.

West, R.G. Marx's hypotheses on the length of the working day. *JPE* 91 (April 1983) 266-281.

Wilensky, H. The moonlighter: a product of relative deprivation. *IR* 3 (October 1963).

Winston, G. An international comparison of income and hours of work. *R.E. Stats.* 48 (February 1966) 28-39.

8 Additional Topics on Labour Supply

As pointed out in Killingsworth (1983) the area of labour supply within labour economics has undergone dramatic changes in the late 1970s and early 1980s. In large part this has reflected the application of standard but sophisticated techniques of microeconomics and econometrics to analyse the various dimensions of labour supply. In fact, many of the procedures in econometrics developed as applications in the labour supply area. For example, they developed to handle econometric problems associated with the discrete nature of the labour force participation decision and the advent of large microeconomic data sets (where the individual person is the unit of observation) and panel or longitudinal data sets (which follow the same individual over a period of time). These developments in labour supply include fixed costs, discontinuities, sample selection bias, nonlinearities in budget constraints and dynamic life-cycle models.

FIXED COSTS

In the absence of any fixed costs associated with engaging in labour market activities, the reservation wage is the slope of the individual's indifference curve at zero hours of work. This slope is given by W_r, the slope of the line RR' which is tangent to the indifference curve U_0 at the point E corresponding to zero hours of work in Figure 8.1(a). (Because the line RR' is downward sloping, the reservation wage is the absolute value of the slope.)

If the individual's market wage was below the reservation wage W_r then the person would not engage in labour market activities. The individual would maximize utility by moving to the "corner solution" at point E in Figure 8.1(a).

If the market wage exceeds the reservation wage W_r then the individual will enter the labour market since the returns from engaging in labour market activity exceed the individual's valuation of their time in nonlabour market activities (their reservation wage, W_r). Their amount of labour supplied will be determined in the usual fashion by the tangency of their highest attainable indifference curve and budget constraint.

Fixed Money Costs

As illustrated by such works as Cogan (1981), Hausman (1980) and Smith (1980), there may be fixed money costs associated with entering the labour market and these "start-up" costs may be independent of the number of

Figure 8.1 Labour Supply and Fixed Costs

(a) No Fixed Costs

(b) Fixed Money Costs

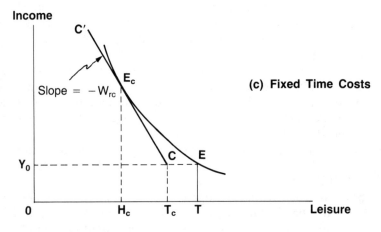

(c) Fixed Time Costs

hours worked. Such costs for a prospective employee could include day care, buying a car to drive to work, buying or renting accommodation closer to work, or the purchase of special clothing. (Fixed costs for *employers* can also be important and will be analysed subsequently as they affect the demand for labour.) Such fixed costs for workers are incurred only if the worker engages in labour market activity; they can be avoided by not participating in the labour force.

Such fixed money costs are analogous to a vertical drop in the individual's budget constraint immediately upon entering the labour market. This is depicted by the line EM in Figure 8.1(b). That is, immediately upon engaging in labour market activities the individual incurs the fixed costs $m = EM$ which are analogous to a drop in income of EM. (The point M is slightly to the left of the vertical line ET to indicate that the costs are incurred only if one engages in labour market activity; that is, moves to the left of T.) These fixed costs are avoided if one does not engage in labour market activity but remains at E.

In the presence of such fixed money costs, the individual's reservation wage is depicted by the slope of the line MM' in Figure 8.1(b). This is the minimum wage above which one would enter the labour market. It is the wage at which one would be indifferent between engaging in labour market activities at E_0 and engaging in non-labour market activities at E. As in the previous case, depicted in Figure 8.1(a), market wages below the reservation wage would not induce labour force participation because the individual would be better off by engaging in non-labour market activities at E, attaining utility level U_0. Market wages above the reservation wage would induce labour force participation and the amount of work would be determined by the tangency of the new higher indifference curve and the higher budget constraint (not shown in the diagram).

Clearly the individual's reservation wage in the presence of fixed money costs is greater than the person's reservation wage in the absence of these fixed costs. This is illustrated in Figure 8.1(b) by the fact that the slope of the line MM' is greater than the slope of the individual's indifference curve at the point E, the latter slope being the person's reservation wage in the absence of fixed costs. (This can be formally proved by the fact that the line MM' is tangent to U_0 at the point E_0 which is to the left of E on the same indifference curve, and the indifference curve becomes steeper as one moves to the left of E because of the hypothesis of diminishing marginal rate of substitution.) Simply stated, fixed costs associated with entering the labour market increase the reservation wage by making labour market work less attractive than nonlabour market activities such as household work, retirement or leisure.

Fixed Time or Commute Costs

Fixed costs can also occur in the form of commuting time associated with getting to work. If it takes one hour to get to work and another to return home from work, then two hours per day are used up in commute time. This cost is fixed in the sense that it is independent of the hours of work; it can be avoided only by not participating in the labour market.

Such fixed costs are akin to taking a fixed amount of time out of each day before time is allocated to earning income in the labour market. This is illustrated in Figure 8.1(c) by the distance $TT_c = EC$. Labour market income is not earned until one moves to the left of C, and works in the labour market (assuming, of course, that the commute time is not directly compensated by the employer).

In the presence of such fixed commute costs, the individual's reservation wage is given by the slope of the line CC' in Figure 8.1(c). It is the minimum wage above which one would enter the labour maket; it is the wage at which one would be indifferent between working in the labour market at E_c, and engaging in nonlabour market activities at E. Market wages below W_{rc} would not induce labour force participation because the individual would attain a higher level of utility, U_0, by engaging in non-labour market activities at E. Market wages above W_{rc} would induce labour force participation and the amount of work would be determined by the tangency of the potential income constraint and the highest attainable indifference curve (not shown in the diagram).

As with fixed money costs, the individual's reservation wage, W_{rc}, is greater in the presence of fixed commute costs than in the absence of such fixed costs. The latter reservation wage in the absence of fixed commute costs is given by W_r, the slope of the individual's indifference curve at zero hours of work (point E in Figure 8.1(c)). Intuitively, the reservation wage is higher in the presence of fixed commute costs because the disutility of engaging in labour market activity is increased when commute costs have to be incurred. Thus, an increase in commute costs will increase reservation wage and decrease the probability of participating in the labour force.

HOURS OF WORK AND DISCONTINUITIES IN LABOUR SUPPLY

The previous discussion focused on the effect of fixed money and commute costs on the individual's reservation wage and subsequently on their labour force participation decision. Fixed costs were seen to raise reservation wages and hence discourage labour force participation. Fixed costs can also have an impact on the *hours of work* dimension of labour supply. This impact is more complicated than the labour force participation dimension.

The left panel of Figure 8.2(a) indicates the reservation wage as the slope of the indifference curve at zero hours of work (i.e., at the point E). The right panel indicates a conventional labour supply schedule as derived from the income-leisure choice framework as discussed previously. In the absence of any fixed costs, the reservation wage in the labour supply diagram would be the height of the labour supply schedule at zero hours of work. It is the minimum wage above which one would enter the labour

Figure 8.2   Labour Supply Discontinuities

(a) No Fixed Costs

(b) Fixed Money Costs

(c) Fixed Time Costs

market and supply positive hours of work. For market wages above the reservation wage, positive hours of work would be supplied as depicted by the labour supply schedule. (At higher wages this schedule may become backward-bending, as the income effect becomes larger and begins to exceed the substitution effect.)

Figure 8.2(b) depicts the situation in the presence of fixed money costs associated with labour market work. The left panel shows an initial equilibrium at E_0 with hours of work H_0 when there are no fixed costs. In this situation, the market wage, as shown by the slope of the budget constraint EE', exceeds the reservation wage and hence the person works H_0 hours.

The existence of fixed money costs of m = EM associated with entering the labour market is akin to a reduction in non-labour income to $Y_0 - m$. This shifts the budget constraint down in a parallel fashion since market wages have not changed. If leisure is a normal good, this pure income effect, from the reduced income, increases hours of work from H_0 to H_m. Tracing this through for various possible wage levels would yield the hours-of-work supply schedule, S_m, in the right-hand panel of Figure 8.2(b). This hours-of-work schedule is to the right of the original schedule, S_0, when there are no fixed costs because one has to work more hours to make up for the income loss associated with the fixed costs.

In addition to increasing hours of work for those who are participating in labour market activity, fixed costs also create a discontinuity in the labour supply schedule. This can be seen in Figure 8.2(b). The distance TH_m in that diagram indicates the number of hours of work below which it would not be worthwhile to enter the labour market given the reservation wage W_{rm} created by the fixed costs EM. It is not possible to amortize the fixed costs of entering the labour force over so few hours; hence, there is a discontinuity in labour supply over that region. Geometrically, it is not possible for there to be a tangency between the budget constraint MM' and the indifference curve U_m in the region E_mE. This is so because the slope of MM' is always greater than the slope of the indifference curve to the right of E_m.

This discontinuity over the range of TH_m hours translates into the distance OH_m in the labour supply diagram of Figure 8.2(b). (The distance OH_m in the right panel of Figure 8.2(b) equals the distance TH_m in the left panel.) The discontinuity OH_m in the labour supply diagram illustrates the range of hours for which it is not worthwhile entering the labour force given the fixed costs associated with entry. Such part-time work does not enable one to amortize the fixed costs of entry over so few hours. This illustrates how fixed costs discourage part-time work.

In summary, fixed money costs of entering the labour force increase reservation wages and this in turn decreases labour force participation. However, for those who do participate, hours of work will be increased. The fixed money costs also create a discontinuity in labour supply, making part-time work less likely. Intuitively, the fixed money costs make entering the labour force less attractive, especially for a few hours; however, once in the labour force, the individual will work more hours to compensate for the loss of income from the fixed money costs. Clearly, fixed costs have a complicated effect on the various dimensions of labour supply.

One would expect a similar pattern for an increase in fixed *time* or commute costs associated with labour market work. However, this case is complicated by the fact that commute time is time not available for labour market or other activities. The left panel of Figure 8.2(c) indicates the situation where the initial equilibrium E_0 with no fixed costs implies hours of work of H_0. Fixed commute costs of $T_cT = EC$ reduce the time available to allocate to labour market work or other activities like leisure. As with fixed money costs this involves an inward shift of the budget constraint in a parallel fashion since wages have not changed. This pure income effect leads to reduced purchases of all normal goods including leisure. Total hours spent in labour market work *and* commute time increase from H_0 to H_c. However, hours worked in the labour market are only T_cH_c since TT_c is commute time. Hours worked actually decrease since T_cH_c is less than TH_0. This is so because H_0H_c is less than TT_c, since the reduction in the individual budget constraint associated with the increased commute time TT_c is allocated between reduced leisure H_0H_c and a reduction in labour market income Y_TY_C. That is, $H_0H_c < TT_c$, and subtracting the common distance H_0T_c from each side yields $H_0H_c - H_0 T_c < TT_c - H_0T_c$ or $T_cH_c < TH_0$.

In essence, the increase in fixed commute costs associated with going to work will increase the *total* time spent in labour market and commuting activity for those who participate in the labour market. However, the increased commute time does not lead to an equivalent increase in labour market work since some of the wealth reduction associated with the increased commute time is absorbed by a reduction in the demand for other goods and services. Hence, hours of work actually decrease even though total work time plus commute time increases. This is illustrated by the leftward shift in the labour supply schedule in Figure 8.2(c). This is in contrast to fixed money costs which increase hours of work for those who participate in labour market activities.

The fixed commute costs also create a discontinuity in labour supply. In Figure 8.2(c) the discontinuity is illustrated by the segment T_cH_c which shows the hours for which it would not be worthwhile to enter the labour market since they would be too few to enable one to amortize the fixed commute costs. Such costs discourage part-time work.

This corresponding discontinuity is illustrated by the distance OH_c in the labour supply diagram of Figure 8.2(c). It is the range of hours over which it is not worthwhile to enter the labour force given the fixed commute time.

In summary, fixed commute costs like fixed money costs associated with entering the labour market will reduce the probability of participating in the labour force. For those who do participate, total hours spent commuting *and* at work will increase as commute time increases; however, hours spent at work by itself will actually decrease. This is so because the reduced wealth associated with the additional commute time will be allocated to reduced income as well as reduced leisure. Hence the total time allocated to work plus commuting will not increase by as much as the commute time increases and hours of work will thereby fall. In addition, there will be discontinuity in labour supply as part-time work becomes less attractive since it does not enable one to amortize the fixed commute time costs over sufficiently long hours.

EFFECT OF DAY CARE SUBSIDY

The importance of fixed costs can be illustrated by analysing the impact of day care subsidies on both the labour force participation and the hours-of-work decision. To simplify the exposition it will be assumed that day care costs are fixed upon entering the labour force and the subsidy eliminates these costs. Also, the impact of taxes needed to finance the day care subsidies is ignored.

By removing the fixed costs associated with day care, subsidies would reduce reservation wages. This in turn would induce labour force participation amongst those who otherwise found the fixed day care costs to be too inhibiting a barrier to labour force participation. Even part-time work may be attractive since there would no longer be a need to amortize the fixed day care costs over longer working hours.

For those who are already participating in the labour force the day care subsidy would not affect their participation decision; that is, it would never cause them to leave the labour force. This is so because if they were already participating then their reservation wage was already below their market wage, hence, lowering their reservation wage would only strengthen their decision to participate in the labour market.

The day care subsidy, however, would induce those who already were participating in the labour force to work fewer hours. This is so because the subsidy is like a demogrant, given to those who have children in day care. This causes them to buy more of all normal commodities including leisure; hence, the reduction in hours worked. Alternatively stated, by eliminating the fixed cost of day care, the subsidy reverses the effect of a fixed money cost as illustrated in Figure 8.2(b). That is, the subsidy would shift the labour supply schedule back from S_m to S_0, reducing hours of work and eliminating the discontinuity that made it unattractive to work part-time.

In summary, subsidies to day care can have a complicated effect on the various dimensions of labour supply, encouraging labour force participation and part-time work, but reducing the hours of work for those already participating (assuming the subsidies are not on a per-hour basis). The net effect on total hours of work is therefore ambiguous. Obviously, making the subsidy available only to those who are not already participating in the labour force would ensure that total hours of work would increase. However, this can create inequities (and some interesting politics!) because similar groups who are already participating in the labour force would not receive the subsidy.

CORNER SOLUTIONS AND CENSORING

In the previous discussion, individuals whose market wage was below their reservation wage were simply lumped together and treated as non-participants in the labour force. In terms of Figure 8.1(a), they were assumed to be at the "corner solution," or point E, since their marginal rate of substitution between income and leisure at E (i.e., slope of indifference curve or reservation wage) was greater than their market wage. All that we knew of these individuals was that the point of tangency between their indifference curve and budget line was not in the range of positive work hours.

Such individuals can be thought of as desiring to work negative hours of labour market work; however, all we can observe is that they do zero hours of labour market work. The notion of negative hours of labour market work can be thought of as an aversion to engaging in labour market work or a desire to engage in household work or other non-labour market activities. When we observe that individuals are not participating in the labour market we only know that their market wage is less than their reservation wage. We do not know if they are marginally indifferent between participating or not (i.e., their point of tangency is near E) or if they are extremely unlikely to enter the labour market unless their market wage increased dramatically (i.e., their point of tangency is far to the right of E).

This notion of desired negative hours of work is illustrated in Figure 8.3 which is simply an extension of Figure 8.1(a) designed to show the hypothetical tangency of the budget constraint and an indifference curve, when that tangency is in the region of negative desired hours of work (i.e., when the wage is below the individual's reservation wage). For this hypothetical individual, the desired equilibrium would be at E_d involving negative desired hours of work, H_n, and income of Y_n; i.e., if it were possible to buy additional leisure time at the market wage W_l, the individual would give up the income $Y_0 Y_n$ for the additional time TH_n. This situation could be a combination of having a low market wage and/or preferences against

Figure 8.3   Corner Solution and Negative Desired Hours

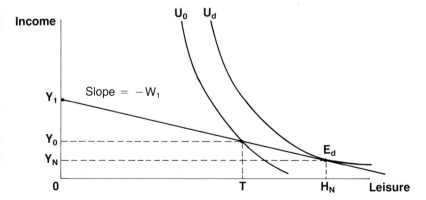

labour market work. Clearly, a higher market wage line emanating upward and to the left of E could induce the person to enter the labour force (i.e., yield a tangency with an indifference curve in the range of positive hours to the left of E). Alternatively, different preferences (i.e., different-shaped indifference curves) could yield a tangency to the budget line EY_1 to the left of E. Given the wage rate W_1 and the individual's preferences, however, their desired hours of work is negative at TH_n and to attain this they would be willing to give up income of Y_0Y_n.

All that we usually observe for such individuals, however, is that they are not participating in the labour market since data on labour supply basically indicates whether an individual is participating in the labour force, and if so, for how many hours of work. That is, we observe only points E (i.e., nonparticipants whose actual hours of work is zero) and tangencies to the left of E (i.e., hours of work for those who participate). All persons who have hypothetical tangencies to the right of E are simply aggregated together at the corner solution E as nonparticipants with zero hours of work.

In this situation where we do not have data on the individual's desired hours of work, the dependent variable in studies of labour supply, but we have information on their characteristics or explanatory variables (market wage and other relevant variables), the sample is said to be censored. If we do not have information on their behaviour that is under examination (i.e. dependent variable) nor on the characteristics believed to determine that behaviour (i.e., explanatory variables) the sample is said to be truncated with respect to those observations. This would be the case, for example, if all high-wage individuals are excluded from eligibility in an income maintenance program in which case we would not have information on their characteristics or behaviour or numbers.

SAMPLE SELECTION BIAS

A number of implications can flow from the fact that we do not observe desired hours of work for those who are not participating in the labour force. One such implication is that estimated relationships between hours of work and explanatory variables believed to determine hours of work may be biased if they are estimated only from the observed data on those who are working positive hours. This select sample of workers may be different from a random draw of the population in terms of unobservable characteristics such as preferences for labour market work versus household work. In such circumstances inferences as to the expected behaviour of a random draw from the population, based upon the observed behaviour of those who are working positive hours, can be misleading unless special statistical techniques are used.

For example, it might be found that a one percent increase in wages led to a two percent increase in the expected hours of work of those who were already in the labour market. But this need not imply that the same relationship would prevail for a random draw from the population who may or may not be a labour force participant. The sample of those who are working may be systematically different in terms of unobservable characteristics than those who are not working in the labour market; that is in fact why one group may be sorted into labour market activities and another group into other activities. Inferences based on the estimated relationship from the subsample of workers may be subject to what is termed sample-selection bias.

Diagrammatic Illustration

The bias can be illustrated diagrammatically. In Figure 8.4, hours of work, H, are measured on the vertical axis, and the wage, W, an individual can expect to receive is measured on the horizontal axis. At this stage we assume that information on each individual's expected wage is available; this assumption will later be relaxed. Assume that the population consists of nine individuals, with expected wages and hours of work represented

Figure 8.4 Sample Selection Bias

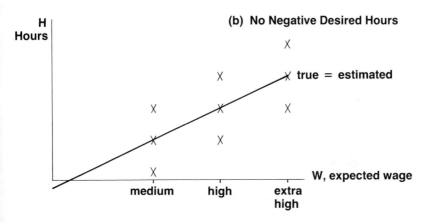

by the X's. Also, assume that the nine individuals can be grouped into three wage levels, low, medium and high. Their variation in hours of work *within* each wage level (i.e., deviations from the true line) is attributable to unobservable characteristics that cannot be measured and hence directly controlled for in statistical analysis. For example, the three persons (X's) above the true line are people with unusually high preferences for labour market work, those below the line have unusually low preferences for such work and those on the line have average preferences for labour market work. On average, the relationship between hours of work and expected wages turns out to be positive as exhibited by the true line. This is akin to an upward-sloping labour supply schedule when wages are exhibited on the vertical axis and hours on the horizontal axis, and corresponds to the situation where the substitution effect dominates the income effect so that wage increases lead to more hours of work. Figure 8.4 reverses the axes because it is more common to portray the dependent variable on the vertical axis and the independent or explanatory variable on the horizontal axis.

The true line, based upon all nine observations, indicates what would happen, on average, to desired hours of work if wages increased. Desired hours of work is the equilibrium concept reflecting the optimizing decision of the individual. Desired hours can be negative as illustrated by the low-wage individual who falls below the horizontal axis.

However, in estimating the observed or actual (as opposed to desired) relationship between wages and hours of work, the only data on hours of work that is available is for the eight observations with positive hours of work. We do not observe the desired hours of work for that person who wishes negative hours. The estimated relationship is therefore based on the sample of the eight observations with positive actual hours of work.

In our particular example, the estimated line is "tilted clockwise" relative to the true line because the estimated line ignores the one low-wage observation with negative preferences toward labour market work. The estimated relationship is based upon a sample of persons who *disproportionately* have positive preferences for labour market work at each expected wage level. That is, of the eight persons in the sample from which the line is estimated, three have unusually positive preferences for labour market work (i.e., are above the true line), three have average preferences (are on the true line) but only two have negative preferences (are below the true line). The third observation with negative preferences (below the horizontal axis) is excluded from the sample altogether. Of crucial importance, that observation is excluded from the sample precisely because of the negative preference for labour market work. If that person had average or above-average preferences then he or she would be in the sample which is used to derive the estimated line.

The sample of eight from which the estimated relationship is derived is therefore systematically different from the total population of nine, in that the sample disproportionately consists of persons with positive preferences for labour market work. That is in fact why many of them are in the labour market working positive hours. This sample is said to be subject to a sample selection bias in the sense that it is not a random sample drawn from the population of potential workers and is therefore not representative of that population. It is a sample based upon the selection rule that to be included in the sample, the person must work a positive number of hours. The sample selection bias comes about because those persons with positive hours of work disproportionately have greater preferences for work than do those who are not working in the labour market. Relative to those who are not working, those who work in the labour market systematically differ in terms of the unobservable variable — preferences for labour market work.

This difference is important because the unobservable preference is correlated with the decision to work which itself is systematically related to wages. That is, within the sample of eight workers the low-wage workers are disproportionately represented by those with above-average preferences for labour market work. The one person with negative preferences and a low wage is excluded from the sample altogether. If the unobservable preferences were not correlated with the decision to work there would not be a difference between the estimated and true relationships.

For example, if the population consisted of the nine individuals in the bottom panel, Figure 8.4(b), then the estimated line would have the same slope whether it is based upon the nine observations, or if the three medium-wage or three high-wage observations were excluded. This is so because the unobservable preferences (deviations of the observations about the true line) are not correlated with the decision to work. That is, the remaining sample of six in either case would have two persons with above-average preferences for labour market work and two with below-average preferences (the same proportions as in the omitted group); hence, a sample selection bias would not occur since the selected sample would not differ from the population in terms of the unobservable preferences. This is so because the unobserved preferences are not correlated with the decision to work, which was used as a sample selection criterion.

Prime-Age Males and Married Women

This highlights the fact that sample selection bias need not always be a problem when select samples are used to make inferences about population behaviour. For example, if prime-age males tend to be participating in the labour force and work a standard workweek then their situation may correspond to the bottom panel Figure 8.4(b). Few of them are at the margin of entering or leaving the labour force; that is, few are at zero or negative desired hours of work. In such circumstances, their hours-of-work response to a wage change may be estimated from a sample of workers with positive hours. Such a sample may give an accurate portrayal of the expected response of a random draw of all prime-age males (just as the estimated line of Figure 8.4(b) is an accurate portrayal of the true line).

Conversely, the situation for married women may be more like the situation portrayed in the top panel, Figure 8.4(a). Many married women, who may expect to receive a low wage if they enter the labour market, may be marginally indifferent between engaging in labour market work and household work. In such circumstances those who had a preference for labour market work disproportionately would be engaging in labour market tasks. Thus the estimated relationship between hours of work and expected wages based on the sample of those who work positive hours would be based on a biased sample of persons who are disproportionately labour market oriented in terms of unobservable characteristics like preferences. The estimated relationship may look more like the estimated line in Figure 8.4(a) in which case it would underestimate the true additional hours of work that would be associated with a wage increase for a randomly selected married woman.

Explanation of Bias in Terms of Response

This example can also be used to illustrate why the estimated relationship gives a smaller hours-of-work response than the true relationship in this case. We earlier indicated that the estimated line was "tilted clockwise" relative to the true line because it disproportionately reflected (was "pulled up" by) the positive preference for labour market work at the low-wage end (the observation with the negative preference for labour market work at that end having been excluded from the sample of participants). An alternative way of understanding the smaller hours-of-work response to a wage change based on the estimated relationship is to examine how hours of work *change* when wages *change*.

For illustrative purposes, assume that wages increase so that in Figure 8.4(a) low-wage persons become medium-wage, the medium become high and the high become extra-high. This means that the three observations in the low-wage category displace the three in the medium-wage category, the three in the medium displace the three in the high, and the three in the high move up to extra-high. On average, this would be reflected by movements along the true response line and the one low-wage individual with negative desired hours would now be a medium-wage person with small positive desired hours, observed as actual hours. The true response of that individual (in terms of the equilibrium concept of desired hours of work) is given by the true line. However, in terms of actual hours of work (which is all that is observed) it will appear that the individual went from *zero* hours to small positive hours; the change from *negative desired* hours to zero is not observed. Thus the estimated response (which does not include the change from negative desired to zero actual hours) underestimates the true response of desired hours of work.

The true hours-of-work response of married women, for example, may be larger than that observed when the relationship is estimated on the sample of those who work in the labour market since those who work only a few hours may have made a large response from negative desired hours to their desired positive hours. All we observe is that they appear to have gone from zero hours to a few actual, observed hours; in reality, their true response is larger, being from (unobserved) negative desired to positive (observed) actual hours. Thus, the true labour supply response of married women to a wage change may be larger than their response estimated from the sample of labour force participants only.

Appropriate Measure

This also highlights that the appropriate measure of labour supply response depends upon the question one wants answered. If one wanted to know the expected increase in hours of work associated with a wage increase *for those who are already participating* in the labour market, then the true response is appropriate. It would reflect the response of those observations who are already participating in the labour force (i.e., above the horizontal axis in Figure 8.4(a)). Similarly, if one wanted to know the response of *desired* hours, to include changes in the desired hours of those who are not working, the *true* response is appropriate. However, if one wanted to know the increase in *actual* hours that would be associated with a wage increase, whether those additional hours come from those who are already participating *or from those who will enter the labour force* in response to the wage change, then the *estimated* relationship (based upon nonparticipants being given zero hours of work) is appropriate even though it gives a smaller response than the true relationship.

To ascertain the actual increase in hours, whether from existing participants or from new entrants, the estimated relationship is appropriate because it reflects the fact that the actual (observed) increase in hours is less than the desired (unobserved) increase for those who also enter the labour force in response to the wage increase. For example, the actual increase in hours for the individual below the horizontal axis of Figure 8.4(a), in response to a wage increase from the low to medium category, would only be the observed hours of work above the horizontal axis. The increase in desired hours up to the horizontal axis would not be recorded as part of the hours response to the wage increase. This is appropriate, however, if one is interested in the actual observed response for potential participants as well as for those who are already participating in the labour force.

Clearly, the appropriate measure of labour supply responsiveness depends upon the questions one wants answered. If one is interested in the change in desired hours or in actual hours for those already participating, then the true relationship is correct. However, if one is interested in the change in actual observed hours for both participants and those who may enter, then the estimated relationship is appropriate.

Correcting for Selection Bias

When sample selection bias is likely to be important because a substantial number of observations are likely to be on the margin of being in or out of the select sample (e.g., married women on the margin of participating in labour market or household work), the obvious question is how to estimate the true relationship given that we only have data on actual hours of work and not desired hours. An explanation of this procedure (e.g. Heckman 1979) requires an understanding of econometrics beyond the prerequisites of this text. However, the procedure basically involves estimating the probability of being in the select sample (participating in the labour force in this case). Information from these predicted probabilities is then used to construct an artificial variable (called the inverse of Mill's ratio). This term is then used to correct the estimated relationship that is based on the select sample, to get a relationship corrected for selectivity bias. With the addition of the selectivity bias correction term one can convert the estimated line of Figure 8.4(a) to the true line.

Other Examples

The previous discussion illustrated the sample selection bias that can occur when one tries to make inferences about the hours-of-work behaviour of a random individual based upon estimates made from a select sample of individuals who differ from the population in terms of unobservable characteristics. The bias occurs because these observable characteristics (preferences for labour market work in the previous example) are important determinants of being in the select sample; that is, people may sort themselves into the select sample in part based upon these unobservable characteristics.

Other examples of selection bias abound in the empirical literature of labour economics; in fact it has been a virtual growth area in recent years. In some instances the selection bias occurs because the individuals sort themselves into the select sample on the basis of unobservable characteristics, in other instances they may be selected by employers, and in other instances by the researcher. The important point is that the selection is not random; that is, the nature of the sample used by the researcher is itself endogenously determined by underlying forces, and the analysis of the data must take into account this endogeneity. While many of the examples are referred to elsewhere in the text, some are recapitulated here to illustrate their common features.

In the previous analysis, *expected* wages were discussed as an explanatory determinant of hours of work. This independent variable was depicted on the horizontal axis of Figure 8.4. Obviously this variable is not observed for persons who do not participate in labour market activities. One solution is to use an observed variable like education to serve as a proxy for the unobserved expected wage; the hypothesis being that, on average, more highly educated people would have a higher expected wage. Obviously this is an imperfect proxy, however, since education can reflect other factors.

Another solution is to estimate the wage that nonparticipants could expect to earn in the labour market if they did participate. This could be done by estimating the relationship between the wages of participants and their wage-determining characteristics and using this information to simulate the wage that nonparticipants could expect to earn if they were to participate in the labour market. However, labour force participants may be systematically different from nonparticipants not only in terms of observable characteristics (which can be controlled for in statistical analysis) but also in terms of unobservable characteristics (which are not directly controlled for). For example, participants may be more highly motivated or have a comparative advantage in labour market tasks; that may be part of the reason that they are sorted into such tasks either by themselves or by employers. If that is the case then their actual wage may be higher than the expected wage that a nonparticipant of similar *observable* characteristics could expect to receive upon participating in the labour market. That is, labour force participants may be systematically different than nonparticipants in terms of unobservable characteristics; hence, the earnings of participants may give a biased estimate of what nonparticipants with the same observable characteristics could expect to earn if they entered the labour market.

Formally, this sample selection bias can be corrected by the same three-step procedure outlined earlier to correct the bias in hours-of-work estimates. First, estimate the probability of being in the labour force, using the full sample of data from participants and nonparticipants. Second, use this information to construct a new variable — formally called the inverse of Mill's ratio. Third, include this new variable in estimating the determinants of wages, based on the select sample of participants. The resulting estimates will be corrected for the sample selection bias that occurs because wages are estimated on the selected sample of participants only. These corrected estimates of the determinants of wages can then be used to get estimates of what nonparticipants could expect to earn if they participated in the labour market.

Other similar examples abound. Migrants may be different from non-migrants in terms of unobservable variables like motivation; hence, it may be inaccurate to use the earnings of the select sample of migrants to simulate what comparable nonmigrants (in terms of observable characteristics) could earn if they were to migrate. Union workers may be systematically different from nonunion workers in terms of unobservable characteristics, especially if employers hire from a queue of applicants for the high-wage union jobs or they alter the job requirements. Hence, it may be inaccurate to use the earnings of the select sample of union workers to estimate what comparable nonunion workers (comparable in terms of observable characteristics) would earn if they were unionized. Never-married females may be different from never-married males in terms of unobservable characteristics like career orientation. Hence it is likely to be inappropriate to use the earnings of the sample of never-married males (who may be less career oriented) to estimate what never-married females could expect to earn if they were paid like comparable males, where comparable is again defined in terms of observable but not unobservable characteristics.

The issue of sample selection bias can also be important in determining the true impact of various legislative activities on labour market behaviour. For example, the impact of an equal pay or equal employment opportunity law may be ascertained by comparing the wages or occupational distribution of males and females in jurisdictions with and without such legislation, after controlling for other observable variables that may affect wages and the occupational distribution. However, jurisdictions with and without such legislative initiatives may also differ in terms of unobservable factors such as discriminatory attitudes that can affect the wages and occupational distribution of females. In fact, such unobservable differences can also account for the differences in legislative initiatives. In such circumstances it may be the different attitudes, and not the independent effect of the legislative initiatives, that account for the difference in the labour market behaviour of women. That is, it could be erroneous to infer the effect of legislative initiatives to the population at large, when the effect of such legislative initiatives is based on estimates from the select sample of jurisdictions with the policy initiative in place. The select sample may be different from the population at large in terms of unobservable characteristics that influence behaviour.

As with the other examples, it would be possible to get estimates of the impact of the policy initiatives by correcting for the selectivity bias. This again requires estimating the determinants of the legislative initiative based on the full sample of jurisdictions with and without the initiative. This in turn is used to derive the correction factor which is included as a determinant of the legislative impact when that impact is based on estimates from the select sample of those jurisdictions with the legislation in place. This should provide an unbiased estimate of the expected effect of the legislation if it is adopted by any jurisdiction.

Clearly the sample selection procedure has a wide variety of applications and it can be very important from a theoretical, empirical and policy perspective. As well, it rekindles a challenge for labour economists; that challenge involves incorporating an understanding of why certain institutional features of labour markets arise and persist. Conventionally in labour economics we regard institutional features such as unions and legislation as exogenously given or determined outside of the labour market. Their impact on various elements of labour market behaviour is then examined. However, the sample selection literature reminds us that this may give a biased estimate of their impact if the existence of these institutional features is determined in part by unobservable factors. In such circumstances we must regard these institutional features as endogenous, that is to explain their existence in terms of other predetermined or exogenous explanatory variables. This information is useful not only to explain why such institutional arrangements arise and change, but also to yield an unbiased estimate of the true impact of these institutional arrangements on other elements of labour market behaviour.

Alternatively stated, the sample selection bias literature reminds us that to fully understand the impact of certain institutional features of labour markets it is necessary to understand why these institutional arrangements arise in the first place. This challenge provides the opportunity to formally incorporate the analysis of the determinants of institutional features of labour markets into the larger picture of labour market analysis. Only then can we properly understand why these institutional features exist and their true impact.

NONLINEARITIES IN BUDGET CONSTRAINTS

In the conventional income-leisure choice framework, the budget constraint was linear (i.e., a straight line). This corresponds to the assumption that wages were constant or independent of hours of work or income. That is, working the first hour yielded the same income as the second hour and so forth. The picture was altered, however, with the introduction of such factors as income maintenance programs, overtime premiums, moonlighting and fixed costs. These changes were shown to have potentially substantial impacts on various dimensions of labour supply. They can also have impacts on the appropriate methodology for analysing labour supply and on the estimation of income and substitution effects (Hausman (1980)). Before illustrating these issues it is useful to introduce some microeconomic terminology.

A budget constraint is said to be nonconvex if a line segment joining two points in the budget choice set can fall outside of the set. Figure 8.5 illustrates four nonconvex budget constraints. Clearly in all cases, the dashed line joining two points within the choice set falls outside of the set of feasible choices. This is in contrast to budget constraints that are convex such as a linear budget constraint with a constant wage and no fixed costs, or a nonlinear budget constraint that reflects wages net of a progressive income tax,[1] or one that reflects a lower moonlighting rate in one's second job. In the latter cases, a straight line drawn between any two points in the feasible choice set (i.e., within the budget constraint) will always be within the constraint.

When the budget constraint is nonconvex, the previously discussed "local reservation wage" approach to analysing labour force participation decisions is inappropriate. That decision rule indicated that the individual would participate in the labour force if the market wage exceeded the reservation wage at zero hours of work; otherwise the individual would not participate. In the presence of nonconvexities in the budget constraint, however, that decision rule could be erroneous in that it may not be consistent with utility maximization.

[1] If the individual faces a fixed gross hourly wage rate (i.e. independent of hours worked), the net or after-tax wage rate will decline as hours of work and therefore total income increases providing the tax system is progressive. This will result in a net-of-tax potential income constraint that is convex. The opposite case, which results when the income tax system is regressive, is shown in Figure 8.5(a).

Figure 8.5   Nonconvex Budget Constraints

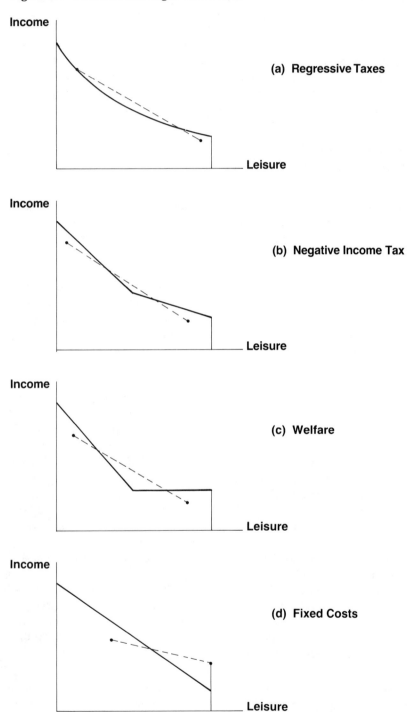

This is illustrated in Figure 8.6 which portrays the nonconvex budget constraint associated with a welfare program requiring the recipient to give up a dollar of welfare for every dollar earned in the labour market. This 100 percent implicit tax implies a *net* market wage of zero (the horizontal portion of the budget constraint) until all the welfare payments are exhausted, in which case the individual returns to the normal market wage line. Clearly the individual's local reservation wage, W_r, (at zero hours of work) is greater than the net market wage, W_0. Hence, by following the reservation wage decision rule the individual would not participate in the labour force, and would receive utility U_0. However, in this particular case the individual could attain a higher level of utility at U_p, by participating in the labour force and working H_p hours (work measured from right to left).

In this case the local reservation wage rule is inconsistent with global utility maximization because, by following the reservation wage rule, the individual is optimizing only with respect to the choices around zero hours of work. In that local region it does not appear to be worth entering the labour market because the disutility associated with an hour of work (the slope of the indifference curve or W_r) is greater than the return to work (the net wage of zero). However, by examining the wider set of choices around H_p hours of work it clearly pays to enter the labour market. After welfare is exhausted, the returns to work become sufficiently high to compensate for the disutility of work. This need not always be the case. The utility isoquant U_0 could become sufficiently steep that it always remains above the budget constraint so that E_0 is the global utility maximizing equilibrium. However, the nonconvexity of the budget constraint raises the *possibility* that the local reservation wage rule is inconsistent with utility maximization.

In the presence of nonconvexities in the budget constraint it is clearly important for the individual to examine the full range of choices that are available before decisions are made. This entails the equivalent of calculating the level of utility associated with the various combinations of wages and nonlabour income that are available and choosing the highest level of utility.[2]

For example, in Figure 8.6 the individual would hypothetically estimate the level of utility, U_0, associated with the net market wage, W_0, and nonlabour market income of E_0 associated with the welfare payment if the individual does not work. Then the individual could estimate the level of utility, U_p, associated with the market wage, W, and the nonwage income,

---

[2] These are termed indirect utility functions (when utility is expressed as a function of income and prices) as opposed to direct utility functions (where utility is expressed as a function of components like income and leisure that give rise to utility). When the direct utility function is maximized, the optimal amount of goods and leisure chosen will be functions of their prices and income. Therefore, these prices and income could be substituted in for the optimal goods and leisure, yielding utility (indirectly) to be a function of income and prices.

Figure 8.6   Local Reservation Wage Versus Utility Comparisons

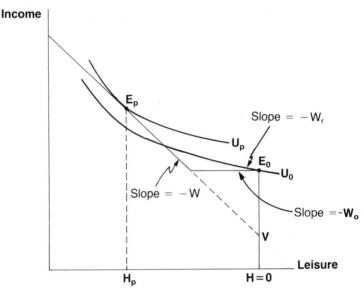

V, received from sources other than welfare.[3] Once these hypothetical calculations are made, the individual would compare the utility levels U_0 and U_p and choose the highest level of utility, in this particular case U_p.

In general, if the budget constraint is not convex, a local optimum such as E_0 need not be the global optimum. In such circumstances it is necessary to compare possible optimal points throughout the feasible set to ensure a global optimum. Informally stated, it is necessary for individuals to assess all of their options before decisions are made. By focusing only on small changes about their existing state, individuals may miss their wider range of opportunities. It follows that researchers analysing labour supply behaviour must take account of the fact that local optima are not necessarily global maxima in the presence of nonconvex budget constraints.

DYNAMIC LIFE-CYCLE MODELS

The previous discussion was couched in terms of static comparisons at a given point in time. Different equilibria were compared (a procedure termed comparative statics) assuming changes in income or relative prices that emanated exogenously from outside of the system, for example, from a change in taxes or transfer payments.

---

[3] This nonwage income V (termed "virtual" income) is the level of nonwage income that the person would have to have, in combination with the known constant market wage, W, to yield a given level of utility, in this case the level of utility, U_p, associated with participating in the labour market. Alternatively stated, virtual income is the hypothetical nonwage income associated with extending the market wage line to zero hours of work.

In a dynamic system, where changes are occurring over time and some may be anticipated and others not anticipated, the income and substitution effects that emanate from such income and price changes are more complicated. MaCurdy (1981) deals with many of these complications, and some of the simpler ones can be illustrated with a diagram based upon that source.

Figure 8.7 illustrates two hypothetical age-wage profiles, indicating how wages may at first increase over the life cycle and then decline later. The higher profile depicts the situation where an individual gets a higher wage at each and every age. The small "blip" in the higher profile illustrates the situation where an individual receives a temporary one-time only, unanticipated wage increase at age t. There are three possible sources of wage changes occurring in this diagram and each have different income and substitution effects and hence would lead to different labour supply responses. For illustrative purposes the three wage changes from A to B, B to C and C to D are assumed to be of the same magnitude; as illustrated by the same vertical distance.

Figure 8.7   Dynamic Life-Cycle Wage Changes

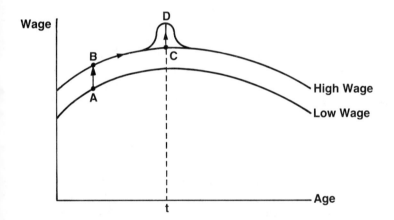

A→B Permanent Unanticipated Wage Increase (smallest labour supply response)

B→C Evolutionary Anticipated Wage Increase (largest labour supply response)

C→D Transitory, Unanticipated Wage Increase (medium labour supply response)

The difference between A and B reflects two persons whose wages differ by a permanent amount at each and every age in their life cycle. That difference would be associated with conventional income and substitution effects working in the opposite direction. That is, the high-wage individual at B would have a higher opportunity cost of leisure and hence work more (substitution effect). However, that individual would also have a higher expected lifetime income and hence be able to afford more leisure and work less (income effect). Since the income and substitution effects work in the opposite direction, the labour supply of the high-wage individual may be greater or less than the labour supply of the lower-wage individual over their lifetime.

The wage increase from B to C along an individual's given wage profile is an *evolutionary* wage change associated with aging over the life cycle. To the extent that such wage changes are fully anticipated and known with certainty, they will not create a leisure-inducing income effect as they occur. Rather, the income effect is spread over the life cycle, independent of when the wage change occurs. The evolutionary wage change, however, does have a substitution effect making leisure more expensive (and hence inducing work) in the years of peak earnings in one's career. Because there is no leisure-inducing income effect, the labour supply response to anticipated evolutionary, life-cycle wage changes (termed the intertemporal substitution response) will be larger than the labour supply response, at a given age (i.e., not adding up over the life cycle), to permanent unanticipated differences like the wage profile shift from A to B, the latter labour supply response being muted by the leisure-inducing income effect.

The wage difference between C and D represents a transitory, one-time wage difference between two individuals whose wage profiles are otherwise similar (both high wage profiles) except at age t. It may be associated, for example, with a period of overtime pay that is not expected to be repeated. This wage difference will have the usual work-inducing substitution effect at year t since the income forgone by not working is very high. There will also be a small leisure-inducing income effect spread over the life cycle associated with the fact that the individual with the higher wage at D will have a slightly higher lifetime wealth because of the transitory wage difference. Because the wage difference is transitory and not permanent, however, the labour supply response to the transitory wage difference at age t will be larger than the labour supply response to a permanent wage difference as between A and B, at age t, because the latter has a stronger more permanent leisure-inducing income effect. Basically, individuals with the higher transitory wage at D will be able to afford to work slightly less over their life cycle; however, they will likely work more at the particular age t to take advantage of the high temporary wage.

Clearly the three different sources of wage differences outlined above have different income effects associated with whether the wage differences are permanent or temporary and anticipated or not anticipated. The different income effects, in turn, imply different labour supply responses to the wage differences. The anticipated evolutionary wage change from B to C has a pure substitution effect and is not offset by any leisure-inducing income effect. Hence it will have the largest positive labour supply response to a wage change. The transitory wage difference between C and D mainly has a work-inducing substitution effect; however, there is a mild offsetting leisure-inducing income effect spread over the life cycle. The permanent wage difference between A and B, at a given age, in contrast has a larger offsetting leisure-inducing income effect and hence will have the smallest labour supply response to a wage increase (in fact, that response may be negative). The labour supply responsiveness to a wage change may thereby be ordered as the largest emanating from an evolutionary wage change (pure substitution effect), a medium response emanating from a transitory wage change (mainly substitution but slight offsetting income effect) and the smallest and possibly negative response emanating from a permanent wage change (reflecting offsetting substitution and income effects).

Clearly, in a dynamic life cycle context the income and substitution effects emanating from a wage change can differ depending upon whether the wage change is permanent or temporary, and anticipated or unanticipated. This in turn means that the labour supply response will differ upon the source of the wage increase in a dynamic life-cycle setting.

QUESTIONS

1. Illustrate the effect of both fixed money and time costs on the individual's reservation wage, participation and hours-of-work decision.
2. Why might an increase in fixed time costs have a different effect than fixed commute costs on hours worked in the labour market?
3. Discuss the possible effects of fixed money and fixed time costs on the decision to work part time.
4. Analyse the effect, on female labour supply, of the following policy initiatives:
   (a) increasing the income tax deduction for childcare expenses;
   (b) changing the deduction to a credit;
   (c) direct subsidies to daycare centres.
5. Discuss the extent to which estimates of female wages, based upon data on females who are participating in the labour force, may give biased estimates of the expected wage that a nonparticipant may receive if she enters the labour market. How would you handle the problem?
6. Discuss the extent to which there may be a sample selection bias in using the wages of migrants to infer the expected wage of nonmigrants if they migrated, or in using the wages of union members to infer the expected wage of nonunion workers if they were to change union status. Give other examples of where sample selection bias may be prominent.
7. What is meant by a nonconvex budget set? Indicate why the "local reservation wage" rule for analysing labour force participation decisions is inappropriate when the income-leisure choice budget set is nonconvex. Indicate why an indirect utility function approach is appropriate under these, and in fact, under any circumstances. When would the two approaches give the same answer?
8. Discuss the labour supply response, in a dynamic life-cycle context, to the following wage changes: a permanent unanticipated wage increase; an evolutionary anticipated wage increase; a transitory, unanticipated wage increase.

REFERENCES AND FURTHER READINGS

Abbott, M. and O. Ashenfelter. Labour supply, commodity demand, and the allocation of time. *R.E. Studies* 43 (October 1976) 389-411 and correction 46 (October 1979) 567-569.

Blundell, R. and I. Walker. Modelling the joint determination of household labour supplies and commodity demands. *EJ* 92 (June 1982) 351-364.

Browning, M., A. Deaton and M. Irish. A profitable approach to labor supply and commodity demands over the life cycle. *Econometrica* 53 (May 1985) 503-543.

Cogan, J. Fixed costs and labor supply. *Econometrica* 49 (July 1981) 945-963.

Cotterman, R. The role of assets in labor supply functions. *EI* 19 (July 1981) 495-505.

Coyte, P. The supply of individual hours and labour force participation under uncertainty. *EI* 24 (January 1986) 155-172.

Deaton, A. and I. Muellbauer. Functional forms for labor supply and commodity demands with and without quantity restrictions. *Econometrica* 49 (November 1981) 1521-1532.

Dickinson, J. Parallel preference structures in labor supply and commodity demand: an adaptation of the Gorman polar form. *Econometrica* 48 (November 1980) 1711-1725.

Eaton, J. and R. Quandt. A model of rationing and labour supply. *Economica* 50 (Aug. 1983) 221-234.

Eaton, J. and H. Rosen. Labor supply, uncertainty and efficient taxation. *JPubEc* 14 (December 1980) 365-374.

Elliot, J. and K. Sherony. Employer search activities and short-run aggregate labor supply. *SEJ* 52 (January 1986) 693-705.

Ham, J. Estimation of a labour supply model with censoring due to unemployment and underemployment. *R.E. Studies* 49 (July 1982) 335-354.

Hausman, J. The effect of wages, taxes, and fixed costs on women's labour force participation. *JPubEc* 14 (December 1980) 161-194.

Heckman, J. Shadow prices, market wages and labor supply. *Econometrica* 42 (July 1974) 679-694.

Heckman, J. Sample selection bias as specification error. *Econometrica* 47 (Jan. 1979) 153-162.

Heckman, J. and T. MaCurdy. A lifecycle model of female labour supply. *R.E. Studies* 47 (Jan. 1980) 47-74.

Hutchens, R. Layoffs and labor supply. *IER* 24 (February 1983) 37-56.

Joerding, W. Lifetime consumption, labor supply and fertility: a complete demand system. *EI* 20 (April 1982) 255-276.

Keeley, M. et al. The estimation of labor supply models using experimental data. *AER* 68 (December 1978) 873-887.

Killingsworth, M. *Labor Supply*. Cambridge: Cambridge University Press, 1983.

Killingsworth, M. and J. Heckman. Female labor supply: a survey. *Handbook of Labor Economics*. Vol. 1. O. Ashenfelter and R. Layard (eds.). New York: Elsevier, 1986.

Lancaster, T. and A. Chesher. An econometric analysis of reservation wages. *Econometrica* 51 (November 1984) 1661-1676.

Link, C. and R. Settle. A simultaneous-equation model of labor supply, fertility and earnings of married women: the case of registered nurses. *SEJ* 47 (April 1981) 977-989.

MaCurdy, T. An empirical model of labor supply in a life-cycle setting. *JPE* 89 (December 1981) 1059-1085.

MaCurdy, T. A simple scheme for estimating an intertemporal model of labor supply and consumption in the presence of taxes and uncertainty. *IER* 24 (June 1983) 265-290.

Pencavel, J. Labor supply of men: a survey. *Handbook of Labor Economics*. Vol. 1. O. Ashenfelter and R. Layard (eds.). New York: Elsevier, 1986.

Rivi Kanbur, S. Labour supply under uncertainty with piecewise linear tax regimes. *Economica* 50 (Nov. 1983) 379-394.

Smith, J. (ed.) *Female labor supply*. Princeton: Princeton University Press, 1980.

Snow, A. and R. Warren, Jr. Price level uncertainty, saving, and labor supply. *EI* 24 (January 1986) 97-106.

Wales, T. Labour supply and commuting time. *Journal of Econometrics* 8 (October, 1978) 215-226.

Wales, T. and A.D. Woodland. Estimation of household utility functions and labor supply response. *IER* 17 (June 1976) 397-410.

Wales, T. and A.D. Woodland. Estimation of the allocation of time for work, leisure, and housework. *Econometrica* 45 (January 1977) 115-132.

Wales, T. and A.D. Woodland. Labour supply and progressive taxes. *R.E. Studies* 46 (January 1979) 83-95.

Wales, T. and A. Woodland. Sample selectivity and the estimation of labor supply functions. *IER* 21 (June 1980) 437-468.

Zabalza, A. The CES utility function, non-linear budget constraints and labour supply: results on female participation and hours. *EJ* 93 (June 1983) 312-330.

Part II

Labour Demand

CHAPTER 9

Demand for Labour in Competitive Labour Markets[1]

The general principles which determine the demand for any factor of production apply also to the demand for labour. In contrast to goods and services, factors of production are demanded not for final use or consumption but as inputs into the production of final goods and services. Thus the demand for a factor is necessarily linked to the demand for the goods and services that factor is used to produce. The demand for land suitable for growing wheat is linked to the demand for bread and cereal, just as the demand for construction workers is related to the demand for new buildings, roads and bridges. For this reason, the demand for factors is called a "derived demand."

In discussing firms' decisions regarding the employment of factors of production, economists usually distinguish between short-run and long-run decisions. The short run is defined as a period during which one or more factors of production — referred to as fixed factors — cannot be varied, while the long run is defined as a period during which the firm can adjust all of its inputs. During both the short and long runs, the state of technical knowledge is assumed to be fixed; the very long run refers to the period during which changes in technical knowledge can occur. The amount of calendar time corresponding to each of these periods will differ from one industry to another and according to other factors. These periods are useful as a conceptual device for analysing firm decision-making rather than for predicting the amount of time taken to adjust to change.

By the demand for labour we mean the quantity of labour services the firm would choose to employ at each wage. This desired quantity will depend on both the firm's objectives and its constraints. Usually we will assume that the firm's objective is to maximize profits. Also examined is the determination of labour demand under the weaker assumption of cost minimization. The firm is constrained by the demand conditions in its product markets, the supply conditions in its factor markets, and its production function which shows the maximum output attainable for various combinations of inputs, given the existing state of technical knowledge. In

---

1 This chapter does not deal directly with the extensive macroeconomic literature on how the demand for labour varies over the business cycle in response to changes in output, real wages, and the price of other inputs. This literature has been useful in understanding productivity and employment and hours-of-work changes over the business cycle. Hamermesh (1976) refers to much of this literature and uses it to provide estimates of the elasticity of demand for labour based on time series data.

the short run the firm is further constrained by having one or more factors of production whose quantities are fixed.

The theory of labour demand examines the quantity of labour services the firm desires to employ given a market-determined wage rate or given the labour supply function the firm faces. In some circumstances, however, the employer and employees may negotiate explicit, or reach implicit, contracts involving both wages and employment. When this is the case, the wage-employment outcomes may not be on the labour demand curve because the contracts will reflect the preferences of both the employer and the employees with respect to both wages and employment. Explicit wage-employment contracts are discussed in Part IV on unions and implicit wage-employment contracts are discussed in Parts V and VI.

CATEGORIZING THE STRUCTURE OF PRODUCT AND LABOUR MARKETS

Because the demand for labour is derived from the output produced by the firm, the way in which the firm behaves in the product market can have an impact on the demand for labour, and hence ultimately on wage and employment decisions. In general, the firm's product market behaviour depends on the structure of the industry to which the firm belongs. In decreasing order of the degree of competition, the four main market structures are: (1) perfect competition, (2) monopolistic competition, (3) oligopoly, and (4) monopoly.

Whereas the structure of the product market affects the firm's derived demand for labour, the structure of the labour market affects the labour supply curve that the firm faces. The supply curve of labour to an individual firm shows the amount of a specific type of labour (e.g. a particular occupational category) that the firm could employ at various wage rates. Analogous to the four product market structures there are four labour market structures. In decreasing order of the degree of competition it faces in hiring labour, these factor market structures are: (1) perfect competition, (2) monopsonistic competition, (3) oligopsony, and (4) monopsony. (The "opsony" ending is traditionally used to denote departures from perfect competition in factor markets.)

The product and labour market categorizations are independent in that there is no necessary relationship between the structure of the product market in which the firm sells its output and the labour market in which it buys labour services. The extent to which the firm is competitive in the product market (and hence the nature of its derived demand for labour curve) need not be related to the extent to which the firm is a competitive buyer of labour (and hence the nature of the supply curve of labour that it faces). The two *may* be related, for example if it is a large firm and hence dominates both the labour and product markets, but they need not be related. Hence for *each* product market structure, the firm can behave in at least four different ways as a purchaser of labour. Thus there are at least sixteen different combinations of product and labour market structure that can bear on the wage and employment decision at the level of the firm.

In general, however, the essence of the wage and employment decision by the firm can be captured by an examination of the polar cases of perfect competition (in product and/or factor markets), monopoly in the product market, and monopsony in the labour market. We will begin by examining the demand for labour in the short run under conditions of perfect competition in the labour market.

DEMAND FOR LABOUR IN THE SHORT RUN

The general principles determining labour demand can be explained for the case of a firm that produces a single output (Q) using two inputs, capital (K) and labour (N). In the short run the amount of capital is fixed at $K = K_o$, while the quantity of labour services can be varied by changing either the number of employees or hours worked by each employee (or both). For the moment we do not distinguish between variations in the number of employees and hours worked; however, this aspect of labour demand is discussed subsequently. Also discussed later is the possibility that labour may be a "quasi-fixed factor" in the short run.

The demand for labour in the short run can be derived by examining the firm's short-run output and employment decisions. Two decision rules follow from the assumption of profit maximization. First, because the costs associated with the fixed factor must be paid whether or not the firm produces (and whatever amount the firm produces), the firm will operate as long as it can cover its variable costs (i.e. if total revenue exceeds total variable costs). This is an example of the "bygones are forever bygones" principle; fixed costs are sunk costs, and their magnitude should not affect what is the currently most profitable thing to do.

The second decision rule implied by profit maximization is that, if the firm produces at all (i.e. is able to cover its variable costs), it should produce the quantity Q^* at which marginal revenue (MR) equals marginal cost (MC). That is, the firm should increase output until the additional cost associated with the last unit produced equals the additional revenue associated with that unit. Because marginal revenue is a constant or decreasing function of output and marginal cost rises with output (due to diminishing marginal productivity), expanding output beyond the point at which MR = MC will lower profits because the addition to total revenue will be less than the increase in total cost. Producing a lower output would also reduce profits because, at output levels below Q^*, marginal revenue exceeds marginal cost; thus increasing output would add more to total revenue than to total cost, raising profits.

The profit-maximizing decision rules can be stated in terms of the employment of inputs rather than in terms of the quantity of output to produce. Because concepts such as total revenue and marginal revenue are defined in terms of units of output, the terminology is modified for inputs.

The total revenue associated with the amount of an input employed is called the total revenue product (TRP) of that input; similarly, the change in total revenue associated with a change in the amount of the input employed is called the marginal revenue product (MRP). Thus the profit-maximizing decision rules for the employment of the variable input can be stated as follows: (1) the firm should produce providing the total revenue product of the variable input exceeds the total costs associated with that input; otherwise the firm should shut down operations, and (2) if the firm produces at all, it should expand employment of the variable input to the point at which its marginal revenue product equals its marginal cost.

The short-run employment decision of a firm operating in a perfectly competitive labour market is shown in Figure 9.1. In a competitive factor market the firm is a price taker; i.e. the firm can hire more or less of the factor without affecting the market price. Thus in a competitive labour market the marginal (and average) cost of labour is the market wage rate. The firm will therefore employ labour until its marginal revenue product equals the wage rate, which implies that the firm's short run labour demand curve is its marginal revenue product of labour curve. For example, if the wage rate is w_0 the firm would employ N_0^* labour services. However, the firm will shut down operations in the short run if the total variable cost exceeds the total revenue product of labour, which will be the case if the average cost of labour (the wage rate) exceeds the average revenue product of labour. Thus at wage rates higher than w_1 in Figure 9.1 (the point at which the wage rate equals the average product of labour) the firm would choose to shut down operations. It follows that the firm's short-run labour demand curve is its marginal revenue product of labour curve below the point at which the average and marginal product curves intersect (i.e. below the point at which the ARP_N reaches a maximum).

Figure 9.1   The Firm's Short-Run Demand for Labour

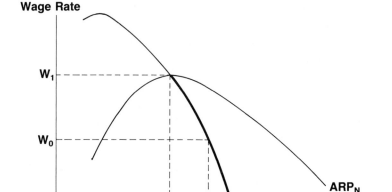

The short-run labour demand curve is downward-sloping because of diminishing returns. Although the average and marginal products may initially rise as more labour is employed, both eventually decline as more units of the variable factor are combined with a given amount of the fixed factor. Because the firm employs labour in the range in which its marginal revenue product is declining, a reduction in the wage rate is needed to entice the firm to employ more labour. Similarly, an increase in the wage rate will cause the firm to employ less labour, thus raising its marginal revenue product and restoring equality between the marginal revenue product and marginal cost.

At this point, it may be worth highlighting a common misconception concerning the reason for the downward-sloping demand for labour. The demand is for a given homogeneous type of labour; consequently, it does *not* slope downwards because, as the firm uses more labour, it uses poorer quality labour and hence pays a lower wage. It may well be true that when firms expand their work-force they often have to use poorer quality labour. Nevertheless for analytical purposes it is useful to assume a given, homogeneous type of labour so that the impact on labour demand of changes in the wage rate for that type of labour can be analysed. The change in the productivity of labour that occurs does so because of changes in the amount of the variable factor combined with a given amount of the fixed factor, not because the firm is delving more into the reserve of less qualified labour.

WAGES, THE MARGINAL PRODUCTIVITY OF LABOUR AND THE PRODUCT MARKET

The demand schedule of a profit-maximizing firm which is a wage taker in the labour market is the locus of points for which the marginal revenue product of labour equals the wage rate. The marginal revenue product of labour (MRP_N) equals the marginal revenue of output (MR_Q) times the marginal physical product of labour (MPP_N). Thus there is a relationship between wages and the marginal productivity of labour.

The marginal revenue of output depends on the market structure in the product market. The two polar cases of perfect competition and monopoly are discussed here. A perfectly competitive firm is a price taker in the product market. Because the firm can sell additional (or fewer) units of output without affecting the market price, the marginal revenue of output equals the product price; i.e. for a competitive firm $MRP_N = MR_Q \cdot MPP_N = p \cdot MPP_N$. Because it is the product of the market price and the marginal product of labour, this term is referred to as the value of the marginal product of labour; i.e., $p \cdot MPP_N = VMP_N$. A firm that is competitive in both the product and labour markets will thus employ labour services until the value of the marginal product of labour just equals the wage; i.e. the demand for labour obeys the equation

$$p \cdot MPP_N = VMP_N = w \qquad (9.1)$$

Equation (9.1) follows from the MR = MC rule for profit maximization; the VMP_N is the increase in total revenue associated with a unit increase in labour input while the wage w is the accompanying increase in total cost. Alternatively stated, the labour demand curve of a firm that is competitive in both the product and labour markets is the locus of points for which the real wage w/p equals the marginal physical product of labour.

The polar case of non-competitive behaviour in the product market is that of monopoly. In this situation the firm is so large relative to the size of the product market that it can influence the price at which it sells its product: it is a price-setter, not a price-taker. In the extreme case of monopoly, the monopolist comprises the whole industry: there are no other firms in the industry. Thus, the industry demand for the product is the demand schedule for the product of the monopolist.

As is well known from standard microeconomic theory, the relevant decision-making schedule for the profit-maximizing monopolist is not the demand schedule for its product, but rather its marginal revenue schedule. In order to sell an additional unit of output, the monopolist has to lower the price of its product. Assuming that it cannot differentiate its homogeneous product to consumers, the monopolist will also have to lower the price on all units of its output, not just on the additional units that it wishes to sell. Consequently, its marginal revenue — the additional revenue generated by selling an additional unit of output — will fall faster than its price, reflecting the fact that the price decline applies to intra-marginal units of output. The marginal revenue schedule for the monopolist will therefore lie below and to the left of its demand schedule. By equating marginal revenue with marginal cost so as to maximize profits, the monopolist will produce less output and charge a higher price (as given by the demand schedule, since this is the price that consumers will pay) than if it were a competitive firm on the product market.

This aspect of the product market has implications for the derived demand for labour. The monopolist's demand for labour curve is the locus of points for which

$$MR_Q \cdot MPP_N = MRP_N = w \qquad\qquad (9.2)$$

The differences between Equation 9.1 and 9.2 highlight the fact that when the monopolist hires more labour to produce more output, not only does the marginal physical product of labour fall (as is the case with the competitor), but also the marginal revenue from an additional unit of output, MR_Q, falls. This latter effect occurs because the monopolist, unlike the competitor, can sell more output only by lowering the product price and this in turn lowers revenue. Because both MPP_N and MR_Q fall when N increases in Equation 9.2, then the monopolist's demand for labour falls faster than it would if it behaved as a competitive firm in the product market, in which case only MPP_N would fall, as given in Equation 9.1.

DEMAND FOR LABOUR IN THE LONG RUN

In the long run the firm can vary all of its inputs. For expositional purposes we will continue to assume two inputs, labour (N) and capital (K) and one output (Q); however, the general principles apply to firms which employ many inputs and produce multiple outputs. As in the previous section, the demand for labour is derived by varying the wage rate that the firm faces for a given homogeneous type of labour, and tracing out the profit-maximizing (or cost-minimizing) quantity of labour that will be employed by the firm.

For conceptual purposes, the firm's production and employment decisions are usually examined in two stages. First, the minimum cost method of producing any level of output is examined. Second, given that each output will be produced at minimum cost, the profit-maximizing level of output is chosen.

Isoquants, Isocosts and Equilibrium

The first stage (cost minimization) is depicted geometrically in Figure 9.2. The top part of the diagram, Figure 9.2(a), gives the firm's isoquant Q_o, which shows the various combinations of labour N and capital K, that can produce a given level of output Q_o, via the firm's production function that can be written in general form as $Q = Q(K,N)$. The slope of the isoquant exhibits a diminishing marginal rate of substitution between the inputs. That is, in the upper left segment when an abundance of capital is used, a considerable increase in the use of capital is required for a small reduction in the use of labour, if output is to be maintained. In the lower right segment when an abundance of labour is used, labour is a poor substitute for capital, and considerable labour savings are possible for small increases in the use of capital. In the middle segment of the isoquant, labour and capital are both good substitutes. Successively higher isoquants or levels of output, such as Q_1, can be produced by successively larger amounts of both inputs.

Figure 9.2(b) illustrates the firm's budget constraint or isocost line K_mN_m, depicting the various combinations of capital and labour the firm can employ, given their market price and the expenditures of the firm. Algebraically, the isocost line is $C = rK + wN$ where r is the price of capital and w the price of labour, or wage rate.[2] The position and shape of the isocost line can be determined by solving for the two intercepts or end points and the slope of the line between them. From the isocost equation, for fixed prices r_o and w_o, these end points are $N_m = C/w_o$ when $K = 0$, and $K_m = C/r_o$ when $N = 0$. The slope is simply minus the rise

---

2 If the firm rents its capital equipment, the cost of capital is the rental price. If the firm owns its capital equipment, the implicit or opportunity cost of capital depends on the cost of the machinery and equipment, the interest rate at which funds can be borrowed or lent and the rate at which the machinery depreciates. In the analysis which follows, we will assume the firm is a price taker in the market for capital.

Figure 9.2   Isoquants, Isocost, and Equilibrium

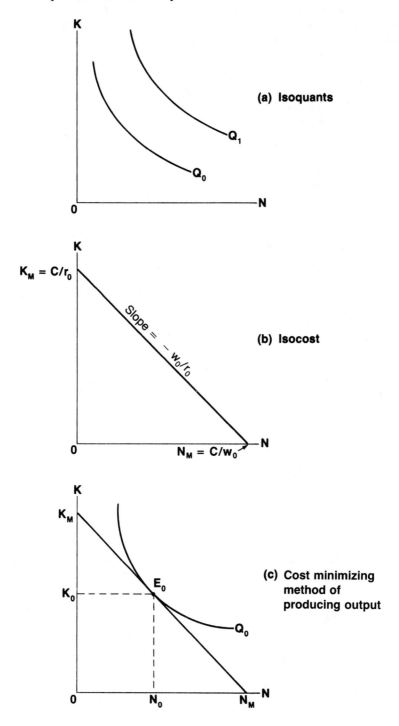

divided by the run or $-[C/r_o \div C/w_o] = -w_o/r_o$, that is, the price of labour relative to the price of capital. This is a straight line as long as w amd r are constant for these given types of labour and capital, which is the case when the firm is a price taker in both input markets.

A profit-maximizing firm will maximize the output that can be produced for a given level of cost, or alternatively it will minimize the cost for a given level of output. Figure 9.2(c) combines the isoquants and isocost to illustrate the maximum output (isoquant) that the firm can attain given its resource expenditure constraint (isocost). This is clearly E_o where the isocost is tangent to the isoquant. The determination of the profit-maximizing level of output (the output at which marginal revenue equals marginal cost) is not shown in the diagram. What is shown is how to produce any output, including the profit-maximizing output, at minimum cost.

At E_o, the cost-minimizing amounts of labour and capital, respectively used to produce Q_o units of output, are N_o and K_o. If Q_o is the profit-maximizing output, this gives us one point on the demand curve for labour, as depicted later in Figure 9.3. That is, at the wage rate w_o the firm employs N_o units of labour.

Deriving the Firm's Labour Demand Schedule

The complete labour demand schedule, for the long run when the firm can vary both capital and labour, can be obtained simply by varying the wage rate and tracing out the new, equilibrium, profit-maximizing amounts of labour that would be employed. This is illustrated in Figure 9.3. For example, if total cost is held constant an increase in the wage rate from w_o to w_1 would rotate the isocost line downwards as in Figure 9.3(a). This is so because if the firm spent all of its expenditures on capital it would be at the same maximum point $K_m = C/r_o$. However, if it spent all of its budget on the higher priced labour then the maximum amount of labour it could employ would be reduced to a point like $N_n = C/w_1$ corresponding to the higher price of labour. Since $w_1 > w_o$ then $N_n < N_m$. Also, the slope of the new budget constraint would be greater than the original; that is, $w_1/r_o > w_o/r_o$.

As depicted in Figure 9.3(b), given the higher wage rate w_1, the firm will maximize profits by moving to a lower level of output Q_1, operating at E_1 and employing N_1 units of labour. This yields a second point on the firm's demand curve for labour depicted in Figure 9.3(c). That is, a lower level of employment N_1 corresponds to the higher wage rate w_1.

To complete the explanation of the firm's response to a wage increase, Figure 9.4 shows how the profit-maximizing output levels (Q_o and Q_1 in Figure 9.3(b)) are determined. The wage increase shifts up the firm's marginal and average cost curves. In a perfectly competitive industry, each firm reduces output which raises the market price of the product. In the new equilibrium the output of each firm and total output are lower than in the original equilibrium. The monopolist responds to the increase in

Figure 9.3 Deriving the Labour Demand Schedule

(a) Isocost rotation from wage increase

(b) New profit maximizing output and derived labour demand

(c) Derived labour demand schedule

costs by raising the product price and reducing output. The analysis of the intermediate market structures (monopolistic competition and oligopoly) is similar; in general an increase in costs, ceteris paribus, leads to an increase in the product price and a reduction in output. Note, however, that although the firm moves to a lower isoquant (Q_0 to Q_1 in Figure 9.3(b)), its total costs may increase (as shown in Figure 9.3(b)) or decrease. Producing a lower output tends to reduce total costs, but the higher wage tends to raise total costs. The net effect therefore depends on the magnitude of these offsetting forces. In this respect the analysis of the response of the firm to an increase in an input price is not exactly analogous to the response of the consumer to a commodity price increase. In consumer theory, income (or total expenditure on goods) is assumed to be exogenously determined; thus a change in the price of one good rotates the budget constraint as in Figure 9.3(a). In the theory of the firm, total cost (or total expenditure on inputs) is endogenous rather than exogenous and depends on the profit-

Figure 9.4   The Effect of a Cost Increase on Output

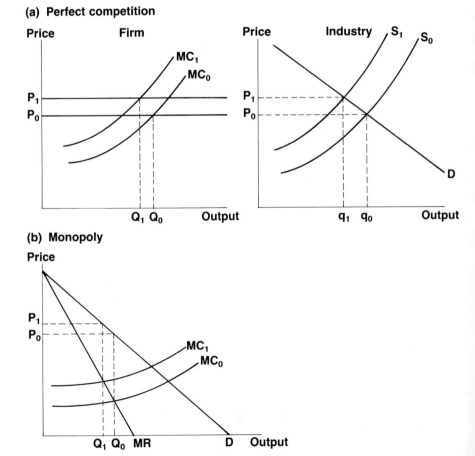

(a) Perfect competition

(b) Monopoly

maximizing levels of output and inputs given the output and input prices. As these change, total costs may change, as depicted in Figure 9.3(b).

Clearly one could trace out the full demand schedule by varying the wage rate and observing the profit-maximizing amounts of labour that would be employed. Economic theory predicts that the demand schedule is downward-sloping (that is, higher wages are associated with a reduced demand for labour) both because the firm would substitute cheaper inputs for the more expensive labour (substitution effect), and because it would reduce its scale of operations because of the wage and hence cost increase (scale effect). For conceptual purposes it is useful to examine these two effects.

Separating Scale and Substitution Effects of a Wage Change

Figure 9.5 illustrates how the wage increase from w_o to w_1 can be separated into its component parts — a substitution effect and a scale or output effect. The negative substitution effect occurs as the firm substitutes cheaper capital for the more expensive labour, therefore reducing the quantity of labour demanded. When labour is a normal input, the negative scale effect occurs as a wage increase leads to a higher marginal cost of production which, in turn, reduces the firm's optimal output and hence derived demand for labour. Thus the scale and substitution effects reinforce each other to lead to an unambiguously inverse relationship between wages and the firm's demand for labour.[3]

The scale effect can be isolated by hypothetically compensating the firm for its lost output so that it would operate on the original isoquant Q_o. This is illustrated by the hypothetical isocost line that is parallel to the new isocost w_1/r_o, but tangent to the original isoquant Q_o at E_s. The only difference between E_s and E_1 is the scale of operation of the firm (Q_o as opposed to Q_1), since the relative price of labour and capital are the same; that is, both are w_1/r_o. Therefore, $N_s - N_1$ can be thought of as the scale

---

3 Nagatani (1978) proves that this is true even when labour is an inferior factor of production; that is, when the firm's production function is such that less labour is employed when the firm expands output. When labour is an inferior factor of production and wages increase, the firm's marginal cost of production actually decreases. This occurs because, after the wage increase, in order to expand production the firm uses less of the more expensive labour and more of the relatively cheaper capital. The decreased marginal cost of production then leads to an increased optimal output which, in the case of the inferior factor, means less labour employed. In essence, the reverse effect from output to employment in the case of inferior factors is negated by the reverse effect on the firm's marginal cost schedule.

This can be illustrated more rigorously by examining what happens to the firm's costs as wages increase. The firm's total cost function can be written as $TC_Q = wN + rK$ and marginal cost is $MC_Q = \partial TC/\partial Q = w\partial N/\partial Q + r\partial K/\partial Q$. The change in marginal cost that results from a wage change is therefore $\partial MC_Q/\partial w = \partial N/\partial Q$. If N is a normal factor of production, then by definition $\partial N/\partial Q > 0$ and therefore $\partial MC_Q/\partial w > 0$. That is, the usual scale effect is in operation: a wage increase leads to higher marginal cost, which results in reduced output and hence a lower derived demand for labour.

However, if N is an inferior factor, then $\partial N/\partial Q < 0$ and therefore $\partial MC_Q/\partial w < 0$ because $\partial N/\partial Q = \partial MC_Q/\partial w$. The scale effect then operates as follows: a wage increase reduces marginal cost, which results in increased output and, because of the inferiority of the factor, a lower derived demand for labour. Thus, the change in the derived demand for labour that results from the firm's changing its scale of output in response to the wage increase is unambiguously negative.

Figure 9.5   Substitution and Scale Effects of a Wage Change

effect — the reduction in employment that comes about to the extent that the firm reduces its output in response to the wage increase. Except in the unusual circumstance in which labour is an inferior input, the scale effect works through the following scenario: wage increases imply cost increases, which lead to a reduced optimal scale of output, which in turn leads to a reduced demand for labour.

The difference between E_o and E_s, on the other hand, is simply due to the different slopes of the isocost lines. They both represent the same output, Q_o. Consequently, the difference between E_o and E_s reflects the pure substitution of capital for labour to produce the same output, Q_o. Therefore, $N_o - N_s$ can be thought of as a pure or compensated substitution effect, representing the substitution of relatively cheaper inputs for the inputs whose relative price has risen. Both scale and substitution effects work in the same direction to yield an unambiguously downward-sloping demand schedule for labour.

For capital, the substitution and scale effects of an increase in the wage rate work in opposite directions. The substitution effect (E_o to E_s) increases the demand for capital as the firm uses more capital and less labour to produce a given level of output. However, the reduction in output from Q_o to Q_l causes a reduction in demand for all normal inputs; thus the scale effect (E_s to E_l) reduces the demand for capital. The overall or net effect on capital thus depends on which of the two effects is larger. In general, an increase in the wage may cause the firm to employ more or less capital.

THE RELATIONSHIP BETWEEN THE SHORT- AND LONG-RUN LABOUR DEMAND

The division of the firm's response to a wage change into the substitution and scale effects is also useful in understanding the difference between the short- and long-run labour demand. In the short run the amount of capital is fixed; thus there is no substitution effect. The downward-sloping nature of the short-run labour demand curve is a consequence of a scale effect and diminishing marginal productivity of labour. In the long run the firm has the additional flexibility associated with varying its capital stock. Thus the response to a wage change will be larger in the long run than in the short run, ceteris paribus. This relationship is illustrated in Figure 9.6. The initial long-run equilibrium is at E_0. The short-run response to the wage increase from w_0 to w_1 involves moving to a new equilibrium at E_1. Here the firm is employing less labour (N_1 versus N_0) but the same amount of capital (K_0). In the long run the firm also adjusts its capital stock from K_0 to K_1, shifting the short-run labour demand curve to the left. The new long-run equilibrium is at E_2. The long-run labour demand curve consists of the locus of points such as E_0 and E_2 at which the firm has optimally adjusted employment of both labour and capital given the wage rate and other exogenous variables.

Figure 9.6   The Demand for Labour in the Short Run and Long Run

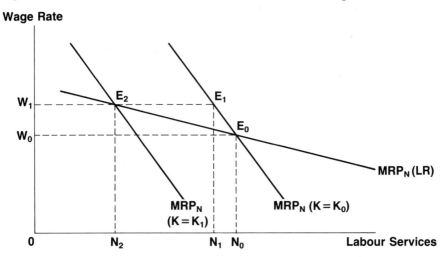

LABOUR DEMAND UNDER COST MINIMIZATION

Economic analysis generally assumes that firms in the private sector seek to maximize profits. However, organizations in the public and quasi-public sectors — such as federal, provincial and municipal public administration,

Crown corporations, and educational and health institutions — generally have other goals. These goals will determine the quantity of output or services provided and the amount of labour and other productive inputs employed. Although the factors that determine the output of these organizations may vary, such organizations may seek to produce that output efficiently; i.e., at minimum cost.

The distinction between the scale and substitution effects is useful in analysing the demand for labour in these circumstances. An organization whose output of goods and/or services is exogenously determined but which seeks to produce that output at minimum cost will respond to changes in wages by substituting between labour and other inputs. That is, with output fixed (determined by other factors) there will be a pure substitution effect in response to changes in the wage rate. Labour demand will therefore be unambiguously downward sloping but more inelastic than that of a profit-maximizing firm because of the absence of an output effect.

Although a cost-minimizing organization will respond to a wage increase by substituting capital for labour, its total expenditure on inputs (total costs) will nonetheless rise. This aspect is illustrated in Figure 9.5. The equilibrium E_s involves greater total costs than the original equilibrium E_o. The increase in total costs is, however, less than would be the case if the organization did not substitute capital for labour in response to the wage increase (i.e. if the firm remained at the point E_o in Figure 9.5).

Mathematical Exposition*

The analysis of labour demand can also be carried out using mathematics. Profits π are defined as total revenues $R(Q)$ minus total costs, or

$$\pi(Q) = R(Q) - wN - rK \tag{9.3}$$

and the production function

$$Q = Q(N,K) \text{ where } \frac{\partial Q}{\partial N} > 0 \text{ and } \frac{\partial Q}{\partial K} > 0 \tag{9.4}$$

The firm is assumed to be a price taker in the input markets; hence w and r are treated as fixed or exogenous variables. In the short run the capital input is also fixed at $K = K_o$.

In the short run the firm will choose labour in order to

$$\text{Max } R(Q(N,K_o)) - wN - rK_o$$
$$\{N\}$$

The necessary condition for a maximum is

$$\frac{dR}{dQ}\frac{\partial Q}{\partial N}(N,K_o) - w = 0 \tag{9.5}$$

$$\text{or} \quad MR_Q \cdot MPP_N = w \tag{9.6}$$

This is the condition discussed previously; the firm should employ labour until the marginal revenue product of labour MRP_N equals the wage rate. The marginal revenue product is the marginal revenue of output MR_Q times the marginal physical product of labour MPP_N.

For firms that operate in a perfectly competitive output market, $R(Q) = p \cdot Q$ where p is fixed so $dR(Q)/dQ = p$; i.e., the marginal revenue of output is simply the product price. Thus (9.6) becomes

$$p \cdot MPP_N = VMP_N = w \qquad (9.7)$$

Unlike the competitive firm which treats the product price as fixed, the monopolist recognizes that the product price and output are negatively related; that is,

$$R(Q) = p(Q) \cdot Q \text{ where } dp/dQ < 0 \qquad (9.8)$$

The monopolist thus employs labour until

$$MRP_N = [p(Q) + Q\frac{dp}{dQ}]\frac{\partial Q}{\partial N} = w \qquad (9.9)$$

The term in square brackets on the left hand side is the marginal revenue of output MR_Q; $MR_Q < p(Q)$ because $dp/dQ < 0$. If price p is fixed ($dp/dQ = 0$), equation (9.9) simplifies to (9.7).

In the long run the firm chooses N and K to

Max $R(Q(N,K)) - wN - rK$
{N,K}

The necessary conditions for a maximum are:

$$\frac{dR}{dQ}\frac{\partial Q}{\partial N} - w = 0 \qquad (9.10)$$

$$\frac{dR}{dQ}\frac{\partial Q}{\partial K} - r = 0 \qquad (9.11)$$

Thus each input is employed to the point at which its marginal revenue product equals its price.

ELASTICITY OF DEMAND FOR LABOUR

The previous analysis indicated that the demand for labour is a negative function of the wage rate. Consequently, in this static, partial-equilibrium framework, an exogenous increase in wages, other things held constant, would lead to a reduction in the quantity of labour demanded. The exogenous increase in wages, for example, could emanate from a union wage demand, a wage parity scheme, or wage-fixing legislation, such as minimum wages, equal pay, fair-wage legislation or extension legislation. Although there may be offsetting factors (to be discussed later), it is important to realize that economic theory predicts that there will be an adverse employment effect from these wage increases. The magnitude of the adverse employment effect depends on the elasticity of the derived damand for labour. As illustrated in Figure 9.7, if the demand for labour is inelastic (Figure 9.7(a)), then the adverse employment effect is small; if the demand is elastic (Figure 9.7(b)), then the adverse employment effect is large.

From a policy perspective it is important to know the expected magnitude of these adverse employment effects because they may offset other possible benefits of the exogenous wage increase. Consequently, it is important to know the determinants of the elasticity of demand for labour. As originally outlined by Marshall and formalized by Hicks (1963, pp. 241–46 and 374–84), the basic determinants of the elasticity of demand for labour are the availability of substitute inputs, the elasticity of supply of substitute inputs, the elasticity of demand for output, and the ratio of labour cost to total cost. These factors are related to the magnitude of the substitution and scale effects discussed previously. Each of these factors will be discussed in turn, in the context of an inelastic demand for labour (Figure 9.7(a)) which implies a wage increase being associated with a small adverse employment effect.

Figure 9.7 Inelastic and Elastic Demand for Labour

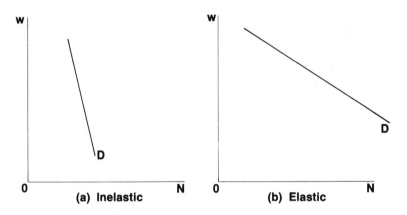

(a) Inelastic (b) Elastic

Availability of Substitute Inputs

The derived demand for labour will be inelastic, and hence the adverse employment effect of an exogenous wage increase will be small, if alternative inputs cannot be substituted easily for the higher-price labour. This would be depicted by an isoquant that is more L-shaped as opposed to a negatively sloped straight line; that is, the marginal rate of technical substitution between other inputs and labour is small. This factor relates to the magnitudes of the substitution effect.

The inability to substitute alternative inputs could be technologically determined, as for example if the particular type of labour is essential to the production process, or it could be institutionally determined, as for example if the union prevents such substitution as contracting-out or the use of non-union labour or the introduction of new technology. Time also is a factor, since in the long run the possibility of substituting cheaper inputs is more feasible.

Examples of workers for whom substitute inputs may not *readily* be available could include construction craftsmen, teachers, and professionals with specialized skills. Even in these cases, however, substitutions are technically possible in the long run, especially when one considers alternative production processes and delivery systems (e.g. prefabricated construction, larger class size with more audio-visual aids, and the use of paraprofessionals).

Elasticity of Supply of Substitute Inputs

The substitution of alternative inputs can also be affected by changes in the price of these inputs. If the substitutes are relatively *inelastic* in supply, so that an increase in the demand for the inputs will lead to an increase in their price, then this price increase may choke off some of the increased usage of these substitutes. In general, this is probably not an important factor, however, because it is unlikely that the firm or industry where the wage increase occurs is such a large purchaser of alternative inputs that it affects their price. Certainly in the long run, the supply of substitute inputs is likely to be more elastic.

Elasticity of Demand for Output

Since the demand for labour is derived from the output produced by the firm, then the elasticity of the demand for labour will depend on the price elasticity of the demand for the output or services produced by the firm. The elasticity of product demand determines the magnitude of the scale effect. If the demand for the output produced by the firm is inelastic, so that a price increase (engendered by a wage increase) will not lead to a large reduction in the quantity demanded, then the derived demand for labour will also be inelastic. In such circumstances, the wage increase can be passed on to consumers in the form of higher product prices without there being much of a reduction in the demand for those products and hence in the derived demand for labour.

This could be the case, for example, in construction, especially non-residential construction where there are few alternatives to building in a particular location. It could also be the case in tariff-protected industries, or in public services where few alternatives are available, or in most sectors in the short run. On the other hand, in fiercely competitive sectors, such as the garment trades or coal mining, where alternative products are available, then the demand for the product is probably quite price-elastic. In these circumstances, the derived demand for labour would be elastic and a wage increase would lead to a large reduction in the quantity of labour demanded.

Ratio of Labour Cost to Total Cost

The extent to which labour cost is an important component of total cost can also affect the responsiveness of employment to wage changes. Specifically, the demand for labour will be inelastic, and hence the adverse employment effect of a wage increase small, if labour cost is a small portion of total cost.[4] In such circumstances the scale effect would be small; that is, the firm would not have to reduce its output much because the cost increase emanating from the wage increase would be small. In addition, there is the possibility that if wage costs are a small portion of total cost then any wage increase more easily could be absorbed by the firm or passed on to consumers.

For obvious reasons, this factor is often referred to as the "importance of being unimportant." Examples of wage cost for a particular group of workers being a small portion of total cost could include construction craftworkers, airline pilots and employed professionals (e.g. engineers and architects) on many projects. In such circumstances their wage increases simply may not matter much to the employer, and consequently their wage demands may not be tempered much by the threat of reduced employment. On the other hand, the wages of government workers and miners may constitute a large portion of the total cost in their respective trades. The resultant elastic demand for labour may thereby temper their wage demands.

Summary of Examples

The previous discussion of the determinants of the elasticity of demand for labour suggested that in some cases the various determinants worked in the same direction to give rise to an inelastic demand. Such could be the case, for example, for many skilled construction trades or airline pilots, where there are few good substitute inputs, the demand for the output is relatively price-inelastic, and labour cost is a small portion of total cost. Consequently, wage demands would be less tempered by the threat of reduced employment.

On the other hand, in sectors like the garment trades or mining, the determinants of the elasticity of demand for labour give rise to an elastic demand. Especially in the long run, substitute inputs are readily available, the demand for the output is relatively price-elastic, and labour cost is a significant portion of total cost. In such circumstances wage demands may be tempered by the possibility of reduced employment associated with the elastic demand for labour. Alternatively, as we will discuss in a later section on unionism, wage demands may be accompanied by complementary policies designed to reduce the adverse employment effect or, as in the case

---

4 Hicks (1963, pp. 245–6) proves formally that this is true as long as the elasticity of demand for the final product is greater than the elasticity of substitution between the inputs; that is, as long as consumers can substitute away from the higher-priced product more easily than producers can substitute away from higher-priced labour. This factor thus depends on the magnitude of both the substitution and scale effects.

of some workers, the adverse employment effect may simply be accepted as a necessary by-product of wage increases.

Empirical Evidence

Clearly, knowledge of the elasticity of demand for particular types of labour is important for policy purposes so as to predict the adverse employment effect that may emanate from such factors as minimum wage and equal pay laws, or wage increases associated with unionization, occupational licensing or arbitrated wage settlements. Estimates of the elasticity of the demand for the particular type of labour being affected would be useful to predict the employment effect of an exogenous wage increase. However, even without precise numerical estimates, judicious statements still can be made based on the importance of the various factors that determine the elasticity of the demand for labour.

Hamermesh (1976) reviewed an extensive empirical literature in the U.S. that can be used to calculate estimates of the elasticity of demand for labour. He concluded that, based largely on private sector data in the U.S., this elasticity ranged from a low of $-.09$ to a high of $-.62$, with a medium estimate of $-.32$, over a time period of one year. That is, a one percent increase in wages would lead to approximately a one-third of one percent reduction in employment after a one-year time period. This adverse employment effect was roughly equally divided between the substitution and scale effect; that is, the substitution and scale elasticities were approximately equal.

Canadian studies have obtained broadly similar estimates. For example, Woodland (1975) estimates labour demand functions for ten broadly defined Canadian industries (agriculture, manufacturing, forestry and mining, and so on) for the 1946–69 period. One labour input and two capital inputs (structures and equipment) are assumed in the empirical analysis. In each of the ten industries, the estimated labour demand curve is downward sloping. Estimated elasticities of labour demand are between zero and 0.5 in most industries. Eight of the ten industries exhibited statistically significant substitution among inputs. Woodland concludes that changes in relative input prices appear to play a significant role in determining the demand for factors of production.

MINIMUM-WAGE LEGISLATION

Minimum-wage laws provide a useful illustration of the practical relevance of our theoretical knowledge of the determinants of the derived demand for labour. In Canada, labour matters usually are under provincial jurisdiction; hence, each province has its own minimum-wage law. Federal labour laws cover approximately 10 percent of Canadian workers. Industries of an inter-provincial or international nature — for example, inter-provincial transportation and telephone communication, air transport, broadcasting, shipping and banks — are under federal jurisdiction. The influence of federal laws may be larger to the extent that they serve as a model for comparable provincial legislation.

The rationale behind minimum-wage laws has not always been clear and explicit. Curbing poverty among the working poor, preventing "exploitation" of the unorganized non-union sector, preventing "unfair" low-wage competition, have all been suggested as possible rationales. In the early days of union organizing, it is alleged, minimum-wage laws were also instituted to curb unionization — in that, if the wages of unorganized labour could be raised through government legislation, there would be less need for unions. As is so often the case with legislation, its actual impact may be different from its intended impact, or at least it may have unintended side effects. Economic theory may be of some help in shedding light on this issue.

Expected Impact

Economic theory predicts that a minimum wage in a competitive labour market will have an adverse employment effect; that is, employment will be reduced relative to what it would have been in the absence of the minimum wage. This is illustrated in Figure 9.8 where w_c and N_c are the equilibrium wage and level of employment, respectively, in a particular competitive labour market. After the imposition of the minimum wage, w_m, employers will reduce their demand for labour to N_m. Thus $(N_c - N_m)$ is the adverse employment effect associated with the minimum wage. In addition to the $(N_c - N_m)$ workers who would not be employed because of the minimum wage, an additional $(N_s - N_c)$ workers would be willing to work in this sector because the minimum wage is higher than the previous prevailing wage. Thus the queue of applicants for the reduced number of jobs is $(N_s - N_m)$, with $(N_c - N_m)$ representing workers laid off because of the minimum wage and $(N_s - N_c)$ representing new potential recruits who are attracted to the minimum-wage jobs.

The adverse employment effect $(N_c - N_m)$ occurs as firms substitute other relatively cheaper inputs for the higher-priced labour, and as they reduce output in response to the higher costs. These are the familiar substitution and scale effects, respectively, that give rise to the downward-sloping demand schedule for labour. (In the short run there would also be a disemployment effect, but the reduction in employment would be less than the long-run effect incorporating the scale and substitution effects.) The adverse employment effect need not mean an increase in measured unemployment: some who lose jobs in the sectors covered by the minimum-wage law may go to the uncovered sectors or drop out of the labour force.[5]

The magnitude of this adverse employment effect depends on the elasticity of the derived demand for labour. If the demand for labour were

---

5 This indicates that minimum-wage laws may affect not only wages and employment in the sectors to which they apply but also in uncovered sectors through their impact on labour supply to these sectors. This aspect of minimum wages is discussed further in a subsequent chapter.

relatively inelastic then the adverse employment effect would be small. Unfortunately, in those sectors most affected by minimum-wage legislation — low-wage industries like textiles, sales, service and tourism — the demand for labour is likely to be fairly elastic, especially in the long run, reflecting the availability of substitute inputs and products as well as the fact that labour costs are often a substantial proportion of the total cost. In addition, since many of these sectors are often thought of as "fiercely competitive," it is unlikely that the minimum-wage cost increases could be absorbed by the industry through a reduction in monopoly profits.

Figure 9.8   Minimum Wage

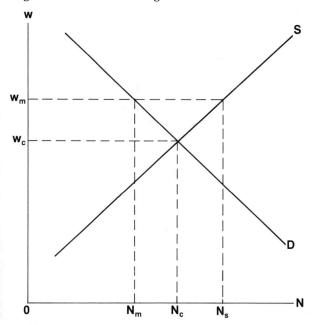

Possible Offsetting Factors

In a dynamic context, other things are changing at the same time as the minimum wage, and these changes may offset, in part at least, the adverse employment effect. For example, the demand for labour could increase perhaps because of an exogenous increase in the demand for output or because of an increase in the price of substitute inputs. While this may mitigate some, or perhaps even all, of the unemployment associated with the minimum wage, it is still true that employment would be even higher were it not for the minimum wage. Hence there is still an adverse employment effect relative to the situation with no minimum wage. This can easily be illustrated in Figure 9.8 by shifting the demand schedule upwards and to the right and tracing out the new level of employment with and without the minimum wage.

It is possible that some of the adverse employment effect may be offset by what could be labelled a "shock effect." Because of the cost pressure associated with the higher minimum wage, employers may be induced into utilizing other cost-saving devices that they should have introduced even without the minimum wage. The minimum wage simply serves as the catalyst for the introduction of cost-saving efficiencies. Similarly labour itself may be induced into becoming more productive, perhaps because of the higher wage or perhaps because of the queue of applicants vying for their jobs. The existence of these shock effects, however, requires that there be some slack in the system; that is, that firms were not maximizing profits or minimizing costs in the first place, because otherwise they would have instituted these possibilities even without the minimum wage.

There are possible situations when employers may be able to absorb the wage cost increases without reducing employment. If the firm were an oligopolist and would lose a substantial share of the market by raising its product price, it might try to absorb the wage cost increase. However, it is likely that the low-wage industries that are most affected by the minimum wage are likely to be competitive rather than oligopolistic.

Similarly, employers who dominate the local labour market may not have to pay a competitive wage rate. In such circumstances the minimum wage may simply compel the employer to pay what would be a competitive wage. (This situation of monopsony and its implications for minimum-wage legislation is developed more formally in Chapter 12.) Once again, however, it is unlikely that the industries that are most affected by minimum wages are those dominated by one or a few employers. Rather, the employers most affected tend to be small in size and competing in a labour market that has large pools of unskilled labour.

Thus while there is the theoretical possibility of these factors offsetting, in part at least, the adverse employment effect of minimum-wage laws, their practical relevance is in question. It is unlikely that they could be of great importance in the long run, especially in those low-wage sectors most affected by minimum wages. This leaves us with the inescapable conclusion that, in all probability, minimum-wage laws reduce employment opportunities. In addition, the impact will fall disproportionately on unskilled workers who are often most in need of work experience. This is the case, for example, with respect to younger workers and women who could utilize employment, even at low wages, as a means to acquire the on-the-job training and labour market experience necessary to move on to higher-paying jobs. For this reason, some would argue that minimum-wage laws actually harm the very people they are allegedly designed to help.

This does not necessarily mean that minimum-wage laws are undesirable, although that probably is the conclusion of most economists. The benefits of the wage increases to some have to be weighed against the costs of reduced employment opportunities to others. In addition, some would argue that even if minimum wages do reduce employment opportunities, it is in jobs that should not exist in the first place. It may be better to have these jobs eradicated and the unemployed workers trained for higher-wage jobs.

Empirical Evidence on Actual Impact

As may be expected, it is difficult to ascertain the actual impact of minimum-wage legislation, largely because so many other factors are also changing over time, and it may take a long time for all of the adjustments to occur. In addition, the adjustment processes may be subtle and difficult to document empirically. For example, a clothing manufacturer, when faced with a minimum-wage increase, may contract-out to households to do specific tasks, such as sewing on buttons or collars, or a restaurant may increase its usage of pre-packaged foods. How does one accurately compare the employment reduction in the clothing establishment or restaurant with the employment creation in the household or the food processing sector, to arrive at a net employment effect of the minimum wage?

In spite of the obvious difficulties, there have been numerous attempts to measure the employment impact of minimum-wage laws, mainly in the United States. After a thorough survey of the empirical evidence up until the late 1960s, Kaufman and Foran (1968) conclude that the overwhelming bulk of evidence supports the predictions of economic theory. Additional empirical evidence since that time seems to continue the support. This is especially the case with the large number of more recent studies — for example Moore (1971), Kosters and Welch (1972), Adie (1973), Katz (1973), Welch (1976), Mincer (1976) and Ragan (1977) — that have documented a significant adverse employment effect on teenagers.

Brown, Gilroy and Kohen (1982) provide a recent survey of the U.S. evidence on the impact of the minimum wage on employment and unemployment. The most frequently studied group is teenage workers (16–19 years of age). Time-series studies typically find that a 10 percent increase in the minimum wage reduces teenage employment by 1 to 3 percent, when other factors are held constant. Cross-section studies provide a wider range of estimated impacts, but most are in the range of a 0 to 3 percent decline in employment for a 10 percent increase in the minimum wage. Less research has been carried out on the impact on young adult workers (20–24 years of age); nonetheless these studies also find a negative impact, albeit smaller than that for teenagers. The impact on adult workers is uncertain. Higher minimum wages for younger workers may increase employment of those adults who are substitutes in production for youth. For other adults, the minimum wage will have the adverse employment impact as depicted in Figure 9.8. The U.S. empirical evidence does not enable one to conclude which of these effects is stronger.

Canadian econometric studies by Cousineau (1979), Fortin and Phaneuf (1979), Maki (1979), Swidinsky (1980) and Schaafsma and Walsh (1983) also find significant minimum-wage impacts. (See West and McKee (1980) for a survey of both Canadian and U.S. studies.) Swidinsky (1980), for example, estimates employment elasticities of 0.10 and 0.27 for male and female teenagers respectively; that is, an increase in the minimum wage of 10 percent results in a decline in employment of 1.0 and 2.7 percent for male and female teenagers. Schaafsma and Walsh (1983) estimate larger impacts on teenagers. They also conclude that the minimum wage has a significant adverse employment impact on adult workers.

An alternative empirical procedure is to directly survey firms about the effect of minimum-wage revisions on their work force. The surveys usually concentrate on firms that employ low-wage workers, and typically find no adverse employment consequences of changes in the minimum wage. (See West and McKee (1980, ch. 4) for a discussion of these studies.) The difficulty with this approach is that it does not distinguish between employment changes due to revisions to the minimum wage and those due to other factors. For example, if labour demand is increasing over time, economic theory indicates that increases in the minimum wage may not result in actual reductions in employment, even though the increase in employment will be lower than it would have been in the absence of the minimum-wage changes. Because the responses to minimum-wage revisions are varied, subtle (involving, for example, changes in the firm's product price and in the capital-labour mix), and take place gradually over time, it is important to control for other factors influencing employment. For this reason the survey approach is of little use in assessing the impact of minimum wages.

QUESTIONS

1. The marginal productivity theory of labour demand has been criticized for being unrealistic in its assumptions, and for ignoring a wealth of information available to us from other sources. Evaluate.
2. Why is is the point E_0 in Figure 9.2(c) a stable equilibrium? Depict the firm's expansion path. Depict the isoquant for a firm whose technology is such that it must utilize labour and capital in fixed proportions to produce its output. Depict the scale and substitution effect of a wage decrease in such a circumstance. Depict the firm's expansion path.
3. What is meant by an inferior factor of production? How would the firm's demand for labour be altered if labour were an inferior factor of production?
4. "The firm's demand for labour is a negative function of the wage because, as the firm uses more labour, it has to utilize poorer quality labour, and hence pays a lower wage." Discuss.
5. Discuss the firm's short-run demand for labour when its capital is fixed.
6. Derive the firm's demand schedule for labour if it were a monopolist that could influence the price at which it sells its output. That is, relax the assumption that product prices are fixed and trace through the implications.

7. Why is the firm's demand for labour more inelastic when one considers the general equilibrium feedback from changes in the product price at the industry level?

8. Utilize Figure 9.8 to depict the situation where the demand schedule for labour exogenously shifts upward to the right at the same time as the minimum wage is set at w_m.
   (a) Could the minimum wage be redundant?
   (b) Could employment increase relative to its earlier level of N_c?
   (c) If employment increased, would it be correct to say that minimum wage legislation has an adverse employment effect?
   (d) If so, what is its magnitude?

9. Why might unions support minimum wage legislation?

10. If minimum-wage laws actually harm the people they are designed to assist, can you explain their seeming political popularity?

11. Discuss various problems associated with measuring the employment impact of minimum-wage legislation.

12. Some jurisdictions in Canada have different minimum wages for different groups such as construction workers, learners and probationary workers, and students. Would you support such policies?

13. What alternative policies may be feasible to achieve the objectives of minimum-wage laws?

14. What complementary policies may be desirable to accompany minimum-wage legislation?

15. Evaluate minimum-wage legislation as an anti-poverty device.

16. In terms of personal characteristics, *who* would you expect to be most affected by minimum-wage laws?

17. Evaluate the practical importance of the various possible offsetting factors that could mitigate the adverse employment effect of a minimum-wage increase.

18. Would you support a 20 percent increase in the minimum wage in all jurisdictions in Canada? Why or why not?

19. Based on your knowledge of labour market theory, outline the expected impact of a minimum-wage increase on each of the following:
   (a) employment and unemployment of workers in the sector covered by the minimum wage;
   (b) employment and unemployment of workers in the non-covered sector;
   (c) occupational wage structure;
   (d) union wages;
   (e) labour force participation rates of women and youths.

REFERENCES AND FURTHER READINGS

A. Labour Demand

Archibald, G.C. Testing marginal productivity theory. *R.E. Stats.* 27 (June 1960) 210–213.

Bassett, L. and T. Borcherding. The firm, the industry, and the long-run demand for factors of production. *CJE* 3 (February 1970) 140–144.

Beach, C. and F. Balfour. Estimated payroll tax incidence and aggregate demand for labour in the United Kingdom. *Economica* 50 (Feb. 1983) 35–48.

Bishop, R. A firm's short-run and long-run demands for a factor. *WEJ* (March 1967).

Borjas, G. The substitutability of black, hispanic, and white labor. *EI* 21 (January 1983) 93–106.

Clark, K. and R. Freeman. How elastic is the demand for labor? *R E Stats* 62 (Nov. 1980) 509–520.

Cotterill, P. The elasticity of demand for low wage labour. *SEJ* 41 (January 1975) 520–526.

Diewert, E. A note on the elasticity of derived demand in the n-factor case. *Economica* 38 (1971) 192–198.

Freeman, R. An empirical analysis of the fixed coefficient "manpower requirements" model, 1960–1970. *JHR* 15 (Spring 1980) 176–199.

Freeman, R. and J. Medoff. Substitutions between production, labor and other inputs in unionized and nonunionized manufacturing. *R E Stats* 64 (May 1982) 220–233.

Fuss, M. and M. Denny. The effect of factor prices and technological change on the occupational demand for labour: evidence from Canadian telecommunications. *JHR* 18 (Spring 1983) 161–176.

Gottschalk, P. A comparison of marginal productivity and earnings by occupation. *ILRR* 31 (April 1978) 368–378.

Gould, J.R. On the interpretation of inferior goods and factors. *Economica* 48 (Nov. 1981) 397–406.

Grant, J. and D. Hamermesh. Labor market competition among youths, white women and others. *R E Stats* 63 (Aug. 1981) 354–360.

Grossman, J. The substitutability of natives and immigrants in production. *R E Stats* 64 (Nov. 1982) 596–603.

Hamermesh, D. Econometric studies of labour demand and their application to policy analysis. *JHR* 11 (Fall 1976) 507–525.

Hamermesh, D. The demand for labor in the long run. *Handbook of Labor Economics*, Vol. 1. O. Ashenfelter and R. Layard (eds.) New York: Elsevier, 1986.

Hamermesh, D. and J. Grant. Econometric studies of labour — labour substitution and their implications for policy. *JHR* 14 (Fall 1979) 518–542.

Hicks, J. *Theory of Wages*, 2nd ed. London: Macmillan, 1963, 241–246, 374.

Johnson, G. The demand for labor by educational category. *SEJ* 37 (October 1970) 190–204.

Killingsworth, M. Substitution and output effects on labour demand: theory and policy implications. *JHR* 20 (Winter 1985) 142–152.

Kotowitz, Y. Capital-labour substitutions in Canadian manufacturing 1926–1939 and 1946–1961. *CJE* 1 (August 1968) 619–632.

Lester, R. Shortcomings of marginal analysis for wage-employment problems. *AER* 37 (March 1946) 63–82.

Machlup, F. Marginal analysis and empirical research. *AER* 36 (September 1946) 519–528.

Maurice, S. Long run factor demand in a perfectly competitive industry. *JPE* 80 (November/December 1972) 1271–1279.

Meza, D. de. Perverse long-run and short-run factor demand curves. *Economica* 48 (Aug. 1981) 299–304.

Nagatani, K. Substitution and scale effects in factor demands. *CJE* 11 (August 1978) 521–526.

Nickell, S. Dynamic models of labour demand. *Handbook of Labor Economics*, Vol. 1. O. Ashenfelter and R. Layard (eds.). New York: Elsevier, 1986a.

Pissarides, C. The role of relative wages and excess demand in the sectoral flow of labour. *R.E. Studies* 45 (October 1978) 453–468.

Razin, A. A note on the elasticity of derived demand under decreasing returns. *AER* 64 (September 1974) 697–700.

Rosen, S. Substitution and the division of labour. *Economica* 45 (Aug. 1978) 235–250.

Russel, R. On the demand curve for a factor of production. *AER* 54 (1964) 726–732.

Sargent, T. Estimation of dynamic labor demand schedules under rational expectations. *JPE* 86 (December 1978) 1009–1044.

Sato, R. and T. Koizumi. Substitutability, complementarity and the theory of derived demand. *R.E. Studies* 37 (January 1970) 107–118.

Schaafsma, J. On estimating the time structure of capital-labor substitution in the manufacturing sector: a model applied to 1949–1972 Canadian data. *SEJ* 44 (April 1978) 740–751.

Skolnik, M. An empirical analysis of the substitution between engineers and technicians in Canada. *RI/IR* 25 (April 1970) 284–399.

Stoneman, P. The effect of computers on the demand for labour. *EJ* 85 (September 1975) 590–608.

Swan, N. Difference in the response of the demand for labour to variations in output among Canadian regions. *CJE* 5 (August 1972) 373–385.

Symons, J. and R. Layard. Neoclassical demand for labour functions in six major economies. *EJ* 94 (Dec. 1984) 788–799.

Tuckman, H. and C. Chang. Own-price and cross elasticities of demand for college faculty. *SEJ* 52 (January 1986) 735–744.

Woodland, A. Substitution of structures, equipment and labor in Canadian production. *IER* 16 (February 1975) 171–187.

Yeung, P. A note on the rule of derived demand. *QJE* 86 (August 1972) 511–517.

B. Minimum Wage Legislation

Adie, D. Teenage unemployment and real federal minimum wages. *JPE* 81 (March/April 1973) 435–441.

Ashenfelter, O. and R. Smith. Compliance with the minimum wage law. *JPE* 87 (April 1979) 333–351.

Behrman, J., R. Sickles, and P. Taubman. The impact of minimum wages on the distribution of earnings for major race-sex groups: a dynamic analysis. *AER* 83 (September 1983) 766–778.

Beranek, W. The illegal alien work force, demand for unskilled labor, and the minimum wage. *JLR* 3 (Winter 1982) 89–100.

Betsey, C. and B. Dunson. Federal minimum wage laws and the employment of minority youth. *AER* 71 (May 1981) 379–384.

Bloch, F. Political support for minimum wage legislation. *JLR* 1 (Fall 1980) 245–254.

Brecher, R. Minimum wage rates and the pure theory of international trade. *QJE* 88 (February 1974) 98–116.

Brown, C., C. Gilroy and A. Kohen. The effect of the minimum wage on employment and unemployment. *JEL* 20 (June 1982) 487–528.

Brown, C., C. Gilroy and A. Kohen. Time-series evidence of the effect of the minimum wage on youth employment and unemployment. *JHR* 18 (Winter 1983) 3–31.

Campbell, C. and R. Campbell. State minimum wage laws as a cause of unemployment. *SEJ* 35 (April 1969) 323–332. Comment by E. Jones and R. White and reply 37 (January 1971) 366–373.

Cotterill, P. and W. Wadycki. Teenagers and the minimum wage in retail trade. *JHR* 11 (Winter 1976) 69–85.

Cousineau, J.-M. Impact du salaire minimum sur le chomage des jeunes et des femmes au Quebec. *RI/IR* 34 (No. 3, 1979) 403–417.

Cox, J. and R. Oaxaca. The political economy of minimum wage legislation. *EI* 20 (October 1982) 533–555.

Donner, A. and F. Lazar. *Minimum Wage Policy*. Ottawa: Department of Manpower and Immigration, 1976.

Eccles, M. and R.B. Freeman. What! Another minimum wage study? *AER* 72 (May 1982) 226–232.

Ferris, J. Information and search: an alternative approach to the theory of minimum wage. *EI* 20 (October 1982) 490–510.

Flug, K. and O. Galor. Minimum wage in a general equilibrium model of international trade and human capital. *IER* 27 (February 1986) 149–164.

Fortin, P. Minimum wage in Quebec: price-employment and redistributive effects. *RI/IR* 34 (No. 4, 1979) 672–673.

Fortin, P. and C. Phaneuf. Why is the unemployment rate so high in Canada? Paper presented at the Canadian Economics Association meeting, Saskatoon, May 1979.

Goldfarb, R. Quantitative research on the minimum wage, *MLR* 98 (April 1975) 44–46.

Gramlich, E. Impact of minimum wages on other wages, employment and family incomes. *BPEA* (No. 2, 1976) 409–462.

Grenier, G. On compliance with the minimum wage law. *JPE* 90 (February 1982) 184–187.

Grossman, J. The impact of the minimum wage on other wages. *JHR* 18 (Summer 1983) 359–378.

Hamermesh, D. Minimum wages and the demand for labor. *EI* 20 (July 1982) 365–380.

Hashimoto, M. Minimum wage effects on training on the job. *AER* 72 (December 1982) 1070–1087.

Imam, M. and J. Whalley. Incidence analysis of a sector-specific minimum wage in a two-sector Harris-Todaro model. *QJE* 100 (Feb. 1985) 207–224.

Johnson, H. Minimum wage laws: a general equilibrium analysis. *CJE* 2 (November 1969) 599–603.

Johnson, W. and E. Browning. The distributional and efficiency effects of increasing the minimum wage: a simulation. *AER* 73 (March 1983) 204–211.

Katz, A. Teenage employment effects of state minimum wages. *JHR* 8 (Spring 1973) 250–256.

Kau, J. and P. Rubin. Voting on minimum wages. *JPE* 86 (April 1978) 337–342.

Kaufman, J. and T. Foran. The minimum wage and poverty. *Towards Freedom From Want*. Madison, Wis.: Industrial Relations Research Association, 1968.

Kaufman, R. Nepotism and the minimum wage. *JLR* 4 (Winter 1983) 81–89.

Keyes, W.A. The minimum wage and the Davis Bacon Act: employment effects on minorities and youth. *JLR* 3 (Fall, 1982) 399–413.

Kosters, M. and F. Welch. The effects of minimum wages on the distribution of changes in aggregate employment. *AER* 62 (June 1972) 323–332.

Leffler, K. Minimum wages, welfare and wealth transfers to the poor. *Journal of Law and Economics* 21 (October 1978) 345–348.

Linneman, P. The economic impacts of minimum wage laws: a new look at an old question. *JPE* 90 (June 1982) 443–469.

Lovell, M. The minimum wage, teenage unemployment and the business cycle. *WEJ* 10 (December 1972) 414–427. Comments by A. Fisher and D. Adie and L. Gallaway and reply 11 (December 1973) 514–537.

Maki, D. The effect of changes in minimum wage rates on provincial unemployment rates, 1970–1977. *IR* 34 (1979) 418–429.

Mattila, J. The effects of extending minimum wages to cover household maids. *JHR* 8 (Summer 1973) 365–382.

Maurice, S. Monopsony and the effects of an externally imposed minimum wage. *SEJ* 41 (October 1974) 283–287.

McCulloch, J. The effect of a minimum wage law on the labour-intensive sector. *CJE* 7 (May 1974) 316–318.

McKee, M. and E. West. Minimum wage effects on part-time employment. *EI* 22 (July 1984) 421–428.

McKenzie, R. The labour market effects of minimum wage laws: a new perspective. *JLR* 1 (Fall 1980) 255–264.

Mercier, J. Les effets du salaire minimum sur l'emploi des jeunes au Quebec. *RI/IR* 40 (No. 3, 1985) 431–456.

Metzger, M.R. and R.S. Goldfarb. Do Davis-Bacon minimum wages raise product quality? *JLR* 4 (Summer, 1983) 265–272.

Meyer, R. and D. Wise. The effects of minimum wage on the employment and earnings of youth. *JOLE* 1 (January 1983) 66–100.

Migné, J. Salaire minimum ou quand le diable se fait moine. *RI/IR* 32 (No. 3, 1977) 310–320.

Mincer, J. Unemployment effects of minimum wages. *JPE* 84 Part 2 (August 1976) S87–S104.

Mixon, J. The minimum wage and voluntary labor mobility. *ILRR* 32 (October 1978) 67–73.

Moore, T. The effect of minimum wages on teenage unemployment rates. *JPE* 79 (July/August 1971) 897–902.

Ragan, J. Minimum wages and the youth labor market. *R.E. Stats.* 59 (May 1977) 129–136.

Schaafsma, J. and W. Walsh. Employment and labour supply effects of the minimum wage: some pooled time-series estimates from Canadian provincial data. *CJE* 16 (February 1983) 86–97.

Schweinberger, A. Employment subsidies and the theory of minimum wage rates in general equilibrium. *QJE* 92 (August 1978) 361–374.

Sellekaerts, B. and S. Welch. An econometric analysis of minimum wage non-compliance. *IR* 23 (Spring 1984) 244–259.

Silberman, J. and C. Durden. Determining legislative preferences on the minimum wage. *JPE* 84 (April 1976) 317–329.

Solon, G. The minimum wage and teenage unemployment: a reanalysis with attention to serial correlation and seasonality. *JHR* 20 (Spring 1985) 292–297.

Starr, G. Minimum wage fixing. *ILR* 120 (Sept./Oct. 1981) 545–562.

Stigler, G. The economics of minimum wage legislation. *AER* 36 (June 1946) 358–367.

Swidinsky, R. Minimum wages and teenage unemployment. *CJE* 13 (February 1980) 158–170.

Swidinsky, R. and D. Wilton. Minimum wages, wage inflation, and the relative wage structure. *JHR* 17 (Spring 1982) 163–177.

Tauchen, G. Some evidence on cross-sector effects of the minimum wage. *JPE* 89 (June 1981) 529–547.

Uri, N. and J. Mixon Jr. The distribution of changes in manufacturing employment and the impact of the minimum wage. *Journal of Econometrics* 7 (February 1978) 103–114.

Uri, N. and J. Mixon Jr. An economic analysis of the determinants of minimum wage voting behaviour. *Journal of Law and Economics* 23 (April 1980) 167–177.

Welch, F. Minimum wage legislation in the United States. *Evaluating the Labor-Market Effects of Social Programs.* O. Ashenfelter and J. Blum (eds.). Princeton: Princeton University Press, 1976.

Welch, F. and J. Cunningham. Effects of minimum wages on the level and age composition of youth employment. *R. E. Stats* 60 (No. 1, 1978) 140–145.

Wessels, W. The effect of minimum wages in the presence of fringe benefits: an expanded model. *EI* 18 (April 1980) 239–313.

West, E.G. and M. McKee. *Minimum Wages: The New Issues in Theory, Evidence, Policy and Politics.* Ottawa: Economic Council of Canada and Institute for Research on Public Policy, 1980.

Zaidi, M. *A Study of the Effects of the $1.25 Minimum Wage under the Canadian Labor (Standards) Code.* Study No. 16, Task Force on Labour Relations. Ottawa: Privy Council Office, 1970.

Zucker, A. Minimum wages and the long-run elasticity of demand for low wage labor. *QJE* 87 (May 1973) 267–277.

10 Labour Demand, Quasi-Fixed Costs and Worksharing

Compared to the growth of material on labour supply, the area of labour demand has been relatively neglected by labour economists, especially during the 1970s. The imbalance in textbooks often simply reflects the fact that a number of topics like hours of work and labour force participation have both supply and demand dimensions and they are somewhat arbitrarily dealt with under the supply dimension if supply is discussed first. As well, new developments like the economics of fertility, family formation, household production theory and human capital theory just happened to deal with dimensions of labour supply, albeit quality and quantity dimensions that conventionally had not been emphasized by labour economists. Large microdata sets on labour supply and statistical procedures to analyse them became available at the same time as the considerable policy interest in determining the work incentive effects of various income maintenance programs. In addition, many topics of labour demand, such as the short-run demand for labour over the business cycle, have been dealt with more in the macroeconomics literature, in part to try to understand problems of unemployment and productivity growth.

In recent years, however, there has been some reemphasis on restoring a balance between the area of labour supply and demand in labour economics. In part, this reflects a desire to better understand certain key policy issues such as alternative work schedules, part-time work, overtime work and the persistence of unemployment, all of which have a labour demand component (from the employer's perspective) as well as a labour supply component (from the employee's perspective). An important ingredient in many of these topics is the quasi-fixed nonwage labour costs that are incurred by employers when they hire labour. Such costs are discussed in Oi (1962), Ehrenberg and Schumann (1982), and Hart (1984a, 1984b) and in the Canadian context, in Meltz, Reid and Swartz (1981), and Reid (1985).

QUASI-FIXED NONWAGE LABOUR COSTS

General Definition

Employers can expand their labour input by expanding the number of employees, the hours per employee or both. The way in which they expand will depend upon the relative costs of the different options.

Variable costs of labour vary with the *total* hours of labour employed, whether the increase in total hours comes from an increase in the number of employees or from an increase in the hours per employee. Variable labour costs are independent of the number of employees. For example, if the only cost of labour is the hourly wage rate, then costs will increase by the same percentage whether the labour input is expanded by increasing employment or hours per employee by a given percent. In such circumstances the firm would be indifferent between whether the labour input was expanded by increased employees or hours per employee. Wage costs are therefore a variable labour cost.

Other labour costs, however, are quasi-fixed costs in the sense that they are incurred per employee and are independent or largely independent of the hours of work per employee. They may be *pure* quasi-fixed costs in the sense that they are fixed per employee and are completely independent of the hours of work of each employee. Or they may be *mixed* variable and quasi-fixed costs in that they increase more rapidly for a given proportionate increase in the number of employees as opposed to hours per employee. In either circumstance, the firm would no longer be indifferent between whether the labour input (employees times hours per employee) expanded by increasing the number of employees or the hours per employee. Increasing the number of employees would be more costly given the quasi-fixed costs.

Examples of Quasi-Fixed Costs

At the hiring stage, firms incur quasi-fixed costs associated with the recruiting, hiring and training of new workers. These costs are independent of the hours the employees subsequently work. Under such circumstances there is an obvious incentive to try to amortize these fixed costs over longer hours and a longer worklife of these employees rather than to hire new employees and incur their additional fixed costs.

Expected termination costs themselves have a fixed cost component in the sense that at the *hiring stage* the firm may anticipate having to incur such costs should they subsequently lay off or dismiss the worker. Such costs become expected quasi-fixed costs at the hiring stage even though they may not be incurred until a subsequent period. Expectations of such costs are incurred when a new employee is hired but they do not increase, at least by the same proportion as wage costs, when an existing employee works additional hours.

As indicated in Meltz, Reid and Swartz (1981) and Reid (1985, p. 163) employers' contributions (payroll taxes) to certain income maintenance programs may also have an element of fixed costs, when such contributions have a ceiling. Employer contributions to workers' compensation and public pensions, for example, have an annual income ceiling, and unemployment insurance a weekly earnings ceiling below which contributions are a certain percent of earnings and beyond which they are zero. Thus, once this ceiling is reached, it pays employers to work these people additional hours since no further payroll taxes are incurred, rather than to hire new employees and incur such payroll taxes. These payroll taxes are variable costs up until the ceiling, and thereafter they become fixed costs creating the incentive to work existing employees more hours so as to amortize these costs.

Similarly, employment standards legislation often requires employees to have been employed for a certain minimum period before they are eligible for such benefits as paid holidays and advance notice of termination. Once the employee reaches this minimum period then these benefits become fixed costs for the employer; they are independent of the additional hours worked by the employee. As with other fixed costs, they encourage the employer to work existing employees longer hours and they discourage the hiring of new employees for whom such costs will be incurred.

Employers' contributions to life insurance and medical and dental plans can also have a quasi-fixed cost component to the extent that they are fixed per employee. In such circumstances costs are increased by hiring a new employee but not when an existing employee works more hours.

Not all fringe benefits are ones that have a quasi-fixed component. Some, like employer-sponsored occupational pension plans, may have employer contribution based on a percent of earnings. In such circumstances the employers' contributions are proportional to earnings and are the same whether the labour input increases through an increase in the number of employees or hours per employee. The same situation prevails for vacation pay that is a percent of earnings.

General Effect of Quasi-Fixed Costs

The effect of such quasi-fixed costs is to increase the marginal cost of hiring an additional worker (sometimes termed the extensive margin of adjustment) relative to the marginal cost of working an existing worker longer hours (sometimes termed the intensive margin of adjustment). The quasi-fixed costs distort the labour expansion decision of the firm away from employment and towards more hours so as to avoid the quasi-fixed costs. Alternatively stated, the firm will want to amortize its fixed costs over the existing workforce for as long as possible rather than to hire new workers and incur the quasi-fixed costs. This is especially so for skilled workers where such quasi-fixed costs may be especially large, mainly because of training costs.

Just as on the supply side of the market fixed money costs of work reduced the probability that an individual would enter the labour market but would increase the hours of work conditional upon having entered, so would quasi-fixed costs of employment have a differential effect on the demand side. Employers would be reluctant to hire more workers (and incur the fixed costs), but once the workers are hired, the employers would like to work them longer hours so as to amortize the fixed costs.

Fixed costs of employment alter the firm's hiring and layoff decisions, making these longer-term in nature. If the firm must incur some hiring and training costs when a new employee is hired, the firm will not hire' the employee unless the addition to revenue is at least as great as the addition to costs, including the hiring and training costs. However, as long as the employee is expected to remain with the firm for several periods, it is not essential that the additional revenue equal or exceed the additional costs each period. Rather, the firm will continue hiring additional workers until the present value of additional future revenues equals the present value of additional costs. Thus rather than hiring until the current wage equals the current value of marginal product (the employment rule discussed previously, summarized in equation 9.1), the profit-maximizing employment rule becomes

$$H + T + \sum_{t=0}^{N} \frac{W_t}{(1+r)^t} = \sum_{t=0}^{N} \frac{VMP_t}{(1+r)^t} \tag{10.1}$$

where $H + T$ are hiring and training costs (assumed to be incurred in the first period for simplicity),

W_t is the wage rate in period t,

VMP_t is the expected value of the marginal product in period t,

r is the firm's discount or interest rate, and

N is the expected length of employment.

The left-hand side of equation 10.1 is the present value of the marginal costs of hiring an additional worker and the right-hand side is the present value of the marginal revenue.

Several implications of equation 10.1 are worth noting. The hiring decision depends on the firm's expectations about the future, in particular the expected duration of employment, expected wage rates and expected product market conditions (which determine the value of the marginal product of labour in future periods). Another implication is that, because of the hiring and training costs on the left-hand side of equation 10.1,

$$\sum_{t=0}^{N} \frac{VMP_t}{(1+r)^t} > \sum_{t=0}^{N} \frac{W_t}{(1+r)^t} \tag{10.2}$$

Thus when hiring an additional worker the firm must anticipate that the value of the marginal product will exceed the wage in most, if not all, future periods. As will be seen below, this prediction of the theory has implications for the firm's layoff behaviour in response to unanticipated changes in demand.

Some Phenomena Explained by Fixed Costs

The existence and growth of such fixed costs may help to explain, in part at least, the existence and growth of a number of labour market phenomena. The desire of employers to work their existing work-force overtime, in spite of overtime premium wage rates and possible fatigue effects, may be explained in part by the fact that fixed costs make it relatively cheaper to work the existing work-force longer hours rather than hiring new workers. Ehrenberg and Schumann (1982, p. 14), for example, discuss a number of studies, based on United States data, indicating that employers' use of overtime hours are positively related to the ratio of their quasi-fixed employment cost to their overtime premium.

Quasi-fixed costs of employment may also explain, in part, the popularity of temporary help agencies and contracting-out. Employers avoid the quasi-fixed costs of hiring new employees when they contract-out or engage the services of temporary help agencies. As with the use of overtime hours, this can be a particularly important way of meeting new demand that may be temporary.

The layoff behaviour of firms will also be affected by quasi-fixed costs of employment. Once an employee has been hired and trained, the associated costs become sunk costs. Because these costs cannot be recovered, they will not influence the firm's decision-making with respect to its existing work-force (for whom the hiring and training expenses have been incurred), even though they will influence decisions regarding potential employees (for whom the expenses have not been incurred).

At the time an employee is hired, the firm anticipates that the present value of future marginal products will exceed the present value of future wage costs, as shown in equation 10.2. This excess of the value of the worker's contribution to the firm over the cost of that worker creates a "buffer" which reduces the risk that the worker will be laid off. In particular, even if there is an unanticipated decline in product demand, reducing the value of the marginal product of labour, the firm may nonetheless choose to not lay off any employees because the present value of the revenue associated with an employee, although lower than anticipated, remains higher than the present value of the costs. Because of the unanticipated decline in demand, the firm's return on its investment in hiring and training costs will be lower than expected; however, the return may still be positive, indicating that it is worthwhile retaining the employee. This will be the case especially if the decline in demand is believed to be temporary in nature, or if workers who are temporarily laid off may not be available for recall when demand returns to normal levels. In such circumstances the company may rationally engage in "labour hoarding" of such workers in a cyclical downturn and they may pay deferred compensation or seniority-related wages or benefits to discourage their experienced workers from leaving.

Fixed costs of employment can also explain the observation that layoff rates are much higher among low-skilled than high-skilled workers. Considerable evidence exists that hiring and training costs are significantly larger for high-skilled workers. Thus they have a larger "buffer" (excess of value of marginal product over wage rate) protecting them from unanticipated declines in demand compared to unskilled and semi-skilled workers.

Quasi-fixed costs may also foster the segmentation of labour markets into a protected sector (where employment stability is relatively guaranteed so as to amortize the quasi-fixed costs) and a sector that cannot compete for these jobs because firms would have to incur additional fixed costs upon hiring such workers. In essence, once an employee has been hired and trained, the firm is not indifferent between an existing employee and an otherwise identical potential employee.

To the extent that fixed costs inhibit the hiring of new workers (at the extensive margin), employers may try to meet their labour demand needs by expanding not only at the intensive margin of more hours, but also at the intensive margin of a greater *intensity* of work effort. That is, employers may try to work their existing work-force not only longer hours but also harder, rather than hiring new workers. Just as labour supply had quality and quantity dimensions so does labour demand, and these various dimensions may be affected by relative prices including fixed costs.

Quasi-fixed costs may also explain some of the employers' resistance to engage in worksharing practices. For example, having all of the companies' employees work a four-day as opposed to five-day workweek, and hiring twenty percent more employees at the same wage, would increase labour costs if there were quasi-fixed costs associated with hiring the new employees. Similarly, having two workers engage in job sharing (e.g., by each working half of the week) would increase the quasi-fixed costs because of the additional employee. Such costs may also make it more expensive to engage part-time employees unless there are compensating offsets in the wage component or in some of the quasi-fixed costs like fringe benefits.

WORKSHARING AND JOB CREATION

With the recent high levels of unemployment increasing attention has been paid to worksharing as a way to create jobs, or at least to share the scarce number of jobs that seem to be available. This emphasis has been buttressed by workers' preferences for flexible worktime arrangements, in part because of the growth of the two-earner family and the changing age and sex composition of the work-force.

Reduced work time could come in a variety of forms including delayed entry into the labour force, early retirement, a shorter workweek, reduced overtime or increased vacation time. The key question is: would any of these reductions in the worktime of some individuals lead to new jobs for other individuals?

Overtime Restrictions

In recent years the question has become extremely important with respect to reductions in the workweek especially through restricting the use of overtime. The paradox of some workers working overtime, seemingly on a regular basis, while other workers in the same community and often in the same plant are on layoff, has led to increasing pressure to restrict the use of overtime. This restriction could come in a variety of forms: reducing the standard work week beyond which an overtime premium must be paid, increasing the overtime premium, establishing or reducing the statutory maximum hours that are allowed, making it more difficult to get special permission to exceed the statutory limit when exemptions are allowed, or granting workers the right to refuse overtime. Changes in any or all of these features of overtime legislation could be used to restrict the use of overtime.

Unfortunately we have very little empirical evidence on the extent to which changes in any of these features of overtime legislation would change the demand for overtime hours. Ehrenberg and Schumann (1982) provide empirical evidence based on United States data indicating that an increase in the overtime premium from time-and-one-half to double-time would reduce the use of overtime hours. However, the relationship was not overwhelmingly conclusive, being statistically insignificant for the manufacturing sector.

Overtime Restriction and Job Creation

Even if overtime hours can be reduced by policy changes like raising the overtime premium, there remains the question of the extent to which reductions in the use of overtime would translate into new jobs. On this issue there is also considerable controversy. Ehrenberg and Schumann (1982, p. 15) estimate that this reduction in the use of overtime that would result from a double-time premium could translate into an employment increase in the neighbourhood of three to four percent, assuming that the overtime hours reduction would be converted directly to new full-time positions. They indicate that this is an upper bound, however, because it ignores a number of the following adjustments that are likely to occur in response to increases in the overtime premium.

For example, firms may not comply fully with the legislation and some workers whose overtime hours were restricted may moonlight. More importantly, although firms may substitute new employees for the more expensive overtime hours, they would also reduce their *overall* demand for labour because it is now more expensive and because the demand for the firm's output will be reduced as it passes some of the cost increase on to consumers in the form of higher product prices. These are, respectively, the familiar substitution and scale effects that occur in response to an increase in the price of a factor of production.

As well, there may be productivity changes that affect the number of new jobs created if hours of work are reduced. If fatigue effects make overtime hours less productive than the hours of work of new workers or rehires, then the number of new jobs created will be diminished because the overtime hours can be replaced by fewer regular hours. Reid (1985, p. 163), for example, cites European evidence suggesting that the productivity improvements associated with a reduced workweek may reduce the employment-creating potential of a reduced workweek by one-half. That is, productivity would be sufficiently higher under the shorter workweek so that the same output could be maintained with half as many hours in the new jobs to replace the reduced hours of the shorter workweek.

Whether this seemingly large productivity offset would be permanent and apply to reductions in overtime hours (as opposed to the standard workweek of everyone) remains an open question. Overtime hours may be more susceptible to fatigue effects but workers who work the overtime may already be the most productive of all workers; that is in fact why they are asked to work overtime. If that is the case, then reducing the overtime hours of the most productive workers may have the potential for creating a larger number of jobs for less productive workers, albeit at an obvious cost — a cost that could reduce the job-creating potential because of the substitution and scale effects discussed previously.

The job-creating potential of a reduction of overtime hours also may be offset by the fact that persons who are unemployed or on layoff (who are likely to be less skilled) may not be good substitutes for persons working overtime (who are likely to be more skilled). Unfortunately, the empirical literature that provides evidence on the substitutability between factors of production does not provide information on that point. That literature provides evidence on the substitutability between employment and hours of work of the labour force in general. And it provides some evidence on the substitutability between different groups of labour (e.g., skilled and unskilled, or females and youths). However, it does not do both simultaneously. Formally stated, we do not have estimates of the elasticity of substitution between overtime *hours* of skilled workers and the *employment* of less-skilled workers. In the absence of such information it is difficult to know by how much the job creation potential of reduced overtime hours would be offset by the fact that additional hours of new recruits or even those on layoff may not be good substitutes for reduced hours of those who work overtime.

The job-creating potential of reduced hours of work is further complicated by the fact that in the long run there are not really a fixed number of jobs in the economy. In fact, the notion that there is a fixed number of jobs is known as the "lump-of-labour fallacy." It is a fallacy because it ignores the fact that people who hold jobs have other effects on the economy (known as general equilibrium effects). For example, they may increase aggregate demand through their increased disposable income and they may reduce aggregate wages augmenting the supply of labour. Both of these effects would enhance employment by these groups being in the labour market.

Thus, while an individual who takes a job or works long hours at a particular establishment may be taking a job from someone else who could work at that establishment, this need not be the case for the economy as a whole. What is true for a given establishment may be a fallacy for the economy as a whole. Perhaps this is best illustrated by the example of the increased labour force participation of females. Few analysts today would say that every job taken by a female means one less job for a male. Even though that may be true for a particular job in a particular establishment (just as a job taken by a male means that particular job is not occupied by a female) it is not true for the economy as a whole. Females working in the labour market also create demands for other goods and services, especially those formerly produced in the household. This in turn creates jobs elsewhere.

In essence, a job held by one person does not mean that another person does not have a job. This applies to jobs held by females, by older workers who do not retire or by persons who work long hours or overtime. Conversely, restricting their work in particular establishments (e.g., by mandatory retirement or by restricting overtime) may open up some new jobs in that establishment but this may not lead to more jobs in the economy as a whole when one considers the general equilibrium effects as previously discussed.

For all of these reasons, the job-creating potential of various forms of worksharing is regarded with some scepticism. This is compounded by the fact that some regard worksharing basically as unemployment sharing, with the fear that any reduced measured unemployment that occurs may take the pressure off governments to follow appropriate policies to reduce unemployment. Nevertheless, as Reid (1985) points out, in times of cyclically high unemployment, worksharing may be a viable temporary method to share the scarce jobs until appropriate aggregate policies can restore the economy towards full employment. In addition, it would be important to remove any impediments that may prevent the parties from entering into otherwise mutually beneficial voluntary worksharing arrangements.

Reducing Barriers to Employment Sharing

Reid (1985, p. 163) suggests a number of changes in public policy that could reduce the unintended barriers to employment sharing that are created by these policies. As indicated previously, the ceilings on payroll taxes for workers' compensation, public pensions or unemployment insurance make it more attractive for employers to work their existing employees longer hours once the ceiling on the payroll tax has been reached, since no further taxes then have to be paid. Having the premiums based on hourly earnings with a ceiling based on hourly earnings would remove the bias against hiring new workers. Similarly, prorating employer contributions to medical, dental and life insurance plans according to hours worked, rather than having fixed contributions per employee, would reduce their existing bias against employment sharing.

QUESTIONS

1. Explain the factors that affect the firm's choice between the number of employees and hours per employee.
2. Firms often respond to decreases in demand by laying off some of their workforce. However, some groups of workers are more likely to be laid off than others. Provide an explanation for this phenomenon.
3. Explain how payroll taxes such as those used to help finance unemployment insurance, the Canada and Quebec Pension Plans and workers' compensation may affect the firm's choice between workers and hours. How could these taxes be structured in order not to affect this choice?
4. Would it ever be rational for a firm to retain an employee whose current marginal revenue product is less than their current wage? Explain.
5. "In the absence of hiring, training and other fixed costs of employment, the firm does not need to forecast the future when making employment decisions. However, in the presence of these fixed costs the firm's employment decision necessarily involves planning for and forecasting of the future." Discuss.
6. Many European countries have legislation regarding severance pay which makes termination of employees costly to employers. What impact would introducing such legislation have on employer behaviour relating to dismissals and new hires? What groups in society are likely to benefit from introducing this type of legislation? What groups are likely to lose?

REFERENCES AND FURTHER READINGS

AFL-CIO. Shorter hours: tool to combat unemployment. *Labour and the National Economy*, W. Bowen (ed.). New York: Norton, 1965.

Bell, D. Labour utilization and statutory non-wage cost. *Economica* 49 (August 1982) 335–344.

Chiswick, C. The elasticity of substitution revisited: the effects of secular changes in labour force structure. *JOLE* 3 (October 1985) 490–507.

Cuvillier, R. *The Reduction of Working Time*. Geneva: International Labour Organisation, 1984.

Disney, R. and E. Szyszczak. Protective legislation and part-time employment in Britain. *BJIR* 22 (March 1984) 78–100.

Ehrenberg, R. Absenteeism and the overtime decision. *AER* 60 (June 1970) 352–357.

Ehrenberg, R. Heterogeneous labour, the internal labour market and the dynamics of the employment-hours decision. *Journal of Economic Theory* 3 (March 1971) 85–104.

Ehrenberg, R. The impact of the overtime premium on employment and hours in U.S. industry. *WEJ* 9 (June 1971) 199–207.

Ehrenberg, R. *Fringe Benefits and Overtime Behavior: Theoretical and Economic Analysis*. Lexington, Mass.: D.C. Heath, 1972.

Ehrenberg, R.G. and P.L. Schumann. *Longer Hours or More Jobs? An Investigation of Amending Hours Legislation to Create Employment*. Ithaca: New York State School of Industrial and Labor Relations, Cornell University, 1982.

Fitzroy, F. and R. Hart. Hours, layoffs and unemployment insurance funding: theory and practice in an international perspective. *EJ* 95 (September 1985) 700–713.

Garbarino, J. Fringe benefits and overtime as barriers to expanding employment. *ILRR* 17 (April 1964) 426–442.

Hamermesh, D. Factor market dynamics and the incidence of taxes and subsidies. *QJE* 95 (December 1980) 751–764.

Hart, R. *The Economics of Non-Wage Labor Costs.* London: Allen and Unwin, 1984a.

Hart, R. *Shorter Working Time: A Dilemma for Collective Bargaining.* Paris: O.E.C.D., 1984b.

Hart, R. *Working Time and Employment.* London: Allen and Unwin, 1986.

Hoel, M. Employment and allocation effects of reducing the length of the workday. *Economica* 53 (February 1986) 75–85.

Laudadio, L. and M. Percy. Some evidence in the impact of non-wage labour costs on overtime work. *RI/IR* 28 (March 1973) 397–403.

Leslie, D. Hours and overtime in British and United States manufacturing industries. *RJIR* 14 (July 1976) 194–201.

Mann, B. Capital heterogeneity, capital utilization and the demand for shiftworkers. *CJE* 17 (August 1984) 450–470.

Meltz, N., F. Reid and G. Swartz. *Sharing the Work: An Analysis of the Issues in Worksharing and Jobsharing.* Toronto: University of Toronto Press, 1981.

Northrup, H., J. Wilson and K. Rose. The twelve hour shift in the petroleum and chemical industries. *ILRR* 32 (April 1979) 312–326.

Oi, W. Labour as a quasi-fixed factor. *JPE* 70 (December 1962) 538–555.

Reid, F. UI-assisted worksharing as an alternative to layoffs: the Canadian experience. *ILRR* 35 (April 1982) 319–329.

Reid, F. Reductions in work time: an assessment of employment sharing to reduce unemployment. *Work and Pay: The Canadian Labour Market*, W.C. Riddell (ed.) Toronto: University of Toronto Press, 1985.

Rosen, S. Short-run employment variation in class I railroads in the U.S., 1937–1964. *Econometrica* 36 (October 1968) 511–529.

Van Ginneken, W. Employment and the reduction of the work week: a comparison of seven European macro-economic models. *ILR* 123 (January 1984) 35–52.

Part III

Equilibrium in Nonunion Labour Markets

11 *Wages and Employment in Competitive Labour Markets*

Once labour demand and the various aspects of labour supply are determined, we can analyse their interaction in determining the equilibrium price and quantity of labour — wages and employment, respectively. In this chapter we analyse the interaction of labour supply and demand when the firm is competitive in the labour market in which it purchases labour inputs. The firm may be operating in a competitive or non-competitive (monopoly, oligopoly, monopolistic competition) product market. In the next chapter we analyse the situation when the firm is not competitive in the labour market. Throughout the analysis we are assuming that labour is selling its services on an individual basis; in Part IV we will analyse the situation of collective bargaining via unionization.

In dealing with the interaction of supply and demand in various market structures, it is important to be specific about the level of aggregation that is being analysed. In this section we deal with the level of aggregation of the individual firm, and consequently focus on the firm as the decision-making unit. Later we will deal with higher levels of aggregation such as the occupation, industry, region and economy as a whole.

COMPETITIVE PRODUCT AND LABOUR MARKETS

We first examine the case in which the firm is a competitive seller of its output on the product market and a competitive buyer of labour in the labour market. In essence, the firm is so small relative to both markets that it can sell all of the output it wants at the going price of the product, and it can buy all of the labour it wants at the going wage rate. The firm is both a price- and wage-taker: it cannot influence either the product price or the wage rate.

This situation is depicted in Figure 11.1(a) and (b) for two competitive firms. In both cases, their supply schedules for a given homogeneous type of labour are perfectly elastic (horizontal) at the market wage rate, w_c. The firms are wage-takers not wage-setters, and consequently can employ all of the labour they want at this market wage rate.

The market wage rate for this specific, homogeneous type of labour is determined by the interaction of supply and demand in the aggregate labour market as depicted in Figure 11.1(c). This aggregate labour market could be a regional labour market for a particular occupational category of labour. For example, it could be the Halifax labour market for junior accounting clerks. By assuming that the firms are in the same region and are hiring the same homogeneous occupational type of labour, we are able to minimize the intervening influence of these factors on the wage determination process, and to thereby focus on the issue of wage and employment determination at the disaggregate or microeconomic level of the firm. In subsequent chapters on wage structures, these assumptions are relaxed sequentially and the resultant wage structures analysed.

Figure 11.1   Competitive Product and Labour Markets

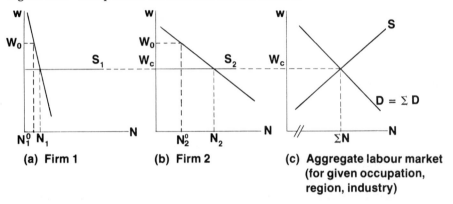

(a) **Firm 1**   (b) **Firm 2**   (c) **Aggregate labour market (for given occupation, region, industry)**

The demand schedules for labour in the two firms are simply the schedule of the value of the marginal products of labour, defined as the marginal physical product of labour times the price at which the firms can sell their products. (These were derived formally in Chapter 9.) Since the firms are assumed to be competitive sellers of their products, then their product prices are fixed at p_1^* and p_2^*. Only if the firms are selling the same output would their product prices have to be the same; otherwise p_1^* need not equal p_2^*. The magnitude and the elasticity of the demand for labour also are depicted as being different simply to highlight that the market wage is the same irrespective of these factors. The demand schedules simply determine the level of employment in each firm: in this case N_1 and N_2 units of labour, respectively in firms one and two.

The market demand curve, as depicted in Figure 11.1(c), is simply the summation of the demand curves of the individual firms, such as those shown in Figures 11.1(a) and 11.1(b). Conceptually the market demand curve can be obtained as follows. For any specific wage rate, such as w_0 in Figure 11.1, determine the quantity of labour that each firm in the market would wish to employ. For the two firms depicted in Figures 11.1(a) and 11.1(b), these quantities are N_1^0 and N_2^0 respectively. Adding these quantities gives the total market demand at that wage rate. Repeating this process for all wage rates traces out the market labour demand curve.

In summary, when the firm is a competitive buyer of labour, it faces a perfectly elastic supply of labour at the market wage. When the firm is a competitive seller of its output on the product market, it regards the price at which it sells its output on the product market as fixed, and its derived demand for labour schedule is the value of the marginal product of labour, defined as the marginal physical product of labour times the fixed price at which the firm sells its output. Because the labour supply schedule to the firm is perfectly elastic at the market wage rate, the intersection of the firm's labour supply and demand schedules determines the employment level of the firm for that particular type of labour — wages are determined elsewhere, specifically in the aggregate industry labour market for that particular type of labour.

SHORT RUN VERSUS LONG RUN

The previous analysis was based on the long-run assumption that the firm could get all of the labour it needed at the market-determined wage rate. That is, in order to expand its work-force it need only hire additional workers at the going wage rate: there is no need to increase wages to attract additional workers.

In the short run, however, even a firm that is competitive in the labour market may have to raise its wages in order to attract additional workers. This situation, in the literature, is often referred to as "dynamic monopsony" (Baily 1975). In such circumstances the firm's short-run labour supply schedule could be upward-sloping, as depicted by the schedule S_s in Figure 11.2. In the short run, in order to expand its work-force so as to meet an increase in the demand for labour from D to D', the firm may have to pay higher wages, perhaps by paying an overtime premium to its existing work-force or by paying higher wages to attract local workers within the community. The resultant expansion of the work-force can be depicted as a movement up the short-run supply curve in response to the new higher wage of w_s, occasioned by the increase in the demand for labour from D to D'.

In the longer run, however, a supply influx of other workers will be forthcoming because the firm is paying an above-market wage (i.e. $w_s > w_c$) for that particular type of labour. The supply influx may not be instantaneous, but may occur in the long run because it may come from other firms or perhaps from outside of the labour force, and such adjustments take time.

The new supply influx in response to the higher wage could be depicted by the S_s' supply schedule of labour. The supply influx would depress the temporarily high, short-run wage of w_s back to its long-run level of w_c. Thus the long-run supply of labour schedule to the firm, S_1, can be thought of as a locus of long-run equilibrium points, traced out by various

Figure 11.2   Short-Run and Long-Run Labour Supply Schedules to Firm

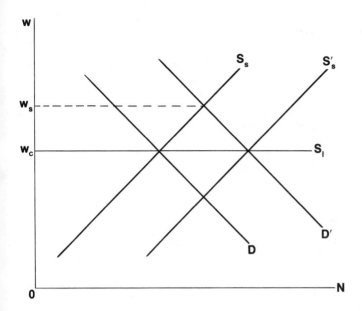

shifting short-run supply schedules of the firm, as the firm tries to expand its work-force.

In essence, temporary wage increases above the competitive norm are consistent with the firm being a competitive buyer of labour in the long run. In fact, short-run wage increases may be a sign that the market is behaving competitively, in that they can be a market signal for the supply response that ensures that the market is competitive, in the longer run.

MONOPOLY

As discussed in Chapter 9, the structure of the product market has implications for the derived demand for labour. Since the monopolist's marginal revenue schedule lies below its demand schedule, then the monopolist's derived demand for labour schedule also lies below the schedule that would prevail if the firm behaved as a competitive firm in the product market. As given by Equation 9.7 in Chapter 9, the labour demand schedule for the competitive firm on the product market is given by:

$$w^* = MPP_N \cdot p_Q^* = VMP_N \text{ [competitor]} \qquad (9.7)$$

This was derived from the more general equation

$$w^* = MPP_N \cdot MR_Q = MRP_N \text{ [monopolist]} \qquad (9.6)$$

which applies to the monopolist since its output price is not fixed. Rather, for the monopolist, marginal revenue is the relevant factor.

The difference between Equations 9.7 and 9.6 highlights the fact that when the monopolist hires more labour to produce more output, not only does the marginal physical product of labour fall (as is the case with the competitor), but also the marginal revenue from an additional unit of output, MR_Q, falls. This latter effect occurs because the monopolist, unlike the competitive firm, can sell more output only by lowering the product price and this in turn lowers marginal revenue. Because both MPP_N and MR_Q fall when N increases in Equation 9.6, then the monopolist's demand for labour falls faster than it would if it behaved as a competitive firm in the product market, in which case only MPP_N would fall, as given in Equation 9.7.

The difference between the labour demand schedule for a monopolist and the schedule that would prevail if the firm were competitive in the product market is illustrated in Figure 11.3. For illustrative purposes the supply schedule of labour is depicted as upward-sloping, perhaps reflecting a short-run situation whereby the firm has to raise wages temporarily to attract additional labour. The labour demand schedule for the competitive firm on the product market would be $D_c = MPP_N \cdot P_Q = VMP_N$. The labour demand schedule for the monopolist is $D_m = MPP_N \cdot MR_Q = MRP_N$. Since $MR_Q < P_Q$ then D_m lies below D_c.

Figure 11.3 Monopolist Demand for Labour

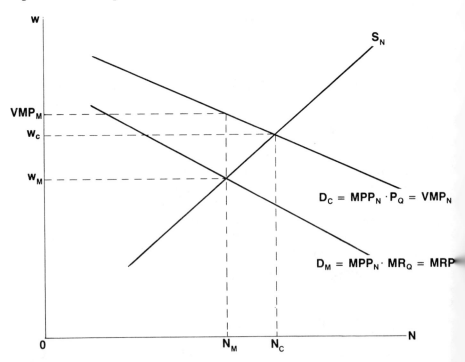

The interaction of the labour supply and demand schedules determines the equilibrium wage and employment of the firm. For the monopolist this is w_m and N_m respectively. If this firm were competitive in the product market, its wages and employment would be w_c and N_c respectively. Thus the monopolist pays a lower wage, $w_m < w_c$, and employs less labour, $N_m < N_c$, than if it were competitive in the product market. In addition it pays workers a wage less than the value of the marginal product of labour since $w_N < VMP_M$ at N_m. This latter difference has been termed a measure of the Pigouvian exploitation of labour, equal to $VMP_M - w_m$ per worker or $(VMP_M - w_m) N_m$ for the firm's total work-force.

If the monopolist in the product market were competitive in the labour market, then it would face a perfectly elastic labour supply schedule at the going wage rate. In such circumstances it would pay the market-determined wage rate. Its reduced labour demand schedule $(D_m < D_c)$ would imply that the monopolist employs less labour than it would if it behaved competitively in the product market, and that it pays a wage equal to the marginal revenue product of labour, but less than the value of the marginal product of labour.

MONOPOLY AND THE ELASTICITY OF DEMAND FOR LABOUR: TECHNICAL DIGRESSION*

At this point it may be worth digressing on a common misconception concerning the elasticity of demand for the output and hence the derived demand for labour from a monopolist. By definition, a monopolist is the only producer of a particular product or service. Consequently it is tempting to think of the demand for the monopolist's output as being price inelastic (and hence its derived demand for labour as being inelastic) because consumers are unable to purchase the particular output elsewhere.

This ignores the fact, however, that consumers need not always consume the particular output produced by the monopolist. Consumers can usually purchase alternative goods or substitutes, and will do so as the price charged by the monopolist increases. In essence, the monopolist is the industry, and the demand for industry output need not be inelastic, but will depend on such factors as the cost and availability of substitutes from other industries.

Not only is it the case that the demand for the output of the monopolist need not be inelastic: in fact, the monopolist will operate on the elastic portion of its demand schedule. This can be demonstrated rigorously as follows.

As previously given in Equation 9.3, the profit function for the monopolist is

$$\pi = p(Q)Q - wN - rK \tag{11.1}$$

The monopolist maximizes profits by selling output until there are no additional profits to be made: that is, until $\partial\pi/\partial Q = 0$. Differentiating Equation 11.1 partially with respect to Q and setting this equal to zero, yields

$$\partial p/\partial Q \cdot Q + p = w \, \partial N/\partial Q + r \, \partial K/\partial Q \qquad (11.2)$$

That is, marginal revenue equals the marginal cost of an additional unit of output. Defining the elasticity of output with respect to price as $\theta_{Qp} = \partial Q/\partial p \cdot p/Q$, then $1/\theta = \partial p/\partial Q \cdot Q/p$ and therefore $p/\theta = \partial p/\partial Q \cdot Q$. Substituting this into Equation 11.2 and defining the right-hand side as marginal cost, yields

$$p(1 + 1/\theta) = MC \qquad (11.3)$$

Assuming that the marginal cost of output is positive, $MC > 0$, then for the monopolist

$$p(1 + 1/\theta) > 0 \qquad (11.4)$$

This will be true only when the monopolist operates on the elastic portion of its demand curve: that is, when $\theta < -1$. (This latter statement can be proven by multiplying both sides by $1/p$, subtracting one from both sides, and then inverting and hence reversing the sign.)

An intuitive explanation for why the monopolist will operate on the elastic portion of its demand curve is as follows. Suppose the monopolist were to operate on the inelastic portion. In this range, marginal revenue is negative; thus, by raising price and reducing output total revenue will increase. Total costs will decline when output is reduced. Thus whenever product demand is inelastic the monopolist can increase profits by raising price and reducing output. The profit-maximizing position must therefore be on the elastic portion of the product demand curve.

DEPARTURES FROM MARKET WAGES

In theory, the previous analysis has little implication for the wages that monopolists will pay relative to the wages paid by firms that are competitive in the product market. This is so because the firm's behaviour in the product market need not be related to the way the firm behaves in the labour market. Specifically, if the firms are competitive in the labour market then they all face a perfectly elastic supply schedule for labour in the labour market; that is, they are wage-takers, not wage-setters. In such circumstances firms facing different product market structures pay the same market wage.

There are reasons to believe, however, that some firms may pay wages somewhat above or below the equilibrium market wage even though the labour market is approximately competitive in nature. Without analysing these factors in the context of a formal model, they can be enumerated qualitatively. Some of these factors are related to product market structure; that is, they serve to imply that monopolists will pay more or less than the market wage. Other factors are unrelated to product market structure; that is, they imply that some firms may depart from the market wage while others — perhaps in the same industry or region — will not.

One factor discussed previously is the length of the decision horizon. A firm wishing to expand its labour force quickly may choose to pay a wage premium even though in the longer run the firm could maintain its labour force by paying the market wage. Similarly a firm planning to contract employment could pay a lower wage for several periods even though this policy would not be feasible in the long run.

Firms may pay above-market wages to reduce turnover, encourage employee work effort, discourage shirking, boost worker morale, and discourage the formation of unions. These factors are discussed more formally subsequently under the topic of "efficiency wages." Because turnover is costly to the firm, especially in the presence of significant hiring and training costs, it may be rational to pay a wage premium in order to discourage employees from quitting. Related to this aspect, paying a higher wage will provide the firm with a larger pool of applicants from which to choose. This may enable the firm to employ the most productive workers or those least likely to quit in the future. Receiving a wage higher than they could earn elsewhere may boost employee morale and encourage work effort or at least discourage shirking. This will especially be the case if employees caught shirking are fired and must then work at the lower alternative wage. Rather than engage in costly monitoring of employees, firms may find that a combination of above-market wages and limited monitoring is more cost-efficient. Because firms and industries differ according to such factors as the costs of turnover, the ability and need for monitoring of work effort and the importance of worker morale, we would expect a variety of wage rates to be observed on the basis of these "efficiency wage" considerations. In these circumstances the market wage can be thought of as the average of the various observed wages, with some firms paying higher wages because of high turnover costs, costly monitoring procedures, or a high probability of unionization while other firms pay lower wages because the opposite conditions prevail.

Turning to aspects related to the product market, one factor suggesting that the monopolist would pay greater-than-market wages is that the monopolist has monopoly profits, and labour — especially if organized — may be able to appropriate some of these profits. Alternatively stated, the monopolist may be under less pressure to be cost-conscious and hence may more readily yield to wage demands. Being sensitive to their public image, monopolists may also pay higher wages as a way of buying the image of being a good employer. This may especially be the case if the monopolist is regulated and subject to the review of a regulatory agency.

By virtue of simply being a large firm (even though it may be a small employer of certain types of labour), monopolists may also pay high wages. This could be the case, for example, if large firms must use formal methods to evaluate job applicants and hence they pay a high wage so as to have a queue of applicants from which to formally evaluate. In addition, large firms may have to pay a wage premium to compensate for the rigid work schedules and mass production techniques associated with large size or to substitute for costly monitoring. Finally, by virtue of their size, large firms may have to follow administratively determined wage policies: unable to pay each worker its marginal product, such firms may pay wages approximating the productivity of the more productive workers within the group. In this way they minimize the risk of losing their more productive workers at a cost of having to pay slightly higher than average wages.

The previously discussed factors suggest why monopolists may pay high wages if they are competitive buyers of labour. Each of these factors, however, could also be associated with lower-than-average wages being paid by monopolists. For example, although monopoly profits could enable the monopolist to pay high wages, they could also enable them to resist wage demands, perhaps by holding out longer against strike activity. In terms of preserving its public image, especially if regulated, monopolists may want to be model employers by paying high wages, but they may also want to appear as cost-conscious to the consuming public and to regulatory agencies. By virtue of their size, monopolists may also be able to pay lower-than-average wages, for example, if their size provided employment security or ample opportunities for advancement, or if turnover was less costly to them because of the availability of standby work-forces.

Clearly the various factors that affect the wage determination process do not yield unambiguous predictions on whether a firm will pay above or below average wages. Consequently, as is so often the case in economics, we must appeal to the empirical evidence to ascertain the net impact of the variety of factors. This evidence will be examined in a subsequent chapter on inter-industry wage differentials where factors such as the degree of concentration in the product market, the threat of unionization, firm size and the costs of turnover, are viewed as determinants of wages.

MONOPOLISTIC COMPETITION AND OLIGOPOLY

In between the polar cases of competition and monopoly in the product market are a variety of intermediate cases. Firms can be monopolistically competitive, a situation characterized by many firms the actions of which do not affect other firms, but with products that are differentiated in some way giving the firm some discretion in its price-setting. In such circumstances the demand for the firm's product is not perfectly elastic, as is the competitive case, but rather has some degree of inelasticity reflecting the fact that if the firm raises its price it will not lose all of its market, and if it lowers its price it will not gain all of the market.

In such circumstances the firm has some discretion with respect to being able to pass wage increases on to customers in the form of price increases. Such cost increases need not put these firms out of business:

they will retain a segment of the market given that their product is differentiated in some fashion. The degree of differentiation of their product determines the degree to which wage-cost increases can be passed on to the consumer. If its product is not well differentiated, then this firm approaches the competitive norm, in which case a wage-cost increase confined to the firm (and not to other firms in the industry) could put the firm out of business. If the product is well differentiated, then this firm approaches the monopolistic norm, in which case it can be thought of perhaps as a local industry.

The end results of monopolistic competition are qualitatively the same as for monopoly, since the firm has a degree of inelasticity to the demand schedule for its product. Consequently, it has a derived marginal revenue schedule with all of the implications that this has for wage determination. While qualitatively similar to monopoly, the situation of monopolistic competition is quantitatively different because there are limits imposed by other firms with similar, albeit perhaps not identical, products and services.

To a certain degree, in the short run at least, most firms can be thought of as having a slight degree of discretion with respect to price setting. Specifically, they could raise their prices slightly without losing all of their market instantly. Custom, habit persistence, lack of knowledge, and transactions costs would ensure that these firms retain some of their customers. In the longer run, however, such firms may not want to exercise these quasi-monopoly powers because of the entailed loss of customers. In essence, once the optimal degree of such quasi-monopoly powers is exercised, then the firm will be as cost-conscious with respect to wages as would other firms. In other words, monopoly power — even a slight degree of monopoly power — may enable firms to pay a higher than average wage. But once this wage premium is paid, they will respond as do other firms to changes in the wages they face.

Between the polar cases of monopoly and competition lies a variety of product-market structures termed oligopoly. Such industries are characterized by few firms that produce sufficiently similar products that the actions of one firm will affect the other firms. Consequently the firms will react to the actions of the other firms. In theory, there is an infinite number of ways in which the firms can react; consequently, there is a large number of possible ways to categorize oligopoly situations. (This in fact is one of the criticisms of oligopoly theory: is it a theory, or a set of *ad hoc* descriptions of various situations?)

For example, there may be an asymmetry between how the other oligopolists will respond to price increases and decreases on the part of an oligopolist that changes its price. For price increases the other firms may not react; consequently, the firm loses a substantial share of the market. For price decreases, however, the other firms may respond by lowering their own prices; consequently this firm does not gain a substantial share of the market, but suffers because it has lowered its price. Because of the dire consequences no matter which way they change their price, oligopolists would try to absorb wage changes before altering their price, and hence output, and hence employment decisions. For this reason there is a range of wage changes that would not be associated with employment changes for the oligopolist.

This implies, for example, that minimum wage increases, over a limited range, may be absorbed by oligopolists rather than passed on to consumers in the form of higher product prices and hence reductions in the derived demand for labour. Similarly union wage increases, over a certain range, may not lead to adverse employment effects if they are confined to specific oligopolistic firms. However, if all of the oligopolistic firms were affected similarly, they would probably all react with a common price increase and the usual adverse employment effect would ensue. This is one situation when it may be advantageous for unions to divide and conquer, gaining wage increases selectively in particular oligopolistic firms that would be reluctant to respond with price increases. Rather, the wage-cost increases may be absorbed from oligopoly profits.

CONCLUDING OBSERVATIONS ON NON-COMPETITIVE PRODUCT MARKETS

Clearly the way in which a firm behaves in the product market can affect the way it behaves in the labour market. Since the firm's demand for labour is derived from the demand for the product or service produced by the firm, then whether the firm is a price-setter or a price-taker can influence its employment and *possibly* wage determination.

The term *possibly* is used with respect to the wage determination process because as long as the firm is competitive in the labour market — and it can be competitive in the labour market and not competitive in the product market – then it would have to pay at least the going wage for labour. This fact is important because it suggests that there may be an upward bias towards higher wages in firms that are not competitive in the product market. This upward bias occurs because non-competitive forces in the product market usually have an indeterminate impact on the wages they would pay to their employees. However, the forces of competition in the labour market would ensure that non-competitive firms in the product market do not pay below the competitive wage. These same forces, however, may be ignored by non-competitive firms that pay greater-than-market wages, perhaps out of monopoly or oligopolistic profits.

For example, if a monopolist did not pay the market wage, it might not be able to recruit any work-force. Consequently, the forces of competition in the labour market ensure a floor on wages paid by the monopolist. However, if the monopolist paid a greater-than-market wage out of monopoly profits, the same forces of competition need not ensure a ceiling. That is, the excess supplies of applicants could be ignored by the monopolist, who may be under less pressure to be cost conscious. Because competitive pressures in the labour market ensure a floor, but not necessarily a ceiling on wages paid in non-competitive sectors of the product market, there may be an upward bias to wages paid in these sectors.

QUESTIONS

1. Monopoly and monopsony go hand in hand. Discuss.
2. "Given the variety of ways of classifying the firm's behaviour in the product and labour markets, and the various possible types of collusive action on the part of labour, we really have no theory of labour market behaviour. Rather, we have a series of explanations corresponding to the variety of ways employers and employees can act in the labour market. This is more description than good theory." Discuss.
3. Based on the demand schedules as given in Figure 11.1, what would happen to the respective labour demand schedules for firms 1 and 2 if they both became monopolists in their respective product markets? What would happen to the wages they pay? What would happen to the labour demand schedule in the aggregate labour market, and hence the wage and employment in that market?
4. For Figure 11.1, make up a hypothetical example for firms one and two with their differing labour demand schedules and indicate the reasons for the shape of their particular schedules.
5. What would happen to the analysis of this chapter if firm 2 in Figure 11.1 began to dominate the aggregate labour market and became a wage-setter rather than a wage-taker?
6. Strictly speaking, the analysis depicted in the diagram of Figure 11.1 is incorrect since the supply-of-labour schedule would not be the firm's relevant decision-making schedule, if it affected the wage rate. Discuss.
7. It is deceptive to say that monopolistic firms do not behave as competitive firms. Both are simply maximizing profits subject to the constraints they face. However, the monopolist simply faces different constraints and this leads to different outcomes. Discuss.
8. Pigouvian exploitation of labour would not persist in the long run because employees would simply move to places where they were paid the value of the marginal product of their labour. Discuss.
9. Since the monopolist, by definition, is the only producer of its output, consumers cannot substitute other outputs, and consequently the demand for the product produced by the monopolist is price-inelastic. This in turn makes the monopolist's derived demand for labour inelastic, which in turn means that the monopolist will pay a greater-than-competitive wage. Discuss.
10. It is not possible to say on theoretical grounds whether monopolists will pay higher or lower wages than competitive firms. Discuss.
11. In the field of industrial organization, considerable advances have been made in analysing the impact of various constraints, imposed by regulatory agencies, on the price and output decision of regulated firms, especially in the transportation, communications and utilities indus-

tries. The field of labour market economics, however, has not kept pace in analysing the impact of these various constraints for the wage and employment decision of such regulated firms. Correct this imbalance . . . and if successful, submit your paper to a reputable economics journal.

12. We really have no theory of non-competitive pricing. Rather, we have a series of *ad hoc* stories corresponding to all of the different possible cases between the competitive and monopolistic norms. Consequently it is more fruitful to examine the implications of these two polar norms and to treat the non-competitive cases as gravitating towards one or other of the norms. Discuss.

13. Set up a hypothetical product demand schedule for an oligopolist whose price decrease would be met by other oligopolists, but whose price increase would not be matched, leading to a reduction in market share. Derive the marginal revenue schedule. Explain why the large drop in marginal revenue occurs where it does and discuss the implication of this drop for the firm's labour demand schedule.

14. Wage fixing, for example via minimum wage or union wage increases, may not have an adverse employment effect if the employer is an oligopolist with a kinked demand curve for its product. This is especially the case if it applies disproportionately to one or a few of the oligopolists rather than to all. Discuss.

15. Competition in the labour market ensures a competitive floor on wages but not necessarily a competitive ceiling. Competition in the product market is necessary to ensure a competitive ceiling. Consequently there is an upward bias to the wages paid by firms that are not competitive in the product market. Discuss.

REFERENCES AND FURTHER READINGS

(This section does not contain references to the extensive literature on the role of non-competitive product market conditions on the determination of aggregate money wages. This is contained in the references in Chapter 27 on Wage-Price-Unemployment Trade-Offs and the Phillips curve. Related references on inter-industry wage determination also are contained in Chapter 21.)

Alcian, A. and R. Kessel. Competition, monopoly and the pursuit of pecuniary gain. *Aspects of Labor Economics*. Princeton: Princeton University Press, 1962.

Baily, M.N. Dynamic monopsony and structural change. *AER* 65 (June 1975) 338–49.

Brown, W., J. Hayles, B. Hughes and L. Rowe. Product and labour markets in wage determination: some Australian evidence. *BJIR* 22 (July 1984) 169–176.

Carroll, T. and D. Ciscel. The effects of regulation on executive compensation. *R E Stats* 64 (August 1982) 505–509.

Dalton, J. and E. Ford. Concentration and professional earnings in manufacturing. *ILRR* 31 (April 1978) 379–384.

Dalton, J. and E. Ford. Concentration and labor earnings in manufacturing and utilities. *ILRR* 31 (October 1977) 45–60.

Hanushek, E. Alternative models of earnings determination and labour market structures. *JHR* 16 (Spring 1981) 238–259.

Hendricks, W. The effect of regulation on collective bargaining in electric utilities. *Bell Journal of Economics* 6 (Autumn 1975) 451–465.

Hendricks, W. Unionism, oligopoly and rigid wages. *R E Stats* 63 (May 1981) 198–205.

Jones, J. and L. Laudadio. Wage differentials and market imperfection: some cross section results in Canadian manufacturing industries. *RI/IR* (No. 3, 1975) 408–421.

Kowka, J. Monopoly, plant and union effects on worker wages. *ILRR* 36 (January 1983) 251–257.

Landon, J. The effect of product market concentration on wage levels. *ILRR* 23 (January 1970) 237–247.

Lawrence, C. and R. Lawrence. Manufacturing wage dispersion: an end game interpretation. *BPEA* (No. 1, 1985) 47–106.

Lawrence, C. and R. Lawrence. Relative wages in U.S. manufacturing: an endgame interpretation. *BPEA* (1985) 47–106.

Levinson, H. Unionism, concentration and wage changes. *ILRR* 20 (January 1967) 198–205.

Mishel, L. Product markets, establishment size and wage determination. *IRRA* (December 1982) 447–454.

Mitchell, D. Shifting norms in wage determination. *BPEA* (No. 2, 1985) 575–599.

Moore, T. The beneficiaries of trucking regulation. *The Journal of Law and Economics* 21 (October 1978) 327–344.

Nakao, T. Wages and market power in Japan. *BJIR* 18 (November 1980) 365–368.

Pusel, T. Profitability, concentration and the interindustry variation in wages. *R.E. Stats.* 62 (May 1980) 248–253.

Richards, D. Wages and the dominant firm. *JLR* 4 (Spring 1983) 177–182.

Ross, S. and M. Wachter. Wage determination, inflation and the industrial structure. *AER* 63 (September 1973) 675–692.

Wachtel, H. and C. Betsey. Employment and low wages. *R.E. Stats.* 54 (May 1972) 121–129.

Weiss, L. Concentration and labor earnings. *AER* 56 (March 1966) 96–117.

Yandle, B. The wages of regulation. *JLR* 5 (Fall 1984) 435–439.

CHAPTER

12 *Monopsony in the Labour Market*

In Chapter 11 we examined the wage and employment decision when the firm is both a competitive seller of its output in the product market and a competitive buyer of labour in the labour market. We also relaxed one of those assumptions — that of a competitive seller of its output — and examined the labour market implications when the firm is a non-competitive seller of its output, but still a competitive buyer of labour in the labour market. In this chapter the assumption of being a competitive buyer of labour is relaxed. So as to trace out the implications of this single change, termed monopsony, the firm is still assumed to be a competitive seller of its product. The results of relaxing both assumptions simultaneously — that of competition in the labour market and the product market — follow in a straightforward fashion from the results of each separate case.

SIMPLE MONOPSONY

The situation in which a firm is sufficiently large relative to the size of the local labour market that it influences the wage at which it hires labour is referred to as monopsony. The monopsonist is a wage-setter, not a wage-taker. In order to attract additional units of labour, the monopsonist has to raise wages; conversely, if it lowers the wage rate it will not lose all of its work-force.

Consequently the monopsonist faces an upward-sloping labour supply schedule rather than a perfectly elastic labour supply schedule at the going wage, as was the case when the firm was a competitive buyer of labour. This labour supply schedule shows the average cost of labour for the monopsonist because it indicates the wage that must be paid for each different size of the firm's work-force. Since this same wage must be paid for each homogeneous unit of labour, then the wage paid at the margin becomes the actual wage paid to all of the workers, and this same average wage is paid to all.

The firm's labour supply or average-cost-of-labour schedule is not its relevant decision-making schedule. Rather, the relevant schedule is its *marginal* cost of labour which lies above its average cost. This is so because when the firm has to raise wages to attract additional units of labour, in the interest of maintaining internal equity in the wage structure it also has to pay that higher wage to its existing work-force (intra-marginal workers). Thus the marginal cost of adding an additional worker equals the new wage plus the addition to wage costs imposed by the fact that this new higher wage must be paid to the existing work-force. Consequently, the marginal cost of adding an additional worker is greater than the average cost, which is simply the wage.

This situation can be depicted by a simple hypothetical example. Suppose the monopsonist employed only one worker at a wage of one dollar per hour. Its average cost of labour would be the wage rate of one dollar. This would also be its marginal cost: that is, the extra cost of hiring this worker. If the monopsonist wanted to expand this type of work-force, however, it would have to pay a higher wage of, for example, 1.20 dollars to attract an additional worker. Its average cost of labour is the new wage of 1.20 dollars (i.e. (1.20 + 1.20)/2); however, the marginal cost of adding the new worker is the new wage of 1.20 dollars *plus* the additional .20 per hour it has to pay the first worker in order to maintain internal equity in the wage structure. Thus the marginal cost of the second worker is 1.40 dollars per hour, which is greater than the average cost or wage of 1.20 dollars. If a third worker cost 1.40 dollars, then the average cost or wage of the three workers would be 1.40 dollars, while the marginal cost of adding the third worker would be 1.80 dollars, composed of 1.40 dollars for the third worker plus the additional .20 dollars for each of the other two workers. (This example is further extended in the first three columns

Figure 12.1   Monopsony

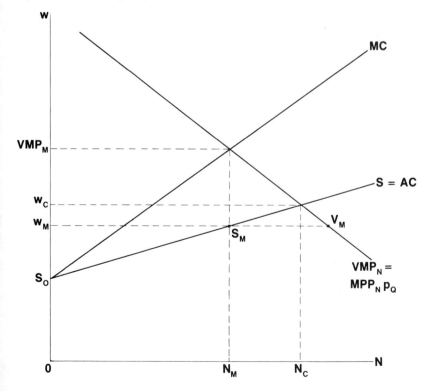

of Table 12.1, which is presented later to show the impact of minimum wages on a monopsony situation.)

The monopsony situation is illustrated diagrammatically in Figure 12.1. The essence of monopsony is that the firm faces an upward-sloping supply schedule for labour and hence has a marginal cost-of-labour schedule that lies above the supply or average cost schedule. The firm maximizes profits by hiring labour until the marginal cost of an additional unit of labour just equals the marginal revenue generated by the additional unit of labour. Marginal revenue is given by the VMP schedule in this assumed case of the firm being a competitive seller of its product. This equality of marginal cost and VMP occurs at the employment level N_m.

The VMP curve for the monopsonist is not really its demand curve for labour in the sense of showing the various quantities of labour that will be demanded at various wage rates. This is so because the monopsonist does not pay a wage equal to the VMP of labour. For example, in Figure 12.1 at the wage w_m, the quantity of labour demanded is N_m, not $w_m V_m$, as would be the case if VMP were a demand schedule equating w with VMP. In essence, the demand for labour is determined by the interaction of the MC and VMP schedules and this depends on the shape of the supply schedule (and hence the MC schedule) as well as the VMP schedule. This line of reasoning is analogous to that underlying the fact that a product market monopolist has no supply curve for its product.

IMPLICATIONS OF MONOPSONY

The level of employment, N_m, associated with monopsony is lower than the level, N_c, that would prevail if the monopsonist behaved as a competitive buyer of labour, equating the supply of labour with the demand. The monopsonist restricts its employment somewhat because hiring additional labour is costly since the higher wages have to be paid to the intra-marginal units of labour.

For N_m units of labour, the monopsonist pays a wage of w_m as given by the supply schedule of labour. The supply schedule shows the amount of labour that will be forthcoming at each wage and, for a wage of w_m, then N_m units of labour will be forthcoming. This wage is less than the wage, w_c, that the monopsonist would pay if it employed the competitive amount of labour N_c. The monopsonist wage is also less than the value of the marginal product of N_m units of labour. That is, the monopsonist pays a wage rate that is less than the value of the output produced by the additional unit of labour (although the value of that output does equal the marginal cost of producing it). This monopsony profit or difference between wages and the value of marginal product of labour has been termed a measure of the monopsonistic exploitation of labour, equal to $VMP_m - w_m$ per worker or $(VMP_m - w_m) N_m$ for the monopsonist's work-force. This monopsony profit accrues to the firm because its wage bill, $w_m N_m$, is less than the market value of the marginal output contributed by the firm's labour force, $VMP_m N_m$.

Because the value of the marginal product of labour for the monopsonist is greater than the value of the marginal product if that firm hired competitively ($VMP_m > VMP_c$, the latter of which equals w_c) then welfare to society would be increased by transferring labour from competitive to monopsonistic labour markets. This seemingly paradoxical result — an increase in welfare by expanding non-competitive markets relative to competitive markets — occurs simply because the value of the marginal product of labour is higher in the monopsonistic market. In effect, transferring labour is akin to breaking down the barriers giving rise to monopsony: it is allocating labour to its most productive use.

Although monopsony leads to a wage less than the value of the marginal product of labour, it is also true that intra-marginal workers are receiving a seller's surplus; that is, the wage they are paid, w_m, is greater than their reservation wage as indicated by the supply schedule. The existing work-force up until N_m units of labour is willing to work for the monopsonist for a wage that is less than the wage, w_m, they are paid. The wage that they are willing to work for is illustrated by the height of the labour supply schedule, which reflects their preferences for this firm and their opportunities elsewhere. However, to the extent that they are all paid the same wage, w_m, then the existing work-force receives a seller's surplus or economic rent equal to the triangle $S_oS_mw_m$.

This is why the term monopsonist exploitation of labour should be used with care. It is true that the monopsonist pays a wage less than the value of the marginal product of labour. However, it is also true that the monopsonist pays a wage greater than the reservation wage (opportunity cost, supply price) that intra-marginal employees could get elsewhere for their labour.

A final implication of monopsony is that there will be equilibrium vacancies (equal to $V_m - S_m$ in Figure 12.1) at the wage paid by the monopsonist. In other words the monopsonist would report vacancies at the wage it pays, but it will not raise wages to attract additional labour to fill these vacancies. In this sense the vacancies are an equilibrium, since there are no automatic forces that will reduce the vacancies. The monopsonist would like to hire additional labour *at the going wage* since the value of the marginal product exceeds the wage cost of an additional unit. However, because the higher wage would have to be paid to intra-marginal units of labour, the value of the marginal product just equals the marginal cost, and that is why there are no forces to reduce the vacancies. The monopsonist is maximizing profits by having vacancies. It does not reduce the vacancies because it would have to raise wages to do so and the marginal cost of doing so is more than the marginal revenue.

CHARACTERISTICS OF MONOPSONISTS

As long as there is some inelasticity to the supply schedule of labour faced by a firm, then that firm has elements of monopsony power. To a certain extent most firms may have an element of monopsony power in the short run, in the sense that they could lower their wages somewhat without losing all of their work-force. However, it is unlikely that they would exercise this power in the long run because it would lead to costly problems of recruitment, turnover, and morale. Facing an irreversible decline in labour demand, however, firms may well allow their wages to deteriorate as a way of reducing their work-force.

In the long run, monopsony clearly will be less prevalent. It would occur when the firm is so large relative to the size of the local labour market that it influences wages. This could be the case, for example, in the classic one-industry towns in isolated regions. Such firms need not be large in an absolute sense: they are simply large relative to the size of the small local labour market, and this makes them the dominant employer. Monopsony may also be associated with workers who have particular preferences to remain employed with the monopsonist. In such circumstances, wages could be lowered and they would stay with the monopsonist because their skills or preferences are not transferable.

Thus a mining company could be a monopsonist, even if it were reasonably small, if it were located in an isolated region with no other firms competing for the types of labour it employed. The same company could even be a monopsonist for one type of labour — for example, miners — while having to compete for other types of labour — for example, clerical workers. Conversely, an even larger mining company might be a competitive employer of miners if it were situated in a less isolated labour market and had to compete with other firms. It is size relative to the local labour market that matters, not absolute size.

Monopsony may also be associated with workers who have specialized skills (specific human capital) that are useful mainly in a specific firm, or with workers who have particular preferences to remain employed with a specific firm. Because their skills or preferences are not completely transferable, such workers are tied to a single employer with a degree of monopsony power. Contractual arrangements in professional sports, for example, effectively tie the professional employee to a specific employer (team), giving the employer a degree of monopsony power. At a minimum the employer need pay a salary only slightly higher than the player's next-best-alternative salary, which would be considerably less. In practice a much higher salary is usually paid in order to extract maximum performance. When players are free agents, as for example when different leagues compete, the resultant salary explosions attest to the fact that the competitive salary is much higher than the monopsonist salary.

The professional sports example illustrates the important fact that, although monopsonists pay less than they would if they had to compete for labour, they need not pay low wages. In fact, unique specialized skills are often associated with high salaries, albeit they might even be higher if there were more competition for their rare services. Monopsony does not imply low wages: it only implies wages that are lower than they would be if there were competition for the particular skills.

PERFECT MONOPSONISTIC WAGE DIFFERENTIATION

The previous discussion focused on what could be labelled *simple monopsony* — a situation where the monopsonist did not differentiate its work-force but rather paid the same wages to all workers of the same skill, both marginal and intra-marginal workers. In terms of Figure 12.1, all workers were paid the wage, w_m, even though intra-marginal workers would have worked for a lower wage as depicted by their supply price. The resultant seller's surplus or economic rent (wage greater than the next-best-alternative) is appropriated by the intra-marginal workers.

This highlights another implication of monopsony. The monopsonist may try to appropriate this seller's surplus by differentiating its otherwise homogeneous work-force so as to pay each worker only their reservation wage. If the monopsonist were able to do this for each and every worker, the result could be labelled *perfect monopsonistic wage differentiation*. In this case the supply schedule would be its average cost of labour *and* its marginal cost, because it would not have to pay the higher wage to the intra-marginal workers. In such circumstances the discriminating monopsonist would hire up to the point N_c in Figure 12.1.

In fact there is an incentive for the monopsonist to try to expand its work-force by means that would make the cost of expansion peculiar only to the additional workers. In this fashion the monopsonist could avoid the rising marginal cost associated with having to pay higher wages to intra-marginal workers. Thus monopsonists may try to conceal the higher wages paid to attract additional labour so as not to have to pay their existing work-force the higher wage. Or they may try to use non-wage mechanisms, the costs of which are specific to only the new workers. Moving allowances, advertising or other more expensive job search procedures, and paying workers for paper qualifications that are largely irrelevant for the job, are all ways in which monopsonists may try to expand their work-force without raising wages for all workers.

IMPERFECT MONOPSONISTIC WAGE DIFFERENTIATION: APPLICATION TO SEX DISCRIMINATION

There may also be situations where monopsonists are unable to differentiate *each* worker so as to pay each only their reservation wage, but are able to differentiate between broad groups of otherwise homogeneous workers. This situation could be termed *imperfect monopsonistic wage differentiation*. In such circumstances the monopsonist only has to pay the same wage *within* groups: different wages can persist *between* groups. Such may be the case, for example, with respect to male and female workers, the example that will be pursued in this section.

The conditions necessary for imperfect monopsonistic discrimination are first that the markets for the different types of labour can be separated (otherwise the low-wage workers would simply move to the high-wage market), and second that there are different supply elasticities in each market (otherwise there are no monopsony rents for the firm to exploit). The importance of these two factors as preconditions for monopsony will become clearer as the analysis progresses.

The situation of imperfect monopsony is depicted in Figure 12.2 for a hypothetical example of a male and female work-force for the firm. For illustrative purposes, males and females are assumed to be equally productive so that there is one VMP schedule for the combined male and female work-force. However, the employer is able to segment or differentiate the male and female work-force from each other. In other words, while there is internal competition within each work-force, there is not competition between the male and female work-forces. The lower supply schedule for females relative to males reflects their lower reservation wage, which in turn may reflect poor employment opportunities elsewhere as well as a low subjective evaluation of their own labour market worth.

Although the labour supply schedules in Figure 12.2 appear parallel, the wage elasticities for different employment levels may be different, whether the curves are parallel or not. Specifically, wage elasticity is defined as $\Theta = \partial N / \partial w \cdot w/N$, and this depends not only on the slope of the supply schedule, $\partial N / \partial w$, but also on where the firm is on the supply schedule, w/N. For females, as will be demonstrated later, w is lower than males and N is higher; consequently w/N is smaller and female labour supply therefore more inelastic.

This lower elasticity for females could prevail for a variety of reasons. Females may have fewer employment opportunities elsewhere and they may be tied to the area of their husband's employment. Household responsibilities and commuting problems may tie them to a single particular local firm. Household and institutional discrimination, especially in educational institutions, may mean that they have been unable to accumulate continuous work experience or labour-market-oriented skills that would lead to competition for their services. In such circumstances, female labour supply to an individual firm may be more inelastic than male labour supply.

Since the supply schedules for both males and females are upward sloping, the employer will have a derived marginal cost schedule which lies above each supply schedule. This reflects the fact that the employer has to pay higher wages to expand each work-force, and because of competition *within* each group it has to pay these higher wages to the intramarginal workers within the group. The total marginal cost schedule, mc_T, is obtained by *horizontally* summing the male and female marginal cost schedules, because this indicates the total amount of labour that can be obtained for a given marginal cost. In other words as the firm expands its homogeneous work-force, it would do so first by hiring only females because their marginal cost is below that of males. However, at some point,

Figure 12.2   Imperfect Monopsonistic Wage Differentiation Between Males and Females

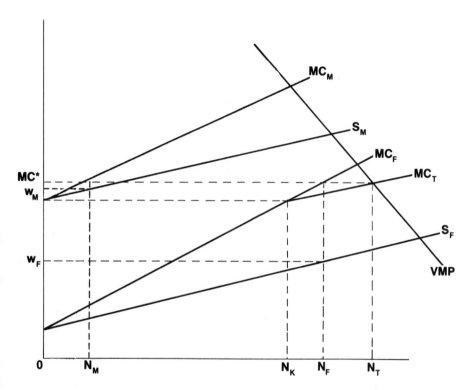

N_k in Figure 12.2, the marginal cost of female labour would just equal that of male labour and the firm would expand by hiring a mixture of males and females, always keeping its marginal cost as low as possible. At this point, N_k, the total marginal cost schedule is kinked downwards, reflecting the fact that it is a weighted average of the male and female marginal cost schedules.

The profit-maximizing employer will hire labour until the marginal cost (MC_T) just equals marginal revenue (VMP_N). This occurs at the employment level N_T in Figure 12.2. This total work-force will consist of N_m males and N_f females because only here will the marginal cost of females just equal the marginal cost of males, and both will equal the common equilibrium marginal cost, MC^* (i.e. $MC_f = MC_m = MC^*$).

Male wages, w_m, are given by the height of the male supply schedule for N_m units of male labour, and female wages, w_f, are given by the height of the female supply schedule for N_f units of female labour. Male wages exceed female wages for the same assumed homogeneous type of labour and this is an equilibrium condition since the firm is maximizing profits by equating marginal cost with marginal revenue. Even though female wages are always lower than male wages over the relevant range of the supply schedules in this diagram, the firm would not hire exclusively females, because the marginal cost of doing so is not always below that of males. And it is the marginal cost of labour, not always the wage, that is relevant for profit maximization.

Imperfect monopsonistic wage differentiation of this form can explain what otherwise appears to be a contradiction in the theory of discrimination: the persistence of a male-female wage differential for equally productive workers, and the persistence of a mixed work-force. These phenomena appear to be contradictions to competitive theory because, under competition, firms would hire only low-wage females and this would increase the demand for females relative to males until the male-female wage differential disappeared. If some firms could resist competitive pressures and satisfy their desire to discriminate by paying higher wages to males, then males would gravitate to these employers and females would gravitate to non-discriminating employers. Discrimination would thereby lead to all-male or all-female work-forces in different firms (and presumably the lower-cost female firms expanding relative to the higher-cost male firms). That male-female wage differentials and mixed work-forces seem to persist, therefore, appears at odds with competitive pressures. They are consistent, however, with imperfect monopsonistic wage differentiation.

Even here, however, there should be competitive pressures at work to break down the segmentation that enables males and females to be considered as two separate pools of labour, with females having a lower reservation wage. In essence, competition from other employers, facilitated by improved labour market information, should serve to raise the wage opportunities for females with other firms, and this would raise the female labour supply schedule of Figure 12.2, mitigating against monopsonistic wage discrimination.

MATHEMATICAL EXPOSITION*

The results of the previous section can be demonstrated more rigorously by the use of mathematics. The profit function for the monopsonist is:

$$\pi = pQ(M,F) - w_m(M)M - w_f(F)F \tag{12.1}$$

The firm is still assumed to be a competitor in the product market, so that p is fixed. However, reflecting the fact that monopsonists are wage-setters and have to raise wages to attract additional labour, male and female wages are positively related to their respective employment levels. The profit-maximizing firm employs additional labour until $\partial\pi/\partial M = \partial\pi/\partial F = O$ which , for males, implies

$$p\partial Q/\partial M = w_m + M\cdot\partial w_m/\partial M \tag{12.2}$$

— that is, the value of the marginal product of male labour (left-hand side) equals its marginal cost (right-hand side). Marginal cost in turn is the male wage rate plus the adjustment in that wage rate for the M intra-marginal units of male labour.

The wage elasticity of supply of male labour to the firm is defined as

$$\theta_m = \partial M/\partial w_m \cdot w_m/M \tag{12.3}$$

Inverting, multiplying by w_m and adding w_m to each side yields

$$w_m(1 + 1/\theta_m) = w_m + M \cdot \partial w_m/\partial M \tag{12.4}$$

— which is the right-hand side of Equation 12.2. Substituting Equation 12.4 into 12.2 yields:

$$p\partial Q/\partial M = w_m(1 + 1/\theta_m) \tag{12.5}$$

The same derivation for females yields:

$$p\partial Q/\partial F = w_f(1 + 1/\theta_f) \tag{12.6}$$

Under profit maximization, the values of the marginal product of males and females are equal; that is, $p\partial Q/\partial M = p\partial Q/\partial F$. Therefore, from Equations 12.5 and 12.6

$$w_m(1 + 1/\theta_m) = w_f(1 + 1/\theta_f) \tag{12.7}$$

For $w_m > w_f$, it must be the case that $(1 + 1/\theta_m) < (1 + 1/\theta_f)$. Subtracting one from each side yields $1/\theta_m < 1/\theta_f$, and multiplying by θ_f yields $\theta_f/\theta_m < 1$, which implies $\theta_f < \theta_m$. That is, for $w_m > w_f$ it must be the case that $\theta_m > \theta_f$: at their equilibrium levels of employment, male labour supply to the firm must be more elastic than female labour supply.

Equation 12.7 also illustrates why the labour supply elasticities have to be different for the male-female wage differential to persist. If $\theta_f = \theta_m$ then $w_m = w_f$.

MINIMUM WAGES AND MONOPSONY

Monopsony also has interesting implications for the employment impact of an exogenous wage increase, for example, from minimum wages, unionization, equal pay laws or other forms of wage fixing. Specifically, over a specified range, an exogenous wage increase may actually *increase* employment in a monopsonistic firm. This seemingly paradoxical result can be illustrated by an example of a minimum wage increase faced by a monopsonist. The proposition first will be demonstrated rigorously, and then explained heuristically and by way of an example.

Formal Exposition

Figure 12.3 illustrates a monopsonistic labour market with w_o being the wage paid by the monopsonist for N_o units of labour with a value of marginal product of VMP_o. With the imposition of an exogenous wage increase, perhaps from minimum wages, to w_1, the new labour supply schedule to the firm becomes horizontal at the minimum wage. This is so because the firm cannot hire at wages below the minimum wage. Thus the firm's labour supply schedule becomes w_1S_1S: to the right of S_1 it becomes

Figure 12.3   Monopsony and a Minimum Wage

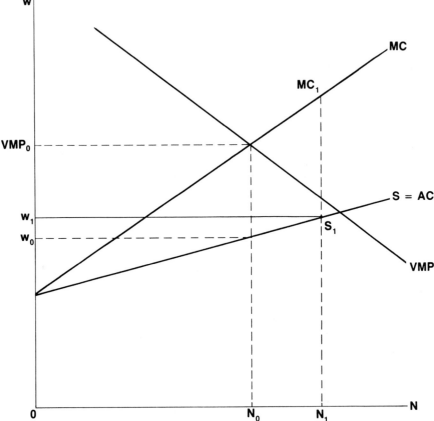

the old supply schedule because firms can pay higher than the minimum wage.

The relevant marginal cost schedule, therefore, becomes $w_1 S_1 MC_1 MC$. It is the same as the labour supply schedule for the horizontal portion $w_1 S_1$ because both marginal and intra-marginal workers receive the minimum wage and consequently marginal cost equals average cost equals the minimum wage. Similarly, to the right of S_1 the marginal cost schedule becomes the old marginal cost schedule $MC_1 MC$ reflecting the relevance of the portion of the old supply schedule $S_1 S$. The jump in marginal cost between S_1 and MC_1 occurs because when the firm expands its work-force beyond N_1 units of labour it has to raise wages to do so and the wage increase applies to all intra-marginal workers who previously were receiving the minimum wage.

After the imposition of the new minimum wage, the monopsonist would equate MC with MR (i.e. VMP) and hence employ N_1 units of labour at the minimum wage w_1. Wages have increased from w_0 to w_1 and, paradoxically, employment has increased from N_o to N_1. In fact, for wage increases up to VMP_o, employment would increase, reaching a maximum increase for wages at the intersection of the supply and VMP schedules.

Heuristic Explanation

Why would wage increases ever lead to employment increases on the part of the firm? It really does not make intuitive sense that a firm would ever respond to a wage increase by employing more labour. The answer to this seeming paradox lies in the fact that the minimum wage negates or makes redundant a certain portion of the firm's supply and marginal cost of labour schedule. Faced with the new constraint of the minimum wage, the firm no longer need concern itself, at least up to a point, with the fact that if it wants more labour it will have to raise wages and pay these higher wages to all workers. In other words it is no longer inhibited in its employment expansion by the rising marginal cost of such expansion. Consequently it will expand employment because although the wage it pays is higher, the marginal cost of expansion is lower since it already pays the minimum wage to its intra-marginal workers.

This does not mean that the monopsonist would welcome a minimum wage increase because then it wouldn't have to worry about the rising marginal cost of labour. The minimum wage obviously reduces profits to the monopsonist, otherwise it would have self-imposed a minimum wage without the need for legislation. The monopsonist is simply responding to a different set of constraints: the minimum wage constraint simply leads to more employment, at least over a limited range of wage increases.

Hypothetical Example

The response of a monopsonist to a minimum wage increase is illustrated in the hypothetical example of Table 12.1. The symbols refer to those in Figure 12.3. The firm's labour supply schedule is given in column (2) with hypothetical increments of .20 dollars per hour necessary to attract an additional worker. The resultant marginal cost schedule is given in column (3), rising faster than the average wage cost because of the necessity to pay intra-marginal workers the extra wage. In the absence of the minimum wage the monopsonist would equate MC with VMP and hence employ four workers.

With the imposition of a minimum wage equal to 2.00 dollars per hour, the firm's labour supply schedule becomes as in column (4). For the seventh worker the minimum wage is redundant, since that worker would not work for less than 2.20 dollars per hour, as indicated earlier in column (1). With the minimum wage the firm's new marginal cost of labour schedule becomes as in column (5). It is constant at the minimum wage for up until six workers because the firm simply pays the minimum wage to all workers. There is a large jump in MC associated with the seventh worker, however, because to acquire the seventh worker the firm has to pay not

TABLE 12.1
HYPOTHETICAL EXAMPLE OF MONOPSONIST
RESPONDING TO MINIMUM WAGE

Units of Labour	No Minimum Wage		Minimum Wage		Value of Marg. Prod.
	Wages	Marg. Cost	Wages	Marg. Cost	
N	S = AC	MC	w_1S_1S = AC	$w_1S_1MC_1MC$	VMP
(1)	(2)	(3)	(4)	(5)	(6)
1	1.00	1.00	2.00	2.00	3.00
2	1.20	1.40	2.00	2.00	2.50
3	1.40	1.80	2.00	2.00	2.30
4	1.60	2.20	2.00	2.00	2.20
5	1.80	2.60	2.00	2.00	2.00
6	2.00	3.00	2.00	2.00	1.80
7	2.20	3.40	2.20	3.40	1.60

only the 2.20 dollars for that worker but also an additional .20 dollars for each of the previous six workers for a total of 3.40 dollars (i.e. 2.20 + 6(.20)).

Given the new marginal cost schedule associated with the minimum wage, the firm will equate MC with VMP by employing five workers. The minimum wage increase results in an increase in employment from four to five workers.

Monopsony profits before the minimum wage were (VMP − w)N = (2.20 − 1.60)4 = 2.40 dollars per hour. After the minimum wage they are reduced to zero in this particular case because the minimum wage was set exactly equal to the VMP of the fifth unit of labour. (In Figure 12.3, for example, there still would be some monopsony profits even after the minimum wage.)

Practical Importance

While in theory minimum wage increases can lead to employment increases in situations of monopsony, in practice the importance of this factor depends on the extent to which monopsony is associated with workers who are paid below minimum wages. Earlier it was pointed out that monopsonists may well pay high wages even though these wages are not as high as they would be if there were more competition for these workers. Low-wage labour markets that are most dramatically affected by minimum wages tend to be in the garment and textile trades and in the service sector, especially hotels, restaurants and theatres. Employers in these sectors tend to be small and the pool of low-wage labour from which they draw large. Consequently, the conditions giving rise to monopsony are not prevalent. There may be isolated instances of one-industry towns where the minimum wage would have an impact on otherwise monopsonistic wage determination. However, it is unlikely that these conditions are sufficiently prominent to negate the usual adverse employment effect that economic theory predicts will emanate from minimum wage increases.

EVIDENCE OF MONOPSONY

Empirical evidence on the prevalence of monopsony is both scant and at times contradictory. In an early study, Bunting (1962) computed concentration ratios of the percentage of the local labour force employed by the largest firms in 1948. He finds little evidence of monopsony power associated with concentration.

Some more recent studies, however, have found evidence of monopsony in some particular labour markets. Landon and Baird (1971) test for the existence of monopsony in the market for U.S. teachers by regressing the starting salary of teachers on a measure of monopsony (number of school districts in the county) and a variety of variables designed to control for ability to pay (per capita income and the percentage of income raised locally) and willingness to pay (tax rate). The starting salary of teachers was used to approximate a homogeneous group of minimally qualified teachers. All variables were statistically significant except for the tax rate. The regression coefficient for the monopsony variable indicated that a one percent increase in the number of school districts in the county gave rise to a 116 dollar increase in the starting salary for teachers. That is, the more competition for the teachers, the greater their salary: conversely the less competition and the greater the monopsony, the less their salary.

If these results are correct, one policy implication is that decentralization would lead to higher starting salaries because of the increased competition, while consolidation of school districts would lead to reduced salaries because the consolidated districts would act like monopsonists. Thus one would expect school boards and taxpayers to support consolidation so as to have more bargaining power against teachers. Conversely one would expect teachers to support decentralization to increase the competition for their services.

In a study of the market for nurses in the U.S., Cohen (1972) regresses the wages of registered nurses relative to an index of competitive wages in the community on variables reflecting monopsony power of the firm. An index of competitive wages was used to control for regional and other factors that could legitimately affect wages. The monopsony variables included a concentration ratio indicating the percentage of beds in the area provided by the four largest hospitals, and a dummy variable to reflect the existence of a nursing school in the area. Theoretically one would expect wages to be negatively related to the concentration variable (because concentration implies monopsony power) and the nursing school variable (because of the attachment of nurses to areas with a nursing school). The regression results confirmed these expectations. Registered nurses receive lower salaries, relative to the competitive wage in the community, in areas that are dominated by a small number of hospitals and where a nursing school is present. The latter variable simply reflects the fact that nurses are often reluctant to leave an area that has a nursing school: their resultant immobility, and hence excess supply in such an area, depresses their wages.

Additional empirical evidence of monopsony in the market for nurses in the U.S. is found in other studies, notably Hurd (1973), Yett (1970), and Link and Landon (1976). These studies suggest that some of the perennial shortage of nurses may be explained by the prevalence of monopsony power in hospitals.

Although the empirical evidence is by no means conclusive, there does appear to be evidence of monopsony in at least some particular labour markets. Scully (1974) finds evidence of monopsony in professional baseball, especially among the "star" players. Further evidence for newspaper printing employees and construction workers is found in Landon (1970) and Landon and Pierce (1971). The extent to which these results can be generalized, even within the occupations where some monopsony was found, remains an open question. In addition, the extent to which it was monopsony power, rather than other factors, that reduced wages could be open to debate.

In theory, however, it is unlikely that monopsony can be an extremely important factor in the long run. Improved communications, labour market information, and labour mobility make the isolated labour market syndrome, necessary for monopsony, unlikely at least for large numbers of workers. It is also true that as these factors improve over time, monopsony should diminish.

QUESTIONS

1. Combine the results of Chapter 11 on monopoly in the product market with Chapter 12 on monopsony in the labour market and illustrate the wage and employment determination process. Is it necessary that monopoly be accompanied by monopsony? Is it possible that the two conditions could go together?
2. If the monopsonist is a wage-setter and not a wage-taker then it can set wages in whatever fashion it wants. Discuss.
3. Monopsonists are at a disadvantage relative to competitive buyers of labour because, when the monopsonist wants to expand its work-force, it has to raise wages while the competitive buyer can get all the labour it wants at the going wage. Discuss.
4. The monopsonist has an upward-sloping labour supply schedule because when it expands its work-force it has to use better quality labour and hence has to pay a higher wage. Discuss.
5. The monopsonist's demand for labour depends on its elasticity of labour supply. Illustrate this proposition in Figure 12.1 by drawing both a more elastic and a more inelastic supply schedule through the point S_m.
6. Explain why the monopsonist has no unique demand schedule for labour.
7. Is it possible for a multi-million dollar professional sports player to be subject to monopsonistic exploitation of labour? Is it possible for workers who are subject to monopsonistic exploitation of labour to be re-

ceiving an economic rent on the sale of their labour market services? Could workers who are receiving an economic rent for their services ever be considered disadvantaged workers?

8. Monopsonists are not necessarily evil: they are simply acting like any other firms when they maximize profits subject to constraints. It is just that the constraints they face are different and this enables them to make a monopsony profit per worker equal to the difference between the wage they pay and the value of the marginal product of labour. The solution to this problem is therefore to alter the constraints faced by monopsonists. Discuss.

9. If the economic rent of $S_oS_mw_m$ in Figure 12.1 were taxed away from the workers, what would happen to the equilibrium employment of the monopsonist? Specifically, would these workers go elsewhere if only their earnings in this particular employment were taxed? Similarly, if the monopsonist appropriates this surplus, what would happen to its employment?

10. Discuss various ways in which monopsonists may try to differentiate their work-force so as to appropriate any economic rent or seller's surplus of their workers.

11. Based on your knowledge of professional sports contracts, discuss ways in which monopsony behaviour may be exhibited.

12. One of the conditions necessary for monopsonistic wage discrimination against females as a group is that their labour supply to the firm must be more inelastic than that of males, at their respective wages and employment. Would you expect this to be the case, and why?

13. Based on the diagram of Figure 12.2, the slopes of the male and female labour supply schedules appear to be the same. How is it then that female labour supply must be more inelastic than male labour supply for the wages of females to be less than the wages of males in this situation of imperfect monopsonistic wage discrimination?

14. Based on the respective supply schedules of males and females in Figure 12.2, if other firms began to compete with this monopsonist for labour, what type of labour would they probably hire and what would this do to the respective supply schedules of this monopsonist? Specifically, would it be able to keep differentiating its pools of labour in the face of such competition?

15. The equilibrium of Figure 12.2 is unstable in the long run because, if the monopsonist is paying males a higher wage than equally productive females, it would obviously try to replace its costly male work-force with a less costly female work-force. Discuss.

16. Indicate how imperfect monopsonistic wage discrimination between males and females can explain the persistence of a male-female wage differential for equally productive workers and the persistence of a mixed work-force within a firm. Could monopsony explain the persistence of these phenomena throughout the aggregate economy?

17. In the case of imperfect monopsonistic wage differentiation (as illus-

trated in Figure 12.2), would the monopsonist ever hire an all female work-force? Why are the male and female marginal cost schedules not vertically summed to get a total marginal cost schedule? Would this monopsonist ever report vacancies of male and female labour at the going wage and, if so, exactly what is the measure of the vacancies for each?

18. The fact that a minimum wage, over a specific range, may actually increase employment for a monopsonist illustrates the proposition that a monopsonist does not have a demand curve for labour in the usual sense. For if it did, then a wage increase would have to be accompanied by a reduction in employment. Discuss.

19. Explain heuristically why a minimum wage increase, over a certain range, would lead to a monopsonist actually increasing employment. Given this possibility, could the monopsony argument be relied upon to negate the critics of minimum wage legislation who argue that minimum wages will have an adverse employment effect and hence harm some of the very people they were designed to help? Could minimum wages ever be applied selectively to monopsony situations? Could wage fixing via unionization be applied more selectively?

20. Based on Figure 12.2, trace through the impact of equal pay for equal work legislation, assuming that the firm could not lower male wages.

21. Based on Figure 12.3, discuss the favourable impact on resource allocation of setting a minimum wage at the intersection of the S and VMP schedules. Heuristically, in what sense are resources allocated more efficiently at that point than at the monopsonist's equilibrium? If the monopsonist followed a policy of perfect wage differentiation in the absence of the minimum wage, what would be the implications for resource allocation? Compare the income distribution consequences of the two alternatives of minimum wages and perfect wage differentiation.

22. Based on the data of Table 12.1, how many units of labour would the monopsonist employ if it acted as a perfectly discriminating monopsonist? What are the consequences for efficient resource allocation?

23. Trace through the implications of the firm acting as an oligopsonist with a kinked supply curve; that is, where wage increases would be met by other oligopsonists but wage decreases would not, so that substantial losses of employment would result.

24. According to Link and Landon (1976, p. 151), "clear evidence of a relation between depressed wage levels and monopsony or oligopsony can be isolated empirically in labour markets such as nursing where highly specialized training is required, where the cross-elasticity of supply between occupations is small, where substantial inter-area variations in monopsony power are present, and where limited geographic mobility exists in the labour market." Discuss how each of these factors could lead to monopsony or oligopsony power being exercised.

25. Cohen (1972, p. 43) estimated the following equation to test for the existence of monopsony in the nursing market:

$$w_N/w_C = 3.69 - 0.30CR - 0.02NS$$

where w_n is the starting wage of registered nurses (in dollars per hour), w_c is an index of competitive wages in the area, CR is a concentration ratio giving the percentage of beds in the area provided by the four largest hospitals, and NS is a dummy variable coded one if the hospital has a nursing school, zero otherwise.

Use this equation to predict the starting salaries of registered nurses in the following three cases, assuming throughout that the competitive wage index is unity (approximately the sample mean):
(a) competitive case when CR = .20 and NS = 0;
(b) typical case when CR = .60 and NS = 0;
(c) oligopsony case when, for example, CR = .80 and NS = 1;
(d) monopsony when, for example, CR = 1.00 and NS = 1.

REFERENCES AND FURTHER READINGS

Altman, S. The structure of nursing education and its impact on supply. *Empirical Studies in Health Economics*, H. Klarman (ed.). Baltimore: Johns Hopkins Press, 1970.

Altman, S. *Present and Future Supply of Registered Nurses*. Washington: Dept. of Health, Education and Welfare, 1971. Chapter II, Appendix A.

Archibald, G. The factor gap and the level of wages. *Economic Record* 30 (November 1954) 187–199.

Arrow, K. and W. Capron. Dynamic shortages and price rises: the engineer-scientist case. *QJE* (May 1959) 292–307.

Baily, M. Dynamic monopsony and structural change. *AER* 65 (June 1975) 338–349.

Bronfenbrenner, M. Potential monopsony in labor markets. *ILRR* 9 (July 1956) 577–588.

Bunting, R. *Employer Concentration in Local Labor Markets*. Chapel Hill, N.C.: University of North Carolina Press, 1962.

Cohen, H. Monopsony and discriminating monopsony in the nursing market. *Applied Economics* 4 (March 1972) 39–48.

Devine, E. Manpower shortages in local employment. *AER Proceedings* 59 (May 1969) 538–546.

Ehrenberg, R. Heterogeneous labor, minimum hiring standards, and job vacancies in public employment. *JPE* 81 (November/December 1973) 1442–1450.

Fellner, W. Prices and wages under bilateral monopoly. *QJE* 61 (1947).

Hall, W. Unionization, monopsony power, and police salaries. *IR* 16 (February 1977) 94–100.

Hieser, R. Wage determination with bilateral monopoly in the labour market: a theoretical treatment. *ER* 36 (March 1970) 55–72.

Hirshleifer, J. An exposition of the equilibrium of the firm: symmetry between product and factor analysis. *Economica* 29 (August 1962) 263–268.

Hurd, R. Equilibrium vacancies in a labor market dominated by non-profit firms: the shortage of nurses. *R.E.Stats.* 55 (May 1973) 234–240.

Ioannides, Y. and C. Pissarides. Monopsony and the lifetime relation between wages and productivity. *JOLE* 3 (January 1985) 91–100.

Landon, J. and R. Baird. Monopsony in the market for public school teachers. *AER* 61 (December 1971) 966–971. Comment by R. Thornton and reply, *ILRR* 28 (July 1975) 574–578.

Landon, J. and W. Peirce. Discrimination, monopsony, and union power in the building trades: a cross section analysis. *IRRA* 24 (December 1971) 254–261.

Link, C. and J. Landon. Monopsony and union power in the market for nurses. *SEJ* 41 (April 1975) 649–659.

Link, C. and J. Landon. Market structure, nonpecuniary factors and professional salaries: registered nurses. *Journal of Economics and Business* 28 (Winter 1976) 151–155.

Mai, C. and J. Shih. Employment effect under monopsony wage discrimination. *SEJ* 49 (July 1982) 242–245.

Maurice, S. Monopsony and the effects of an externally imposed minimum wage. *SEJ* 41 (October 1974) 283–287.

Nelson, P. The elasticity of labor supply to the individual firm. *Econometrica* 41 (September 1973) 853–866.

Persky, J. and H. Tsang. Pigouvian exploitation of labor. *R.E.Stats.* 56 (February 1974) 52–57.

Raimond, H. Free agents' impact on the labour market for baseball players. *JLR* 4 (Spring 1983) 183–193.

Robinson, J. *The Economics of Imperfect Competition.* London: Macmillan, 1933, Reprinted 1965, 211–228.

Rottenberg, S. The baseball players' labor market. *JPE* (June 1956) 242–258.

Scully, G. Pay and performance in major league baseball. *AER* 64 (December 1974) 915–930.

Yett, D. Causes and consequences of salary differentials in nursing, *EI* 7 (March 1970) 78–99.

Yett, D. The chronic shortage of nurses: a public policy dilemma. *Empirical Studies in Health Economics*, H. Klarman (ed.). Baltimore: Johns Hopkins Press, 1970.

13 Institutionalism, Dualism and Radicalism

Throughout this part we have emphasized the interaction of supply and demand in alternative market structures as being crucial in determining wages and employment. There have always been schools of thought, however, that have de-emphasized, and at times attacked, the notion of these market forces as being important factors in wage and employment determination. The severity of the criticism of the economic factors has ranged from saying that they play an important but minor role, to saying that they are distinctly subservient to other political-institutional factors, to the more radical critiques that argue that the economic framework simply masks the forces of power and class conflict that are the real determinants of wages and employment.

While it is always hazardous to try to categorize alternative perspectives and paradigms, they are labelled here as institutionalism, dualism, and radicalism. While there are some basic differences between these perspectives, they have as a common thread a critique of the neoclassical paradigm. In what follows an attempt will be made to summarize each of these schools of thought with respect to their criticism of neoclassical theory, their own contribution, and their own strengths and shortcomings.

INSTITUTIONALISM

The institutionalist tradition in labour economics is one that plays down the economic forces and emphasizes the roles of individuals, institutions, custom and socio-political factors. It tends to emphasize descriptive realism as being more important than abstract, theoretical reasoning. The case-study and real-world observations are emphasized as being important in understanding the behaviour of the labour market.

The institutionalist tradition is evident in the work of Lester (1946) who attacked the assumptions of economics and its emphasis on marginal analysis as being unrealistic. He argued for empirical testing of the assumptions often employed in economics. For example, in responding to interviews and questionnaires, employers said that they did not use marginal analysis in their everyday business decisions and that they seldom responded to wage increases by reducing employment. Lester interpreted this as a rejection of conventional economic analysis.

Conventional economics was not without its defence. Machlup (1946) stressed the fact that it was the predictions and not the assumptions of theory that mattered, and that simplifying assumptions were necessary to deduce generalizations about labour market behaviour. For example, as discussed subsequently, the assumption of perfect mobility is a simplifying assumption that enables predictions about long-run wage differentials. It can be relaxed, and the implication for wage differentials examined. In addition, it may not be so unrealistic if one remembers that all that is required for the implications of economic analysis is that some workers at the margin of decision (not all workers) be mobile or, at times, have the threat of mobility.

The neoclassical paradigm can also be defended on the basis that it is operational and leads to empirically verifiable propositions. In defending the use of abstractions such as profit maximization on the part of firms and utility maximization on the part of individuals, Rottenberg (1956, p. 45) states: "complex motivation of real life does not destroy the truism of simple motivational behaviour in the abstract neoclassical model of the labour market. Other things equal, it can be a correct description of real life behaviour to say that workers make job choices with reference to relative prices."

The institutional tradition is also evident in the work of Arthur Ross (1956). He argued that wages are determined by "conscious human decision rather than by impersonal market forces" and that to understand union wage policy we must understand the internal policy aspect of the union — "what kind of organism it is, how it functions, and what is the role of leadership." Above all, Ross emphasized the interdependence of the wage structure and the importance of "equitable comparisons" as a criterion for wage determination.

The institutionalist tradition has continued in the writings of those who emphasized the importance of segmentation in labour markets. These writings in particular were the forefront of the more current work on dual labour markets. Kerr (1954), for example, coined the phrase "Balkanization of labour markets" to describe what he felt was a trend towards the increased segmentation of the labour market into a variety of non-competing groups. In his view firms were becoming increasingly divorced or insulated from the competitive forces of the external labour market. They recruited from this labour market only at the lower "ports of entry." Most jobs were filled from internal promotion from the firm's "internal labour market." Consequently administered rules and internal company policies governing the internal labour market were more important than competitive economic forces that were important only for the seldom-used external labour market.

Dunlop (1957) also emphasized the importance of segmentation with the concepts of "job clusters" and "wage contours." Job clusters were occupational groupings with common wage-making characteristics so that wages within the clusters were highly interdependent. The clusters were linked together by technology, administrative rulings of the firm, or social custom. Wage contours referred to the stable wage relationships between certain firms that were linked together by similar product markets, labour markets, or custom. Thus the wage of an individual worker was dependent upon the job cluster of the occupation and on the wage contour of the firm. These clusters and contours defined the relevant comparisons for the actual wage determination process. Key wage settlements spilled over onto other jobs within the same cluster and onto other firms within the same contour. Thus, institutional forces which determined the nature of the job clusters, wage contours, key settlements and spillover effects were seen as being of prime importance in the wage determination process.

The institutionalist framework, with its impressive list of contributors, has given insight into the real-world behaviour of labour markets. It has been rich in classification and in describing the peculiarities of the labour market. However, it has not really provided an *analysis* of the basic forces that lie behind the everyday actions of labour and management. Consequently, it has seldom given rise to empirically testable implications that are capable of empirical confirmation or refutation. As such its contribution has not been cumulative. Rather, its insights have been incorporated into labour market analysis in a rather *ad hoc* fashion, often to explain particular anomalies.

In recent years, a literature has emerged applying Hirschman's (1970) concepts of exit and voice to the labour market. Exit refers to the traditional competitive response of leaving unsatisfactory market situations for more acceptable ones; voice refers to alternative means (e.g. complaint, protest, or suggestions) to improve unsatisfactory market situations. While the concepts of exit and voice can be subject to many of the criticisms of institutional economics, they do provide some interesting insights into labour market behaviour.

According to Hirschman, traditional economics regards exit, or the threat of exit, as the basic pressure that ensures that competition will provide goods and services efficiently: if they are not provided, then customers will exit and shop elsewhere. There are situations, however, where exit is not feasible, perhaps because it is a costly process or because of brand loyalty. In such circumstances, consumers may use voice ranging from constructive suggestion to severe protest. Most important, the possibility of exit reduces the necessity to use voice. From a policy perspective, Hirschman's analysis therefore implies that the usual economic solution of attaining efficiency through increased competition (exit) works against the possibility of attaining efficiency through mechanisms involving voice.

This has interesting implications for the analysis of labour markets since it suggests that increased competition and mobility (exit) — the panacea of economists — may reduce the use of voice as a way of handling labour market problems. As Freeman (1976) points out, collective bargaining can be viewed as the institutional embodiment of voice in the labour market. It therefore can serve as a viable alternative to the costly use of exit as a way of handling labour market problems.

Johnson's (1975) perspective on the impact of unions can also be viewed in the context of exit versus voice. Traditional economic analysis regards the union as a causal factor gaining higher wages for union members, largely through the threat of exit (withdrawal of services). Johnson raises the possibility, however, that causality works the other way. That is, for various reasons some firms and industries simply pay a greater-than-market wage, perhaps because it is important for them to reduce turnover and to have a queue of applicants from which to hire. Workers that are fortunate enough to be hired in this sector will not use exit to improve their situation because they cannot do better elsewhere. Because exit is not effective for them, they turn to voice in the form of collective bargaining and unionization to achieve other objectives (e.g. due process), knowing that they will be remaining in the firm for a long time. In essence, high wages reduce exit and encourage voice, raising the intriguing possibility that high wages lead to unionization rather than vice versa.

Clearly the exit, voice, and loyalty concepts raise some interesting issues, especially with respect to the advantages and disadvantages of various forms of exit as opposed to voice and loyalty as general ways of achieving efficiency and reconciling efficiency objectives with other objectives. In particular, they raise the possibility that many institutional arrangements can be regarded as efficient ways of utilizing voice in the labour market. These issues are discussed further in Part IV on unions.

The efficiency wage literature, which has emerged in recent years, is also relevant to the institutionalist tradition. One of the criticisms of neoclassical economic theory made by institutionalists was the prediction of a single equilibrium wage in a competitive labour market. Data collected by institutionalists and others indicated that a distribution of wages often existed in markets in which employers were sufficiently small relative to the market that they should not have any monopsony power (i.e. an essentially competitive labour market). Furthermore, this wage distribution was often found to be quite stable over time, suggesting that its existence could not be accounted for by factors such as imperfect information or shifts in demand and supply. As discussed previously, the efficiency wage literature can explain the existence of a distribution of wages in an otherwise competitive labour market if there are differences across firms in such factors as the costs of turnover, the ability to monitor work effort and the ability of the firm to screen out the most productive workers. Because many of these factors are likely to remain stable over time, the associated wage distribution is also predicted to remain stable.

DUALISM

The institutionalist tradition has also re-emerged in recent years in the works of a number of economists who characterize the labour market as being segmented into two main parts, the primary or core, and the secondary or peripheral labour market. An excellent review of this literature, with emphasis on its applicability to the Canadian environment and its usefulness in analysing Canadian human resource issues, is contained in Smith (1976).

Characteristics of Segmented Markets and Their Work-force

The characteristics of the primary and secondary labour markets are given in Doeringer and Piore (1971, p. 165):

> Jobs in the primary market possess several of the following characteristics: high wages, good working conditions, employment stability, chances of advancement, equity, and due process in the administration of work rules. Jobs in the secondary market, in contrast, tend to have low wages and fringe benefits, poor working conditions, high labour turnover, little chance of advancement, and often arbitrary and capricious supervision. There are distinctions between workers in the two sectors which parallel those between jobs: workers in the secondary sector, relative to those in the primary sector, exhibit greater turnover, higher rates of lateness and absenteeism, more insubordination, and engage more freely in petty theft and pilferage.

Of crucial importance in the analysis of segmented labour markets is the role of the internal labour market of individual firms in the primary sector. Within each internal labour market, well-developed hierarchies and stable employment relationships develop that are of mutual benefit to both management and workers. The job security and opportunities for career advancement that are so important to workers are also of value to management as ways of retaining a work-force that has accumulated enterprise-specific skills and informal on-the-job training. In such circumstances, firms will try to reduce turnover cost by paying high wages, granting job security, and providing career advancement.

Within the internal labour market, the allocation of labour is determined by administrative rules and custom. Competitive forces, emphasized by neoclassical economics, have only a minor influence in determining broad limits within which administered and customary wage and employment policies are carried out.

Reasons for Segmentation

Reasons for the segmentation of labour markets are difficult to disentangle from the characteristics of the markets because cause and effect are interrelated. In essence, segmentation prevails because it produces characteristics in workers that sustain the segmentation. A veritable Catch 22 situation prevails as workers are trapped in the secondary labour market in part because of their poor work habits: their poor work habits in turn result in part from their being employed in the secondary labour force. Cause and effect are unclear. But what is clear is the cumulative nature of the problem and the inherent difficulty of breaking out of the secondary labour market. In essence, segmentation becomes self-perpetuating.

To an extent segmentation may be historically determined and sustained by forces of custom and tradition. Well established patterns emerge and these become accepted norms. As Doeringer and Piore (1971, p. 85) state with respect to the wage determination process: "Any wage rate, set of wage relationships, or wage-setting procedure which prevails over a period of time tends to become customary; changes are then viewed as unjust or inequitable, and the work group will exert economic pressure in opposition to them." Thus segmentation becomes self-perpetuating through the forces of custom and tradition.

A dual labour market can also result from forces which lead some firms to pay above-market wages. This possibility is examined more formally in Part IV on unions. The higher wages may be negotiated via collective bargaining or be set by the employer to reduce turnover or encourage employee work effort. Because of the higher wage, employment is reduced below the level that would prevail in the absence of unionization or efficiency wage considerations. As a result, labour supply to other sectors is increased, reducing wages in these sectors. The consequence is a high-wage sector, in which workers are well paid because they are represented by a union or because paying a high wage is in the firm's interest, and a low-wage sector, in which union organization is difficult or in which firms have little incentive to pay above-market wages to reduce turnover, provide work incentives and so on.

Institutional and legal factors can also foster segmentation in labour markets. Unions, especially craft unions, can create barriers to entry into the primary (often unionized) labour market via such devices as the hiring hall, nepotism, and lengthy apprenticeship programs. Professional associations also create barriers to entry and prevent competition via occupational licensing and the control of paraprofessional substitutes. Discrimination can be an effective barrier preventing minority groups from moving from the secondary to the primary labour market.

Social legislation may foster segmentation, usually as an unintended side effect. For example, termination of employment legislation, experience rating under unemployment insurance, ceilings on the payroll tax used to finance social security – all of which result in quasi-fixed costs being associated with each employee — encourage firms to work their existing work-force longer hours (to spread the fixed costs) rather than to hire additional employees which would result in additional fixed costs. The existing work-force becomes protected from the competition of other workers because of these legislated fixed costs associated with hiring additional workers. These legislated quasi-fixed costs are compounded by the normal fixed costs associated with the recruitment, hiring and training of new workers. To a certain extent employers may minimize these quasi-fixed costs by contracting out for work in the secondary labour market which does not have these high fixed costs, often because the legislation is inapplicable to small employers and to the self-employed. In essence, legislation that results in quasi-fixed costs of employment fosters segmentation by discouraging employers from hiring potential recruits from the secondary labour market, especially if their work habits are such that turnover may be high and hence the fixed costs are lost.

The impact of such legislation in fostering segmentation is illustrated most dramatically in the so-called "black markets" that are alleged to have developed as a way of avoiding the legislation. Especially in response to the difficulty of laying off workers, but also in response to minimum wage and other legislation, employers have at times responded by purchasing semi-finished inputs from households or by contracting out to households to do specific tasks (e.g. sew on buttons, assemble a minor part). Veritable "cottage industries" develop which are not covered by legislation that creates fixed costs of employment, nor by safety laws, child labour laws, nor any other labour standards for that matter. In addition, the job of quality control, supervising, and monitoring the labour input is left up to the household, with firms simply buying or not buying the output. Markets develop and operate in unusual forms, and employers and employees adjust to legislation in subtle fashions!

Policy Implications of Segmented Labour Markets

Concerns for issues of public policy arise from the segmented labour market analysis for reasons of both distributive equity and allocative efficiency. Equity concerns arise because workers trapped in the secondary labour market tend to be disadvantaged workers, often caught in a vicious circle of poverty, and experiencing other problems associated with discrimination and poor working conditions. Efficiency concerns arise because of the costs associated with immobility of labour and barriers to entry.

As Smith (1976, p. 27) points out, as a general policy prescription the dual and segmented labour market analysis suggests a re-emphasis towards the structural aspects of labour demand and away from the structural aspects of labour supply and from macroeconomic full employment policies. Macroeconomic full employment policies to raise the level of aggregate demand are dismissed as helping mainly workers in the primary labour market, with at best a minor trickling-down effect on those in the secondary market, and a loosening of the barriers that prevent workers from moving from the secondary to the primary market. As Smith (1976, p. 28) concludes: "policies to maintain high, stable levels of aggregate demand have beneficial but limited effects in the dual theory."

Similarly, human capital policies that alter the structure of labour supply are not regarded by dual labour market analysts as viable ways of improving the earnings of workers in the secondary labour markets. Thus improved education, training, mobility and labour market information — the traditional human capital factors — are dismissed largely on the grounds that they do little to improve earnings because they do not necessarily enable those in the secondary labour market to enter the primary labour market. In essence, improving the characteristics of workers via human resource development will do little if this is not accompanied by policies that alter the structure of labour demand so that these workers obtain jobs in the primary labour market.

After rejecting aggregate demand (full employment) and structural supply (human capital) policies, proponents of the dual labour market analysis suggest the structure of labour demand as being the most important determinant of the wages and working conditions of workers in the secondary labour market. The structure of labour demand is reflected in the characteristics of the industry, occupation, region and firm in which workers find themselves. That is, the structure of labour demand in the secondary labour market reflects declining demand, low profitability, fierce competition in the product market, and competitive pressures from other sources of labour supply. Thus it is the characteristics of markets more than the characteristics of the workers themselves that are taken as being responsible for the low wages of the working poor in the secondary labour market.

Proponents of dual labour market analysis, therefore, recommend de-emphasizing human resource policies — the panacea of the 1960s — and recommend improvements in the characteristics of the markets in which low-wage workers find themselves. This could be done basically in two ways. One is to *extend* the protection, high wages and good working conditions of workers in the primary labour market to workers in the secondary labour market. This could be accomplished by wage fixing (e.g. minimum wages, equal pay laws), labour standards legislation, the encouragement of unionization and collective bargaining in the secondary labour market, and by policies such as unemployment insurance that would increase the bargaining power of workers in the peripheral sector. Wherever these policies have adverse side effects, perhaps on the employment opportunities of low-wage workers, they would have to be rectified by complementary programs, such as perhaps public employment.

A second device to improve the labour market situation in which low-wage workers find themselves is to break down the barriers that prevent movement from the secondary to the primary labour market. In particular, anti-discrimination laws may be effective, as would the removal of unnecessary educational or occupational licensing requirements. In general, however, not much hope is held out for these policies because there is the possibility that even if secondary sector workers get jobs in the primary sector, they will still be treated as secondary workers. In addition, many of the protective features and job security of the primary labour market are regarded as desirable, and removing these features would be like "throwing out the baby with the bath water." Hence, the emphasis on extending the benefits of the primary labour market into the secondary labour market.

Strengths and Weaknesses of Dualism

An overall evaluation of the usefulness of dual labour market analysis is both difficult and perhaps premature. It may be premature because much of the work appeared in the 1960s and sufficient time has not passed to judge its usefulness. Nevertheless, it is a continuation of the institutionalist tradition that has always been a part — at times the only part — of labour market analysis.

On the positive side, the dualist (and institutionalist) approach has often exposed observers to the harsh realities of the operations of labour markets and has emphasized that low wages may be a result of the characteristics of the labour market in which workers operate as well as (or rather than) the characteristics of the workers themselves. This highlights the fact that the poverty of the working poor may be a fault of the economic system as well as (or rather than) of individual workers themselves. Dualism has also provided a wealth of descriptive information, classification devices and, most importantly, insights into the real-world operation of labour markets, especially for the working poor.

These very contributions, however, are at the root of the weaknesses of dual labour market analysis. In its over-concern for descriptive detail, and in documenting reality, the dual labour market analysis has fallen short of providing a coherent and systematic analysis of the basic causal forces that underly the everyday actions of labour market participants. The emphasis on descriptive case studies and the in-depth analysis of particular local labour markets also has suffered from an inability to generalize the results. In essence, the dual labour market analysis has been long on description and classification and short on cumulative theoretical analysis from which one could derive testable implications capable of empirical acceptance or refutation.

To a certain extent this may be an unfair criticism since it comes from the very paradigm — neoclassical economics with its emphasis on cumulative theory and empirical implications capable of empirical scrutiny — that the dual labour market analysis criticizes. Nevertheless, unless dual labour market analysis moves beyond description and classification, it is unlikely to do more than supplement more traditional economic analysis as a way of understanding labour market behaviour.

As an example, one of the fundamental weaknesses of dual labour market analysis is its failure, at least at this stage, to explain how the barriers between the primary and secondary labour markets can persist in the long run against competitive forces. Why can't workers move, in the long run, from the secondary to the primary labour market, and why don't employers recruit in the secondary labour market knowing that they could obtain abundant labour at low wages? It is not enough to *describe* the barriers: it is also necessary to *explain* why they exist and how they can persist over time. Without a theory of cause and effect, policy prescriptions are, at best, hazardous.

This suggests that a fruitful approach would be to try to explain the causal factors that give rise to the institutional barriers that separate the primary and secondary labour markets. In other words, whereas economics traditionally regards institutional factors and administrative policies as constraints (and then analyses their impact, especially on efficiency), perhaps more understanding could be had by regarding them as rational (and perhaps efficient) outcomes of employer and employee interaction, given the peculiarities of the labour markets. In formal terms, what may be needed is a theory of institutions and administrative arrangements, rather than simply regarding them as exogenously given. This was suggested in our earlier discussion of the importance of voice as opposed to exit, and it is in the spirit of the work of Addison and Burton (1978, p. 221), who have argued that the "labour market phenomena that have been labelled as 'institutional', non-market phenomena by institutionalists — comparative group monitoring and collective bargaining, internal labour markets and seniority practices — may be seen . . . as institutional arrangements adopted by market participants because of the efficiency of such arrangements."

RADICALISM

An alternative perspective on labour market economics is found in the recent radical neo-Marxian writings as discussed, for example, in the works of Samuel Bowles (1972), Richard Edwards, Michael Reich and Thomas Weisskopf (1972), Herbert Gintis (1970, 1971), David Gordon (1972), Bennet Harrison (1972), and Howard Wachtel (1971, 1972). Probably the best summary of the radical perspective, giving an explicit comparison with the orthodox neoclassical and the dual labour market perspectives, is contained in Gordon (1972).

As Gordon (1972, p. 53) points out:

> Radical economic theory . . . has not yet been pulled together into a fully embellished theoretical system. Individual strands of radical economic analysis have begun to interweave, but many of the features of the eventual fabric have not become entirely clear. So far, much of the analysis has not even been precisely formulated, much less published; it continues to flow through conversations, letters and unpublished notes.

This makes a review of the radical perspective difficult; nevertheless, some common threads interweave through their analysis.

Following Marx, radicals emphasize that *economic classes* emerge as a result of the particular way in which productive activity is organized: under capitalism, the working class and capitalists emerge, with each group developing a strong subjective identification with its own class. Because of technological change and growth, an *economic surplus* develops over and above the subsistence level necessary to sustain and maintain the economic system. *Class conflict* arises over the division of this economic surplus. Under the current state of capitalism, this surplus tends to be appropriated by the capitalist owners of the means of production and they use the surplus to ensure their continued *power*. In particular, they use the instruments of the *state* (e.g. police, education, granting agencies, tax-transfer schemes) to ensure that effective power remains in their hands. These policies could include the granting of concessions to the working class, largely as a way to buy support, co-opt insurgence, and defuse protest.

Over time, however, capitalism develops *internal contradiction* — in essence, it contains the seeds of its self-destruction. In particular, competition, efficiency and the specialization of labour are necessary for the survival of capitalism, but these very factors dehumanize and alienate the work-force, strengthening class consciousness amongst exploited workers. Eventually, their plight will become intolerable and they will act in a concerted fashion to gain the effective power necessary to improve their position.

Radicals, therefore, emphasize the importance of class power in economic relationships. In particular, Gordon (1972, p. 64) argues that there are really two stages in the determination and distribution of income. First, the share of total income that goes to workers as opposed to capitalists depends on the relative power of the two groups. Second, once that share is determined by power relationships, then the amount that a given worker gets within the working class depends on the individual's productivity, which in turn varies with the personal characteristics and capacities of the worker (as emphasized by human capital theory) and the characteristics of the job (as emphasized by dualism). Thus, to the conventional concepts of the quality of labour supply as emphasized by human capital theorists, and the structure of labour demand as emphasized by dual labour market analysts, radicals have added the concept of class power as an important factor in the determination and distribution of income. To cite Gordon (1972, p. 65): "The worker's final wage thus depends *both* on his individual productivity *and* on the relative power of the class to which he belongs. The radical theory thus combines the radical concept of class with orthodox notions of supply and demand."

As a general policy prescription, therefore, radicals tend to emphasize the importance of the development of class consciousness amongst workers and of fundamental changes in the power relationships between workers and capitalists. Specific policies to change these power relationships are not usually spelled out clearly, but what is clear is the radicals' belief that most of the policy recommendations that flow from traditional economic analysis, or from the dual labour market perspective, are ineffective without radical changes in power relationships.

AN OVERALL ASSESSMENT

Any overall assessment of the various competing paradigms — neoclassical, institutional, dual, and radical — is made difficult by the political overtones that surround any perspective. In addition, some of the writings — those of Lester Thurow (1969) for example — are difficult to categorize because they contain elements of various paradigms. The matter is further complicated by the fact that the dual and new radical perspectives have not been subject to the test of time. And when they are judged, it is probably through the perspective of the reigning paradigm — neoclassical economics — with its emphasis on theory that yields implications capable of empirical acceptance or rejection. The extent to which this is a fair test is an open question, especially since the empirical testing itself is geared to the neoclassical paradigm with its emphasis on marginal analysis.

Each of the perspectives certainly does give insights into our understanding of labour market behaviour. Neoclassical economics, with its emphasis on income and relative prices as they affect various facets of labour supply and labour demand in alternative market structures, certainly has provided a systematic and consistent theoretical explanation for various aspects of observed labour market behaviour. This is especially the case when it has been modified to incorporate realistic factors such as uncertainty, transaction costs, and lack of information. Institutionalism, with its emphasis on the importance of individuals, institutions, custom and sociopolitical factors, has reminded us of the importance of these factors, especially as they interact in that most peculiar of markets — the labour market. In addition, some perspectives of voice versus exit, for example, have suggested the possibility that certain institutional features of the labour market are rational efficient responses to peculiarities of the labour market. Dualism has continued the institutional tradition and has focused on the structure of labour demand that segments the labour market into essentially two non-competing groups in the primary and secondary labour markets. Radicalism adds the importance of power relationships in a system of inherent class conflict.

While there certainly is no consensus as to which paradigm provides us with the greatest understanding of labour market behaviour, there is certainly more agreement that the insights from all of the paradigms have been useful. As a general proposition it is probably correct to say that the basic neoclassical economic paradigm has not been replaced — at least not yet — by any of the alternatives. Nevertheless, they have been useful in pointing out its possible weaknesses and in pressuring it to analyse institutional phenomena, labour market segmentation, and power relationships — all of which seem to be particularly important in labour markets. The extent to which the neoclassical paradigm is sufficiently adaptable remains an open — and interesting — question.

QUESTIONS

1. "By emphasizing descriptive realism, especially with respect to the assumptions of economics and the motivation of labour and management, institutional labour economics must be correct and therefore more useful in our understanding of labour market behaviour." Discuss.
2. "Because it assumes perfect information, perfect mobility and zero transaction costs, conventional microeconomics has no applicability to the labour market." Discuss.
3. Discuss the meaning of the following terms as used in labour market

analysis: internal versus external labour markets; job clusters; wage contours, key settlements and spillover effects; and exit, voice, and loyalty.

4. Briefly outline the characteristics of the primary and secondary labour markets, and the characteristics of the workers in each. Is there a parallel in the literature on product markets as described in the field of industrial organization?

5. Discuss the main forces that give rise to the segmentation of the primary from the secondary labour market, according to the proponents of dual labour markets. Over time would we expect these forces to increase or decrease, and why?

6. Document a variety of internal administrative rules or company personnel policies that apply to the internal labour market. To what extent might these be an efficient response to the peculiarities of the labour market rather than simply inefficient institutional constraints?

7. Compare and contrast the *general* policy implications that flow from each of the following paradigms — neoclassical, institutional, dual, and radical. What would each say about the usefulness of the following specific policies:
   (a) minimum-wage legislation;
   (b) equal pay legislation;
   (c) unemployment insurance;
   (d) training programs;
   (e) job creation in the public sector.

8. "It is tempting to argue that each of the various labour market paradigms has a role and that different paradigms may be necessary to analyse different phenomena. However, it is intellectually unsatisfactory to utilize paradigms in such an *ad hoc* fashion so as to 'fit the facts' of each case. If a set of forces are important then they should apply as basic determinants of a variety of phenomena at a variety of levels." Discuss.

9. The use of voice has been suggested as an alternative to exit as a way of dealing with some labour market problems. Discuss various forms of exit and voice and discuss their costs and benefits.

10. 'One of the problems of relying on voice is that the free market will provide an insufficient amount of voice because it has public good characteristics; that is, the benefits of voice are available to a wide group of persons (while the costs may be born by those who provide the voice) and the market does not automatically extract payment from those who benefit, to reward those who bear the cost." Discuss the extent to which this is true. To the extent that it is true, are there institutional arrangements to make all those who benefit pay so as to reward those who bear the cost?

11. In his evaluation of the usefulness of the dual labour market approach in the Canadian context, David Smith (1976, p. 3) suggests that it highlights the following areas for further research: barriers to job choice

arising from restrictions to entry into many types of jobs; the effect on job choice of behavioural traits induced by the work environment and peer groups; the extent to which on-the-job training is more of a socialization process than a costly investment, and the role of discrimination in this process; analysis of types of internal labour markets created by economic organizations and the integration of this analysis with economic theory developed primarily for external labour markets. Discuss briefly how our understanding of each of these areas could be furthered by the application of dual and/or conventional labour market analysis.

REFERENCES AND FURTHER READINGS

Addison, J. and J. Burton. Wage adjustment processes: a synthetic treatment. *BJIR* 16 (July 1978) 208–223.

Alexander, A. Income, experience and the structure of internal labour markets. *QJE* 88 (February 1974) 63–85.

Barron, J. and M. Loewenstein. On employer-specific information and internal labor markets. *SEJ* 52 (October 1985) 431–445.

Bishop, C. Hospitals: from secondary to primary labour market. *IR* 16 (February 1977) 26–34.

Bosanquet, N. and P. Doeringer. Is there a dual labour market in Great Britain? *EJ* 83 (June 1973) 421–435.

Bowles, S. Unequal education and the reproduction of the social division of labour. *The Capitalist System*, R.C. Edwards, M. Reich and T.E. Weisskopf, eds. Englewood Cliffs, N.J.: Prentice-Hall, 1972.

Cain, G. The challenge of dual and radical theories of the labour market to orthodox theory. *AER Proceedings* 65 (May 1975) 16–22.

Dickens, W.T. and K. Lang. A test of dual labor market theory. *AER* 75 (December 1985) 792–805.

Doeringer, P. and M. Piore. *Internal Labour Markets and Manpower Analysis*. Lexington, Mass.: Heath, 1971.

Doeringer, P. and M. Piore. Unemployment and the "dual" labour market. *Public Interest* 38 (Winter 1975) 67–79.

Donner, A. and F. Lazar. An econometric study of segmented labour markets and the structure of unemployment: the Canadian experience. *IER* 14 (1973) 312–327.

Dunlop, J. The task of contemporary wage theory. *The Theory of Wage Determination*, J. Dunlop, ed. New York: St. Martin's Press, 1957.

Edwards, R., M. Reich and T. Weisskopf. *The Capitalist System*. Englewood Cliffs, N.J.: Prentice-Hall, 1972.

Flanagan, R. Segmented market theories and racial discrimination. *IR* 12 (October 1973) 253–273.

Freeman, R. Individual mobility and union voice in the labour market. *AER Proceedings* 66 (May 1976) 361–368.

Gintis, H. Education, technology, and the characteristics of worker productivity. *AER Proceedings* (May 1971) 266–279.

Gordon, D. *Theories of Poverty and Underemployment*. Lexington, Mass.: Heath, 1972.

Harrison, B. *Education, Training and the Urban Ghetto*. Baltimore: Johns Hopkins, 1972.

Hirschman, A. *Exit, Voice and Loyalty*. Cambridge, Mass.: Harvard University Press, 1970.

Kerr, C. The balkanization of labour markets. *Labour Mobility and Economic Opportunity*, E. Wight Bakke et al., eds. Cambridge, Mass.: M.I.T. Press, 1954.

Lester, R. Shortcomings of marginal analysis for wage-employment problems. *AER* 36 (March 1946) 63–82.

Machlup, F. Marginal analysis and empirical research. *AER* 36 (September 1946) 519–554.

Malcolmson, J. Work incentives, hierarchy and internal labor markets. *JPE* 92 (June 1984) 486–507.

McNabb, R. and G. Psacharopoulos. Further evidence on the relevance of the dual labor market hypothesis for the U.K. *JHR* 16 (Summer 1981) 442–448.

Mellow, W. Equilibration in the labor market. *SEJ* 45 (July 1978) 192–204.

Meng, R. An empirical test for labour market segmentation of males in Canada. *IR* 24 (Spring 1985) 280–287.

Merrilees, W. Labour market segmentation in Canada: an econometric approach. *CJE* 15 (August 1982) 458–473.

Miyazaki, H. The rat race and internal labour markets. *Bell Journal of Economics* 8 (Autumn 1977) 394–418.

Osberg, L., R. Muzany, R. Apostle and D. Clairmont. Job mobility, wage determination and market segmentation in the presence of sample selection bias. *CJE* 19 (May 1986) 319–346.

Osterman, P. An empirical study of labour market segmentation. *ILRR* 28 (July 1975) 508–523.

Piore, M.J. Fragments of a "sociological" theory of wages. *IRRA* (December 1972) 286–295.

Ross, A. *Trade Union Wage Policy*. Berkeley: University of California Press, 1956.

Rottenberg, S. On choice in labor markets. *ILRR* 9 (January 1956) 183–199. Comment by R. Lampman and reply, 9 (July 1956) 629–641.

Smith, David. *The Dual Labour Market Theory: A Canadian Perspective*. Kingston: Queen's University Industrial Relations Centre, 1976.

Taubman, P. and M. Wachter. Segmented labour markets. *Handbook of Labour Economics* Vol. 1. O. Ashenfelter and R. Layard (eds.). New York: Elsevier, 1986.

Thurow, L. *Poverty and Discrimination*. Washington: Brookings, 1969.

Wachtel, H. Capitalism and poverty in America: paradox or contradiction? *AER Proceedings* 62 (May 1972) 187–194.

Wachter, M. Primary and secondary labour markets: a critique of the dual approach. *BPEA* (No. 3, 1974) 637–694.

Williamson, O., M. Wachter and J. Harris. Understanding the employment relation: an analysis of idiosyncratic exchange. *Bell Journal of Economics* 16 (Spring 1975) 252–278.

Part
IV

Unions

CHAPTER

14 *Union Growth and Incidence*

The three chapters in this part examine labour market equilibrium in situations where wages, employment, and working conditions are determined by collective bargaining between employers and unions. Previous chapters discussed the nature of labour market equilibrium when both firms and workers act on an *individual* basis. In these circumstances, the individual labour supply decisions of employees and the labour demand choices of employers interact to determine wages, employment and other working conditions. In labour markets in which unions play a role, the distinguishing feature is that the conditions of employment are determined by *collective* rather than individual action. That is, the union negotiates with the employer on behalf of the workers as a group. As is the case in nonunion organizations, individual employees who are dissatisfied with wages and working conditions may quit or threaten to quit to seek employment elsewhere (the "quit threat"); however, in unionized establishments the main mechanism for bringing pressure to bear on the employer is the threat of the collective withdrawal of labour (the "strike threat").

Unions are collective organizations whose primary objective is to improve the well-being of their members. In Canada, this objective is met primarily through collective bargaining with the employer. The outcome of this process is a collective agreement specifying wages, non-wage benefits such as those relating to pensions, vacation time and health and medical expenses, and aspects of the employment relation such as procedures relating to hiring, promotion, dismissal, layoffs, overtime work, and the handling of grievances.

There are two basic types of unions. Craft unions represent workers in a particular trade or occupation; examples are found in the construction, printing, and longshoring trades. Industrial unions represent all the workers in a particular industry regardless of occupation or skill; examples are found in the automobile, steel, and forest industries.

In addition to their collective bargaining activities, unions play a role in social and political affairs. Close ties between unions and social democratic political parties are common, especially in Western Europe. In Canada the union movement provides financial and other support for the New Democratic Party. Unions also seek to influence the government in power, and accordingly have been involved in various forms of consultation and collaboration with governments and, in some cases, representatives of the business community. Although these and other political and social aspects of unions are important and deserve study, the major function of Canadian unions is to represent their members' interests in collective bargaining with employers, and it is this aspect of unions which is studied here.[1]

This chapter begins with a brief discussion of the nature and significance of unions and collective bargaining in Canada. The extent of unionization in the labour force, how this has changed over time, how it compares with other countries, and the legal framework governing unionization and collective bargaining are described. We then examine the determinants of the extent and incidence of unionization in the economy: what factors result in some groups of workers being represented by a union while other groups of workers remain unorganized? The following chapters are devoted to understanding the economic consequences of unions and collective bargaining.

UNIONS AND COLLECTIVE BARGAINING IN CANADA

For a significant fraction of the Canadian labour force, wages and other conditions of employment are determined by collective bargaining. Table 14.1 provides several measures of the quantitative significance of unions and collective bargaining in the labour market. Over time, an upward trend is evident in all these measures. Union membership as a proportion of the civilian labour force increased from about 9 percent in 1921 to over 30 percent in 1983. Union membership as a proportion of (civilian) non-agricultural paid workers — a measure which excludes from consideration the self-employed and those employed in agriculture, who are generally not eligible for unionization — has increased from 18 to 40 percent over the same period. Both these measures tend to understate the extent of union organization in the economy because not all those covered by collective agreements are union members. (As is explained below, Canadian labour legislation provides that, once certified, the union is the exclusive bargaining representative for all employees in the bargaining unit, whether or not they are union members.) As Table 14.1 indicates, in recent years about 58 percent of workers in firms with 20 or more employees are covered by collective agreements.[2]

1 For discussion of the social and political aspects of unions and collective bargaining see Anderson and Gunderson (1982), Banting (1986) and Riddell (1986).
2 Unfortunately the statistics on union membership and collective agreement coverage are not strictly comparable. The collective agreement coverage survey covers only about 40 percent of the labour force, excludes establishments with fewer than 20 employees, and, among included establishments, the survey has a higher response rate in larger enterprises. Because unions are much more common in larger enterprises, the latter two factors imply that the reported coverage of 58 percent in 1981 overstates the extent of collective bargaining.

TABLE 14.1
UNION MEMBERSHIP AND COLLECTIVE AGREEMENT COVERAGE IN CANADA, 1921-83

Year	Union Membership (000s)	Union Membership As a Percentage of Civilian Labour Force	Union Membership As a Percentage of Non-Agricultural Paid Workers	Proportion of Workers in Firms with 20 or More Employees Covered by Collective Agreements		
				Total	Non-Office	Office
1921	313	9.4	16.0			
1926	275	7.5	13.6			
1931	311	7.5	15.3			
1936	323	7.2	16.2			
1941	462	10.3	18.0			
1946	832	17.1	27.9			
1951	1029	19.7	28.4	38.9		
1956	1352	24.5	33.3	28.7		
1961	1447	22.6	31.6	47.5	62	13
1966	1736	24.5	30.7	43.5	58	14
1971	2231	26.8	33.6	51.5	65	28
1976	3042	30.6	37.3	57.4	72	37
1981	3487	30.6	37.4	58.8	73	38
1983	3563	30.6	40.0	58.6	73	38

Sources: Union membership: Canada, Department of Labour, *Labour Organization in Canada* and *Labour Gazette* (1975).
Collective agreement coverage: Canada, Department of Labour, *Working Conditions in Canadian Industry* and *Labour Gazette* (1957).

The influence of unions may extend further than is suggested by these measures of the extent of union organization or "union density." As Table 14.1 shows, the extent of unionization is much higher among non-office than office employees. The wages and benefits negotiated for production workers may set a standard for nonunion office employees in the same establishment. More generally, union agreements may influence the wages and working conditions of unorganized workers in the same industry, urban area, or region.

THE LEGAL FRAMEWORK

Union representation and collective bargaining in Canada are regulated by an elaborate legal framework. The evolution of this framework reflects the changing social attitudes toward the role of unions and collective bargaining in Canadian society, and has played a role in the increase in union organization evident in Table 14.1. In general terms, the law with respect to collective bargaining in Canada has passed through three main phases. (For a more detailed description of the evolution of Candian labour legislation see Weiler, 1986.) In the first phase, the period mostly prior to Confederation, the law discouraged collective bargaining. Judges interpreted the common law to hold that collective action by employees constituted a criminal conspiracy. There were also other criminal and civil constraints on both individual and group action by workers. In the second phase, which began in the 1870s, the law was "neutral" with respect to collective bargaining. In particular, the Trade Unions Act of 1872, amendments to criminal law, and other legislative actions removed many of the restrictions on union formation and the collective withdrawal of labour. This neutral stance lasted in Canada until the enactment in 1944 of the National War Labour Order, Order-in-Council P.C. 1003, after which labour law facilitated union formation and, in turn, encouraged the spread of collective bargaining. P.C. 1003, which was partly modelled on the National Labor Relations Act (the Wagner Act) of 1935 in the United States, provided most private sector employees with the right to union representation and collective bargaining, established certification procedures, provided a code of unfair labour practices primarily intended to prevent employers from interfering with employees' right to union representation, and established a labour relations board to administer the law. Thus, in the post-World War II period, legislation encouraged collective bargaining.

These three phases in the history of collective bargaining applied primarily to the private sector. With the passage of the Public Service Staff Relations Act (PSSRA) in 1967 at the federal level and similar acts at provincial levels, governments encouraged collective bargaining and union formation in the public sector, which was also an area of rapid growth in employment.

The Canadian labour relations policy which emerged in the 1940s had the following central features (Weiler, 1986):

(1) workers who met the statutory definition of employee had the right to join and form unions;
(2) collective bargaining rights were protected under unfair labour practices legislation, which prohibited acts by both employers and unions to discourage or interfere with the employees' prerogative to bargain collectively;
(3) a system of defining appropriate bargaining units and certifying bargaining representatives was established;
(4) once certified, the union became the exclusive bargaining representative of all employees in the bargaining unit;
(5) unions and employers were required to bargain in good faith;
(6) these rights and obligations were administered and enforced usually by a labour relations board, but in some cases in court.

This Wagner Act framework was combined with the traditional Canadian labour policy, expressed in the Industrial Disputes Investigation Act of

1907 and subsequent legislation, of regulating the use of work stoppages. These features included:

(1) compulsory postponement of strikes and lockouts, coupled with compulsory mediation and/or conciliation procedures;

(2) prohibition of strikes or lockouts during the term of the collective agreement coupled with a requirement that each collective agreement provide some alternative means for the resolution of disputes concerning the interpretation and application of the agreement;

(3) while the content of the collective agreement was left largely to the parties, Ottawa and the provinces increasingly began to require certain items to be included in collective agreements, such as a recognition clause, a no-strike/no-lockout clause, a clause providing for a peaceful mechanism to resolve disputes arising during the term of the agreement, and provision for a date of termination of the agreement.

Another important aspect of the legal framework is the division of powers between the federal and provincial governments over labour legislation. The Constitution Act, 1867, has been interpreted by the courts as implying that jurisdiction over labour relations matters rests primarily with the provinces. Federal jurisdiction is limited to about 10 percent of the labour force — federal public servants, employees of federal Crown corporations and those employed in rail, air, shipping and truck transportation, banks, broadcasting, uranium mines, and grain elevators.

FACTORS INFLUENCING UNION GROWTH AND INCIDENCE

Inspection of Table 14.1 reveals that during the past six decades union growth in Canada has been substantial but erratic. In some periods union membership declined in absolute terms (1921-31), in others it increased absolutely but declined relative to the labour force (1956-66), while in others union membership grew substantially more rapidly than the labour force (1941-46; 1966-76). The causes of union growth — both the upward trend and the variations around the trend — have long been a subject of scholarly research and debate. There are also significant cross-sectional differences in the extent of unionization — across countries, industries, regions and occupations — which call for an explanation.

Table 14.2 shows the extent of union organization in several countries. Union density in Canada is higher than in Japan and the U.S.A., but lower than in Australia and most European countries. These data also indicate that during the past two decades both union membership and employment have been growing at a relatively rapid rate in Canada. Particularly noteworthy is that in Canada union membership has been growing at a higher rate than the labour force (so that union density has been rising) while the opposite is the case in the United States. (For further discussion of these divergent trends see Meltz, 1985, Kumar, 1986, and Riddell, 1986.)

The extent of union organization in Canada varies considerably by industry, occupation, sex and region.[3] Table 14.3 shows the variation across broad industrial groups. A majority of workers in forestry, construction and transportation, communication and utilities are union members, while in mining and manufacturing a significant minority of employees belong to unions. The service sector is a picture of extremes, with almost 70 percent of public administration unionized yet very little unionization in private sector services (trade, finance, insurance and real estate). Occupational differences are also substantial. About one-half of full-time workers in blue-collar occupations (such as logging, mining, processing, assembling and repairing, construction trades, and transport equipment operating and ma-terial handling) were union members in 1981. The proportion organized was lower in white-collar occupations: managerial and professional (37 percent), clerical (29 percent), service (27 percent) and sales (9 percent). In almost all occupations the proportion of females who were union members was substantially lower than for males. Finally, there are also regional differences, with Newfoundland being the most heavily unionized prov-ince, followed by British Columbia and Quebec; Alberta and Prince Edward Island are the least unionized.

TABLE 14.2
UNION MEMBERSHIP GROWTH AND DENSITY IN SELECTED
COUNTRIES, 1961-81

Country	Membership as a Percent of Wage and Salary Earners			Average Annual Growth Rate in Union Membership
	1961	1971	1981	1961-81
Australia	59	53	56	2.4
Canada	30	31	35	4.6
Japan	34	34	35	2.2
Sweden	63	76	89	3.1
United Kingdom	43	50	58	1.1
United States	30	30	25[a]	1.7
West Germany	31	37	42	2.0

Sources: Union membership: Australia, Commonwealth Bureau of Census and
   Statistics, *Official Yearbook of the Commonwealth of Australia*; Canada,
   Department of Labour, *Labour Organizations in Canada*; Japan, Statistics
   and Information Department, *Yearbook of Labour Statistics*; Sweden,
   National Bureau of Statistics, *Statistical Abstract of Sweden*; United
   Kingdom, Department of Employment, *Employment Gazette*; United States,
   Bureau of Labor Statistics, Director of National Unions and Employee
   Associations; West Germany, Federal Republic of Germany, *Statistiches
   Jahrbuch*. Wage and salary earners: OECD, *Labour Force Statistics*.
Notes: Differences in data definitions and measurement procedures across
   countries imply that these statistics should be interpreted cautiously.
[a]1980 estimate.

3 For a more detailed discussion of the current structure and organization of unions in Canada see Kumar,
   1986, on which some of the following is based.

TABLE 14.3
UNION ORGANIZATION BY INDUSTRY, CANADA, 1981

Industry	Union Membership as a Percentage of Total Employment
Agriculture	—
Forestry	56
Mining	36
Construction	54
Manufacturing	44
Transportation, Communication and Utilities	53
Trade	9
Finance, Insurance and Real Estate	3
Public Administration	69

Source: Statistics Canada, *Corporations and Labour Unions Returns Act,* 1983.

Explaining these differences in unionization — over time and across industries, regions and occupations — is of considerable interest for its own sake. As discussed subsequently, this understanding is also important in interpreting research findings on the consequences of unions. Indeed, a central theme of recent research has been that union/nonunion status and the wage and non-wage effects of unions are jointly determined. That is, unionization may result in higher wages and improved working conditions, but also higher wages as well as other factors related to higher wages may make unionization more likely to occur.

The growth and incidence of union organization can be analysed using a demand and supply framework.[4] The demand for union representation emanates from employees and depends on the expected benefits and costs of union representation. The supply of union representation emanates from the organizing and contract administration activities of union leaders and their staff. These demand and supply forces are discussed in turn.

On the demand side the potential benefits of union representation may include higher wages and non-wage benefits, greater employment security (through protection from dismissal other than for cause) and protection from arbitrary treatment by management. Potential costs include direct costs such as union dues and time devoted to union activities, potential loss of income in the event of a work stoppage, and costs associated with the employer's actions, should the employer be willing and/or able to attempt to discourage unionization. Several factors may be net benefits or costs depending on the individual employee's circumstances. Higher wages will benefit those who retain union jobs but may reduce employment opportunities of others. Unions typically alter procedures for determining

---

4 This approach can be traced to Berkowitz (1954), Ashenfelter and Pencavel (1969) and Pencavel (1971). There is also a substantial institutional and historical literature on the causes of union growth. For a summary and assessment of this literature see Blum (1968).

promotions and layoffs — usually placing more emphasis on seniority — which will enhance some workers' opportunities and reduce those of others.

On the supply side, administering the contracts covering existing union members and organizing new (or previously nonunion) workplaces are costly activities. Unions need to allocate their scarce resources to the activities that are expected to yield the greatest return, measured in terms of the union's objectives. Success in organizing new workplaces and in maintaining membership and union representation in existing organizations will depend on a variety of factors including the resources devoted to contract administration and organizing drives, the activities of employers, and the economic and policy environment.

This demand and supply framework provides a useful conceptual model for analysing the extent of union organization at a point in time and changes in unionization over time. The central concept is that the extent of unionization depends on the choices made by employees, the organizational and contract administration activities of union leaders, and the actions of employers. Those enterprises in which a majority of the employees perceive substantial net benefits from being represented by a union and in which the actions of the employer will not significantly reduce these benefits will have a high demand for unionization, and vice-versa. The supply of union organizational and contract administration effort will be high to those enterprises in which the per-worker cost of organization and representation is low. The interaction of these demand and supply forces determines an equilibrium extent of union organization at a point of time. Some enterprises will be organized while others — because of either low demand or high organizational costs — will remain unorganized. Changes over time in the factors influencing demand and supply will result in changes in union density.

Empirical Evidence

This demand and supply framework was used as the basis for econometric analyses of union growth in the United States by Ashenfelter and Pencavel (1969) and the United Kingdom by Pencavel (1971). Subsequently, Bain and Elsheikh (1976a) carried out an extensive econometric study of union growth in Australia, Sweden, Great Britain, and the United States. Empirical studies by Swidinsky (1974), Bain and Elsheikh (1976b), Abbott (1982) and Kumar and Dow (1983) have applied and extended this approach in the Canadian setting. There have also been a number of U.S. and U.K. studies of the cross-sectional incidence of unionization according to such factors as industry, enterprise and personal characteristics, region, and legislative jurisdiction. Although this literature will not be reviewed in detail here, the main findings and their consistency with the demand and supply framework are briefly discussed.

Several factors suggested by the demand and supply framework have been investigated in empirical studies:

Social attitudes towards unions and collective bargaining

Both the receptiveness of employees to union representation and the resistance of employers may be affected by the prevailing attitudes regarding the role of unions and collective bargaining in society, a factor which is, however, difficult to measure. In their U.S. study, Ashenfelter and Pencavel (1969) find that the percentage of Democrats in the House, a measure of pro-union sentiment, has a significant effect on U.S. union growth. Because society's attitudes toward unions tend to be reflected in labour legislation and its administration, measures of the legal regime (discussed below) capture social attitudes to some degree.

The legislative framework governing unionization and collective bargaining

Legislation governing the right of workers to act collectively and the machinery for administering and enforcing these rights are likely to exert an important influence on the demand for and supply of union representation. However, it must be recognized that labour relations legislation and its administration themselves reflect certain unobservable factors such as society's attitudes toward unions; in the absence of good measures of social attitudes, it will be difficult to determine the independent impact of the legislation. Further, union growth and a legislative environment that is conducive to union growth both may be joint manifestations of underlying societal attitudes. Without favourable attitudes, legislation may not have an independent influence.

The changes in the Canadian legislative framework described earlier have lowered the cost to employees of collective action and have increasingly restricted the employer's ability to attempt to discourage unionization. The former increases the demand for unions by raising the net benefits to workers of union representation; the latter increases the supply by lowering the costs of organizing and representing workers. The legislative changes are therefore predicted to have encouraged union growth. Although this trend in labour legislation and its administration has occurred gradually over time, particularly important changes took place in the 1870s (e.g. the Trade Unions Act of 1872), the early 1900s (the Industrial Disputes Investigation Act of 1907 contained an implicit form of union recognition by banning strikes or lockouts over recognition issues), the 1940s (the enactment of P.C. 1003 gave workers the right to form and join unions and made illegal a number of employer practices previously used to discourage collective bargaining; similar legislation was enacted in most provinces following the Second World War and the end of federal emergency powers), and in the 1960s (the extension to public sector employees of the right to collective bargaining).

Examination of Table 14.1 suggests that the changes in the legislative framework around 1944 and 1967 have had a positive impact on union growth in Canada. Econometric studies by Abbott (1982) and Kumar and Dow (1983) support the view that labour legislation has had a significant effect on the union growth process. In addition, the divergent patterns of union growth in Canada and the United States since the 1960s has been argued to be associated to a considerable extent with differences between the two countries in labour relations legislation and its enforcement (Weiler, 1983, 1984; Meltz, 1985).

Other economic and social legislation

The extent of union organization may also be affected by other economic and social legislation, although the direction of the effect is ambiguous. The setting (and raising) of employment standards such as those with respect to minimum wages, overtime premiums, statutory holidays, workplace health and safety, notice of layoff, and severance pay may narrow the gap in wages and working conditions between organized and unorganized workers, thus reducing the demand for unionization. On the other hand, such policies may have aided union growth by reducing competition from the lower labour costs that otherwise would have prevailed in the nonunion sector in the absence of extending such benefits to unorganized workers through employment standards. Social programs such as those respecting public pensions, medical and health care, and unemployment insurance may also have offsetting effects. Neumann and Rissman (1984) have suggested that the provision of certain welfare benefits by governments in the United States accounts for some of the decline in union strength there. In Canada, however, union density rose during the postwar period, an era of rapid expansion of the welfare state and significant increases in employment standards.

Aggregate economic conditions

Early institutional economists such as Commons (1918) emphasized the role of the business cycle in the growth of unions. Subsequent econometric studies have investigated the influence of such variables as the unemployment rate, the rate of growth of employment that is eligible for unionization, and the rate of price inflation. The general finding that the rate of union growth varies directly with the rate of growth of employment that is eligible for unionization is consistent with several hypotheses, including: (1) employer resistance to union formation is lowest when product demand is high and the labour market is tight, and (2) the ability of unions to secure wage and benefit increases (and thus the perceived net benefits of being represented by a union) is highest when there is excess labour demand. However, even in the absence of these cyclical effects, a positive relationship between union growth and growth in employment eligible for unionization is expected. Employment growth in existing organized enterprises will result in an increase in the unionized labour force unless the employees decide to decertify the union. In addition, some new enterprises and their employees will have characteristics (discussed below) which make them likely to become organized.

Although the above reasons suggest that union growth will be pro-cyclical in nature, the experience of the Great Depression — during and subsequent to which the union movement displayed strong growth, especially in the United States — led Ashenfelter and Pencavel (1969) to hypothesize that severe business contractions will raise worker discontent which in turn will be a spur to unionization, perhaps with a lag. Although U.S. studies generally find that union growth is positively related to the severity of past recessions, Canadian evidence on this issue is mixed (Abbott, 1982; Kumar and Dow, 1983).

Time series studies also generally find that union growth varies directly with the rate of price inflation. This finding is consistent with the hypothesis that unions are viewed by workers as an effective vehicle for maintaining real wages.

Industry and enterprise characteristics

As Table 14.3 shows, there are substantial differences across industries in the extent of union organization. Cross-sectional studies carried out in the United States and Great Britain have found that union density tends to be higher in industries with larger firms or establishments, in more concentrated industries, in industries with more capital-intensive production processes and in industries with more hazardous jobs (Ashenfelter and Johnson, 1972; Lee, 1978; Bain and Elsheikh, 1979; Duncan and Stafford, 1980; Hirsch, 1982; Leigh, 1982; Hirsch and Berger, 1984).

These results can be interpreted using the demand-supply framework. The demand for union representation is likely to be higher in larger establishments because individual action becomes less effective the larger the group; and the need for formal work rules, communications, and grievance procedures is greater in larger organizations. In addition, the per-worker cost of union organizing is lower in larger establishments. Industries with hazardous jobs are also likely to be characterized by greater demand for a collective "voice" to represent workers' interests in the internal regulation of workplace health and safety.

Capital intensity may be associated with several effects. As with job hazards, capital-intensive production processes may entail greater need for a collective voice relating to the organization and flow of work — aspects such as the speed of assembly lines, scheduling of shifts, and overtime regulations. In addition, high capital intensity implies that labour costs are a small fraction of total costs. This tends to make labour demand more inelastic and thus increases the potential wage gains from unionization.

The finding that more concentrated industries tend to be more heavily unionized may reflect several factors. Concentrated industries typically have significant barriers to entry; there is thus less threat of nonunion competition in the form of new entrants. In addition, unions may enable workers to share in the excess profits or rents earned by the established firms. Organizing costs may also be lower in more concentrated industries.

Because of these differences across industries in the extent of union organization, changes over time in the economy's industrial structure will be accompanied by changes in union density, other things equal. In Canada and most other industrialized countries, significant changes in industrial structure have occurred in the postwar period: employment has grown rapidly in services-producing industries and the share of service sector employment incrased substantially; goods-producing industries (manufacturing and construction) have experienced slower employment growth and a decline in the share of total employment; employment in agriculture both declined absolutely and relative to the share of total employment; and other primary industries (mining, forestry, fishing and trapping) have experienced positive employment growth but declining shares of total employment.

These trends in the industrial composition of employment have had offsetting effects on union growth. Several factors tend to increase union density: the decline in employment in agriculture, an industry with little unionization; and the rapid growth in employment in public administration (employees of the federal, provincial, and municipal governments), a sector which has become extensively unionized since the mid-1960s. However, other changes in industrial structure have tended to reduce the extent of union organization in the economy: declining employment shares in manufacturing, mining, and forestry, sectors with above average unionization; and increases in the share of employment in trade, finance, insurance, real estate, and other private sector services, industries with low degrees of unionization.

Personal characteristics

A number of personal characteristics affect the propensity to be a union member or to be represented by a union. Part-time workers and workers with intermittent labour force attachment are less likely to be organized. For these individuals, the net benefits of union representation — especially in the form of seniority provisions, pension benefits and other forms of deferred compensation — are lower than is the case with full-time workers and employees with a permanent labour force attachment. The costs of organizing part-time workers and workers with intermittent labour force attachments may also be high. Largely because they are more likely to work part-time and have tended to have less permanent attachment to the labour force, women are less likely to be represented by a union than men.

As noted earlier, the extent of union organization is much higher among blue-collar than white-collar workers. Blue-collar workers are more likely to demand union representation because of less identification with management and possibly greater need for a collective voice in the determination of working conditions.

Age and experience have also been found to be related to the propensity to be organized in a number of studies (Antos, Chandler and Mallow, 1980; Farber and Saks, 1980; Duncan and Stafford, 1980; Hirsch and Berger, 1984). Although there are some conflicting results, this relationship appears to be concave; that is, the propensity to choose union representation at first increases, reaches a maximum, and subsequently decreases with age and/or experience. This result is consistent with the view (discussed in detail below) that, when members' preferences differ according to some characteristic like age, unions tend to represent most closely the preferences of members in the middle of the distribution of preferences (i.e. the median member).

An individual's position in the earnings distribution may also affect the net benefits of being represented by a union. As explained subsequently, unions tend to increase the wages of those at the lower end of the wage distribution by a relatively large amount and those in the upper tail of the wage distribution by a relatively small amount. Thus individuals whose earnings would be above average in the absence of a union are less likely to favour union representation.

Summary

In summary, the growth of unions over time and the extent of union organization across industries, regions, occupations, and employee characteristics are systematically related to a number of economic, social, and legal variables. These observed relationships are generally consistent with the demand-supply framework, which appears to provide a valuable conceptual device for understanding the growth and incidence of unions.

QUESTIONS

1. Account for the differential growth of unionization between Canada and the United States in recent years.
2. "Differential legislative structures may account for some of the differential union growth between Canada and the U.S.; however, that begs the question of why the legislative structures are different. That is, legislation should be regarded as an endogenous variable and its existence explained." Discuss.
3. Discuss differences in the concepts of union density based on union membership and the proportion of the workforce that is covered by a collective agreement. What accounts for the differences in the magnitude in Canada? Which of the two best measures the significance of unions in the determination of wages and working conditions?
4. Outline the main legislative initiatives in Canada that have facilitated the development of unionization and collective bargaining.
5. "Any theory of union growth must be able to explain not only its long-run trend and short-run cyclical variation, but also why unionization varies across countries and across industries, regions and occupations within a country." Discuss.
6. Given the determinants of unionization, discuss the future prospects for union growth in Canada.
7. The extent of unionization in Canada varies from one province to another. Discuss the factors which account for these differences.
8. Discuss the general factors that would explain the differences in union density across industries shown in Table 14.3.

9. Ashenfelter and Pencavel (1969) carry out an econometric analysis of the determinants of union growth in the U.S. between 1900 and 1960. Would their estimated equation over-predict, accurately predict or under-predict the subsequent union growth in the U.S.? If you believe their equation would under- or over-predict the subsequent growth, what variable or variables may be omitted?

REFERENCES

Abbott, M.G. An Econometric Model of Trade Union Membership Growth in Canada, 1925-1966. Princeton University, Industrial Relations Section, Working Paper 154, September 1982.

Abowd, J.M. and H.S. Farber. Job Queues and the Union Status of Workers. ILRR 35 (April, 1982) 354-367.

Anderson, J. and M. Gunderson (eds.). Union-Management Relations in Canada. Don Mills, Ontario: Addison-Wesley, 1982.

Antos, J.R., M. Chandler and W. Mellow. Sex Differences in Union Membership. ILRR 33 (January 1980) 162-169.

Ashenfelter, O. and G.E. Johnson. Unionism, Relative Wages and Labor Quality in U.S. Manufacturing Industries. IER 13 (October 1972) 488-508.

Ashenfelter, O. and J.H. Pencavel. American Trade Union Growth: 1900-1960. QJE 83 (August 1969) 434-448.

Bain, G.S. and F. Elsheikh. Union Growth and the Business Cycle: An Econometric Analysis. Oxford: Blackwell, 1976a.

Bain, G.S. and F. Elsheikh. Trade Union Growth in Canada: A Comment. RI/IR 31 (No. 3, 1976b) 482-490.

Bain, G.S. and F. Elsheikh. An Inter-Industry Analysis of Unionisation in Britain. BJIR 17 (July 1979) 137-157.

Banting, K.G. (ed.). The State and Economic Interests. Toronto: Royal Commission on the Economic Union and Development Prospects for Canada and University of Toronto Press, 1986.

Berkowitz, M. The Economics of Trade Union Organization and Administration. ILRR 7 (July 1954) 575-592.

Bloch, F. The endogeneity of union membership in a pay model. IER 23 (October 1982) 695-676.

Blum, A.A. Why Unions Grow. Labor History 9 (Winter 1968) 39-72.

Commons, J.E. et al. History of Labor in the United States, I. New York: Macmillan, 1918.

Duncan, G. and D. Leigh. The endogeneity of union status: an empirical test. JOLE 3 (July 1985) 385-402.

Duncan, G. and F. Stafford. Do union members receive compensating wage differentials? AER 70 (June 1980) 335-371.

Farber, H.S. The determination of the union status of workers. Econometrica 51 (September 1983) 1417-1438.

Farber, H.S. Right-to-work laws and the extent of unionization. JOLE 2 (July 1984) 319-352.

Farber, H. and D. Saks. Why workers want unions: the role of relative wages and job characteristics. JPE 88 (April 1980) 349-369.

Hirsch, B.T. The interindustry structure of unionism, earnings, and earnings dispersion. ILRR 36 (October 1982) 22-39.

Hirsch, B.T. and M.C. Berger. Union membership determination and industry characteristics. *SEJ* 50 (January 1984) 665-679.

Kokkelenberg, E.C. and D.R. Sockell. Union membership in the United States, 1973-1981. *ILRR* 38 (July 1985) 497-543.

Kumar, P. Union Growth in Canada: Retrospect and Prospect. *Canadian Labour Relations*, W.C. Riddell (ed.). Toronto: Royal Commission on the Economic Union and Development Prospects for Canada and University of Toronto Press, 1986.

Kumar, P. and B. Dow. Econometric Modelling of Union Membership Growth in Canada, 1935-1981. Queen's University, Industrial Relations Centre, 1983.

Lee, Lung-Fei. Unionism and wage rates: a simultaneous equations model, with qualitative and limited dependent variables. *IER* 19 (June 1978) 415-434.

Leigh, J.P. Are unionized blue collar jobs more hazardous than nonunionized blue collar jobs? *JLR* 3 (Summer 1982) 349-357.

Meltz, N. Labour Movements in Canada and the United States: Are They Really That Different? *Challenges and Choices Facing American Labor*, T. Kochan (ed.). Cambridge, Mass.: MIT Press, 1985.

Neumann, G.R. and E.R. Rissman. Where have all the union members gone? *Journal of Labor Economics* 2 (April, 1984) 175-192.

Pencavel, J.H. The demand for union services: an exercise. *ILRR* 24 (January 1971) 180-190.

Riddell, W.C. (ed.). *Labour-Management Cooperation in Canada*. Toronto: Royal Commission on the Economic Union and Development Prospects for Canada and University of Toronto Press, 1986.

Sheflin, N., L. Troy and C.T. Koeller. Structural stability in models of American trade union growth. *QJE* 96 (February 1981) 77-88.

Swidinsky, R. Trade union growth in Canada: 1911-1970. *RI/IR* 29 (No. 3, 1974) 435-450.

Weiler, J. The Role of Law in Labour Relations. *Labour Law and Urban Law in Canada*, I. Bernier and A. Lajoie (eds.). Toronto: Royal Commission on the Economic Union and Development Prospects for Canada and University of Toronto Press, 1986.

Weiler, P. Striking a new balance: freedom of contract and the prospect for union representation. *Harvard Law Review* 98 (December 1984) 351-420.

Weiler, P. Promises to Keep: Securing workers' rights to self-organization under the NLRA. *Harvard Law Review* 96 (June 1983) 1769-1829.

15 Union Preferences, Efficient Contracts and Bargaining Theory*

The previous chapter was concerned with explaining which organizations are unionized and which are nonunion. We now turn to the behavioural implications of unionization and collective bargaining. In order to understand and predict the consequences of collective bargaining we begin by examining union objectives and the constraints unions face in attempting to achieve those objectives. Then we examine the firm's objectives and constraints and how the two parties interact to determine collective bargaining outcomes. Much of this chapter focuses on the determination of wages and employment. Various non-wage aspects of employment — such as grievance procedures, seniority provisions, workplace health and safety and fringe benefits — are discussed in the next chapter.

THEORY OF UNION BEHAVIOUR

The economic analysis of firms and households begins from the assumption that the decision maker maximizes an objective function subject to the constraints imposed on the agent by the economic environment. Private sector firms are usually assumed to maximize profits subject to the production function (which summarizes the technical possibilities available to the firm), the demand conditions in the product markets, and the supply conditions in the markets for inputs. This is the theory that underlies the demand for labour discussed in Part II of this book. It is a theory rich in testable implications, and one which has generally been found to accord with the available evidence. Similarly, the household is assumed to maximize utility (which depends on the quantities consumed of various goods, including leisure) subject to the budget constraint (which depends on the prices of goods and the wage rate). This is the theory that underlies the demand for goods and services in product markets and the theory of labour supply discussed in Part I of this book. This theory is also rich in testable implications, and has generally been found to be consistent with the evidence on household behaviour.

Economists have generally agreed that an understanding of union behaviour and its consequences must likewise begin with a theory of union objectives. The union can then be assumed to maximize its objective or utility function subject to the constraints imposed on the union and its members by the economic environment. However, our ability to characterize union preferences has long been and remains controversial. The major aspects of this controversy were debated several decades ago by Dunlop (1944) and Ross (1948). Dunlop advocated an "economic" approach in which the union is modelled as attempting to maximize a well-defined objective function subject to labour market constraints. (The specific objective function suggested by Dunlop is discussed below). Ross criticized this approach and argued that union decision making can only be understood by treating the union as a political institution. Although this debate has not been fully resolved, the modern approach to union behaviour recognizes some merit in both positions in that the union is modelled as attempting to maximize a well-defined objective function but attention is paid to the political nature of union decision making.

UNION OBJECTIVES

Unions are collective organizations whose leaders represent members of the bargaining unit — the rank-and-file — in collective bargaining with the firm. Union objectives refer to the goals of the organization. These need not be identical to the objectives of the individual members or to those of the union leaders. Three factors influence the relationship among the preferences of the members, the union leaders and those of the union as a whole: (1) the information available to the rank-and-file about the available options, (2) the nature of the union's political decision-making process, and (3) the degree of homogeneity of the individual members' preferences. If the rank-and-file are well-informed and the union's decision-making processes are highly democratic, then the union leaders will make choices that have the support of a majority of the members. (Otherwise they will be quickly replaced). In these circumstances, the union's objectives are those which a majority of the rank-and-file would favour. However, asymmetric information or imperfectly democratic decision-making processes may allow the union leaders to pursue their own objectives to some degree. In these circumstances the objectives of the members and those pursued by the union may differ.

The degree of homogeneity of individual members' preferences is another important factor. If the rank-and-file have very similar preferences it will be easy for the union leaders to determine the group's preferred choices. However, if preferences differ significantly across individuals or groups of individuals the task of the union leaders is more difficult and selecting an option that will be supported by a majority may require considerable skill and judgement.

In our discussion of union preferences we will initially examine the simplest case in which members' preferences are homogeneous and information flows and union decision-making processes are such that union leaders are not able to pursue their own objectives. The implications of relaxing these assumptions will be examined subsequently.

Although various union objectives have been postulated, most involve two key aspects — the wages and employment of union members (abstracting from the various non-wage aspects of working conditions for the moment). This suggests a union objective or utility function whereby utility is a positive function of both the wage rate and the employment of union members (and which may also depend on other variables as discussed below). Combinations of the wage rate and employment which are equally satisfactory to the union — the union's indifference or iso-utility curves — must be downward sloping in wage-employment space because a higher wage is needed to compensate for lower employment and vice versa. Furthermore, it is plausible to hypothesize that union preferences display a diminishing marginal rate of substitution between wages and employment; that is, holding utility constant, the union will be less willing to accept a wage reduction in return for a given increase in employment the higher the level of employment, and vice versa. This implies that the union utility function is quasi-concave; i.e., that the indifference curves have the convex shape displayed in Figure 15-1.

Union objectives are likely to depend on several additional variables. One is the overall price level, or the cost of living. Clearly what matters to the workers (and thus to the union leaders) is the real wage rate. A 10 percent increase (or decrease) in the nominal wage rate accompanied by a 10 percent increase (or decrease) in the price level leaves the workers' real income and therefore consumption and leisure possibilities unchanged. Union utility is also likely to depend on the alternative wage (i.e. the wage rate that union members could earn if employed elsewhere). Few workers will be willing to bear the costs of union representation (union dues and

Figure 15.1   Union Objectives and Constraints

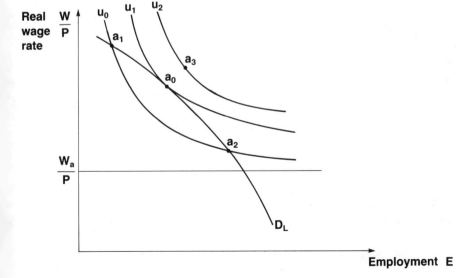

other costs discussed earlier) unless their compensation is equal to or greater than that available elsewhere for comparable work. For this reason the alternative (real) wage is shown as a lower bound to the union's indifference curves in Figure 15-1.

Summarizing this discussion, the union's objective function can be written:[1]

$$u(\cdot) = u(w, E; w_a) \tag{15.1}$$

where $u(\cdot)$ is union utility

w is the real wage rate; i.e. $w = \dfrac{W}{P}$ where W is the nominal wage

w_a is the alternative real wage

P is the aggregate price level

and E is the number of union members employed.

The utility function $u(\cdot)$ is hypothesized to have the following properties:

(P1) increasing in w and E, i.e. $u_w > 0$, $u_E > 0$, where the subscript denotes a partial derivative;

(P2) homogeneous of degree zero in W, W_a and P; i.e. if each of W, W_a and P changes by the same proportion union utility is unchanged;

(P3) quasi-concave in w and E; i.e. the marginal rate of substitution between w and E is decreasing.

The alternative wage has two effects which work in opposite directions. Increases in w_a make the union members better off because they will be able to earn more income should they be temporarily or permanently laid off from the union job. For this reason we would expect $u(\cdot)$ to be increasing in w_a. However, increases in w_a raise the benchmark wage needed to maintain the relative attractiveness of the union job. In this sense *union* utility is decreasing in w_a (holding w and E constant).

In using the term "employment" we have not distinguished between hours worked and number of employees. Implicitly hours worked are held constant, so that employment refers to the number of workers. This assumption is innocuous at this stage, but needs to be relaxed when examining issues such as work-sharing versus layoffs in response to temporary reductions in demand. Also, we have not discussed how the size of the union membership is determined. Rather, we have taken union membership as exogenously determined and have examined the members' preferences regarding wages and employment given the membership size. More generally, however, membership size will matter to both the union leadership and the existing union members — the former because a larger membership implies more dues revenue and possibly more power and prestige and the latter because a larger membership may imply reduced employment op-

---

1 In writing the utility function (15.1) we have distinguished between the arguments of the function over which the union exercises some choice (w and E) and those which are exogenously determined (w_a).

portunities, depending on how scarce jobs are rationed when employment demand is insufficient. The joint determination of membership size and union preferences with respect to wages and employment raises some complex issues which are examined subsequently. In the meantime, then, we take union membership as exogenously determined.

Some special cases

As noted earlier, various union objective functions have been suggested in the literature on union behaviour. Several of these are special cases of the utility function specified in equation (15.1) above; and examining these may increase our understanding of union objectives.

Maximize the wage rate W

This would imply that the union places no weight on employment; i.e. that the indifference curves are horizontal straight lines as shown in Figure 15-2(a). Although this may seem implausible, the notion that, in negotiating wages, unions do not take into account the employment consequences of higher wages has a long tradition including the influential work of Ross (1948), and is often stated by union leaders today.

Maximize employment E

This is the opposite extreme of the previous objective, and implies indifference curves which are vertical straight lines as shown in Figure 15-2(b).

Maximize the (real) wage bill wE

This objective, proposed by Dunlop (1944), implies that the indifference curves are rectangular hyperbolae as shown in Figure 15-2(c). (wE = a constant is the equation of a rectangular hyperbola). It has the advantage that the union attaches weight to both wages and employment. The wage bill is, of course, total labour income. It may appear plausible that union members would attempt to maximize their total income, especially if there is some mechanism for sharing the income between employed and unemployed members. The main defect of this objective function is that it disregards the alternative wage; indeed it implies that the union may be willing to allow the wage to fall below W_a in exchange for higher employment.[2]

Maximize (real) economic rent $(w - w_a)E$

This objective is analogous to profit-maximization for a monopolist; the alternative wage is the opportunity cost to each union member so economic rent is analogous to total revenue (wE) minus total cost ($w_a E$). In this case the indifference curves are rectangular hyperbolae with respect to the new origin (w_a, O), as shown in Figure 15-2(d).

This objective is probably the most plausible of the group, in that it hypothesizes that the union members seek to maximize their "total return,"

---

2 To avoid this difficulty, Dunlop (1944) suggested that the union maximize the wage bill subject to a "membership function" which shows the wage rate needed to attract a given number of union members. The membership function is analogous to a labour supply function.

Figure 15.2 Union Objectives: Some Special Cases

(a) Maximize wage rate

(b) Maximize employment

(c) Maximize wage bill

(d) Maximize economic rent

given what they could earn elsewhere. Again, the objective is most plausible when there is some mechanism for sharing the income between employed and unemployed union members.

Union preferences: an example

Under certain conditions an explicit union objective function can be derived. One formulation of union preferences that has been widely used recently is based on the following assumptions:

(A1) Union members have identical preferences $u(w)$ where $u(\cdot)$ is the individual member's utility function and w is the real wage.

(A2) The size of the union membership M is exogenously determined.

(A3) If $E < M$ (i.e. not all union members are employed in union jobs), layoffs are determined by random draw.

(A4) Those members (temporarily) laid off from their union job can obtain employment (or unemployment insurance benefits) at the alternate real wage w_a.

Under these assumptions, the expected utility of each union member is given by:

$$U(w, E; w_a) = \frac{E}{M} u(w) + (1 - \frac{E}{M}) u(w_a) \tag{15.2}$$

where $\quad \dfrac{E}{M}$ = probability of being employed in a union job

$\qquad u(w)$ = utility if employed in a union job at wage w

$\qquad 1 - \dfrac{E}{M}$ = probability of being laid off from the union job

$\qquad u(w_a)$ = utility when laid off

Because each union member's expected utility is given by (15.2), the union can be assumed to maximize the expected utility of a typical member; i.e. (15.2) is the union's objective function in these circumstances.

This union objective function has the properties discussed previously:

(P1) Increasing in w and E. Note that it is also increasing in w_a.

(P2) Homogeneous of degree zero in W, W_a, and P.

(P3) Quasi-concave in w and E.

Proof of P1 and P2 is straightforward. To check P3, note that the slope of an indifference curve is given by

$$\frac{dw}{dE} = - \frac{[u(w) - u(w_a)]}{u'(w) \cdot E} < 0 \tag{15.3}$$

Thus $\dfrac{d^2w}{dE^2} > 0$, so the union's preferences exhibit diminishing marginal rate of substitution between wages and employment.

As noted by Oswald (1982), the union objective function (15.2) can also be justified by an alternative set of assumptions which do not require the assumption that layoffs are randomly determined. (Layoffs are typically in reverse order of seniority in union settings; thus the random layoffs assumption is questionable). Specifically, if the union has utilitarian preferences (i.e. the union maximizes the sum of the individual member's utilities) then under the assumptions A1, A2 and A4 above the union objective function is given by

$$U^*(w, E; w_a) = E u(w) + (M - E) u(w_a) \tag{15.4}$$

Note that the only difference between (15.2) and (15.4) is the size of the union membership M which appears in the denominator of (15.2). Since M is exogenously determined, (15.4) is equivalent to (15.2). That is, maximizing $U^*(\cdot)$ will yield identical choices of w and E as maximizing $U(\cdot)$.

UNION PREFERENCES: SOME ADDITIONAL CONSIDERATIONS

The task of deriving union objectives from the preferences of the constituent members is relatively straightforward under the simplifying conditions assumed above: (1) members' preferences are homogeneous, (2) union leaders are constrained by democratic decision-making processes and the availability of information from pursuing their own objectives and (3) union membership is exogenously determined. Relaxing these assumptions raises a number of considerations which are at the forefront of current research on the economics of union behaviour.

Heterogeneous preferences

The preferences of individual union members may differ for a variety of reasons. The union may represent several groups of employees with different occupations or skills. Industrial unions often contain highly skilled employees (usually a minority) in addition to semi-skilled and unskilled workers. Alternatively, workers performing similar jobs may differ according to a number of personal characteristics such as age, seniority, marital status, and alternative employment opportunities. Individual preferences may depend in a systematic way on these characteristics. For example, older workers may desire a greater emphasis on pensions and other forms of deferred compensation and less emphasis on current earnings in the total compensation package. Those with good alternative employment opportunities (high w_a's) may prefer a higher union wage than those with limited opportunities, for given levels of employment security. If layoffs take place in accordance with seniority, more senior workers may wish to place more emphasis on wages and less emphasis on employment in union objectives. Clearly these sources of heterogeneity may be important in particular settings and the economic analysis of union behaviour should be able to account for their implications.

The conditions under which heterogeneous individual preferences can be aggregated into a group or social objective function is a central issue in the theory of public choice. One well-known result is the median voter model which states that when choices over a single variable are made in a democratic fashion (i.e. by voting among alternatives) then under certain conditions the group's preferences will be identical to those of the median voter. The reason is that the outcome preferred by the median voter will defeat all others in a sequence of pairwise elections. In the union context this result implies that if, for example, the members' preferences with respect to the wage rate depend on the worker's seniority, the union's objective function will be that of the member with the median seniority (i.e. that individual for whom half the members are more senior and half the members are less senior).

The conditions under which the median voter model holds are fairly stringent: (1) preferences must be defined over a single variable (e.g. the wage in the union setting) and (2) utility as a function of this variable must be single-peaked (i.e. attain a single global maximum, with no local maxima). The second condition will hold if the members' utility functions are concave, a common assumption in economic analysis under uncertainty. However, the first condition is more problematic in that it states that, with heterogeneous members, union preferences over multiple objectives (wages, employment, non-wage benefits, working conditions) cannot be derived from the assumption of pairwise voting among alternatives except under very special (and generally implausible) conditions. This "single issue" condition does not rule out deriving a union objective function over wages in which each member takes into account the employment consequences of their preferred wage (e.g. by having the firm choose employment given the wage and realized demand conditions). This case has been analysed by Blair and Crawford (1984). However, the single issue condition does raise questions about the existence of a union objective function defined over both wages and employment when members' preferences are heterogeneous.

When the above conditions do not hold, a voting equilibrium will generally not exist; i.e., no single set of outcomes will defeat all others in a sequence of pairwise elections. In these circumstances, the organization's choice will depend on factors such as the order in which alternatives are presented for voting.

Clearly the assumptions of the median voter model do not apply precisely in the union setting. Unions typically do not choose among alternatives by conducting a sequence of pairwise votes. Most choices are made by union leaders who are elected periodically by the membership. In addition, the union leaders often face tradeoffs among several alternatives such as wages, non-wage benefits, and employment. Nonetheless when union members' preferences are heterogeneous the median voter model may predict union behaviour reasonably well. Union leaders wishing to remain in office will adopt positions that a majority of the membership support. When the members can be ordered by a preference-related factor such as age or seniority the choices of the median member, because of their central position in the distribution of preferences, may be more likely to receive majority support than any other set of choices.

Union leaders vs. union members

Unions, like societies, generally do not make choices in a fully democratic fashion in the sense of conducting a referendum each time a decision must be made. Rather, union leaders are elected to implement policy and their position of authority may allow them to pursue their own interests to some extent. Furthermore, because they specialize in contract administration and collective bargaining with the employer, union leaders generally have greater access than members to information regarding the feasible options. In addition, the information that is received by the rank-and-file can be filtered to some degree by the leadership.

These observations suggest that union leaders may be able to pursue their own interests — such as maximizing dues revenue, expanding the union's membership and influence, and raising their own personal income. Nonetheless, the desire to remain in office (and perhaps other considerations) does constrain the leaders from deviating too far from the wishes of the membership. How binding these constraints are may well vary according to individual circumstances. A theory of union preferences based solely on the wishes of the members may not be able to account for all aspects of union behaviour in all settings. Nonetheless, it may provide a good approximation to observed behaviour.

Union membership and union objectives

Changes in union membership may alter union preferences. For example if employment in the industry or firm is expanding rapidly, not only will membership size increase but the age and seniority of the median member will probably fall. The union's objectives, according to the median voter model, will adjust to reflect the wishes of the younger, less senior worker. The opposite is likely to occur in declining sectors.

In formulating wage policy, the current union membership also influences the size of future membership and thus future union preferences. If the union pursues a high-wage policy, future membership will be reduced as employers substitute capital for labour and consumers substitute less expensive products. Thus union preferences may not be stable over time, but may depend on the wage policies adopted. The conditions under which membership will tend to grow or shrink remains an interesting area for future research.

UNION CONSTRAINTS

The union cannot choose whatever wage and employment outcomes it desires, but most negotiate with the firm and must also take into account the consequences for its members of the outcomes of these negotiations. Initially we will assume that the two parties negotiate over the wage rate, leaving the firm free to choose the level of employment at whatever wage rate is agreed upon by collective bargaining. (The possibility of negotiating over both wages and employment is discussed subsequently.) In these circumstances, the firm will choose the level of employment that maximizes profits given the negotiated wage; i.e. will choose employment according to the labour demand curve.[3] It follows that when the firm can unilaterally determine employment the union is constrained by the firm's labour de-

---

3 In the public and non-profit sectors the labour demand curve is derived under different assumptions about the organization's objective; e.g., cost minimization. In these circumstances the demand curve shows the cost-minimizing level of employment for each wage rate.

mand curve. That is, the firm's labour demand curve is analogous to a budget constraint for the utility-maximizing union.

In this situation, the union's preferred wage-employment outcome is the point a_O in Figure 15-1, where the iso-utility curve u_1 is tangent to the labour demand curve. Wage-employment combinations such as a_1 and a_2 are attainable but the union prefers a_O to a_1 and a_2. Outcomes such as a_3 are not attainable if the firm can choose employment.

The firm will prefer wage-employment outcomes at which profits (π) are higher to those at which profits are lower. The firm's iso-profit curves — combinations of wage rates and employment which yield equal profits — are shown in Figure 15-3. Note that lower curves imply higher profits; that is, $\pi_3 > \pi_2 > \pi_1 > \pi_O$. This is so, because for any given level of employment, say E^*, profits are higher when wages are lower, other things equal.

Each curve attains a maximum at the point at which the iso-profit curve and the demand for labour curve intersect. This is so because if we fix the wage at, say, w^*, then profits must be highest at c because D^L shows the profit-maximizing quantity of E at each wage. Thus, as the firm increases employment from e to f to c, π must increase (i.e. the firm must be moving to iso-profit curves with higher profit levels), reflecting the fact that each additional worker hired adds more to total revenue than to total cost (i.e. MRP > W where MRP is the "Marginal Revenue Product," the change in total revenue that results when one additional employee is hired). Similarly, as the firm increases employment from c to g to h, π must fall, reflecting the fact that for $E > E^*$, MRP < W (i.e. each additional employee adds less to total revenue than to total costs).

It is important to recognize that although the firm is maximizing profits at each point on the labour demand curve, the firm is not indifferent amongst these points because each corresponds to a different level of profits. The higher the wage rate, the lower the maximum attainable level of profits.

Because profits rise as the firm moves down and to the right along D_L, the firm will prefer lower points on D_L to higher points. However, the firm is constrained by the fact that it cannot pay wages below the alternative wage that employees could get elsewhere. Thus in Figure 15-4 I_f (I for "ideal") is the firm's preferred (w,E) combination while I_u is the union's preferred (w,E) combination. The bargaining range is the interval $[w_a,w_u]$. The firm would not want the wage rate to fall below w_a, and the union would not want a wage higher than w_u because a higher wage would not be worth the reduction in employment. Within the bargaining range, however, higher wages make the union better off and the firm worse off (and vice versa).

The bargaining range may be further limited by the need for the firm to earn a normal rate of return (zero economic profits) in order to remain in business, a constraint analogous to the requirement that employees receive a wage at least equal to that available elsewhere. The iso-profit curve corresponding to zero economic profits is shown as π_o in Figure 15-4;

thus if the wage were higher than w_o the firm would go out of business. The wage at which profits are zero (w_o) may be above or below the union's preferred wage, w_u. (In a competitive equilibrium w_o and w_a coincide, and there is no scope for raising wages without forcing some firms to shut down operations). When w_o is below w_u, the upper limit to the bargaining range is w_o.

Figure 15.3 The Firm's Iso-Profit Curves

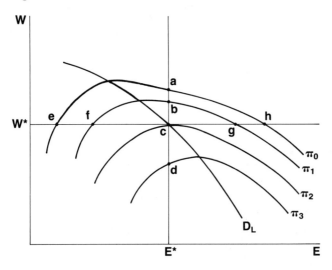

The theory outlined thus far does not predict a unique wage and employment outcome, but rather predicts that the wage rate will lie somewhere in the bargaining range $[w_a, w_u]$ with the corresponding level of employment being determined according to the labour demand function. To complete the theory we require an explanation of the determination of the bargaining outcome arrived at by the two parties. This requires a theory of bargaining, a subject taken up later. First we examine two closely related possibilities: (i) that the union may attempt to alter the constraint and (ii) that the firm and union may bargain over both wages and employment, rather than leaving the latter to be unilaterally determined by the firm. In addition, the way unions can achieve their objectives by restricting supply is also discussed.

RELAXING THE DEMAND CONSTRAINT

Through collective bargaining with the employer, the union will attempt to reach a wage-employment outcome as close as possible to its preferred outcome I_u. However, unions can also enhance the set of available options by altering the constraint — either increasing labour demand or making the demand for labour more inelastic, so that increases in wages will have less severe consequences for employment. Various union practices attempt to achieve these results. With respect to the goal of making labour demand more inelastic, recall that the elasticity of labour demand depends on (i) the elasticity of product demand, (ii) the elasticity of substitution between labour and other inputs, (iii) the share of labour in total costs, and (iv) the elasticity of labour supply of other inputs. Union activity is thus often directed at restricting substitution possibilities by consumers in product markets and by employers in labour markets, the latter including the substitution of nonunion for union labour in addition to the substitution of capital and other inputs for labour. Some restrictions come about through collective bargaining with the employer, while others are achieved by influencing public policy.

Figure 15.4   The Firm's and Union's Preferred Wage-Employment Outcomes and the Bargaining Range

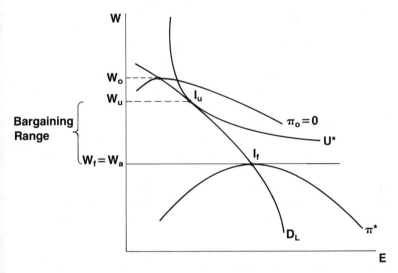

Because of the derived nature of labour demand, some attempts to alter the constraint focus on the product market. These include: support for quotas, tariffs, and other restrictions on foreign competition in order to reduce the number of substitutes for union-produced goods and services (observed, for example, in the Canadian auto, textile, and shoe industries); opposition to deregulation which generally enhances product market competition and may facilitate entry by nonunion competitors (observed, for example, in the communications and transportation industries); advertising of the product (e.g. union label on beer); and union attempts to organize all the firms in an industry in order to minimize substitution of nonunion-produced for union-produced goods and services.

Other union policies focus on the labour market. Unions are generally strong supporters of various forms of wage-fixing for nonunion labour such as minimum wage laws and "fair wage" provisions in government contracts. Raising the wage of nonunion workers reduces the potential for substitution of nonunion for union labour — both directly through arrangements such as contracting out of work by unionized employers and indirectly by the growth of nonunion firms at the expense of union firms. Advocating fair wages for unorganized employees and higher minimum wages for both organized and unorganized workers may also be viewed by the union movement as an effective method of raising the living standards of the labour force and increasing labour's share of national income. Union support for full employment policies may reflect similar desires; such support can also be viewed as an attempt to increase labour demand generally, including the demand for union labour, as well as reducing the size of the pool of unemployed workers competing for jobs and thus weakening the position of employed union members.

Attempts to alter the constraint can have offsetting effects; in these circumstances the union's optimal strategy will depend on the magnitude of the opposing effects. For example, raising the wages of unorganized workers limits the potential for substitution of nonunion for union labour, but may also reduce the incentive for these workers to organize. The growth paths adopted by early craft unions also illustrate opposing effects. Some craft unions remained narrowly focused, representing a small group of highly skilled workers. An advantage of this arrangement is that the earnings of these workers often account for a small fraction of total cost. Other craft unions expanded to cover semi-skilled and unskilled workers in the same enterprise and industry in order to minimize the substitution among different types of labour that would occur in response to an increase in the wage of the highly skilled group.

The potential for labour market substitution can also be reduced by restrictions on labour supply — such as limited immigration and control of entry through occupational licensing and apprenticeship arrangements. Restrictions on labour supply into the occupation or trade are most frequently employed by craft unions and professional associations such as those representing doctors and lawyers. Unions also attempt to limit the employer's substitution possibilities by negotiating contract provisions such as those relating to technological change, contracting out of work and work practices. This feature of collective bargaining involves the two parties in the negotiation of contracts relating to both wages and employment, a topic examined next.

EFFICIENT WAGE AND EMPLOYMENT CONTRACTS

Because unions generally care about the employment prospects of their members, we would expect the union to use its bargaining power to negotiate over employment as well as wages. Of course, the employer may resist this attempt because agreeing to certain levels of employment will have implications for the firm's profits. Nonetheless, if the union and its members care enough about employment, they may be willing to accept a lower wage in exchange for higher levels (or greater security of) employment. In these circumstances, the union and the firm may discover that an agreement with respect to both wages and employment is to their mutual advantage. Such an arrangement may be explicit (i.e. contained in the collective agreement) or implicit (i.e. an understanding that both parties respect).

In general, the firm and union can each benefit from negotiating a contract covering *both* wages and employment rather than having the firm choose employment subject to a fixed wage. That is, wage-employment outcomes on the labour demand curve imply unexploited "gains from trade" and thus are inefficient in the Pareto sense. (Recall that an outcome is said to be *Pareto-efficient* or *Pareto-optimal* if no individual or group of individuals can be made better off without making some individual or group of individuals worse off).

This is illustrated in Figure 15-5. Starting at points on the labour demand curve such as A and B, it is possible to make one or both parties better off by moving to outcomes in the respective hatched areas. At A' both the union and firm are better off than at A, while at A" the union is better off than, and the firm as well off as, at A. Note that at A" it is not possible to move in any direction that does not make at least one party worse off. Thus A" is a Pareto-efficient wage-employment outcome. It is characterized by the union's indifference curve being tangent to the firm's iso-profit curve. This is a necessary condition for an efficient wage-employment arrangement. (A formal derivation of this condition is provided below.)

The reasoning underlying this condition is as follows. The slope of the indifference curve measures the union's willingness to trade off wages against employment, holding utility constant. That is, it shows the largest wage reduction the union would accept in exchange for an increase in employment of one unit. Similarly the slope of the iso-profit curve measures the firm's ability to substitute between wages and employment while holding profits constant. That is, it shows the minimum wage reduction the firm would require in exchange for an agreement to increase employment by one unit. When these slopes are not equal, unexploited gains from trade must exist. That is, by increasing employment by one unit and reducing the wage by more than the minimum the firm would require to maintain constant profits but less than the union would accept to maintain constant utility, both parties are made better off.

The locus of the Pareto-efficient wage-employment outcomes is called the "contract curve" and is shown as CC' in Figure 15-5. When the union cares about wages and employment (i.e. if the indifference curves are downward-sloping), the contract curve must lie to the right of the labour demand curve. This follows from the fact that the iso-profit curves are upward-sloping to the left of the labour demand curve, have a slope of zero where the two intersect, and are downward-sloping to the right of the labour demand curve. Thus the tangency conditions can only be met to the right of the labour demand function, where both the iso-profit and iso-utility curves slope downwards.

In summary, both the firm and the union can benefit from negotiating a wage-employment outcome on the contract curve. Of course, the two parties will have differing views about which particular outcome on the contract curve should be chosen. Moving up CC', the union becomes better off and the firm worse off, and vice versa. As before, there is a bargaining range and where the parties end up within that range depends on their relative bargaining strengths. The lower limit of the bargaining range is determined as before; the firm would not want the wage rate to be lower than would be required to attract workers. The upper limit is determined by a zero economic profit condition; in general the union would not want wages and employment set at a level which caused the firm to cease operations.

Figure 15.5   Efficient and Inefficient Wage-Employment Contracts

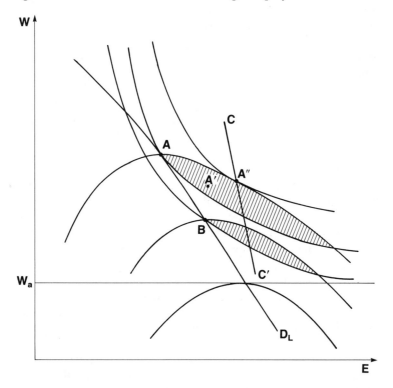

Several implications follow from this analysis. Perhaps the most important implication is that the two parties have an incentive to negotiate wage-employment arrangements which may appear to be wasteful. Outcomes on the contract curve must involve the firm employing more labour than the firm would choose on its own, given the wage rate; i.e. hiring redundant personnel or spreading a given number of tasks among more workers. Such outcomes can be enforced by work rules of various kinds — arrangements which are often referred to as restrictive work practices or featherbedding. The above analysis shows why such practices may be to the mutual advantage of the employer and the union.

A second important implication is that, in the context of efficient contracts, the negative (partial) relationship between wages and employment may not hold. The contract curve may be vertical or upward- or downward-sloping. Thus it need not be the case in this setting that higher wages imply reduced employment, and vice versa. A more powerful union will generally be able to achieve higher wages *and* employment than a less powerful union, other things equal. (The meaning of the term union power is discussed further in the next chapter.) Nonetheless, any particular union ultimately faces a tradeoff between wages and employment, even when the contract curve is upward-sloping, because the union is ultimately constrained by the need for the employer to earn a satisfactory level of profits in order to continue producing. Thus the union is constrained by the locus of wage-employment combinations that yield this satisfactory level of profits, illustrated by the iso-profit curve π_0 in Figure 15-4, a locus which is downward-sloping to the right of the demand curve.

Obstacles to reaching efficient contracts

While there is an incentive for firms and unions to bargain over both wages and employment and reach an outcome on the contract curve, there are also reasons for believing that outcomes on the labour demand curve may be more likely. One reason is that the information needed to recognize that there are unexploited gains from trade may not be available to both parties. For example, suppose the two parties are currently located at point A in Figure 15-5. As long as each has some information about the other side's preferences, then both will recognize that they are both better off at A' than at A. What this requires is the firm knowing something about the union's willingness to trade off wages against employment, and similarly for the union. However, if neither party trusts the other then each may be unwilling to reveal information about their preferences to the other, perhaps because of a fear that the other will later use this information to their own advantage. Indeed, there may even be an incentive to misrepresent one's preferences in bargaining situations; i.e., not to "tell the truth, the whole truth, and nothing but the truth." In these circumstances it may be difficult for the two bargainers to recognize a Pareto-improving change.

Also, while an agreement over wages is easily enforced, an agreement about employment may be difficult (i.e., costly) to enforce. Some enforcement mechanism is needed to prevent the firm from "cheating" on the agreement; this follows from the fact that at each wage rate the firm's profits are highest at the level of employment given by the labour demand curve. Thus even though both sides are better off on the contract curve, given the negotiated wage rate the firm always has an incentive to cut employment.

If the demand for labour is expected to remain constant during the contract period (the period during which the collective bargaining agreement is in effect), then an agreement about employment should not be difficult to enforce. Presumably the union can keep track of its employed members and if the firm is caught cheating (e.g., not replacing a worker who quits, retires or is fired) the union will act accordingly (e.g., a strike, slowdown, etc.). However many collective agreements cover a period of two or more years (almost all provide for a duration of at least one year) so that it is unlikely that labour demand will remain constant over the contract period. Thus an agreement concerning employment would have to specify the level of employment for each of the many sets of circumstances that may prevail in the future.[4] This is the case for such factors as the future state of the product market and the costs of other inputs for the firm. From the workers' point of view, important variables would be the cost of living and wages in other firms and industries. Clearly it may be very difficult and expensive to negotiate and enforce such a "contingent" agreement, depending on the different states of nature that may prevail.

The obstacles to negotiating efficient wage-employment contracts are often evident in concession bargaining. Unions have generally been reluctant to engage in concession bargaining unless job guarantees are part of the package, recognizing that without such guarantees the concessions may save few union jobs and may simply lead to higher firm profits. Firms are often reluctant to make explicit employment guarantees because of potential changes in product and labour market conditions.

Since an agreement covering all possible contingencies is unlikely to be workable, the two sides may try to approximate such an arrangement. This can be accomplished by tying employment to the output of the firm or to the use of other inputs. The most common such arrangement is to specify the minimum number of employees to be used for a given task; examples of such provisions are observed in railroads (size of freight train crews), airlines (number of pilots per aircraft), teaching (class size provisions) and musical performances (minimum size of orchestra). (Some of these provisions may also reflect other objectives such as safety.) Such rules may not be difficult to enforce; further, they have the advantage that they allow the firm to adjust employment in response to fluctuations in the demand for the firm's product, yet oblige the firm to hire more employees in each state of demand than the firm would choose on its own.

The practice of negotiating work rules that restrict the firm's ability to control employment can thus be interpreted as a mechanism for approximating an efficient contract. In effect the unconstrained demand curve

4 If D_L shifts, so does the set of Pareto-efficient (w,E) combinations. Even if an agreement for a specific level of employment could be enforced, there is no incentive for the two parties to reach such an agreement if the demand or supply of labour is expected to shift.

D_L is replaced by a constrained demand curve D_L^C which shows the firm's profit-maximizing level of employment given the work rules implicitly or explicitly agreed to by the two parties (see Figure 15-6). Although this constrained demand curve is unlikely to coincide exactly with the contract curve, for each outcome on D_L there is a Pareto-superior outcome on D_L^C.

Previously we noted that if the union is constrained by the labour demand curve, it is in the union's interest to shift the demand curve to the right or make it more inelastic. What wasn't clear was why the firm would accede to such requests. A primary insight of the analysis in this section is that featherbedding rules or restrictive work practices which force the firm to operate to the right of the unconstrained labour demand curve can be to the mutual advantage of both parties.

Efficient vs. inefficient contracts: summary

Two alternative models of the determination of wages and employment in unionized settings have been outlined. The first — which can be termed the "labour demand curve model" — involves the two parties negotiating the wage rate and the firm unilaterally setting employment. The alternative model — the contract curve model — involves the two parties negotiating over both wages and employment. Which of these two models applies in any particular setting is an empirical question. The observation that both parties can improve their welfare by negotiating both wages and employment suggests strong incentives to reach an outcome on the contract curve and provides an explanation of negotiated work rules as a rational response to these incentives. However, in many settings, employment is unilaterally determined by the firm and work rules appear to play a minimal role. This suggests that in many settings the costs of monitoring and enforcing an efficient contract are too high, given the variability in demand, to make this type of arrangement worthwhile.

Figure 15.6   Inefficient, Approximately Efficient and Efficient Contracts

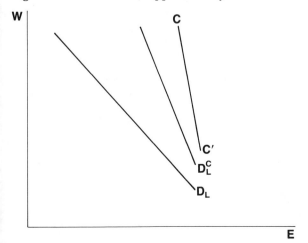

MATHEMATICAL EXPOSITION

Much of the above analysis can be stated succinctly using mathematics. Union preferences are given by $U(w, E; w_a)$ where $w = \dfrac{W}{P}$ is the real wage received by employed union members, w_a is the real alternative wage and E is total employment of union members. Hours of work are assumed fixed for the purposes of simplicity. With the capital stock fixed in the short run, the firm's total revenue is a function of the variable factor and is written as R(E). This notation is general enough to allow for various product market conditions. For example, if the firm is a perfect competitor in the product market then

$$R(E) = p{\cdot}Q = p{\cdot}f(E) \tag{15.5}$$

where p is the market price of the product and $Q = f(E)$ is the short-run production function. The case of a monopolist in the product market is

$$R(E) = p(Q){\cdot}Q = p(f(E)){\cdot}f(E) \tag{15.6}$$

where p(Q) is the monopolist's product demand function.

Short-run or variable profits are given by

$$\Pi(E) = R(E) - W{\cdot}E \tag{15.7}$$

Since the aggregate price level P is exogenous to the individual firm, maximizing nominal and real profits are equivalent. Real profits are given by

$$\pi(E) = r(E) - w{\cdot}E \tag{15.8}$$

where $\pi = \dfrac{\Pi}{P}$ and $r({\cdot}) = \dfrac{R({\cdot})}{P}$.

Using Shepherd's lemma, the short-run labour demand function is obtained by differentiating the variable profit function with respect to employment:

$$r'(E) - w = 0 \tag{15.9}$$

where $r'(E) = \dfrac{d}{dE} r(E)$ is the marginal revenue product of labour.

When the firm chooses employment, the union's preferred wage-employment outcome is the solution to the following constrained maximization problem:

Max U(w, E; w_a)
{w,E}

subject to r'(E) − w = 0

Substituting in the constraint yields the unconstrained maximization problem:

Max U(r'(E), E; w_a)
{E}

The necessary condition for a maximum is:[5]

$$U_w r''(E) + U_E = 0 \tag{15.10}$$

where $U_w = \dfrac{\partial U}{\partial W}$ and $U_E = \dfrac{\partial U}{\partial E}$ This condition can be written as

$$-\frac{U_E}{U_w} = r''(E) \tag{15.11}$$

The left-hand side is the slope of a union iso-utility curve and the right-hand side is the slope of the labour demand function. Thus (15.11) states that the union's indifference curve must be tangent to the labour demand function, as shown in Figure 15-1.

The firm's iso-profit curves are defined by

$$r(E) - wE = \pi_0 \tag{15.12}$$

where π_0 is a constant. The slope of an iso-profit line is thus given by

$$\frac{dw}{dE} = \frac{(r'(E) - w)}{E} \tag{15.13}$$

Thus $\dfrac{dw}{dE} \gtreqless 0$ according to $r'(E) - w \gtreqless 0$ $\tag{15.14}$

That is, the iso-profit curves have a positive slope to the left of the labour demand curve, a slope of zero where they intersect the labour demand curve, and have a negative slope to the right of the labour demand curve. This is the shape shown in Figure 15-3.

The locus of Pareto-efficient contracts is obtained as the solution to the following constrained maximization problem:

Max $(U(w, E; w_a)$
{w,E}

subject to $r(E) - wE = \pi_0$

where π_0 is an arbitrary constant. The necessary conditions for a maxium simplify to

$$-\frac{U_E}{U_w} = \frac{(r'(E) - w)}{E} \tag{15.15}$$

The left-hand side is the slope of the union's iso-utility curves and the right-hand side is the slope of the firm's iso-profit curves. Thus the contract curve is the locus of points at which the iso-profit and iso-utility curves are tangent, as shown in Figure 15-5.

Because the iso-profit curves slope downward only to the right of the

---

5 It is straightforward to verify that the sufficient condition for a maximum requires that the union's indifference curves be more convex to the origin than the labour demand function.

labour demand curve, the contract curve must lie to the right of the labour demand curve. This result can also be seen from rewriting (15.15):

$$r'(E) = w - E \cdot \frac{U_E}{U_w} < w \tag{15.16}$$

That is, efficient contracts are characterized by the marginal revenue product of labour being less than the wage rate.

The slope of the contract curve can be obtained by differentiating (15.15):

$$\frac{dw}{dE} = \frac{U_E + E\, U_{EE} + r''(E)\, U_w + (r'(E) - w)\, U_{wE}}{U_w - E\, U_{Ew} - U_{ww}\, (r'(E) - w)} \tag{15.17}$$

Because both the numerator and denominator of (15.17) may be either positive or negative, the contract curve may be upward- or downward-sloping or vertical.

Two special cases are worth examining. The first is the case in which the union maximizes economic rent:

$$U(w, E; w_a) = (w - w_a)E \tag{15.18}$$

In this case it can be verified from (15.15) that the contract curve is given by

$$r'(E) - w_a = 0 \tag{15.19}$$

Thus the efficient level of employment is independent of the union wage; the contract curve is vertical. Furthermore, the level of employment is identical to that which would be chosen by a firm facing the market wage w_a. This situation is illustrated in Figure 15-7(a).

Another explicit union objective function is the expected utility formulation discussed previously:

$$U(w, E; w_a) = \frac{E}{M} u(w) + (\frac{M-E}{M}) u(w_a) \tag{15.20}$$

In this case the contract curve is given by

$$r'(E) - w = \frac{u(w) - u(w_a)}{u'(w)} \tag{15.21}$$

Thus the contract curve intersects the labour demand curve at $w = w_a$.

The slope of the contract curve is obtained by differentiating (15.21):

$$\frac{dw}{dE} = -\frac{u'(w)\, r''(E)}{u''(w)\, [r'(E) - w]} \tag{15.22}$$

Since $r'(E) - w < 0$ and $r''(E) < 0$, the contract curve is upward-sloping providing the workers are risk-averse ($u''(w) < 0$). This example is shown in Figure 15-7(b).

EMPIRICAL APPLICATIONS

Compared to the large number of empirical studies of the product demand and labour supply behaviour of households and of the production and cost behaviour of firms, the number of studies of wage and employment determination in unionized labour markets is very limited. Nonetheless, following pioneering research by Farber (1978) and Dertouzos and Pencavel (1981), a number of studies have been carried out recently. Although the literature remains at an embryonic stage of development, it is worthwhile discussing here what has been learned and what remains to be discovered about union wage and employment policy.

Empirical applications of the theory of union wage and employment determination face several obstacles:
(1) choosing an appropriate specification of union preferences,

Figure 15.7   (a) Efficient Contracts under Rent Maximization

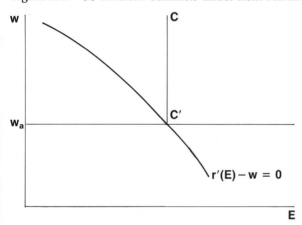

(b) Efficient Contracts under the Expected Utility Formulation

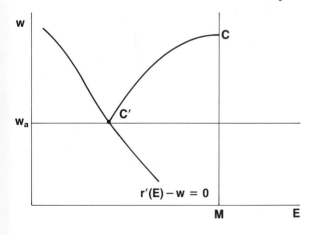

(2) the presence of two alternative models of wage and employment determination which are plausible on a priori grounds,

(3) the need for a theory of firm-union bargaining to predict the specific wage-employment outcome chosen by the parties.

These are clearly major challenges. As noted previously, the issue of whether it is appropriate to characterize unions as attempting to maximize an objective function has long been a matter of scholarly debate. With respect to (2) and (3), the studies by Farber (1978), Dertouzos and Pencavel (1981), Pencavel (1984) and Carruth and Oswald (1986), assume that observed wage-employment outcomes lie on the labour demand curve and that the union is sufficiently powerful that it can achieve its preferred outcome, I_u in Figure 15-4. Another group of studies — including Brown and Ashenfelter (1986), MaCurdy and Pencavel (1986) and Martinello (1985) — have addressed the question of whether observed wage and employment outcomes are more consistent with the labour demand or contract curve models. These two groups of studies are examined in turn.

The Dertouzos and Pencavel study focuses on the International Typographical Union (ITU), a once-powerful closed shop union representing printers. The employers are mostly newspaper firms. Recently there have been important technological changes in the industry (computer typesetting, etc.) and employment has fallen drastically. The period studied, 1946-65, is before these drastic changes to the collective bargaining setting.

Dertouzos and Pencavel argue that the union has a dominant power position, and that this justifies the assumption that the union can determine the wage. The union's power derives mainly from the vulnerability of local newspaper firms to a prolonged period of non-production. This vulnerability results from several factors: (1) the product can't be stored, (2) both advertisers and subscribers have various alternative media they can turn to in the event of a strike, (3) it is often costly and difficult to regain former subscribers and advertisers after a strike. They suggest that the absence of any strikes over this period reflects the dominant power position of the union and the "mature" bargaining relationship that exists.

The union is known to be one of the most democratic of American unions. Union leadership is passed around among members. Thus there is little reason to believe that the objectives of union leaders and members differ. There is also considerable homogeneity in the union membership.

Union organization parallels that of the product market which is geographically segmented. There are about 1000 local organizations, and bargaining over remuneration is carried out at the local level. The Central Federation is concerned with broad issues (e.g., union's jurisdiction over printing occupations, adaptation to technological change).

Empirical implementation requires specifications of the union objective function and the labour demand function. The former is assumed to take the "Stone-Geary" form:

$$U(w, E) = (w - \gamma)^\theta (E - \delta)^{1-\theta} \tag{15.22}$$

where w = real wage rate, E = employment, and γ, δ, θ are parameters. γ and δ can be interpreted as the "minimum required levels" of the real wage and employment respectively. (This follows from the fact that utility approaches zero as w approaches γ or E approaches δ). θ is a parameter reflecting the weight placed on real wages vs employment by the union. (If $\theta = 0$ the union cares only about employment; if $\theta = 1$ the union cares only about wages.) Thus the estimated value of θ, $\hat{\theta}$, will indicate the relative weights put on employment and wages by the ITU.

The objective function 15.22 nests several hypotheses about union behaviour as special cases:

1. Maximize wage rate: $\quad\quad \gamma = 0, \delta = 0, \theta = 1$
2. Maximize employment: $\quad \gamma = 0, \delta = 0, \theta = 0$

3. Maximize wage bill: $\quad\quad\, \gamma = 0, \delta = 0, \theta = \dfrac{1}{2}$

4. Maximize total economic rent: $\gamma = w_a$ (alternative wage)
$$\delta = 0$$
$$\theta = \frac{1}{2}$$

Thus it is possible to test each of these hypotheses by testing whether the estimated parameters differ significantly from these values.

The demand for labour is assumed to depend linearly on the wage rate, price of newsprint, price of capital (machinery and equipment), output (measured by advertising lineage sold), and a dummy variable for mergers between newspaper firms.

For the union local examined in the most detail, the Cincinnati Post, Dertouzos and Pencavel estimate that $\theta = 0.21$, which is significantly greater than zero and significantly less than 0.5. This indicates that the union cares about both wages and employment, but that relatively more weight is put on employment. Tests of the special cases resulted in the rejection of both wage bill maximization and maximization of economic rents, with the former being strongly rejected. They also found that the estimated value of γ was significantly greater than zero, suggesting that there is a minimum acceptable real wage, possibly equal to the alternative wage. However, no evidence of a minimum acceptable level of employment was found (i.e. the estimated value of δ was not significantly different from zero.)

Dertouzos and Pencavel also analyse the wage-employment outcomes attained by the ITU in several other cities. They find evidence of considerable variation in union preferences (i.e. different values of θ, δ, and γ). In subsequent research using an alternative specification for union preferences, Pencavel (1984) finds that larger union locals have preferences which are approximately those of rent maximization while smaller locals place more weight on employment.

Farber (1978) analyses the wage and employment behaviour of the

United Mine Workers in the U.S. bituminous coal industry over the period 1946-73. The union is a dominant force in the industry due to the fragmented market structure (large number of essentially competitive firms), and is thus assumed to be able to dictate the wage. However, the union is constrained by the position and shape of the labour demand curve which depend on substitution: (1) between coal and other fuels in the product market, (2) between labour and other inputs in coal production, and (3) between union-produced and nonunion-produced coal. These various forces are incorporated in the specification of the model.

With respect to union preferences, Farber assumes a variant of the expected utility formulation described earlier. Thus union members are uncertain about whether they will be employed at the union wage; those not employed in a union mine receive the alternative wage. Members' preferences also are allowed to differ with respect to age because of retirement benefits, which are more important to older miners. The union's objective is taken to be that of maximizing the expected utility of the median-aged member.

Farber's estimates imply that the union places a relatively high weight on employment relative to wages and benefits, higher than would be implied by wage bill or economic rent maximization. Other findings included the following: (1) union members valued $1 worth of non-wage benefits (e.g. health and medical benefits) more than $1 in wages; this may be because non-wage benefits are not taxed, (2) union wage policy was estimated to be most sensitive to the alternative wage and the age distribution of the membership, and to a lesser extent to non-labour costs (e.g. transport costs); union wage policy was not sensitive to shifts in the demand for coal.

Other studies based on the labour demand model also find that unions place a relatively high weight on employment. Carruth and Oswald (1986) analyse the National Union of Mineworkers in the United Kingdom over the period 1950-80, using the expected utility formulation of union preferences. The estimates imply that the union places less weight on employment than its U.S. counterpart, the United Mine Workers, but nonetheless a high weight relative to that on wages. Martinello (1985) analyses the behaviour of the International Woodworkers of America (IWA) in the British Columbia forest products industry. Although his primary objective is to compare the performance of the labour demand and contract curve models, his estimates for the labour demand model (assuming the union can set the wage) also imply that the union places a relatively high weight on employment.

On the basis of these studies, there appears to be agreement on several issues: (1) both employment and wages are important to unions, (2) union preferences display diminishing marginal rate of substitution between wages and employment, (3) union preferences are sensitive to the alternative wage, (4) unions generally place relatively more weight on employment than wages, (5) wage bill maximization is uniformly rejected as a union objective function, and (6) economic rent maximization is rejected in the majority of cases. In assessing these conclusions, it is important to keep in mind that only a small number of unions have been analysed using modern econometric methods and that the conclusions are conditional on some key assumptions, in particular that the union can dictate the wage and the firm unilaterally sets employment.

The task of testing between the contract curve and labour demand models has been addressed in recent papers by Brown and Ashenfelter (1986), MaCurdy and Pencavel (1986) and Martinello (1985). The first two studies are based on the ITU in the United States and the latter on the IWA in Canada. Brown and Ashenfelter assume that the union's objective is to maximize economic rents. In these circumstances, the contract curve is vertical and the union wage will be independent of the alternative wage. Brown and Ashenfelter find that the union wage is not independent of the alternative wage, thus rejecting either the contract curve model or the assumption of rent maximization. The analysis of MaCurdy and Pencavel suggests that perhaps the latter should be rejected. Their test uses the prediction that if outcomes lie on the labour demand curve, the wage will equal marginal revenue product, while if outcomes lie on the contract curve, the wage rate will exceed the marginal revenue product. Martinello performs a similar, though more general, test. Both studies conclude that the contract curve model provides a better explanation of observed wage-employment behaviour than the labour demand curve model. This suggests that in these cases the unions have been able to negotiate work rules that constrain the firm to employ more union members at the union wage than the firm would choose on its own.

Perhaps the most important aspect of union wage and employment determination that is not addressed by the above studies is the incorporation of firm-union bargaining in the empirical analysis. In general, the labour demand and contract curve models predict a range of possible wage-employment outcomes rather than a unique outcome. In order to determine the particular settlement the parties will reach we require a theory of bargaining, a subject to which we now turn.

THEORY OF BARGAINING

Bargaining theory is concerned with predicting the outcome in any particular bargaining situation, and explaining what factors this outcome depends on. Because of the importance of bargaining in many aspects of life, bargaining theory has received considerable attention from social scientists. There is not yet, however, any single widely accepted theory of bargaining. In this section we examine some important contributions, with particular emphasis on their implications in the collective bargaining setting.

Although each bargaining situation may be unique, all share some common features: there is a set of possible outcomes, with minimum acceptable outcomes for each party; because agreement is voluntary, neither party will agree to an outcome worse than their minimum acceptable outcome. Whether the parties bargain over wages alone or over wages and employment, there is a set of feasible outcomes, with upper and lower limits representing the minimum outcomes acceptable to the union and the firm. This type of situation is illustrated in Figure 15-8(a). The point $d = (d_1, d_2)$ shows the utility of each party if no agreement is reached; this is referred to as the "disagreement" or "threat" point. Neither party will agree to an outcome worse than d and each can threaten to impose this outcome on the other by failing to agree. The set S consists of feasible outcomes in which one or both parties is better off than they would be without an agreement. This diagram illustrates the bargaining situation in utilities space because what ultimately matters to each party is the satisfaction obtained from an agreement. However, the parties do not bargain over utilities but rather over outcomes such as wages and employment and in some cases the analysis is best carried out in terms of these outcomes.

In bargaining there are incentives for both co-operation and conflict. The incentives for co-operation are evident from the fact that there are various feasible outcomes that make both parties better off than if no agreement is reached. As long as the employees' utility is at least as great as they can obtain elsewhere and the employer's profits at least as great as can be earned elsewhere, both sides are better off continuing the employment relationship. Indeed, the two parties have an incentive to co-operate at any Pareto-inferior outcome, such as the point (u_0, f_0) in Figure 15-8(a), because both can gain from this process. The incentives for conflict arise because, once all Pareto-improvements have been realized, such as at the point (u_1, f_1) in Figure 15-8(a), actions which make one party better off result in the other becoming worse off. Further, the recognition by each party that the other benefits from reaching an agreement may create an incentive to threaten the other with non-agreement. For example, recognizing that the firm is better off with outcome f_1 than d_2, the union may threaten the firm with non-agreement unless the firm agrees to the outcome (u_1, f_1). Alternatively the firm may threaten non-agreement unless the union agrees to (u_2, f_2). Because of these incentives for both co-operation and conflict, most bargaining situations contain an uneasy mixture; on the one hand, recognition of the importance of reaching agreement and, on the other, attempts to mislead, out-manoeuvre or otherwise gain advantage over the other party.

SOLUTIONS TO THE BARGAINING PROBLEM

A number of solutions to the bargaining problem have been proposed. These can be classified into two groups: theories of the bargaining process and theories of the bargaining outcome. The former not only predict the outcome but also model the process by which that outcome is reached. The latter model the bargaining outcome, by specifying a number of properties or axioms which the outcome should obey. Leading examples of each type are outlined below.The theories described here assume full information; each party knows the set of feasible payoffs or outcomes, the preferences of the other side, and therefore the set of feasible utility outcomes, S in Figure 15-8. However, this does not imply that there is no uncertainty; although each party is aware of the outcomes available to itself and the other party, it may well be uncertain about what the other will do. As is common in uncertain situations, the parties are assumed to maximize expected utility.

Figure 15.8(a)   The Bargaining Problem

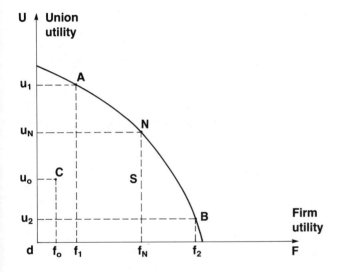

Figure 15.8(b)   The Nash Solution and the Independence of Irrelevant Alternatives Axiom

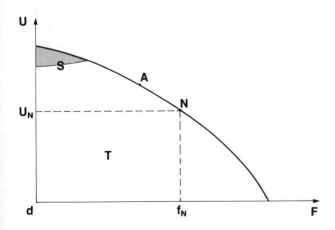

Nash's Bargaining Theory

Following the publication by Von Neumann and Morgenstern in 1944 of the *Theory of Games and Economic Behaviour*, the Princeton mathematician John Nash proposed a solution to the bargaining problem which is still widely used today. Nash (1950) specified four axioms that the solution should obey:

(A1) Pareto-efficiency: only Pareto-efficient bargains will be agreed to.

(A2) Symmetry: if the feasible bargaining set S is symmetric (i.e. if it doesn't matter which party's utility is measured on which axis), the solution will give equal utility increments (relative to the disagreement outcome) to each party.

(A3) Transformation invariance: the solution is not altered by linear transformations of the utility function of either party.

(A4) Independence of irrelevant alternatives: Suppose that the solution to the bargaining problem has been reached for a particular bargaining set S; for example, the point A in Figure 15-8(b). Then the solution will not be altered if some outcomes other than A are unavailable (such as the shaded area in Figure 15-8(b)). That is, if A is the solution with the bargaining set S then A will also be the solution if the same two players face the bargaining set T (S less the shaded area).

The first axiom can be regarded as a natural consequence of the rationality of the two bargainers and the full information assumption. Why would they agree to an outcome such as (u_0, f_0) when both can be made better off at outcomes such as (u_1, f_1) and (u_N, f_N)? The second axiom can be viewed as stating that the bargaining power of each side is reflected in the nature of the set of feasible bargaining outcomes and the disagreement outcome. If the set of bargaining outcomes is symmetric, the two parties must be equally powerful because they both stand to gain or lose equally from agreement or non-agreement. Thus the solution should reflect this equality of bargaining power, and give each an equal gain from agreement.

The third axiom states that the units in which utility is measured should not matter. Utility functions simply represent an individual's preference ordering of outcomes, and any pair of functions that order outcomes in the same way are equally valid for this purpose. In expected utility theory, cardinal utility functions are needed; any linear transformation of a cardinal utility function will preserve the ordering and therefore be a valid utility function. The measurement of temperature is analogous; the fahrenheit and centigrade scales are equally valid measures of temperature, one being a linear transformation of the other. Because this axiom states that the actual numerical scale used to measure utility is arbitrary, its main consequence is to rule out interpersonal comparisons of utility.

The fourth axiom has probably been the most controversial. According to this axiom, if the parties chose the outcome A from all the alternatives in the set S, then the same outcome should be chosen from the set T because the only difference between the two situations is the absence of the outcomes in the shaded area, outcomes which have already been rejected in favour of A by the two bargainers. An analogy in the case of individual decision making is the following. You go out to a restaurant for dinner, and are told by the waiter that there are three choices: chicken in a mustard sauce, veal with a chanterelles sauce and salmon with a cucumber sauce. You decide to order the veal. The waiter subsequently informs you that they are out of salmon. Would you want to change your order? Obviously not — you chose veal over salmon and chicken, so should choose veal over chicken alone. Whether this reasoning applies in a two-person bargaining situation is a more complex question — which is why the axiom has generated controversy.

Nash's (1950) remarkable result was that assumptions A1 to A4 imply a unique solution to any bargaining situation — the outcome that maximizes the product of the two parties' utility increments from the disagreement point; i.e. maximizes $(U - d_1) (F - d_2)$. The Nash solution is shown as the point N in Figure 15-8. Geometrically, the Nash outcome maximizes the area within the set S; i.e. the area $du_N Nf_N$ in Figures 15-8(a) and (b) exceeds the area of any other rectangle contained in the bargaining set.

A number of other axiomatic theories of the bargaining outcome have been proposed; Roth (1979) provides a survey of these theories and Roth and Malouf (1979) and others have tested these competing theories in experimental settings. The Nash solution predicts the outcomes of some bargaining experiments well; however, in other situations the outcomes appear to contradict axiom A3, and a theory that assumes the parties make interpersonal utility comparisons predicts outcomes better than the Nash solution.

It can be debated whether the axiomatic approach constitutes a positive or normative theory of bargaining. The approach proceeds by stating properties that the solution ought to obey, and therefore may be more appropriate for the analysis of arbitration decisions (i.e. decisions about what the outcome ought to be) than collective bargaining outcomes. For the latter purpose, theories that explicitly model the bargaining process may be more appropriate. It should be noted, however, that although the axiomatic theories do not specify the process by which the outcome is reached, they may be consistent with one or several such processes. For example, in an early contribution to the theory of bargaining, Zeuthen (1930) proposed a model of the concession behaviour of each party. The assumed concession process results in the outcome that maximizes the product of the two utility increments, an outcome identical to the Nash solution. Recent contributions have provided more general theories of the bargaining process, and these are examined next.

Rubinstein's Bargaining Theory

In an important contribution, Rubinstein (1982) obtains a solution to the bargaining problem using some concepts of non-co-operative game theory.

The type of bargaining situation analysed by Rubinstein has the following characteristics. The two bargainers take turns making offers. If an offer is accepted, the process ends; if the offer is not accepted the other party will have the opportunity to make an offer in the next period. However, delay is costly to both sides. Each period the total "pie" to be shared by the two parties gets smaller. This situation is illustrated in Figure 15-9. As before, there is a bargaining set which shows the outcomes available to each party. In the first period this is the set bounded by du_1f_1. However, if an agreement is not reached in the first period, the set of utility outcomes available in period two shrinks to that bounded by du_2f_2. Similarly in period three the bargaining set becomes du_3f_3, and in period four the only feasible outcome is the disagreement point $d = (u_4, f_4)$. In general it may require delay of more than four periods in order to reach the situation where both parties gain nothing from an agreement (if, indeed, this situation is ever reached); the assumption that this outcome is reached quickly is made simply for ease of illustration.

As before, both parties are assumed to possess full information about the bargaining situation. That is, each knows the size of the "pie" available to be shared in the first period, the other party's preferences and the costs of delay (or disagreement) to both sides. Thus each can infer the nature of the bargaining set they will face in subsequent periods.

Each party is assumed to be concerned only with its own self-interest; i.e. it wants to obtain the highest possible utility from the bargain, and cares only about the outcome, not how it was reached. Also, each behaves rationally (and expects the other to do likewise) in the sense that neither will believe threats that would not be in the interest of the threatening party to carry out. For example, suppose it is the union's turn to make an offer in period 1. The union could offer $A = (u_A, f_A)$ and threaten to refuse to accept or make any future offers unless the outcome A is accepted. If the firm believed the threat, it would accept because f_A is better than f_4, which is what the firm would receive if the offer A is rejected and the union carries out the threat. However, the threat is not credible. Suppose the firm rejects the offer. In period 2 the bargaining set becomes du_2f_2 and if the firm offers the outcome B, the union will accept because u_B is better than u_3, the best outcome the union could obtain in the next period. For this reason, the firm knows that the union's threat in period 1 is not credible and it will therefore not believe it.

We can now turn to the solution. Suppose that in the initial period it is the union's turn to make an offer. Rubinstein's analysis predicts that the union will offer and the firm will accept the outcome (u_R, f_R); that is, the Rubinstein outcome is the point R in Figure 15-9. To see why this solution is predicted to occur, we proceed by backward induction. In the second period it will be the firm's turn to make an offer and in the third period the union's turn. In the fourth period there is nothing left to be shared. Now look at the situation facing the union in period 3. Both parties recognize that the best the firm can attain next period is the outcome f_4.

Figure 15.9(a)   Rubinstein's Solution to the Bargaining Problem

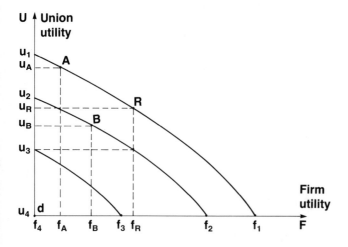

Figure 15.9(b)   The Effect of Delay Costs on the Rubinstein Outcome

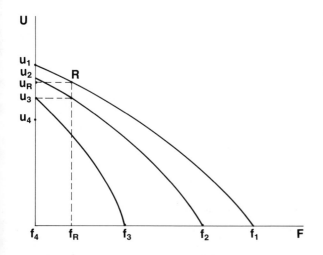

Thus in period 3 the firm will accept any offer equal to or better than f_4. The union would therefore offer (u_3, f_4) and the firm would accept. Now go back to the situation facing the firm in period 2. The firm knows that the best the union can expect next period is u_3. Thus the firm won't offer more than u_3; i.e., will make an offer in the interval between (u_3, f_R) and (u_4, f_2). However, the firm also knows that next period the union will offer and the firm will accept (u_3, f_4). Thus in period 2 the firm will offer and accept (u_3, f_R). Now go back to period 1 and the union's choice of offers. The same analysis leads to the conclusion that the union will offer and the

Figure 15.9(c)   The Effect of a Proportional Change in Disagreement Costs on the Rubinstein Solution

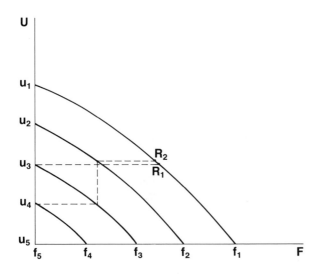

firm will accept (u_R, f_R). Thus the point $R = (u_R, f_R)$ is the bargaining outcome; the costs of delay and the rational behaviour of the two parties result in an agreement that avoids incurring any disagreement costs.

Clearly delay costs play an important role in generating agreement in the Rubinstein model. The existence of these costs — and the fact that both parties are aware of them — gives each some power over the other. For this reason the relative magnitude of delay costs exerts an important influence on the negotiated outcome. This result is illustrated in Figure 15-9(b). The bargaining set du_1f_1 is identical to that in Figure 15-9(a), as are the delay costs to the firm (measured by the outcomes f_1, f_2, f_3 and f_4). However, the union's disagreement costs are less than in Figure 15-9(a), as indicated by the outcomes u_1, u_2, u_3 and u_4. As a consequence, the outcome predicted by Rubinstein's theory is more favourable to the union and less favourable to the firm.

It is important to recognize that *relative* disagreement costs determine the extent to which the negotiated outcome favours one party or the other. By holding constant the firm's disagreement costs and lowering the union's in the comparison between the situation in Figures 15-9(a) and (b), the union's relative delay costs declined. The consequence is a more favourable outcome for the union and a less favourable outcome for the firm. However, suppose the disagreement costs fall by the same proportion for both parties, leaving relative costs unchanged. This situation is shown in Figure 15-9(c). Two bargaining situations are depicted in the same diagram. In the first case the outer boundary of the bargaining set is u_1f_1 in the first period, u_2f_2 in the second period, and so on, reaching the disagreement point (u_5, f_5)

in the fifth period. In the second bargaining situation, disagreement costs are proportionally higher for both parties; the boundary of the bargaining set is u_1f_1 in the first period, u_3f_3 in the second, and the disagreement point in the third period. In both cases the firm makes the first offer. The solution is essentially unchanged by the proportionate increase in delay costs, illustrating the reason for emphasizing the role of relative disagreement costs in bargaining outcomes.

As a description of the collective bargaining process, the Rubinstein model is highly simplified. For example, in most bargaining situations either party can make an offer in any period. Nonetheless, this theory captures important aspects of collective bargaining, in particular the role played by the costs of delay or disagreement in bringing about a negotiated settlement. The negotiations process itself consumes scarce resources; thus the sooner an agreement is reached the lower the direct negotiations costs to each party. But the major disagreement costs are those associated with attempts of one side to bring pressure to bear on the other to make concessions. Although there are a variety of relatively inexpensive (and possibly also ineffective) methods for exerting pressure on the other party (e.g. work-to-rule actions, refusal to work overtime), the primary mechanism is the strike or lockout.

The strike involves the collective withdrawal of union labour in an attempt to halt or sharply curtail production. The lockout denies union members access to their normal job and source of income. Both types of work stoppage impose costs on the employer and the employees represented by the union (and also possibly on third parties). The firm loses profits and the workers lose income. In addition to the costs incurred during the strike or lockout, there may be costs of a more permanent nature. Clearly rational bargainers (and perhaps even irrational bargainers) will, in the negotiations process, take into account the magnitude of the costs that they and the other party will bear in the event of a strike or lockout. Rubinstein's theory confirms our intuition that the relative size of the costs of a work stoppage will be an important determinant of the negotiated settlement. Further, it is not necessary for a strike or lockout to occur in order for the costs associated with a work stoppage to influence the outcome.

UNION BARGAINING POWER

The term "bargaining power" arises frequently in discussions of firm-union bargaining. Like many terms that are widely used, the precise meaning is not always clear. In this section we contrast two possible meanings of union bargaining power. For simplicity we assume that the two parties negotiate over wages alone, leaving the firm to set employment. The extension of these ideas to the case of bargaining over wages and employment is straightforward.

One meaning of bargaining power is related to the elasticity of labour demand. A union facing an inelastic demand for labour can raise wages substantially with only minor adverse employment consequences. This notion of bargaining power is associated with the *willingness* to increase wages; other things equal, the more inelastic the demand for labour, the more willing is the union to raise the wage rate.

An alternative notion of bargaining power is associated with the *ability* to raise wages. According to this meaning of the term, a powerful union is one that can obtain a negotiated outcome close to its most preferred outcome. This aspect of union power depends not on the elasticity of labour demand but primarily on the relative costs of disagreement to each party.

Because these two aspects of bargaining power depend on different variables, it is possible for a union to be powerful according to one definition but weak according to another. This possibility is illustrated in Figure 15-10. Panel (a) shows a union that is willing to raise wages substantially but unable to do so; the negotiated wage w_c is considerably below the union's preferred wage w_u. Panel (b) shows a union that can obtain its preferred outcome but is not willing to raise wages substantially because of the employment consequences. Of course, in some circumstances a union may be powerful (or weak) according to both meanings. However, neither aspect of bargaining power alone ensures that the negotiated union wage will be substantially higher than the alternative wage.

UNION POWER AND LABOUR SUPPLY

Most unions attempt to improve the wages and working conditions of their members directly by bargaining with the employer, and the strike threat is their primary source of bargaining power. However, craft unions and professional associations can raise the wages and working conditions of their members indirectly by controlling labour supply. For these organizations, restrictions on the supply of labour can constitute an important source of union power.

Restricting Supply: Craft Unions

By restricting the supply of labour, unions can raise wages artificially relative to the situation where competition prevailed in the supply of labour. Craft unions generally have sought to raise the wage of their members by controlling entry into their craft through the apprenticeship system, discrimination, nepotism, high union dues, and such devices as the closed shop (the worker has to be a member of the union *before* being hired, i.e. the union controls the hiring hall). Because the supply of labour to the craft is reduced, wages will rise above the wage that would prevail in the absence of the craft restrictions.

Needless to say the craft union will try to control the whole trade; otherwise the benefits of the supply restriction would also go to nonunion craft workers. Hence the importance to the union of apprenticeship licens-

Figure 15.10   Alternative Aspects of Union Power

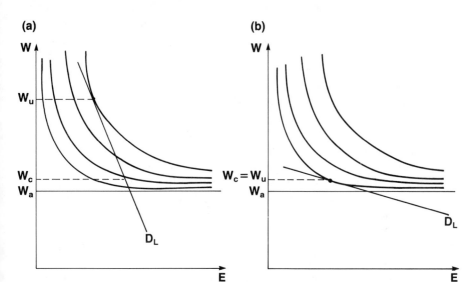

ing, the closed shop, the union shop (the worker has to join the union after a probationary period of employment), or the agency shop (the worker must pay union dues but need not be a member of the union).

At the artificially high union wage rate, the quantity of labour supplied will exceed the quantity demanded. To the extent that the union controls entry, the scarce jobs can be rationed to the large number of workers who would like the jobs by such devices as discrimination, nepotism, or high union dues. To the extent that employers have a say in who is hired, they may ration jobs on the basis of discrimination or nepotism, but they may also ration on the basis of productivity-related factors such as education or training or experience. While these productivity-related factors obviously are useful requirements for employers, they may be set *artificially* high because the employer has an excess supply of applicants, given the higher unionized wage.

Restricting Supply: Professional Associations

Professional associations can also behave much like craft unions in their control over labour supply, largely through the processes of occupational licensing and certification. This setting of standards is deemed necessary, ostensibly to protect the public interest in circumstances where it is important but difficult for the consuming public to judge the quality of the professional service. The job of governing the profession has usually gone to the profession itself — hence the term self-governing professions — because only members of the profession were deemed qualified to set standards. Traditionally, this has occurred in the stereotypic professions such as medicine and law, where an uninformed clientele purchases complex services from a self-employed professional. Increasingly, however, professionals are becoming employed on a salaried basis and the rationale for self-governing powers for salaried professionals can be questioned when the employer can provide an effective mediator between the consuming public and the salaried professional.

The techniques of occupational control utilized by professional associations usually involve occupational licensing or certification. Under certification only those with the professional certificate have the right to use the professional designation or title; that is, they have a *reserve-of-title certification*. However, other practitioners are allowed to practise in the profession, albeit they cannot use the certified title. Under licensing, only those with the professional licence can practise; that is, they have the *exclusive right-to-practise licence*. Clearly the exclusive right-to-practise licence involves more control over the occupation than the reserve-of-title certification; hence, it is sought after by most professional and quasi-professional groups.

Under licensing the supply of labour to the occupation is restricted only to those with the licence. Under certification the supply restrictions are less severe in the sense that others can practise in the profession, although competition is restricted because others cannot use the professionally designated certification. Whatever the impact on the quality of the service performed, the supply of labour to the occupation is restricted and wages rise accordingly. In this sense, professional associations like craft unions raise the wages of their members.

Although they receive higher wages, members of the profession may bear costs associated with the occupational licensing requirements. Such costs could include lengthy education periods as well as practical training periods, such as internship for doctors or articling for lawyers. There is a danger, however, in that the *incumbent* professionals may try to have the brunt of the licensing costs born by *new* entrants into the profession. This could be accomplished by having increasingly stringent education or training requirements as a qualification for entry into the profession, with so-called "grandfather" clauses exempting those who are already practising. In this fashion, the new entrants bear more of the licensing costs (they will do so as long as the wage premium outweighs these costs), the existing practitioners who control the profession benefit from the restricted competition, and the consuming public gets increasingly qualified practitioners, albeit at a higher cost. Restricting grandfather clauses, or having licensing requirements set by persons other than existing practitioners, could go a long way to correct this potential abuse of occupational licensing.

QUESTIONS

1. Discuss the reasons why the objectives of union leadership may differ

from the objectives of the rank-and-file. Discuss the implications of such differences.

2. Draw the union indifference curves (iso-utility curves) for the following situations:
   (a) wages and employment are perfect substitutes.
   (b) there is a minimum wage below which union members will not go in order to increase employment.
   (c) at the current level of employment within the union, unions attach more disutility to a given employment reduction than the utility they attach to a corresponding employment increase.
   (d) as their wealth increases, union members attach more weight to job security than to real income gains.
   (e) the union objective is to minimize its wage bill.
   (f) the union objective is to maximize total economic rent.

3. Discuss the effect of an increase in the alternative wage rate on the utility of the union.

4. Discuss why union members may differentiate in their preferences between hours of work and employment. What are the implications for union preferences?

5. Discuss the implications of unions being a democratic institution, reflecting the preferences of the median unon voter. Why would the preferences of the median voter dominate in such a situation? What are the implications for minority rights within the union?

6. Discuss the error in the following statement: "Because the firm is minimizing profits at each point on its demand curve, it is indifferent amongst these points."

7. Discuss the constraints that limit the "bargaining range" between unions and employers.

8. "If unions engage in concession bargaining to maintain job security they should specifically bargain for a specific level of security to be associated with their wage concessions rather than simply agreeing to the concessions and allowing the firm to choose the level of employment." Discuss.

9. Discuss various ways in which unions may try to make the demand for labour more inelastic so as to minimize any adverse effect emanating from any wage increase.

10. Discuss why efficient wage and employment contracts are not on the firm's labour demand curve. That is, show how both labour and management potentially could be better off by agreeing to wage and employment combinations that are not on the firm's labour demand curve.

11. What determines where the parties will settle on the contract curve? Could the indeterminacy of where the parties will be on the contract curve ever prevent this from arriving at an efficient contract?

12. Discuss how certain featherbedding rules may be efficient and sustain themselves in a competitive market environment. Does this mean that firms will never try to "buy out" such seemingly inefficient practices?

13. Some trade unionists have agreed that wage concessions have not preserved jobs. Use the material developed in this chapter to illustrate how this concern may be legitimate.

14. Discuss the obstacles that unions and management may face in arriving at efficient wage-employment contracts.

15. Show that if the union's objective is to maximize economic rent and if the firm and the union negotiate an efficient contract, then the contract curve will be vertical and employment will equal the level that would occur if the employer could unilaterally set employment and if a wage taker were facing the alternative wage.

16. "The main foe of any union is various forms of substitution, not the firm."
    (a) Explain the various forms of substitution that unions need to be aware of in formulating their bargaining objectives, and elaborate on the relationship between these forms of substitution and union bargaining power.
    (b) The United Mine Workers studied by Farber (1978) had two instruments for affecting the monetary returns to and employment of their members — the hourly wage rate and the output tax (tax per ton of coal produced), the proceeds from which were distributed to members. Under what circumstances would the use of these two instruments allow the union to achieve outcomes that could not be achieved by affecting the wage rate alone?

17. Indicate conditions under which one may expect unions to have a substantial impact on the wages of their members.

18. Craft unions and professional associations will affect the wages of their members in a different manner than will industrial unions. Discuss, and indicate why this may be the case.

19. If craft unions or professional associations are able to raise the wages in their trades above the competitive norm, excess supplies of applicants would result. Discuss how the scarce jobs may be rationed.

20. Self-government is an anachronism for salaried as opposed to self-employed professionals Discuss.

21. Distinguish between occupational licensing and certification. Give examples of each.

22. If occupational licensing is necessary, the only group that could be entrusted not to abuse the powers of licensing would be the alumni of the profession, or at least members who were about to retire. Only they have knowledge about the profession, without having a self-interest in abusing the power of licensing. Existing practitioners, while knowledgeable about the profession, have a self-interest to restrict entry by putting unnecessarily costly entry requirements on new entrants into the profession. New entrants may not find it in their self-interest to put unnecessary restrictions on their entry into the profession, but they do not yet have sufficient knowledge about the profession and what is required for proper qualifications. The general public, while

having an interest in ensuring quality performance without unnecessary restrictions, may not be able to judge what requirements are necessary for professional competence. Only alumni have knowledge of the profession without having a self-interest in excessive quality restrictions; consequently, they are the persons who should be entrusted with the powers of occupational licensing, if it is necessary. Discuss.

23. Restrictions on the use of grandfather clauses would go a long way in reducing the abuses of occupational self licensing. Discuss.

24. Indicate why incumbent practitioners in a profession may want to put excessive restrictions on entry into the profession.

REFERENCES

Atherton, W.N. *Theory of Union Bargaining Goals*. Princeton, NJ: Princeton University Press, 1973.

Blair, D.H. and D.L. Crawford. Labor union objectives and collective bargaining. *QJE* 99 (August 1984) 547-566.

Brown, J. and O. Ashenfelter. Testing the efficiency of employment contracts. *JPE* 94 (July 1986) S40-S87.

Card, D. Efficient contracts with costly adjustment: short-run employment determination for airline mechanics. *AER* 76 (December 1986) 1045-1071.

Carruth, A.A. and A.J. Oswald. Miners' wages in post-war Britain: an application of a model of trade union behavior. *EJ* 95 (December 1985) 1003-1020.

Dertouzos, J.N. and J.H. Pencavel. Wage and employment determination under trade unionism: the international typographical union. *JPE* 89 (December 1981) 1162-1181.

Dunlop, J.T. *Wage Determination Under Trade Unions*. New York: Macmillan, 1944.

Eberts, R.W. and J.A. Stone. On the contract curve: a test of alternative models of collective bargaining. *JOLE* 4 (January 1986) 66-81.

Eden, B. Trading uncertainty, enforcement and labor unions. *EI* 23 (October 1985) 637-650.

Farber, H.S. Individual preferences and union wage determination: the case of the united mine workers. *JPE* 86 (October 1978) 923-942.

Farber, H.S. The analysis of union behavior. *Handbook of Labor Economics*, O. Ashenfelter and R. Layard (eds.) Amsterdam: North Holland, 1986.

Grossman, G. Union wages, temporary layoffs, and seniority. *AER* 73 (June 1983) 277-290.

Grossman, G. International competition and the unionized sector. *CJE* 17 (August 1984) 541-556.

Gylfason, T. and A. Lindbeck. Union rivalry and wages. An oligopolistic approach. *Economica* 129-140.

Hall, R.E. and D.M. Lilien. Efficient wage bargains under uncertain supply and demand. *AER* 69 (December 1979) 868-879.

Hicks, J.R. *The Theory of Wages*. 2nd edn. New York: Macmillan, 1963.

Hollander, A. and R. Lacroix. Unionism, information disclosure and profit-sharing. *SEJ* 52 (January 1986) 706-717.

Johnson, G.E. Economic analysis of trade unionism. *AER Papers and Proceedings* 65 (May 1975) 23-28.

Kotowitz, Y. and F. Mathewson. The economics of the union-controlled firm. *Economica* 49 (November 1982) 421-434.

Lazear, E.P. A competitive theory of monopoly unionism. *AER* 83 (September 1983) 631-643.

Martin, D.L. *An Ownership Theory of the Trade Union.* Berkeley, CA.: University of California Press, 1980.

McDonald, I. and R. Solow. Wage bargaining and employment. *AER* 71 (December 1981) 896-908. Also, comments and reply 74 (September 1984) 755-761.

Macurdy, T. and J. Pencavel. Testing between competing models of wage and employment determination in unionized markets. *JPE* 94 (July 1986) S3-S39.

Martinello, F. Wage and Employment Determination in a Unionized Industry: The IWA in the B.C. Wood Products Industry. Carleton University, Working Paper No.1 84-09, March 1984.

Nash, J.F. The bargaining problem. *Econometrica* 18 (April 1950) 155-162.

Oswald, A. The microeconomic theory of the trade union. *EJ* 92 (September 1982) 576-595.

Oswald, A.J. Efficient Contracts Are on the Labor Demand Curve: Theory and Facts. Princeton University, Industrial Relations Section, Working Paper 178, July 1984.

Oswald, A.J. The economic theory of trade unions: an introductory survey. *Scandinavian Journal of Economics* 87 (No. 2, 1985) 160-193.

Pencavel, J.H. The tradeoff between wages and employment in trade union objectives. *QJE* 99 (May 1984) 215-232.

Pencavel, J.H. Wages and employment under trade unionism: microeconomic models and macroeconomic applications. *Scandinavian Journal of Economics* 87 (No. 2, 1985) 197-225.

Rees, A. *The Economics of Trade Unions*, 2nd ed. Chicago, IL: University of Chicago Press, 1977.

Reid, J.D. Labor unions in the American economy: an analytical survey. *JLR* 3 (Summer 1982) 277-294.

Ross, A.M. *Trade Union Wage Policy.* Berkeley: University of California Press, 1948.

Roth, A.E. *Axiomatic Models of Bargaining.* New York: Springer-Verlag, 1979.

Roth, A.E. and M. Malouf. Game theoretic models and the role of information in bargaining. *Psychological Review* 86(6) (November 1979) 574-594.

Rubinstein, A. Perfect equilibrium in a bargaining model. *Econometrica* 50(1) (January 1982) 97-110.

Sampson, A. Employment policy in a model with a rational trade union. *EJ* 93 (June 1983) 297-311.

Shah, A. Wage/job security contracts and unionism. *SEJ* 51 (January 1985) 849-859.

Svejnar, J. Bargaining power, fear of disagreement and wage settlements: theory and empirical evidence from U.S. industry. *Econometrica* 54 (September 1986) 1055-1078.

Swidinsky, R. Bargaining power under compulsory unionism. *IR* 21 (Winter 1982) 62-72.

Viscusi, V.K. Unions, labor market structure, and the welfare implications of the quality of work. *JLR* 1 (Spring 1980) 175-192.

Von Neumann, J. and O. Morgenstern. *Theory of Games and Economic Behaviour.* Princeton, N.J.: Princeton University Press, 1944.

Warren-Boulton, F.R. Vertical control by labour unions. *AER* 67 (June 1977) 309-322.

Zeuthen, F. *Problems of Monopoly and Economic Warfare.* London: G. Routledge and Sons, 1930.

16 Union Impact on Wage and Nonwage Outcomes

This chapter focuses on the impact of unions on various labour market outcomes. We begin by examining the impact of unions on the wages of their members and on the wages of other employees. The final part of the chapter discusses various non-wage consequences of unions — including their impact on fringe benefits, productivity, firm profitability, turnover (quits and layoffs), income distribution and the allocation of resources.

UNION WAGE IMPACT

The impact of unions on wages has received more attention from economists than any other aspect of union behaviour. Most of the empirical research has been directed at measuring the union-nonunion wage differential, the (percentage) difference in wages between union and otherwise comparable nonunion workers. Our discussion of this research begins by outlining the relevant theoretical background and explaining some of the conceptual and measurement issues involved; we then proceed to a summary of the main empirical findings and a discussion of how these empirical results should best be interpreted.

Theoretical background

In many respects, the basic theory of the union wage impact is similar to that underlying the impact of other wage-fixing arrangements such as minimum wages. However, there are some unique aspects of union wage determination and these will emerge in what follows. We first examine the union wage impact in the simplest setting, and subsequently introduce additional complications.

In the analysis of union wage and employment determination in the previous chapter, the union workers' alternative wage — which in many situations may be taken to be the nonunion wage — was taken as exogenously given. At this stage, however, it is important to recognize the impact of unions not only on the wages of union members but also on the wages of others. This requires a general equilibrium model. Most of the basic principles can be illustrated with a two-sector model, as shown in Figure 16-1(a). The two sectors A and B can be thought of as two different industries or regions employing the same type of labour, which is assumed to be homogeneous. There is a sufficiently large number of firms and workers that, in the absence of unions, the labour market is competitive.

The equilibrium wage in the absence of collective bargaining is therefore w_0. (If there are differences in the desirability of jobs in the two sectors, a compensating wage differential would exist in equilibrium; allowing for this possibility would not affect the analysis other than to make it more complex.) Now suppose a union organizes the workers in sector A and is able to raise the wage to w_u. Employment in sector A will therefore decline to E_1^A. (We are assuming here that the firm can unilaterally set employment; the possibility of wage-employment outcomes to the right of the labour demand curve is discussed below.) The workers who are unable to obtain (or retain) employment in sector A will search for jobs in sector B, increasing labour supply to that sector by a = $E_0^A - E_1^A$. The additional labour supply depresses the wage in sector B, resulting in a new equilibrium wage of w_n. Employment expands to E_1^B, an increase (the amount b in Figure 16-1(a)) which is smaller than the reduction in employment in sector A. The difference (a − b in Figure 16-1(a)) is due to the upward-sloping supply of labour to the economy; as the market wage falls in sector B, some individuals drop out of the labour force, the market wage falling below their reservation wage.

In this economy the union-nonunion wage differential would be $d = \dfrac{w_u - w_n}{w_n}$. Note that this is greater than the difference between the union wage w_u and the wage union members would receive in the absence of unionization (w_0). The difference arises because the higher wages associated with unionization force more workers to seek employment in the unorganized sector, depressing wages there.

According to this basic two-sector model, the magnitude of the union-nonunion differential depends on: (1) the elasticity of labour demand in each sector, (2) the ability of the union to raise wages in the organized sector, and (3) the elasticity of labour supply.

This basic model is consistent with the notion of a dual labour market. The primary sector (A) consists of firms or industries that have characteristics — such as establishment size, concentration in the product market, stability of employment, and the nature of production — that make unionization likely. The secondary sector (B) consists of firms or industries with the opposite characteristics. The reduction in employment in the primary sector (relative to what employment would be in the absence of wage increases associated with unionization) creates a widening of the wage gap between the two sectors as those who cannot obtain employment in the unionized sector crowd into the nonunion labour market, depressing wages even further in the secondary sector. These low wages may in turn be a source of many of the employment-related phenomena — such as high absenteeism and frequent turnover — characteristic of the secondary sector.

Contrary to the belief that union wage increases tend to depress the wages of unorganized workers is the perspective, often advanced by practitioners, that nonunion firms may raise the wages of nonunion labour in order to compete with unionized firms for the work-force. In addition,

Figure 16.1 (a) Union Wage Impact in a Two-Sector Model

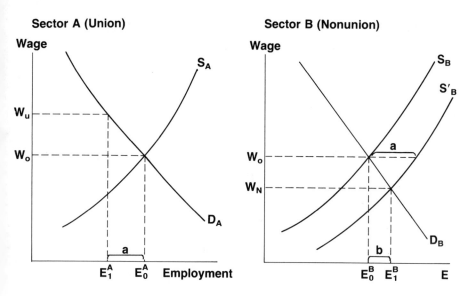

(b) Union Wage Impact with a Threat Effect

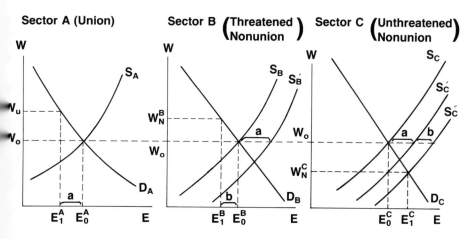

firms with both union and nonunion workers may raise the wages of nonunion labour in order to preserve traditional wage differentials. While this belief has intuitive appeal, especially because comparability appears to be so important in wage determination, it ignores the market factors — in particular the supply influx from workers who cannot get jobs in the unionized sector — that would enable employers to pay lower wages to nonunion labour. In essence, there may not be a need to compete with the unionized sector because there is a large pool of labour to hire that cannot get jobs in the high-wage unionized sector. It is true that the unionized

(c) Union Wage Impact with a Vertical Contract Curve

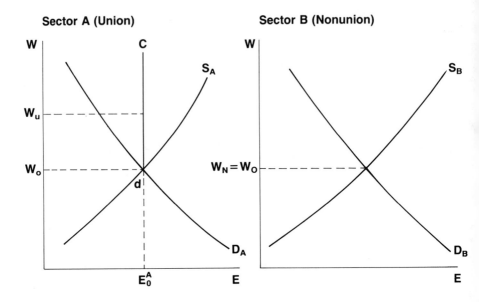

Sector A (Union)   **Sector B (Nonunion)**

(d) Union Wage Impact with Wait Unemployment

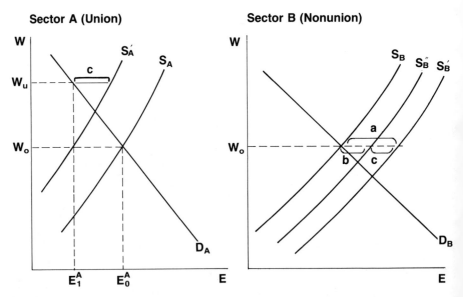

Sector A (Union)   **Sector B (Nonunion)**

sector may get the top applicants because of the high wages, and it is true that the reserve of labour may dry up in periods of prosperity (hence compelling the nonunion sector to pay higher wages), but it is also true that those who cannot get jobs in the union sector are a supply influx into the nonunion sector, and this lowers wages in that sector.

Nonetheless it is true that *some* nonunion employers may raise wages in order to reduce the threat of their employees choosing to become unionized. This threat effect will be greater if the union wage premium is high, the nonunion sector is easy to organize, the potential union is aggressive, or the employers have a strong aversion to unionization. In such circumstances, nonunion employees may be paid close to the union wage (perhaps even higher if the firm has a strong aversion to unionization) and provided with similar working conditions as union workers. Such employees could receive the benefits of unionization without bearing such costs as union dues or possible strike costs. However, such benefits may be precarious in that they hinge on the willingness of employers to provide them.

To illustrate the operation of the threat effect, we need to distinguish between those firms that choose to pay higher wages to avoid unionization — perhaps because of a strong aversion to unionization or because they are easy to organize — and those that will choose to pay the lowest wage needed to attract labour. This situation is shown in Figure 16-1(b). As before, the equilibrium in the absence of collective bargaining is the wage w_O in each sector. The establishment of a higher union wage w_u causes some employers (sector B) to raise wages to w_N^B, despite the supply of individuals willing to work at lower wages. (w_N^B may be above or below the union wage, depending on the employer's aversion to unionization.) Employment declines in sectors A and B; thus wages fall further in sector C than in the absence of the threat effect. In dual labour market analysis, sector C would be identified as the secondary labour market.

The impact of the threat effect on the union-nonunion wage differential is ambiguous. The nonunion wage is a weighted average of w_N^B and w_N^C with weights being the employment in each sector. This average nonunion wage may be higher or lower than the nonunion wage that would prevail in the absence of a threat effect, w_N in Figure 16-1(a).

Two additional theoretical points should be noted; these can be explained using the basic two-sector model. One is the possibility that the firm and union will negotiate wage-employment outcomes to the right of the labour demand curve, for reasons discussed previously. Figure 16-1(c) illustrates the case in which the parties negotiate outcomes on a vertical contract curve. (This can also be interpreted as an attempt to approximate an upward-sloping contract curve.) In these circumstances, the higher union wage is not associated with reduced employment in the union sector and therefore with depressed wages in the nonunion sector. The union-nonunion differential in this case is identical to the difference between the union wage and the wage union members would earn in the absence of collective bargaining.

The final complication to be discussed is that of "wait" or "queue" unemployment. The rationale behind this phenomenon can be understood by returning to the two-sector model illustrated in Figure 16-1(a). In that case it was assumed that all of the workers unable to obtain jobs in the union sector would seek employment in the nonunion sector. However, because union jobs pay relatively well, it may be rational to wait for a union job to turn up rather than seek employment elsewhere. This strategy is most likely to be sensible when there is rapid turnover in the union sector (so that union jobs become available fairly frequently) and when it is difficult to queue for a union job while employed. When these conditions apply, some individuals may choose to remain attached to the union sector, albeit unemployed. As a consequence, the increase in supply to the non-union sector will be less than the reduction in employment in the union sector; compare Figures 16-1(a) and (d). The union-nonunion wage differential will be smaller than in the case of no queuing unemployment, though higher union wages nonetheless have some depressing effect on the wages of nonunion workers.

Higher union wages may also affect the demand for labour in the two sectors. This outcome is most likely to occur when the sectors constitute two groups of firms — possibly one group easy to organize and the other difficult to organize — in the same industry. Unless offset by higher labour productivity (a possibility discussed later) the union-nonunion wage differential may enable nonunion firms to expand their market share at the expense of union firms, thus shifting the demand for nonunion (union) labour to the right (left). The final equilibrium in this case will generally involve a smaller union-nonunion wage differential than that shown in Figure 16-1(a).

The above analysis of the union wage impact was based on several simplifying assumptions, including a homogeneous labour force and competitive labour markets (in the absence of collective bargaining). Several implications follow from relaxing these assumptions. With several different types of workers, changes in the wages of any one group will generally alter the wages of other groups. If union and nonunion workers are employed in the same firm or industry, an increase in union wages will increase (reduce) the demand for nonunion labour if the two groups are substitutes (complements) in production, and therefore increase (reduce) the wages of nonunion workers in that firm or industry. In addition, the wages of nonunion workers may be affected by various forms of wage-fixing such as minimum wage rates and fair wage provisions, many of which are supported by unions to reduce competition based on lower nonunion wages. In these circumstances the wage in the unorganized sector may not decline sufficiently to absorb the workers displaced by higher wages in the union sector. Jobs will be rationed in both sectors and there will be a number of individuals willing to work at existing wage rates but unable to find employment.

In summary, collective action (in particular the strike threat) will generally enable unions to raise wages relative to a hypothetical labour market equilibrium without unions, thus creating a wage differential between union and comparable nonunion workers. The magnitude of this differential depends not only on the ability and willingness of unions to raise wages but also on the impact on the wages of nonunion workers. Clearly the various factors discussed above can be at work simultaneously affecting the wages of nonunion workers, and since they do not all work in the same direction, economic theory does not provide unambiguous predictions of the effect of unions on the wages of nonunion workers. The wages of some nonunion workers may increase because of the increased demand for substitute nonunion labour, as a result of the threat effect, in response to legislative wage-fixing, or as part of the nonunion sector adjusts to restore old wage relativities. In contrast, some nonunion wages may decrease because of a decrease in the demand for complementary inputs, or because of the supply influx into the nonunion sector created by the reduced employment opportunities in the unionized sector. Ultimately, the impact of unions on the wages of nonunion workers is an empirical proposition.

Some problems in measuring the union wage impact

Attempts to measure the union-nonunion wage differential face a number of problems, the most important being those of controlling for other wage-determining factors and separating cause and effect.

In estimating a *pure* union-nonunion wage differential, it is important to control for other wage-determining factors so as to be able to attribute the differential purely to unionization. If, for example, unionized establishments tend to utilize more skilled labour than non-unionized establishments, it is crucial to control for these skill differentials. Otherwise, the union-nonunion wage differential may simply reflect the skill differential, not a pure union impact on wages. Controlling for differences in labour quality between the union and nonunion sectors is especially important because, as indicated earlier, if unionized establishments have to pay a wage that is greater than the competitive wage, they will have a queue of applicants and will be able to hire the "cream of the crop" of workers. Union firms faced with higher labour costs may also try to increase the job assignment, for example by increasing the pace of work; however such adjustments are likely to be resisted by the union.

In these circumstances it is extremely important to control for differences in the characteristics of workers and job assignments. Otherwise these omitted variables are likely to impart an upward bias because the union-nonunion wage differential would reflect better quality workers and perhaps more onerous job assignments in the union sector in addition to the pure wage impact of unions. Empirical studies try to control for labour quality differences (for example, by including variables such as education, training, and experience in multiple regression analyses); however, some factors affecting labour quality (e.g. motivation, work effort, and reliability) may not be observed by researchers. Information relating to the pace of work and job assignments is also often unavailable, although some studies (e.g. Duncan and Stafford, 1980) have been able to control for these factors. Most studies are able to include only crude controls (such as occupation, industry, and region) for the characteristics of the job. Thus it is not clear that the available data enables researchers to *fully* control for differences in productivity-related factors, although as will be explained below the quality of the available data has steadily improved.

There is also the problem of sorting out cause and effect in studies of the union impact. Usually the argument is advanced that unions cause higher wages. However, there is the possibility that cause and effect also works in the opposite direction. That is, some firms may simply be high-wage firms, perhaps because they are trying to reduce the turnover of workers with firm-specific human capital, or because they want to be known as a model employer, or because they want a queue of applicants from which to hire. Unionization may be more likely to emerge in high-wage sectors because they are easier to organize or because the workers may be more likely to demand union representation. Workers in these firms will be reluctant to leave because wages are so high. Knowing that they want to stay in the high-wage establishment, and knowing that they will probably stay there for a considerable period of time because of the high wages, they may turn to devices to try to improve the everyday work conditions of the job. One such device may be unionization with its emphasis on due process, regulating the work environment, and administered rulings that provide a degree of certainty and security for the unionized workers.

In Hirschman's (1970) terminology, the restriction of "exit" increases the use of "voice." In this case, voluntary quitting (exit) is reduced because of the high wages, and hence workers seek to have more of a say (voice) in their job by collective bargaining.

This possibility of cause and effect working in both directions suggests that some of the wage advantage of union establishments may not be due to unions, but may be attributed to other factors; in fact, unionism itself emerges because of the wage advantage. This suggests that econometric studies of the impact of unions should be based on simultaneous equation models, which allow wages to be a function of unionism as well as unionism to be a function of wages.

EMPIRICAL EVIDENCE ON UNION WAGE IMPACT

In varying degrees the numerous empirical studies of the wage impact of unions have attempted to deal with the measurement problems just discussed. Research has passed through several phases. Early studies based on aggregate data (e.g. industry or region) have given way to those using data based upon the individual worker as the unit of observation. Recent studies have attempted to account for the joint determination of the extent of unionization and the union wage impact and for unobserved quality differences between union and nonunion workers. Much of the research has been carried out in the U.S.A. and our summary reflects this fact.

Early studies

The classic work of H. Gregg Lewis (1963) both reviewed and reanalysed the existing literature in the United States and provided new estimates up to 1958. While there was considerable variation in the estimated impact of the studies reviewed by Lewis, he attributed much of the variation to methodological differences. Lewis' estimate of the union-nonunion differential, based on his own work and a reanalysis of earlier studies, was approximately 10-15 percent for the U.S. economy as a whole, being larger in recessions and smaller in the boom phase of the business cycle. This estimate of a 10-15 percent differential was associated with an increase in the average union wage of 7 to 11 percent and a decrease in the average nonunion wage of approximately 3 or 4 percent.

Data availability imposed important limitations on these early studies. Because separate union and nonunion wage series were not available, the union-nonunion differential often had to be inferred from the average wage and the extent of unionization. This inference can be made only under certain restrictive assumptions; thus the estimates should be treated with caution.

Since Lewis' work there have been numerous additional studies, most utilizing new data sets where the unit of observation is the individual establishment or worker. Estimates of the union-nonunion wage differential based on individual cross-sectional data have tended to be higher than the 10-15 percent recorded by Lewis. These studies thus suggested that the union wage impact is higher than was previously believed. However, this conclusion is subject to the qualification that some of the difference between union and nonunion wages (after controlling for other wage-determining factors such as education, age, and experience) may be a reflection of reverse causality and/or unmeasured quality differences between union and nonunion workers. Recent research has focused on these issues.

Modeling union incidence and impact

A number of recent studies have attempted to account for the joint determination of union status and the union wage impact. Ashenfelter and Johnson (1972), who were the first to formally deal with the simultaneity issue, used aggregate U.S. time series data. They found that higher wages make unionization more likely, and that the estimated union wage impact is considerably smaller when the two-way causality is taken into account. Most subsequent studies have applied simultaneous equation methods with individual data. In addition, these authors often include a selectivity bias correction term to account for the possibility that the sample is not randomly generated with respect to union status; that is, some individuals have unobserved characteristics that make them more likely to be represented by a union than others.

Unfortunately the application of these more sophisticated techniques has not resulted in greater consensus about the magnitude of the average union wage impact. Indeed, the range of estimates produced by these studies is very wide, evidently a reflection of the sensitivity of simultaneous equations estimates to differences in specification and possibly the sensitivity of adjustments for selectivity bias.

Longitudinal studies

Another recent development has been the availability of longitudinal or panel data which provide observations on the same individuals over time. With longitudinal data, person-specific characteristics which are conventionally unobservable (e.g. reliability, work effort, and motivation) can be assumed to be fixed or constant for each individual over time, thus providing a natural way of controlling for the effects of such characteristics. This is in contrast to conventional cross-section estimates, which compare different individuals at the same point in time, and which can only control for differences in observed characteristics like education, training, experience, and union status. To the extent that these variables are correlated with unobserved variables that also influence wages then the cross-section estimates may not give a pure estimate of the impact of unions. Longitudinal data controls for the unobserved variables in a natural fashion and identifies the union impact from the wage change for those individuals who *change* union status. Essentially the estimated differential is an average of the earnings gain of those who moved from nonunion to union jobs and the earnings loss of those who moved from union to nonunion jobs, after controlling for other observable factors.

Longitudinal analyses in the United States (e.g. Mellow, 1981; Mincer, 1983; Moore and Raisian, 1983; Chamberlain, 1984) find that the estimated union-nonunion wage differential is about 10 percent, substantially smaller than suggested by cross-sectional estimates. Indeed, when cross-sectional analyses are carried out on the same data sets, the estimated differentials are approximately double those obtained using data on those who change union status. This finding suggests that unobserved (by the researcher) differences in worker quality between union and nonunion workers exist and are quantitatively significant; if true, this conclusion has important implications for the interpretation of not only observed earnings differences between organized and unorganized workers but also observed differences in labour productivity between the two sectors.

Even the longitudinal data has some deficiencies. There is evidence of substantial error in the measurement of union status which may bias downward the estimated union-nonunion wage impact (Freeman, 1984). Thus the estimated average wage impact of 10 percent may be too low. In addition, the number of individuals changing status is typically only 3-5 percent of the total sample, resulting in small and possibly unrepresentative samples. Furthermore, the facts that those individuals who change status may not be typical individuals and that changes in union status may themselves be associated with other unobservable factors suggest that it would be hazardous to rely exclusively on the estimates from longitudinal studies.

Summary of average impact in United States

Clearly important advances have taken place in the measurement of the union wage impact, a reflection of improved data sources and more sophisticated econometric methods. The accumulated U.S. evidence indicates that there is a statistically significant difference between the wages of union and otherwise comparable nonunion workers — probably in the order of 10 to 20 percent for the economy as a whole after controlling for observed and unobserved worker characteristics other than union status. In a major extension of his earlier work, Lewis (1986) reviews almost 200 empirical studies of the impact of unions on wages in the United States. He concludes that the average union-nonunion wage differential over the period 1967-79 was 15 percent. However, there remains uncertainty about the magnitude of the union-nonunion wage differential when the joint determination of unionization and its impact is taken into account.

Canadian evidence

Canadian studies of the union wage impact are summarized in Table 16-1. Studies using aggregate industry data, plant level data, and individual data have been carried out. The estimates are broadly similar to those obtained in comparable U.S. studies. Average differentials (for the samples used) generally lie in the 10-25 percent range. The much higher estimates obtained by Robinson and Tomes (1984) appear to be due primarily to the nature of the sample (hourly paid workers). Their estimates are also sensitive to the selectivity bias correction, as is the case in several U.S. studies.

One difference between the Canadian and U.S. evidence is that reported in the single Canadian study using longitudinal data. Grant, Swidinsky and Vanderkamp (1983) estimate an economy-wide average differential of 20-25 percent, much higher than U.S. studies based on longitudinal data. Unlike the U.S. studies, Grant et al. obtain similar estimates when they carry out a cross-sectional analysis on their data. The reasons for these substantial differences are unclear and remain an important issue for future research.

VARIATION IN THE UNION WAGE IMPACT

As would be expected on theoretical grounds, the estimated union-nonunion wage differential varies considerably across firms, industries, and workers. The average differential also varies over time. A number of generalizations about these variations emerge from the empirical literature, although for most generalizations there are exceptions in particular studies.

TABLE 16.1
ESTIMATE OF THE UNION/NONUNION WAGE DIFFERENTIAL IN CANADA

Author	Time Period	Estimated Differential (%)	Characteristics of Sample; Other Comments
1. Kumar (1972)	1966	17-23	Unskilled workers in manufacturing; aggregate data
2. Starr (1973)	1966	10-15	Unskilled male workers in Ontario manufacturing; disaggregate data (base wage rates at plant level)
3. Grant and Vanderkamp (1980)	1971	15	Individual data; "union member" includes membership in professional associations
4. MacDonald and Evans (1981)	1971-76	16	Aggregate industry data; 30 manufacturing industries
5. MacDonald (1983)	1971-79	20	Aggregate industry data; 30 manufacturing industries
6. Grant, Swidinsky and Vanderkamp (1983)	1969-71	20-25	Individual longitudinal data, annual earnings; "union membership" includes professional associations; selectivity bias correction
7. Robinson and Tomes (1984)	1979	Private sector 34 Public sector 27	Individual data on hourly paid workers; selectivity bias correction
8. Simpson (1985)	1974	18.6	Microdata on wage rates for narrowly defined occupations; selectivity bias correction
9. Kumar and Stengos (1985)	1978	10	Union and nonunion earnings data, by industry

The union-nonunion wage differential tends to be larger when a high proportion of the relevant jurisdiction (industry, occupation, region) is organized. The relationship, however, is nonlinear; once a certain proportion of the jurisdiction is unionized, further increases have little additional effect on the differential. These findings can be interpreted in terms of two aspects of union power discussed previously: the elasticity of demand for union labour and the threat effect. As the fraction of the industry (or occupation or region) unionized increases, the possibilities for the substitution of nonunion for union labour decline, reducing the elasticity of demand for union labour. However, as more of the industry is organized, the remaining nonunion firms may face a higher possibility that their workforce will organize and thus will tend to raise their wages. The gap between union and comparable nonunion workers in the same jurisdiction will thus not continue to widen, and may even narrow. (This latter finding is reported by MacDonald and Evans, 1981.)

Firm or establishment size has also been found to be positively related to both union and nonunion wages in the majority of studies. The relationship is considerably stronger for nonunion workers; thus the wage differential between union and comparable nonunion workers declines with firm or establishment size. This outcome may reflect several forces. Unions usually attempt to standardize wage rates across firms and occupations — to "take wages out of competition" — which implies raising wages more in smaller firms, given the positive relationship between wages and firm size in the absence of unionization. Further, the threat of union organization is generally higher (due to reduced organizational costs per prospective member) in larger firms. Thus larger nonunion firms are more likely to match union wage scales than their smaller counterparts.

Large differences in the estimated union-nonunion differential are usually found to exist across occupations and industries. The impact is higher for blue-collar workers than for white-collar workers (because their sample is restricted to hourly paid workers, the estimates obtained by Robinson and Tomes, 1984, are largely for blue-collar workers); higher in non-manufacturing than manufacturing industries; and it can be exceptionally high in certain specific sectors such as construction. Skilled workers typically gain less from unionization than their semi-skilled and unskilled counterparts, although there are specific examples of skilled trades — usually organized in craft unions — that exhibit large earnings differentials. Simpson (1985) provides a detailed analysis of skill differences in the union impact with Canadian data; some of his estimates are shown in Table 16-2. The estimated union-nonunion differentials decline almost monotonically with skill level; indeed, in the most skilled categories, nonunion wages exceed union wages. This outcome may largely reflect the fact that in many unions — especially industrial unions — skilled workers constitute a minority with little influence on the union's wage policy.

An alternative perspective on the relationship between union and nonunion wages and skill level is shown in Figure 16-2. (It should be understood that all other wage-determining factors are held constant.) Wages increase with skill level in both sectors; however, the increase is more gradual under collective bargaining, and at high skill levels the union may even fall below the nonunion wage. This type of relationship applies to a number of productivity-related characteristics (e.g. experience, education) in addition to skill. Simply stated, union wages are typically found to be less responsive to the personal characteristics of workers. The relationship between earnings and such factors as age, experience, education, and even marital status is weaker (i.e. age-earnings profiles are flatter, albeit higher) in the organized sector. When fringe benefits — which are typically of greater benefit to older, more experienced workers — are included together with wages this outcome is weaker, at least with respect to age and experience, but nonetheless remains.

One personal characteristic to which union and nonunion wages are approximately equally responsive is gender. Lewis (1986) surveys 48 U.S. studies dealing with the impact of unions on male and female wages; the union-nonunion wage differential for females is generally estimated to be similar to that for males. However, as noted by Freeman and Leonard (1985), there is evidence of a larger differential for females in the public sector. Although the union-nonunion differential for females is approximately the same as that for males, females benefit less from unionization because they are significantly less likely to be represented by a union than males.

TABLE 16.2

ESTIMATES OF THE UNION-NONUNION PERCENTAGE WAGE DIFFERENTIAL BY SKILL LEVEL, CANADA, 1974

Skill Level	All Industries	Manu- facturing	Non- Manufacturing	Public Sector[a]	Private Sector
1 (Low)	33.2	26.5	33.7	12.0	32.9
2	28.9	17.1	29.6	2.9	28.7
3	18.1	11.0	22.6	2.3	19.1
4	17.9	3.3	23.4	−1.0	19.0
5	12.4	−1.9	14.9	4.8	10.2
6	13.1	14.1	9.5	−24.3	15.0
7 (High)	−10.7	−11.1	−14.2	−33.4	−9.4
All Skill Levels	18.6	11.5	20.9	−10.6	18.9

Source: Wayne Simpson, The impact of unions on the structure of Canadian wages: an empirical analysis with microdata. *Canadian Journal of Economics* 18 (February 1985), 164-81.

Note: [a]Includes workers in health and education as well as public administration.

In the United States the union wage impact tends to be smaller in the public than in the private sector (Mitchell, 1983; Freeman, 1986). This finding may appear somewhat surprising, given that the elasticity of labour demand is generally estimated to be lower in the public sector. However, there are other important differences between the two sectors, and these may account for the observed behaviour. Unlike their private sector counterparts, many U.S. public sector employees do not have the right to strike. Thus the *willingness* of public sector workers to raise wages may be higher than in the private sector, but their *ability* to do so may be lower. In addition, union-nonunion wage differentials for the private sector workers most alike

Figure 16.2 The Relationship Between Union and Nonunion Wages and Personal Characteristics

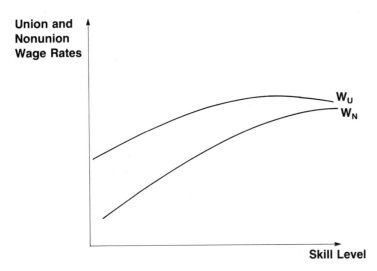

the majority of those in the public sector — those in white-collar, service sector employment — are significantly lower than for employees in blue-collar, goods-producing jobs. Thus, once one controls for the nature of employment, the public-private sector differences in union impacts narrow considerably. Finally, for reasons discussed in Gunderson (1984), public sector unions may have a larger impact on fringe benefits and working conditions than their private sector counterparts.

Canadian evidence, although limited, generally supports the conclusion that the union wage impact is smaller in the public sector. Robinson and Tomes (1984) find modestly lower differentials for hourly paid workers in the public sector (27 percent versus 34 percent in the private sector); however, only a minority of public sector workers are paid on that basis. As shown in Table 16-2, Simpson (1985) concludes that union-nonunion wage differentials are significantly lower in the public than private sector for each skill group. Indeed, the differentials for higher skill groups in the public sector are sufficiently negative that unionized public sector workers are estimated to earn *less* than comparable nonunion public sector workers, while unionized private sector employees earn substantially more than their nonunion counterparts. These studies therefore suggest that the positive earnings differential observed between comparable public and private sector employees arises because of the much greater extent of union organization in the public sector.

In his earlier work, Lewis (1963) concluded that unionism has probably lowered the wages of nonunion workers, this effect accounting for about 3 to 4 percentage points of the total estimated differential of 15 percent. Subsequent studies utilizing better data (Kahn, 1978, 1980) also reach this conclusion; however, the overall average effect masks considerable variability, with some groups such as nonunion white males receiving a large wage increase from unionism. This outcome suggests the operation of both the threat and labour supply effects of union wage increases, as analysed previously.

Lewis also concluded that the union-nonunion wage differential varies cyclically, widening in recessions and narrowing in booms; that is, union wages are less responsive to variations in economic and labour market conditions than nonunion wages. This behaviour partly results from the fact that collective agreements typically provide for fixed nominal wage rates — often for durations of two to three years — and these agreements overlap each other. At any point in time, only the fraction of union contracts being renegotiated are able to respond to changes in economic conditions. In the nonunion sector, agreements are implicit rather than explicit and wages can be adjusted in response to variations in economic conditions. However, even if union wage contracts were renegotiated frequently and did not provide for fixed durations (as is the case for example in Great Britain), union wages may well exhibit less cyclical variation than nonunion wages. For reasons discussed subsequently, unions are likely to prefer employment reductions to wage reductions as a method of responding to temporary reductions in labour demand.

Recent U.S. research has generally supported Lewis' conclusion that the union-nonunion wage differential varies counter-cyclically, although some conflicting results have been reported for the past two decades. The growth of cost-of-living-allowance clauses in collective agreements during this period is one factor that may have altered the cyclical behaviour of union wage rates. Because the price level varies pro-cyclically (in the absence of supply shocks), indexing union wages to the cost of living tends to increase their responsiveness to variations in aggregate economic conditions.

Canadian evidence on the time series behaviour of the union-nonunion wage differential is extremely limited. As can be seen from Table 16-1, nine years (1971-1979) is the longest period for which estimates are available. MacDonald (1983) finds the differential rose almost continuously during this period from 16.4 percent in 1971 to 22.8 percent in 1979. Because this was a period of generally rising unemployment and increasingly slack economic conditions, these results are broadly consistent with the hypothesis that the union wage impact varies counter-cyclically. U.S. studies (e.g. Mitchell, 1980; Johnson, 1984) also find substantial growth in the union-nonunion wage differential during the decade of the 1970s.

UNION WAGE IMPACT: CONCLUDING COMMENTS

There is substantial evidence of a significant wage differential between union and nonunion workers who are otherwise comparable in terms of observable characteristics. Based on a relatively limited number of Canadian studies, the average differential appears to be approximately 10 to 25 percent, similar in magnitude to estimates based on U.S. data. The earnings gap between union and comparable nonunion workers varies across industries, firms, regions, occupations and over time with aggregate economic conditions.

Although exceptions can be found in particular studies, a number of generalizations emerge from the substantial body of empirical research on the wage impact of unions:

(1) The overall impact of higher wages in the union sector is a somewhat lower average wage in the nonunion sector, consistent with additional labour supply to nonunion firms because of reduced employment opportunities in unionized enterprises. However, there is considerable variability in the effect on nonunion workers, with some gaining from higher union wages and others losing.

(2) In unionized enterprises, wage differences among workers who differ according to various productivity-related personal characteristics — such as education, age, experience, skill, and marital status — are smaller than in nonunion enterprises, and evidently smaller than they would be in the absence of unionization. Thus the financial "return" to additional amounts of these attributes — e.g. years of education or experience — is generally lower with collective than individual bargaining.

(3) The union-nonunion wage differential is generally higher in the private than the public sector, higher in small firms and enterprises, higher for blue-collar than white-collar workers, higher when a large proportion of the relevant jurisdiction is organized, and higher in recessions than booms.

Canadian empirical evidence is consistent with these conclusions; however, only a handful of studies have been carried out with Canadian data and there is considerable scope for further research.

Clearly a great deal has been learned about the effects of unions on wages. Nonetheless, several unresolved issues remain:

(1) On theoretical grounds there is reason to believe that unionized firms will respond to higher wages and the concomitant larger queue of applicants by hiring higher "quality" workers. The extent to which estimated union-nonunion differentials reflect this difference in labour quality rather than a pure differential remains largely unknown. U.S. evidence from longitudinal studies suggests that unobserved personal characteristics may account for a substantial proportion — perhaps as much as one-half — of the estimated wage differential. However, the differences between longitudinal and cross-sectional analyses could be due to other factors.

(2) Unionized firms may also respond to higher wages by attempting to increase the job assignment. Although empirical studies have generally been able to control for a variety of measured worker characteristics, few have been able to control for attributes of the job. Some studies

have concluded that estimated union-nonunion differentials partly reflect compensating differentials for more hazardous jobs, faster work pace, more structured work settings and less flexible working hours (Duncan and Stafford, 1980; Leigh, 1982).

(3) Uncertainty exists regarding the extent to which earnings differences between union and comparable nonunion workers are caused by unions raising their members' wages as opposed to unions being more likely to exist in firms that would choose to pay relatively high wages even in the absence of unions.

UNIONS, WAGE DISPERSION AND THE DISTRIBUTION OF INCOME

As documented by Freeman (1980, 1982), there is significantly less wage dispersion among union workers than among comparable nonunion workers. This smaller variance is related to several aspects of union wage policy noted above. Unions tend to reduce wage differentials among workers that differ according to factors such as skill, age, experience, and seniority. Unions also attempt to standardize the wages of similar workers across establishments, especially those in the same industry or region. Further, unions have a larger impact on the wages of blue-collar than on white-collar workers. These policies imply that unions typically raise the wages of those at the lower end of the pay scale proportionally more than those at the upper end. As a result, the union wage distribution is both to the right and less dispersed than the nonunion distribution, as shown in Figure 16-3.

Although wage dispersion is substantially lower in the union than in the nonunion sector, it does not necessarily follow that unionism is associated with reduced wage dispersion in the economy as a whole. By creating a wage differential between union and comparable nonunion workers, unions also increase the variability of earnings relative to a hypothetical economy without collective bargaining. Because of these offsetting factors — lower wage dispersion within the union sector but greater inequality between union and nonunion workers — the direction of the overall impact of unionism on the wage distribution is indeterminate. Studies by Hyclak (1979, 1980), Freeman (1980) and Quan (1984) indicate that in the United States the net effect of unionism is to reduce wage dispersion. Unfortunately there is no Canadian evidence on this aspect of the impact of unions.

UNION IMPACT ON RESOURCE ALLOCATION AND ECONOMIC WELFARE

Because they alter wages and employment, unions affect the allocation of labour and other resources in the economy. The nature and magnitude of this effect depends on several factors discussed previously in the context of the union wage impact. As before, the consequences of unions are studied by comparing the situation with unions to a hypothetical economy without unions.

Figure 16.3   Wage Dispersion in the Union and Nonunion Sectors

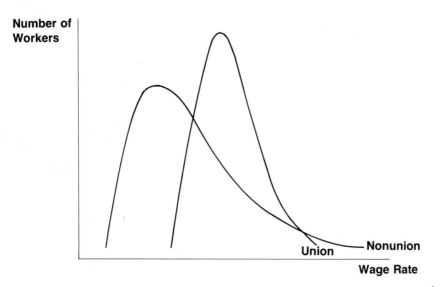

Figure 16-4 shows the allocative consequences of the union wage impact in a simple two-sector general equilibrium model in which outcomes are on the labour demand curve and the supply of labour to the economy is completely inelastic. With homogeneous workers and competitive labour markets, the equilibrium in the absence of unions implies a common wage (w_0) in both sectors. Because of the higher union wage w_u, employment declines to E_1^u in the union sector and increases to E_1^N in the nonunion sector, reducing the wage there to w_N. With inelastic labour supply the increase in employment in the nonunion sector ($E_0^N E_1^N$) equals the reduction in employment in the union sector ($E_1^u E_0^u$).

These changes in wages and employment result in an inefficient allocation of society's resources and a reduction in the total output and income generated by the economy. The magnitude of this allocative inefficiency can be illustrated using the fact that, because the labour demand curve is the marginal revenue product curve, the area under the labour demand curve equals the total value of the output produced. Thus the value of the output produced by the union sector declines by E_1^u a b E_0^u as a result of the union wage impact, while the value of output produced by the nonunion sector increases by E_0^N d f E_1^N. Total income declines by E_1^u a b E_0^u minus E_0^N d f E_1^N, an amount equal to the sum of the two hatched areas cab and edf. (This follows from the fact that the area E_1^u c b E_0^u equals the area E_0^N d g E_1^N and the area def equals the area dgf, assuming a linear demand curve.)

An alternative way of viewing the losses is to distinguish between deadweight or real resource losses and transfer losses, the latter of which represent a redistribution, not a loss, of output or income. For example, the loss of output E_1^u a b E_0^u in the union sector consists of two components: the loss of income E_1^u c b E_0^u to the displaced workers (which is a transfer loss since employers and ultimately customers are not paying that amount), and a real resource or deadweight loss abc which represents what consumers are willing to pay for the output over and above what the workers were willing to accept to produce the output. When the displaced workers move to the union sector ($E_1^u E_0^u = E_0^N E_1^N$), their income is reduced from E_1^u c b E_0^u in the union sector to E_0^N e f E_1^N in the nonunion sector. They therefore lose income of edgf. However, edf of that is a gain to the rest of society reflecting their value of the output E_0^N d f E_1^N over and above what they have to pay for the additional output E_0^N e f E_1^N. Therefore, the only real resource loss is dgf, which equals edf given a linear demand curve. Thus the total real output loss is abc plus def: the former represents what consumers are willing to pay for the loss of output in the unionized sector over and above what workers required to produce that output; the latter represents the loss associated with the fact that the output increase is valued less in the nonunion sector than the output loss in the union sector. The sum of these two components constitutes the welfare loss from union wage fixing in an otherwise competitive market.

This reduction in the value of total output is referred to as a "dead weight loss" because it is not offset by a benefit elsewhere. The misallocation of labour resources occurs because higher wages and reduced employment in the union sector push other workers into less-productive and more poorly paying jobs in the nonunion sector. As a result there are too few workers employed in the union sector and too many in the nonunion sector. The use of other resources is also affected. Relative to an efficient allocation of resources, firms will respond to the wage differential by utilizing excessively capital-intensive production techniques in the union sector and excessively labour-intensive techniques in the nonunion sector.

The existence and magnitude of a deadweight loss associated with the union wage impact depend on several factors discussed earlier: the elasticity of labour supply, the amount of queuing unemployment, and the extent to which firms and unions negotiate wage-employment outcomes to the right of the demand curve. Depending on these various factors, the magnitude of the reduction in total output may be lower or higher than that shown in Figure 16-4. For example, in the situation depicted in Figure 16-1(c) in which union wages and employment lie on a vertical contract curve, employment in the two sectors is identical to that which would occur in a competitive labour market equilibrium and no misallocation of labour resources results. In these circumstances, the higher union wage

Figure 16.4 The Union Wage Impact and Allocative Inefficiency

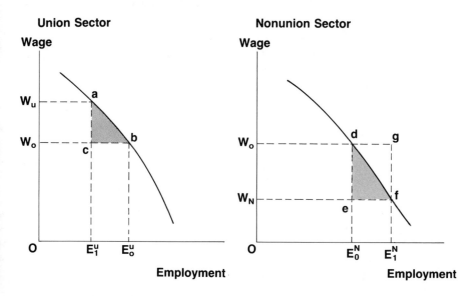

alters the distribution of income (increasing labour's share) but not total income. On the other hand, an additional output loss will occur if some individuals leave the labour force because the nonunion wage falls below their reservation wage and/or some individuals choose to remain unemployed hoping to receive a union job.

The potential allocative inefficiency associated with the union wage impact was illustrated using as a reference point an economy in a competitive equilibrium. From this starting point, any distortion such as monopoly in the product market or wage fixing in the labour market will result in a misallocation of resources and a reduction in total income. However, if the starting point is an economy with existing distortions, then it is not necessarily the case that adding another distortion (e.g. union wage impact) will cause a reduction in society's economic welfare. (This is the central proposition of the "Theory of Second Best" associated with Lipsey and Lancaster, 1958). The Canadian economy contains numerous distortions which would cause it to deviate from a first best (Pareto-optimal) allocation of resources in the absence of unions; therefore it is an empirical question as to whether the union wage impact improves or worsens allocative efficiency.

Early estimates of the deadweight loss, such as that of Rees (1963), were based on fairly crude methods and did not take into account other distortions in the economy. These studies estimated the loss for the United States to be about 0.15 percent of GNP when the union-nonunion wage differential was 15 percent. More recently, De Fina (1983) reports estimates based on a computational general equilibrium model of the U.S. economy incorporating several existing distortions. De Fina estimates the deadweight loss to be about half that of earlier studies; when the union-non-union wage differential is 15 percent, the loss is less than 0.1 percent of GNP, while a differential of 25 percent produces an estimated loss of 0.2 percent of GNP. The deadweight loss may be somewhat higher in Canada than in the United States owing to the higher union density. However, on the basis of the U.S. studies it appears unlikely to be substantially greater than 0.2 percent of GNP, or about 850 million dollars per year at 1984 levels of national income.

UNION IMPACT ON NON-WAGE OUTCOMES

Unions bargain for a wide range of factors in addition to wages, and a more complete understanding of the economic and social consequences of unions will emerge from examining these other outcomes of collective bargaining. We begin by discussing the impact of unions on fringe benefits and proceed to working conditions, quit and layoff behaviour, and productivity and profitability.

Unions and Fringe Benefits

Non-wage or fringe benefits refer to employer payments such as those for pensions, medical and life insurance, vacations, holidays, and sick leave. Omitting these benefits understates both the cost of labour to the employer and the benefit received by the employee; thus total compensation is the relevant measure for both labour demand and supply decisions. The omission of fringe benefits would not bias estimates of the impact of unions on the total compensation of union and nonunion workers if non-wage benefits were the same proportion of total compensation in both sectors. However, evidence indicates that non-wage benefits account for a greater proportion of total compensation among union than nonunion enterprises; i.e., unions tend to have a greater impact on fringe benefits than on wages. This implies that estimated union-nonunion differentials understate the total compensation gap between organized and unorganized workers.

Table 16.3 provides information on wage and non-wage compensation in Canada. Fringe benefits are divided into those which are legally required and those which are voluntary or negotiated. Legally required benefits account for similar proportions of total compensation in both sectors; however, voluntary/negotiated non-wage benefits account for a higher proportion of total compensation in unionized firms. In this sample, fringe benefits are 75 percent higher in unionized firms, while wage rates differ by about 30 percent between union and nonunion firms. The largest gap occurs with pension and health benefits. These data are not adjusted for other factors which may cause wages and non-wage benefits to differ between union and nonunion firms. However, empirical analyses with U.S. data (e.g. Freeman, 1981) indicate that significant differences between the two sectors remain after controlling for other factors.

TABLE 16.3

WAGE AND NON-WAGE BENEFITS IN UNION AND NONUNION FIRMS, CANADA, 1978[1]

Component of Compensation	Union Firms		Nonunion Firms		Union-nonunion Differential
	$/Yr.	%	$/Yr.	%	
Total Compensation	16,977	100.0	12,323	100.0	37.8
Pay for time worked[2]	13,192	77.7	10,159	82.4	29.9
Fringe Benefits (Total)	3,786	22.3	2,164	17.6	75.0
Legally Required Benefits[3]	1,043	6.1	651	5.3	60.2
Voluntary/Negotiated Benefits	2,743	16.2	1,513	12.3	81.3
Paid Absence[4]	1,634	9.6	1,085	8.8	50.6
Pension and Health[5]	699	4.1	248	2.0	181.9
Miscellaneous[6]	410	2.4	180	1.5	127.8

Source: Statistics Canada, *Employee Compensation in Canada*, 1980.

Notes: [1] Based on a survey of employers with 100 or more employees. Data are for wage earners only.

[2] Includes basic straight time pay, commissions, overtime and shift premium pay.

[3] Includes Canada and Quebec Pension Plans, workers' compensation, provincial medicare, and unemployment insurance.

[4] Paid holidays, sick leave and vacation pay.

[5] Private pension and other benefit plans.

[6] Includes COLA, bonuses, severance pay, and taxable benefits.

There are numerous reasons why all parties — employees, employers and governments — may prefer fringe benefits over wages as a form of compensation. (These are discussed in more detail in a subsequent chapter.) Workers may prefer fringe benefits because they are often not taxable or taxes are deferred; in addition there may be economies of scale and administrative simplicity associated with group purchases. Employers may benefit from the fringe benefits provided to employees to the extent that they facilitate the planning and operation of the production process, provide appropriate work incentives, and reduce turnover. In periods of wage control both parties may favour compensation via non-wage benefits. Governments may prefer fringe benefits (and hence grant favourable tax treatment) because private sector expenditures on items like pensions, workers' compensation, and unemployment insurance may reduce pressure for government expenditures in these areas.

While there are these reasons for the existence and growth of fringe benefits, the question remains as to why their magnitude is greater in the union than the nonunion sector. There are several theoretical reasons why this is so.

To the extent that union workers are made better off by unionization, they can afford to buy more of everything, including fringe benefits. Thus if the income elasticity of demand for non-wage benefits exceeds unity, union workers will devote a larger share of total income to fringe benefits than comparable nonunion workers. Compounding this effect is the fact that the price of non-taxable fringe benefits falls as income (and therefore the marginal tax rate) rises.

The union's role in articulating its members' preferences regarding non-wage benefits may also affect the share of total compensation devoted to fringe benefits. As discussed previously, because of their political nature unions can be expected to represent the wishes of the median union voter. In contrast, nonunion employers will design their compensation packages to appeal to the marginal worker — the employee on the verge of joining or leaving the firm — who is likely to be younger and more mobile than the member of median age or seniority. Because the demand for such fringe benefits as pensions and life, accident and health insurance increases with age, seniority, and family responsibilities, compensation packages in unionized enterprises are thus expected to devote a greater share to these non-wage benefits.

Fringe benefits in the form of deferred compensation are also expected to be more prevalent in unionized establishments. As discussed in a subsequent chapter, employers may prefer deferred compensation because of favourable work incentive effects (employees will work diligently in order to retain their jobs and thus receive the deferred payment later in their careers) and because it reduces turnover (employees who quit lose some or all of their deferred compensation — for example, pensions and vacation rights). Deferred compensation will be attractive to employees if they are given a sufficiently high wage to compensate for some of it being deferred (and hence its receipt being uncertain), and/or if they are provided with sufficient guarantees that employers will ultimately pay the deferred wages. Such guarantees are more binding when they are provided in a collective agreement which, for example, protects against arbitrary dismissal. Thus deferred compensation arrangements are expected to be more acceptable to union than nonunion employees, other things equal.

Freeman's (1981) empirical analysis indicates that unionism increases fringe benefits both directly and indirectly (through higher levels of compensation for union workers). This suggests that the tendency of unions to represent the preferences of the median or inframarginal worker and the increased acceptability of deferred compensation to workers protected by a collective agreement help account for the increased significance of non-wage benefits in the union sector.

Union impact on working conditions

In addition to their impact on wages and fringe benefits, unions affect a variety of working conditions. These changes may reflect both the collective bargaining objectives pursued by the union and the firm's response to the higher labour costs associated with unionism.

Union workplaces tend to be governed much more by various rules than comparable nonunion settings. Collective agreements typically stipulate such factors as the way grievances are to be handled, the role of company service, and the scheduling of worker hours. Nonunion enterprises, although not without their own bureaucratic procedures such as personnel policies, tend to be less rules-oriented, and to exhibit more worker and management flexibility.

In addition to a more structured work setting and less flexible hours, there is also evidence that unionized environments are characterized by a faster work pace. This may reflect the fact that unionism is more likely to occur in response to such working conditions or that employers are able to respond to the union wage effect by changing the conditions of work. Without being able to disentangle the true cause and effect, Duncan and Stafford (1980) estimate that about two-fifths of the union-nonunion wage differential reflects a compensating wage for these more onerous working conditions. This conclusion is relevant to interpreting empirical evidence not only on union-nonunion wage differences, but also on productivity differences between union and nonunion workers, discussed subsequently.

Union impact on turnover and mobility

Unions also affect various aspects of labour market turnover and mobility — quits, layoffs, rehires, promotions, and terminations. Numerous U.S. studies (e.g. Freeman, 1980a, 1980b; Blau and Kahn, 1983) have found that the quit rate is significantly lower among union workers than comparable nonunion workers. In part this reflects the reluctance of workers to leave the higher-wage union environment. However, even after controlling for differences in wages, union workers quit less frequently than their nonunion counterparts.

There may be several explanations for this phenomenon. As discussed previously, deferred compensation is more prevalent in union enterprises; such benefits provide an extra inducement to remain with the employer. Causality may also operate in the other direction. Deferred compensation such as pensions and vacations tied to length of service is more attractive to individuals who expect to remain with the firm for a long time. Thus this type of compensation tends to act as a sorting or screening mechanism, attracting to union firms workers who are less likely to quit (and vice versa in nonunion firms).

The lower quit propensity among union workers can also be interpreted as reflecting their substitution of a "voice" mechanism for an "exit" mechanism (Freeman, 1980; Freeman and Medoff, 1984). Union employees dissatisfied with their working conditions can attempt to bring about improvements through collective bargaining, while the main mechanism available to dissatisfied workers in nonunion enterprises is the threat of seeking employment elsewhere.

Unions also affect the use of temporary layoffs, hours reductions and wage reductions as mechanisms for responding to short-term fluctuations in demand. Collective agreements typically provide for a fixed nominal wage rate, possibly indexed to the cost of living but rarely indexed to other variables such as the state of the firm's product demand. With wages fixed, union firms rely more heavily on layoffs and recalls to respond to temporary fluctuations in demand than otherwise comparable nonunion firms, who make greater use of adjustments in wages and hours of work (Medoff, 1979; Blau and Kahn, 1983). In addition, seniority receives more weight in determining the order of layoffs and recalls in union firms. These differences in adjustment behaviour are consistent with the view that unions tend to represent the preferences of the median member. Having substantial seniority, such workers are unaffected by layoffs except in the case of extremely large reductions in the work-force. In contrast, nonunion employers respond to the preferences of the marginal worker. Being younger and less senior, such workers would prefer that all workers take a reduction in wages and/or hours rather than some workers being laid off in reverse order of seniority.

Internal mobility also differs between union and nonunion employees and organizations. Promotion decisions depend much more on seniority in union than nonunion organizations, as do decisions about employee terminations (Medoff and Abraham, 1982; Blau and Kahn, 1983). As with layoffs, the greater weight given to seniority in these organizational decisions can be seen as reflecting the preferences of the median union member.

Union impact on productivity and profitability

Although the impact of unions on various aspects of productivity has been debated for a long time, the subject received little quantitative analysis until recently. This recent literature has confirmed that unions can have both positive and negative effects on productivity, so that the overall impact depends on the magnitude of various offsetting factors.

In discussing the impact on productivity it is important to distinguish between the effects that occur directly as the outcome of collective bargaining and those that occur indirectly in the form of a behavioural response to higher wages. It is also important to recognize that unions may affect productivity not only in unionized firms but also elsewhere in the economy.

Economic theory predicts that firms will respond in several ways to the increase in labour costs associated with unionization. Relative to their nonunion counterparts, union firms will utilize more capital and other inputs and less labour per unit of output. Union employers will also attempt to hire more productive workers, and may try to increase job assignments and the pace of work.

Each of these responses to the union wage impact tends to raise labour productivity (output per worker) in the union sector and lower labour productivity in the nonunion sector. Thus a union-nonunion productivity comparison that does not control for differences in the amount of capital per worker, productivity-related worker characteristics, and the nature of the job assignment may well conclude that union workers are more productive than their nonunion counterparts. Although this conclusion would be correct, it would not follow that unions benefit society as a whole by raising worker productivity. For example, as discussed previously, the union wage impact and its consequences for the allocation of labour and other resources results in a reduction in society's total output and income, even though output per worker in the union sector rises. Similarly, society as a whole will, in general, not benefit from distributing the labour force such that unionized firms employ the more productive workers and nonunion firms the less productive. For these reasons, empirical analyses have attempted to determine whether unions and collective bargaining have direct effects on productivity in addition to those which arise as a consequence of the union wage impact. Such direct impacts, if positive do imply a social benefit; if negative they imply a social loss.

A common belief is that unions reduce productivity directly by inducing work stoppages and by negotiating restrictive work rules which compel the employer to use excessive amounts of union labour and/or prevent the employer from introducing technological innovations. However, as emphasized by Freeman and Medoff (1979, 1984), unions may also have positive effects on productivity by reducing turnover, improving morale and cooperation among workers, improving communications between labour and management, and by "shocking" management into more efficient practices.

Turnover is generally costly to firms because of expenses associated with hiring and training new workers to replace experienced personnel. While some turnover costs — for example, expenditures on job advertising — may not affect measured productivity, others — for example, existing personnel devoting less time to their own tasks and more to training new workers — do have this effect. In addition, lower turnover implies greater incentives for firms to engage in on-the-job training which enhances productivity. For these reasons, the lower quit rate in union enterprises is expected to result in higher productivity than in otherwise comparable nonunion enterprises. As discussed earlier, the differential in turnover can in turn be partly attributed to the union-nonunion wage differential and partly to the direct impact of collective bargaining.

Unions may affect employee morale, the amount of cooperation among workers, and communications between labour and management in several, possibly offsetting, ways. Employee morale may be enhanced through better wages, benefits and working conditions, by providing workers with a mechanism for expressing their collective preferences, and by negotiating grievance, dismissal and other procedures which protect workers from arbitrary treatment by management. Better morale may in turn raise productivity, although it is also possible that grievance procedures can be abused by workers — resulting in management and employee time being devoted to trivial matters — and that making dismissal more difficult may reduce work effort and protect the incompetent. By making promotions much more dependent on seniority, unions may increase the amount of cooperation among workers because there will be less competition among employees for advancement. On the other hand, competition among workers for promotion may also enhance work effort and thus raise productivity. Unions also provide a formal mechanism for communication between workers and management, and these communications channels can be used to provide the firm with information about potential improvements in production techniques, product design and the organization of the workplace. However, the union-management relationship can also become adversarial, with the consequence that there is less communication between the firm and its employees about potential improvements than in nonunion organizations.

Some analysts have also suggested that unionization — and the accompanying increase in labour costs — may shock the firm into adopting more efficient production and management techniques. This "shock effect" hypothesis assumes the existence of organizational slackness or inefficiency prior to unionization and is therefore consistent with satisficing behaviour on the firm's part, but not with optimizing behaviour (profit maximization and/or cost minimization). Although logically separate, the shock effect is difficult to distinguish empirically from the response of an optimizing firm to a change in relative factor prices — in this case, implementing a variety of changes in production techniques, hiring practices and job assignments which result in the more efficient utilization of union labour.

In summary, economic theory suggests a variety of mechanisms through which unions may affect productivity. Because there exist mechanisms that tend to both raise and lower productivity, the net impact is ambiguous. Empirical studies have found evidence of both positive and negative net impacts, suggesting that in some circumstances the productivity-enhancing mechanisms dominate while in others the opposite occurs. To the extent possible, studies have attempted to control for such factors as differences in capital per worker and in productivity-related worker characteristics such as education and experience. The purpose, then, is to estimate the direct impact of unions on productivity, i.e., to exclude those effects which are a consequence of the union-nonunion wage differential.

Broadly based studies using aggregate data have generally produced inconclusive results. Using cross-sectional data for U.S. manufacturing industries, Brown and Medoff (1978) found a large positive union impact on productivity when certain strong assumptions were made regarding the technology of production in union and nonunion firms, but found no statistically significant impact under more general assumptions. With pooled time series cross-section data for Canadian manufacturing industries, Maki (1983) obtains results which are even more sensitive to econometric specification, being positive when the Brown-Medoff assumptions are imposed but significantly negative under more general conditions. Adding to the conflicting results, Warren (1985) finds evidence of a negative union impact on productivity using aggregate U.S. time series data.

Empirical studies based on more disaggregated data generally appear to be much less sensitive to changes in specification. Using a large sample of individual U.S. firms, Clark (1984) estimates a small negative union impact on productivity. The growing number of econometric studies of individual industries provides evidence of both positive and negative impacts. In detailed studies of the U.S. cement industry, Clark (1980a, 1980b) finds that union labour was 6 to 8 percent more productive than nonunion labour, an amount which approximately offset the higher labour costs associated with the union wage impact. Large productivity effects have been estimated in residential and office construction (Mandelstamm, 1965; Allen, 1984), a sector in which the union-nonunion wage differential is also substantial. However, union and nonunion labour are estimated to be equally productive in the construction of schools (Allen, 1984). The difference may be due to the high degree of competition in residential and office construction relative to that for schools. Consistent with the hypothesis that product market competition plays an important role in the impact of unions on productivity is the general finding that there is no union-nonunion productivity differential in the provision of public sector services such as municipal libraries (Ehrenberg, Sherman and Schwarz, 1983) hospital services (Sloan and Adamache, 1984), and building department services (Noam, 1983).

Labour-management relations also appear to be an important determinant of labour productivity. The dramatic productivity decline in Canadian postal services was evidently caused by a sharp deterioration in labour-management relations (Read, 1982). U.S. studies of unionized automobile plants (Katz, Kochan and Gobeille, 1983) and paper mills (Ichniowski, 1984) find that productivity is negatively related to the number of grievances, a measure of labour-management relations. Perhaps the strongest evidence of the importance of these factors is that of Freeman, Medoff and Connerton (1979) who estimate that in the U.S. bituminous coal industry, union labour went from being significantly more to substantially less productive than nonunion labour during the period 1965-75, a reversal which they attribute to changes in labour relations.

Management response to unionization may also play a significant role. In his study of cement plants that became unionized, Clark (1980a) found that existing managers were replaced with new managers who were less paternalistic or authoritarian, and who placed more emphasis on controlling costs, setting production standards and improving communication and monitoring. This adjustment can be interpreted either as a "shock effect" or as an optimizing firm's substitution of higher quality managerial input in response to an increase in the relative price of production labour.

In summary, the impact of unions on productivity, long a controversial issue, has received considerable attention recently. Evidence on the average economy-wide impact is inconclusive. However, in specific industries union labour has been found to be more productive, in some cases substantially so, than comparable nonunion labour. This productivity differential persists after controlling for differences in capital per worker and observed productivity-related worker characteristics, differences which can be attributed to the union-nonunion wage differential. However, the existence of a positive union impact on productivity is by no means assured. The direction and magnitude of the effect appears to depend on the management response to unionization, the quality of labour-management relations and perhaps the degree of product market competition.

The conclusion that in some industries union labour is significantly more productive than comparable nonunion labour will no doubt surprise those who believe that, by restricting management flexibility and negotiating various work rules, unions reduce production efficiency. Sceptics are correct in claiming that several interpretations can be given to such evidence. Unions may organize the most productive firms in the industry, perhaps because these are the most profitable and have the greatest potential for wage gains. Alternatively, as discussed previously in the context of the union wage impact, there may be unobserved differences in worker characteristics and/or job assignments which account for observed productivity differences. However, it also may be the case that, for the various reasons discussed above, union representation makes otherwise comparable workers more productive.

One interesting consequence of a positive union productivity effect is that it may explain the coexistence of both union and nonunion firms in the same industry. In a perfectly competitive industry unions must either organize all the firms in the industry (and credibly threaten to organize potential entrants) or the cost-increasing consequences of the higher union wages must be offset by higher productivity. When barriers to entry or other factors enable firms to earn above-normal profits, it is not essential that union wage gains be offset by the higher productivity of union labour. In these circumstances unions may be able to capture some of the economic rents that would otherwise accrue to the firm's managers and/or owners. Empirical evidence indicates that this in fact occurs. Despite differences in data sources, measurement of profitability and methodology, numerous U.S. studies are unanimous in concluding that union firms are less profitable than comparable nonunion firms. The available Canadian evidence, although somewhat inconclusive, is generally consistent with this finding (Maki and Meredith, 1986).

The conclusion that unions are associated with lower profits implies that owners and managers of firms are rational in generally opposing unionization, despite the possible existence of a positive union impact on labour productivity. In an interesting U.S. study, Ruback and Zimmerman (1984) find that the effect of unionization on firm profits is anticipated by stock market participants. Equity values fell significantly when an application for a union representation election was announced. The decline was substantially higher in those cases in which the union subsequently achieved certification, suggesting that investors were also able to anticipate the outcome of the representation vote.

QUESTIONS

1. Discuss the various wage structures and wage levels that unions can affect.
2. Discuss the various ways in which unions can affect the wages of *non-union* labour.

   Why may one expect the skill level of union workers to be different from the skill level of nonunion workers? What does this imply about union-nonunion wage differentials? Why may one expect high wages to cause unionism, as well as vice versa, and what does this imply about union-nonunion wage differentials?

   Why may the union-nonunion wage differential not reflect the impact of unions on the wages of their members relative to what their wage would be in the absence of unionism?
3. If you expect the wage impact of unions to differ systematically with respect to certain conditions (e.g., extent of unionization in the industry or extent of concentration in the product market), how would you capture the interaction effect in a regression equation designed to measure the impact of unions?
4. The following union impact equation was estimated by Starr (1973, p. 56, Equation 11.3):

   $W = .361\ CA + .00403\ CA{\cdot}U + .00377\ CA{\cdot}CR - .01228\ CA{\cdot}RLC$ + other control variables where W is the male base wage rate in the establishment; CA represents the existence of a union in the establishment (coded one if the establishment has a collective agreement, zero otherwise); U represents the percentage of the industry that is unionized; CR represents industry concentration; and RLC is the ratio of wage labour cost to value added.

   (a) Theoretically justify the use of each of these explanatory variables.
   (b) What sign would you expect for each regression coefficient?
   (c) Why are the explanatory variables entered in the equation in that particular fashion: that is, multiplied by CA?
   (d) What is the effect on wages of being unionized as opposed to non-unionized?
   (e) Evaluate this effect at the following mean values of the explanatory variables: $\overline{U} = 57.6$, $\overline{CR} = 7.8$, $\overline{RLC} = 36.1$.
   (f) Compare this union impact in an establishment with the impact that would occur if the industry in which the firm operated was completely unionized, other things being equal.
   (g) Compare the union impact of part (e) with the impact that would occur if the ratio of wage labour cost to value added were only 20 percent as opposed to the average of 36.1 percent.
5. Discuss why the union wage impact may vary according to such factors

as industry, occupation, the stage of the business cycle and the size of the firm.

6. Discuss the pros and cons of using longitudinal data to estimate the impact of unions.
7. Discuss why wage dispersion may differ between comparable union and non-union workers.
8. Discuss the effect of unionization on the efficient allocation of resources. How would you measure these "welfare" effects?
9. Discuss the effect of unions on fringe benefits and working conditions.
10. Discuss the various ways in which unions may affect productivity.
11. Indicate how the average union non-union wage differential, estimated from micro data based upon the individual as the unit of observation can be decomposed into two component parts: one part attributable to their different wage determining characteristics and the other due to different prices for the same characteristics.
12. In their article "The Two Faces of Unionism," R. Freeman and J. Medoff state:

    "According to our recent research on the subject, treatment of unions as organizations without solidaristic or purposive values, whose sole function is to raise wages, is seriously misleading. While unions appear to raise wages above competitive levels, they also have significant nonwage effects which influence diverse aspects of modern industrial life. By providing workers with a voice both at the work place and in the political arena, unions can and do positively affect the functioning of the economic and social systems."

    Elaborate and assess this claim.
13. For each part, classify the statement as either true, partly true but incomplete, or false and explain your reasoning:
    (a) Unions tend to raise wages for unionized workers and lower wages for most non-union workers. Thus unions tend to increase the amount of income inequality in the economy.
    (b) A powerful union is one for which the costs of a strike to the firm are very high, while a weak union is one for which costs of a strike are low.
    (c) Empirical research has found that unionized labour is more productive than comparable nonunion labour. This proves that unions increase the total value of output in the economy.
    (d) Unions can't raise wages in competitive industries because firms earn zero economic profits in equilibrium in these industries.

REFERENCES

Addison, J. and A. Barnett. The impact of unions on productivity. *BJIR* 20 (July 1982) 145–162.

Allen, S. Trade unions, absenteeism and exit voice. *ILRR* 37 (April 1984) 331-345.

Allen, S.G. Trade unionized construction workers are more productive. *QJE* 99 (May 1984) 251-274.

Ashenfelter, O. and G.E. Johnson. Unionism, relative wages, and labour quality in U.S. manufacturing industries. *IER* 13 (October 1972) 488-508.

Blakemore, A., J. Hunt and B. Kiker. Collective bargaining and union membership effects on the wages of male youths. *JOLE* 4 (April 1986) 193-211.

Blau, F.D. and L.M. Kahn. Unionism, seniority, and turnover. *IR* 22 (Fall 1983) 362-373.

Borjas, G. Job satisfaction, wages, and unions. *JHR* 14 (Winter 1979) 21-40.

Brown, C. and J. Medoff. Trade unions in the production process. *JPE* 86 (June 1978) 355-378.

Chamberlain, G. Multivariate regression models for panel data. *Journal of Econometrics* 18 (January, 1982) 5-46.

Christensen, S. and D. Maki. The union wage effect in Canadian manufacturing industries. *JLR* 2 (Fall 1981) 355-368.

Clark, K. The impact of unionization on productivity: a case study. *ILRR* 33 (July 1980) 451-469.

Clark, K. Unionization and productivity. *QJE* 95 (December 1980) 613-640.

Clark, K. Unionization and firm performance. *AER* 74 (December 1984) 893-919.

Connerton, M., R.B. Freeman and J.L. Medoff. Industrial Relations and Productivity: A Study of the U.S. Bituminous Coal Industry. Harvard University, mimeo, 1983 revision.

DeFina, R.H. Unions, relative wages, and economic efficiency. *JOLE* 1 (October 1983) 408–429.

Duncan, G. and D. Leigh. Wage determination in the union and non-union sectors: a sample selectivity approach. *ILRR* 34 (October 1980) 24-34.

Duncan, G. and F. Stafford. Do union members receive compensating wage differentials? *AER* 70 (June 1980) 335-371.

Eberts, R. Union effects and teacher productivity. *ILRR* 37 (April 1984) 346-358.

Ehrenberg, R.G., D.R. Sherman and J.L. Schwarz. Unions and productivity in the public sector: a study of municipal libraries. *ILRR* 36 (January 1983) 199-213.

Freeman, R.B. Unionism and the dispersion of wages. *ILRR* 34 (October 1980) 3-23.

Freeman, R.B. The exit-voice trade-off in the labour market: unionism, job tenure, quits and separations. *QJE* 94 (June 1980) 643-673.

Freeman, R.B. The effect of unionism on worker attachment to firms. *JLR* 1 (Spring 1980) 29-62.

Freeman, R.B. The effect of unionism on fringe benefits. *ILRR* 34 (July 1981) 489–509.

Freeman, R.B. Union wage practices and wage dispersion within establishments. *ILRR* 36 (October 1982) 3-21.

Freeman, R.B. Longitudinal analyses of the effects of trade unions. *JOLE* 2 (January, 1984) 1-26.

Freeman, R.B. Unionism comes to the public sector. *JEL* 24 (March 1986) 41-86.

Freeman, R.B. and J.S. Leonard. Union maids: unions and the female workforce. National Bureau of Economic Research Working Paper No. 1652. June 1985.

Freeman, R. and J. Medoff. The two faces of unionism. *The Public Interest*. (Fall 1979) 69-93.

Freeman, R. and J. Medoff. The impact of the percentage organized on union and non-union wages. *R. E. Stats* 63 (November 1981) 561-572.

Freeman, R.B. and J.L. Medoff. The impact of collective bargaining: can the new facts be explained by monopoly unionism? *New Approaches to Labor Unions*, J.D. Reid, Jr. (ed.), Greenwich, CT: JAI Press, 1983.

Freeman, R.B. and J.L. Medoff. *What Do Unions Do?* New York, NY: Basic Books, 1984.

Grant, E.K., R. Swidinsky and J. Vanderkamp. Union-Non-Union Differentials in Annual Earnings: An Empirical Study Using Canadian Longitudinal Micro Data 1969-71. University of Guelph, mimeo, April 1983.

Grant, E.K. and J. Vanderkamp. The effects of migration on income: a micro study with Canadian data, 1965-71. *CJE* 13 (August 1980) 381-406.

Gunderson, M. The Public/Private Sector Controversy. *Conflict or Compromise: The Future of Public Sector Industrial Relations*, M. Thompson and G. Swimmer (eds.). Montreal: Institute for Research on Public Policy, 1984. 1-44.

Hirsch, B.T. and A.N. Link. Unions, productivity and productivity growth. *JLR* 5 (Winter 1984) 29-38.

Hirschman, A.O. *Exit, Voice and Loyalty*. Cambridge, MA: Harvard University Press, 1970.

Hyclak, T. The effect of unions on earnings inequality in local labour markets. *ILRR* 33 (October 1979) 77-84.

Hyclak, T. Unions and income inequality: some cross-state evidence. *IR* 19 (Spring 1980) 212-215.

Ichniowski, C. Industrial Relations and Economic Performance: Grievances and Productivity. National Bureau of Economic Research Working Paper 1367, June 1984.

Johnson, G.E. The determination of wages in the union and non-union sectors. *BJIR* 15 (July 1977) 211-225.

Johnson, G.E. Changes over Time in the Union-Non-union Wage Differential in the United States. *The Economics of Trade Unions: New Directions*, J. Rosa (ed.), Boston, MA: Kluwer-Nijhoff, 1984.

Jones, E.B. Union/non-union differentials: membership or coverage? *JHR* 17 (Spring 1982) 276-285.

Kahn, L.M. The effects of unions on the earnings of non-union workers. *ILRR* 31 (January 1978) 205-216.

Kahn, L.M. Union spillover effects on unorganized labour markets. *JHR* 15 (Winter 1980) 87-98.

Kahn, L.M. The effect of collective bargaining on production technique: a theoretical analysis. *JLR* 5 (Winter 1984) 1-12.

Kalachek, E. and F. Raines. Trade unions and hiring standards. *JLR* 1 (Spring 1980) 63-76.

Karier, T. Unions and monopoly profits. *R.E. Stats* 67 (February 1985) 34-42.

Katz, H.C., T.A. Kochan and K.R. Gobeille. Industrial relations performance, economic performance, and QWL programs: an interplant analysis. *ILRR* 37 (October 1983) 3-17.

Killingsworth, M. Union-nonunion wage gaps and wage gains. *R.E. Stats* 65 (May 1983) 332-336.

Kuhn, P. Union productivity effects and economic efficiency. *JLR* 6 (Summer 1985) 229-248.

Kumar, P. Differentials in wage rates of unskilled labour in Canadian manufacturing industries. *ILRR* 26 (October 1972) 631-645.

Kumar, P. and T. Stengos. Measuring the union relative wage impact: a methodological note. *CJE* 18 (February 1985) 182-189.

Lee, Lung-Fei. Unionism and wage rates: a simultaneous equations model with qualitative and limited dependent variables. *IER* 19 (June 1978) 415-434.

Leigh, J.P. Are unionized blue collar jobs more hazardous than non-unionized blue collar jobs? *JLR* 3 (Summer 1982) 349-357.

Lewis, H.G. *Unionism and Relative Wages in the United States: An Empirical Inquiry.* Chicago, IL: University of Chicago Press, 1963.

Lewis, H.G. Union relative wage effects: a survey of macro estimates. *JOLE* 1 (January 1983) 1-27.

Lewis, H.G. *Union Relative Wage Effects: A Survey.* Chicago: University of Chicago Press, 1985.

Lipsey, R.G. and J. Lancaster. The general theory of second best. *R.E. Studies* 24 (December 1956) 11-32.

Macdonald, G.M. The size and structure of union — non-union wage differentials in Canadian industry: corroboration, refinement and extension. *CJE* 16 (August 1983) 480-485.

Macdonald, G. and J. Evans. The size and structure of union — non-union wage differentials in Canadian industry. *CJE* 14 (May 1981) 216-231.

Maki, D.R. The effects of unions and strikes on the rate of growth of total factor productivity in Canada. *Applied Economics* 15 (February 1983) 29-41.

Maki, D.R. Trade unions and productivity: conventional estimates. *RI/IR* 38 (No. 2, 1983) 211-225.

Maki, D. and S. Christensen. The union wage effect re-examined. *RI/IR* 35 (No. 2, 1980) 210-229.

Maki, D. and L. Meredith. The effect of unions on profitability: Canadian evidence. *RI/IR* 41 (No. 1, 1986) 54-68.

Mandelstamm, A.B. The effects of unions on efficiency in the residential construction industry: a case study. *ILLR* 18 (July 1965) 503-521.

Medoff, J.L. Layoffs and alternatives under trade unions in U.S. manufacturing. *AER* 69 (June 1979) 380-395.

Medoff, J.L. and K.G. Abraham. The role of seniority at U.S. workplaces: a report on some new evidence. Cambridge, Mass. *NBER* Working Paper No. 618, 1981.

Mellow, W. Unionism and wages: a longitudinal analysis. *R.E. Stats* 63 (February 1981) 43-52.

Mincer, J. Union effects: wages, turnover, and job training. *New Approaches to Labor Unions*, J.D. Reid, Jr. (ed.), Greenwich, CT: *JAI Press*, 1983.

Mitchell, D. Some empirical observations of relevance to the analysis of union wage determination. *JLR* 1 (Fall 1980) 193-216.

Mitchell, D. Union — non-union wage spillovers. *BJIR* 18 (November 1980) 372-376.

Mitchell, D.J.B. Unions and wages in the public sector: a review of recent evidence. *Journal of Collective Negotiations* 12 (4) (1983) 337-353.

Moore, W., R. Newman and J. Cunningham. The effect of the extent of unionism on union and non-union wages. *JLR* 6 (Winter 1985) 21-44.

Moore, W. and J. Raisian. Cyclical sensitivity of union/non-union relative wage effects. *JLR* 1 (Spring 1980) 115-132.

Moore, W.J. and J. Raisian. The level and growth of union/non-union relative wage effects, 1967-1977. *JLR* 4 (Winter 1983) 65-80.

Mulvey, C. and J. Abowd. Estimating the union/non-union wage differential: a statistical issue. *Economica* 47 (February 1980) 73-80.

Noam, E.M. The effect of unionization and civil service on the salaries and productivity of regulators. *New Approaches to Labor Unions*, J.D. Reid, Jr. (ed), Greenwich, CT: *JAI Press*, 1983.

Parsley, C. Labor union effects on wage gains. *Journal of Economic Literature* 18 (March 1980) 1-31.

Pencavel, J.H. The distributional and efficiency effects of trade unions in Britain. *BJIR* 15 (July 1977) 137-156.

Pencavel, J.H. and C.E. Hartsog. A reconsideration of the effects of unionism on relative wages and employment in the United States, 1920–1980. *JLE* 2 (April 1984) 193-232.

Podgursky, M. Unions, establishment size and intra-industry threat effects. *ILRR* 39 (January 1986) 277-284.

Polachek, S.W. and E.P. McCutcheon. Union effects on employment stability: a comparison of panel versus cross–sectional data. *JLR* 4 (Summer 1983) 273-288.

Quan, N. Unionism and the size distribution of earnings. *IR* 23 (Spring 1984) 270-277.

Raisian, J. Union dues and wage premiums. *JLR* 4 (Winter 1983) 1-18.

Read, L.M. Canada Post, a case study in the correlation of collective will and productivity. *Research on Productivity of Relevance to Canada*, D.J. Daly (ed.), Ottawa: Social Science Federation of Canada.

Rees, A. The effects of unions on resource allocation. *Journal of Law and Economics* 6 (October 1963) 69-78.

Robinson, C. and N. Tomes. Union wage differentials in the public and private sectors: a simultaneous equations specification. *JOLE* 2 (January 1984) 106-127.

Rosen, S. Trade union power, threat effects and the extent of organization. *R.E. Studies* 36 (April 1969) 185-196.

Rosen, S. Unionism and the occupational wage structure in the United States. *IER* 11 (June 1970) 269-286.

Ruback, R. and M. Zimmerman. Unionization and profitability: evidence from the capital market. *JPE* 92 (December 1984) 1134-1157.

Schmidt, P. Estimation of a simultaneous equations model with jointly dependent continuous and qualitative variables: the union-earnings question revisited. *IER* 19 (June 1978) 453-465.

Schmidt, P. and R.P. Strauss. The effect of unions on earnings and earnings on unions: a mixed logit approach. *IER* 17 (February 1976) 204-212.

Shah, A. Job attributes and the size of the union/non-union wage differential. *Economica* 51 (November 1984) 437-446.

Simpson, W. The impact of unions on the structure of Canadian wages: an empirical study with micro data. *CJE* 18 (February 1985) 164–181.

Slichter, S.H., J.J. Healy and E.R. Livernash. *The Impact of Collective Bargaining on Management*. Washington, DC: Brookings Institution, 1960.

Sloan, F.A. and K.W. Adamache. The role of unions in hospital cost inflation. *ILRR* 37 (January 1984) 252-262.

Solnick, L. The effect of blue-collar unions on white-collar wages and fringe benefits. *ILRR* 38 (January 1985) 236-243.

Starr, G.E. *Union-Non-union Wage Differentials: A Cross-Sectional Analysis.* Toronto: Research Branch, Ontario Ministry of Labour, 1973.

Stewart, M. Relative earnings and individual union membership in the United Kingdom. *Economica* 50 (May 1983) 111-126.

Toner, B. The unionism and productivity debate: an employee opinion survey in Ireland. *BJIR* 23 (July 1985) 179-202.

Viscusi, W.K. Strategic behavior and the impact of unions on wage incentive plans. *JLR* 3 (Winter 1982) 1-12.

Voos, P. and L. Mishel. The union impact on profits: evidence from industry price-cost margin data. *JOLE* 4 (January 1986) 105-133.

Warren, R.S., Jr. The effect of unionization on labor productivity: some time series evidence. *JLR* 6 (Spring 1985) 199-207.

Wessels, W. The effects of unions on employment and productivity: an unresolved contradiction. *JOLE* 3 (January 1985) 101-108.

Part
V

Wage Structures

17

Compensating Wages: Applications to Fringe Benefits and Risk

In previous chapters we discussed labour demand and various aspects of labour supply and how they interact in alternative market structures to determine the wages and employment of a homogeneous group of labour. In the chapters of this section we focus on the wage *differentials* that arise when jobs and job characteristics are not homogeneous, but differ because of positive characteristics like fringe benefits, negative characteristics like risk, and that differ by occupation, industry, region, and personal characteristics.

FRINGE BENEFITS AND TOTAL COMPENSATION

Any analysis of wages and wage structures is complicated by the fact that wages are only one aspect of the total compensation associated with a job. In particular, fringe benefits (indirect labour costs) are a large and increasing component of total compensation.

This is illustrated in Table 17.1. Between 1957 and 1984 fringe benefits as a percentage of direct labour costs (wages) increased from 16.4 to 32.4 percent. This approximate doubling in percentage terms tended to occur across most of the categories of fringe benefits, so that the ranking of the components remained the same, with pay for time not worked, and pension and welfare plans being the largest components, although the latter grew the slowest.

The existence and growth of fringe benefits are interesting phenomena to try to explain, especially given the basic economic proposition that unconditional cash transfers (e.g. wages) are more efficient than transfers-in-kind (e.g. fringe benefits). This economic proposition follows from the fact that recipients who receive cash could always buy the transfers-in-kind if they wanted them, but they are better off because they could buy other things if they wanted them more. Applied to fringe benefits, why wouldn't employees and employers prefer wage compensation since it would enable employees to buy whatever fringe benefits they want rather than being given some they may not value?

There are obviously a variety of possible reasons for the existence and growth of fringe benefits. They are usually not taxed and, as taxes have increased over time, this increasingly makes fringe benefits a preferred

TABLE 17.1
FRINGE BENEFITS:[1] COMPONENTS AND CHANGES OVER TIME

Fringe Benefit Categories	$ Per Worker		% of Wages	
	1957	1984	1957	1984
Pay For Time Not Worked	287	4107	6.7	14.9
Pension and Welfare Plans	272	2639	6.4	9.4
Payments Required By Law[2]	87	1175	2.0	4.4
Bonuses, Profit-Sharing, Other	55	1036	1.3	3.7
Total Fringe Benefits	701	8957	16.4	32.4

Notes: [1]Figures are for all industries. Separate figures for manufacturing and non-manufacturing are not dramatically different.
[2]Includes workers' compensation, unemployment insurance and Canada/Quebec pension plans.
Source: 1957: Industrial Relations Counselors Service Inc., *Fringe Benefit Costs in Canada*, Toronto, 1957.
1984: Thorne Stevenson and Kellogg, *Employee Benefit Costs in Canada*, Toronto, 1984.

form of compensation. (This does raise the question, however, of why governments should want to offer tax advantages to fringe benefits over wages.) There may be economies of scale, and administrative economies for group purchases through the employer of such things as pension and insurance plans. However, many of these economies still could be had through completely voluntary group plans. There is the possibility that workers think they are receiving fringe benefits free in the sense that, if they did not have the fringe benefits, their wages would not rise by a corresponding amount. This possibility, of course, can be true in times of wage controls to the extent that fringe benefits are exempt or more difficult to control. More likely, workers simply prefer fringe benefits because it is an easy way of purchasing benefits that they value. In some cases, like increased vacations and holidays with pay, it is a way of institutionalizing the increased purchase of more leisure that accompanies their growing wealth.

Employers may have accepted the increased role of fringe benefits for reasons that are beneficial to them. Paid vacations and holidays, for example, enable the planning of the production process more than if the workers' desire for increased leisure came in the form of lateness, absenteeism, work slowdowns, or turnover. Similarly, workers' compensation and unemployment insurance and health insurance can reduce the need for employers to have contingency plans for workers in industrial accidents or subject to layoffs or health problems. In addition, some fringe benefits may alter the behaviour of workers in a fashion that is preferred by the employer. Subsidized cafeterias can reduce long lunch hours and keep employees in the plant, the provision of transportation can ensure that workers get to work on time, company health services can reduce absenteeism and provide a check on a worker's health, and pensions and other seniority-related fringe benefits may reduce unwanted turnover. Employers may also prefer fringe benefits because they reduce turnover and provide work incentives. Non-wage benefits such as company pension plans and seniority-based vacation pay represent deferred compensation in that these benefits are received later in the employee's career. Workers who leave the firm early in their careers do not receive these benefits. With some of their compensation in the form of deferred benefits, existing employees will be less likely to quit in order to seek or accept employment elsewhere. In addition, deferred compensation raises the cost of being fired for poor work, absenteeism, and so on, thus strengthening work incentives. These effects of deferred compensation on turnover and work incentives are discussed further in Chapter 24.

Deferred compensation can also act as a sorting or screening device, enabling the employer to hire those workers who are most likely to remain with the firm. Employers for whom turnover is very costly — perhaps because of the costs of hiring and training new workers — can screen out those potential employees who do not expect to remain with the firm for an extended period by making deferred compensation a significant proportion of total compensation, a compensation package that is most attractive to potential employees who expect to remain with the firm for a long period of time. Such screening mechanisms are especially valuable when the employer is unable to determine *ex ante* which job applicants are likely to leave the firm after a brief period and which are likely to remain with the firm.

Governments may also prefer fringe benefits (and hence grant favourable tax treatment) because they may reduce pressures for government expenditures elsewhere. Employer-sponsored pensions may reduce the need for public pensions; contributions to the Canada (or Quebec) Pension Plan may reduce the need for public care for the aged, at least for the aged who have worked; and increased contributions for unemployment insurance directly reduce the amount the government has to pay to this fund. In addition, many fringe benefits are part and parcel of the whole package of increased social security, and hence the reasons for their growth are caught up with the reasons for the growth of the whole welfare state.

PURPOSES OF WAGES AND WAGE STRUCTURES

The discussion of wage determination is complicated by the fact that wages and wage structures are called upon to serve a variety of purposes in our economy. Wage structures are the relative prices of labour that are utilized to allocate labour to its most productive and efficient use and to encourage human capital development — education, training, mobility, job search — into areas yielding the highest return. Wages are also the price that compensates workers for undesirable job characteristics and hence they ensure that the supply of and demand for such characteristics are in balance. In addition wages are an important component of family income and hence may have an important role to play in the achievement of an equitable distribution of income. Our macroeconomic objectives of full employment, price stability, and a viable balance of payments can also be affected by wage developments, just as wage determination is affected by the macroeconomic environment.

There is a complex nexus between wages and productivity. Usually we think of high wages being the result of high productivity that can come about, for example, through various forms of human capital formation, or through technological change. (With respect to the latter factor, wage increases are one way of distributing the gains of general productivity improvements; price reductions are another.) However, there is the possibility of cause and effect working the other way as well. That is, high wages may induce productivity improvements through improved morale, health, and intensity of work effort, as well as by reductions in absenteeism and turnover. In addition wage increases may induce efficient changes elsewhere in the system — changes that should have occurred earlier but that would not occur without the shock induced by a wage change.

The matter is further complicated by the fact that wages and wage structures serve a social role, in that prestige is associated with wages; hence, the importance of *relative* positions in the wage hierarchy and the importance of key comparison groups. The social role of wages is further heightened by the fact that labour services are inseparable from the person who provides the services: hence, the importance of the human element in labour market analysis.

Clearly wages and wage structures are called upon to serve a variety of often conflicting roles in our economic system in particular, and in our social system in general. Perhaps this is why there is so much emotive conflict over various policies — such as minimum wages or wage controls or equal pay legislation — that affect wages.

THEORY OF COMPENSATING WAGES

Just as wages are but one component of the total compensation package and hence are expected to be lower, other things equal, when fringe benefits are higher, so do wages serve the purpose of compensating employees for undesirable working conditions or for negative or costly attributes associated with a particular job. Such conditions include an unsafe or unhealthy work environment, long commute time, undesirable working hours, lengthy training or other human capital requirements, and even the need for workers with discriminatory preferences to work in an integrated work environment. As illustrated subsequently, many of these characteristics are associated with particular occupations, industries, regions or firms and hence form part of the rationale for wage structures associated with these factors. In this chapter, the theory of compensating wages is illustrated with respect to compensating wages associated with the risk of injury or illness that can result from an unsafe or unhealthy work environment — an area where the theory has seen considerable development and empirical application.

Single Firm's Isoprofit Schedule

Figure 17.1a illustrates a single firm's isoprofit schedule, I, defined as the various combinations of wages and safety that the firm can provide and

Figure 17.1   Employer's Isoprofit Schedules and Offer Curve

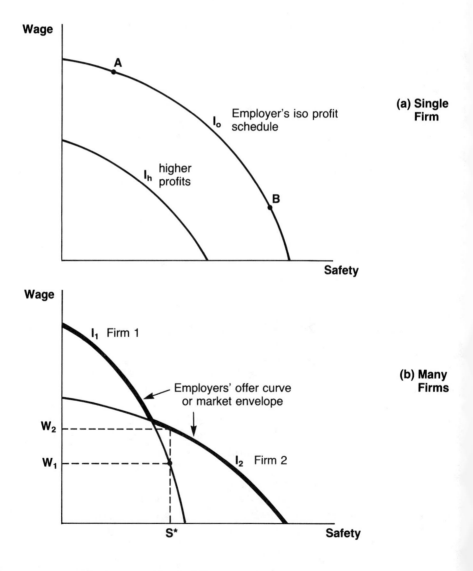

maintain the same level of profits. For the firm, both wages and a safe work environment are costly to provide; hence, the negative trade-off between the two. That is, the firm can provide more safety and maintain profits only if it can pay a lower wage. The isoprofit schedule exhibits a diminishing marginal rate of transformation between wages and safety. That is, in the upper left portion, like at point A, where the firm is providing little safety, it can provide additional safety in a relatively inexpensive fashion with minor basic changes in its safety technology (e.g. better lighting, signs, guard rails). It is in a stage of increasing returns with respect to the provision of safety. In such circumstances, the firm can provide these inexpensive safety features without requiring much of a wage reduction in order to maintain a constant profit level. That is, the isoprofit schedule is relatively flat.

Conversely, in the bottom right segment as at point B, where the firm is providing considerable safety, it can provide additional safety only through the introduction of more sophisticated and costly safety procedures. It is in a stage of diminishing returns in the provision of safety, having already exhausted the cheapest forms of providing safety. That is, as the firm moves from left to right on the horizontal axis and provides additional safety, it will start with the cheapest forms of safety provision and then move to the more expensive. In such circumstances, it will require an even larger compensating wage to compensate for its additional safety costs, in order to maintain the same level of profits. That is, the isoprofit schedule will become steeper as more safety is provided and the firm moves from point A towards B.

Lower isoprofit schedules like I_h in Figure 17.1a imply higher levels of profits. That is, profits are the same at all points along I_h just as they are the same at all points along I_o. However, profits are higher along I_h than I_o. This is so because to the firm both wages and safety are costly to provide. Hence, providing both lower wages and lower safety means higher profits.

Different Firms with Different Safety Technologies

Different firms can have different abilities to provide safety at a given cost. Hence different firms may have differently shaped isoprofit schedules even for the same level of profit (e.g., even if they all operate at the competitive level of zero excess profits).

Figure 17.1b illustrates the isoprofit schedules for two firms (or industries, or occupations). Firm 1 exhibits rapidly diminishing returns to providing a safe work environment. Additional safety can only be provided if wages drop quite rapidly to compensate for the safety costs, if profits are to be maintained. This could be the case, for example, for firms in sectors that are inherently dangerous, such as mining or logging. In contrast, Firm 2 may be in an inherently safer industry and hence be able to provide high levels of safety without having to pay a high compensating wage to maintain profits. Equilibrium requires that profits be the same in firms 1 and 2 and a competitive equilibrium ensures that excess profits are reduced to zero (i.e., $I_1 = I_2 = 0$).

The outer limits of the two isoprofit schedules (bold line), given the employers' *offer* curve or market *envelope* curve, show the maximum compensating wages that will be offered in the market for various levels of safety. Points within the envelope will not prevail in the market because they will always be dominated by points on the envelope. For example, for a given level of safety, S^*, Firm 2 is able to offer the compensating wage W_2 and maintain its given level of profit, I_2. Firm 1, in contrast, can only offer the compensating wage, W_1, and stay in business under the zero excess profit condition. Hence, Firm 2's offer will dominate Firm 1's offer for levels of safety, like S^*, to the right of the intersection of the isoprofit schedules; Firm 1's offer will dominate to the left of the intersection. In other words, assuming perfect competition, workers would always go to employers that offer the highest compensating wage for every level of safety; hence, only points on the outer segments of the isoprofit schedules will prevail in a competitive market.

Single Individual's Preferences

As with any other items they value, individuals will have preferences for wages and safety. These preferences can be illustrated by a typical indifference or isoutility curve showing various combinations of wages and safety that yield the same level of utility, as depicted in the top panel, Figure 17.2a. The curvature of the isoutility curve illustrates a diminishing marginal rate of substitution between wages and safety. That is, at points in the upper left segment such as A where the individual does not have a very safe work environment, that individual would likely be willing to give up considerable wages to get a slightly safer work environment. Hence the indifference curve is steep. Conversely, at points such as B where the individual has a safe work environment, the individual may not be willing to give up much in the form of wages to obtain additional safety. Hence, the isoutility curve is relatively flat. Higher indifference curves, like U_h, indicate higher levels of utility since the individual has more of both wages and safety, both of which yield utility.

Different Individuals with Different Risk Preferences

Different individuals may have different risk preferences and hence may show a different willingness to give up safety in return for a compensating risk premium in the form of higher wages. Figure 17.2b illustrates a more risk-averse and a less risk-averse individual. As indicated at the point of intersection of the two schedules, the more risk-averse individual requires a larger compensating wage in return for giving up some safety and accepting a riskier work environment.

Figure 17.2   Worker Isoutility Curves

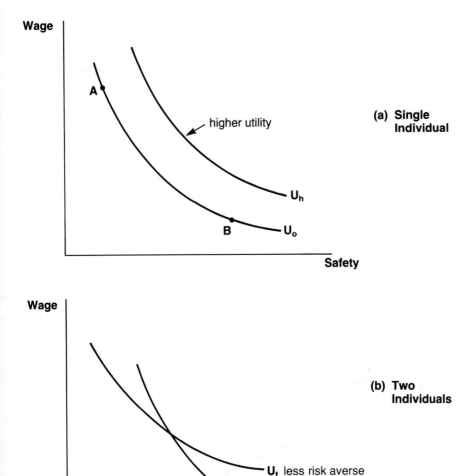

Equilibrium with Single Firm, Single Individual

Figure 17.3a illustrates the market equilibrium for a single firm and single individual as the point of tangency, E_c, between the firm's isoprofit schedule, I_c, and the individual's isoutility curve U_c. This is an equilibrium because the compensating wage, W_c, required by the worker for the level of safety, S_c, is just equal to what the firm is willing to offer for that level of safety. For movements to the left of S_c, the additional wage that the in-

Figure 17.3   Market Equilibrium

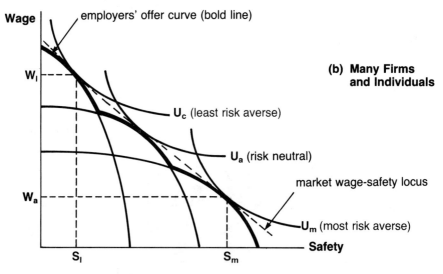

dividual requires for accepting more risk (i.e., slope of the isoutility curve) is greater than what the firm is willing to give (i.e., slope of the isoprofit schedule) in order to maintain the same competitive profit level. Conversely, for movements to the right, what the worker is willing to give up for additional safety is insufficient to compensate the employer so as to maintain the same competitive profit level.

Higher isoutility curves are not attainable for the worker, because they would lie outside of the feasible choice set as dictated by the employer's isoprofit schedule, I_c, which gives the competitive level of profits.

Higher isoprofit schedules would imply profits that are below the competitive level. Conversely, under competitive conditions, individuals would not have to accept combinations of lower wages and safety that would put them on isoutility curves below U_c (and employers on isoprofit schedules that are closer to the origin, implying profits above the competitive norm) because workers could move to firms that would offer higher compensating wages and still maintain competitive profits. Of course, if firms could offer lower combinations of wages and safety (e.g., if worker mobility were restricted or they did not know the risk to which they were exposed), then workers would be on lower isoutility curves and firms would have higher profits.

Equilibrium with Many Firms and Individuals

Figure 17.3b illustrates the market equilibrium that will prevail when there are many firms and individuals. Assuming perfect competition, individuals will sort themselves into firms (occupations, industries) of different risks (i.e., along the market envelope schedule) and receive differing compensating wages for the different levels of risk. The least risk-averse individual, for example, will enter a high-risk firm in order to get the higher wage, W_1, associated with the low level of safety, S_1. Conversely, the most risk-averse individual will enter the low-risk work environment and accept the lower wage, W_m, in order to have the safe work environment, S_a.

The set of tangencies between the various isoprofit and isoutility schedules gives the various equilibrium combinations of wages and safety that will prevail in the market. This is termed the wage-safety locus (dashed line in Figure 17.3b). The *slope* of that locus of wage-safety combinations gives the change in the wage premium that the market yields for *differences* in the risk of the job. The slope of that line can change for different levels of safety. It is determined by the interaction of workers' preferences and the firms' technology for safety, and these basic underlying determinants may change with the level of safety. The only restriction on the slope of the line is that it be negative, reflecting the fact that compensating wages are required for reductions in safety, given worker aversion to risk and the fact that safety is costly to firms.

The fact that the slope of the wage-safety locus can change magnitude but not direction means, for example, that the compensating wage premium required for *additional* risk may be very high in an already risky environment. Whether that is true, however, is an empirical proposition since it depends upon whether there are sufficient workers willing to take that risk in return for the higher wage, and whether firms could reduce the risk in ways that are less costly than paying a wage premium for workers to accept the risk.

In such circumstances of perfect information and competition (assumptions that will be relaxed later), the market will pay a compensating wage premium for undesirable working conditions, such as risk. This will induce workers to sort themselves into jobs depending upon their aversion to risk. It will also induce employers to adopt the most cost-effective safety standards (not necessarily the safest) since they can save on compensating wages by increasing their safety. In this fashion the need of employers to carry on production in a manner that may involve some risk, is required to confront the equally compelling need of workers for desirable working conditions, and vice versa. The price that mediates these competing objectives is the compensating wage paid for the undesirable working conditions.

Obviously, the markets for each and every characteristic are likely to be "thin" (i.e., involve few buyers and sellers). For example, a worker who wants (and is willing to pay for) a job that is reasonably safe, close to home, and that allows flexible working hours, may not have a large set of jobs to choose from. Of course, if enough workers want those characteristics, then employers will find it is in their interest to provide them, because of the lower wages they can pay in return for providing the desired work characteristics. Nevertheless, it is easy to see that there may not be a large number of buyers and sellers for each and every characteristic, and hence the shadow price yielded by the market for each characteristic may not be the same as the competitive price that would prevail if there were many buyers and sellers for *each* characteristic.

ALTERNATIVE PORTRAYAL

The previous analysis was portrayed in terms of conventional indifference curve analysis with wages and safety — both of which are valued by employees — displayed on the axes. Following the insurance literature, the analysis is often portrayed in wage-*risk* space with risk portrayed on the horizontal axis. Since risk is negatively valued by employees this will obviously alter the portrayal; nevertheless, the same conclusions follow.

In Figure 17.4 the upward-sloping isoprofit schedules illustrate how firms can pay higher wages and maintain profits if risk can be increased because reductions in risk (increases in safety) are costly. The curvature of the isoprofit schedules exhibits diminishing returns; that is, as risk is reduced to very low levels in a firm it becomes extremely costly to reduce risk further and hence a larger wage reduction is necessary to maintain profits. The employers' offer schedule (bold line) indicates the maximum compensating wage that will be offered in the market for each level of risk. Points on employers' isoprofit schedules below that line will be dominated by points on the offer curve. Higher offer schedules yield lower profits since firms have to pay a higher compensating wage for every level of risk.

Worker indifference curves slope up because workers require a higher compensating wage to remain indifferent to the additional risk. Their curvature illustrates a diminishing marginal rate of substitution between wages and risk; that is, for a given individual to accept more risk and remain indifferent, an ever-increasing compensating wage is required to compen-

Figure 17.4   Wage-Risk Space Portrayal

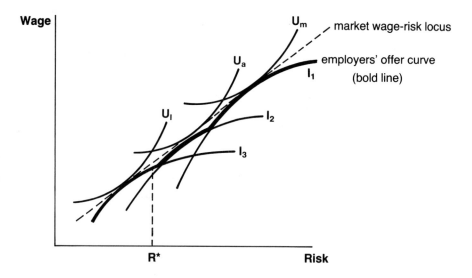

sate for the increasing risk. Different individuals have different aversions to risk, as illustrated by the different indifference curves. As depicted at the intersection of the indifference curve for the most risk-averse (U_m) versus the least risk-averse (U_l) individual, the risk-averse individual requires a higher compensating wage to accept additional risk.

Individuals will sort themselves into different firms (occupations, industries) on the basis of their willingness to accept risk in return for a compensating wage. The locus of tangencies between worker indifference curves and the employers' offer schedule will trace out the market wage-risk locus illustrating the varying wage premium the market will yield for different levels of risk. The market wage-risk locus can be of any configuration except that it slopes upwards, indicating the assumptions that workers require a compensating wage for additional risk and reductions in risk are costly for employers.

EFFECT OF SAFETY REGULATION

Perfectly Competitive Markets

The effect of safety regulation depends critically upon whether markets are operating properly or not to compensate workers for occupational risk. In markets that are operating perfectly the effect of regulation may be perverse. This is illustrated in Figure 17.5a. For a single representative firm and individual, the competitive equilibrium is given at E_c, with the wage, W_c, being paid for the level of safety, S_c. In the absence of any external effects on third parties for which the market does not extract appropriate

Figure 17.5   Responses to Safety Standard

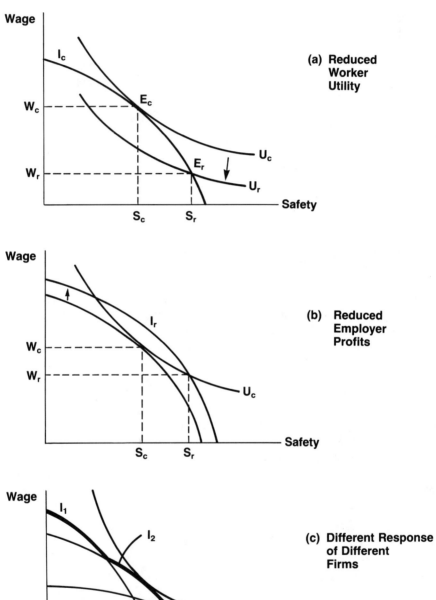

(a) Reduced Worker Utility

(b) Reduced Employer Profits

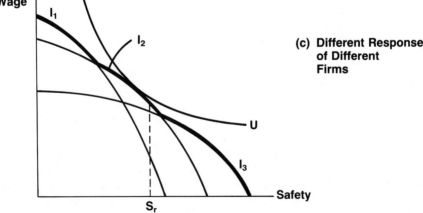

(c) Different Response of Different Firms

compensation, the level of safety, S_c, can be considered socially optimal in the sense that the price mechanism, through compensating wages, ensures that neither employers nor employees want to move from the level of safety, S_c. By moving from S_c neither party can be made sufficiently better off to compensate the other party so that they are no worse off.

A regulatory agency that required the parties to increase the level of safety to S_r would actually make one or both parties worse off, in this particular situation of perfectly competitive markets. This is illustrated in Figure 17.5a, where the firm remains on its isoprofit schedule (it has to if this is the competitive level of zero excess profits) and the individual worker is on a lower level of utility U_r, with compensating wage W_r. The worker's level of utility under regulation is lower (i.e., $U_r < U_c$), because the worker is not voluntarily willing to accept the wage reduction from W_c to W_r in return for the safety increase from S_c to S_r; if given the choice the worker would return to E_c. In this particular example, the firm was no worse off after the regulation (i.e., on the same isoprofit schedule) but the worker was worse off (i.e., on a lower indifference curve). If the firm originally had excess profits it could absorb the cost increase associated with the safety regulation and not go out of business. In such circumstances the worker need not be worse off after the regulation. This is depicted in Figure 17.5b, where the firm moves to a higher isoprofit schedule, I_r, (with lower profits because it is experiencing both higher wage and safety costs) and the worker stays on the same isoutility curve. The worker still receives a reduction in the compensating wage from W_c to W_r, but this is exactly offset by the increase in safety, so that utility remains constant at U_c. In this case, the firm bears the cost of the safety regulation by taking lower profits.

Realistically, the cost of the safety regulation will likely be borne by both workers in the form of compensating wage reductions and firms in the form of lower profits, their respective shares depending upon their relative bargaining powers.

Not all firms will be affected in the same fashion. For some, the safety regulation may be redundant since they are already meeting the standard. Others may be put out of business, unless their work-force accepts wage concessions. This is illustrated in Figure 17.5c for three firms that are as- sumed to be operating under a competitive profit constraint so that excess profits are zero (i.e., $I_1 = I_2 = I_3 = 0$). For Firm 3, a uniform safety standard of S_r would be redundant since it is already providing a safer work envi- ronment than required by the standard; that is, the relevant portion of its isoprofit curve making up part of the market wage envelope always lies to the right of S_r. Firm 2 could meet the standard and stay in business only if its work-force were willing to provide wage concessions (and hence a lower level of utility) for the firm to stay on its zero profit isoprofit schedule. (For simplicity only the isoutility curve for a representative worker of Firm 2 is shown.) Firm 1 would go out of business because its isoprofit schedule is below that of Firm 2 in the relevant region of the safety standard S_r. That is, for the minimal level of safety, S_r, Firm 2 could offer a higher compensating wage than Firm 1 and still stay in business. Workers in Firm 1 would go to Firm 2 if the standard were improved, even though they would prefer to be in Firm 1 with no standard. This competitive analysis, of course, assumes that Firm 2 can absorb the workers, with no adverse general equilibrium effects.

While this analysis suggests that the application of a uniform safety standard has the desirable effect of weeding out firms whose safety technology is such that they cannot meet the standard, it must be remembered that they were able to pay a sufficiently high wage to attract certain workers who were willing to accept the inherent risk. By imposing a uniform standard, the regulators are saying that firms that cannot meet the standard will not be able to operate no matter how much they are able to pay to have workers willingly accept the risk.

Imperfect Information

The previous analysis assumed perfect information about the level of safety involved. Such an assumption, however, may be unrealistic in situations where employers may have a vested interest in not disclosing information about health hazards, and where the latency period before an occupational disease shows up can be very long. In such circumstances, workers may think that they have a higher level of safety, and hence, utility, for the compensating wage they receive.

This situation is depicted in Figure 17.6. For a given compensating wage, W_a, associated with an actual level of safety, S_a, workers may perceive their level of safety to be greater at S_p. Their (mis)perceived level of utility would be U_p, while their actual level would be U_a. In such circum-

Figure 17.6 Effect of Imperfect Information

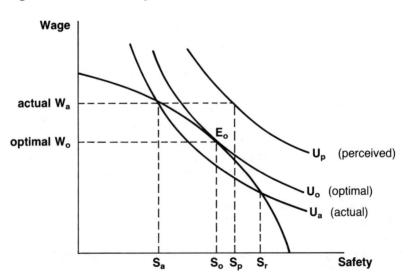

stances, any imposed safety standard between S_a and S_r could improve workers' utility without making employers worse off since they would be on the same or a lower isoprofit schedule (lower schedules representing higher profits). The optimal standard would be at the point of tangency, E_o, between the employer's isoprofit schedule and the employee's highest attainable indifference curve.

Providing the parties the correct information would also lead to the optimal amount of safety because workers would increase their utility by moving to offers in the range of the offer curve between S_a and S_r. Ultimately, they would arrive at E_o, accepting the wage reduction from W_a to W_o in return for the increase in safety from S_a to S_o. With full information, market forces can also lead to the optimal amount of safety.

Rationale for Regulation

If a perfectly competitive market with proper information can lead to the socially optimal amount of safety at the workplace, why does regulation persist, especially since it runs the risk of making both employers and employees worse off? While no easy answer to this question exists, a number of plausible explanations can be given, in addition to the possibility that it may simply be a well-meaning mistake. First, information is not perfect and may be hidden by employers or improperly discounted by workers. Second, competition may not prevail for the buying and selling of each and every job characteristic, including safety in the work environment. Workers simply may not have much choice in the risk of their work. Third, workers who opt for risk in return for a high wage may not pay the full cost of their decisions to the extent that the state bears some of the medical or workers' compensation costs if the risk comes to fruition. Fourth, society may feel that workers ought not to have to sell their health and safety to make a living, even if they are willing to do so. If regulating safety means a lower compensating wage, then it may be best to try to take care of that problem through other income maintenance schemes. Fifth, the willingness of workers to accept some risk in return for a compensating wage premium may be dictated by the existing amount of risk to which they are currently exposed. If that risk is reduced by law for everyone, they may actually prefer the new level of risk even though earlier they were unwilling to accept the wage reduction to achieve the reduced risk. Although economists tend to regard preferences as given, preferences in fact may be influenced by our existing state. Lastly, there may be the feeling that the market simply may not yield the compensating wages necessary to ensure the socially optimal amount of safety.

EMPIRICAL EVIDENCE ON COMPENSATING WAGES

Obtaining empirical evidence on the existence of compensating wages for undesirable working conditions is difficult because of the problem of controlling for the myriad of positive and negative job characteristics to isolate the separate effect of one characteristic. This is compounded by the fact that situations of strong employee bargaining power often have high wages, good fringe benefits, and good working conditions. While there still could be a trade-off between wages and a better work environment, there is often insufficient variation in the data to identify the trade-off with any degree of precision.

In some cases the trade-off may be direct and explicit. For example, collective agreements or company pay policy may specify a premium for underground as opposed to above-ground mining, or for the night shift as opposed to the day shift. Premiums for an isolation allowance or even hazard pay may be explicitly mentioned with the explicit price stated.

In other circumstances, however, the compensating pay premium is not explicitly given but rather is embedded as part of an individual's wage rate and hence is an implicit or "shadow" price associated with the job characteristic. It can be estimated only by comparing wages in jobs that are similar except for the one characteristic. Given that jobs involve a multiplicity of characteristics this is not an easy task and usually requires fairly sophisticated statistical procedures.[1]

A number of such studies have estimated compensating wages for undesirable job characteristics such as the risk of being unemployed (Adams 1985, Li 1986), the uncertainty of pension receipts (Smith 1981, Schiller and Weiss 1980), the mandatory requirement to work overtime (Ehrenberg and Schumann 1984), and retirement characteristics (Ehrenberg 1980). The most extensive literature in this area pertains to compensating wages for the risk of injury or death on the job. These studies have been plagued by a number of econometric problems that are typical of statistical work in economics.

For example, in addition to higher wages being paid to compensate for undesirable working conditions, cause and effect may work the other way as undesirable working conditions may result from lower wages. That is, low-wage individuals can't afford to buy a safe work environment and the forgone income from an accident is less to them. These income and substitution effects, respectively, cause them to buy less occupational health and safety. Failure to account for such reverse causality can lead to a simultaneous equation bias in the estimates of compensating wages for work hazards. Simultaneous equation techniques to account for the two-way causality have been employed in only a few such studies (e.g., Chelius 1979 and McLean, Wendling and Neergeard, 1978).

---

[1] Conventionally, this is done by multiple regression analysis which enables isolating the effect of one variable while controlling for the effect of the other variables included in the regression. In this case, wages are regressed on various wage-determining factors including job characteristics and human capital factors. The resulting regression coefficients for the job characteristics (e.g., risk) give the change in wages associated with a unit change in the job characteristic, holding constant the effect of all other variables included in the regression equation. The regression coefficients are therefore the shadow price (compensating wage premium) associated with changes in the job characteristic, such as risk. Such a wage equation is termed a hedonic wage equation.

Problems of "errors-in-variables" may also exist, especially in those studies that relate an *individual's* wage to an *aggregate* measure of risk such as the injury rate in the person's industry or occupation. Such aggregate measures of risk are likely to be subject to considerable random error as a proxy for the risk that an individual will face in that occupation. Econometrically, it can be shown that this will lead to an underestimation of the compensating wage paid for risk.

Omitted variable bias may also exist to the extent that crucial variables that affect wages and that are also correlated with risk are not controlled for in the measurement of the wage-risk trade-off. For example, bargaining power of workers (as represented by unionization) may lead to high wages and low risk. Failure to control for this factor may mean that there appears to be little or no wage premium paid for the risk. In reality the low wages in risky jobs may reflect the fact that workers with little bargaining power end up in jobs of low wages and high risk. The low wages in risky jobs may reflect the disproportionate absence of bargaining power of workers in those jobs, not the absence of a wage premium for risk. One method to control for such difficult-to-measure variables as preferences or an individual's bargaining power is to use longitudinal or panel data that follows the same individual over time so that such factors can be assumed to be relatively constant or fixed over time (e.g., Brown 1980).

Sample-selection bias problems may also prevail to the extent that wage-risk premiums are estimated on a subsample of risky jobs, perhaps because actuarial data is available only on risky occupations (e.g. Thaler and Rosen (1975)). In such circumstances, the risk premiums obtained from the subsample of risk-taking individuals may not give an accurate estimate of the compensating wage paid for a random worker.

Such econometric problems are typical of the applied econometrics literature; hence, the econometric evidence on compensating wages for occupational risk is likely to be neither more nor less reliable than typical econometric estimates. Reviews of such evidence are contained in Smith (1979), Gunderson and Swinton (1981), and Digby and Riddell (1986). The general consensus appears to be that compensating wage premiums are paid for work hazards and they increase with the seriousness of the risk. That is, they are larger for risks of death than for risks of injury and, for risks of injury, they are larger for permanent than for temporary injuries. In fact, for less serious injuries, compensating wage premiums often do not exist. A limited amount of evidence also suggests that the compensating wage premiums are reduced when the risk is partly covered by workers' compensation systems, and that compensating wage premiums are larger in union than in nonunion environments.

POLICY IMPLICATIONS

A number of policy implications associated with compensating wage differences for undesirable job characteristics have already been discussed.

In particular, competitive markets can yield the optimal amount of these characteristics, with compensating wages being the price that equilibrates markets. This ensures that the need of employers to carry on production in a manner that may involve undesirable working conditions is required to confront the need of workers for desirable conditions, and vice versa. This also implies, for example, that the optimal amount of safety is not zero; people are seldom willing to pay the price of attaining that otherwise desirable state.

In such competitive markets, regulations setting a uniform standard, such as a health and safety standard, run the risk of making the parties worse off, largely because compensating wages will adjust in a fashion that workers themselves would not have accepted for the improved working conditions. If there is imperfect information, or markets fail for other reasons, then regulation can make workers better off.

To the extent that wage premiums fully compensate workers for the expected risk of a job, then compensating them if the risk comes to fruition can involve double compensation. Of course, once this is anticipated by the parties, then the compensating wage premium itself will fall, and be paid only for the uncompensated risk. Thus, the compensating wage paid for the risk of injury or of being unemployed will be smaller, respectively, in situations of workers' compensation and unemployment insurance.

Empirical estimates of the compensating wage paid for the risk of death have been used to provide estimates of the "value of life." This phrase is somewhat of a misnomer since the estimates really reflect what people are willing to pay (as revealed through the market) to reduce the risk of death by a certain percentage. This is then extrapolated to arrive at the total price they would be willing to pay to reduce the risk of death to zero. These values are arrived at through impersonal transactions as people reveal how much in wages they are willing to give up to reduce their risk of death. These are not the values that people would attach to the *certainty* of saving a *specific* life, a value that would likely be incalculable.

For policy purposes such estimates have been used to compensate victims, or their survivors, for the loss of life or limb. They have also been used in decisions on how much resources to devote to life-saving activities or on the appropriate safety standards to set in industry. Rightly or wrongly, economics with its emphasis on trade-offs enters into many socially sensitive issues.

The notion that a job involves a set of positive and negative characteristics, each with its own implicit price, also has important implications for the analysis of wage differentials by such factors as occupation, industry, or region. As shown subsequently, the wage that is associated with each of these factors can have a component that reflects the compensating wage premiums paid for certain undesirable characteristics associated with each occupation, industry, or region. This will be important for understanding the existence and persistence of inter-occupation, inter-industry, and inter-regional wage structures.

REFERENCES AND FURTHER READINGS

A. Fringe Benefits

Bailey, W. and A. Schwenk. Employer expenditures for private retirement and insurance plans. *MLR* 95 (July 1972) 15-19.

Brinker, P.A. Labor union coercion of employees: the use of fringe benefits. *JLR* 4 (Summer, 1983) 249-256.

Dye, R. and R. Antle. Self-selection via fringe benefits. *JOLE* 2 (July 1984) 388-411.

Ehrenberg, R. *Fringe Benefits and Overtime Behavior.* Lexington, Mass.: D.C. Heath, 1971.

Garbarino, J. Fringe benefits and overtime as barriers to expanding employment. *ILRR* 17 (April 1964) 426-442. Comment by R. MacDonald and reply 19 (July 1966) 569-572.

Green, F., G. Hadjimatheou and R. Smail. Fringe benefit distribution in Britain. *BJIR* 23 (July 1985) 261-280.

Hameed, S. Employment impact of fringe benefits in Canadian manufacturing sector: 1957-1965. *RI/IR* 28 (No. 2, 1973) 380-396.

Hawkesworth, R. Fringe benefits in British industry. *BJIR* 15 (November 1977) 396-402.

Jain, H. and P. Janzen. Employee pay and benefit preferences. *RI/IR* 29 (No. 1, 1974) 99-110. Also, 32 (No. 3, 1977) 449-451.

Laudadio, L. and M. Percy. Some evidence of the impact of non-wage labour cost on overtime work and employment. *RI/IR* 28 (No. 2, 1973) 397-404.

Lester, R. Benefits as a preferred form of compensation. *SEJ* 33 (April 1967) 488-495.

Mabry, B. The economics of fringe benefits. *IR* 12 (February 1973) 95-106.

Macdonald, B. The design of a fringe benefit costing program. *RI/IR* 28 (October 1973) 799-807.

Mitchell, O. Fringe benefits and labour mobility. *JHR* 17 (Spring 1982) 286-298.

Mitchell, O. Fringe benefits and the cost of changing jobs. *ILRR* 37 (October 1983) 70-78.

Oi, W. Labor as a quasi-fixed factor of production. *JPE* 70 (December 1962) 538-555.

Pencavel, J. Alternative methods of remuneration. *Research in Labor Economics*, R. Ehrenberg (ed.). Greenwich, Conn.: JAI Press, 1977.

Perlman, R. Observations on overtime and moonlighting. *SEJ* 32 (October 1966).

Rice, R. Skill, earnings and the growth of wage supplements. *AER* 61 (May 1966) 583-592.

Schultz, L. Ruminations on the benefit package. *RI/IR* 28 (No. 4, 1973) 849-858.

Solnick, L. Unionism and fringe benefit expenditures. *IR* 17 (February 1978) 102-107.

Veendrop, E. and B. Wilbratte. Hourly wages, piece rates, fringe benefits, and the allocation of labor services. *SEJ* 46 (January 1980) 852-862.

Woodbury, S. Substitution between wage and non wage benefits. *AER* 73 (March 1983) 166–182.

B. Compensating Wages and Application to Occupational Safety

Adams, J. Permanent differences in unemployment and permanent wage differentials. *QJE* 100 (February 1985) 29-56.

Arnould, R.J. and L.M. Nichols. Wage-risk premiums and workers' compensation: a refinement of estimates of compensating wage differentials. *JPE* 91 (April 1983) 332-340.

Arthur, W. The economics of risks to life. *AER* 71 (March 1981) 54-64.

Atrostic, B.K. The demand for leisure and nonpecuniary job characteristics. *AER* 72 (June 1982) 428-440.

Brown, C. Equalizing differences in the labour market. *QJE* 94 (February 1980) 113-134.

Chelius, J. The control of industrial accidents. *Law and Contemporary Problems* 38 (Autumn 1979) 700-729.

Dardis, R. The value of a life: new evidence from the marketplace. *AER* 70 (December 1980) 1077-1082.

Digby, C. and W.C. Riddell. Occupational health and safety in Canada. *Canadian Labour Relations*, W.C. Riddell (ed.). Toronto: University of Toronto Press, 1986, pp. 285-320.

Dillingham, A. and R. Smith. Union effects on the evaluation of fatal risks. *IRRA* (December 1983) 270-277.

Dorsey, S. Employment hazards and fringe benefits: further tests for compensating differentials. In *Safety and the Work Force*. J. Worral, ed. Ithaca, N.Y.: ILR Press, 1983.

Dorsey, S. and N. Walzer. Workers' compensation, job hazards, and wages. *ILRR* 36 (July 1983) 642-654.

Duncan, G. Earnings functions and nonpecuniary benefits. *JHR* 11 (Fall 1976) 462-483.

Duncan, G.J. and B. Holmlund. Was Adam Smith right after all? Another test of the theory of compensating wage differentials. *JOLE* 1 (October 1983) 366-379.

Eberts, R. and J. Stone. Wages, fringe benefits, and working conditions: an analysis of compensating differentials. *SEJ* 52 (July 1985) 274-280.

Ehrenberg, R. Retirement system characteristics and the compensating wage differentials in the public sector. *ILRR* 33 (July 1980) 470-484.

Ehrenberg, R. and P. Schumann. Compensating wage differentials for mandatory overtime. *EI* 22 (October 1984) 460-478.

Evans, R. and R. Weinstein. Ranking occupations as risky income prospects. *ILRR* 35 (January 1982) 252-259.

Fishbuck, P. Discrimination on nonwage margins: safety in the West Virginia coal industry, 1906-1925. *EI* 23 (October 1985) 651-670.

Gerking, S. and W. Wierick. Compensating differences and interregional wage differentials. *R.E. Stats.* 65 (August 1983) 483-486.

Gunderson, M. and K. Swinton. *Collective Bargaining and Asbestos Dangers in the Workplace*. Ontario Royal Commission on Asbestos, 1981.

Leigh, J.P. Racial differences in compensating wages for job risks. *IR* 20 (Fall 1981) 318-321.

Leigh, J.P. Are unionized blue collar jobs more hazardous than nonunionized blue collar jobs? *JLR* 3 (Summer 1982) 349-358.

Li, E. Compensating differentials for cyclical and noncyclical unemployment: the interaction between investors' and employees' risk aversion. *JOLE* 4 (April 1986) 277-300.

Low, S. and L. McPheters. Wage differentials and the risk of death: an empirical analysis. *EI* 21 (April 1983) 271-280.

Lucas, R.E.B. Hedonic wage equations and psychic wages in the returns to schooling. *AER* 67 (Sept. 1977) 549-558.

Luntz, H. The role of compensation in health and safety at work. *The Journal of Industrial Relations* 23 (September 1981) 383-396.

Marin, A. and G. Psacharopoulos. The reward for risk in the labor market: evidence from the U.K. and a reconciliation with other studies. *JPE* 90 (August 1982) 827-853.

Marshall, J.M. Gambles and the shadow price of death. *AER* 74 (March 1984) 73-86.

McLean, R., W. Wendling and P. Neergaard. Compensating wage differentials for hazardous work: an empirical analysis. *Quarterly Review of Economics and Business* 18 (Autumn 1978) 97-107.

Mellow, W. Worker differences in the receipt of health and pension benefits: extending the analysis of compensation differentials. *IRRA* (December 1981) 16-25.

Mishan, E.J. Evaluation of life and limb: a theoretical approach. *JPE* 79 (July/August 1971) 687-705.

Olson, C. An analysis of wage differentials received by workers on dangerous jobs. *JHR* 16 (Spring 1981) 167-185.

Rea, S. Workmen's compensation and occupational safety under imperfect information. *AER* 71 (March 1981) 80-93.

Rosen, S. Hedonic prices and implicit markets: product differentiation in pure competition. *JPE* 82 (January 1974) 34-55.

Rosen, S. The theory of equalizing differences. *Handbook of Labour Economics*, Vol. 1. O. Ashenfelter and R. Layard (eds.). New York: Elsevier, 1986.

Schiller, B. and R. Weiss. Pensions and wages: a test for equalizing differences. *R.E.Stats.* 62 (Nov. 1980) 529-538.

Smith, R. Compensating wage differentials and public policy: a review. *ILRR* 32 (April 1979) 339-352.

Smith, R.S. Compensating differentials for pensions and underfunding in the public sector. *R.E.Stats.* 63 (Aug. 1981) 463-467.

Thaler, R. and S. Rosen. The value of saving a life: evidence from the labor market. *Household Production and Consumption*, N. Terleckyj (ed.). New York: National Bureau of Economic Research, 1975, pp. 265-302.

Viscusi, W. Kip. Labor market valuations of life and limb: empirical evidence and policy implications. *Public Policy* 29 (Summer 1978) 359-386.

Viscusi, W. Kip. Wealth effects and earnings premiums for job hazards. *R.E. Stats.* 60 (Autumn, 1978) 408-416.

Viscusi, W. Kip. Job hazards and worker quit rates: an analysis of adaptive worker behaviour. *IER* 20 (February 1979) 29-58.

Viscusi, W. Kip. *Employment Hazards*. Cambridge, Massachusetts: Harvard University Press, 1979.

Viscusi, W. Imperfect job risk information and optimal workmen's compensation benefits. *J Pub Ec* 14 (December 1980) 319-338.

Worral, J.D. and R.J. Butler. Health conditions and job hazards: union and nonunion jobs. *JLR* 4 (Fall, 1983) 339-348.

18 Human Capital Theory: Applications to Education and Training

In the previous section on labour supply we emphasized the *quantity* aspects of labour supply, ranging from family formation to labour force participation to hours of work. Labour supply also has a *quality* dimension encompassing human capital elements such as education, training, labour market information, mobility and health. In addition, in the previous chapter on compensating wages, we indicated that compensating wages may have to be paid to compensate workers for the costly process of acquiring human capital like education or training. The hedonic wage approach developed in that chapter can be applied to costly attributes necessary to do a job, just as it can be applied to negative job attributes like risk.

While the economics of education and health economics are often the subject matter of separate courses and textbooks, they — along with training, job search, and mobility — have a common theoretical thread: that of human capital theory. This chapter presents the basic human capital theory and applies it mainly to the areas of education and training. The acquisition of labour market information in connection with the job search process is discussed in Chapter 26 on unemployment. Mobility is discussed in chapter 20 in the context of regional wage structures.

HUMAN CAPITAL THEORY

The essence of human capital theory is that investments are made in human resources so as to improve their productivity and therefore their earnings. Costs are incurred in the expectation of future benefits: hence, the term "investment in human resources." Like all investments, the key question becomes: is it economically worthwhile? The answer to this question depends on whether or not benefits exceed costs by a sufficient amount. Before dealing with the investment criteria whereby this is established, it is worthwhile to expand on the concepts of costs and benefits as utilized in human capital theory. In this chapter, only the basics are touched upon. A wealth of refinements and precise methodological techniques is contained in the extensive literature on human capital theory and its application.

In calculating the costs of human capital, it is important to recognize not only direct costs, such as books or tuition fees in acquiring university education, but also the opportunity cost or income forgone while people acquire the human capital. For students in university or workers in lengthy training programs, such costs can be the largest component of the total cost. The evaluation of these opportunity costs can prove difficult because it requires an estimation of what the people would have earned had they not engaged in human capital formation.

In addition, it is important to try to distinguish between the consumption and the investment components of human capital formation, since it is only the investment benefits and costs that are relevant for the investment decision. In reality this separation may be difficult or impossible — how does one separate the consumption from the investment benefits of acquiring a university degree? Nevertheless, the distinction must be made qualitatively, if not quantitatively, especially in comparing programs where the consumption and investment components may differ considerably.

A distinction must also be made between private and social costs and benefits. Private costs and benefits are those that accrue to the parties making the investment and as such will be considered in their own calculations. Social costs and benefits are all those that are accrued by society, including not only private costs and benefits but also any third-party effects or externalities that accrue to parties who are not directly involved in the investment decision. Training disadvantaged workers, for example, may yield an external benefit in the form of reduced crime, and this benefit should be considered by society at large even though it may not enter the calculations of individuals doing the investment.

A further distinction can be made between real costs and benefits as opposed to pecuniary or distributional or transfer costs and benefits. Real costs involve the use of real resources, and should be considered whether those resources have a monetary value or not. Pecuniary or transfer costs and benefits do not involve the use of real resources, but rather involve a transfer from one group to another: some gain while others lose. While it may be important to note the existence of such transfers for specific groups, it is inappropriate to include them in the calculation of social costs and benefits since, by definition, gains by one party involve losses by another. For example, the savings in unemployment insurance or social assistance payments that may result from a retraining program are worthy of noting, and for the unemployment insurance fund they may be a private saving, yet from the point of view of society they represent a reduction in a transfer payment, not a newly created real benefit.[1] Similarly, the installation of a retraining facility in a community may raise local prices for construction facilities, and this may be an additional cost for local residents: yet it is a pecuniary cost since it involves a transfer from local residents to those who raised the prices. While such a transfer may involve a loss to local residents,

---

[1] This discussion ignores the possible real resource costs involved in operating and financing unemployment insurance or social assistance programs. If savings in unemployment insurance or social assistance payments reduce the real resources required to operate and finance these programs, then a real externality is involved in addition to the transfer externality.

it is not a real resource cost to society as a whole, since it represents a gain for other parties.

From the point of view of the efficient allocation of resources, only real resource costs and benefits matter. Transfers represent offsetting gains and losses. However, from the point of view of distributive equity or fairness, society may choose to value those gains and losses differently. In addition, costs and benefits to different groups may be valued differently in the economic calculus.

Thus, in the calculation of the benefits from a training program, it is conceivable to weigh the benefits more for a poor disadvantaged worker than an advantaged worker. The appropriate weighting scheme obviously poses a problem, but it could be based on the implicit weights involved in other government programs or perhaps in the progressive income tax structure, or it could simply be based on explicit weights that reflect a pure value judgement.

Care must also be exercised in imputing a macroeconomic impact from investment programs. It is often tempting, for example, to multiply the benefits of some program to capture the multiplier effect as the investment sets up further rounds of spending throughout the economy. Or it is tempting to document the employment expansion that may accompany a particular investment program. The error in this reasoning occurs because it ignores the fact that the opportunities forgone, as resources were devoted to this particular investment rather than to some other one, also have a multiplier and employment creation effect. It is true that the multiplier effects may be different in magnitude (for example, if they involve different leakages into imports), and they may occur in different regions. While these factors may be worthy of note, they do not justify the imputation of a multiplier effect for all human capital investments. This is especially the case since, in general, fiscal policy is available with its multiplier effects to alter the levels of aggregate demand in the economy.

EDUCATION

The main elements of human capital theory can be outlined by considering decisions relating to investment in education. This decision is illustrated in Figure 18.1 which shows alternative income streams associated with different levels of education: incomplete high school (10 years of education at age 16), high school completion (age 18), and university or college degree (age 22). These three outcomes are used for illustration only; in general we may regard "years of education" as a continuous variable, each year being associated with a lifetime income stream. The earnings in each year are measured in present value terms to make them comparable across different time periods.

The shapes of the earnings streams (or "age-earnings profiles") reflect two key factors. First, for each profile, earnings increase with age but at a decreasing rate. This concave shape reflects the fact that individuals gen-

Figure 18.1 Education and Alternative Income Streams

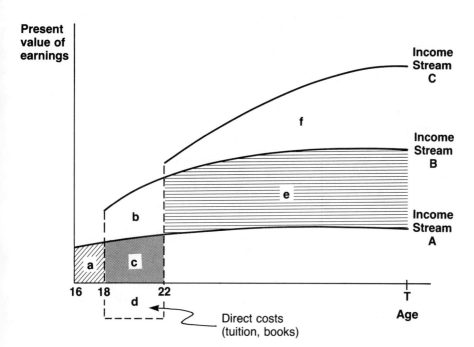

erally continue to make human capital investments in the form of on-the-job training and work experience once they have entered the labour force. This job experience adds more to their productivity and earnings early in their careers due to diminishing returns to experience. Second, the earnings of individuals with more years of education generally lie above those with fewer years of education. This feature is based on the assumption that education provides skills which increase the individual's productivity and thus earning power in the labour market. Because of the productivity-enhancing effect of work experience, individuals with more education may not begin at a salary higher than those in their age cohort with less education (and therefore more experience). Nonetheless, to the extent that education increases productivity, individuals with the same amount of work experience but more education will earn more, perhaps substantially more.

Which lifetime income stream should the individual choose? To address this question we will initially make several simplifying assumptions:
(1) the individual doesn't receive any direct utility or disutility from the educational process
(2) hours of work (including work in acquiring education) are fixed
(3) the income streams associated with different amounts of education are known with certainty
(4) individuals can borrow and lend at the real interest rate r.

These assumptions are made to enable us to focus on the salient aspects of the human capital investment decision. The first assumption implies that we are examining education purely as an investment, not a consumption, decision. The second assumption implies that the quantity of leisure is the same for each income stream, so that they can be compared in terms of income alone. Assumption three allows us to ignore complications due to risk and uncertainty. The fourth assumption — often referred to as "perfect capital markets" — implies that the individual can base the investment decision on total lifetime income, without being concerned with the timing of income and expenditures. The consequences of relaxing these simplifying assumptions are discussed below.

In these circumstances, the individual will choose the quantity of education that maximizes the net present value of lifetime earnings. Once this choice is made, total net lifetime earnings (or human capital wealth) can be distributed across different periods as desired by borrowing and lending.

As illustrated in Figure 18.1, human capital investment involves both costs and benefits. The costs include both direct expenditures such as tuition and books and opportunity costs in the form of forgone earnings. For example, in completing high school the individual forgoes earnings equal to the shaded area 'a' associated with income stream A. The benefits of completing high school consist of the difference between earnings streams A and B, equal to the areas 'b + e' in Figure 18.1. For a high school graduate contemplating a university education, the additional costs include the direct costs (area 'd') and forgone earnings equal to area 'b + c', while additional benefits equal the earnings associated with income stream C rather than B (area 'f'). As Figure 18.1 is drawn, a university education yields the largest net present value of lifetime income. However, for another individual with different opportunities and abilities, and therefore different income streams, one of the other outcomes might be best.

The rule for optimal human capital investment can be expressed in a number of alternative, but equivalent, ways. Two common ways of stating this decision rule are illustrated in Figure 18.2. One is in terms of marginal rather than total costs and benefits: the individual should increase years of education until the present value of the benefits of an additional year of education equals the present value of the additional costs. In terms of Figure 18.1, for a high school graduate facing income stream B, the marginal benefits of a university education consist of the area 'f' while the marginal costs consist of the area 'b + c + d'. Marginal benefits generally decline with years of education due to diminishing returns to education and the shorter period over which higher income accrues. Marginal costs rise with years of education because forgone earnings increase with educational attainment. The point at which marginal benefits equal marginal costs yields the maximum net present value of lifetime earnings.

Human capital decisions, like those involving financial and physical capital, are also often expressed in terms of the rate of return on the

Figure 18.2

(a) Marginal Benefits Equal Marginal Costs

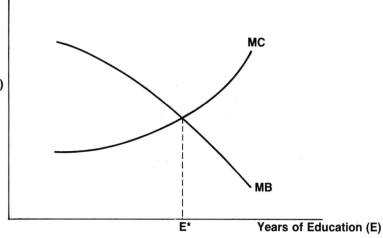

(b) Internal Rate of Return Equals Market Interest Rate

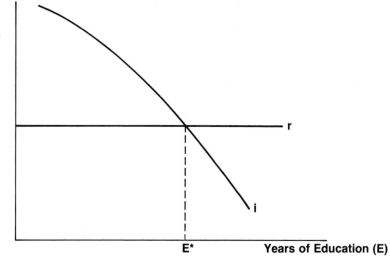

investment. For any specific amount of education, the internal rate of return (i) can be defined as the discount rate that would make the net present value of earnings equal to zero. This is the implicit rate of return earned by an individual acquiring that amount of education. The optimal strategy is to continue investing as long as the internal rate of return exceeds the market rate of interest r, the opportunity cost of financing the investment. Because the present value of marginal benefits and marginal costs are declining and increasing functions, respectively, of years of education, the internal rate of return falls as educational attainment rises. The point at which i = r yields the optimal quantity of human capital.

Perhaps the most obvious implication of the theory is that human capital investments should be made early in one's lifetime. Educational investments made at later stages earn a lower financial return because forgone earnings increase with work experience and because of the shorter period over which higher income is earned. A related implication is that individuals who expect to be in and out of the labour force — perhaps in order to raise children — have less financial incentive to invest in education and will earn a lower return on any given amount of human capital investment.

This framework can be used not only to explain human capital investment decisions but also to predict the impact of changes in the economic and social environment and in public policy on levels of education. For example, changes in the degree of progressivity of the income tax system are predicted to alter levels of educational attainment. Because optimal human capital investment decisions are based on real after-tax income, an increase in the progressivity of the income tax system would shift down high income streams (such as C in Figure 18.1) relatively more than low income streams (such as A), thus reducing the demand for education. Similarly, policies such as student loans programs alter the total and marginal costs of education, and thus levels of educational attainment.

Not all individuals have or obtain sufficient information to make the detailed calculations needed to determine the optimal quantity of education. Nonetheless, people do take into account costs and benefits when making decisions, including those with respect to human capital investments. Consequently, as is frequently the case in economic analysis, models that assume rational decision making may predict the behaviour of individuals quite well, especially the average behaviour of large groups of individuals. Optimization errors that result in a specific individual's choice of education deviating from the optimum level tend to offset each other and thus have little effect on the average behaviour of large groups of individuals.

Decisions relating to investment in education are also complicated by the fact that the simplifying assumptions used in the above analysis may not hold in practice. The process of acquiring education may directly yield utility or disutility. The existence of this consumption component does not imply that the investment aspect is irrelevant; however, it does indicate that human capital decisions may not be based on investment criteria alone. Individuals who enjoy learning will acquire more education than would be predicted on the basis of financial costs and benefits, and vice versa for those who dislike the process of acquiring knowledge. The decision continues to be based on costs and benefits, but these concepts need to be broadened to include non-financial benefits and costs.

In addition to increasing one's future earnings, education may open up a more varied and interesting set of career opportunities, in which case job satisfaction would be higher among those with more education. The consequences may be even more profound; for example, the acquisition of knowledge may alter peoples' preferences and therefore future consumption patterns, possibly enhancing their enjoyment of life for a given level of income. In principle these aspects — to the extent that they exist — can be incorporated in the theory, but they clearly present challenges for measurement and empirical testing. Similarly, the returns to education are unlikely to be known with certainty so that investment decisions must be based on individuals' expectations about the future. Because some alternatives may be less certain than others, attitudes toward risk will also play a role. Risk-neutral individuals will choose the amount of education that maximizes the expected net present value of lifetime earnings, while risk-averse individuals will place more weight on expected benefits and costs that are certain than those that are uncertain.

Financing is generally an important aspect of any investment decision. In the case of human capital investments financing is particularly problematic because one cannot use the value of the human capital (i.e. the anticipated future earnings) as collateral for the loan. In contrast, machinery and equipment, land, and other physical assets can be pledged as loan collateral. There is therefore a fundamental difference between physical and human capital in terms of the degree to which "perfect capital markets" prevail. In the absence of subsidized tuition, student loan programs and similar policies, the problems associated with financing human capital investments could prevent many individuals from choosing the amount of education that would maximize their net present value of lifetime earnings. Even in the presence of these policies, borrowing constraints may exert a significant influence on decisions regarding education.

This discussion of human capital theory has focused on the private costs and benefits of education because these are the relevant factors affecting choices made by individuals. However, the acquisition of knowledge may also affect third parties, in which case the social costs and benefits may differ from their private counterparts. These issues are discussed further below in the context of public policy towards education.

Education and Market Equilibrium

The income streams shown in Figure 18.1 represent hypothetical alternatives available to a given individual. In order to understand the relationship between income and education we need to study the interaction between individuals' preferences regarding different levels of education and employers' preferences with respect to workers with different amounts of human capital. This interaction determines market wage rates associated with different levels of education and employment of workers with various amounts of human capital. The nature of the market equilibrium is very similar to that analysed in the previous chapter in terms of compensating wages for risk, the difference being that human capital is a positive attribute affecting the productivity of workers while risk is a negative characteristic associated with jobs. Because of the similarity, our treatment in this chapter will be brief.

Figure 18.3 shows indifference curves for two different types of workers (A and B workers) and isoprofit curves for two different types of firms (α and β firms). Two types of each group are assumed purely for illustration. Employees differ in their preferences for education versus income because of such factors as differences in tastes for acquiring knowledge, learning ability, utility or disutility derived directly from the educational process, and need or ability to borrow to finance human capital investments. Because human capital is costly to acquire, both types of employee require a higher wage to induce them to obtain more education. Type A workers have a stronger preference for education, as reflected in the shape of their indifference curves U_A. Holding utility constant, a larger wage increase is required to induce B workers to undertake an additional year of education than is the case for A workers.

Firms' isoprofit curves will be upward-sloping, as depicted in Figure 18.3, if workers with more human capital are more productive. Holding profits constant, a higher wage can be paid to more educated employees due to their greater productivity. (Otherwise the isoprofit curves would

Figure 18.3 Education and Market Equilibrium

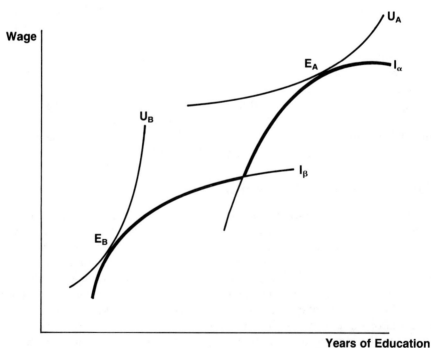

be horizontal straight lines.) However, firms differ in the value of more educated workers to the production and marketing of their product. More educated workers are more valuable to the type α firms as reflected by the shape of their isoprofit curves I_α. Holding profits constant, α firms can pay a larger wage increase to workers with an additional year of education than is the case for β firms.

In competitive equilibrium firms earn zero excess profits (normal rate of return). Thus if I_α and I_β are the isoprofit curves corresponding to zero profits, the outer limits of these two isoprofit curves (bold lines) constitute the employers' offer curve showing the maximum wage that can be paid for different levels of education consistent with competitive equilibrium. Market equilibrium occurs at points E_A and E_B. This equilibrium has two important properties. First, workers who invest more in human capital receive a compensating differential for doing so. The magnitude of the compensating differential depends on both the preferences of different types of workers regarding income and education and the technology of production and market opportunities of firms. Second, employees with the strongest preferences for education are matched with employers for whom education is most valuable. This sorting equilibrium is Pareto-optimal. Both A and B types of workers are better off employed with the α and β firms respectively than would be the case if they switched to the other firm type.

Empirical Evidence

Figure 18.4 shows age-earnings profiles for four educational categories of Canadian males: (i) eight years or less of elementary schooling (ELEM), (ii) nine to thirteen years of elementary and secondary schooling (HS), (iii) some post-secondary education but not a university degree (Some Post-HS), and (iv) university degree (UNIV). Studies of the relationship between education and earnings are usually confined to males because of the empirical problems associated with the intermittent labour force participation of females.

As these data indicate, there is a strong relationship between education and lifetime earnings. The income streams of those with more education generally lie above the streams of those with less education. Two additional patterns are evident. First, earnings increase with age and thus labour market experience until age 40 to 50 and then decline somewhat. As noted previously, this concave relationship between age and earnings is generally attributed to the accumulation of human capital in the form of on-the-job training and experience, a process which displays diminishing returns. Second, earnings increase most rapidly to age 40 or 50 for those individuals with the most education. Thus the salary differential between groups with different amounts of education is much wider at ages 40 to 50 than at ages 20 to 30.

Data on earnings by age and education can be used together with

Figure 18.4

(a) Earnings by Age and Education, Canadian Males, 1971/73

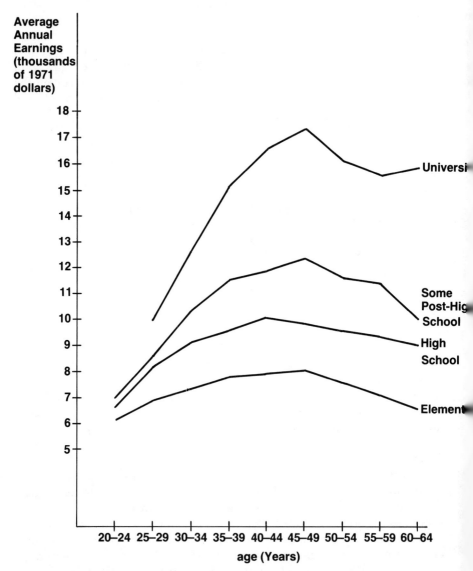

Notes: 1. Earnings are average annual earnings of full-year, full-time males in 1971 dollars. Full-year, full-time workers are defined as those who worked 50 or more weeks and usually worked full weeks.

2. Panel (a) uses the average of 1971 and 1973 earnings while panel (b) uses the average of 1979 and 1981 earnings.

3. Education categories are defined as follows:
   (i) ELEM: eight years or less of elementary schooling
   (ii) HS: nine to thirteen years of elementary and secondary schooling

Figure 18.4

(b) Earnings by Age and Education, Canadian Males, 1979/81

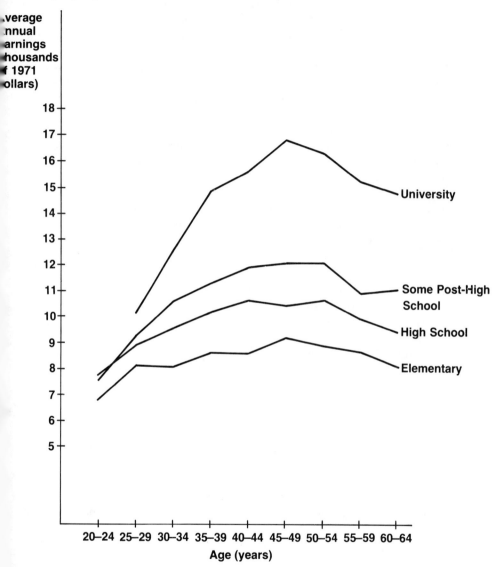

(iii) Some Post-HS: some post-secondary education, but not a university
      degree
(iv) UNIV: university degree.

Source: M.D. Dooley, "The overeducated Canadian? Changes in the relationship
      among earnings, education, and age for Canadian men: 1971-81." *Canadian Journal of Economics* 19 (February 1986) 142-159.

information on direct costs to calculate the rate of return on investments in education. Such calculations can be useful to individuals wishing to know, for example, whether a university education is a worthwhile investment. They can also be useful input into public policy decisions. In particular, efficient resource allocation requires that investments in physical and human capital be made in those areas with the greatest return.

Studies of the monetary returns to investments in education during the late 1960s and early 1970s generally concluded that rates of return were substantial, especially for an undergraduate university degree or less (Stager, 1972). Private after-tax returns were usually estimated to be in the 10-15 percent range. There is some evidence that rates of return increased during the 1960s. Mehmet's (1977) estimates indicate a significant increase in the rate of return to 22 percent in 1969 followed by a modest decline to 18 percent in 1971. During the 1970s the returns to education declined (Dooley, 1986). This development is evident in Figure 18.4. Comparison of the age-earnings profiles for 1971/73 (panel a) and 1979/81 (panel b) reveals that the largest increases in earnings occurred for those groups with the least education. For those with some post-high school, earnings were approximately unchanged between 1971/73 and 1979/81, while for those with a university degree, earnings actually declined slightly. Using 1981 data, Vaillancourt and Henriques (1986) estimate private after-tax rates of return to university education in Canada ranging from 7 to 14 percent, depending on the region and length of degree program (3- or 4-year). These estimates also indicate that monetary returns to education declined significantly during the 1970s.[2]

In the U.S., the financial return to a university or college degree also declined during the 1970s. One explanation of this phenomenon is the substantial increase in the proportion of the population going to university, particularly the entry into the labour force of the "baby boom" generation during the 1970s (Welch, 1979). Welch (1979) argues that the effects on relative earnings of the large baby boom cohort will be temporary, and that earnings differentials among workers with different amounts of education will return to their previous levels as the baby boom generation gains work experience. In contrast, Freeman (1976, 1980) argues that the demand for educated workers has also declined, so that not all of the change in relative earnings can be attributed to temporary developments on the supply side.

Dooley (1986) examines these competing explanations in the Canadian setting using data for the period 1971-81. He concludes that the entry of the large baby boom cohort during this period did lower earnings growth for this group, but that this demographic effect cannot account for the

---

[2] As noted by Krashinsky (1987), the Vaillancourt-Henriques estimates need to be interpreted with some care because they are based on a comparison of only two groups: those without university education (which includes those with elementary, high school and some post-high school education) and those with a university degree (which includes those with post-graduate degrees).

observed narrowing of earnings differentials by level of education. Dooley's results thus suggest that demand-side forces may also have played a role; unless these forces are reversed, some of the decline in the return to education may be permanent in nature.

In concluding this discussion of the empirical evidence relating to education and earnings, several observations should be made. The returns to education discussed here are restricted to the private monetary benefits. Additional benefits to the individual — such as any enjoyment derived directly from acquiring knowledge, a more varied and interesting career, or even an enhanced ability to enjoy life — would increase the private returns to education. Further, the social returns to education may differ from the private returns for a variety of reasons. It is also important to note that these estimates provide the *average* rate of return for all those making a particular educational investment. Policies such as those relating to the allocation of resources should be based on *marginal*, not average, calculations; that is, for social efficiency funds should be allocated among various physical and human capital investments such that the social rate of return on the last dollar invested in each project is equal.

The calculated returns to education are based on cross-sectional data (different individuals at a point in time). This procedure will be accurate if the age-earnings profiles for each educational category are approximately constant over time, apart from overall earnings growth affecting all groups. To the extent that earnings differentials by education narrow or widen over time, the actual realized return to educational investments will be smaller or larger than that estimated on the basis of cross-sectional data.

The empirical analysis of the relationship between education and earnings is usually carried out by estimating an "earnings function" in which the dependent variable is (the logarithm of) earnings and the explanatory variables are various determinants of earnings such as age, experience, marital status, hours worked and educational attainment (often measured by years of education). One potential determinant that is difficult to control for is ability, by which we mean ability in the workplace, not learning ability (though these may be correlated). If more able individuals are also more likely to invest in education, some of the estimated return to education may in fact be a return to innate ability. A number of U.S. studies have controlled for ability through the use of measures such as I.Q. scores — which may measure learning ability better than ability in the workplace. Estimated returns to education are only modestly lower, suggesting that serious bias is not introduced by the omission of ability as an explanatory variable (Griliches, 1977).

Nonetheless, the role of ability in the relationship between education and earnings remains controversial. A central aspect of the debate is the hypothesis that higher education may act as a filter, screening out the more able workers rather than enhancing productivity directly. According to this "signalling/screening hypothesis," workers may use education to signal unobserved ability while firms use education to screen workers (Arrow,

1973; Spence, 1973, 1974). Such an outcome can arise when employers can't observe ability directly (perhaps even some time after hiring) and when the costs of acquiring education are lower for those workers with greater ability; otherwise, both able and less able workers will invest in education and employers' beliefs about the correlation between ability and education won't be confirmed. In these circumstances, education may yield a private return (more able individuals can increase their earnings by investing in education) but its social return consists only of its role in sorting the more from the less able rather than directly increasing productivity as in human capital theory.

Empirical tests of the signalling/screening hypothesis have not been conclusive (Riley, 1979; Lang and Kropp, 1986). The pure signalling model in which education has no impact on productivity does not appear capable of explaining observed behaviour (Rosen, 1977). Professional educational programs such as those in medicine, law and engineering clearly are more than elaborate screening devices. However, educational programs may act as a filter to some degree. Furthermore, as discussed by Davies and MacDonald (1984), the informational role of education in terms of matching individuals' interests and abilities may be significant, albeit difficult to measure.

TRAINING

Like education, training is a form of investment in human capital in which costs are incurred in the present in the anticipation of benefits in the future. The benefits accrue because training imparts skills which raise the worker's productivity and thus value in the labour market.

In this section, we focus on some *economic* aspects of training rather than on an institutional description of training in Canada: the latter is discussed, for example, in Davies (1986). The main focus of our analysis is to shed light on the following questions: Who pays for training? Is a government subsidy warranted? How should training be evaluated?

Who Pays?

In his classic work on the subject, Becker (1964, pp. 11-28) distinguishes between *general* training and *specific* training. General training is training that can be used in various firms, not just in firms that provide the training. Consequently, in a competitive market, firms will bid for this training by offering a higher wage equal to the value of the training. Since competition ensures that the trainee reaps the benefits of general training in the form of higher earnings, then the trainee would be willing to bear the cost of training as long as benefits exceed costs. If a company were to bear the cost of such training they would still have to bid against other companies for the services of the trainee.

This argument is illustrated in Figure 18.5(a). In the absence of training, the individual can earn the alternative wage W_a equal to the value of

Figure 18.5   Costs, Benefits, and Financing of Training

(a) Costs and Benefits of Training

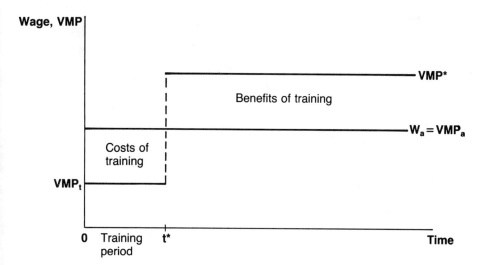

(b) Specific Training as a Shared Investment

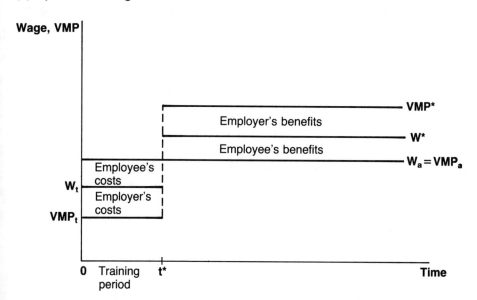

Figure 18.5 (continued)

(c) Earnings Growth with Gradual Training

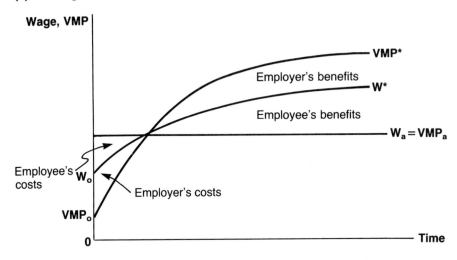

marginal product without training (VMP_a). During the training period the value of the worker's output is VMP_t (which could be zero). After training the worker's value to *any* firm in this labour market rises to VMP^*. The costs and benefits are as shown. If the investment is worthwhile, the employee can finance the training and earn the benefits by being paid a wage equal to the VMP at each point in time; i.e., the worker receives $W_t = VMP_t$ during training and $W^* = VMP^*$ after the training period. The firm could incur the costs and hope to reap the benefits by paying the worker W_a before and after training. However, because the employee can earn W^* elsewhere, the firm's strategy won't work. Thus, in the absence of bonding arrangements (such as are used for limited periods in the armed forces for certain types of general training such as pilot training), general training will be financed by employees.

With specific training, however, the training is useful only in the company that provides the training. Consequently, other companies have no incentive to pay higher earnings for such training and the trainee would not bear the cost because of an inability to reap the benefits in the form of higher earnings. The sponsoring company, however, would bear the cost providing they exceed the benefits. In addition, the sponsoring company would not have to pay a higher wage for those persons with specific training since other firms are not competing for such trainees.

This case is also illustrated in Figure 18.5(a). The firm pays the alternative wage W_a during and after training, incurring costs of $W_a - VMP_t$ during the training period and receiving benefits of $VMP^* - W_a$ after the completion of training.

Specific human capital may also be a shared investment. This arrangement is particularly likely when there is some uncertainty about the continuation of the employment relation due to shifts in labour demand affecting the worker's VMP and shifts in supply affecting the alternative wage W_a. If the sponsoring company pays for the specific training, as shown in Figure 18.5(a), it faces the risk that the employee may quit at some point after the training period, thus reducing the employer's anticipated return on the investment. Because the worker is receiving no more than the alternative wage, the cost of quitting is low. Even a small increase in W_a could cause the worker to go elsewhere. However, the cost to the company is high because the trained employee is worth more to the firm than he or she is being paid. In these circumstances, the sponsoring company may pay trainees a wage premium to reduce their turnover and hence to increase the probability that the company will recoup its investment costs. To compensate for the wage premium, the firm may lower the wage paid during the training period, in which case the two parties share the costs and benefits of training.

This situation is shown in Figure 18.5(b). The firm pays $W_t < W_a$ during the training period and $W^* > W_a$ after training. Both parties incur costs and reap benefits as shown. The shared investment minimizes the risk that either party will wish to terminate the employment relation because both the employer and employee are earning rents after the completion of training. The employer's rents of $VMP^* - W^*$ each period reduce the risk that the employee will be laid off due to a decline in demand. Only when the worker's value to the firm falls below W^* will the firm consider layoffs. The employee's rents of $W^* - W_a$ each period reduce the risk that the employee will quit in response to an improvement in labour market opportunities. Only when the alternative wage rises above W^* will the employee consider quitting.

This analysis indicates that specific human capital investments provide an incentive for firms and workers to maintain their employment relationship in the face of external shocks to demand and supply. The return on the shared investment acts like "glue" keeping the two parties together. These incentives for long-term employment relationships and their consequences are discussed further in Chapter 26 in the context of labour market turnover and implicit contracts.

In competitive markets, then, trainees will pay for general training whereas specific training investments may be paid by the sponsoring company or shared by the two parties. The form of payment may be subtle, as, for example, when trainees in an apprenticeship program forgo earnings by accepting a lower wage rate during the training period, or when companies forgo some output from workers when they provide them with on-the-job training.

The sharp distinction made in panels (a) and (b) of Figure 18.5 between the training and post-training periods may not hold in practice. Much on-the-job training is informal and takes place gradually as employees learn different facets of their job and its place in the overall organization. In these circumstances, earnings can be expected to rise gradually, as shown in Figure 18.5(c), rather than abruptly. The concave shape of the earnings profile reflects the assumption that there are diminishing returns to on-the-job training and work experience. As noted previously, this shape is typical of age-earnings profiles (see Figure 18.4).

In practice the distinction between general and specific training can be difficult to make. Training often contains elements of both. Even training that is geared to the specific production processes of a particular firm often contains elements that are transferable and the completion of such training can serve as a *signal* to firms that the trainee is capable of learning new skills even if the particular skills themselves are not transferable. On the other hand, general training that is provided in a particular firm may be somewhat more useful in the sponsoring company simply because the trainee is more familiar with that company. Nonetheless, the distinction between general and specific training is useful for conceptual purposes. Furthermore, although training usually contains a mixture of the two forms, occupations and industries will differ in the proportion of training that is general versus specific. Differences across occupations and industries in such factors as earnings growth and layoff and quit rates can therefore be explained in terms of differences in the amount of training and the proportions of general and specific training.

Appropriate Role of Government

If trainees will pay for and benefit from general training and sponsoring companies and employees will share the costs and benefits of specific training, why should governments be involved in the training process? In other words, are there situations when the private unregulated market does not provide a socially optimal amount of training?

This possibility may exist for trainees who cannot afford to purchase training (perhaps by accepting a lower wage during the training period) and who cannot borrow because of an inability to use their human capital (future earnings) as collateral for a loan. Subsidies to training the disadvantaged may be particularly appealing to taxpayers who prefer to support transfer programs that are associated with work activity. Recent concern with the working poor who work full time but at a wage that is too low to yield a level of income above the poverty line also suggests the possibility of supporting training programs for disadvantaged workers.

The private market may also yield a less than socially optimal amount of training to the extent that training generates external (spillover, third-party) benefits that are not paid for in the market. In such circumstances firms and individuals would have no incentive to consider such benefits in their investment calculations and consequently may under-invest in training. Externalities may exist in the form of vacuum effects when trainees move up the occupation ladder and vacate a job that is filled by a member of the unemployed, or they may exist in the form of complementary multiplier effects as trainees reduce structural bottlenecks that previously resulted in the unemployment of related workers.

A sub-optimal amount of general training may also be provided by companies where on-the-job training is a natural by-product of their production process. Workers simply acquire training in their everyday work tasks. However, because it is difficult to know how much training they are acquiring and at what cost, they may be reluctant to pay for such training. In such circumstances, training may have public-good characteristics in that the training is available to all workers and yet it is difficult to exclude those who don't pay for the training. To be sure, only those who are willing to work for lower wages could be hired (and in this way non-payers are excluded). However, the indirect nature of the training makes it difficult for the purchasers to know how much training they are acquiring.

At the macroeconomic level, training may also yield benefits to the general public in the sense of helping the economy achieve such goals as growth, full employment, price stability, a viable balance of payments, and a more equitable distribution of income. As an anti-cyclical device to reduce the inflation-unemployment trade-off, training may be effective in absorbing some of the unemployed during a recession and in providing supplies of skilled workers when structural bottlenecks may otherwise lead to inflation.

QUESTIONS

1. Discuss the analogy between physical and human capital.
2. How would you evaluate the extent to which your acquiring a university education is a sound investment economically? Be precise in the information you would require and exactly what you would do with it.
3. You have been asked to evaluate an on-the-job training program in a particular company. Specify exactly what sort of information you require and what you would do with it.
4. The federal government supports a variety of human resource programs including education, training, mobility, labour market information and health. Could you suggest any techniques that may be useful to suggest how resources should be allocated to the various functions?
5. Should governments subsidize human resource programs? If so, why? Be precise in your answer by indicating where, if anywhere, the private market may fail to yield a socially optimal amount of human resource development.
6. Assume that you are deciding whether or not to acquire a four year university degree. Your only consideration at this moment is the degree as an investment for yourself. Costs per year are tuition fees $600, and books $100. The government also pays to the university an equivalent amount to your tuition fees to cover the real cost. If you didn't go to university, you would have earned $6,000 per year as an acrobat. With a university degree, however, you know that you can earn $10,000 per year as an acrobat. Because of the nature of your chosen occupation,

your time horizon for the investment decision is exactly 10 years after university; that is, if the investment is to be worthwhile, it must be so within a 10 year period after graduation. The market rate of interest is 5%. Would you make the investment in a degree?

7. Compare the virtues of on-the-job versus institutional training.

8. Give an example of each of the following as errors in a cost-benefit calculation: ignoring opportunity cost; failing to discount benefits; double counting; considering sunk cost with no alternative value; ignoring a real externality; considering a pecuniary externality; and ignoring consumption benefits.

REFERENCES AND FURTHER READINGS

A. Human Capital Theory and Cost Benefit Evaluations

[Additional readings in this area can be found in the bibliographies in the following entries.]

Becker, G. *Human Capital and the Personal Distribution of Income*. Ann Arbor, Michigan: Institute of Public Administration and Department of Economics, 1967.

Becker, G. *Human Capital*. New York: National Bureau of Economic Research, 1964.

Blaug, M. The empirical status of human capital theory. *Journal of Economic Literature* 14 (September 1976) 827-856.

Bossiere, M., J. Knight and R. Sabot. Earnings, schooling, ability, and cognitive skills. *AER* 75 (December 1985) 1016-1030.

Bound, J., Z. Griliches and B. Hall. Wages, schooling and I.Q. of brothers and sisters: do the family factors differ? *IER* 27 (February 1986) 77-106.

Butler, R. The effect of education on wages — hedonic makes selectivity bias (sort of) simpler. *EI* 22 (January 1984) 109-120.

Coyte, P. Specific human capital and sorting mechanisms in labor markets. *SEJ* 51 (October 1984) 469-480.

Donaldson, D. and B. Eaton. Specific human capital and shared investments again. *CJE* 10 (August 1977) 474-475.

Dooley, M. The overeducated Canadian? Changes in the relationship among earnings, education, and age for Canadian men: 1971-1981. *CJE* 19 (February 1986) 142-159.

Eastman, S. Uncertainty and the time profile of wages. *CJE* 10 (August 1977) 472-473.

Eaton, J. and H. Rosen. Taxation, human capital, and uncertainty. *AER* 70 (September 1980) 705-715.

Garen, J. The returns to schooling: a selectivity bias approach with a continuous choice variable. *Econometrica* 52 (September 1984) 1199-1218.

Griliches, Z. Wages of very young men. *JPE* 84 (August 1976) 569-586.

Griliches, Z. Estimating the returns to schooling: some econometric problems. *Econometrica* 45 (January 1977) 1-22.

Hansen, W.L. (ed.). *Education, Income and Human Capital*. New York: National Bureau of Economic Research, 1970.

Heckman, J. and G. Sediacek. Heterogeneity, aggregation and market wage functions: an empirical model of self-selection in the labor market. *JPE* 93 (December 1985) 1077-1125.

Jones, E. and J. Long. Part-week work and human capital investment by married women. *JHR* 14 (Fall 1979) 563-578.

Journal of Political Economy, Supplement, 70, Part 2 (October 1962).

Kenny, L. The accumulation of human capital during marriage by males. *EI* 21 (April 1983) 223-231.

Kiker, B. and R. Roberts. The durability of human capital: some new evidence. *EI* 22 (April 1984) 269-281.

Kniesner, T., A. Padilla and S. Polachek. The rate of return to schooling and the business cycle. *JHR* 13 (Spring 1978) 264-277.

Lee, L. Health and wage: a simultaneous equation model with multiple discrete indicators. *IER* 23 (February 1982) 199-222.

MacDonald, G. The impact of schooling on wages. *Econometrica* 49 (September 1981) 1349-1359.

McMahon, W. and A. Wagner. Expected returns to investment in higher education. *JHR* 16 (Spring 1981) 274-285.

Mincer, J. Investment in human capital and personal income distribution. *JPE* 66 (August 1958) 281-302.

Nitzan, S. and J. Paroush. Investment in human capital and social self protection under uncertainty. *IER* 21 (October 1980) 547-558.

Rosen, S. Human capital: a survey of empirical research, *Research in Labor Economics*, R. Ehrenberg (ed.). Greenwich, Conn.: JAI Press, 1977.

Rosenzweig, M., J. Morgan, A. Blinder. An exchange: On the appropriate specification of human capital models. *JHR* 11 (Winter 1976) 3-27.

Schultz, T. Investment in human capital. *AER* 51 (March 1961) 1-17.

Shaw, K. A formulation of the earnings function using the concept of occupational investment. *JHR* 19 (Summer 1984) 319-340.

Thurow, L. *Investment in Human Capital*. Belmont, California: Wadsworth, 1970.

Tomes, N. Religion and the rate of return on human capital: evidence from Canada. *CJE* 16 (February 1983) 122-138.

Tomes, N. The effects of religion and denomination on earnings and the returns to human capital. *JHR* 19 (Fall 1984) 472-488.

Vijverberg, W. Consistent estimates of the wage equation when individuals choose among income-earning activities. *SEJ* 52 (April 1986) 1028-1042.

Wachtel, P. The effect in earnings of school and college investment expenditures. *R.E. Stats.* 68 (August 1976) 326-331.

Walsh, J. Capital concept applied to man. *QJE* (February 1935) 255-285.

Weisbrod, B. The valuation of human capital. *JPE* 69 (October 1961) 425-437.

Welland, J. Schooling and ability as earnings complements. *CJE* 13 (May 1980) 356-367.

Willis, R. Wage determinants: a survey and reinterpretation of human capital earnings functions. *Handbook of Labour Economics*, Vol. 1. O. Ashenfelter and R. Layard (eds.). New York: Elsevier, 1986.

B. Education

Arrow, K.J. Higher education as a filter. *Journal of Public Economics* 2 (1973) 193-216.

Bound, J., Z. Griliches and B.W. Hall. Wages, schooling and I.Q. of brothers and sisters: do the family factors differ? *IER* 27 (February, 1986) 77-105.

Davies, J.B. Training and skill development. *Adapting to Change: Labour Market Adjustment in Canada*, W.C. Riddell (ed.). Toronto: University of Toronto Press, 1986, 163-220.

Davies, J.B. and G.M.T. MacDonald. *Information in the Labour Market: Job-Worker Matching and Its Implications for Education in Ontario.* Toronto: Ontario Economic Council, 1984.

Dooley, M.D. The overeducated Canadian? Changes in the relationship among earnings, education, and age for Canadian men: 1971-1981. *CJE* 19 (February 1986) 142-159.

Freeman, R.B. *The Overeducated American.* New York: Academic Press, 1976.

Freeman, R.B. The facts about the declining economic value of college. *JHR* 15 (1980) 124-142.

Globerman, S. Formal education and the adaptability of workers and managers to technological change. *Adapting to Change: Labour Market Adjustment in Canada,* W.C. Riddell (ed.). Toronto: University of Toronto Press, 1986, 41-70.

Griliches, Z. Estimating the returns to schooling: some econometric problems. *Econometrica* 45 (January 1977) 1-22.

Griliches, Z. and W.M. Mason. Education, income, and ability. *JPE* 80 (May/June, 1972).

Hause, J.C. Earnings profile: ability and schooling. *JPE* 80 (May/June 1972).

Krashinsky, M. The returns to university schooling in Canada: a comment. *CPP* 13 (June 1987) 218-221.

Lang, K. and D. Kropp. Human capital versus sorting: the effects of compulsory attendance laws. *QJE* 101 (August 1986) 609-624.

Mehmet, O. Economic returns on undergraduate fields of study in Canadian universities: 1961 to 1972. *RI/IR* 32 (1977) 321-339.

Riley, J.G. Testing the educational screening hypothesis. *JPE* 87 (Supplement, 1979) S227-52.

Spence, A.M. Job market signalling. *QJE* 87 (1973) 353-374.

Spence, A.M. *Market Signaling: Informational Transfer in Hiring and Related Screening Processes.* Cambridge, Mass.: Harvard University Press, 1974.

Stager, D. Allocation of resources in Canadian education. *Canadian Higher Education in the Seventies,* S. Ostry (ed.). Ottawa: Information Canada, 1972.

Stager, D. Economics of higher education: research publications in English in Canada, 1971 to 1981. *Canadian Journal of Higher Education* 12 (1982) 17-28.

Taubman, P.J. and T.J. Wales. Higher education, mental ability and screening. *JPE* 81 (January 1973) 28-55.

Vaillancourt, F. and I. Henriques. The returns to university schooling in Canada. *CPP* 12 (September 1986) 449-458.

Welch, F. Effects of cohort size on earnings: the baby boom babies' financial bust. *JPE* 87 (Supplement, 1979) 565-598.

Wilkinson, B.W. Elementary and secondary education policy in Canada: a survey. *CPP* 12 (December 1986) 535-572.

C. Training

Adams, A. The stock of human capital and differences in post-school formal occupational training for middle-aged men. *SEJ* 44 (April 1978) 929-936.

Ashenfelter, O. Estimating the effect of training programs on earnings. *R.E. Stats.* 63 (February 1978) 47-57.

Bartel, A. and G. Borjas. Specific training and its effects on the human capital investment profile. *SEJ* 44 (October 1977) 333-341.

Block, F. (ed.). Evaluating manpower training programs, *Research in Labor Economics,* Supplement 1. Greenwich, Conn.: JAI Press, 1976.

Borus, M. *The Economic Benefits and Costs of Retraining.* Lexington, Mass.: D.C. Heath, 1971.

Davies, J.B. Training and skill development. *Adapting to Change: Labour Market Adjustment in Canada*, W.C. Riddell (ed.). Toronto: University of Toronto Press, 1986, 163-219.

Donaldson, D. and B. Eaton. Firm-specific human capital: a shared investment or optimal entrapment? *CJE* 9 (August 1976) 462-472. Comment by S. Eastman and reply 10 (August 1977) 472-475.

Freeman, R. Occupational training in proprietary schools and technical institutes. *R.E. Stats.* 56 (August 1974) 310-318.

Goodman, R. Hiring, training and retraining the hard-core. *IR* 9 (October 1969) 54-66.

Gunderson, M. Determinants of individual success in on-the-job training. *JHR* 8 (Fall 1973) 472-484.

Gunderson, M. Retention of trainees: a study with dichotomous dependent variables. *Journal of Econometrics* 2 (May 1974) 79-93.

Gunderson, M. Training subsidies and disadvantaged workers: regression with a limited dependent variable. *CJE* 7 (November 1974) 69-82.

Gunderson, M. The case for government supported training. *RI/IR* 29 (December 1974) 709-726.

Holtman, A. Joint products and on-the-job training. *JPE* 79 (July-August 1971) 929-931.

Holtman, A. On-the-job training, obsolescence, options and retraining. *SEJ* 38 (January 1972) 414-417.

Holtman, A. and V.K. Smith. Uncertainty and the durability of on-the-job training. *SEJ* 44 (July 1977) 36-42. Also, an extension, 45 (January 1979) 855-857.

Maki, D. The direct effect of the occupational training of adults program on Canadian unemployment rates. *CJE* 5 (February 1972) 125-130.

Mehmet, O. A critical appraisal of the economic rationale of government subsidized manpower training. *RI/IR* 25 (No. 3, 1970) 568-580.

Mehmet, O. Evaluation of institutional and on-the-job manpower training in Ontario. *CJE* 4 (August 1971) 362-373.

Meltz, N. Manpower policy: nature, objectives, perspectives. *RI/IR* 24 (January 1969) 38-43.

Meltz, N. Identifying sources of imbalance in individual labour markets. *RI/IR* 31 (No. 2, 1976) 224-246.

Mincer, J. On-the-job training: costs, returns and some implications. *JPE* Supplement, 70, Part 2 (October 1962) 50-79.

Newton, K. A countercyclical training program for Canada. *RI/IR* 26 (No. 4, 1971) 865-889.

Newton, K. The rationale for government involvement in manpower training in Canada: theory and evidence. *RI/IR* 32 (No. 3, 1977) 399-414.

Oatey, M. The economics of training. *BJIR* 8 (March 1970) 1-21.

Piore, M. On-the-job training and adjustment to technological change. *JHR* 3 (Fall 1968) 435-449.

Scott, L. The economic effectiveness of on-the-job training. *ILRR* 23 (January 1970) 220-236.

Simpson, W. An econometric analysis of industrial training in Canada. *JHR* 19 (Fall 1984) 435-451.

Solie, R. Employment effects of retraining the unemployed. *ILRR* 21 (January 1968) 210-225.

Somers, G. *Retraining the Unemployed*. Madison: University of Wisconsin Press, 1968.

Stromsdorfer, E. Determinants of economic success in retraining the unemployed: the West Virginia experience. *JHR* 3 (Spring 1968) 139-158.

Tabbush, V. Investment in training: a broader approach. *JHR* 12 (Spring 1977) 252-257.

Thirwell, J. Government manpower policies in Great Britain: their rationale and benefits. *BJIR* 10 (July 1972) 165-179.

Thomas, B., J. Moxham, and J. Jones. A cost benefit analysis of industrial training. *BJIR* 7 (July 1969) 231-264.

Truesdell, L. Determinants of the demand for manpower training. *RI/IR* 30 (No. 3, 1975) 424-434.

White, W. On-the-job screening and investment in general and specific training. *SEJ* 47 (July 1980) 14-20.

19 Occupational Wage Structures

As the *Canadian Classification and Dictionary of Occupations* (1971) — hereafter termed the CCDO — indicates, the term occupation denotes the "kind of work performed" (p.xiii); that is, "the term 'occupation' is used to refer to a number of jobs that have the same basic work content, even though they may be found in a number of different establishments or industries" (p.xv).

The occupational wage structure refers to the wage structure between various occupations or occupation groups. The occupation groups can be broadly defined, as for example, one of the 23 CCDO two-digit major groups such as managerial, clerical, sales, service or processing. Or they can be one of the 496 four-digit codes for which Census data is often available or a narrowly defined occupation, such as one of the 6700 seven-digit occupations, for example, typist (4113-126) or arc-welder (8335-138).

The average wage in an occupation, and the changes in that wage relative to the wages in other occupations, will reflect the forces of labour supply and demand in the occupations. Before analysing the basic determinants of these forces, it may be worth highlighting, at the outset, the differences between the various concepts of labour supply that have been developed so far.

The *individual's* labour supply schedule reflects the income-leisure choice decision on the part of the individual. Its shape depends upon the relative importance of income and substitution effects induced by a wage change. The labour supply schedule that the *firm* faces for a given occupation reflects the extent to which the firm is a wage-setter or a wage-taker. Monopsonistic firms face an upward-sloping labour supply schedule, whereas competitive buyers of labour face a perfectly elastic supply of labour schedule at the going wage rate as that wage is determined in the more aggregate labour market for the occupation. That wage rate for the *occupation*, and its relation to wages in other occupations, is the subject of this chapter.

DETERMINANTS OF OCCUPATIONAL SUPPLY AND DEMAND

Figure 19.1 illustrates the occupational wage differential (skill differential) that exists between two hypothetical occupations, for example skilled welders and unskilled labourers. The demand schedules for each occupation

Figure 19.1 Occupational Wage Differential

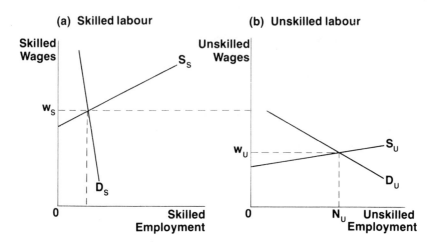

are simply the aggregation of the demand schedules of the various firms that utilize each type of labour. They could be large or small, elastic or inelastic, depending on the circumstances.

The supply schedules for each of the occupations are upward-sloping, reflecting the fact that higher wages are required to attract additional workers into the occupations, away from other occupations, or from non-labour market activities. The higher wages are often necessary to attract additional workers because of different worker preferences for the various occupations, or because of increasing costs associated with acquiring the skills necessary to do the work. Those who prefer the occupation or who have a natural talent for doing the work would enter at the lower wages; higher wages would be necessary to attract those who did not have a preference for the occupation or who could do the work only by a more costly acquisition of the skills.

The supply schedule, therefore, can be thought of as reflecting a ranking of actual and potential workers in the occupation, where those who most prefer the occupation or who have an innate talent for it are ranked at the beginning (and hence require a lower wage to enter), and those who least prefer the occupation or for whom the acquisition of the skills would be more costly are ranked at the end (and hence require the higher wage to enter). If all preferences were identical and there were no increasing costs associated with entering the occupation, then the supply schedule would be perfectly elastic at the going wage for the occupation.

The degree of elasticity of the supply schedule to each occupation also depends on the responsiveness of alternative sources of labour supply which, in turn, depends upon such factors as labour market information and mobility, training requirements, immigration, and the general state of the economy. For example, in the short run, the labour supply schedule to an occupation may be inelastic (and hence a demand increase would lead to more of a wage increase than an employment increase) for a variety of reasons: potential recruits to the occupation are not yet aware of the high wages; they have to be trained to enter the occupation; fulfilling some of the occupational demand through immigration takes time; and the labour market is presently tight, so there is no ready surplus of labour from which to draw.

In the long run, however, most of these factors would adjust to the new demands and the labour supply schedule to the occupation would be more elastic. It may not be perfectly elastic if the new sources of supply are more costly than the original sources. However, in the long run if all of the supply responses had sufficient time to adjust, and if the new sources of supply were not more costly than the original sources, then any inelasticity to the labour supply in an occupation would reflect the different preferences of workers, which would result in a need to raise wages to attract workers who do not have a strong preference for the occupation.

REASONS FOR INTER-OCCUPATIONAL WAGE DIFFERENTIALS

Given the basic determinants of occupational supply and demand, economic theory predicts that the forces of competition will ensure an equal present value of net advantage at the margin in the long run across all occupations. If this does not prevail, then competition ensures that workers at the margin of decision will move from jobs of low net advantage to ones of high net advantage. This does allow for considerable variation in the occupational wage structure to reflect such factors as the non-pecuniary aspects of the job, the human capital skills brought to the job, intra-marginal rents for scarce talents, short-run adjustments, and non-competitive forces.

Thus the occupational wage differential portrayed in Figure 19.1 could persist even in the long run and in the face of competitive forces. In such circumstances, however, it would reflect a compensating wage differential for differences between the occupations in the non-pecuniary aspects of the job, differences in human capital costs associated with each job, or economic rents associated with scarce talents. In the short run it could also reflect short-run adjustments, and even in the long run it could reflect the absence of competitive forces.

Each of these factors will be discussed in turn. In order to focus on the effect of the one factor by itself we will assume that all other aspects of the job are the same, so that the resulting occupational wage differential reflects only the one set of factors under examination.

Compensating Differences for Non-pecuniary Aspects of Job and Human Capital Requirements

Occupations differ in their non-pecuniary characteristics, such as pleasantness, safety, responsibility, fringe benefits, seasonal or cyclical stability, and the certainty of their return. As discussed in the previous chapter on compensating wage differentials occupational wage differentials may exist, therefore, to compensate for these non-pecuniary differences. As Adam Smith (1937, p. 100) observed over two hundred years ago:

> The five following are the principal circumstances which, so far as I have been able to observe, make up for a small pecuniary gain in some employments, and counter-balance a great one in others: first, the agreeableness or disagreeableness of the employments themselves; secondly, the easiness and cheapness, or the difficulty and expense of learning them; thirdly, the constancy or inconstancy of employment in them; fourthly, the small or great trust which must be reposed in those who exercise them; and fifthly, the probability or improbability of success in them.

Adam Smith's reference to the expense of learning how to do a job reminds us that part of the wage paid in a particular occupation may reflect a compensating wage premium to compensate workers for the costly acquisition of human capital necessary to do a particular job. A competitive wage premium would be one that just yields a competitive rate of return on the investment in human capital.

Endowed Talents and Economic Rents

Individuals may also be *endowed* with skills that are valued in the marketplace, in which case the wage premium that is paid to them reflects their natural embodiment of these skills rather than their costly acquisition of the skills. The individual may be endowed with a skill that is useful in a variety of occupations (e.g. strength, dexterity or intelligence) or one that is unique to one or a few (e.g. ability to sing or put the puck in the net).

Economic theory predicts an equality of net advantage *at the margin* associated with each job. Competition ensures this equality at the margin. However, this does not prevent some members of an occupation from receiving an economic rent defined as the difference between what they are paid in their occupation and what they would earn in their next best alternative. This economic rent or seller's surplus is illustrated in Figure 19.1(a) as the area of the triangle below the market wage w_s and above the supply schedule S_s. This is an economic rent or seller's surplus because the reservation wage depicting what workers could get in alternative occupations (including non-labour market activities) is given by the height of the labour supply schedule. However, the actual wage, w_s, is determined by the intersection of the supply and demand schedules. To the extent that this actual wage is paid to all workers in the occupation, intra-marginal workers receive an economic rent and hence have a strong preference to remain in this occupation. Because it is a surplus payment over and above what is necessary to keep the worker in the occupation, it can be taxed away without affecting the allocation of resources to the occupation.

It is because of the existence of economic rents and the high returns to a scarce talent that the prediction of economic theory — equality of net advantage at the margin across all occupations — becomes deceptive, even though it is true. The phrase may imply that all occupations are equally advantageous and that none are any more attractive than others. Clearly this is not true: many occupations can be more attractive than others, but they can be unattainable because of the talents they require. Competitive forces simply ensure that no *additional* gains in net advantage can be made by leaving or entering an occupation: the equality is at the margin. Competitive forces do not ensure that all occupations are equally attractive or that people in some occupations would not prefer to be in others that are presently unattainable to them.

For example, the average salary of a professional hockey player may be ten times that of a university professor. Even if all university professors wanted to be hockey players, they may not possess the talent to do so. There could be an equality of net advantage at the margin — that is no *additional* net advantage to be had — even though all university professors longed to be hockey players. It would be deceptive to say that both occupations were equally advantageous: it is more accurate to say that no additional advantages are to be had by occupational mobility. The net advantages associated with being a hockey player may be unattainable to most and in this sense there are no additional gains in net advantage to be had. Thus it must be emphasized that economic theory predicts an equality of net advantage at the margin, which means simply that no additional net advantage can be attained by further occupational change.

Short-Run Adjustments

The equality of net advantage at the margin predicted by competitive economic theory is one that would prevail in the long run, defined as the time period that is sufficiently long for all adjustments that are going to occur to have occurred. Thus occupational wage differentials could reflect, in part at least, the price signal that induces the supply response that is part of the long-run adjustment process.

For example, assume that the wages of a particular skilled job are twice those of an unskilled job. This is an equilibrium wage differential in the sense that there are no competitive forces that would alter the differential: there is an equality of net advantage at the margin for each occupation. Now assume a permanent exogenous increase in the demand for skilled workers, perhaps because of technological change. In the short run, the supply schedule to the skilled occupation may be fairly inelastic because of a long training period required to do the skilled work. Thus wages would rise in this occupation and this would be a short-run signal for workers in other occupations to acquire the skills necessary to work in the skilled occupation. The old equality of net advantage has now tipped in favour of the skilled occupation because the wage advantage has increased: there now are gains in net advantage to be had by acquiring the skills necessary to work in the skilled occupation.

In response to the short-run wage premium in the skilled occupation, new workers will enter this occupation and this increased supply will reduce the wage premium until it is just large enough to restore an equality of net advantage at the margin: that is, until no further gains in net advantage are possible. This wage adjustment process may be buttressed by the fact that mobility into this skilled occupation may reduce the supply of labour in the other occupations, and this would serve to increase their wages.

The new equality of net advantage may or may not be associated with the old occupational wage differential whereby skilled workers received twice the wage of unskilled workers. This depends on the preferences of workers in the occupations (i.e. on the slopes of the supply schedules to each occupation). If the skilled occupation had an upward-sloping supply schedule, and therefore higher wages were necessary to attract the additional workers, the new skill differential may be greater than two to one. The skilled workers who were already in the occupation (intra-marginal workers) would receive an additional rent because they were willing to work in the occupation at the old wage but now receive the new higher wage that was necessary to expand the number of workers in the occupation.

Non-competitive Factors

Up to this point we have focused on how the forces of competition would ensure an equality of net advantage at the margin across all occupations and how this could give rise to inter-occupational wage differentials to reflect such factors as non-pecuniary differences, requirements for human capital or natural talents, and short-run adjustments. The occupational wage structure may also reflect the fact that in some instances the forces of competition may be weakened or absent. In such circumstances, non-competitive factors prevent the complete supply response that would ensure that wages adjust to ensure an equality of net advantage at the margin.

The extreme version of the importance of non-competitive factors is in the dual or segmented labour market as discussed earlier. According to that perspective, competition has only a minor influence on wage structures, with the forces of custom and tradition and administered rulings being much more important.

Even within the neoclassical economic perspective, as well as the dual labour market one, there are forces that can thwart some of the impact of competition. In particular, occupational licensing on the part of professional associations, by regulating entry into the profession, can effectively lead to a reduction in the supply of labour to the occupation and hence artificially high salaries. Unions, especially craft unions through the hiring hall and apprenticeship requirements, can also exclude people from some occupations and crowd them into others, raising wages in the former and depressing them in the latter.

Other policies may work directly on wages rather than indirectly through the supply of labour. Minimum wage legislation would affect low-wage occupations and equal pay for equal work laws would affect wages in female-dominated occupations. Wage controls would have an ambiguous effect. To the extent that low-wage workers are exempt then the occupational wage structure may narrow; however, to the extent that it is more difficult to enforce at high income levels, then the structure may widen. Legislation setting fair wages in jobs on government contracts may fall differently on different occupations: in particular, its effect may be most important on occupations in construction jobs where such laws are more prominent. Wage extension legislation that extends the results of negotiated wage settlements throughout an industry may also affect occupations differently. Any or all of these factors may thwart the forces of competition, and this would be reflected in the wage structure between occupations.

Unions may also have an impact on the occupational wage structure, with their effect depending upon the differential impact of the union by occupation and on the extent to which the occupation is unionized. To the extent that unions have obtained larger relative wage gains for their less-skilled members — perhaps through equal absolute wage increases — then they may have narrowed the occupational wage structure. However, if the extent of unionization (and professional associations) is greater in high-wage occupations then this would widen the occupational wage structure. This is compounded by the fact that if union wages lead to an adverse employment effect, then some of those so affected may compete for jobs in the low-wage occupations, widening the structure even further. The impact of unions on the occupational wage structure, therefore, is ultimately an empirical proposition.

Clearly, there are a variety of socio-legal-institutional factors that can work against the forces of competition in the labour market. In fact, many of these factors arose as a response to the results of competitive market forces. Since their impact falls differently on different occupations, they will obviously affect the inter-occupational wage structure.

SECULAR OR LONG-RUN CHANGES IN THE OCCUPATIONAL WAGE STRUCTURE

Meltz and Stager (1979a) indicate that there was a tendency for the Canadian inter-occupational wage structure to narrow from 1931 to 1951, and to remain roughly constant and perhaps even widen slightly from 1951 to 1971. However, the current occupational wage structure is still more narrow than in 1931. While this is the overall trend for all occupations, individual occupations showed marked differences in their trends, reflecting the different supply and demand conditions.

Changes in the demand for different occupations often are not regarded as important determinants of occupational differentials in the long run, because demand changes would lead to short-run wage changes, which would in turn lead to supply responses. As long as labour supply to an occupation is fairly elastic in the long run, demand changes would lead to changes in employment, not wages.

However, there may be times when demand changes can lead to more permanent changes in the occupational wage structure. If, for example, demand increases are continuous and not fully anticipated, they may give rise to a constant series of wage increases to attract additional labour. The maturation of industrialization that has gone on since the 1930s, for example, may be associated with a slower growth in the demand for skilled craft workers and an increase in the demand for the less skilled blue- and white-collar jobs associated with automation and mechanization. Cyclical narrowing of the occupational wage structure associated with business cycle expansions may also lead to more permanent effects if it becomes difficult to re-establish the old occupational wage structure for institutional reasons.

Demand factors also may permanently affect the occupational wage structure if there are different supply elasticities to different occupations. In particular, if the long-run supply to less skilled occupations is more inelastic than the long-run supply to the more skilled occupations, then even equal demand increases in both would lead to greater wage increases in the less skilled occupations and hence a narrowing of the wage structure. It is possible, for example, that the labour supply schedule is relatively inelastic for low-wage occupations (higher wages are necessary to attract additional workers) because of a reluctance to do unskilled work and because of a preference for a more pleasant work environment which is usually associated with skilled jobs. This could be reinforced by a ratchet effect if workers who become exposed to the skilled jobs develop a reluctance to return to unskilled trades.

On the supply side, there are reasons to believe that much of the long-run narrowing of the occupational wage structure, at least up until the 1950s, can be explained by exogenous increases in the supply of skilled workers and decreases in the supply of unskilled. Changes in these factors since the 1950s may also explain the cessation of the narrowing and the possible recent widening.

Increases in the supply of skilled labour have been associated with a variety of factors. Most aspects of human capital formation — training, education, mobility and labour market information — have become cheaper to the *individual* with massive government provision or support of these programs, and they have become more affordable with our increased family income over time. Improved communication in general, and employment services in particular, have improved information and mobility. Immigration has been increasingly restricted to skilled occupations and many supply restrictions (the hiring hall, occupational licensing, apprenticeship schemes) have been reduced or made redundant with the ascendancy of mass production and industrial unions over craft unions.

In addition to this exogenous increase in the supply of skilled workers which would serve to reduce skilled wages, there has been a decrease in the supply of unskilled workers which would serve to raise the wages of unskilled workers. Immigration has been reduced over time and it has increasingly become skill oriented, therefore reducing this pool of unskilled labour. With the diminution of the farm population, rural to urban migration is no longer a source of unskilled labour. Legislation limiting child labour and establishing compulsory school attendance has reduced the supply of young unskilled labour. Social programs that reduce the incentive to work — welfare, unemployment insurance, public pensions — may also reduce the supply of unskilled labour.

Over time minimum wage laws may also have increased, thereby raising the wages of unskilled workers relative to skilled workers. Unions may also serve to compress the occupational wage structure, especially if they follow policies of equal absolute, rather than relative, gains for their members. The increased importance of industrial as opposed to craft unions would serve to strengthen the tendency of unions to compress the occupational wage structure.

In recent years, dramatic demographic changes, documented earlier, have occurred in the composition of our labour force. Specifically, there have been large influxes of female workers, particularly married women, and of younger workers as the baby boom population entered the labour market. In general, many of these workers were unskilled and this increase in the supply of unskilled labour may have contributed to a widening of the occupational wage structure. In addition, there is the possibility that the cessation of the narrowing in the 1950s and 1960s may reflect the long-run forces working themselves out. That is, prior to the 1950s, the occupational wage structure may have been narrowing as a result of a series of unanticipated transitory demand increases (associated for example with World War II and the post-war demand) and the long-run supply responses never fully worked themselves out until after the 1950s.

SHORT-RUN OR CYCLICAL CHANGES IN OCCUPATIONAL WAGE STRUCTURES

In addition to its long-run trend patterns, the occupational wage structure exhibits pronounced changes in the short run over the business cycle or in response to unusual events such as war. In particular, the occupational wage structure or skill differential tends to narrow in tight labour markets associated with periods of prosperity or war, and the wage structure tends to widen in recessions. As with the long-run changes, these cyclical changes must be explicable by changes in the demand and supply of labour, or in changes in wage fixing or job content over the business cycle.

Reasons for Widening During Recession

During a recession there is a maintenance of the demand for skilled labour but a decrease in the demand for unskilled workers, and hence a widening of the skill differential. As discussed previously in Chapter 10, this occurs because skilled workers are associated with greater fixed recruiting and hiring costs than unskilled workers. Firms are therefore reluctant to lay off their skilled workers for fear of losing the fixed costs by not being able to rehire their skilled workers when prosperity returns. In addition, as Reder (1955) points out, recessions are associated with shorter production runs and skilled workers are better able to adapt to the variety of tasks associated with shorter production runs.

During a recession there is also an increase in the supply of unskilled workers relative to skilled workers. This occurs, as Reder (1955) indicates, because skilled workers, who were retained for reasons discussed earlier, are moved down the internal queue or occupational ladder, having the same effect as an increase in the supply of unskilled workers and therefore depressing unskilled wages even further. Many of the unskilled workers, on the other hand, are laid off and enter the reserve of unemployed where they exert a further depressing influence on unskilled wages because the firm can always hire unskilled workers from the queue of unemployed.

Reasons for Narrowing During Prosperity

During periods of tight labour markets, associated for example with prosperity or war, the previous scenario is reversed. Demand for unskilled workers rises relative to the demand for skilled workers, and the supply of skilled workers increases. Unskilled wages therefore rise more rapidly than skilled wages and the occupational wage structure narrows.

The demand for unskilled workers rises more rapidly than the demand for skilled workers because the firm already has the reserve of skilled workers that it retained during the previous recession. There is, therefore, no need to raise skilled wages to attract additional skilled workers from the outside. However, the firm will increase its demand for unskilled workers from the external labour market and will have to raise unskilled wages to attract these workers from the small pool of unemployed that has dwindled because of the tight labour market. This would also enable unskilled workers to obtain the compensating wage differential that would normally be associated with the unpleasant nature of many unskilled jobs.

Periods of prosperity are also associated with longer production runs that enable production processes to be broken down into a series of repetitive tasks that can be done by unskilled labour. This may also increase the demand for unskilled relative to skilled labour.

On the supply side, during periods of tight labour markets there is an increase in the supply of skilled workers relative to unskilled. According to Reder (1955), this occurs because hiring and job standards are relaxed and firms utilize many of their unskilled workers to perform skilled tasks. In effect, the content of the skilled jobs becomes diluted and a lower wage rate in these skilled occupations results.

These short-run changes can have longer-run effects in that, once unskilled workers are exposed to doing some of the skilled tasks, they may accumulate experience and on-the-job training in these tasks. In addition, they may develop a preference for some of the better working conditions that are often associated with skilled tasks. Thus a short-run narrowing of the occupational wage structure may encourage a longer-run narrowing, even though the initial short-run stimuli are gone. As indicated earlier, this may account for some of the long-run narrowing that has occurred.

SOME CONCLUDING OBSERVATIONS

The occupational wage structure has exhibited both long-run trend patterns and short-run variation. It seems possible to explain both the long- and short-run patterns by basic forces of supply and demand, coupled with institutional factors such as minimum wages and unions. Nevertheless, to a certain extent the explanations appear as *ad hoc* responses that have been devised after the fact, to explain the facts. Consequently, the explanations have not been subject to rigorous empirical tests based on data that was not used to derive the explanation itself.

What is needed on the theoretical side is a more consistent theoretical explanation that will encompass *all* aspects of occupational wage structures: the reasons for their magnitude at any given point in time, their long-run changes over time, and their short-run changes over business cycles and in response to unusual events. What is needed on the empirical side is more discriminating empirical tests that will enable the rejection of some hypotheses and the acceptance of others. Until the theory can be improved and the evidence tested more rigorously, we should regard with caution our various explanations for the behaviour of occupational wage structures. Without an adequate theoretical explanation, policy prescriptions are, at best, hazardous.

QUESTIONS

1. Discuss the interrelationship between occupational wage structures and other wage structures, particularly wage differentials by industry, region and personal characteristics. Why does the interrelatedness make it difficult to talk about such a thing as a pure occupational wage differential? Illustrate by an example.
2. Discuss the differences between inter- and intra-occupational wage differentials.
3. Discuss the various factors that determine the shape of the labour supply schedule for an occupation. Give an example of an occupation that may have an elastic supply schedule and one that may have an inelastic one, and indicate why this is so. If both occupations received an equal increase in the demand for their labour, what would happen to the skill differential between the two occupations?
4. "Economic theory predicts that all occupations yield an equal net ad-

vantage. This is patently not so and therefore economic theory is wrong."
Discuss.

5. Discuss the expected impact on wages, and hence the wage structure, of each of the following policies:

   (a) an increase in unionization;
   (b) an increase in public subsidies to education, training, job search and mobility;
   (c) wage-price controls;
   (d) child labour laws;
   (e) laws governing the minimum age one can leave school;
   (f) a reduction in rural-urban migration;
   (g) a reduction in immigration;
   (h) an exogenous influx into the labour force of younger workers and married women;
   (i) an increase in workers' compensation;
   (j) an increase in industrial safety regulations:
   (k) a reduction in the seasonal nature of construction work and a more even phasing of construction activity over the business cycle;
   (l) more strict control of entry into the medical profession;
   (m) a reduction of featherbedding on the part of unions.

6. Just as in computing the aggregate price index it is important to net out the effect of quality change over time, so in computing the aggregate wage index we should net out changes in the quality of labour and in the characteristics of jobs. Otherwise we won't know how much, if any, an increase in the aggregate wage level is attributable to quality change or to changes in the work environment as opposed to a pure wage increase. How do you think these factors — labour quality and job environment — have changed over time, and how would this affect our aggregate wage level?

7. "The purpose of human resource programs is to increase the elasticity of labour supply to an occupation." Discuss.

8. "One of the problems in recent years is that the occupational wage structure has narrowed so much that there is little incentive to acquire skills or to engage in job search or mobility." Discuss.

9. Discuss the strengths and weaknesses of the coefficient of variation and the skill differential as measures of the occupational wage structure. Discuss some alternative measures. Make up a hypothetical example of an occupational wage structure and compute the coefficient of variation. Compute the skill differential for each occupation, defined as the ratio of the wage in each occupation to the average wage of all occupations.

10. Discuss the possible long-run narrowing of the occupational wage structure that has gone on over the last fifty years. Why may this narrowing have stopped, at least between 1950 and 1970? What do you think the structure would be like in the future and why?

11. Discuss the reasons for the short-run fluctuations in the skill differential

over the business cycle and in response to tight labour markets associated with war. How might these factors also alter the long-run wage structure?

12. "We really don't have a consistent theory that can explain both the long-run and short-run changes in the occupational wage structure. Rather, we have a series of *ad hoc* explanations (stories?) that have often arisen, after the facts, to explain the facts." Discuss.

13. "There is little policy interest in analysing occupational wage structures because they have no normative significance by themselves. They are simply the result of the interplay of various market and institutional forces. If these forces are undesirable, then they should be curbed for that reason, not because of any impact that they may have on the occupational wage structure. For this reason, when told that occupational wage structures have narrowed over the last fifty years and that they narrow at the peak of the business cycle, an appropriate response is — so what?" Discuss.

REFERENCES AND FURTHER READINGS

Boskin, M. A conditional logit model of occupational choice. *JPE* 82 (March/April 1974) 389-398.

Brown, W., J. Hayles, B. Hughes and L. Rowe. Occupational pay structures under different wage fixing arrangements. *BJIR* 18 (July 1980) 217-230.

Bruce, C. and J. Cheslak. Sources of occupational wage differentials in a competitive labour market. *RI/IR* 33 (No. 4, 1978) 621-640.

De Meza, D. Wage uncertainty, expected utility and occupational choice. *IER* 25 (October 1984) 757-762.

Fogel, W. Occupational earnings: market and institutional influences. *ILRR* 33 (October 1979) 24-35.

Hawkesworth, R. The movement of skill differentials in the U.K. engineering industry. *BJIR* 16 (November 1978) 277-286.

Kerr, C. Wage-relationships — the comparative impact of market and power forces. *The Theory of Wage Determination*, John Dunlop (ed.). New York: St Martin's Press, 1957, 173-193.

Kumar, P. Differentials in wage rates of unskilled labor in Canadian manufacturing industries. *ILRR* 26 (October 1972) 631-645.

Kumar, P. and M. Coates. Occupational earnings, compensating differentials and human capital: an empirical study. *CJE* 15 (August 1982) 442-457.

Meltz, N. and D. Stager. *The Occupational Structure of Earnings in Canada 1931-1975*. Anti-Inflation Board Report. Ottawa: Supply and Services, 1979a.

Meltz, N. and D. Stager. Trends in the occupational structure of earnings in Canada 1931-1971. *CJE* 12 (May 1979b) 312-315.

Ostry, S. A note on skill differentials. *SEJ* 29 (January 1963) 231-234.

Peitchinis, S. Occupational wage differentials in Canada, 1939-1965. *Australian Economic Papers* 8 (June 1969) 20-40.

Reder, M. The theory of occupational wage differentials. *AER* 45 (December 1955) 833-852.

Reder, M. Wage structure theory and measurement. *Aspects of Labor Economics*. Princeton: Princeton University Press, 1962.

Rosen, S. Unionism and the occupational wage structure in the United States. *IER* 11 (June 1970) 269-286.

Schoeplein, R. Secular changes in the skill differential in manufacturing, 1952-1973. *ILRR* 30 (April 1977) 314-324.

Smith, A. *The Wealth of Nations.* Toronto: Random House, 1937.

Walsh, W. The short-run behaviour of skilled wage differentials. *ILRR* 30 (April 1977) 302-313.

Wilkinson, B. Present values of lifetime earnings for different occupations. *JPE* 74 (December 1966) 556-572.

CHAPTER 20

Regional Wage Structures and Geographic Mobility

The existence of pronounced regional wage differentials is a well documented fact in Canada as in most economies. As with most wage structures, however, what is less well known are the reasons for the differentials and the extent to which a pure geographic wage differential would persist in the very long run. The problem is compounded by the fact that regional wage structures tend to reflect a variety of other wage structures, notably those by industry, occupation, and personal characteristics of the workers; hence, it is difficult to isolate what could be considered a pure inter-regional wage differential, independent of other wage differentials.

ECONOMIC DETERMINANTS OF REGIONAL WAGE DIFFERENTIALS

Economic theory predicts that the forces of competition would ensure an equality of net advantage at the margin associated with identical jobs in each region. That is, if the non-wage aspects of employment (including the probability of obtaining employment) were the same, competition would ensure that wages for the same job would be the same across all regions. Competitive forces could operate in the form of workers moving from the low-wage regions to the high-wage regions, or in the form of firms moving from high-wage regions to low-wage regions to minimize labour cost. As workers leave the low-wage region, the reduced supply would raise wages, and as firms enter the low-wage region, the increased demand would also increase wages. The converse would happen in the high-wage region and the process of the mobility of labour and/or capital would continue until an equality of net advantage were restored in the long run.

To the extent that different people have different geographic preferences, the supply of labour for a given occupation in a particular region may not be perfectly elastic. That is, for a region to expand its work-force, higher wages may have to be paid to attract workers from other regions. This could obviously be the case in the short run, but it may also be the case in the long run to the extent that geographic preferences exist. In such circumstances, some workers may be receiving location rents in the sense that they would prefer to remain in a particular region even if wages were lower.

The equality of net advantage at the margin predicted by economic theory does allow for considerable variation in the inter-regional wage structure; however, as with inter-occupational wage differentials that variation would have to reflect compensating differences, short-run adjustments, or non-competitive factors. Each of these will be discussed in turn.

Compensating Differences

The compensating differences are most obvious and they include wage compensation for such factors as cost of living, remoteness, and climate. They may even include compensation for non-priced externalities such as pollution and congestion. Obviously the compensating factors need not work in the same direction. Urban workers may receive a wage premium to compensate for pollution or congestion externalities, or a higher cost of living: they would obviously not receive it for remoteness.

In addition, the compensating factors need not be valued the same by all workers. The compensating wage is paid to get the marginal worker into the region. Intra-marginal workers may not require the full compensating factor — after all, they were in the region in the first place, even before the compensating wage was paid the marginal worker — and yet because of competition for their services, they are paid the full compensating premium. As indicated earlier, these intra-marginal workers would be receiving location rents because of their geographic preference.

Short-Run Adjustments

Short-run inter-regional wage differentials could also be present. In fact such short-run differentials are signals that are necessary to induce the mobility that will lead to a long-run equilibrium. The key questions concerning the appropriateness of the economic explanation for short-run wage differentials then become: does mobility move in the direction predicted by economics (that is, from low- to high-wage regions), and does this process serve to reduce the differential?

The adjustment process can take a long time because the costs of geographic mobility can be large, involving not only the direct costs of moving, but also the psychic costs associated with such factors as leaving a familiar cultural, linguistic and geographic environment. In addition, the factors giving rise to the adjustments may change slowly but continuously over time. For example, the decline of the fishing and maritime trade may be a slow but constant sequence of demand declines, reducing the derived demand for labour in the Maritime region. The supply response would be very slow, usually involving younger workers who would not have built up as strong regional attachments as older ones. By the time the supply response has occurred, a further demand decline occurs, and the adjustment process continues.

In essence, a long-run equality of wages is not achieved because of a series of short-run adjustments that continue in the same direction. Even if they are fully anticipated by workers, their supply response cannot be immediate. The system may be in constant long-run disequilibrium, although in a series of short-run equilibria. Thus inter-regional wage differentials could persist for a long period of time, although economics predicts that the forces of competition (mobility of capital and labour) should respond to these differentials, and that this should serve to reduce them.

Non-competitive Factors as Barriers to Mobility

Not only is geographic mobility hindered by the barriers that arise because of the high direct and psychic costs of moving, but also it can be hindered by artificial barriers and by public policies that have an indirect, and perhaps unintentional, impact on mobility.

Occupational licensing, for example, can hinder geographic mobility. Some provinces may not recognize training done in other jurisdictions, others may have residency requirements, and others may even require citizenship. In addition, trade unions that control hiring (i.e. have the "hiring hall") can require that people who have worked in the zone be hired first, hence discouraging others from entering the zone. While these policies do achieve other objectives, they also reduce the effectiveness of inter-regional mobility as a force to reduce inter-regional wage differentials.

Social transfer programs that try to reduce income disparities will obviously have different regional impacts and this could reduce regional mobility. In such circumstances governments are faced with a basic dilemma: as they use transfer programs to reduce income inequality, they reduce part of the incentive for people to engage in regional mobility, unless the transfer programs are conditional upon geographic mobility. Regional expansion policies can encourage capital to move into low-income areas, but this also reduces the mobility of labour from that region and hence reduces some of the market forces that would reduce inequalities. Obviously these policies can achieve other important objectives — noticeably, perhaps, a more equitable distribution of regional income — but they do have the effect of reducing the effectiveness of geographic mobility as a force to reduce geographic wage differences.

MIGRATION DECISION

As the previous section indicates, economic theory predicts that the forces of competition would serve to reduce pure regional wage differentials so that they reflect compensating differences, short-run adjustments, or non-competitive factors. Those forces of competition were the movement of capital from high- to low-wage areas, and the movement of labour from low- to high-wage areas.

This latter movement — geographic mobility or migration — can be treated as a human capital decision, the determinants of which are discussed in Chapter 18. That is, geographic mobility will occur as long as the marginal benefits exceed the marginal costs to the individuals making the decision. Benefits can include such factors as expected income (which in turn can be a function of earnings and job opportunities as well as transfer payments), climate, and the availability of social services. Costs can include the usual costs of information-seeking and moving, as well as the psychic costs associated with geographic moves. In addition the migration decision may depend on one's ability to finance the move — a problem that is particularly acute in human capital theory because one cannot legally use human capital (e.g. the larger expected earnings) as collateral to finance any necessary loan.

The human capital framework provides a variety of empirically test-able propositions concerning the mobility decision. Other things being equal, relative to older workers, younger workers would tend to engage in more job mobility because they have a longer benefit period from which to recoup the costs, their opportunity cost (forgone income) of moving is lower as are their direct costs if they do not have a home to sell or family to move, and their psychic costs are probably lower becauase they have not established long ties in their community. In addition, they may not be locked in by seniority provisions or pensions that are not portable.

Although older persons who are about to retire may move to get the benefits of a better climate, potential workers would move towards job opportunities: that is, to areas of low unemployment or to centres where there is a large stock of jobs available. In addition, economic theory predicts that geographic mobility would be pro-cyclical, increasing at the peak of a business cycle when job opportunities are more abundant, and decreasing in a recession when jobs are scarce.

Mobility in and out of Quebec would be expected to be lower than in other regions of Canada because of language and cultural differences. In addition, as Grant and Vanderkamp (1976, p. 87) indicate, distance is an inhibiting factor because it increases moving costs and uncertainty as well as the psychic costs associated with being uprooted from one's familiar environment.

EMPIRICAL EVIDENCE ON INTERNAL MIGRATION

Empirical evidence tends to verify the implications of migration as a human capital decision. In the Canadian context, this is evident in the work of Courchene (1970, 1974), Laber and Chase (1971), Mansell and Copithorne (1986), McInnis (1970), and in the extensive work of John Vanderkamp (1968, 1971, 1972, 1973, 1976 and 1986).

Grant and Vanderkamp (1976), for example, confirm that migrants typically move from low-income, high-unemployment regions to high-income, low-unemployment regions, and that they are more likely to move to a nearby region so as to minimize the moving and psychic costs asso-ciated with a more distant move. They also confirm that mobility is greater for younger than older workers, migration to and from Quebec tends to be substantially lower than for other regions, and migration increases with prosperity and decreases in recession.

With respect to the impact of migration, they find that it does improve the income position of the migrant considerably and that it reduces regional disparities. Grant and Vanderkamp (1976, pp. 88-89) conclude: "The overall impression is one of a labour market adjustment process that works in the right direction; but the adjustment is rather sluggish and by no means the caricature of frictionless market adjustments. . . . It is quite clear that the migration process contributes to the elimination of regional disparities." They attribute much of the slowness of the adjustment process to the large distances in Canada, to the language and cultural differences, and to the fact that many of the demand changes that set off the adjustments (for example, the decline in coal-mining, shipbuilding and fishing in the Maritimes) have been protracted and continuous.

Clearly both the causes and consequences of the migration decision are in line with the predictions of economic theory. That is, geographic mobility responds to the costs and benefits associated with migration, and the process of migration tends to reduce the regional disparities that induced the migration decision. The extent to which the process would ever completely eliminate *pure* regional earnings differentials remains an open and probably empirically unverifiable proposition, given the near impossibility of completely controlling for the impact of other wage structures, as well as compensating factors, short-run adjustments, and non-competitive forces.

INTERNATIONAL MIGRATION

The decision to migrate internationally also can be viewed as a human capital decision that depends upon benefits and costs. In this decision, the non-economic constraints are even more important, however, because imigration is strictly regulated and hence subject to political decisions of the host economy. These political decisions, however, often are a function of the economic environment.

In Canada, for example, immigration currently is regulated through a point system whereby a large percentage of the points are given for such factors as education, training, previously arranged employment, and possession of skills that are in high demand and short supply. Clearly the control of immigration is highly job-oriented and it can be turned on and off depending upon economic conditions.

Immigration into Canada also tends to be pro-cyclical. That is, in prosperous times immigration tends to be large, and in periods of recession and high unemployment it is small. This is attributed to the fact that in periods of high unemployment, immigration officials may tighten up on the influx, and new immigrants may be less prone to enter. The importance of the economic environment is further illustrated by the fact that new immigrants have chosen to settle in the more prosperous regions and urban centres of Canada.

As with the internal migration decision, international migration is strongly influenced by economic factors in the direction predicted by economic theory. What is less clear is the impact of immigration itself on wage differentials. To the extent that recent Canadian immigration has been restricted to skilled groups, this augmentation of skilled labour should serve to reduce skill differentials. In addition, since immigration has gone to the more prosperous regions, it should serve to reduce interregional wage differentials.

BRAIN DRAIN

From a policy perspective, one of the most interesting and controversial aspects of international migration is the issue of the so-called brain drain. The problem arises because countries, especially less-developed ones, may lose their most-skilled labour to the more-developed countries. It is the skilled workers that tend to leave because they can afford to do so, they have the knowledge of foreign opportunities (perhaps acquired while studying abroad), and they can usually amass sufficient points to enter the host country.

The problem is especially acute with countries that heavily subsidize the education and training of their workers. In such circumstances, the home countries bear the cost of the education, and the skilled emigrant reaps all of the benefits in the form of higher earnings in the host country. In many circumstances these skilled workers are the very persons that the developing economy can least afford to lose.

The brain drain often occurs when students from less-developed economies go to more-developed economies for advanced education and training. The psychic costs associated with the cultural and environmental change have already been incurred, and the direct cost of education or training is often borne by the home country. By definition, the income opportunities are greater in the more-developed host country and hence the temptation to stay.

For countries that are net losers of highly skilled labour, there are some possible remedies, but they all involve other problems. Having the individuals themselves pay for their own education and training would at least ensure that they were paying the costs for the benefits they could receive if they emigrate. However, especially in developing economies, this may hinder large numbers of otherwise poor people from acquiring the education or training. Placing an "exit tax" equal to the amount of the human capital cost borne by the state is theoretically possible, but practically difficult to enforce, and it may be politically unpopular as it becomes compounded with issues of human rights. Recruiting your own students abroad and encouraging their return is a policy that is utilized, but it does have costs and it may be vacuous if viable job opportunities cannot be provided. Providing job opportunities at high wages, of course, is easier said than done, especially in countries that have followed a conscious policy of minimizing wage differentials, possibly for equity reasons. Clearly, as in so many elements of public policy, a variety of delicate trade-offs are involved.

QUESTIONS

1. Discuss the problems associated with calculating what could be considered a pure inter-regional wage differential. What does economic theory imply about the existence of such a differential?

2. Discuss the competitive forces that should work to reduce inter-regional wage differentials.

3. The economic model of migration has been criticized for predicting that the forces of competition would reduce regional disparities. Some have argued that disparities would increase as the best people leave for the better job alternatives, and as capital flows to the already expanding sector. Discuss.

4. "Equity of net advantage at the margin does not imply that everyone is equally happy with their geographic location." Discuss.

5. It could be argued that market forces will not prevent cities from growing beyond a socially optimal size because pollution or congestion externalities associated with city growth are not accounted for through the market mechanism. Discuss the extent to which wage adjustments may reflect these externalities. Will the wage adjustments ensure a socially optimal city size?

6. "Even though we may not be able to make empirical statements about the magnitude of a pure geographic wage differential, we can empirically test how the geographic wage structure will *change* in response to changes in its determinants." Discuss.

7. "Long-run changes in the demand for labour should not affect the inter-regional wage structure to the extent that they are fully anticipated." Discuss.

8. Discuss the variety of artificial barriers that can impede geographic mobility in a country like Canada. Should these barriers be removed?

9. Discuss the ways in which government social transfer programs may decrease or increase geographic mobility. To the extent that they decrease mobility, should they be removed? Are there ways of mitigating their adverse effects on geographic mobility?

10. Discuss the extent to which the migration decision is a human capital decision. To the extent that it is a human capital decision, what does this tell us about the determinants of migration? Derive some empirically testable hypotheses from the human capital model of migration.

11. "Internal and international migration are essentially different decisions because international migration involves political boundaries and therefore controls which take it out of the economic realm." Discuss.

12. Would you expect geographic mobility to be greater for younger or older workers and why?
13. Discuss the extent to which empirical evidence for Canada supports the economic analysis of the migration decision, both internally and internationally.
14. What impact would immigration be expected to have on wage structures in the host country?
15. Discuss what is meant by the brain drain, why it arises, and possible solutions to the problem.

REFERENCES AND FURTHER READINGS

A. Regional Wage Structures

Behman, S. Interstate differentials in wages and unemployment. *IR* 17 (May 1978) 168-188.

Denton, F. *An Analysis of Interregional Differences in Manpower Utilization and Earnings.* Staff Study No. 15. Ottawa: Economic Council of Canada, 1966.

Economic Council of Canada. *People and Jobs: A Study of the Canadian Labour Market.* Ottawa: Information Canada, 1976.

Gerking, S. and S. Wierick. Compensating differences and interregional wage differentials. *R.E. Stats.* 65 (August 1983) 483-486.

Hanushek, E. Regional differences in the structure of earnings. *R.E. Stats.* 55 (May 1973) 204-213.

Johnson, G. Wage theory and inter-regional variations. *IR* 6 (May 1967) 321-337.

McInnis, M. The trend of regional income differentiation in Canada. *CJE* 1 (May 1968) 440-470.

Morony, J. Factor prices, factor proportions and regular factor endowments. *JPE* 78 (January/February 1970) 158-164.

Newman, R. Dynamic patterns in regional wage differentials. *SEJ* 49 (July 1982) 246-254.

Polzen, P. State and regional wage differences. *SEJ* 38 (January 1972) 371-378.

Reza, A. Geographical differences in earnings and unemployment rates. *R.E. Stats.* 60 (May 1978) 201-208.

Sahling, H. and S. Smith. Regional wage differentials: has the South risen again? *R.E. Stats.* 65 (February 1983) 131-134.

Scully, G. Interstate wage differentials: a cross-section analysis. *AER* 59 (December 1969) 757-773.

Stiglitz, J. Wage determination and unemployment in LDCs. *QJE* 88 (May 1974) 194-227.

Ulman, L. Labour mobility and the industry wage structure in the postwar United States. *QJE* (February 1965) 73-97.

Wonnacott, R. Wage levels and employment structure in United States regions: a free trade precedent. *JPE* 72 (August 1964) 414-419.

Zaidi, M. Structural unemployment, labor market efficiency and the intra-factor allocation mechanisms in the United States and Canada. *SEJ* 35 (January 1969) 205-213. Comment by B. Mabry and reply 39 (October 1972) 307-310.

B. Geographic Mobility, Migration and the Brain Drain

Ault, D., G. Rautman and T. Stevenson. Some factors affecting mobility in the labor force for academic economists. *EI* 20 (January 1982) 104-132.

Bellante, D. The North-South differential and the migration of heterogeneous labor. *AER* 69 (March 1979) 166-175.

Berry, R.A. and R. Soligo. Some welfare aspects of international migration. *JPE* 77 (September/October 1969) 778-794.

Bhagwati, J. (ed.). *The Brain Drain and Taxation*. Amsterdam: North Holland, 1976.

Bhagwati, J. and M. Partington. *Taxing the Brain Drain*. Amsterdam: North Holland, 1976.

Bhagwati, J. et al. The brain drain: a symposium. *Journal of Development Economics* 2 (September 1975) 193-378.

Blomqvist, A. International migration of educated manpower and social rates of return to education in LDCs. *IER* 27 (February 1986) 165-174.

Bohning, W. International migration in Western Europe. *ILR* 118 (July-August, 1979) 401-414.

Borjas, G. Assimilation, changes in cohort quality and the earnings of immigrants. *JOLE* 3 (October 1985) 463-489.

Canto, V. and F. Udwadia. The effect of immigration quotas on the average quality of migrating labor and income distribution. *SEJ* 52 (January 1986) 785-793.

Carliner, G. Wages, earnings and hours of first, second, and third generation American males. *EI* 18 (January 1980) 87-102.

Chiswick, B. The earnings of white and coloured male immigrants in Britain. *Economica* 47 (February 1980) 81-88.

Chiswick, B. Is the new immigration less skilled than the old? *JOLE* 4 (April 1986) 168-192.

Comay, Y. The benefits and costs of study abroad and migration. *CJE* 3 (May 1970) 300-308.

Comay, Y. Determinants of return migration: Canadian professionals in the U.S. *SEJ* 37 (January 1971) 318-322.

Comay, Y. Influences on the migration of Canadian professionals. *JHR* 6 (Summer 1971) 333-344.

Comay, Y. The migration of professionals: an empirical analysis. *CJE* 5 (August 1972) 419-429.

Courchene, T. Interprovincial migration and economic adjustment. *CJE* 3 (November 1970) 550-576.

Courchene, T. *Migration, Income and Employment: Canada 1965-1968*. Montreal: Howe Research Institute, 1974.

Crowley, R. An empirical investigation of some local public costs of in-migration to cities. *JHR* 5 (Winter 1970) 11-23.

Da Vanzo, J. Repeat migration in the United States: who moves back and who moves on? *RE Stats* 65 (November 1983) 552-559.

De Freitas, G. The earnings of immigrants in the American labor market. *IRRA* (December 1981) 58-59.

Denton, F. and B. Spencer. Some aspects of economic adjustments through migration flows. *EJ* 84 (December 1974) 868-885.

Dunlevy, J. and D. Bellante. Net migration, endogenous incomes and the speed of adjustment to the North-South differential. *RE Stats* 65 (February 1983) 66-75.

Ethier, W. International trade and labor migration. *AER* 75 (September 1985) 691-707.

Ethier, W. Illegal immigration: the host country problem. *AER* 76 (March 1986) 56-71.

Falaris, E. Migration and regional wages. *SEJ* 48 (January 1982) 670-686.

Farber, S. A labour shortage model applied to the migration of college professors. *JHR* 10 (Fall 1975) 482-499.

Farber, S. A directional flow migration model. *SEJ* 45 (July 1978) 205-217.

Farber, S. Post-migration earnings profiles: an application of human capital and job search models. *SEJ* 49 (January 1983) 693-705.

Grant, E.K. and J. Vanderkamp. *The Economic Causes and Effects of Migration: Canada 1965-1971.* Ottawa: Economic Council of Canada, 1976.

Grant, E.K. and J. Vanderkamp. The effects of migration on income: a micro study with Canadian data 1965-1971. *CJE* 13 (August 1980) 381-406.

Graves, P. Income and migration reconsidered. *JHR* 14 (Winter 1979) 112-121.

Green, A. *Immigration and the Postwar Canadian Economy.* Toronto: Macmillan, 1976.

Greenwood, M. Research on internal migration in the United States. *Journal of Economic Literature* 13 (June 1975) 397-433.

Greenwood, M. and G. Hunt. Migration and interregional employment redistribution in the United States. *AER* 74 (December 1984) 957-969.

Grossman, J. Illegal immigrants and domestic employment. *ILRR* 37 (January 1984) 240-251.

Herzog, H., Jr., and A. Schlottmann. Labor force migration and allocative efficiency in the United States: the roles of information and psychic costs. *EI* 19 (July 1981) 459-475.

Herzog, H., Jr., and A. Schlottmann. Migrant information, job search and the remigration decision. *SEJ* 50 (July 1983) 43-56.

Hunt, J. and J. Kau. Migration and wage growth: a human capital approach. *SEJ* 51 (January 1985) 697-710.

Johnson, G. The labour market effects of immigration. *ILRR* 33 (April 1980) 331-341.

Johnson, G. The theory of labour market intervention. *Economica* 47 (August 1980) 309-330.

Kaluzny, R. Determinants of household migration. *R.E. Stats.* 57 (August 1975) 269-274.

Kau, J. and C. Sirmans. New, repeat, and return migration: a study of migrant types. *SEJ* 43 (October 1976) 1144-1148. Comment by J. Da Vanzo and reply 44 (January 1978) 680-689.

Kleiner, M.R. Gay and K. Greene. Barriers to labor migration: the case of occupational licencing. *IR* 21 (Fall 1982) 383-391.

Kwok, V. and H. Leland. An economic model of the brain drain. *AER* 72 (March 1982) 91-100.

Langley, P. The private gains to long distance migration in the United States. *EJ* 89 (March 1979) 120-126.

Laber, G. and R. Chase. Interprovincial migration in Canada as a human capital decision. *JPE* 79 (July/August 1971) 795-804.

Liu, B. Differential net migration rates and the quality of life. *RE Stats* 57 (August 1975) 329-337. Comment by Larson and Wilford and reply 62 (February 1980) 157-162.

Mansell, R.L. and L. Copithorne. Canadian regional economic disparities: a survey. *Disparities and Interregional Adjustment.* Toronto: University of Toronto Press, 1986, pp. 1-51.

Milne, D. Migration and income opportunities for blacks in the South. *SEJ* 46 (January 1980) 913-917.

Mincer, J. Family migration decisions. *JPE* 86 (October 1978) 749-776.

Mueser, P. A note on simultaneous equations models of migration and employment growth. *SEJ* 52 (October 1985) 516-522.

Nakosteen, R. and M. Zimmer. Migration and income: the question of self-selection. *SEJ* 46 (January 1980) 840-851.

Navratil, R. and J. Doyle. The socioeconomic determinants of migration and the level of aggregation. *SEJ* 43 (April 1977) 1547-1559.

Polachek, S. and F. Horvath. A life cycle approach to migration. *Research in Labor Economics*, R. Ehrenberg (ed.). Greenwich, Conn.: JAI Press, 1977.

Preston, L. Research on internal migration in the United States. *Journal of Economic Literature* 13 (June 1975) 397-433.

Robinson, C. and N. Tomes. Self-selection and interprovincial migration in Canada. *CJE* 15 (August 1982) 474-502.

Rodriguez, C. On the welfare aspects of international migration. *JPE* 83 (October 1975) 1065-1072.

Rosenbluth, G. Wage rates and the allocation of labour. *CJE* 1 (August 1968) 566-582.

Schlottmann, A. and H. Herzog. Home economic conditions and the decision to migrate: new evidence for the U.S. labor force. *R.E. Studies* 48 (April 1982) 950-961.

Schroeder, L. Interrelatedness of occupational and geographical labour mobility. *ILRR* 29 (April 1976) 405-411.

Schwartz, A. Interpreting the effect of distance on migration. *JPE* 81 (September/October 1973) 1153-1169.

Schwartz, A. Migration, age and education. *JPE* 84 (August 1976) 701-720.

Scott, A. The recruitment and migration of Canadian social scientists. *CJE* 33 (November 1967) 495-508.

Scott, A. and H. Grubel. The international flow of human capital. *AER* 56 (May 1966) 268-274. Comment by N. Aitken and reply 58 (June 1968) 539-547.

Scott, A. and H. Grubel. The international movement of human capital: Canadian economists. *CJE* 2 (August 1969) 375-388.

Sjaastad, L. The costs and returns of human migration. *JPE* 70 (October 1962) S80-S93.

Starr, S. In search of a rational immigration policy. *CPP* 1 (Summer 1975) 328-342.

Steinnes, D. Causality and migration. *SEJ* 45 (July 1978) 218-226.

Usher, D. Public property and the effects of migration upon other residents of the migrants' countries of origin and destination. *JPE* 85 (October 1977) 1001-1020.

Vanderkamp, J. Interregional mobility in Canada: a study of the time pattern of migration. *CJE* 1 (August 1968) 595-608.

Vanderkamp, J. The effect of out-migration on regional employment. *CJE* 3 (November 1970) 541-549.

Vanderkamp, J. Migration flows, their determinants and the effects of return migration. *JPE* 79 (September/October 1971) 1012-1031.

Vanderkamp, J. Return migration: its significance and behaviour. *WEJ* 10 (December 1972) 460-466.

Vanderkamp, J. *Mobility Behaviour of the Labour Force*. Special Study No. 16. Ottawa: Economic Council of Canada, 1973.

Vanderkamp, J. The role of population size in migration studies. *CJE* 9 (August 1976) 508-516.

Vanderkamp, J. The efficiency of the interregional adjustment process. *Disparities and Interregional Adjustment*, K. Norrie (ed.). Toronto: University of Toronto Press, 1986, pp. 53-108.

Vasegh-Daneshvary, N., H. Herzog, Jr. and A. Schlottmann. College educated immigrants in the American labor force: a study of locational behavior. *SEJ* 52 (January 1986) 818-831.

Webb, M. Migration and education subsidies by governments: a game-theoretic analysis. *J Pub Ec* 26 (March 1985) 249-262.

Wilkinson, B. *Studies in the Economics of Education*. Ottawa: Department of Labour, 1965.

Winer, S.L. and D. Gauthier. *Internal Migration and Fiscal Structure*. Ottawa: Economic Council of Canada, 1982.

Wong, K. The economic analysis of internal migration: generalization. *CJE* 19 (May 1986) 357-362.

Young, G. The choice of dependent variable for cross-section studies of migration. *CJE* 8 (February 1975) 93-100.

21 Inter-Industry Wage Differentials

As the Canadian *Standard Industrial Classification* (1970) manual indicates, industrial designations refer to the principal kind or branch of economic activity of establishments in which individuals work. The industries may be broadly defined sectors, as, for example, agriculture, mining, manufacturing, construction, transportation, trade and public administration. Or they may be more narrowly defined. For example, within the non-durable manufacturing sector there are food and beverage, tobacco, rubber, textile and paper industries. The inter-industry wage structure indicates the wage differential between industries, however broadly or narrowly defined.

THEORETICAL DETERMINANTS OF INTER-INDUSTRY WAGE DIFFERENTIALS

The average wage in an industry will reflect a variety of factors, including the occupational composition and personal characteristics of the work-force, and the regional domination of some industries. Consequently, pure inter-industry wage differentials are difficult to calculate because they reflect other wage structures, notably those by occupation, region and the personal characteristics of the work-force.

If we could net out the effect of these other wage structures, however, so that we were comparing wages across industries for the same occupation, the same type of worker, and the same region, then the pure inter-industry wage differential would reflect only the different characteristics of the industry. Many of these different wage-determining characteristics are similar to the ones analysed as determinants of the inter-occupational wage structure — non-pecuniary aspects of the jobs in each industry, short-run adjustments, and non-competitive forces. If there are no differences in any of these aspects, competitive forces should ensure that all industries pay the same wage for the same type of labour.

This is illustrated in Figure 21.1(a), which deals with a given homogeneous type of labour that differs only in so far as it is employed in either industry 1 or 2. If there are no differences between the industries in the non-pecuniary aspects (e.g. safety, pleasantness) or in their non-competitive aspects (e.g. monopoly, unionization), then economic theory predicts an equality of compensation between the two sectors in the long run. This

Figure 21.1 Inter-industry Wage Structure for a Given Homogeneous Type of Labour

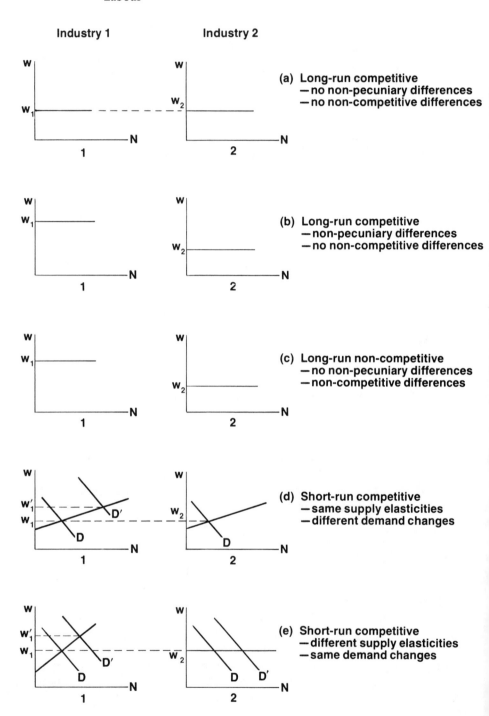

Industry 1   Industry 2

(a) Long-run competitive
    — no non-pecuniary differences
    — no non-competitive differences

(b) Long-run competitive
    — non-pecuniary differences
    — no non-competitive differences

(c) Long-run non-competitive
    — no non-pecuniary differences
    — non-competitive differences

(d) Short-run competitive
    — same supply elasticities
    — different demand changes

(e) Short-run competitive
    — different supply elasticities
    — same demand changes

is ensured by the mobility of labour towards higher paying industries, or by the entry of new firms into lower paying industries. In the short run, of course, this may not occur and hence there is some inelasticity to the supply of labour, as in Figures 21.1(d) and 21.1(e). In the long run there may also be some inelasticity to the extent that non-pecuniary or non-competitive differences are related to the employment in the industry.

The basic general determinants of the inter-industry wage structure, therefore, are non-pecuniary and non-competitive differences between the industries in the long run, and adjustment factors in the short run. Each of these will be examined in turn.

Compensating Wages for Non-pecuniary Aspects

Industries, like occupations, can differ in the non-pecuniary aspects of the job. Some industries, for example, may be associated with unpleasant or unsafe work conditions, or with seasonal or cyclical employment. These conditions would require a compensating wage payment to attract workers into the industry. Thus workers in the same occupation and region, and with the same demographic characteristics, could receive different wages for being in different industries. This is illustrated in Figure 21.1(b) where Industry 1 is required to pay the compensating wage premium.

Casual empiricism does not always confirm the expectation that compensating wage premiums would have to be paid to attract workers to less desirable industries. On the surface it appears that industries with undesirable working conditions are often associated with low wages rather than a compensating wage premium. This is certainly the story portrayed in our earlier discussion of dual labour market analysis.

Unfortunately, in the real world, it is difficult to disentangle all of the wage-influencing forces at work. The poor wages *and* working conditions in some industries may be a result of other factors, such as a declining demand or a lack of unionization. Economics simply predicts that even within the low wage sector of our economy, and when all other factors are held constant, inter-industry wage differentials could exist to compensate for inter-industry differences in the non-pecuniary aspects of the jobs in the various industries. Even this proposition, however, may be disputed by many, especially proponents of the dual labour market analysis. In addition, empirical testing is made difficult because of the near impossibility of controlling for the various other wage-determining factors.

Non-competitive Factors

There also may be a variety of non-competitive factors that could affect the inter-industry wage structure. The degree of monopoly power of the firms in the industry may affect wages; however, as discussed in Chapter 11, theoretical considerations alone do not indicate unambiguously whether monopolistic firms would pay higher or lower wages than firms in competitive industries. To the extent that both have to compete in the same labour market, irrespective of the way they compete in the product market, then non-competitive industries would not be able to pay *below* the going wage. However, their non-competitive conditions may enable them to pay *more* than the going wage: hence, the presumption that non-competitive industries may pay higher wages for the same type of labour.

The ability of non-competitive sectors to pay higher wages will more likely be translated into higher *actual* wages by non-competitive institutional forces in the labour market itself. Such devices include wage-fixing laws (minimum wages, equal pay, fair wage laws and extension legislation), occupational licensing, and unions (to be discussed in a subsequent chapter). To the extent that these factors affect different industries in a different manner, they will also affect the inter-industry wage structure.

Minimum-wage laws would obviously affect low-wage industries, such as personal services (laundries, hotels, restaurants and taverns), retail trade, and parts of non-durable manufacturing, especially clothing. Equal pay laws would affect those industries with a high proportion of females (and which also are often low-wage), for example, non-durable manufacturing, retail trade, services and finance, insurance and real estate. Fair wage laws and wage extension laws tend to be most important in the construction sector. Occupational licensing and unionization tend to be more prominent in high-wage industries — in part, of course, because they may have raised wages in those industries.

Figure 21.1(c) illustrates the situation where Industry 1 pays a higher wage for the same type of labour as in Industry 2 because of non-competitive factors. Industry 1, for example, may have monopoly profits that were converted into higher wages because of a high degree of unionization. This may persist in the long run because the non-competitive forces prevent the forces of competition from equalizing wages.

The forces of competition, however, may work in a subtle fashion over the long run. In particular, coupled with having to pay a higher wage, firms in Industry 1 would be able to recruit the "cream of the crop" within each occupation and they may even be able to change the non-pecuniary aspects of their job, for example, by requiring more responsibility or more rigorous work assignments. Hence, skill differentials and non-pecuniary differentials can change in response to the non-competitive differentials (unless of course they are controlled by the non-competitive factors), and the extent to which the inter-industry wage differential reflects pure non-competitive forces becomes more difficult to evaluate.

Short-Run Demand Changes

Just as with the occupational wage structure, the inter-industry wage structure may reflect short-run changes in the demand for labour, derived from changes in the demand for the output of a particular industry. Thus a short-run increase in the demand for the output of a particular industry may lead to an increase in the derived demand for labour in that industry.

To the extent that the supply of labour to the industry is somewhat inelastic in the short run (it may take time to attract new workers), then that industry would experience wage increases.

In the long run, however, the supply of labour to the industry would probably be fairly elastic as the short-run wage increases would attract new workers. Unlike the supply of labour to an *occupation*, which may be inelastic because of training cost, preferences for other occupations, or because of innate talents for particular skills, the long-run supply of labour to an *industry* should be fairly elastic because there are usually minimal costs to changing industries (unlike changing occupations or regions), and because preferences for particular industries are probably less strong than preferences for a particular occupation or region.

To the extent that the supply of labour to an industry is perfectly elastic in the long run, changes in the demand for labour would lead to employment changes, not wage changes, in the industry. However, to the extent that non-pecuniary returns may decrease or non-competitive factors increase as employment increases in an industry, the supply of labour to the industry may be somewhat inelastic even in the long run. In these circumstances, long-run changes in demand may lead to changes in the inter-industry wage structure as well as to employment changes.

Short-run changes in aggregate demand associated with business cycle fluctuations may also have a differential impact across industries. This could emanate from the fact that aggregate demand changes very often imply different disaggregate demand changes by industry (Figure 21.1(d)): construction, for example, is cyclically sensitive. The different impact across industries may also emanate from the differing abilities of industries to expand or contract their work-forces without changing wages — the differing supply elasticities illustrated in Figure 21.1(e). Thus, even faced with the same demand change, industries may respond with different wage changes to expand or contract their work-force. Low-wage industries, for example, may have a fairly elastic supply determined by minimum wages, downward wage rigidity, and by competitive pressures exerted by the pool of unemployed. For them, fluctuations in demand would simply lead to employment changes, whereas higher-wage industries may have to adjust their wage policy. If this were the case, the inter-industry wage structure would be positively related to the business cycle, expanding during economic expansions and contracting during economic contractions.

The prediction that *inter-industry* wage structures would be *positively* related to cyclical conditions is not in contradiction to our earlier prediction that the *inter-occupational* wage structure would be *negatively* related to the business cycle. As long as we are dealing with pure wage structures, the two are independent and they can therefore respond to the same cyclical pressures differently.

In particular, with respect to the inter-occupational wage structure, it is the higher skilled wages that remain relatively fixed over the cycle for reasons outlined earlier. Therefore, the skill differential w_s/w_u will decrease during prosperity because w_u increases and w_s remains relatively constant. However, with respect to the inter-industry wage structure it is the low-wage industry that has the rigid wages for reasons outlined earlier. Therefore, the inter-industry wage differential w_h/w_l (with h and l being high- and low-wage industries respectively) would increase when w_h increases and w_l remains constant during prosperity. This is illustrated by a hypothetical example in the questions at the end of the chapter.

EMPIRICAL EVIDENCE

The previously discussed theoretical determinants of industry wages should explain the magnitude of inter-industry wage differentials and the reasons for their changes over time, both in the long run and short run. Unfortunately, this is an area where there is little consensus on how to interpret the empirical results. This in part reflects the continuing debate between institutionalists and neoclassical economists over the relative importance of market and non-market forces in the wage determination process. And it reflects the difficulty in empirical work of controlling for the effect of intervening variables so that one is examining a relatively pure inter-industry wage differential.

Magnitude of Inter-Industry Wage Differentials

Empirical evidence does suggest the existence and persistence of inter-industry wage differentials for the same type of labour. Based on extensive analysis of Canadian data, Kumar (1974, p. 33) concludes: "In Canada, some industries pay higher wage rates than others to workers of similar skill: significant inter-industry differentials exist for unskilled labour as well as for skilled workers. . . . There has been little change in the relative position of industries in the inter-industry wage hierarchy." Ostry and Zaidi (1979, p. 353) also document the stability of the ranking of industries in terms of their wages, but they indicate that in the long run (e.g. over forty years) there is considerable pliability. Thus high-wage industries tend to remain high-wage industries, although their position can change over long periods of time. This reflects the fact that the long-run determinants of inter-industry wage differentials — non-pecuniary characteristics of the industries and non-competitive factors that may affect industries differently — are likely to change only slowly. Wage equations, estimated from multiple regression analysis, also typically find the worker's industry to be an important determinant of his wage, even after controlling for the effect of such wage-determining factors as education, experience, sex, occupation, and region.

Empirical Determinants of Inter-Industry Wage Differentials

While there appears to be agreement that inter-industry wage differentials do prevail, there is not agreement on whether these differences are *pure* inter-industry differentials or whether they reflect skill differentials that are not fully controlled for, compensating differentials for differences in the non-pecuniary aspects of the job in each industry, or wage differentials that arise because of non-competitive factors.

On the question of the impact of skill differentials on inter-occupational wage differentials, it is nearly impossible, given the nature of available data, to fully control for this factor. And yet it is crucial to control for skill differentials because, for theoretical reasons outlined earlier, high-wage industries would probably be able to recruit the "cream of the crop" for each occupation. Utilizing a specific occupational group such as unskilled labour or maintenance mechanic may go a long way to *reduce* the effect of different skills levels, but does it completely *eliminate* the effect? Is an unskilled labourer in the furniture industry the same as an unskilled labourer in petroleum refineries, especially if petroleum refineries have to pay high wages for other reasons (e.g. unions extracting monopoly profits) and therefore will be able to hire the best workers for each occupation? Even multiple regression analysis that controls for differences in skill levels by a variety of human capital and personal characteristics variables, may omit less quantifiable factors the importance of which could vary across industries.

In spite of these reservations stemming from the inability of the data to enable the estimation of a pure inter-industry wage differential that fully controls for skill differentials, it is unlikely that skill differentials could account for the *large* inter-industry differentials that persist. Non-pecuniary differences in the nature of the jobs in the industries could be important; however, low-wage industries also tend to be associated with poor working conditions and unstable employment (e.g. Kumar (1974, pp. 54-61)). Non-competitive conditions in the product market of the industry could be important; however, there appears to be no empirical consensus on the effects of various measures of industry concentration on wages in the industry. Differences in the extent and impact of unionization could be important, especially in industries with monopoly profits, and Kumar's (1974, pp. 62-65) work bears this out with Canadian data.

Clearly the extent to which the inter-industry wage structure can be explained on purely economic grounds remains an open question. In part this reflects the inability to utilize existing data to *fully* control for the effect of other wage structures; consequently, the inter-industry wage structure may reflect such factors as skill differences, discriminatory wage differentials, and union-nonunion wage differentials. Certainly economists have *not* been able to demonstrate empirically that once all the legitimate wage-determining factors are controlled for, there are no remaining pure wage differentials across industries.

Changes in the Inter-industry Wage Structure

While economists have not been very successful in explaining the factors that determine the *magnitude* of the inter-industry wage structure, they have been more successful in documenting how it has *changed* over time. As indicated earlier, the ranking has been relatively stable throughout much of the post-World War II period in Canada, although it is more flexible over a longer period of time. The long-run determinants of the inter-industry wage structure, such as non-pecuniary aspects and non-competitive factors, and other wage structures (e.g. occupation and region) that are related to the industry wage structure, change very slowly over time.

In addition, as indicated in Kumar (1974, p. 24) and Ostry and Zaidi (1979, p. 355), the dispersion of the inter-industry wage structure in Canada has also been fairly constant over the long run, an observation that has been documented for other industrialized countries. Thus, the inter-industry wage structure is fairly stable not only in that the dispersion has been fairly constant, but also in that industries tend to maintain their approximate ranking within the constant structure.

In the shorter run, over the business cycle, Ostry and Zaidi (1979, p. 355) find the inter-industry wage structure to be positively related to the business cycle: that is, to widen in boom periods and contract in recessions. This is consistent with the theoretical explanation, outlined earlier, based on the rigidity of wages in low-wage industries.

SUMMARY AND CONCLUDING OBSERVATIONS

Empirically, there are a number of generalizations that can be made about inter-industry wage differentials. They are large, although the magnitude of a pure differential after controlling for other factors remains elusive. In particular, we do not know how much of the inter-industry wage structure can be attributed to a pure differential, and how much to such factors as non-pecuniary and non-competitive differences, or to short-run adjustments.

Over the long run, the inter-industry wage structure has been relatively constant, both in the sense of a constant dispersion, and a relatively constant ranking of industries within the hierarchy, although in the very long run the ranking has exhibited some pliability. This reflects the fact that the basic determinants of the inter-industry wage structure, such as non-pecuniary and non-competitive factors, change very slowly. In addition, as emphasized by dual labour market analysts, custom and tradition may make it very difficult for wage structures to change, even if some of the basic determinants change.

Over the short run, in response to business cycle changes, the inter-industry wage structure tends to be pro-cyclical, expanding in expansions and contracting in contractions. This probably reflects a greater degree of wage rigidity for all occupations in low-wage industries.

While we have been reasonably successful in documenting the magnitude and changes of inter-industry wage structures, we have been less successful in empirically verifying the explanations for these magnitudes and their changes over time. As Ostry and Zaidi (1979, p. 370) conclude after a thorough view of Canadian evidence and the results of other (often contradictory) studies: "The wage structure . . . . is by and large consistent with expectations in its relations with some explanatory variables, while not so consistent with others."

Our inability to consistently explain the reasons for the magnitude and changes in inter-industry wage structures reflects both empirical and theoretical problems. On the empirical side, the available data simply does not enable one to fully control for the impact of the variety of factors at work affecting inter-industry wages and their structure. Consequently, empirical generalizations are often made on the basis of rough associations, and explanations for the phenomena often are provided in an *ad hoc* fashion.

On the theoretical side, the weakness stems from the fact that many of our explanations for the magnitude and the changes in the inter-industry wage structure are ones that are derived from the facts, after the fact. Thus they cannot be subject to empirical testing: since the "theory" is derived from the data, it is bound to be verified. If rejected by a new set of data, however, a new theoretical story emerges. In addition, the theory is not always formulated so as to explain all aspects of inter-industry wage differentials — for example, their magnitude and how that magnitude changes in the long run and the short run — nor to be consistent with other observable phenomena, such as inter-occupational wage differentials.

Clearly this is an unsatisfactory state of affairs, and it is one that has contributed to the schism between neoclassical economists who tend to follow the dictum "theory is truth — don't be fooled by the facts," and institutionalists and others who have amassed an array of facts without a satisfactory explanation for them. Progress is needed on both fronts.

QUESTIONS

1. Discuss how the inter-industry wage structure is intricately mixed with a variety of other wage structures and why this makes it so difficult to estimate a pure inter-industry wage differential.
2. "In a competitive economy, there can be no such thing as a pure inter-industry wage differential in the long run." Discuss.
3. Modify Figure 21.1(a) to reflect the fact that Industry 1 becomes more easy to unionize as employment expands. What would happen to the inter-industry wage structure and how would it change over time if the demand for labour in the two industries increased the same?
4. Modify Figure 21.1 to reflect each of the following factors, and depict the change in the inter-industry wage structure:
   (a) the industry becomes unionized, but the industry is so competitive on the product side that unions are unable to get wage gains;
   (b) the industry becomes monopolized, but the firms still compete in a perfectly competitive labour market;
   (c) the industry becomes monopolized, and the union is able to appropriate some monopoly profits in the form of wage increases.
5. "Even if labour were not mobile, the actions of firms would ensure

that the inter-industry wage structures reflected competitive forces."
Discuss.

6. "The dual labour market literature has amply documented that industries with poor working conditions are also low-wage industries. Therefore, compensating premiums do not exist and traditional labour market analysis must be replaced by an analysis grounded in the realities of the system." Discuss.

7. Would you expect wages to be higher or lower in monopolistic industries than competitive industries and why?

8. "Even if laws or unions can fix wages in an industry above the competitive rate, the resulting queue of applicants will enable employers to hire better quality labour or change the non-pecuniary aspects of the job so as to restore an equality of net advantage." Discuss.

9. Why might the supply of labour to an industry be inelastic in the short run, but elastic in the long run? Could it ever be inelastic in the long run?

10. Why might we expect, roughly speaking, that the supply of labour to an occupation is more inelastic than the supply of labour to an industry?

11. How would you expect the inter-industry wage structure to change over the business cycle? Is this consistent with the behaviour of inter-occupational wage differentials over the cycle?

12. "A theory that requires high skilled wages to be fairly rigid over the business cycle (to explain the cyclical behaviour of the occupational wage structure), but requires wages in low-wage industries to be fairly rigid over the cycle (to explain the cyclical behaviour of the inter-industry wage structure), has problems." Discuss.

13. Consider an economy of only two industries, one high-wage and the other low-wage. Each employs the same number of workers, equally divided between two groups, skilled and unskilled. Skilled workers are identical with each other in the two industries and so are unskilled workers. The low-wage industry pays its skilled labour $4.00 per hour, and its unskilled labour $2.00 during both a recession and an expansion; that is, it has a rigid wage structure. The high-wage industry pays its skilled labour $8.00 per hour in both a recession and an expansion, but it pays unskilled labour $2.00 during recession and $6.00 during expansion; that is, its skilled wages are rigid.

    For the whole economy, calculate the inter-occupational wage differential (ratio of skilled to unskilled wages) in both the recession and the expansion. Calculate the inter-industry wage differential (ratio of high to low industry) for both skilled and unskilled workers in both the recession and the expansion. Why does the inter-occupational wage differential contract in the expansion and the inter-industry differential widen?

14. Document the main empirical generalizations that we have concerning the inter-industry wage structure and its changes.

15. Why might you expect the inter-industry wage structure to be fairly

constant over time, and the ranking of industries within the hierarchy to change only slowly?

16. The inter-industry wage structure reflects both dispersion and ranking within that dispersion. Illustrate how dramatic changes could occur in the ranking of industries without altering the wage structure.

17. "A theory of inter-industry wage differentials must be able to explain why differentials exist and why they change over time, both in the long run and the short run. In addition, it must be consistent with other theories and it must be capable of empirical acceptance or rejection." Discuss with respect to the current state of inter-industry wage theory.

18. What do you think are the greatest gaps in our understanding of inter-industrial wage structures? How would you propose to fill those gaps?

19. "Even if we knew the determinants of the overall inter-industry wage structure, and why it changed, this would be of little policy value since there is not much we could or should do to change that structure. It is the result of the interplay of a variety of market forces and what we want to do is to make sure that the market forces are legitimate (e.g. non-discriminatory, not artificial). Once that is done, then the inter-industrial wage structure is what it is, and nothing more should be done." Discuss.

REFERENCES AND FURTHER READINGS

Anderson, C. Wage spillover mechanisms: a U.S.-Canadian analysis. *IR* (May 1972) 172-183.

Chapman, B. and H. Tan. Specific training and inter-industry wage differences in U.S. manufacturing. *R.E. Stats.* 62 (August 1980) 371-378.

Christofides, L., R. Swidinsky and D. Wilton. A micro-economic analysis of spillovers within the Canadian wage determination process. *R.E. Stats.* 62 (May 1980) 213-221.

Eckstein, O. and T. Wilson. The determination of money wages in American industry. *QJE* 76 (August 1962) 379-414. Comment by T. McGuire and L. Rapping 81 (November 1967) 684-690.

Kumar, P. Differentials in wage rates of unskilled labour in the Canadian manufacturing industries. *ILRR* 26 (October 1972) 631-645.

Kumar, P. *Relative Wage Differentials in Canadian Industries.* Kingston: Queen's University Industrial Relations Centre, 1974.

Lutz, M. The evolution of the industrial earnings structure: the geological theory. *CJE* 9 (August 1976) 473-491.

Lutz, M. Quit rates and the quality of the industrial wage structure. *IR* 16 (February 1977) 61-70. Comment by J.W. Mixon and reply 18 (Winter 1979) 122-125.

Ostry, S. Inter-industry earnings differentials in Canada, 1945-1956. *ILRR* 12 (April 1959) 335-352.

Ostry, S. and M. Zaidi. *Labour Economics in Canada,* 3rd ed. Toronto: Macmillan, 1979.

Pagel, T. Profitability, concentration and interindustry variation in wages. *R.E. Stats.* 62 (May 1980) 248-253.

Pessarides, C. The role of relative wages and excess demand in the sectoral flow of labour. *R.E. Studies* 45 (October 1978) 453-468.

Reuber, G. Wage adjustments in Canadian industry. *R.E. Studies* 37 (October 1970) 449-468.

Rosen, S. On the inter-industry wage and hours structure. *JPE* 77 (April 1969) 249-273.

Ulman, L. Labor mobility and the industrial wage structure in the post-war United States. *QJE* 67 (February 1965) 73-97.

Vanderkamp, J. Industrial mobility: some further results. *CJE* 10 (August 1977) 462-472.

Wabe, S. and D. Leech. Relative earnings in U.K. manufacturing. *EJ* 88 (June 1978) 296-313.

Wachtel, H. Workers management and inter-industry wage differentials in Yugoslavia. *JPE* 80, Part 1 (May/June 1972) 540-560.

Wachtel, M. Cyclical variation in the inter-industry wage structure. *AER* 60 (March 1970) 75-84.

Weiss, L. Concentration and labor earnings. *AER* (March 1956) 96-117.

Yu, E. Economic growth, interindustry flows and wage differential. *SEJ* 46 (January 1980) 925-932.

CHAPTER

22 *Public-Private Sector Wage Differentials*

The issue of public-private sector wage differentials is a topic of inter-industry wage determination since the public sector is simply one of many industries. However, the public sector is singled out for special attention because it is a large sector, it is the subject of policy concern mainly because of strikes and wage settlements, its impact may spill over into the private sector, and it has peculiarities that make wage determination somewhat unique.

As our earlier discussion indicated, the theoretical determinants of inter-industry wage differentials include compensating adjustments for non-pecuniary differences, short-run adjustments, and non-competitive factors. Just as these broad categories provided a convenient framework for ana-lysing the determinants of inter-industry wage differentials, they also are convenient for categorizing the theoretical determinants of the particular inter-industry wage differential examined in this chapter — the public-private sector wage differential.

The public sector can be broadly defined to include education, health and government enterprises, as well as the more narrowly defined gov-ernment employment at the federal, provincial and municipal levels. According to this broad definition, Bird (1978, p. 25) estimates Canadian public sector employment in 1975 to be approximately 2.2 million workers, or 23 percent of the employed labour force. The breakdown of the broad public sector into its component parts as of 1975 is: federal government 18.2%, provincial government 15.8%, municipal government 11.1%, edu-cation 23.8%, hospitals 17.1%, and government enterprises 14.0%. Thus, the various levels of government — the more narrow definition of the public sector — comprise less than half of public sector employees. If one considers most hospital employees and teachers in post secondary edu-cation as provincial employees, then the provincial public sector becomes the largest element of the broad public sector. However one portions the data, the fact remains that the public sector is a large and important employer.

THEORETICAL DETERMINANTS OF PUBLIC-PRIVATE WAGE DIFFERENTIALS

Compensating Adjustments for Non-pecuniary Differences

Inter-industry wage differentials may reflect compensating adjustments for differences in the non-pecuniary aspects of employment across industries. With respect to the private and public sector, non-pecuniary advantages may exist with respect to such factors as job security, fringe benefits, and political visibility. To the extent that these advantages prevail in the public sector, we would expect a correspondingly lower wage to compensate for the advantages. However, to the extent that these advantages are dissipating over time, we may also expect public sector wages to rise relative to those in the private sector to compensate for the loss of these non-pecuniary advantages.

Job Security

Job security often is discussed as being more prevalent in the public than in the private sector. Theoretically this may be the case because job security could be necessary to prevent the abuses of political patronage. That is, without a modicum of job security, civil servants could be replaced each time a new political party came into power, or whenever a politician wanted to gain favour by granting patronage in the form of civil service jobs. To avoid this potential abuse, and to ensure a degree of continuity in the public sector work-force, a degree of job security may be granted.

Job security may also be more prevalent in the public sector because the costs of providing it may be less than in many elements of the private sector. Because of its size (except in some instances at the local level), the public sector has a *portfolio* of jobs in which to reallocate its work-force and it has the means of utilizing personnel policies and motivational techniques that do not require the ultimate sanction of firing a worker. If a worker is not competent at a particular job there usually are other jobs available within the public sector that would enable the worker to perform some, at least minimal, function. In addition, it may be possible within the public sector to grant job security to a *core* of workers because of the feasibility of contracting out for work or of utilizing part-time, casual employees. As well, as long as the public sector is a growth industry it is easier to grant job security.

As with many labour market phenomena that at first glance appear to be inefficient constraints in the market, the existence of a degree of job security for civil servants *may* have elements of being a rational, low-cost, institutional response to a peculiarity of the labour market—in this case, the possible abuse of political patronage, coupled with the relatively low cost of providing job security in the large and expanding public sector.

While there is this theoretical reason to expect job security to be greater in the public sector, and while this certainly appears to be the conventional wisdom, job security appears to be waning, perhaps because of reduced growth, or increased public criticism, or because political patronage is less of a concern. Teachers, part-time and casual employees, and even the core of the civil service no longer appear to have job security.

In addition, while there may still be a degree of *employment* security, this need not imply *job* security. That is, public sector workers may be shifted to different jobs within the public sector, and these may not be the jobs for which they were hired or at which they would prefer to work. This can be the case especially because of the fluctuating nature of much government activity associated with counter-cyclical demand policies, and because many government activities can shift dramatically according to the wishes and whims of political forces.

In summary, while there are theoretical reasons to believe that job security would be greater in the public than private sector, in practice this security may not be as great as conventional wisdom suggests. In addition, it is probably waning relative to job security in the private sector. This has obvious implications for the existence of a public-private sector compensating wage differential and its change over time. Specifically, while the public sector at one time may have been able to pay lower wages in return for a degree of job security, this possibility may be less prevalent today. This would suggest that public sector wages may rise more rapidly than private sector wages to compensate for the relative decrease in job security over time.

Fringe Benefits

Fringe benefits provide another possible source of compensating wage differentials. Specifically, if the public sector provides more generous fringe benefits than the private sector, it should be able to recruit an adequate work-force by paying lower wages. It is total compensation, not simply wages, that is relevant.

As with job security, there are theoretical reasons to suggest that the public sector may pay more liberal fringe benefits. This occurs because in the public sector there are not adequate checks to prevent employers from saving on *current* wage costs by granting liberal retirement benefits and pension schemes, the cost of which may be borne by *future* generations of taxpayers. Fringe benefits that are payable in the future, such as early retirement plans and employer-sponsored pensions, can be viewed as deferred wages in the sense that workers would willingly give up some current wages for these future benefits. Such deferred compensation systems may be a way for the public sector to shift costs to future generations of taxpayers; however (as discussed previously) they also may exist as part of an optimal compensation system to ensure honesty and work effort. Such a system may be especially important in the public sector, to the extent that other mechanisms, such as the threat of dismissal or the monitoring of output, are not available.

In the private sector there is a built-in check to ensure that employers are constrained in their granting of such deferred benefits: eventually they have to meet the obligation of paying for them. However, in the public sector, unless such benefits are fully funded, their costs will be borne by future taxpayers. To the extent that they have little or no say in the current political process, there is no automatic mechanism to prevent public sector employers from saving on current wage costs by granting liberal deferred cost items, such as early retirement or substantial pensions or pensions indexed for future inflation. The only check is the possibility that future generations may not honour such commitments made by their predecessors, or the possibility that local property values may fall to the extent that they reflect the future tax obligations associated with such future cost commitments.

Political Visibility and Access to Rules

Additional non-pecuniary advantages offered by the public sector could include political visibility, access to control over political rules, and the opportunity to provide public service. For some, these factors may be valued for their own end; for others they may be valued as a means to other objectives. For example, some workers may regard a period of public sector employment as a low-wage apprenticeship period that provides them with inside knowledge, access to power sources, and contacts in the political arena. These factors may be of immense value (and hence lead to higher remuneration) in future private sector jobs as consultants, lobbyists, or simply partners in firms that do business with the government or that would benefit from inside political information.

For others, public sector employment may provide "the non-pecuniary satisfaction of doing good" — to use a phrase utilized by Reder (in Hamermesh 1975, p. 28). This could be a reason, for example, for people to do volunteer work for churches or charities, or for some to accept lower salaries in such non-profit institutions. It may be a more prevalent phenomenon throughout the public sector, especially in teaching or health care. The term "public service" means just that to many persons.

Summary of Compensating Factors

The non-pecuniary factors that we have discussed — job security, fringe benefits, and political visibility — generally are ones for which there are theoretical reasons to believe that they would be greater in the public than private sector. Certainly conventional wisdom and casual empiricism seems to suggest this to be the case. To the extent that it is true, the public sector would be expected to have lower wages to compensate for these factors.

While these non-pecuniary factors may be greater in the public than private sector, there are reasons to believe that the gap may be dissipating over time. Certainly this seems to be the case with job security and it may be the case with fringe benefits to the extent that the public sector may have reached diminishing returns with respect to fringe benefits it can provide, and the private sector is now catching up. Even with respect to the opportunity to do public service, attitudes seem to be changing so that public sector jobs are done in return for pay, like most other jobs. To the extent that these non-pecuniary factors have diminished in the public sector, one would expect the wages of public sector workers to rise relative to those of their private sector counterparts.

Short-Run Adjustments

Inter-industry wage differentials may reflect a short-run disequilibrium situation. In fact the disequilibrium wage serves as the signal for new entrants, and this supply response should restore the inter-industry wage structure to its long-run equilibrium level.

This scenario could be relevant to the public sector. In essence, the expansion of the public sector that occurred, especially in the 1950s and 1960s, would lead to increases in the demand for public sector labour and, hence, to increase in their wages. The higher wages would enable public employers to recruit the necessary work-force associated with the expansion of the public sector.

In recent years, however, there are forces at work to suggest that the rapid expansion of the public sector may have ended. Certainly political pressures are mounting as taxpayers show opposition to an ever-expanding role of the public sector. In addition, basic demographic changes may be reducing the demand for public services, especially in education as the baby boom has left the education sector, and in health as family size reduces. Again, this may change in the future as health care for the aged becomes an issue.

Empirical evidence for Canada, in fact, indicates that the rate of expansion of the public sector had levelled off by the 1970s. According to Richard Bird (1978, p. 19): "The fastest growth in total public employment probably occurred during the 1950s. Although this growth continued through the 1960s, it did so at a relatively slower pace and by the 1970s, on most measurements, the growth of public employment levelled off and perhaps even declined." In such circumstances, we would expect public sector wages to be rising relative to private sector wages during the 1950s and 1960s, but for this pattern to stop by the 1970s.

Non-competitive Factors

Inter-industry wage differentials may also reflect non-competitive factors and it is in this area that the differences between public and private sector labour markets become most pronounced. Specific features that have important implications for public-private wage differentials and their changes over time revolve around the fact that the public sector can be characterized as subject to various peculiarities including a political constraint rather than a profit constraint, possible monopsony, an inelastic demand for labour, and a high degree of new unionization. Each of these factors will be discussed in turn, with an emphasis on their implications for public-private wage differentials and their changes over time.

Political Rather than Profit Constraint

The public sector usually is not subject to a profit constraint as traditionally exists in the private sector. Rather, the profit constraint is replaced by an ultimate political constraint and there is the belief that the political constraint is less binding. This occurs because taxpayers are diffuse, often ill-informed, and can exert pressure only infrequently and with respect to a package of issues. Public sector managers also are diffuse in the sense that lines of responsibility are not always well defined and "buck-passing" can prevail. Workers in the public sector, on the other hand, are often portrayed as a unified, distinct interest group providing direct pressure for wage increases. A more serious imperfection of the political process arises from the fact, discussed earlier, that future taxpayers have little or no representation in today's political process.

While these features of the political constraint suggest the possibility that it is less binding than the profit constraint, there still are constraining influences on wage settlements in the public sector. Taxpayer scrutiny is now extremely strong and in fact politicians may gain by appearing to be cost-conscious guardians of the public purse by reducing wage costs. Public sector workers may also be called upon to set an example of moderate wages to curb inflation as was evident in recent wage controls applied to the public sector. Even the alleged diffuse nature of management in the public sector may work against employees; it can be difficult to win wage gains if one doesn't know with whom one is bargaining.

Perhaps the most important feature of the political constraint that works against public sector workers is that, during a strike, tax revenues keep coming in to the public sector even though wage expenditures are reduced and public services are not provided. This is in contrast to the private sector where employers are under considerable pressure to settle because they are losing customers and sales revenues during a strike. To be sure, there can be pressure from taxpayers to have the wage savings go into general tax revenues or into tax reductions because services are not provided. Nevertheless, the fact remains that this political pressure is less stringent than the profit constraint when firms lose customers and revenues during a strike.

Monopsony

To the extent that the government sector is often the dominant employer in particular labour markets, governments may utilize their monopsony power to pay lower wage rates than if they behaved competitively. Political forces may pressure them to act as model employers and not utilize their monopsony power; nevertheless, there is also pressure to be cost conscious and this may lead them to exercise their monopsony power.

In fact, the empirical evidence cited earlier in the chapter on monopsony suggested that for at least two elements of the public sector —

teaching and nursing — there was some evidence of monopsony. The extent to which these results can be generalized for other elements of the public sector, or for the teaching and nursing professions as a whole, remains an unanswered empirical question.

To the extent that monopsony power exists and is exercised in the public sector, public sector wages would be lower than they would be in the absence of monopsony. However, the pressure of monopsony also means that, for a range of wage increases, unions would not have to be concerned about employment reductions. In fact, as illustrated in the chapter on monopsony, wage increases may actually lead to employment increases, suggesting the possibility of a substantial union wage impact in monopsonistic labour markets.

Inelastic Demand for Public Sector Labour
The possibility of a substantial union impact on wages in the public sector is furthered by the possibility that the demand for labour in the public sector may be wage inelastic. In such circumstances unions could bargain for substantial wage increases without worrying about large reductions in the employment of their members. The inelasticity of the demand for labour may occur because non-competitive forces restrict the utilization of substitute inputs as well as substitute services.

Many of the services produced in the public sector are so-called essential services that are not provided in the private sector, and when they are so provided, they are often under governmental regulation. Since consumers (taxpayers) are unable to substitute other services for those provided by the public sector, their demand for these services may be relatively price (tax) inelastic. In essence, wage increases can be passed on to taxpayers in the form of tax increases for the essential services without taxpayers reducing their demand for these services and hence the derived demand for labour.

This is strengthened by the fact that there are often few good inputs to substitute for public sector labour as it becomes expensive. This may reflect the nature of the public sector production function, but it may also reflect the fact that the public sector is heavily professionalized, and professional labour tends to have a degree of control over the utilization of other inputs, including non-professional labour. Often the utilization of other inputs is discouraged because it reduces the "personal touch" that professionals advocate.

While these factors suggest that the demand for public sector labour would be wage inelastic, other factors are at work in the opposite direction. Specifically, the high ratio of labour cost to total cost in many public services suggests that the demand would be elastic. In addition, substitute inputs and services certainly could be utilized, especially in the long run. Even the essentiality of the service may work against public sector employees by restricting their right to strike and reducing public sympathy during a strike. In addition, the employers may lag in the bargaining process, knowing that the essential elements of the service will be maintained and, as indicated earlier, tax revenues are still forthcoming.

Since theory does not indicate unambiguously whether the demand for public sector labour would be elastic or inelastic, we must appeal to the empirical evidence. The evidence, as given in Ehrenberg (1973a) and Ashenfelter and Ehrenberg (in Hamermesh 1975), based on U.S. data, indicates that the demand for labour in the public sector is inelastic, and that the more essential the service, the greater the inelasticity.

Unionization

A final non-competitive factor — recent unionization — may also affect the wages of public sector workers relative to their private sector counterparts. This is especially the case when the unionization is coupled with the other factors discussed in this chapter — the inelastic demand for public sector labour, the possible monopsony in some public sector markets, and the absence of a profit constraint. In addition, the unionization of the public sector is a relatively recent phenomenon, and it is in the early periods of union organizing drives that the union impact on wages tends to be the greatest.

In Canada, this recent growth and high degree of unionization in the public sector is documented, for example, in Cousineau and Lacroix (1977), pp. 4-8, 44-46). Some sectors, like the federal civil service, are organized almost to their full potential. Others, like teaching and health, are now predominantly unionized.

Competitive Floor But Not Ceiling

The previously discussed factors — absence of a profit constraint, monopsony, inelastic demand, and the high degree of recent unionization — all suggested that wage determination may be different between the public and private sectors, and that non-competitive factors may give rise to an inter-industry wage differential between the public and private sectors. Most of the factors, with the exception of monopsony, would appear to favour a non-competitive wage advantage in the public sector, although a variety of subtle constraining influences are present.

However, there is a stronger reason to expect the wage advantage to be in favour of public sector workers. This is so because the forces of competition would ensure that wages in the public sector would not fall much below wages in the private sector for comparable workers. If they did, the public sector would not be in a competitive position to recruit labour, and would experience problems of recruitment, turnover and morale. That is, competition would ensure a competitive *floor* on wages in the public sector.

These same competitive forces, however, need not provide an effective *ceiling* on wages in the public sector. To be sure, if public sector wages exceeded wages of comparable workers in the private sector, there would be queues of applicants and excessive competition for public sector jobs. Nevertheless, employers in the public sector are not under a profit constraint to respond to these disequilibrium signals; they need not lower their relative wage. They *may* not pay an excessive wage if the political constraint is a binding cost constraint; nevertheless, there is no guarantee that this will be the case.

In essence, the forces of competition ensure a floor, but they need not provide an effective ceiling on wages in the public sector. Hence the potential bias, in theory, for wages in the public sector to be in excess of wages in the private sector for comparable workers. The extent to which this potential upward bias exists in practice is an empirical proposition.

EMPIRICAL EVIDENCE

Reflecting the newness of the concern over public-private sector wage differentials, it is only recently that a number of empirical studies have tried to measure such differentials. In general, the studies have tried to control for other legitimate wage-determining factors by multiple regression analysis or by standardizing, by choosing groups that are similar except that one group is in the public sector and the other is in the private sector. While the empirical studies are few in number, they do provide some tentative generalizations. The extent to which these generalizations withstand further scrutiny and the test of time remains an unanswered question.

Decomposition of Public-Private Wage Differentials: Mathematical Exposition

The overall average earnings differential between public and private sector workers can be decomposed into two component parts: a portion due to differences in the endowments of wage-determining factors between the two sectors, and a portion attributable to a pure inter-industry wage differential. The latter can be termed an economic rent or surplus payment because it represents payment for being in a particular industry, after controlling for the effect of the usual wage-determining factors.

This decomposition technique—which will also be utilized in the subsequent chapter on male-female wage differentials — can be illustrated formally. Let y denote the dependent variable (earnings), X the set of usual wage-determining explanatory variables (human capital factors such as education and training, and control variables for such factors as occupation and region), and b the set of regression coefficients estimated from an earnings equation based on individuals as units of observation. In such an earnings equation, the X's can be regarded as the endowments of wage-determining factors and the b's as the pay structure associated with differences in these endowments. The regression coefficient for the education variable, for example, indicates the change in earnings that results from an additional year of education — it is the monetary reward or pay structure associated with the acquisition of additional education.

Separate earnings equations can be estimated for each of the public and private sectors, respectively denoted by the subscripts g (government or public) and c (private or competitive). That is, for the public sector

$$y_g = \Sigma b_g X_g \tag{22.1}$$

and for the private sector

$$y_c = \Sigma b_c X_c \tag{22.2}$$

In regression analysis, the mean of the dependent variable is equal to the regression coefficients times the mean values of the explanatory variables. Therefore,

$$\bar{y}_g = \Sigma b_g \bar{X}_g \text{ and} \tag{22.3}$$

$$\bar{y}_c = \Sigma b_c \bar{X}_c \tag{22.4}$$

Subtracting Equation 22.4 from Equation 22.3 gives the average earnings differential between public and private sector workers: that is,

$$\bar{y}_g - \bar{y}_c = \Sigma b_g \bar{X}_g - \Sigma b_c \bar{X}_c \tag{22.5}$$

Subtracting and adding $\Sigma b_c \bar{X}_g$ to the right-hand side (and therefore not changing the equality) yields

$$\bar{y}_g - \bar{y}_c = \Sigma b_g \bar{X}_g - \Sigma b_c \bar{X}_g + \Sigma b_c \bar{X}_g - \Sigma b_c \bar{X}_c \tag{22.6}$$

which, after collecting terms, yields

$$\bar{y}_g - \bar{y}_c = \Sigma (b_g - b_c) \bar{X}_g + \Sigma b_c (\bar{X}_g - \bar{X}_c) \tag{22.7}$$

The first term on the right-hand side is the differences in pay structure (b's) between public and private sector workers, evaluated for the same wage-determining endowments ($\bar{X}_g$'s). This represents the pure inter-industry wage differential because it arises solely from differences in the way public and private sector workers are paid for the same wage-determining characteristics. The second term on the right-hand side of Equation 22.7 is the difference in the endowments of wage-determining characteristics (X's) between the public and private sector workers, evaluated according to the private sector pay structure (b_c's). Since the private sector pay structure is usually regarded as the competitive norm, it makes sense to evaluate differences in the wage-determining endowments according to that norm.

Obviously it is the first term on the right-hand side of Equation 22.7 that is important for policy purposes since it reflects the economic rent or surplus payment associated with being in one sector as opposed to the other sector. If the public sector pays its workers more than the private sector (that is, the b_g's are greater than the b_c's for similar levels of education, training, and other wage-determining factors (that is for the $\bar{X}_g$'s),. then this will result in a positive surplus payment, $\Sigma (b_g - b_c) \bar{X}_g$. The second expression, on the other hand, is not of policy concern since it represents a differential payment for different endowments of legitimate wage-determining factors, such as human capital. These two components — a surplus payment, and a payment for differences in productivity-related en-dowments — together make up the overall average earnings differential, $\bar{y}_g - \bar{y}_c$, between public and private sector workers.

Estimates of this average earnings differential and its two component parts for full-year, full-time workers are provided in Gunderson (1979b, p. 237) based on 1971 Canadian census data. The public sector is the in-dustry designation of public administration and the private sector is the manufacturing industry. The main results are reproduced in Table 22.1.

Clearly workers in the public sector on average have higher earnings than workers in the private sector. However, much of the differential comes about because workers in the public sector have greater endowments of wage-determining factors such as education. The pure surplus payment or economic rent associated with being employed in the public as opposed to the private sector (column 2) is estimated as $492 or 6.2 percent for males and $383 or 8.6 percent for females. Since there are over twice as many males as females in the public administration category, this would yield a pure public sector earnings advantage of approximately 7 percent overall. These results generally are in line with those reported in Smith's (1977b) comprehensive analysis, which summarizes and updates her application of this decomposition technique in a variety of U.S. studies.

TABLE 22.1
PUBLIC SECTOR EARNINGS ADVANTAGE AND ITS DECOMPOSITION

	Overall Differential	Amount Attributed to	
		Surplus	Endowments
Males			
Dollar Advantage	$737	$492	$245
As percent of private earnings	9.3%	6.2%	3.1%
Females			
Dollar Advantage	$989	$383	$606
As percent of private earnings	22.3%	8.6%	13.7%

Source: Gunderson (1979b, p. 237)

Other Empirical Evidence

These results generally are also consistent with those obtained from other Canadian data sets and employing different statistical methodology. Based on calculations from taxation statistics, the Highly Qualified Manpower Survey, contract data from collective agreements, occupational wage rate surveys of municipal governments, and Pay Research Bureau data, Gun-derson (1978b, p. 127) concludes: "in recent years, the wages of public sector employees in Canada appear to have exceeded those of their private sector counterparts by about five to fifteen percent. This wage advantage appears to have been larger for females than males and for low level as opposed to high level occupations. In fact, for high level occupations evidence suggests that the public sector may not even pay the competitive wage."

This same study suggests a number of other empirical generalizations based on Canadian data. The wage advantage of public sector workers probably is a fairly recent phenomenon, emerging in the late 1960s and 1970s; during the 1950s and early 1960s public sector workers were probably paid a wage less than their private sector counterparts. This time pattern is what one would expect given the demand increases associated with the growth of the public sector in the 1950s and 1960s, and the growth of unionization over that same period. To the extent that these forces have dissipated in recent years, they would no longer be a source of wage increases in the public sector. In fact, more recent evidence indicates the public sector wage advantage to have waned by the 1980s (Gunderson 1984; Wilton 1986).

Wage settlements in the public sector often are quite volatile, even at the aggregate level. However, unusually high settlements in a given year tend to reflect catch-up for low settlements in previous years, or the high wage increases tend to be temporary, dissipating over time. Hence, the importance of utilizing a reasonably long time horizon in comparing wage settlements in the public and private sectors.

Robinson and Tomes (1984) also found that most of the public sector wage advantage in Canada is really a union-nonunion wage advantage reflecting the high degree of unionization of Canadian public sector workers. They were able to determine this through a unique data set that provided information on the union status of both private and public sector workers.

On the monetary value of fringe benefits between the public and private sectors, the empirical evidence is scant and difficult to compare because of different definitions utilized. However, the limited empirical evidence in Canada certainly does not indicate the public sector to be ahead of the private sector. Based on 1976 Canadian data from the Pay Research Bureau, Gunderson (1978b, p. 152) concluded: "all that can really be determined on the basis of the available data is that the value of fringe benefits has increased rapidly in the private sector, and that currently they appear to be roughly comparable to those in the public sector." Based upon more recent data, Daniel and Robinson (1980) also find rough comparability of fringe benefits, being only slightly higher for the public sector as opposed to the private sector. In the United States, however, fringe benefits are a slightly higher proportion of wage costs in the public than the private sector and they have increased more rapidly in the public than the private sector (Smith 1977a and Gunderson 1984). Clearly this is an area where more empirical evidence is needed on a consistent, comparable basis so as to make viable comparisons on a total compensation basis.

Many of the previous empirical generalizations based on Canadian data also are generally true for the United Kingdom and the United States.

This latter evidence — reviewed in Gunderson (1978c) — indicates that by the late 1970s there appeared to be a public sector wage advantage in both the United Kingdom and the United States. As is the case with Canada, this advantage is fairly recent, emerging in the 1970s in the United Kingdom and in the 1960s in the United States. There are differences in the patterns of the wage advantage, however, being larger for public corporations in the United Kingdom, larger at the federal level in the United States, and larger for provincial and municipal employees in Canada. These differences are to be expected, given the ultimate importance of political factors in the wage determination process in the public sector, and the fact that political pressures may differ across countries, over time, and with respect to different elements of the public sector.

A number of recent studies have estimated the relationship between aggregate wage changes, in the public and private sectors, and various measures of the aggregate state of the economy and of the labour market such as inflation and unemployment. The purpose was to see if wages were responsive to the state of the economy. The earliest Canadian evidence in this area tended to indicate that labour market conditions had much less of an influence on public sector wages than on private sector wages (Cousineau and Lacroix 1977). However, more recent work has found both the public and private sectors to be equally responsive to market forces and that there have been no significant spillovers from public to private sector wages. (Auld, Christofides, Swidinsky and Wilton 1980; Auld and Wilton study in Conklin, Courchene and Jones 1985; Wilton 1986; and Riddell and Smith 1982).

SOME POLICY IMPLICATIONS

The previous analysis suggests that the public sector wage advantage that appeared to prevail in Canada in the 1970s has now dissipated. Although there is not precise current data on the issue, it is unlikely that there is currently a substantial public sector wage advantage, if there is one at all. If there is an advantage it is likely to reflect a union wage advantage, not a pure public sector wage advantage per se, the public sector being extensively unionized in Canada. In other words, public sector workers in Canada are likely to be paid similarly to comparable unionized workers in Canada. Including fringe benefits is unlikely to modify this picture substantially, albeit more empirical work in this area would be desirable before firm conclusions could be reached.

In essence, natural forces associated with the reduced growth of the public sector and a trend towards public sector restraint appear to have provided a sufficient check on public sector wages, even in the absence of strict market forces. This does not mean that rents may not exist for certain public sector workers or that unusually high settlements may not occur in certain periods. Rather, it means that rents are not all-pervasive and that unusually high settlements in the public sector tend to dissipate over time.

Draconian measures appear to be unnecessary, especially because the effect of such policies likely would fall disproportionately on females and lower-wage workers since they tend to receive the largest public sector wage advantage.

QUESTIONS

1. Since the public sector is simply one of many industries, public-private sector wage differentials are really a special topic of inter-industry wage differentials. Discuss.

2. Discuss various possible definitions of the public sector.

3. Are there any *theoretical* reasons to believe that job security and fringe benefits may be different in the public and the private sector?

4. Indicate how the various determinants of the public-private sector wage differential may have *changed* during the 1950s and 1960s in Canada and how this may have affected the wage differential over that period.

5. Cousineau and Lacroix (1977, p. 113) indicate: "because of its particular characteristics as an employer, the public sector is particularly 'vulnerable' to the unionization of its employees and to union pressure." Discuss.

6. The fact that wage determination in the public sector ultimately depends on political factors may well work against workers in the public sector, even though we traditionally think that this puts them in a better position than when wages are under the ultimate profit constraint in the private sector. Discuss.

7. Criticisms of public sector wages as being too high often implicitly assume that private sector wages are the correct norm. What is so virtuous about private sector wages given that they can reflect market imperfections, unequal bargaining power, and a variety of non-economic constraints? Discuss.

8. The potential upward bias for wages in the public sector relative to the private sector occurs because the market provides a reasonably effective floor on wages in the public sector but it does not necessarily provide an effective ceiling. Discuss.

9. Based on your knowledge of the determinants of the elasticity of demand for labour, would you expect the demand for public sector labour to be inelastic or elastic and why? Why might one expect the elasticity to differ across different elements of the public sector?

10. Differences in the elasticity of demand for labour between the public and the private sector, by themselves, are not sufficient conditions for a wage differential between the two sectors. Discuss.

11. Ehrenberg (1973) provides empirical estimates of the wage elasticity of demand for public sector labour in the U.S., ranging from -1.00 in public welfare to $-.28$ in health, fire and protection services. What does this imply about the expected employment impact of a wage change in each of these sectors?

12. In Canada, by the mid-1970s, about two-thirds of employees in public administration were unionized compared to about one-third for workers in other industries. Discuss the implication of this phenomenon for public-private sector wage differentials.

13. (a) What variables would you utilize as determinants of wages in a micro wage equation (individual worker is the unit of observation) to be estimated separately for public and private sector workers?

   (b) Why would you want to estimate *separate* wage equations for public and private sector workers rather than a single wage equation for both, with a dummy variable for public as opposed to private sector workers?

   (c) How would you test to see if the underlying wage determination process is different in the two sectors?

   (d) Based on this regression analysis, illustrate formally how one could decompose the overall average earnings differential between the public and the private sector into two components: a portion due to an economic rent or pure surplus payment, and a portion attributable to different endowments of productivity-related factors.

   (e) Which is the portion that public policy is concerned with and why?

   (f) Discuss some possible pitfalls in employing this methodology to estimate a pure public-private sector wage differential.

14. Decompose the overall average public-private sector wage differential by adding and subtracting $\Sigma b_g \bar{X}_c$ to the right-hand side of Equation 22.5. Is this also a reasonable decomposition technique?

15. Just as with measuring a pure impact of unions on relative wages, it is difficult to measure a pure public-private sector wage differential. It is extremely important, but difficult, to control for differences in the quality of labour, and to consider wage spillover effects between the two sectors. Discuss.

16. Estimating a pure public-private sector wage differential is difficult because the choice of sector itself is endogenously determined in that individuals may sort themselves into sectors on the bases of unobservable characteristics that influence wages. In such circumstances, the conventional regression procedure for decomposing the public-private sector wage differential into rents and differences due to observable differences in endowments of wage-determining characteristics does not control for differences in unobservable characteristics. Illustrate the appropriate econometric procedures for correcting for the biases that may result from the differences in unobservable characteristics between workers in the public and private sectors.

17. Why might it not be surprising to find the public-private sector wage differential to differ across components of the public sector, or to differ across various levels of government, or to differ in different countries?

18. In Canada in the year 1975, the rate of increase in base wages in collective agreements was 20.0 percent in the provincial public sector and 21.3 percent in the health-education-welfare sector, compared to

14.4 percent in the private sector. These large increases in particular elements of the public sector apparently triggered public reaction. Why might it be a bit hazardous to react to specific public sector increases in a particular year; that is, why might one expect public sector wage settlements to be more volatile than private sector wages?

19. What current forces are at work to suggest that public sector wage settlements are under pressure to be more moderate now and in the near future?

20. Even if there is a pure public sector wage advantage of 7 percent based on 1971 Canadian Census data, perhaps the appropriate policy response is one of benign neglect. Do you agree or disagree and why?

21. In many instances in the public sector, wages are set by wage arbitration. Discuss the various criteria that you think would be appropriate to utilize in deciding upon the appropriate wage. Indicate any theoretical and practical problems associated with the criteria that you have discussed.

22. If the current generation of taxpayers tries to save on the current public sector budget by granting generous deferred compensation in the form of liberal pensions, how may this affect local property values? Is this a sufficient market check to ensure that the consequences of their decision are internalized by the current taxpayers?

23. Indicate how you would test for whether the determination of aggregate wage changes are more responsive to market forces in the public or private sectors. How would you test for wage spillovers from one sector to the other?

REFERENCES AND FURTHER READINGS

Abbott, M. and T. Stengos. Alternative estimates of union-nonunion and public-private wage differentials in Ontario, 1981. Kingston: Queen's University Industrial Relations Centre, 1987.

Auld, D., L. Christofides, R. Swidinsky and D. Wilton. A microeconomic analysis of wage determination in the Canadian public sector. *J Pub Ec* 13 (June 1980) 369-388.

Asher, M. and J. Popkin. The effect of gender and race differentials on public-private wage comparisons: a study of postal workers. *ILRR* 38 (October 1984) 16-25.

Bartel, A. and D. Lewin. Wages and unionism in the public sector: the case of police. *RE Stats* 63 (February 1981) 53-59.

Bird, R. The growth of the public service in Canada. *Public Employment and Compensation in Canada*, D. Foot (ed.). Toronto: Butterworths, 1978.

Borjas, G. Labor turnover in the U.S. federal bureaucracy. *J Pub Ec* 19 (November 1982) 187-202.

Christensen, S. Collective bargaining in provincial public administration. *RI/IR* 36 (No. 3, 1981) 616-628.

Conklin, D., T. Courchene and W. Jones (eds.). *Public Sector Compensation*. Toronto: Ontario Economic Council, 1985.

Cousineau, J.-M. and R. Lacroix. *Wage Determination in Major Collective Agreements in the Private and Public Sectors*. Ottawa: Economic Council of Canada, 1977.

Daniel, M. and W. Robinson. *Compensation in Canada: A Study of the Public and Private Sectors*. Ottawa, Conference Board, 1980.

Delaney, J., P. Fenstle and W. Hendricks. Police salaries, interest arbitration and leveling effect. *IR* 23 (Fall 1984) 417-423.

Dunson, B. Pay experience and productivity: the government-sector case. *JHR* 20 (Winter 1985) 153-160.

Edwards, L. and F. Edwards. Public unions, local government structure and the compensation of municipal sanitation workers. *EI* 20 (July 1982) 405-425.

Ehrenberg, R. The demand for state and local government employees. *AER* 63 (June 1973a) 366-379.

Ehrenberg, R. Municipal government structure, unionization and wages of fire fighters. *ILRR* 27 (October 1973b) 36-48.

Ehrenberg, R. Heterogeneous labor, minimum hiring standards, and job vacancies in public employment. *JPE* 81 (November/December 1973) 1442-1459.

Ehrenberg, R. and G. Goldstein. A model of public sector wage determination. *Journal of Urban Economics* 2 (1975) 223-245.

Ehrenberg, R. and J. Schwarz. Public sector labour markets. *Handbook of Labour Economics* Vol. 1. O. Ashenfelter and R. Layard (eds.). New York: Elsevier, 1986.

Ferland, G. La politique de remunération dans les secteurs publics et parapublics au Québec. Salary policy in Québec's public and parapublic sectors. *RI/IR* 36 (No. 3, 1981) 475-498.

Feville, P., J. Delaney and W. Hendricks. Police bargaining, arbitration and fringe benefits. *JLR* 6 (Winter 1985) 1-20.

Field, C. and R. Keller. How salaries of large cities compare with industry and federal pay. *MLR* (November 1976) 23-28.

Fogel, W. and D. Lewin. Wage determination in the public sector. *ILRR* 27 (April 1974) 410-431.

Freeman, R. Unionism comes to the public sector. *Journal of Economic-Literature* 24 (March 1986) 41-86.

Freund, J. Market and union influence on municipal employee wages. *ILRR* 27 (April 1974) 391-404.

Grosskopf, S., K. Hayes and T. Kennedy. Supply and demand effects of under-funding pensions on public employee wages. *SEJ* 51 (January 1985) 745-753.

Gunderson, M. Data on public sector wages in Canada. *Public Employment and Compensation in Canada*, D. Foot (ed.). Toronto: Butterworths, 1978a, 107-126.

Gunderson, M. Public-private wage and nonwage differentials in Canada: some calculations from published tabulations. *Public Employment and Compensation in Canada*, D. Foot (ed.). Toronto: Butterworths, 1978b, 127-166.

Gunderson, M. Public sector wage determination: a review of the literature. *Public Employment and Compensation in Canada*, D. Foot (ed.). Toronto: Butterworths, 1978c, 167-188.

Gunderson, M. Wage determination in the public sector: Canada and the U.S. *Labour and Society* 4 (January 1979a) 49-70.

Gunderson, M. Earnings differentials between the public and private sectors. *CJE* 12 (May 1979b) 228-242.

Gunderson, M. Public sector compensation in Canada and the U.S. *IR* 19 (Fall 1980) 257-271.

Gunderson, M. The public/private sector compensation controversy. In *Conflict or Compromise*. Edited by M. Thompson and G. Swimmer. Ottawa: Institute of Research on Public Policy, 1984.

Hamermesh, D. (ed.). *Labor in the Public and Non-Profit Sectors*. Princeton, N.J.: Princeton University Press, 1975.

Katz, H. Municipal pay determination: the case of San Francisco. *IR* 18 (Winter 1979) 44-58.

Lewin, D. Wage parity and the supply of police and firemen. *IR* 12 (February 1973) 77-85.

Lewin, D. Aspects of wage determination in local government employment. *Public Administration Review* 34 (March/April 1974) 149-155.

Mehay, S. and R. Gonzalez. The relative effect of unionization and interjurisdictional competition on municipal wages. *JLR* 7 (Winter 1986) 79-93.

Olson, C. The impact of arbitration on the wages of firefighters. *IR* 19 (Fall 1980) 325-339.

Owen, J. Toward a public employment wage theory: some econometric evidence on teacher quality. *ILRR* 25 (January 1972) 213-222.

Perloff, J. and M. Wachter. Wage comparability in the U.S. postal service. *ILRR* 38 (October 1984) 26-35.

Porter, F. and R. Keller. Public and private pay levels in large labor markets. *MLR* 104 (July 1981) 22-26.

Proulx, P. Comment établir des comparaisons de la rémunération entre les secteurs publics et privés? *RI/IR* 35 (No. 2, 1980) 202-208.

Quinn, J. Postal sector wages. *IR* 18 (Winter 1979) 92-96.

Quinn, J. Wage differentials among older workers in the public and private sectors. *JHR* 14 (Winter 1979) 41-62.

Riddell, W.C. and P. Smith. Expected inflation and wage changes in Canada. *CJE* 15 (August 1982) 377-394.

Robinson, C. and N. Tomes. Union wage differentials in the public and private sectors. *JOLE* 2 (January 1984) 106-127.

Schmenner, R. The determination of municipal employee wages. *R.E.Stats.* 55 (February 1973) 83-90.

Smith, S. Pay differentials between federal government and private sector workers. *ILRR* 29 (January 1976) 179-197. Also comment by W. Bailey and reply 31 (October 1977) 78-87.

Smith, S. Government wage differentials by sex. *JHR* 11 (Spring 1976) 185-199.

Smith, S. Are postal workers over- or under-paid? *IR* 15 (May 1976) 168-176.

Smith, S. *Equal Pay in the Public Sector: Fact or Fantasy*. Princeton, N.J.: Industrial Relations Section, 1977a.

Smith, S. Government wage differentials. *Journal of Urban Economics* 4 (July 1977b) 248-277.

Smith, S. Prospects for reforming federal pay. *AER* 72 (May 1982) 273-277.

Spizman, L. Public employee unions: a study in the economics of power. *JLR* 1 (Fall 1980) 265-273.

Stelluto, G. Federal pay comparability: facts to temper the debate. *MLR* 102 (June 1979) 18-28.

Subbaro, A. Impasse choice and wages in the Canadian federal service. *IR* 18 (Spring 1979) 233-236.

Thompson, M. and J. Cairnie. Compulsory arbitration: the case of British Columbia teachers. ILRR 29 (October 1973) 3-17.

Utgoff, K.C. Compensation levels and quit rates in the public sector. *JHR* 18 (Summer 1983) 394-406.

Weisbrod, B.A. Non-profit and proprietary sector behavior: wage differentials among lawyers. *JOLE* 1 (July 1983) 246-263.

Wellington, H. and R. Winter. The limits of collective bargaining in public employment. *Yale Law Journal* 78 (June 1969) 115-130.

Wellington, H. and R. Winter. *The Unions and the Cities*. Washington: Brookings Institute, 1971.

Williams, C. and G. Swimmer. The relationship between public and private sector wages in Alberta. *RI/IR* 30 (No. 2, 1975) 217-226.

Wilton, D. Public sector wage compensation. In *Canadian Labour Relations*. Edited by W.C. Riddell. Toronto: University of Toronto Press, 1986.

Wise, D. (ed.). *Public Sector Payrolls*. Chicago: University of Chicago Press, 1987.

CHAPTER 23

Discrimination and Male-Female Earnings Differentials

The economic analysis of discrimination provides a good application for many of the basic principles of labour market economics. In addition it indicates the limitations of some of these tools in an area where non-economic factors may play a crucial role. In fact, many would argue that discrimination is not really an economic phenomenon, but rather is sociological or psychological in nature. While recognizing the importance of these factors in any analysis of discrimination, the basic position taken here is that economics does have a great deal to say about discrimination. More specifically, it can indicate the labour market impact of the sociological or psychological constraints and preferences. More important, economics may shed light on the expected impact of alternative policies designed to combat discrimination in the labour market.

Although the focus of this analysis is on sex discrimination in the labour market, it is important to realize that discrimination can occur against various groups and in different markets. Discrimination can occur in the housing market, product market, capital market and human capital market (e.g. education and training), as well as in the labour market. It can be based on a variety of factors including race, age, language, national origin, sexual preference, or political affiliation, as well as on sex.

In order to better understand the economics of sex discrimination, the reasons, sources and forms of sex discrimination are first discussed. Various theories of discrimination are then presented and empirical evidence is given to document the existence of sex discrimination in the labour market. The chapter concludes with a discussion of alternative policies to combat discrimination in the labour market.

DISCRIMINATION: REASONS AND SOURCES

Reasons for Discrimination

Labour market discrimination against females may result because males have a preference for working with or buying from fellow males. This prejudice would be especially strong against females in supervisory positions or in jobs of responsibility.

Discrimination may also occur because of erroneous information on the labour market worth of females. Such erroneous information could come from females who consistently underestimate their own capacity in the labour market or it could come from employers who consistently underestimate the productivity of females. Erroneous information on the part of employers may come from the subjective reports of co-workers or supervisors, or it may be based on sex-biased test scores.

Because information on individual workers is extremely costly to acquire, employers may judge individual females on the basis of the average performance of all females. Statistical and signalling theories of discrimination are discussed in Aigner and Cain (1972), Lundberg and Startz (1983), Phelps (1972) and Stiglitz (1973). Although, from the employers' viewpoint, such statistical judgment may be efficient, it could be inequitable for many individual females.

Males may also discriminate for reasons of job security. To protect their high-wage jobs from low-wage female competition, males would use the forces of governments, unions and business cartels to ensure that power remains in their hands and is used to further their own ends.

Obviously, discrimination can occur for any, or all, of the previously mentioned reasons of preference, erroneous information, statistical judgment, or job security. As we shall see later, the effectiveness of policies designed to combat discrimination often depends on the reasons for the discrimination.

Sources of Discrimination

Labour market discrimination can come from a variety of sources. *Employers* may discriminate in their hiring and promotion policies as well as their wage policies. To a certain extent the forces of competition would deter employers from discriminating since they would forgo profits by not hiring and promoting females who are as productive as their male counterparts. However, profit-maximizing firms do have to respond to pressure from their customers and male employees. For this reason they may be reluctant to hire and promote females, or they may pay females a lower wage than equally productive males. In addition, firms in the large not-for-profit sector (e.g. government, education, hospitals) may be able to discriminate without having to worry about losing profits by not hiring and promoting females.

In addition to discrimination on the part of employers, *male co-workers* may also discriminate for reasons of prejudice, misinformation or job security. Representing the wishes of a male majority, craft unions may discriminate through the hiring hall or apprenticeship system and industrial unions may discriminate by bargaining for male wages that exceed female wages for the same work. Another potential source of discrimination is *customers* who may be reluctant to purchase the services of females or who may not patronize establishments that employ females, especially in positions of responsibility.

THEORIES OF LABOUR MARKET DISCRIMINATION

Alternative theories of sex discrimination in the labour market can be classified according to whether they focus on the demand or supply side of the labour market, or on non-competitive aspects of labour markets.

Demand Theories of Discrimination

Demand theories of discrimination have the common result that the demand for female labour is reduced relative to the demand for equally productive male labour. The decreased demand for female labour would reduce the employment of females and, unless the supply of female labour is perfectly elastic, the decreased demand would reduce the wages of females relative to the wages of equally productive males. How does discrimination lead to a reduction in the demand for female labour?

According to Becker (1971, p. 14), employers act as if $W_f(1 + d_f)$ were the net wage paid to females, male co-workers act as if $W_m(1 - d_m)$ were the net wage they receive when working with females, and consumers act as if $p_c(1 + d_c)$ were the price paid for a product sold by a female. In all cases, the discrimination coefficient, "d," represents the cost, in percent, associated with hiring, working with, or buying from females. For example, a firm that has a discrimination coefficient of .10 and that can hire all the female labour it wants at $2.00 per hour, would act as if it paid 2.00 $(1 + .10) = \$2.20$ each time it hired a female. Clearly such discrimination reduces the demand for females relative to equally productive males.

Arrow (1973) gives a neoclassical theory of discrimination based on the firm's desired demand for labour when the firm maximizes utility (rather than simply profits) and the firm's utility is increased by employing fewer workers from minority groups. Again, this results in a reduced demand for female labour and lower female wages.[1]

The reduced demand for female labour in the discriminatory sector would create excess supply and low female wages in the non-discriminatory sector. As Zellner (1972, p. 157) points out:

> Assuming that discrimination takes the form of a preference for males over comparable females in masculine occupations, it results in a demand curve

---

[1] Arrow's (1973) neoclassical theory of discrimination can be presented formally as follows. Assume that the firm maximizes utility, U, which is a positive function of its profits, Π, and a negative function of the number of females, F, it employs (discrimination). That is $U = u(\Pi, F)$ where the partial derivatives are denoted by $U_\Pi > 0$ and $U_F < 0$ and where $\Pi = P \cdot Q(M + F) - W_m M - W_f F$. For simplicity we have assumed that output, Q, is produced by perfectly substitutable male and female labour of equal productivity so that the output is denoted by the production function $Q(M + F)$. Utility maximizing firms will hire females until $U_F = 0$ which, from the utility function, implies $U_\Pi \Pi_F + U_F = 0$. Since $\Pi_F = PQ_F - W_F$, utility maximization implies $U_\Pi(PQ_F - W_F) + U_F = 0$, which upon rearrangement yields $W_F = PQ_F + U_F/U_\Pi$. Thus female wages will be less than their marginal revenue product, PQ_F, since $U_F < 0$ and $U_\Pi > 0$. In addition, female wages will be less than male wages if males are paid a wage equal to their marginal revenue product.

for women to the left of that which would prevail in this sector in a non-discriminatory situation, thereby lowering female employment in masculine occupations. This reduced demand for women in the masculine sector increases their supply to those occupations in which males are not preferred to females, thus creating a "feminine" sector. Discrimination therefore directly lowers the female wage in masculine occupations by reducing demand for women in this sector, and indirectly lowers the female wage in feminine occupations by increasing their supply to this sector.

The demand for female labour relative to male labour also depends on information concerning their relative productivity. To the extent that employers consistently underestimate the productivity of females, they would correspondingly reduce their demand for female labour. This misinformation on the part of employers may be due to their own ingrained prejudices as well as to erroneous information fostered by male customers and co-workers.

Supply Theories of Discrimination

Supply theories of discrimination have the common result that the supply of female labour is increased by discrimination or, conversely, that the female asking wage is reduced by discrimination.

The crowding hypothesis, as put forth by Fawcett (1918) and Edgeworth (1922), and formalized by Bergmann (1971), implies that females tend to be segregated into "female-type" jobs. The resulting abundance of supply lowers their marginal productivity and hence their wage. Thus, even if females are paid a wage equal to their marginal productivity, their wage will be less than male wages that are not depressed by an excess supply.

In a similar vein, dual labour market theory posits two separate and distinct labour markets. The primary or core labour market (unionized, monopolistic, expanding) provides secure employment at high wages. The secondary or peripheral labour market (non-unionized, highly competitive, declining) is characterized by unstable employment at low wages. Men tend to be employed in the primary labour market, women in the secondary labour market. Prejudice on the part of the dominant group and its desire to exclude female competition will prevent the entry of women into the primary labour market. Unions, occupational licensing, discriminatory employment tests, and barriers to education and training, can all work against the entry of females into the core labour market. Female immobility may also result because of women's stronger ties to the household and their tendency to move to the places of their husbands' employment. For these various reasons, females tend to be crowded into jobs in the secondary labour market with its concomitant unstable employment and low wages. Their low wages and undesirable working conditions in turn create high absenteeism and turnover which further depress wages in the secondary labour market.

Females' attitudes of their own labour market worth also may induce them to lower their asking wage when seeking employment. Because of conditioning in a male-dominated labour market, females may erroneously underestimate their own labour market worth. This would tend to lower female asking (reservation) wages; that is, the female labour supply schedule would be shifted vertically downwards. Employers would naturally foster these attitudes because they lead to lower labour costs.

Non-Competitive Theories of Discrimination

In theory, male-female wage differentials for equally productive workers are inconsistent with competitive equilibrium. As long as females could be paid a wage lower than that of equally productive males, firms that do not have an aversion to hiring females would increase their profits by hiring females. The resultant increased demand for females would bid up their wages, and the process would continue until the male-female wage differential is eliminated. Firms that do not have an aversion to hiring females would be maximizing profits by employing large numbers of females; firms that have an aversion to hiring females would be forgoing profits by employing only males. According to competitive theory, discrimination leads to a segregation of males and females, not wage differentials. It also implies that discrimination should be reduced over time since firms that discriminate will go out of business as they forgo profits to discriminate.

Some would argue that these predictions of competitive economic theory are at variance with the facts. Male-female wage differentials seem to persist, and discrimination does not appear to be declining over time. What then are some of the factors that may explain this persistence in the face of competitive forces?

Arrow (1973, pp. 20-23) attributes the persistence of male-female wage differentials to costs of adjustment and imperfect information. Even if they do acquire the information that profits can be increased by hiring low wage females to do certain jobs performed by higher wage males, firms cannot immediately replace their male workers by an all-female work-force. There are fixed costs associated with recruiting and hiring; consequently, firms want to spread these fixed costs as much as possible by retaining their existing work-force. Firms may replace male turnover by new female recruits, but they would be reluctant to immediately replace their male work-force. In essence, Arrow implies that the long run may be a very long time.

Stiglitz (1973) provides a queuing theory to explain the persistence of male-female wage differentials for equally productive workers. He argues that some firms pay wages greater than competitive market wages in order to reduce turnover, improve morale, or secure the advantages of always having a queue from which to hire workers. Other firms pay greater than competitive wages because of union or minimum wage pressure, or because of a necessity to share monopoly or oligopoly profits with their workers. The resultant higher-than-competitive wage enables these high-wage firms to hire from a queue of available workers. Rationing of the scarce jobs may be carried out on the basis of nepotism or discrimination. Thus, discriminatory wage differentials may exist in a long-run competitive equilibrium when profit-maximizing firms minimize labour costs by paying high wages in order to reduce turnover or improve morale, or because they face institutional constraints such as unions or minimum wage legislation.

As an alternative explanation for the persistence of discrimination, Freeman (1973) argues that discrimination comes mainly from non-competitive sectors, mainly the government and trade unions. Reflecting majority wishes, governments discriminate both in their own hiring practices and in the provision of education and training. In the case of sex discrimination, this would reduce the skill endowment of minorities and reduce the number of professional-managerial females who would hire fellow females. Also reflecting the wishes of a male majority, unions could discriminate against females, especially in apprenticeship and training programs. Freeman also emphasizes the importance of social pressure in sanctioning instances of non-discrimination, especially when profits can be made through discrimination.

In the same vein, Thurow (1969) emphasizes that majority groups use the power inherent in governments, unions and business monopolies to further their own ends through discrimination and segregation. He implies that an alteration in the power structure would do most to improve the economic position of minorities.

A more radical perspective regards discrimination as deliberately fostered by employers as part of a conscious policy of divide-and-conquer (Reich 1978; Roemer 1979). Employers will consciously pit workers against each other and utilize a reserve of unemployed workers as ways of disciplining the work-force and reducing working class solidarity and power. In this perspective, group power is more important than the economic forces of supply and demand in determining wages.

Monopsony is another non-competitive factor that can affect female wages relative to male wages, mainly in two ways. First, if females tend to be employed by monopsonists, their wages will be reduced correspondingly. Because of their immobility (tied to household and to husbands' places of employment), females may not have the effective threat of mobility necessary to receive a competitive wage. Second, monopsonists may try to differentiate their work-force so as to pay the higher wage rate only to some employees. One obvious way of differentiating workers is by sex. Thus, the company may pay higher wages to male employees and yet not have to pay these higher wages to its female employees who do the same work, simply because the female employees do not consider themselves direct competitors with male employees doing the same job. Employers find it in their interest to foster this attitude, since it enables them to maintain the wage differentials based on sex. The formal monopsony model of sex discrimination with separate male-female labour supply schedules was discussed earlier in Chapter 11.

The concept of systemic (not to be confused with systematic) discrimination has been advanced to explain discrimination that may be the unintended byproduct of historically determined practices. It may result, for example, from informal word-of-mouth recruiting networks (the "old-boy system") that perpetrate the existing sex composition of the work-force. Or, it may result from certain job requirements pertaining to height or strength that may no longer serve a legitimate purpose. In situations where wages are institutionally set above the competitive norm, such job requirements may simply serve to ration the scarce jobs and serve little or no function related to productivity.

Productivity Differences: Choice or Discrimination?

Female wages may differ from male wages because of productivity differences that arise from differences in the human capital endowments and differences in the absenteeism and turnover of males and females. The human capital endowments could include *acquired* attributes such as education, training, labour market information, mobility and labour market experience, as well as more *innate* characteristics such as intelligence, strength, perseverance or dexterity. In general there is little reason to believe the endowment of these *innate* characteristics to differ substantially between the sexes, and in an increasingly mechanized society the innate characteristic for which there may be the greatest difference — physical strength — takes on reduced importance. It is in the area of acquired human capital endowments that productivity differences may arise.

Human capital formation will occur until the present value of the marginal benefits (usually in the form of increased earnings) equals the present value of the marginal cost (both direct cost and the opportunity cost of the earnings forgone while acquiring human capital). Because of their dual role in the household and in the labour market, women traditionally have a shorter expected length of stay in the labour market. Consequently, they have a reduced benefit period from which to recoup the costs of human capital formation. In addition, their time in the labour market tends to be intermittent and subject to a considerable degree of uncertainty, thus creating rapid depreciation of their human capital and preventing them from acquiring continuous labour market experience. For this reason it may be economically rational for females (or firms) to be reluctant to invest in female human capital formation that is labour market oriented. This perspective is emphasized, for example, in Mincer and Ofek (1982), Mincer and Polachek (1974), and Polachek (1975b).

The human capital decision therefore may reflect rational choice, but it may also reflect discrimination as well as rational choice subject to discriminatory constraints. Females may be discriminated against in the returns they receive for acquiring human capital as well as in borrowing to finance the cost of human capital formation. In addition, family and peer group pressures may close off certain avenues of human capital formation.

Most important, female responsibility for household tasks may reflect discrimination more than choice. Whatever the reason, females tend to acquire less labour-market-oriented human capital than males, and consequently their wages and employment opportunities are reduced in the labour market. This occurs even if in the labour market there is no discrimination on the part of firms, co-workers or customers. Differences in wage and employment opportunities may reflect productivity differences, which in turn may come about because of rational economic choice as well as discrimination prior to entering the labour market.

Productivity and hence wage differences may also occur because of differences in the absenteeism and turnover of females. This is especially the case if female turnover occurs primarily as a result of leaving the labour force (which would reduce earnings as explained earlier), and male turnover occurs primarily to move to a higher paying job. Higher absenteeism for females would also occur, in large part, because of their household responsibilities, especially care of children. Boulet and Lavallée (1984 p. 67), for example, cite Canadian evidence indicating that while total absenteeism was only slightly higher for females than males without children or with school-age children only, it was about seven times higher for females than males with pre-school age children. In addition to causing lower wages, higher absenteeism and turnover may be the result of low wages: cause and effect work in both directions to reinforce each other.

As with the case of the acquisition of human capital, so with absenteeism and turnover, it is difficult to know how much of the difference in behaviour between the sexes is a matter of economic choice as opposed to discrimination. The fact that the household responsibility of females is so important in these aspects of productivity makes it more understandable that there will be increased pressure for a more equitable division of labour in the household as well as more day-care facilities for children. In addition, in empirical work that attempts to control for productivity differences between males and females, we should be careful in interpreting the productivity adjusted wage and employment patterns as ones that are free of discrimination. The discrimination may simply be occurring outside of the labour market.

EVIDENCE ON MALE-FEMALE EARNINGS DIFFERENTIALS

Empirical studies have employed a variety of techniques to estimate the male-female earnings differential and to see how much of the differential reflects discrimination. The results are quite varied, in part because of different data sources and methodology, but also in part because of an emphasis on different aspects of discrimination. Some studies focus on wage discrimination within the same establishment and occupation; others involve measures of sex discrimination that also reflect the crowding of females into low-wage establishments, occupations and industries; and other studies utilize measures of earnings differentials that could reflect discrimination outside of the labour market, perhaps in educational institutions or in households.

As with many differences in empirical research, it is not that one method is correct and the other incorrect; they simply show different things. Hence, it is important to know exactly what the study is attempting to measure, especially in making comparisons across studies or in utilizing the results for policy purposes. With these qualifications in mind, some generalizations can be made on the empirical evidence, based largely on the Canadian studies referred to in the bibliography. A more detailed analysis of the Canadian studies is contained in Gunderson (1985a). Summaries of U.S. studies are contained in Lloyd and Neimi (1979), Treiman and Hartman (1981), Wilborn (1986) and Cain (1986).

On average, females tend to earn 50 to 60 percent of what males earn in a year. This unadjusted ratio may reflect wage discrimination, the segregation of females into low-wage firms, occupations and industries, as well as differences in productivity-related factors such as education, training, experience, and absenteeism and turnover. Differences in these productivity-related factors may reflect unconstrained choices and they may reflect pre-labour market discrimination, perhaps in educational institutions or in the household.

Unfortunately the evidence does not enable one to state precisely the relative contributions of each and all of these factors to the overall earnings differential. Studies that make some *rough* adjustments find that females who work full-time, and with levels of education, training and experience, and with occupational and industrial distributions similar to those of males, tend to earn approximately 80 percent of what males earn. This is the case, for example, in Ostry (1968), where adjustments were made by examining males and females with similar characteristics, and it is the case in Robb (1978) and Gunderson (1979), where differences in these characteristics were controlled for by multiple regression analysis.[2]

Because of the lack of data, the adjustment factors involved in arriving at the adjusted ratio of .80 are quite crude. In particular, they usually do not reflect differences in such factors as absenteeism or turnover, nor do

---

[2] The methodology — first utilized with U.S. data by Oaxaca (1973), Blinder (1973), and Malkiel and Malkiel (1973) — is identical to that which was formally presented in the previous chapter to decompose the public-private sector wage differential. Separate earnings equations are estimated for males and females. Subtracting the female from the male earnings equations, evaluated at the mean of the explanatory variables, yields

$$\bar{y}_m - \bar{y}_f = \Sigma b_m \bar{X}_m - \Sigma b_f \bar{X}_f$$

Subtracting and adding $\Sigma b_f \bar{X}_m$ from the right-hand side, and collecting terms, yields

$$\bar{y}_m - \bar{y}_f = \Sigma b_m (\bar{X}_m - \bar{X}_f) + \Sigma (b_m - b_f) \bar{X}_f$$

That is, the average male-female earnings differential can be decomposed into two parts: a portion attributable to differences in endowments of wage-determining characteristics (some of which may reflect pre-labour market discrimination), and a portion attributable to different wage payments for the same characteristics (i.e. wage discrimination).

they reflect differences in the extent to which the education or training is labour market oriented, or the extent to which experience is continuous. The possibility that the earnings gap of .20, implied by an adjusted female/male earnings ratio of .80, cannot be fully attributed to wage discrimination (but may reflect other discrimination) is reinforced by studies that utilize data on male-female wage differentials within the same narrowly-defined occupations within the same establishments.

Gunderson (1975), for example, finds the earnings ratio to be approximately .82 in such circumstances.[3] In addition, within incentive pay jobs where pay would be more directly linked with productivity, the earnings ratio averaged .88. To the extent that the incentive pay system reflects productivity, this suggests that the marginal productivity of females averaged 88 percent of males. Much of this difference, of course, may reflect pre-labour market discrimination as well as occupational segregation. (Recall that occupational segregation would result in a lower marginal productivity of females as they were crowded into female-type jobs.) If the marginal physical product of females is 88 percent of males, but their wage averaged only 82 percent of males, the adjusted ratio of female to male earnings for equally productive workers is .93.[4] That is, in the particular data set analysed, females tended to earn 93 percent of what equally productive males earned in the same establishment.

Clearly this adjusted ratio is much higher than the adjusted ratio of approximately .80 implied by regression analysis. The different ratios, however, indicate different things. In particular, the adjusted ratio of .93 suggests that wage discrimination (narrowly defined as unequal pay for equally productive work) within the same narrowly-defined occupations within the same establishments is small — but it does exist. The small magnitude of wage discrimination may be expected because such discrimination is most blatant, and is subject to equal pay laws.

The Ontario *Green Paper on Pay Equity* (1985, p. 10) provides a summary picture of the magnitude of the male-female earnings gap and the factors that contribute to that gap. They indicate that as of 1982, in Ontario, the ratio of female to male average annual full-time earnings was 0.62, implying an unadjusted gap of 0.38. That gap was attributed to the following factors: 0.16 to differences in hours worked; 0.05 to 0.10 to differences in such factors as experience, education and unionization; 0.10 to 0.15 to occupational segregation; and 0.05 to narrowly-defined wage discrimination.

Gunderson (1985a) also suggests a number of generalizations, and policy implications, that emerge from the extensive empirical literature on the male-female earnings gap and its determinants. The more extensive the list of variables used to control for differences in productivity-related

---

[3] The actual measure of the wage differential estimated was the proportionate male-female wage differential $(w_m - w_f)/w_f$ of .22, which implies a female to male wage ratio w_f/w_m of .82.

[4] If w_f/w_m is .82 and $MPP_f/MPP_m = .88$, then $(w_f/w_m)/(MPP_f/Mpp_m) = .82/.88 = .93$. Therefore, $w_f/w_m = .93$ when $MPP_f = MPP_m$.

factors, the smaller the productivity-adjusted earnings gap. However, many of these differences in productivity-related factors themselves may reflect discrimination, perhaps prior to entering the labour market. Also, a discriminatory gap almost invariably remains, thereby suggesting a legitimate need for policy intervention.

The portion of the male-female earnings gap attributable to occupational segregation is larger than the portion attributable to wage discrimination within the same narrowly-defined occupation within the same establishment. This suggests a larger potential role for policy initiatives, discussed subsequently — like equal employment opportunity policies, affirmative action and equal value policies — that can deal with occupational segregation.

Differences in the various dimensions of labour market experience — its quantity, quality and continuity — are an important determinant of the overall earnings gap. The effect of marital status also is important: being married dramatically increases the earnings of males and decreases the earnings of females. These substantial effects of labour market experience and marital status highlight the likely effect of differential household responsibilities in influencing the earnings gap. In effect, because females tend to spend a disproportionate amount of time on household tasks, especially those associated with the bearing and raising of children, this may have an adverse effect on their labour market behaviour, especially on such factors as absenteeism, hours of work, turnover and their willingness to engage in geographic and occupational mobility. This in turn may affect the types of occupations they enter, as well as their remuneration. It also reminds us of the potential importance of policies, such as daycare, that can affect the division of labour within the household.

Other generalizations about the male-female earnings gap include the fact that it is smaller in the public sector than in the private sector. There is more controversy about what has happened to the gap over time. Boulet and Lavallée (1984) indicate that the gap has been narrowing in Canada over the 1970s, in part because of the increased importance of younger workers where the gap is smallest. There is hope that this may be a permanent change because the new female entrants tend to be increasingly committed to continuous labour market participation and their education tends to be more labour market oriented, than was the case for their predecessors.

POLICIES TO COMBAT SEX DISCRIMINATION

Because of the variety of sources and forms of discrimination, policies to combat discrimination have also tended to take on a variety of forms. The main thrusts of public policy have been in the areas of equal pay legislation, equal employment opportunity legislation, affirmative action, policies designed to facilitate female employment, and policies designed to alter attitudes and preferences. Each of these will be discussed in turn.

Equal Pay Legislation

The history, coverage, extent, and enforcement of equal pay in Canada is reviewed in Cook and Eberts (1976), Agarwal and Jain (1978) and Gunderson (1985a). Beginning with Ontario in 1951, all jurisdictions in Canada now have equal pay laws which require equal pay for equal work between males and females. Although there are important differences in the laws of each jurisdiction, they basically require equal pay for *substantially similar* work within the same establishment.

Most jurisdictions follow a *composite approach* which basically requires that the jobs be similar in the composite of the components of skill, effort, responsibilities, and working conditions required for the job. That is, the jobs do not have to be similar in each component; rather, a shortfall in one component can be compensated by more of another component, as long as the composite or package of components is substantially the same. As when market forces determine the pay in a job, this allows the components to be traded off against each other, as long as the composite of the components is substantially the same.

The scope of conventional equal pay legislation is limited by the fact that it deals with only one aspect of discrimination — wage discrimination within an establishment — and as our earlier discussion of the empirical evidence indicated, this is probably a quantitatively small aspect of discrimination. In addition, the enforcement of the law can be difficult because it usually relies upon individuals to complain and because there are problems of interpreting what is meant by equal work, although the courts have interpreted this rather broadly.

Another problem associated with equal pay laws is the possibility, associated with all forms of wage fixing, that they could reduce employment opportunities for females. Faced with having to pay females a higher wage, firms may substitute other factors of production (capital or male labour) for female labour. Or firms may cut back their output or even go out of business because of the higher female wage costs. These are the familiar substitution and scale effects, respectively, predicted by economic theory to result from any wage fixing legislation.

This potential adverse employment effect of equal pay legislation has long been recognized. At the turn of the century, Rathbone (1917, p. 57) writes that equal pay for equal work has been adopted "by the more astute and enlightened of the trade unionists, who see in it an effective way of maintaining the exclusion of women while appearing as the champions of equality between the sexes." In the same vein, Brady (1947, p. 53) writes: "When an extraordinary number of women are added to the labour force in a short period, they are seen as a serious threat to wage levels, and official action on equal pay is the result. . . . The timing, phrasing and interpretation of the orders and laws have made clear . . . that they are designed to protect men, and to prevent the degradation of the wage structure."

Equal pay laws have also been condemned on the grounds that they prevent women from accepting lower wages to obtain on-the-job training which would improve their future wages and employability. To cite Sawhill (1973, p. 394):

> Equal pay laws are not very helpful. Although they may guarantee equal wages to women working side by side with men and although they have obvious moral and symbolic value, they tend to reduce the training alternatives available to women, which is a major source of the sex differential. Much more emphasis needs to be placed on opening up employment opportunities.

Equal Value or Comparable Worth Legislation

In part because of the limited potential for conventional equal pay policies to narrow the overall male-female earnings gap, further legislative initiatives have been advocated on the pay side in the form of equal pay for work of equal value. The phrases equal value, pay equity and comparable worth are usually used interchangeably, although equal value is often used internationally and in Canada. Pay equity is the phrase also used in Canada, although it often refers to the goal rather than the means of achieving that goal. Comparable worth is used most often in the United States.

Existence of Equal Value Legislation

In Canada, equal pay for work of equal value (as opposed to conventional equal pay for equal work) has been in place in Quebec since 1976; however, their cases have tended to be of the conventional equal work type. Since 1978, the principle of equal value has been in place in the federal jurisdiction, which covers approximately 10 percent of the Canadian work-force. In Manitoba, the principle of equal value has been in place for the civil service since 1985. In 1987, Ontario passed equal value legislation for both the public sector and most of the private sector.

In the United States, by the mid-1960s over a dozen states had passed comparable worth legislation covering state employees: however, these laws were rarely enforced (Ehrenberg and Smith 1987b). Only a few states such as Washington State and Minnesota had active comparable worth policies. At the local level a larger number of cities, counties or school districts (mainly in California, Washington and Minnesota) were experimenting with or studying the concept; however, it has yet to be adopted on a widescale basis in the United States. Equal value initiatives have not been prominent in Europe in spite of the fact that a number of European countries have made a token adoption of such policies. In Australia, a form of comparable worth was adopted in 1972 when their national wage awards made by their wage tribunals (which set wages for the majority of workers) eliminated wage differentials across occupations that were designated as predominantly male and predominantly female. However, this decision, which substantially raised the wages of females, was based on legislative fiat not on the results of job evaluation procedures, and hence is not a comparable worth procedure in the conventional sense.

Equal Value Procedures

Equal value policies generally require an equality of pay between jobs of equal value where value is determined by a job evaluation scheme. Such schemes generally involve comparisons between jobs that are designated as predominantly male and predominantly female, where gender predominance is designated, for example, as involving seventy percent or more of either sex. The next step involves the determination of the *factors* such as skill, effort, responsibility, and working conditions that are believed to be the important determinants of the value or worth of a job. For the various jobs, job evaluators then assign point scores for each of these factors. The points are then summed to get a total point score for each job (which implies equal weights for a point score for each of the factors) or different weights could be assigned to the scores of each factor on an *a priori* basis. Predominantly female jobs are then compared to predominantly male jobs of the same total point score, and the wages adjusted to those of the predominantly male jobs. In situations where this equal value approach has been applied, wages in female-dominated jobs typically have been only 80 to 90 percent of wages in male-dominated jobs of the same job evaluation point scores. The jobs can be in different occupations as long as they have the same job evaluation point scores. One case in the federal jurisdiction, for example, involved a comparison of predominantly female librarians with predominantly male historical researchers.

Economic versus Administrative Concepts of Value

This procedure highlights the fact that equal pay for work of equal value involves an *administrative* concept of value, where value is determined by the *average* value of the *inputs*, such as skill, effort, responsibility, and working conditions, that are involved in a job. This is in contrast to the *economic* concept of the value of the marginal product of labour whereby value is determined by the value of the *output* produced by an *additional* unit of labour. The administrative concept of value is akin to the notion of value-in-use (i.e., the average value of inputs) while the economic concept involves value-in-exchange (i.e., marginal contribution to the value of output). According to the economic concept, inputs that are in abundance in supply may have little value-in-exchange (and hence command a low market wage) even though they may have a high value-in-use because they involve substantial average inputs of skill, effort, responsibility and working conditions. This is analogous to the diamond-water paradox whereby diamonds have a high value-in-exchange (because of their scarcity) but water has a low value-in-exchange (because of its abundance) in spite of its high value-in-use.

The equal value concept in fact explicitly rejects the notion that market forces should be the prime determinant of the value and hence pay for jobs. This rejection is based on the belief that market forces reflect discrimination. Even if market forces enable employers to hire workers in predominantly female jobs at rates of pay that are lower than those paid to workers in predominantly male jobs, proponents of comparable worth would argue that such an outcome is socially unacceptable because it reflects discriminatory segregation and the systematic undervaluation of female-dominated jobs. The belief is that females should not have to leave female-dominated jobs to get the same pay as in male-dominated jobs that require the same inputs of skill, effort, responsibility, and working conditions.

In essence, the primacy of market forces of supply and demand is rejected in that the value and hence remuneration of a job is not deemed to be low simply because there is an abundance of labour willing to do the work, or because there is little demand for that type of labour. This is in contrast to the economic emphasis on the market forces of supply and demand to determine the value and hence remuneration of a job.

While there is a sharp contrast between the economic and comparable worth concepts of value, the two concepts do not have to be diametrically opposed to each other. Skill, effort, and responsibility are scarce resources and hence will receive a market premium, just as they are assigned point scores by job evaluators. Similarly, compensating wage premiums are paid in the market for undesirable working conditions, just as they can be assigned point scores by job evaluators. In fact, it is possible to use the premiums that the market yields for the various factors of skill, effort, responsibility, and working conditions, based only on the male-dominated jobs, and then to apply those premiums to weigh the scores of the female-dominated jobs to arrive at the value of those jobs had they been paid the same market premium as the male-dominated jobs. This procedure is termed a "policy capturing approach" in that it is a policy that simply captures the pricing mechanism that is used for the male-dominated jobs and extends it to the female-dominated jobs. Comparable worth approaches can also pay attention to market forces by allowing exceptions for occupations that are in scarce supply.

Clearly market forces do not have to be ignored by the principle of comparable worth, but it is equally clear that the comparable worth concept of value is different from the economic concept of value. The former is an administrative concept of value based upon job evaluation procedures; the latter is based upon market forces of supply and demand.

Rationale for Equal Value Initiatives

Equal value initiatives have been rationalized on the grounds of being able to deal with *both* wage discrimination and occupational segregation — the latter on the grounds that comparisons can be made across different occupations as long as they are of the same value as determined by job evaluation procedures. This is important because occupational segregation generally is believed to be a more important contributor to the overall earnings gap than is wage discrimination, and conventional equal pay can only deal with the latter. Equal value policies have also been rationalized on the grounds of securing redress for those women who do not want to leave predominantly female jobs to get the same pay as predominantly male jobs of the same value as determined by job evaluation procedures.

Scope of Equal Value Initiatives

The scope of equal value policies is potentially large because it enables comparisons across occupations, unlike conventional equal pay policies which enable comparisons only within the same occupations. However, the scope of equal value policies will be limited in a complaints-based system by the fact that it is difficult for individuals or even groups to lodge a complaint under such a complicated procedure. For individuals, the fear of reprisals may also deter complaints. For this reason, supporters of comparable worth have advocated a "proactive system-wide" procedure whereby employers would be required to have a bona fide job evaluation system in place to help achieve pay equity. Even if such a system were in place, the scope of comparable worth would be limited by the fact that comparisons can be made only within the same establishment. This means that comparable worth could not reduce that portion of the overall earnings gap that reflects the segregation of females into low-wage establishments or industries. Based upon U.S. data, for example, Johnson and Solon (1986) indicate that these restrictions mean that even if comparable worth completely eliminated the relationship between wages and the sex composition of an occupation, it would reduce the average male-female earnings gap by only a small amount.

Design Features of Comparable Worth

If comparable worth becomes more prominent as a policy initiative, there are a large number of program design features that will have to be worked out to facilitate the practical implementation of the policy. Such design features include: the definition of gender predominance for comparing male-dominated with female-dominated jobs; the job evaluation procedure for establishing the value of a job; the procedure for relating the job evaluation point scores to the pay of jobs; the procedure for adjusting pay in undervalued jobs and in overvalued jobs; the definition of establishment and of pay itself; the appropriate exemptions if any; and the optimal enforcement procedure including whether a complaints-based or more proactive, system-wide procedure should be followed. These and other design features can have a substantial impact on the scope of equal value initiatives and hence on their positive and negative consequences.

Equal Employment Opportunity Legislation

In contrast to equal pay and equal value policies which deal with pay discrimination, equal employment opportunity legislation — also termed fair employment practices legislation — is designed to prevent discrimination in recruiting, hiring, promotion, and dismissals. The history, coverage, extent, enforcement, and legal issues involved with equal employment laws in Canada are discussed in Cook and Eberts (1976) and Abella (1984).

In general, provincial equal employment opportunity legislation is part of the Human Rights Code of each province. Usually, complaints concerning discrimination in employment are made by the individual party to the Human Rights Commission. An officer of the Commission tries to reach a settlement by conciliation. If this is unsuccessful, a board of inquiry investigates and makes a final decision. Most provinces have appeal procedures to regular courts. Although the Commissions generally act only on complaints, on a more informal basis they can and do persuade employers to increase their quotas of female employees.

In spite of the fact that this procedure is time-consuming and cumbersome, equal employment opportunity legislation does have the virtue of increasing the demand for female labour at the recruiting, hiring and promotion stages. This in turn should increase female wages *and* employment. Unlike equal pay laws which increase female wages at the expense of their employment, equal employment opportunity legislation would work through the market to increase both the wages and employment of females. However, equal employment opportunity legislation is likely to be more beneficial to new recruits or women seeking to change their jobs; it may do little to help incumbent females in their existing jobs.

Some have argued that equal pay and equal employment legislation are complementary, in that one is useless without the other. The argument is that without equal employment opportunity legislation, equal pay would result in employers refusing to recruit, hire and promote females. Similarly, without equal pay, equal employment opportunity legislation would result in employers hiring females but paying them lower wages than equally productive males. However, this ignores the economic argument that the increased demand for females resulting from equal employment opportunity legislation would work through the market to increase female wages. Equal pay may be a natural by-product of equal employment opportunities.

Affirmative Action

While equal employment opportunity legislation is designed to remove discriminatory barriers so as to ensure an equality of *opportunity*, affirmative action is a more intrusive form of intervention, focusing on *results* and not just opportunities. The rationale is that an equality of opportunity is insufficient to compensate for the legacy of a cumulative history of discrimination as well as systemic discrimination that may be the unintended by-product of certain personnel policies. True equality may require some preferential treatment for women, at least on a temporary basis, to ensure an equality of starting points. The hope is that temporary affirmative action programs may break the circle of entrapment whereby women are relegated to low-wage dead-end jobs, which in turn foster labour market behaviour that keeps them in such jobs.

Affirmative action programs involve a number of implementation procedures. First, a data base is established indicating the occupational composition, pay and sex composition of the work-force in the establishment and in the relevant surrounding labour market. Second, internal targets or quotas on the appropriate sex composition of the work-force are set for the establishment, based upon the relevant surrounding labour market. Third, a plan and timetable is established for achieving these targets.

In Canada, affirmative action has largely been on a voluntary basis, encouraged by some governments for their own public employees and encouraged in the private sector through government affirmative action offices. In 1986, the federal government proclaimed Bill C-62, the Employment Equity Act, requiring affirmative action in the federal jurisdiction, which covers about 10 percent of the Canadian work-force. In the United States, in contrast, affirmative action has been actively instituted, as part of the federal Executive Order 11246 of 1965 and its amendments, for employers with federal government contracts (hence, the phrase "federal contract compliance program"). Such affirmative action does not appear to be a policy followed by other countries internationally.

Policies to Facilitate Female Employment

In addition to the various direct policies such as equal pay and equal employment opportunities legislation, and affirmative action, there are a variety of policies that can indirectly affect the employment opportunities and wages of women. These could be labelled *facilitating* policies, in that they are generally designed to expand the range of choices open to women and hence to facilitate their participation in labour market activities in a non-discriminatory fashion.

Currently, women tend to have the primary responsibility for household tasks, especially the bearing and raising of children. This may reflect historical tradition, comparative advantage (which itself may be historically determined), or discrimination within the household. Whatever the origin, this responsibility can create tensions over the equitable division of labour within the household when both parties engage in labour market work.

To minimize some of this tension, and to expand the employment opportunities available to women, facilitating policies have been suggested. Improved availability of day care, flexible working hours, part-time jobs, and childbirth leaves are examples of such facilitating policies. In the interests of equality they would apply to males as well as females, so as to maximize the opportunities of households to allocate their labour amongst various market and non-market alternatives.

Certainly such policies are not without their costs, which could be substantial in some areas such as subsidized day care. Consequently there is legitimate debate over the efficiency of such policies. What is less contentious, from the perspective of economics at least, is that at a minimum such facilitating policies be allowed to emerge in response to market demands. This may require, for example, that day-care expenses be tax deductible or that quality regulations do not restrict excessively the availability of day care. Or it may require that government policies do not discourage flexible working arrangements by increasing quasi-fixed costs of employment which may encourage employers to utilize only a core of male workers.

To a large extent these institutional features — flexible hours, part-time jobs, child-care leaves and day care arrangements — are emerging as endogenous responses to the increased labour market role of women. Their emergence, however, may be subject to impediments reflecting discrimination, government policies designed to achieve other objectives, or simply the slow operation of market forces subject to inertia and fixed costs.

Considerable debate emerges over the appropriate role of public policy in this area. Some would argue that such facilitating policies should be discouraged in order to preserve the traditional sex division of labour. Others argue that public policies should be neutral by simply removing impediments to the emergence of these facilitating policies. Others argue for a more active role — subsidized day care, extended child-care leave — to compensate for discrimination elsewhere in the system, including past discrimination.

The role of protectionist labour standards policies takes on an interesting light in the context of policies designed to facilitate the labour market work of women. Such protectionist policies could include special provisions requiring employers to provide free transportation for women on night shifts, or prohibiting the employment of women in some specific occupations, or restrictions on the hours of work for females. Some may argue that such protective devices would enable women to take on some jobs they would otherwise be reluctant to do. Most would argue that such protective devices simply protect male jobs by reducing the employment opportunities of females and by perpetuating the stereotype of women as in need of outside protection. If such protection is desirable, it should be provided to all workers, male and female, through labour standards laws or collective agreements.

This suggests another institutional arrangement for facilitating the labour market work of females — unionization. The rationale for increasing the role of women in unions is really two-fold. The first is to have women share in the wage and job security gains that unions obtain for their members. In order to obtain these gains, it is not only necessary for women to unionize; they must aspire to powerful positions within the union or at least ensure that their minority rights are guaranteed. The second rationale for increasing the role of women in unions is to ensure effective monitoring of equal pay, equal employment opportunities, and affirmative action. As Brady (1947, p. 57) earlier stated:

> Through increasing participation of women in unions, the women workers, acting in their own interest, can narrow the difference between women's rates and men's rates. The continued study of the character of the work process and of comparative occupational wage rates will define the meaning of "equivalence," "comparability" and "equity" so that the existence of discrimination is proved and its magnitude measured.

Females may be more willing and able to press for equal pay and employment opportunities through the union both because the apparatus is available (shop steward, grievance procedure) and because reprisal by the company is less likely when the worker is protected by a union.

Alter Preferences and Attitudes

Economics traditionally regards tastes and preferences as exogenously given, and then inquires into what happens to the demand for something when such factors as relative prices and income change. In the area of sex discrimination, this is a legitimate inquiry. Equal pay and equal employment opportunity legislation can be viewed as policies designed to raise the "price" of discrimination to those who discriminate. The price in this case is the legal costs which include court costs and the expected fine. The contention is that raising the price of discrimination will reduce the quantity demanded.

In the area of discrimination, however, some have suggested the utilization of public policies designed to alter the basic tastes and preferences that give rise to discrimination, since tastes and preferences of employers, co-workers and customers are an important source of discrimination. The dominant group, for example, may find it important to foster uniform preferences for discrimination and to punish non-discriminators. Preferences are also shaped by the media, the education system, and the socio-economic system in general. Preferences are not immutable over time, nor are they likely to be the same for all firms, employees or customers. For this reason, many anti-discrimination policies are designed to alter basic tastes, preferences and attitudes.

In practice, of course, changing basic tastes and attitudes is a difficult task. Specific policies have been instituted and include: removal of sex stereotyping in schoolbooks, guidance programs and television; provision of information on the labour market performance and attachment of females; and politicization of women to raise their own group awareness. The process will be slow, but many argue that the results at least will be long lasting.

IMPACT OF POLICY INITIATIVES

While there is considerable empirical evidence on the magnitude of the male-female wage differential and its determinants, there is much less evidence on the impact of various policy initiatives. The Canadian evidence is largely restricted to conventional equal pay policies in Ontario, where econometric analysis was unable to discern any impact of such initiatives (Gunderson 1975, 1976a, 1985b).

In the United States, a number of econometric studies have analysed the impact of Title VII (the Equal Employment Opportunity Title) of the Civil Rights Act of 1964, which forbids both wage and employment discrimination. The empirical results are somewhat mixed for most minority groups including females (Gunderson 1985a p. 252). There is more agreement on the effect of affirmative action under the federal contract compliance of Executive Order 11246 (also summarized in Gunderson 1985a p. 254). That legislation did benefit the minority groups to which it was targeted — mainly black males in the earlier years of the program. Much of that benefit, however, came at the expense of losses to other minority groups — mainly white females — to which the program was not targeted in the earlier years. However, when the affirmative action programs began to be more targeted towards females, they too benefited from them. The legislative initiatives also tended to be more effective in an expanding growing economy than in a recession (Beller 1982) and when it was aggressively enforced (Beller 1982; Leonard 1984b).

Ehrenberg and Smith (1987a, 1987b) simulate the potential adverse employment that would result from the widespread application of comparable worth to the public sector in the United States. Based upon the magnitude of the wage adjustments that occurred in a number of comparable worth cases in the United States, they assume that comparable worth would lead to a 20 percent increase in the wages of females in the state and local public sector. Based upon existing estimates of the elasticity of demand for public sector labour, this in turn would yield an employment reduction of only 2 to 3 percent. These adverse employment effects are small because of the existing lack of substitutability between males and females in the public sector. Whether this would be true in the long run when there is sufficient time to substitute away from female-intensive activities remains an unanswered question.

Gregory and Duncan (1981) also estimate the employment effect that resulted from the Australian pay awards emanating from their wage tribunals which set wages for the majority of the work-force. Between 1972 and 1978 those awards led to an increase in the ratio of female to male wages from 0.774 to 0.933. This in turn led to a statistically significant but quantitatively small reduction in the growth of female employment relative to male employment. That is, female employment growth averaged 3.0 percent per year as opposed to the 4.5 percent that would have occurred without the substantial wage increase. Most of the reduced growth occurred in the manufacturing and service sector, not in the public sector where employment growth was relatively insensitive to the wage increases.

Based on U.S. data, Johnson and Solon (1986) estimate the potential effect, on the overall male-female earnings gap, of a comprehensive comparable worth policy that would eliminate the relationship between wages and the sex composition of an occupation. They find that such a policy would reduce the average earnings gap of 0.41 by an amount ranging from 0.03 to 0.08 assuming full coverage, and by less than half of that amount based upon realistic coverage. This small effect occurs because most of the overall earnings gap reflects the segregation of females into low-wage firms and industries, and comparable worth cannot involve comparison across different firms or industries.

This relatively small potential effect of a comprehensive comparable worth policy does not negate the fact that, where comparable worth has been applied, it has resulted in substantial wage adjustments. In such cases in both Canada and the United States, the pay in predominantly female jobs has been about 80 to 90 percent of the pay in predominantly male jobs of the same job evaluation point score, and the comparable worth adjustments have been in the magnitude of two to three thousand dollars for persons in the predominantly female jobs (Gunderson 1984).

Similarly, Sorenson (1986) uses the information from four comparable worth cases in the United States to estimate the hypothetical wage that female-dominated ocupations would have received if they received the same premium as the male-dominated occupations received for their job evaluation point scores. Her results indicate that such an adjustment would have raised the average ratio of female to male earnings from 0.76 to 0.87, thereby closing almost half of the overall gap, at an average cost of about eight percent of payroll. While comparable worth can eliminate a substantial portion of the earnings gap where it is applied, its overall impact will be limited by the fact that it cannot deal with the substantial portion of the gap that arises because females are segregated into low-wage firms and industries, and such segregation is immune to comparable worth or any form of equal pay policy.

Although it is hazardous to draw a conclusion about the impact of the various policy initiatives from such a limited number of studies, some tentative generalizations can be made. The effect of equal pay and equal employment opportunity policies tends to be inconclusive, although there is some evidence that affirmative action policies in the United States have been effective for the target groups to which they have seriously been applied. Comparable worth policies have reduced the earnings gap and resulted in considerable-sized awards in the few situations where they have been applied, albeit on a comprehensive basis their scope will be limited by an inability to deal with the considerable portion of the wage gap that reflects the segregation of females into low-wage establishments and industries. The adverse employment effects associated with substantial wage increases emanating from comparable worth adjustments have been small, probably in part because of small adjustments in the public sector.

It should be kept in mind, however, that estimating the impact of such policy initiatives is extremely difficult, especially given the other dramatic changes that are occurring simultaneously in the female labour market. This is especially the case since the policy initiatives themselves may be a function of the policy problem they are designed to eliminate, and the initiatives may be related to other unobservable factors that are the true cause of the changes in labour market behaviour. Such problems are not unique to these policy initiatives; they apply to estimating the impact of almost any social program.

QUESTIONS

1. "If females are paid a wage equal to their marginal productivity, then sex discrimination in the labour market does not exist." Discuss.
2. "Male-female wage differentials for equally productive workers will not persist in the long run because the forces of competition would remove these differentials." Discuss.
3. If the proportionate male-female wage differential, $(W_m - W_f)/W_f$, is .25, what is the ratio of female to male wages, W_f/W_m?
4. What impact would you expect unions to have on male-female wage differentials and why?
5. How would we expect male-female wage differentials to change over time in response to both short-run cyclical and long-run trend forces?
6. If we adjusted the gross male-female wage differential for all of the productivity-related factors that influence wages (e.g. education, experience, absenteeism, turnover, etc.) and found that the wage gap would be zero if males and females had the same productivity-related characteristics, would this indicate the absence of sex discrimination?
7. What impact would equal pay laws have on the wages and employment of female workers? What impact would equal employment opportunity laws (fair employment laws) have on the wages and employment of female workers?
8. Would you expect sex discrimination to be more prevalent in capitalist or socialist-communist economies and why?
9. For policy purposes does it matter if the reason for discrimination is prejudice, erroneous information, or job security? Does it matter if the main source of discrimination is employers, co-workers, or customers?
10. Does the occupational distribution of women yield any insight into the possible employment effect of policies to raise women's wages via equal pay, minimum wages, or unions? More specifically, are women employed in occupations where the demand for female labour is elastic or inelastic? Are women employed in monopsonistic labour markets?
11. Based on the utility maximization theory given in footnote 1, show that male wages will exceed their marginal revenue product when nepotism exists whereby, other things being equal, the firm's utility is increased when it employs more males.
12. How would one explain the large variation in the male-female earnings gap found in the various Canadian empirical studies? That is, why do some studies find a much larger differential than others?
13. Based on the decomposition technique discussed in footnote 2, indicate how an alternative decomposition could be utilized by subtracting $\Sigma b_m \overline{X}_f$ rather than $\Sigma b_f \overline{X}_m$ from the right-hand side. Which decomposition is correct?
14. Roberta Robb (1978) estimated separate earnings equations for males as well as single females thirty years of age and over and finds wage discrimination to be considerably less than is the case when males are compared to all females. Why might one expect this to be the case?

15. Holmes (1976) finds a substantially higher ratio of female to male earnings in Canada at higher levels of education than at lower levels. Why might this be the case?

16. Would you expect discrimination to be greater in the public sector or in the private sector and why?

17. Based upon your knowledge of the various components of the overall male-female wage, discuss the potential scope of the various possible policy initiatives.

18. Discuss the factors influencing the long-run trend and short-run cyclical variation in the male-female wage gap. What would you expect to happen to the gap in the future and why?

19. Based upon your knowledge of equal value policies, distinguish between the following concepts: pay equity and comparable worth; *a priori* weighting versus a policy capturing approach; complaints-based versus a system-wide, proactive approach.

20. Assume you are a manager of a firm that will be establishing a comparable worth plan and an affirmative action program. What steps would you be taking for each? What steps might you take if you were trying to evade such initiatives and what does this imply about compliance?

21. In designing a viable equal value policy, what steps might you take to minimize any inherent conflict between administrative concepts of value (as implied by job evaluation procedures) and economic concepts of value (as implied by market-determined wages)?

22. Assume that you have used a job evaluation procedure to establish the point scores for a number of male-dominated jobs and a number of female-dominated jobs in your organization. Indicate how you would estimate a pay line between point scores and pay for each of the predominantly male and predominantly female jobs. What is the appropriate functional form for such pay lines? Should they each have an intercept? If the pay in the undervalued female-dominated jobs is to be adjusted should the female pay line be raised to the male pay line (line-to-line adjustment) or should the pay in each female job be raised to the male pay line (point-to-line adjustment) or to some other value such as an average line or the pay of the closest male job? Should interpolation of the pay lines be allowed, within the sample range of the data? Should extrapolation of the pay lines be allowed outside of the sample range of the data?

REFERENCES AND FURTHER READINGS

[References here refer mainly to sex discrimination and theoretical issues pertaining to discrimination. Additional references, especially to race discrimination, are contained in Cain (1986).]

Aaron, H. and C. Lousy. *The Comparable Worth Controversy.* Washington: Brookings Institution, 1986.

Abella, R., (Commissioner). *Report of the Commission on Equality in Employment.* Ottawa: Supply and Services, 1984.

Abowd, J. and M. Killingsworth. Sex discrimination, atrophy, and the male-female wage differential. *IR* 22 (Fall 1983) 387-402.

Agarwal, N. Male-female pay inequity and public policy in Canada and the U.S. *RI/IR* 37 (No. 4, 1982) 780-802.

Agarwal, N. and Harish Jain. Pay discrimination against women in Canada. *ILR* 117 (March-April 1978) 169-178.

Aigner, D. and G. Cain. Statistical theories of discrimination in labour markets. *ILRR* 30 (January 1972) 175-189.

Akerlof, G. Discriminatory, status-based wages among tradition-oriented stochastically trading coconut producers. *JPE* 93 (April 1985) 265-276.

Albelda, R. Occupational segregation by race and gender, 1958-1981. *ILRR* 39 (April 1986) 404-411.

Aldrich, M. and R. Buchele. *The Economics of Comparable Worth*. Cambridge: Ballinger Publishing Company. 1986.

Allison, E. Sex linked earnings differentials in the beauty industry. *JHR* 11 (Summer 1976) 383-390.

Allison, E. Male-female professionals: a model of career choice. *IR* 17 (October 1978) 333-337.

Antos, J. and S. Rosen. Discrimination in the market for public school teachers. *Journal of Econometrics* 3 (January 1975) 123-150.

Arrow, K. Models of job discrimination. *Racial Discrimination in Economic Life*, A. Pascal (ed.). Lexington, Mass.: Lexington Books, 1972.

Arrow, K. Simple mathematical models of race in the labor market. *Racial Discrimination in Economic Life*, A. Pascal (ed.). Lexington, Mass.: Lexington Books, 1972.

Arrow, K. The theory of discrimination. *Discrimination in the Labour Market*, O. Ashenfelter and A. Rees (eds.). Princeton, N.J.: Princeton University Press, 1973.

Ashenfelter, O. Changes in labor market discrimination over time. *JHR* 5 (Fall 1970) 403-430. Comment by H. Terrill 6 (Summer 1971) 384-390.

Ashenfelter, O. and J. Heckman. Measuring the effect of an antidiscrimination program. *Evaluating the Labor-Market Effects of Social Programs*, O. Ashenfelter and J. Blum (eds.). Princeton, N.J.: Princeton University Press, 1976.

Becker, G. *The Economics of Discrimination*. Chicago: University of Chicago Press, 1971.

Beller, A. The economics of enforcement of an antidiscrimination law: Title VII of the Civil Rights Act of 1964. *Journal of Law and Economics* 21 (October 1978) 359-380.

Beller, A. The effect of economic conditions on the success of equal employment opportunity laws. *R.E. Stats.* 62 (August 1980) 379-387.

Beller, A. The impact of equal opportunity policy on sex differentials in earnings and occupations. *AER* 72 (May 1982) 171-175.

Beller, A. Occupational segregation by sex: determinants and changes. *JHR* 17 (Spring 1982) 371-392. Also, comments and reply 20 (Summer 1985) 437-444.

Beller, A. Changes in the sex composition of U.S. occupations, 1960-1981. *JHR* 20 (Spring 1985) 235-250.

Bergmann, B. The effect on white incomes of discrimination in employment. *JPE* 79 (March/April 1971) 294-313.

Blinder, A. Wage discrimination: reduced form and structural estimates. *JHR* 8 (Fall 1973) 436-455.

Block, W. and M. Worker (eds.). *Discrimination, Affirmative Action and Equal Opportunity*. Vancouver: Fraser Institute, 1982.

Bloom, D. and M. Killingsworth. Pay discrimination research and litigation: the use of regression. *IR* 21 (Fall 1982) 318-339.

Borjas, G. Discrimination in HEW. *Journal of Law and Economics* 21 (April 1978) 97-110.

Borjas, G. Biased screening and discrimination in the labor market. *AER* 68 (December 1978) 918-922.

Borjas, G. The measurement of race and gender wage differentials: evidence from the federal sector. *ILRR* 37 (October 1983) 79-91.

Boulet, J.A., and L. Lavallée. *The Changing Economic Status of Women*. Ottawa: Economic Council of Canada, 1984.

Brady, D. Equal pay for women workers. *Annals of the American Academy of Political and Social Science* (May 1947) 53-60.

Brown, R., M. Moon and B. Zoloth. Occupational attainment and segregation by sex. *ILRR* 33 (July 1980) 506-517.

Brown, R., M. Moon and B. Zoloth. Incorporating occupational attainment in studies of male-female earnings differentials. *JHR* 15 (Winter 1980) 3-28.

Buchele, R. and M. Aldrich. How much difference would comparable worth make? *IR* 24 (Spring 1985) 222-233.

Butler, R. Estimating wage discrimination in the labour market. *JHR* 17 (Fall 1982) 606-621.

Butler, R. Direct estimates of the demand for race and sex discrimination. *SEJ* 49 (April 1983) 975-990.

Cain, G. The economic analysis of labour market discrimination: a survey. *Handbook of Labour Economics*, Vol. 1. O. Ashenfelter and R. Layard (eds.). New York: Elsevier, 1986.

Cardwell, L. and M. Rosenzweig. Economic mobility, monopsonistic discrimination and sex differences in wages. *SEJ* 46 (April 1980) 1102-1117.

Carliner, G. Wage differences by language group and the market for language skills in Canada. *JHR* 16 (Summer 1981) 416-426.

Chiplin, B. An alternative approach to the measurement of sex discrimination: an illustration from university entrance. *EJ* 91 (December 1981) 988-997.

Chiplin, B. and P. Sloan. Economic consequences of the Equal Pay Act. *IRJ* 1 (December 1970).

Chiplin, B. and P. Sloan. Sexual discrimination in the labour market. *BJIR* 12 (November 1974) 371-402.

Chiplin, B. and P. Sloan. Equal employment opportunities for women. *IRJ* 6 (Autumn 1975) 20-28.

Chiplin, B. and P. Sloan. *Sex Discrimination in the Labour Market*. London: Macmillan, 1976.

Chiplin, B. and P. Sloan. Male-female earnings differences: a further analysis. *BJIR* 14 (March 1976) 77-81.

Chiplin, B. and P. Sloan. Personal characteristics and sex differentials in professional employment. *EJ* 86 (December 1976) 729-745.

Cook, A. Equal pay: where is it? *IR* 14 (May 1975) 158-176.

Cook, G. and M. Eberts. Policies affecting work. *Opportunity for Choice: A Goal for Women in Canada*. Ottawa: Statistics Canada, 1976, 143-202.

Corcoran, M. and G. Duncan. Work history, labour force attachment, and earnings differences between races and sexes. *JHR* 14 (Winter 1979) 3-20.

Cox, D. Panel estimates of the effects of career interruptions on the earnings of women. *EI* 22 (July 1984) 386-403.

Cussel, F., S. Director and S. Doctors. Discrimination within internal labour markets. *IR* 14 (October 1975) 337-344.

Cymrot, D. Does competition lessen discrimination? Some evidence. *JHR* 20 (Fall 1985) 605-611.

Daymont, T. and P. Andrisani. Job preferences, college major and the gender gap in earnings. *JHR* 19 (Summer 1984) 408-428.

Edgeworth, F. Equal pay to men and women for equal work. *EJ* 32 (December 1922) 431-457.

Ehrenberg, R. and R. Smith. Comparable worth wage adjustments and female employment in the state and local sector. *JOLE* 5 (January 1987a) 43-62.

Ehrenberg, R. and R. Smith. Comparable worth in the public sector. In *Public Sector Compensation*. Edited by D. Wise. Chicago: University of Chicago Press, 1987b.

Elberts, R. and J. Stone. Male-female differences in promotions: EEO in public education. *JHR* 20 (Fall 1985) 504-521.

England, P. The failure of human capital theory to explain occupational sex segregation. *JHR* 17 (Summer 1982) 358-370. Also, comments and reply 20 (Summer 1985) 437-444.

Fawcett, M. Equal pay for equal work. *EJ* 28 (March 1918) 1-6.

Ferber, M. and H. Lowry. The sex differential in earnings. *ILRR* 29 (April 1976) 377-387. Also comment by D. Snyder and P. Hudis and reply 32 (April 1979) 378-386.

Ferber, M. and W. McMahon. Women's expected earnings and their investment in higher education. *JHR* 14 (Summer 1979) 405-420.

Ferber, M. and J. Spaeth. Work characteristics and the male-female earnings gap. *AER* 74 (May 1984) 260-264.

Ferber, M. and A. Westmiller. Sex and race differentials in nonacademic wages on a university campus. *JHR* 11 (Summer 1976) 366-373.

Filer, R.K. Sexual differences in earnings: the role of individual personalities and tastes. *JHR* 18 (Winter 1983) 82-99.

Filer, R. Male-female wage differences: the importance of compensating differentials. *ILRR* 38 (April 1985) 426-437.

Filer, R. The role of personality and tastes in determining occupational structure. *ILRR* 39 (April 1986) 412-424.

Flanders, D. and P. Anderson. Sex discrimination in employment: theory and practice. *ILRR* 26 (April 1973) 938-955.

Frank, R. Family location constraints and the geographic distribution of female professionals. *JPE* 86 (February 1978) 117-130.

Freeman, R. Changes in the labor market for Black Americans, 1948-72. *BPEA* (No. 1, 1973) 67-132.

Freeman, R. Decline of labor market discrimination and economic analysis. *AER* 63 (May 1973) 280-287.

Freeman, R. Labor market discrimination: analysis, findings and problems. *Frontiers of Quantitative Economics*, M. Intriligator and D. Kendrick (eds.). Amsterdam: North Holland, 1974, 501-55.

Fuchs, V. Differences in hourly earnings between men and women. *MLR* 94 (May 1971) 9-15.

Fujii, E. and J. Trapani. On estimating the relationship between discrimination and market structure. *SEJ* 44 (January 1978) 556-567.

Gaumer, G. Sex discrimination and job tenure. *IR* 14 (February 1975) 121-129.

Goldberg, M. Discrimination, nepotism, and long-run wage differentials. *QJE* 79 (May 1982) 307-320.

Goldberger, A. Reverse regression and salary discrimination. *JHR* 19 (Summer 1984) 293-318.

Goldfarb, R. and J. Hosek. Explaining male-female differentials for the same job. *JHR* 11 (Winter 1976) 98-108.

Goldin, C. Monitoring costs and occupational segregation by sex: a historical analysis. *JOLE* 4 (January 1986) 1-27.

Gordon, N. and T. Morton. A low mobility model of wage discrimination — with special reference to sex differentials. *Journal of Economic Theory* 7 (March 1974) 241-253.

Gordon, N., T. Morton and I. Brader. Faculty salaries: is there discrimination by sex, race, and discipline? *AER* 64 (June 1974) 419-427.

Green, C. and M. Ferber. Employment discrimination: an empirical test of forward versus reverse regression. *JHR* 19 (Fall 1984) 557-569.

Greenhalgh, C. Male-female wage differentials in Great Britain: is marriage an equal opportunity? *EJ* 90 (December 1980) 751-755.

Gregory, R. and R. Duncan. Segmented labour market theories and the Australian experience of equal pay for women. *Journal of Post Keynesian Economics* 2 (Spring 1981) 403-428.

Grenier, G. The effects of language characteristics on the wages of Hispanic-American males. *JHR* 19 (Winter 1984) 35-52.

Gunderson, M. Male female wage differentials and the impact of equal pay legislation. *R.E.Stats.* 57 (November 1975) 426-470.

Gunderson, M. Time pattern of male-female wage differentials. *RI/IR* 31 (No. 1, 1976a) 57-71.

Gunderson, M. Work patterns. *Opportunity for Choice: A Goal for Women in Canada*, G. Cook (ed.). Ottawa: Statistics Canada, 1976b, 93-142.

Gunderson, M. The influence of the status and sex composition of occupations on the male-female earnings gap. *ILRR* 31 (January 1978) 217-226.

Gunderson, M. Decomposition of male-female earnings differential: Canada 1970. *CJE* 12 (August 1979) 479-484.

Gunderson, M. *Costing Equal Value Legislation in Ontario*. Toronto: Ontario Ministry of Labour, 1984.

Gunderson, M. Discrimination, equal pay and equal opportunities in the labour market. In *Working and Pay: The Canadian Labour Market*. Edited by C. Riddell. Toronto: University of Toronto Press for the Mcdonald Commission, 1985a.

Gunderson, M. Spline function estimates of the impact of equal pay legislation: the Ontario experience. *RI/IR* 40 (No. 4, 1985b) 775-791.

Gwartney, J. and C. Hawarth. Employer costs and discrimination: the case of baseball. *JPE* 82 (July/August 1974) 873-881.

Gwartney, J. and R. Stroup. Measurement of employer discrimination according to sex. *SEJ* 39 (August 1973) 575-587.

Haessel, W. and J. Palmer. Market power and employment discrimination. *JHR* 13 (Fall 1978) 545-560.

Hartmann, H.I. (ed.). *Comparable Worth: New Directions for Research*. Washington: National Academy Press, 1985.

Hashimoto, M. and L. Kochin. A bias in the statistical estimation of the effects of discrimination. *EI* 18 (July 1980) 478-486.

Hirsch, J. and J. Stone. "New and improved" estimates of qualification discrimination. *SEJ* 52 (October 1985) 484-491.

Hodson, R. and P. England. Industrial structure and sex differences in earnings. *IR* 25 (Winter 1986) 16-32.

Hoffman, E. Faculty salaries: is there discrimination by sex, race, and discipline? *AER* 66 (March 1976) 196-198.

Holmes, R. Male-female earnings differentials in Canada. *JHR* 11 (Winter 1976) 109-112.

Industrial and Labor Relations Review. Symposium on Evaluating the Impact of Affirmative Action. 29 (July 1976) 485-584.

Johnson, G. and F. Stafford. The earnings and promotion of women faculty. *AER* 69 (December 1974) 888-903.

Johnson, G. and G. Solon. Estimates of the direct effects of comparable worth policy. *AER* 76 (December 1986) 1117-1125.

Jones, F. On decomposing the wage gap: a critical comment on Blinder's method. *JHR* 18 (Winter 1983) 126-130.

Kahne, H. Economic perspectives on the role of women in the American economy. *Journal of Economic Literature* 13 (December 1975) 1249-1292.

Killingsworth, M. Comparable worth in the job market: estimating its effects. *MLR* 108 (July 1985) 39-41.

King, A. Is occupational segregation the cause of the flatter experience-earnings profile of women? *JHR* 12 (Fall 1977) 541-549.

Koch, J. and J. Chiemar. Sex discrimination and affirmative action in faculty salaries. *EI* 14 (March 1976) 16-24.

Landes, E. Sex differences in wages and employment: a test of the specific capital hypothesis. *EI* 15 (October 1977) 523-538.

Lazear, E. The narrowing of Black-White wage differentials is illusory. *AER* 69 (September 1979) 553-564.

Leonard, J. Antidiscrimination or reverse discrimination: the impact of changing demographics, Title VII and affirmative action on productivity. *JHR* 19 (Spring 1984a) 145-174.

Leonard, J. Employment and occupational advance under affirmative action. *R.E. Stats.* 66 (August 1984b) 377-385.

Leonard, J. Affirmative action as earnings redistribution: the targeting of compliance reviews. *JOLE* 3 (July 1985) 363-384.

Leonard, J. What promises are worth: the impact of affirmative action goals. *JHR* 20 (Winter 1985) 3-20.

Livernash, E.R. (ed.). *Comparable Worth: Issues and Alternatives.* Washington, D.C.: Equal Employment Opportunity Advisory Panel, 1980.

Lloyd, C. (ed.). *Sex, Discrimination, and the Division of Labor.* New York: Columbia University Press, 1975.

Lloyd, C., E. Andrews and C. Gilroy (eds.). *Women in the Labor Market.* New York: Columbia University Press, 1979.

Lloyd, C. and B. Neimi. *The Economics of Sex Differentials.* New York: Columbia University Press, 1979.

Long, J. Employment discrimination in the federal sector. *JHR* 11 (Winter 1976) 86-97.

Long, J. Public-private sectoral differences in employment discrimination. *SEJ* 42 (July 1975) 89-96.

Lundberg, S. and R. Startz. Private discrimination and social intervention in competitive labor markets. *AER* 73 (June 1983) 340-347.

Madden, J. Economic rationale for sex differences in education. *SEJ* 44 (April 1978) 778-797.

Madden, J. *The Economics of Sex Discrimination*. Lexington, Mass.: Lexington Books, 1972.

Malkiel, B. and J. Malkiel. Male-female pay differentials in professional employment. *AER* 63 (September 1973) 693-705.

Mellor, E. Investigating differences in weekly earnings of women and men. *MLR* 107 (June 1984) 17-28.

Milkovitch, G. The male-female earnings gap: a need for reevaluation. *MLR* 104 (April 1981) 42-44.

Mincer, J. Intercountry comparisons of labor force trends and of related developments. *Journal of Labor Economics* 3 (January 1985 Supplement) S1-S32.

Mincer, J. and J. Ofek. Interrupted work careers: depreciation and restoration of human capital. *JHR* 17 (Winter 1982) 3-24.

Mincer, J. and S. Polachek. Family investment in human capital: earnings of women. *JPE* 82 (March/April 1974) S76-S108. Also comment by S. Sandell and D. Shapiro and reply *JHR* 13 (Winter 1978) 103-134.

Mincer, J. and S. Polachek. Women's earnings reexamined. *JHR* 13 (Winter 1978) 118-134.

Moore, W. and R. Newman. An analysis of the quality differentials in male-female academic placements. *EI* 15 (July 1977) 413-433.

Oaxaca, R. Male-female wage differentials in urban labour markets. *IER* 14 (October 1973) 693-709.

Oaxaca, R. Sex discrimination in wages. *Discrimination in Labor Markets*. O. Ashenfelter and A. Rees (eds.). Princeton, N.J.: Princeton University Press, 1974.

Olson, C. and B. Becker. Sex discrimination in the promotion process. *ILRR* 36 (July 1983) 624-641.

Ontario, *Green Paper on Pay Equity*. Toronto: Attorney General's Office, 1985.

Ontario, *Report of the Consultation Panel on Pay Equity*, Attorney General's Office, 1986.

Oster, S. Industry differences in discrimination against women. *QJE* 89 (May 1975) 215-229.

Osterman, P. Sex discrimination in professional employment: a case study. *ILRR* 32 (July 1979) 451-464.

Osterman, P. Affirmative action and opportunity: a study of female quit rates. *R.E. Stats.* 64 (November 1982) 604-613.

Ostry, S. *The Female Worker in Canada*. Ottawa: Queen's Printer, 1968.

Phelps, E. The statistical theory of racism and sexism. *AER* 62 (September 1972) 659-661.

Polachek, S. Sex differences in college major. *ILRR* (July 1974) 498-508.

Polachek, S. Potential biases in measuring male-female discrimination. *JHR* 10 (Spring 1975a) 205-229.

Polachek, S. Differences in expected post-school investment as a determinant of market wage. *IER* 16 (June 1975b) 451-470.

Polachek, S. Occupational self selection in human capital approach to sex differences in occupational structure. *R.E. Stats.* 63 (February 1981) 60-69.

Polachek, S. Occupational segregation: a defence of human capital predictions. *JHR* 20 (Summer 1985) 437-440.

Ragan, J. and S. Smith. The impact of differences in turnover rates on male-female pay differentials. *JHR* 16 (Summer 1981) 343-365.

Rathbone, E. The remuneration of women's services. *EJ* 27 (March 1917) 55-68.

Reich, M. Who benefits from racism? *JHR* 13 (Fall 1978) 524-544.

Reimers, C. Labor market discrimination against Hispanic and Black men. *R.E. Stats.* 65 (November 1983) 570-579.

Remick, H. (ed.). *Comparable Worth and Wage Discrimination*. Philadelphia: Temple University Press, 1984.

Robb, R.E. Earnings differentials between males and females in Ontario. *CJE* 11 (May 1978) 350-359.

Robb, R.E. Equal pay policy. In *Towards Equity*. Ottawa: Supply and Services, 1985.

Roemer, J. Divide and conquer: micro-foundations of a Marxian theory of wage discrimination. *Bell Journal of Economics* 10 (Autumn 1979) 695-706.

Sandell, S. and D. Shapiro. Work expectations, human capital accumulation, and the wages of young women. *JHR* 15 (Summer 1980) 335-353.

Sandell, S., D. Shapiro, J. Mincer and S. Polachek. An exchange: The theory of human capital and the earnings of women. *JHR* 13 (Winter 1978) 103-134.

Sawhill, E. The economics of discrimination against women: some new findings. *JHR* 8 (Summer 1973) 383-395.

Schrank, W. Sex discrimination in faculty salaries. *CJE* 10 (August 1977) 411-433.

Schwab, S. Is statistical discrimination efficient? *AER* 76 (March 1986) 228-234.

Sgro, P. Factor substitution and discrimination in labor markets. *SEJ* 52 (April 1986) 1103-1114.

Shapiro, D. and L. Shaw. Growth in the labor force attachment of married women: accounting for changes in the 1970s. *SEJ* 50 (October 1983) 461-473.

Shapiro, D. and M. Stelcner. Male-female earnings differentials and the role of language in Canada, Ontario and Quebec, 1970. *CJE* 14 (May 1981) 341-348.

Shapiro, D. and M. Stelcner. Earnings differentials among linguistic groups in Quebec. *IR* 21 (Fall 1982) 365-375.

Shapiro, D. and M. Stelcner. Language legislation and male-female earnings differentials in Quebec. *CPP* 8 (Winter 1982) 106-113.

Siebert, W. and P. Sloane. The measurement of sex and marital status discrimination at the workplace. *Economica* 48 (May 1981) 125-142.

Simiral, M. The impact of the public employment program on sex-related wage differentials. *ILRR* (July 1978) 509-519.

Smith, S. Government wage differentials by sex. *JHR* 11 (Spring 1976) 185-199.

Sorensen, E. Implementing comparable worth: a survey of recent job evaluation studies. *AER Proceedings* 76 (May 1986) 364-367.

Staines, G., R. Quinn, and L. Shepherd. Trends in occupational sex discrimination: 1969-73. *IR* 14 (February 1976) 88-98.

Stewart, M. and C. Greenhalgh. Work history patterns and the occupational attainment of women. *EJ* 94 (September 1984) 493-519.

Stiglitz, J. Approaches to the economics of discrimination. *AER Proceedings* 63 (May 1973) 287-296.

Thurow, L. *Poverty and Discrimination*. Washington: Brookings Institution, 1969.

Treiman, D. *Job Evaluation: An Analytic Review*. Washington, D.C.: National Academy of Sciences, 1979.

Treiman, D., H. Hartman (eds.) *Women, Work and Wages: Equal Pay for Jobs of Equal Value*. Washington: National Academy of Sciences, National Research Council, 1981.

Tzannatos, P. and A. Zabalza. The anatomy of the rise of British female relative wages in the 1970s. *BJIR* 22 (July 1984) 177-194.

Weiss, Y. and R. Gronau. Expected interruption in labour force participation and sex related differences in earnings growth. *R.E. Stats.* 48 (October 1981) 607-620.

Welch, F. Affirmative action and its enforcement. *American Economic Review* 71 (May 1981) 127-133.

Willborn, Steven. *A Comparable Worth Primer.* Lexington: D.C. Heath, 1986.

Zellner, H. Discrimination against women, occupational segregation, and the relative wage. *AER Proceedings* 62 (May 1972) 157-160.

Zincone, L. and F. Close. Sex discrimination in a paramedical profession. *ILRR* 32 (October 1978) 74-85.

CHAPTER 24

Optimal Compensation Systems, Deferred Compensation and Mandatory Retirement

Many features of our compensation system in particular (and personnel policies in general) seem peculiar and inefficient. For example promotion and pay are often based on seniority and not necessarily merit. Workers are often required to retire from specific jobs even though they could carry on many of the necessary functions. Certain individuals receive astronomical pay, certainly relative to what they would receive in their next best alternative activity, even though they appear to be only slightly better performers than others. In many circumstances, pay seems to resemble a prize rather than payment equal to the marginal revenue product of the employee to the firm. Retroactive cost of living adjustments are often made to the pensions of retired workers, even though neither the firm nor the incumbent employees have a formal obligation to the retired workers. In many circumstances wages appear to be in excess of the amount necessary to recruit and retain a viable work-force to the firm.

To some, these examples are simply taken as illustrations of the fact that labour markets do not operate in the textbook fashion predicted by conventional economics. They are regarded as inefficient pay practices or the results of constraints imposed by unions. In recent years, however, basic economic principles have been applied to help explain, in part at least, the existence of various institutional features of labour markets, including compensation systems. An efficiency rationale was sought to explain their survival value. This is part of the trend away from simply regarding these institutional features as exogenously given and examining their impact. It is part of the trend to try to explain these institutional features (i.e., to regard them as endogenous) using basic principles of economics.

AGENCY THEORY AND EFFICIENCY WAGE THEORY

In many instances the theoretical framework that has been applied is part of what is termed principal-agent theory. That perspective deals with the problem of designing an efficient contract between the principal (worker) and the agent (employer) when there are incentives to cheat. The problems are particularly acute when monitoring costs are an issue or there is asymmetric information (i.e., one party has better information than the other and there is no incentive to reveal that information). In such circumstances the parties may try to design contracts that elicit "truth-telling" and that ensure incentive compatibility so that no party has an incentive to cheat on the contract.

In such circumstances the pay of workers need not equal their marginal revenue product to the firm at each and every point in time (a condition economists label the "spot" or "auction market"). Rather their *expected* pay would equal their expected productivity over their expected lifetime with the firm with productivity being broadly defined to include the effect on others. Such circumstances are often characterized by explicit contracts like collective agreements that provide a degree of guarantee of the receipt of payment. Or they are often characterized by implicit contracts that rely largely upon reputation. Where reputation is weak, a compensating wage may be paid for the risk that the contract may be broken. Economists term such markets "contract" markets to highlight the long-term contract nature of the arrangements.

The growing literature on efficient compensation systems is also related to the literature on "efficiency wages" which argues that wages may affect productivity as well as wages being paid according to the value of the marginal product of labour in the firm; that is, causality can run both ways. This efficiency wage literature has had a number of applications. The economic development literature has often emphasized the subsistence wage necessary for basic levels of nutrition. The Marxist literature has emphasized the subsistence wage necessary for the reproduction of the labour force. As discussed in the chapter on the impact of unions, much of the new literature on the impact of unions has emphasized that unions may arise in response to high wages (in addition to the conventional view that unions *cause* higher wages) and that such unions can have a positive influence on productivity. As discussed previously, one possible response to minimum wage legislation (or any other form of wage fixing) is for employers to be "shocked" into more efficient practices; again higher wages induce higher productivity. High pay also enables employers to hire from a queue of applicants and this may serve as a worker discipline device, making the cost of layoff high to the worker, especially if there is a pool of unemployed. Pay (and especially perceptions about the fairness of pay) has long been recognized in the personnel literature as potentially being able to affect productivity. In all of these examples the causality runs in the direction of pay affecting productivity. This supplements the conventional economic emphasis that pay is given in return for the value of the marginal product of labour to the firm. This two-way causality must be recognized in the design of any optimal compensation system.

ECONOMICS OF SUPERSTARS

Optimal compensation systems must also consider the fact that the value of the marginal product of labour may reflect the size of the market as well as the contribution of an employee to the productivity of others. As emphasized by Rosen (1981) small differences in the skill input of certain individuals may get magnified incredibly in the value of the marginal product of the service consumed by the public or co-workers in certain circumstances. This could be the case, for example, in a collectively consumed consumption good like a concert or T.V. performance where the size of the audience does not usually detract from the ability of others to watch. In such circumstances of a common demand, people are willing to pay to hear the best person because the additional price they have to pay to hear the best is shared amongst a large group of collective recipients. The additional *per person* cost of hearing the best person is small because it is shared amongst the large audience. Hence, "the best" person may command a superstar salary that is astronomical relative to the next-best person even though the superstar's ability or skill may only be marginally better than that of the next-best person. Small differences in skill get magnified into large differences in the value of the marginal product of the service when that service can be consumed by a large audience that can share the cost.

Similarly, if an individual can have a positive effect on the productivity of other workers in the job hierarchy then the value of the marginal product of that person's labour to the organization may be high, even if that positive effect is small for each person. A small positive effect on each person can cumulate to a large total effect when the number of affected persons in the organization is large. Hence, we may expect certain executives or talented individuals to receive a much larger salary than the next most talented individual, even though there may not be much difference in the skills of the two individuals. Small differences in skill get magnified into large differences in the value of an individual to an organization when those skills can improve the productivity of a large number of persons. We would also expect such talented individuals to be drawn to large organizations where the benefits of their talent could be spread over larger numbers.

SALARIES AS PRIZES

As pointed out in Lazear and Rosen (1981), executive salaries often seem to resemble prizes to the winners of contests rather than compensation in return for the value of the marginal product of one's services. This is starkly illustrated in the situation of a company that has a number of vice-presidents, all of whom are of roughly comparable ability. However, the one who gets promoted, presumably on the basis of being the best, gets a high increase in salary. The salary difference between the president and the vice-president seems to reflect a prize for winning a contest more than differences in ability or the value of the person to the organization. That is, the president is probably slightly more capable than the vice-president and yet the salary difference seems much more than the ability difference.

Such a compensation system may be efficient, however, if the organization is only able to *rank* its executives according to the value of their contribution to the organization. That is, the organization may be able to say that individual A is better than B who is better than C, and so forth. However, the organization is not able to assess the precise contribution of each individual or by how much the contribution of one individual exceeds that of another. If the organization is able to assess the productivity of the group, then it could pay individual wages equal to the *average* productivity of each person. However, this compensation system may not create much incentive to perform since the individual's pay would be based on the productivity of the group, not the individual. In fact, it may create perverse incentives for individuals, who themselves know that they have below average productivity, to enter the group and get the average pay. This adverse selection procedure (a common problem in markets with asymmetric information) could lead to a situation where the bad workers drive out the good workers.

In order to create performance incentives in such markets, organizations may pay a top salary that resembles a prize to the winner in the group. Even if most are paid a wage equal to the average productivity of the group, there will be an incentive to perform in order to be promoted to win the prize. The organization can judge the winner in order to award the prize because, by assumption, the organization can rank individuals on the basis of their performance, even though it cannot gauge their individual productivity.

Such compensation in the form of prizes may be particularly important for senior persons who otherwise have few promotional opportunities left in their career. There may still be an incentive to perform if one of those promotions means the prize of a large salary increase.

Such compensation systems in the form of prizes can also create perverse incentive structures. For example, they may discourage co-operative behaviour since that could lead to one's competitor receiving the prize, unless of course the organization is able to identify and reward such "team-players." Such compensation systems may even encourage individuals to disrupt the performance of their competitors for the prize so as to enhance their own probability of winning the prize. The firm is also limited in the extent to which it can use prizes since risk-averse individuals would not enter a contest for which the runner-ups (e.g., vice-presidents) would receive nothing. Hence, it must balance the needs to provide an incentive to win a large prize against the needs to guarantee some payment to get people to enter the contest.

DEFERRED WAGES

Evidence

Compensation often appears to be deferred in the sense that wages are above an individual's productivity for the more senior employees (Figure 24.1(a)). Alternatively stated, wages rise with seniority or experience, in-

Figure 24.1   Wage Productivity Profiles

(a) Deferred Wages Contract Market

(b) Spot Market

(c) Deferred Wages with Company Specific Training

(d) General Training

dependent of the individual's productivity. Abraham and Medoff (1982), for example, review a large number of empirical studies and find that such deferred compensation systems are prominent.

The deferred wage aspect would be even larger when one considers the fact that pension accruals become important in the pre-retirement years. That is, for every additional year an individual works, that individual experiences not only a wage increase but also pension increments that are a cost to the employer but a compensation benefit to employees. Pension benefits themselves also can be considered part of the deferred compensation package.

Associated Characteristics

Obviously such deferred compensation systems will exist only in situations where there is some long-term commitment on the part of the firm to continue the contracted arrangements. Otherwise the firm has an incentive to dismiss the employee at the time when the workers' pay begins to exceed their productivity (at the point of intersection, S_B of the pay and productivity schedules of Figure 24.1(a)). Firms that did so, however, would develop a bad reputation and have to pay a higher regular compensating wage in return for the risk that employees may not receive their deferred wage.

Of course, firms that find themselves with an aging work-force with accumulated seniority and few younger workers (perhaps because of a decline in their hiring due to a decline in their product demand), may find it "profitable" to declare bankruptcy and hence sever their deferred wage obligations, especially if they can restructure elsewhere and hire younger workers at a wage less than their productivity. Obviously, if this were known by the new recruits, then a compensating wage would be required for accepting employment in a firm that deliberately restructured to avoid its deferred compensation obligations. However, the true rationale for such bankruptcy can be difficult to detect, especially in situations of asymmetric information where the firm has more information than employees on the true profitability of the firm.

Given the fact that firms have a short-run incentive to renege on the deferred wage obligation when that obligation becomes due, such a compensation system will prevail only when there are certain checks and balances to ensure that the deferred compensation is paid. Such checks and balances include the reputation of the firm, the payment of wages related to seniority, and the fact that unions can ensure a degree of "due-process" to ensure that their members are not arbitrarily dismissed. These checks and balances are characteristic of the longer term "contract market," where a longer term employment relationship is expected, rather than the "spot" or "auction" market, where wages would equal the workers' productivity at each and every point in time (Figure 24.1(b)).

Rationales for Deferred Compensation

Such deferred compensation systems may serve a number of important functions and hence have an efficiency rationale. As emphasized by Lazear (1979), they may ensure honesty and work effort because the worker wants to stay with the company to get the deferred wage. It is like the worker posting a bond (equal to the excess of the worker's productivity over wages when young) that will be returned (in the form of wages in excess of productivity) when the worker has accumulated seniority with the firm. The returning of the bond (deferred compensation) will be done conditional upon the worker having performed satisfactorily after a period over which past performance can be observed. Workers whose performance has not been satisfactory can be dismissed, subject to the checks and balances discussed previously. The greater honesty and work effort that results from such a system enhances productivity and hence provides the means for such workers to receive greater compensation over their expected work life.

Such a compensation system also reduces the need for constant every-day monitoring of the productivity of workers. With deferred wages monitoring can be made on a periodic, retrospective basis (i.e., examining past performance) with the worker being promoted and hence receiving the deferred wage conditional upon satisfactory performance (again subject to the previously discussed checks and balances). In contrast, under the spot market system (Figure 24.1(b)), where wages are equal to productivity at each and every point in time, productivity and performance must be assessed or known on a regular basis in order to compensate accordingly. The paradigm of the spot market is the piece-rate system, where payment is made directly according to output — a system that can exist only where output is easily measured (e.g., sales, logs cut, buttons sewn).

Deferred wages may also reduce unwanted turnover and hence enable firms to recoup their quasi-fixed hiring and training costs that are usually incurred early in the employee's career with the company. Such costs to the firm are illustrated in Figure 24.1(c), by the area above the value-of-marginal product, VMP, line and below the wage line. In order to recoup these costs and amortize them over a longer work life of their employees, firms may want to defer compensation in order to provide employees with an incentive to stay with the firm.

The training here is *company-specific* in the sense that it is usable mainly in the company providing the training. As discussed in the previous chapter on human capital theory, if the training were *generally usable* in other firms then the employee would have the incentive to pay for the training, often in the form of accepting a lower wage during the training program. In this case the trainee's productivity and wage during training ($VMP_t = W_t$ in Figure 24.1(d)) would fall below what their productivity and wage would have been in the absence of training ($VMP_o = W_t$). After the training period, the employee's productivity would increase and, since general training is usable anywhere, so would the trainee's wage (i.e., $VMP_t = W_t$ and both lie above $VMP_o = W_o$ in the post-training period). In the case of general training, where the employee bore the cost of accepting a lower wage during the training period, the company would not have incurred any quasi-fixed costs, and hence would have no incentive to pay a deferred wage, at least for that reason. In such circumstances the wage profile would equal the productivity profile (i.e. $W_t = VMP_t$) as in a spot market. If deferred wages were desirable for other reasons, then they could be superimposed upon the general-training wage profile.

Deferred wages may also exist so as to provide workers with a financial interest in the solvency of the firm. Under the pure spot market of Figure 24.1(b), except for the transactions costs of finding a new job, the employee would be indifferent as to whether the firm went bankrupt since employees would get a wage equal to their productivity elsewhere. With deferred wages, as in Figure 24.1(a), however, the employee stands to lose the deferred wage portion if the firm goes bankrupt. Thus deferred wages, including pension obligations, provide employees with an interest in the financial solvency of the firm. The loss of deferred wages, for example, may be one reason for the larger income losses that are incurred by older workers when they lose their jobs and are displaced to their next-best-alternative employment.

Public sector employers may prefer deferred wages because this arrangement passes costs to future generations of taxpayers, the only check being the willingness of the future generations to honour these commitments. Such deferred compensation may come in the form of more liberal pension benefits or greater job security so that one's *expected* wage (i.e., wage times the probability of receiving the wage) is higher. Deferred wages may also be legitimately needed more in the public than private sector to the extent that honesty is more important in the public sector and to the extent that monitoring and the measurement of current output is more difficult.

Deferred wages may also facilitate the synchronization of income and expenditures over the life cycle. That is, the shortfall of wages below productivity for junior people can be regarded as a form of forced savings, paid out later in the form of wages in excess of productivity in later years. Whether this corresponds to their years of greatest expenditure needs and whether saving in the form of deferred wages is better than private saving through capital markets is an open question. Deferred wages may also correspond to a sense of equity and fairness to employees so that they receive wage increases commensurate with seniority, even if their productivity does not increase or even declines.

Clearly there are a variety of possible rationales for deferred wages that can confer mutual benefits to both employers and employees. Even when the initial benefits would go mainly to employers (e.g., increased work incentives, reduced monitoring costs, reduced unwanted turnover) such benefits would provide the means for them to compensate employees for any adverse effects of deferred wages. Employees could be compensated in the form of a higher lifetime wage profile and more job security. As mentioned previously, employees may also benefit from the lifetime employment aspects of the contract market, from the periodic rather than everyday monitoring, from the due-process and seniority rules that provide security to ensure that deferred wages are paid, and from the possible synchronizing of income and expenditures and the sense of equity and fairness that may be associated with wages based on seniority.

RATIONALE FOR MANDATORY RETIREMENT

To Enable Deferred Wages

While there clearly can be efficiency and equity reasons for deferred wages to exist, such a contractual arrangement requires a termination date for it to exist. Otherwise, employers run the risk of paying wages in excess of productivity for an indefinite period (as illustrated in Figure 24.1(a)). In such circumstances a contractual arrangement involving deferred wages could not persist.

Lazear (1979) argues that mandatory retirement provides the termination date for such contractual arrangements with deferred wages, and he provides empirical evidence indicating that mandatory retirement provisions are more prevalent in situations of deferred wages. The mandatory retirement date, MR in Figure 24.2, provides an equilibrium condition, enabling the expected present value of the wage stream to be equal to the expected present value of the productivity stream to the firm. Without that termination date to the existing contractual arrangement it would be difficult or impossible for the deferred wage contract to exist since the firm would be paying a wage in excess of productivity for an indefinite period. Mandatory retirement is the institutional rule that gives finality to the

Figure 24.2 Mandatory Retirement Age

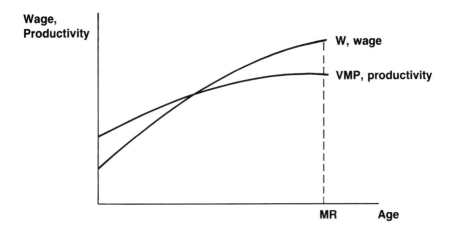

existing contractual arrangement. Viewed in this light, it is an endogenous institutional feature of labour markets that arises for efficiency reasons to allow deferred compensation systems to exist; it is not an exogenously imposed constraint as is often perceived.

As discussed in the previous chapter on retirement, the phrase "mandatory retirement" is somewhat of a misnomer since it does not mean that the person is required to retire from the *labour force*. It means that the existing contractual arrangement is now terminated, and the employee must re-negotiate an alternative arrangement with another employer or with the same employer (the latter being possible under compulsory but not automatic retirement). Presumably any new arrangement would be for a wage commensurate with the worker's productivity and this may involve a substantial wage drop since deferred wages no longer would be paid. This need not be because productivity declines with age; rather it occurs because deferred wages are in excess of productivity for senior employees (in return for wages being below productivity in their early years with the company). In fact, this emphasizes that mandatory retirement need not exist because productivity (correctly or incorrectly) is perceived to decline with age. The appropriate response to such a phenomenon, if it existed, would be wage reductions not requiring that the person must leave the job. Mandatory retirement could be an efficient compensation rule even if productivity continued to increase throughout a worker's working life (as it in fact does in the diagram).

Other Possible Rationales for Mandatory Retirement

In addition to enabling a deferred wage compensation system, other possible rationales may exist for mandatory retirement. It may facilitate work-sharing by opening up promotion and employment opportunities for younger workers. While this may be true in particular firms and industries, as indicated in our previous discussion of worksharing, caution should be used in applying this argument to the economy as a whole so as to avoid the "lump-of-labour fallacy." That is, there need not be a fixed number of jobs in the economy so that the job held by an older worker would mean that a younger worker would not have a job. The younger worker may not have that *particular job*, but by working longer the older worker may be generating other jobs through increased consumption expenditures and through affecting wage levels.

Mandatory retirement may also create a greater degree of certainty about when an employee will retire from a particular job. For employers, this may facilitate planning for new staffing requirements, pension obligations and medical and health expenditures, the latter of which can be quite high for older workers. For workers, the advent of mandatory retirement may encourage pre-retirement planning and preparation of eventual retirement, preparation they may otherwise postpone indefinitely if the retirement date were not fixed. Retirement may also be facilitated by the fact that pensions, as a form of deferred compensation, are prominent in situations of mandatory retirement.

Mandatory retirement also reduces the need for the monitoring and evaluation of older workers and it enables them to "retire with dignity" since they are retiring because of a common retirement rule, not because they are singled out for incompetence. Less productive workers can be "carried" to the retirement age by employers or co-workers because that may be a short period and it is known with certainty. In contrast, without mandatory retirement, the performance of older workers will have to be monitored and evaluated, and dismissals may occur more frequently.

Arguments Against Mandatory Retirement

The arguments against mandatory retirement tend to rest on human rights issues, with mandatory retirement being regarded as a form of age discrimination. The appearance of age discrimination is further enhanced by the fact that employment standards or human rights legislation often has an age limit, not covering workers who are 65 years of age and older. Workers beyond that age have no formal recourse to the law to prevent age discrimination. This apparent sanctioning of mandatory retirement provisions certainly makes the provisions appear as a form of age discrimination. Stereotypes that give rise to discrimination are likely to be as prominent against older workers as against women, racial groups or any other visible minorities.

Even if certain rules may be efficient, they may not be socially justifiable if they discriminate against individuals. Thus even if mandatory retirement creates certainty for employers and employees, and it facilitates retirement with dignity, if this occurs at the expense of some who want to continue working, and are capable of working, it still may be regarded as discriminatory against those individuals.

The abolition of mandatory retirement has also been supported on the grounds of improving the viability of public and private pensions, a growing concern as the aging population puts increasing pressure on pension obligations at the same time as a declining work-force provides fewer persons paying into pension funds. If workers continue to work beyond what was the former retirement age they will be less of a drain on pensions. Of course, this argument assumes that those who continue to work will not draw full pension income, an assumption that is seldom explicitly stated. In fact, many unions tend to be concerned that banning mandatory retirement is simply a veiled excuse to reduce private and public pension obligations.

A Middle Ground

Given the pros and cons of mandatory retirement it is not surprising that the debate over banning mandatory retirement is conducted at an emotive level. The real question, however, is: to what extent should legislation ban

parties from entering into contractual arrangements (like mandatory retirement) that inhibit their freedom at some time in the future, presumably
in return for other benefits such as job and promotion opportunities when
they are younger, pensions when they retire, and the benefits of a deferred
compensation scheme? Clearly legislation sanctions some contracts like
marriage contracts and loan contracts that can inhibit freedom at certain
points in time, presumably because of the other benefits they bring. Yet
the state does forbid other contracts like indentured service or separate
pay or promotion lines for females or racial groups, even if the individuals
themselves are willing to enter into such contractual arrangements. Not
all contractual arrangements are sanctioned by the state, especially if people
can be misinformed or if they can be exploited because of a weak bargaining
position.

One possible solution to prevent the worst abuses of mandatory
retirement and yet to preserve its benefits would be to remove the age
ceiling on anti-discrimination legislation but to exempt bona fide collective
agreements or employees covered by a bona fide pension plan. This would
enable people to enter into arrangements involving mandatory retirement
if they had the protection of a union. Presumably the union would be
informed of the trade-offs involved and it would represent the interests of
its older workers, because all of its members could expect to become older
and subject to any constraints like mandatory retirement. Exempting
employees covered by a bona fide pension plan would ensure that when
workers become subject to the mandatory retirement constraint, they would
retire with an adequate pension.

Such exemptions, however, would allow mandatory retirement to
continue much in its present form since most workers who are currently
subject to mandatory retirement are also protected by a collective agreement
and/or a pension plan. However, it would prevent the potential abuse of
the employer who engages in age discrimination or who requires mandatory retirement but does not provide a pension.

Impact of Banning Mandatory Retirement

As indicated in Gunderson (1983) whatever the pros and cons of mandatory
retirement as a work rule, banning it can be expected to have a variety of
implications on various aspects of the employment relationship. To the
extent that deferred compensation is no longer as feasible, then the wages
of younger workers will rise and the wages of older workers with more
seniority will fall, as wage profiles will now have to more closely approximate productivity profiles (i.e., the profiles will be more like Figure 24.1(b)
than 24.1(a)). The wages of older workers may drop quite substantially to
compensate for any increase in age-related fringe benefit costs like medical
and disability insurance. Those adjustments, in turn, may bring charges
of age discrimination in pay practices. Until such wage adjustments occur,
however, older workers may receive substantial "windfall gains" from the
abolition of mandatory retirement, as their wages could now exceed their

productivity for an indefinite period of time (i.e., beyond MR in Figure 24.2).

Not only will the wage profile "tilt" downwards towards the productivity profile but the whole productivity profile and wage profile will drop to the extent that productivity was enhanced by the deferred wage system, for example, because of enhanced work incentives and reduced monitoring. New efforts will also be made to restore the deferred wage system in a fashion that does not rely upon mandatory retirement for its existence. For example, periodic bonuses may be more prominent. If deferred wages are continued, employee voluntary buy outs or "golden handshakes" may become more prominent to encourage voluntary retirement. Actuarial reductions in pension benefits may also be used to encourage people to voluntarily retire. Pensions themselves may become less prominent to the extent that they were a part of the deferred compensation scheme.

Monitoring and evaluation of workers will likely increase to the extent that it is less feasible to use periodic evaluations based upon past performance. In addition, they will be more necessary to detect early signals of performance in younger workers and to provide documentation in the case of dismissals or wage reduction of older workers so as to avoid age discrimination charges.

The employment and promotion opportunities of younger workers may be reduced in particular jobs when older workers continue past the usual retirement age. The extent to which other job opportunities may open up because of the spending activities of those who remain in the work-force, or because of their effect on wage levels, is an empirical unknown. To the extent that deferred wages are not as prominent, promotion will take on a different meaning, since it will not mean promotion to receive the deferred wage. If wages are now equal to the worker's value of marginal product at each and every stage of the life cycle, then promotion by itself will be less important.

Training will decrease to the extent that deferred wages can no longer exist to discourage the unwanted turnover of those who receive company-specific training. However, training may increase to the extent that the expected benefit period, without mandatory retirement, is longer. Forecasting and planning will be more difficult given the greater uncertainty about retirement ages.

Jobs may be redesigned to accommodate the older workers who stay, but they may also be designed to encourage them to leave. Some dismissals of older workers who otherwise may have been "carried" to the mandatory retirement age will be inevitable, and this will likely increase the amount of litigation over unjust dismissal cases. Layoffs of older workers may also be more prominent to the extent that seniority declines as a work rule that was co-existent with deferred compensation.

These are meant to be simply illustrative of the sorts of adjustments that may occur if one aspect of the intricate employment relationship is changed, in this case if mandatory retirement is abolished. The adjustments may be minor if they are going on already in anticipation of mandatory retirement being banned, or if alternative procedures can arise to enable deferred wages, or if workers continue their trend towards earlier retirement. Nevertheless, we do not know if that trend will continue especially as the proportion of the white-collar work-force grows, as retirement plans have more lead-time to change, as larger numbers of co-workers postpone retirement, and if pensions dissipate. In addition, as discussed in the chapter on retirement, Canadian public pension plans do not have a tax-back feature as exists in the United States, so that Canadian workers may be more prone to postpone retirement than their American counterparts.

Clearly, the current debate over the pros and cons of banning mandatory retirement is not one that is likely to be resolved easily, and if it is resolved in favour of banning mandatory retirement, a number of repercussions are likely to follow. Hopefully, the application of some basic principles of economics can narrow the focus of the debate, though it may also make the issues more complicated than they appear at first glance. At the very least, these principles should provide us with information on the repercussions of a policy change and the alternative and complementary policies that may be desirable.

REFERENCES

Abraham, K. and J. Medoff. Length of service and the operation of internal labour markets. *IRRA* (December 1982) 308-318.

Akerlof, G. Labor contracts as partial gift exchange. *QJE* (Nov. 1982) 543-570.

Arnott, R. and J. Stiglitz. Labor turnover, wage structures and moral hazard: the inefficiency of competitive markets. *JOLE* 3 (October 1985) 434-462.

Burkhauser, R. and J. Quinn. Is mandatory retirement overrated? *JHR* 18 (Summer 1983) 337-358.

Carmichael, L. Does rising productivity explain seniority rules for layoffs? *AER* 73 (December 1983) 1127-1131.

Carmichael, L. Reputations in the labor market. *AER* 74 (September 1984) 713-725.

Chaykowski, R. and C. Beach. Prizes in an industrial union environment. *JLR* 6 (Spring 1985) 181-198.

Donaldson, D. and B.C. Eaton. Person-specific costs of production: hours of work, rates of pay, labour contracts. *CJE* 17 (August 1984) 441-449.

Dye, R. Optimal length of labor contract. *IER* 26 (February 1985) 251-270.

Eaton, C. and W. White. The economy of high wages. *Economica* 50 (May 1983) 175-182.

Frank, R. Are workers paid their marginal products? *AER* 74 (September 1984) 549-571.

Gunderson, M. and J. Pesando. Eliminating mandatory retirement: economics and human rights. *CPP* 6 (Spring 1980) 352-360.

Gunderson, M. Mandatory retirement and personnel policies. *Columbia Journal of World Business* (Summer 1983) 8-15.

Hashimoto, M. Bonus payments, on-the-job training, and lifetime employment in Japan. *JPE* 87 (October 1979) 1086-1104.

Hashimoto, M. and J. Raisian. Employment tenure and earnings profiles in Japan and the United States. *AER* 75 (September 1985) 721-735.

Hashimoto, M. and B. Yu. Specific capital, employment contracts, and wage rigidity. *The Bell Journal of Economics* 11 (Autumn 1980) 536-549.

Johnson, W. The social efficiency of fixed wages. *QJE* 100 (Feb. 1985) 101-118.

Kuhn, P. Wages, effort and incentive compatibility in life-cycle employment contracts. *JOLE* 4 (January 1986) 28-49.

Lapp, J. Mandatory retirement as a clause in an employment insurance contract. *EI* 23 (April 1985) 69-92.

Lazear, E. Why is there mandatory retirement? *JPE* 87 (Dec. 1979) 1261-1284.

Lazear, E. and S. Rosen. Rank-order tournaments as optimum labor contracts. *JPE* 89 (October 1981) 841-864.

Leigh, D. Why is there mandatory retirement? An empirical re-examination. *JHR* 19 (Fall 1984) 512-531.

Medoff, J. and K. Abraham. Experience, performance and earnings. *QJE* 95 Dec. 1980) 703-736.

Ohashi, I. Wage profiles, layoffs and specific training. *IER* 24 (February 1983) 169-181. Comment by L. Carmichael 26 (October 1985) 747-753. Rejoinder by M. Hashimoto 26 (October 1985) 753-754.

Parsons, D. The employment relationship: job attachment, work effort, and the nature of contracts. *Handbook of Labour Economics* Vol. 1. O. Ashenfelter and R. Layard (eds.). New York: Elsevier, 1986.

Rosen, S. The economics of superstars. *AER* 71 (December 1981) 845-858.

Schuster, M. and C. Miller. An empirical assessment of the age discrimination in employment act. *ILRR* 38 (October 1984) 64-74.

Shapiro, D. and S. Sandell. Age discrimination in wages and displaced older men. *SEJ* 52 (July 1985) 90-102.

Tachibanki, T. Further results on Japanese wage differentials: nenko wages, hierarchical position, bonuses, and working hours. *IER* 23 (June 1982) 447-462.

Viscusi, W. Self-selection, learning-induced quits, and the optimal wage structure. *IER* 21 (October 1980) 529-546.

Viscusi, W. Moral hazard and merit rating over time: an analysis of optimal intertemporal wage structures. *SEJ* 52 (April 1986) 1068-1079.

Weitzman, M. Some macroeconomic implications of alternative compensation systems. *EJ* 93 (Dec. 1983) 763-783.

Wright, G. Cheap labor and southern textiles, 1880-1930. *QJE* 96 (Nov. 1981) 605-630.

Part VI

Unemployment and Inflation

25 Unemployment: Meaning and Measurement

With the possible exception of the Consumer Price Index, no single aggregate statistic receives as much attention as the unemployment rate. To a considerable extent this attention reflects concern about the hardship which unemployment may impose on affected individuals and their families and the waste of human resources that may be associated with unemployment. In addition, the unemployment rate is used as a measure of the overall state of the economy and of the degree of tightness (excess demand) or slack (excess supply) in the labour market. However, in spite of this evident interest, there is often confusion about what is meant by our unemployment statistics. This chapter examines the meaning and measurement of unemployment. The causes and consequences of unemployment and the role of public policy in this area are discussed in the following chapter.

MEASURING UNEMPLOYMENT

The unemployed are generally defined as those who are not currently employed and who indicate by their behaviour that they want to work at prevailing wages and working conditions. In Canada, measurement of the unemployed can be obtained from the Labour Force Survey, the Census, or from the number of registrants or claimants in the Unemployment Insurance Commission. While there are these alternative measures, and different ones can be useful for different purposes, the unemployment measure according to the Labour Force Survey is the one that receives the most attention: it is the one that is so often quoted by the press and utilized for general policy purposes.

Labour Force Survey

As indicated in Chapter 5 on Labour Force Participation, the Labour Force Survey in Canada is conducted monthly by Statistics Canada. According to the Labour Force Survey, people are categorized as unemployed if they did not have work but they were available for and actively seeking work. There are some minor exceptions to this general principle. For example, the unemployed also includes persons who were available for work but who were not seeking work because they were on lay-off for six months or less, or they had a new job to start within four weeks. Nevertheless, the general principle remains: to be counted as unemployed, one has to be available for and actively seeking work. That is, in general circumstances, it is necessary to engage in active job search to be classified as unemployed. Individuals who are not employed and who are not actively seeking work (such as students, persons engaged in household work, and retirees) are classified as being out of the labour force.

Persons are categorized as employed if they did any work for pay or profit, including unpaid work on a family farm or business, or if they normally had a job but were not at work because of such factors as bad weather, illness, industrial dispute, or vacation. The employed plus the unemployed make up the labour force, and the unemployment rate is defined as the number of unemployed divided by the labour force.

Census

The Canadian Census, conducted every ten years since 1871, also provides information on the unemployed, at least since 1921. (A smaller census containing more limited information is also conducted in between the 10-year census.) Rather than being based on a sample of the population, the Census is based on the whole relevant population, with detailed information coming from approximately one-third of this population. Consequently, Census data is more comprehensive and provides detailed information on such factors as unemployment by industry and occupation, as well as a wealth of demographic and economic information on the respondents. For this reason the Census data has proven useful in detailed statistical and econometric analysis of labour market behaviour. However, as our earlier discussion on defining the labour force indicated in Chapter 5, the usefulness of the Census data is limited by the fact that it is conducted infrequently and its reliability on labour force issues may be questioned because of the fact that it covers so many issues in addition to labour force activity. In addition, there is a time lag of about two years before the Census data are available, whereas the Labour Force Survey results are available within a few weeks of the survey.

Unemployment Insurance Claimants

A third data source — unemployment insurance claimants — can be used to obtain estimates of the unemployed. However, these estimates are not commonly available and they are not usually cited in the press or utilized for general policy purposes. Comparisons of the number of unemployed according to unemployment insurance figures versus Labour Force Survey figures are given in Naemark (1973) and Cook, Jump, Hodgins and Szabo (1976).

While the number of unemployed according to the Labour Force Survey may be similar to the number claiming unemployment insurance or registered in an unemployment insurance office, the two series generally differ. The number of unemployment insurance claimants may exceed the

Labour Force Survey number because some people may be collecting un-employment insurance but are not actively seeking work. These people could range from persons on maternity leave who are legally entitled to collect unemployment insurance, to persons who traditionally do seasonal work and collect unemployment insurance for part of the year, to outright cheaters who simply don't bother looking or who may even be working illegally. Such persons may be collecting unemployment insurance, but they need not indicate, in the confidential Labour Force Survey question-naire, that they are actively seeking work.

On the other hand, the number of unemployed according to the Labour Force Survey could exceed the number of unemployment insurance claimants. New job seekers, for example, may not be eligible for UI, or the long-term unemployed may have exhausted their benefit period. Some may not be covered by unemployment insurance; others may not register because then they would have to accept a job. They (or their parents who are often the respondents) may still indicate on a Labour Force Survey questionnaire that they are actively seeking work.

Clearly the two series need not be identical since they indicate some-what different things. Because, from a policy perspective, what is usually wanted is an indicator of the number of persons who are available for work and actively seeking work, then the Labour Force Survey figures are the ones that are commonly used.

Canadian Experience

As Figure 25-1 illustrates, Canada's unemployment rate fluctuated widely during the 1921-86 period, to a considerable extent because of cyclical fluctuations in business activity. With the onset of the Great Depression in 1929, the unemployment rate soared from about 3 percent to almost 20 percent. A lengthy period of declining unemployment followed, and dur-ing World War II unemployment fell to very low levels. Following the war, unemployment remained low until the recession of 1957-58. As the econ-omy recovered from the 1957-58 recession, the unemployment rate grad-ually declined, reaching 3.4 percent in 1966. Since that time the overall trend in unemployment has been upward, although fluctuations around the trend have continued to occur. The most significant increases occurred in the recession of 1974-75 and in the severe recession of 1982-83 which resulted in the unemployment rate reaching 11.9 percent, the highest level since the Great Depression. During the economic expansion which fol-lowed the 1982-83 recession, the unemployment rate gradually declined; nonetheless, in 1986 it remained at close to 10 percent, a level which is high by the standards of the postwar period.

The unemployment rate is the most commonly used measure of ag-gregate labour market activity and the degree of labour force utilization. Two alternative measures are the labour force participation rate (the ratio of the labour force to the population of working age, or source population)

Figure 25.1   Unemployment in Canada, 1921-86

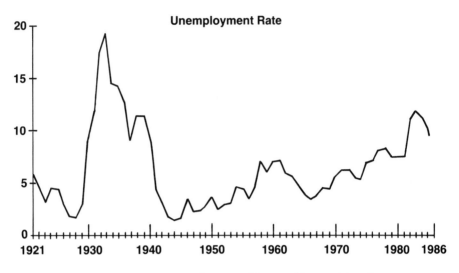

Sources: M.C. Urquhart, ed., *Historical Statistics of Canada* (Toronto: Macmillan,
         1965); and Statistics Canada, *The Labour Force*
         (Ottawa: Statistics Canada, various years).

and the employment rate (the ratio of employment to the source population). These statistics are shown for selected years in Table 25-1. (The years
1956, 1966, 1973 and 1981 correspond to the peak years of the business
cycle in the postwar period.) Because they focus on somewhat different
aspects of labour market activity, these three measures need not always
move together. For example, since 1966 the unemployment rate has risen
sharply, yet at the same time both the fraction of the source population
employed and the fraction in the labour force have risen rather than fallen.
Additional perspective on these divergent patterns is provided by the fourth
column of Table 25-1; the rate of growth of employment between 1966 and
1981 was the most rapid of the postwar period. The combination of rapid
employment growth and rising unemployment rates reflected several phenomena, including the substantial number of youths and women who
entered the labour force, particularly after the mid 1960s. Although employment grew rapidly between 1966 and 1981, the growth in labour supply
was even more substantial; thus the unemployment rate rose.

   Which of these three measures is used for analysing aggregate labour
market activity will depend on the purpose of the analysis. The employment and labour force participation rates focus on the fraction of the source
population which is employed and in the labour force respectively, while
the unemployment rate measures the fraction of the labour force which is
out of work and searching for work. Because this chapter deals with unemployment, the main aggregate statistic referred to is the unemployment

TABLE 25.1
LABOUR FORCE PARTICIPATION, EMPLOYMENT AND
UNEMPLOYMENT, CANADA, 1946–86[1]

Year	Labour Force Participation Rate	Employment Rate	Unemployment Rate	Rate of Growth of Employment[2]
1946	55.0	53.1	3.4	
1956	53.5	51.7	3.4	1.8
1966	57.3	55.4	3.4	2.5
1973	59.7	56.4	5.5	3.0
1981	64.8	59.9	7.5	2.9
1986	65.7	59.4	9.6	2.2

Notes: [1] All statistics are based on the former Labour Force Survey prior to 1966 and the Revised Labour Force Survey from 1966 on.

[2] Civilian employment; growth rates are averages of compound annual increases from the level in the year in the row one line above to the level in the year one line below.

Source: Statistics Canada, *The Labour Force*, various issues, and calculations by the authors.

rate. However, in many circumstances the employment and labour force participation rates may provide useful additional information on labour market developments.

Hidden Unemployment

The measurement of unemployment raises some difficult and controversial issues. Hidden unemployment refers to situations in which individuals may be without work, yet they desire work but are not classified as unemployed according to the official statistics. Perhaps the most significant example — especially during recessions and in regions where few jobs are available — is the "discouraged worker" phenomenon. This refers to individuals who are not employed, who may wish to work at prevailing wages, but who are not actively seeking work because they believe that no work is available. Other examples of hidden or unmeasured unemployment include: individuals still awaiting recall after more than six months on layoff; forms of underemployment, such as individuals working fewer hours than they desire to work or normally work; and those temporarily employed in jobs that do not utilize their skills or training. Each of these examples illustrates the difficulties involved in making a satisfactory distinction between "employment," "unemployment" and "out of the labour force."

As discussed by Kaliski (1984), some evidence on the quantitative significance of hidden unemployment in Canada is available. Since 1979 an annual supplement to the Labour Force Survey has identified those who want work, are available for work, but are not seeking work for "economic reasons." (The remainder of those out of the labour force either do not want work or are not seeking work for "personal reasons.") The two most important economic reasons are "believe no work available" (the discouraged worker phenomenon) and "waiting for recall" (after more than six months on layoff); these account for approximately 1/2 and 1/3 respectively of those not seeking work for economic reasons. The overall amount of hidden unemployment as measured by this "economic reasons" criterion is a small proportion of those classified as out of the labour force but can be substantial in relation to the number of unemployed. For example, in March 1983 there were 1,658,000 unemployed and another 335,000 (about 20 percent of the unemployed) not seeking work for economic reasons (Statistics Canada, *The Labour Force*, 1983). If these individuals had been classified as unemployed rather than out of the labour force, the unemployment rate would have been 15.1 percent rather than 12.6 percent.

Whether individuals not seeking work for economic reasons should be classified as unemployed is a controversial issue. The observation that they are without work and want work (assuming the response to the survey is accurate) argues for including them among the unemployed. According to this view, the fact that they are not actively searching for work may be a rational way to spend their time given a belief (which may be well founded) that no jobs are available. Similarly, waiting more than 6 months for recall may be sensible behaviour rather than wishful thinking, especially if the chances of recall are good and the job to which the individual expects to return is attractive relative to potential alternatives. In contrast, the absence of active job search may indicate a low degree of labour force attachment, justifying the classification "out of the labour force."

These phenomena respond to changes in aggregate economic conditions. The number of discouraged workers increased substantially during the 1982-83 recession and subsequently declined as the economy gradually recovered. The number of individuals awaiting recall after more than six months displayed a similar pattern. As a consequence, the increase in the unemployment rate in recessions is smaller than would be the case if those not seeking work for economic reasons were classified as unemployed. Similarly, the decline in the unemployment rate during the recovery is smaller than would be the case if these individuals were included in the unemployed.

Some evidence on the significance of underemployment is also available from the March supplement to the Labour Force Survey. For example, in March 1983, in addition to the 1,658,000 unemployed and 335,000 not seeking work for economic reasons, there were 427,000 persons working part-time who would have preferred full time work. Once again, the measured unemployment rate may understate the extent of unutilized labour services, especially in recessionary periods.

The major lesson to be learned from this discussion is *not* that the official unemployment rate is a poor measure of unemployment, but rather that the concept of unemployment is not sufficiently well defined that any single measure will suit all purposes. For many purposes the official un-employment measure will be appropriate; however, in other situations this should be supplemented by measures of hidden unemployment and underemployment.

LABOUR FORCE DYNAMICS

Recent research by economists has emphasized the dynamic nature of the labour force. The Labour Force Survey provides a snapshot at a point in time, an estimate of the stock of persons in each labour force state. How-ever, even if the magnitudes of these stocks remain approximately constant from one period to another, it would be a mistake to conclude that little change had taken place in the labour force. In fact, as Figure 25-2 illustrates, the flows between the three labour force states (employment, unemploy-ment, out of the labour force) are large in comparison to the stocks and

Figure 25.2   Labour Market Stocks and Flows, January-February 1981

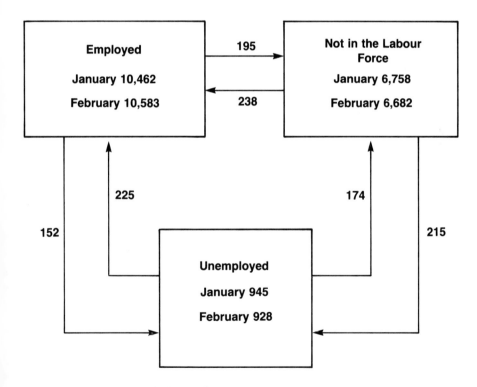

NOTES: 1. All numbers are in thousands.
        2. Parts may not sum to totals due to rounding.
Source: Based on data in Economic Council of Canada, *In Short Supply: Jobs and Skills in the 1980s,* Ottawa: Supply and Services Canada, 1982, Table 6–1.

the gross flows are huge in comparison to net flows. For example, between January and February 1981 the number of unemployed declined only slightly (from 945,000 to 928,000). However, 225,000 individuals, 24 percent of those unemployed in January, became employed between January and February. This large gross flow from unemployment to employment was offset by a movement of 152,000 individuals in the opposite direction; the net flow from unemployment to employment was thus 73,000 (225,000 minus 152,000).

TABLE 25.2

DECOMPOSITION OF UNEMPLOYMENT BY REASON, 1975–1986

Year	Job Losers	Job Leavers	New Entrants	Re-Entrants	Total Rate[1]
Components of Unemployment Rate by Reason for Unemployment					
	(1)	(2)	(3)	(4)	(5)
1975	2.7	1.9	0.4	1.8	6.9
1976	3.3	1.7	0.4	1.8	7.1
1977	4.1	1.7	0.5	1.8	8.1
1978	4.2	1.8	0.5	1.9	8.3
1979	3.6	1.5	0.5	1.9	7.4
1980	3.7	1.5	0.4	1.9	7.5
1981	3.8	1.4	0.4	1.9	7.5
1982	6.5	1.6	0.5	2.3	11.0
1983	7.0	1.6	0.5	2.6	11.9
1984	6.5	1.8	0.5	2.5	11.3
1985	5.8	1.8	0.5	2.4	10.5
1986	5.3	1.7	0.4	2.2	9.6
Distribution of Unemployed by Reason for Unemployment					
	(1)	(2)	(3)	(4)	(5)
1975	39.4	27.8	5.8	26.7	100.0
1976	46.3	23.3	5.6	24.8	100.0
1977	50.5	21.1	5.7	22.7	100.0
1978	50.3	21.1	5.8	22.8	100.0
1979	48.4	20.1	6.1	25.4	100.0
1980	49.7	19.7	5.5	25.2	100.0
1981	50.1	19.0	5.3	25.5	100.0
1982	59.3	15.0	4.4	21.3	100.0
1983	59.3	13.8	4.8	22.0	100.0
1984	57.3	15.5	4.8	22.4	100.0
1985	55.6	17.1	4.4	22.9	100.0
1986	55.5	17.9	4.2	22.5	100.0

Note: [1] May not equal the sum of the rates in the first four columns because of rounding.

Source: Calculated from data given in Statistics Canada, *Historical labour force statistics — actual data, seasonal factors, seasonally adjusted data, 1986*, 71-201 (1987), pp. 31, 156-158.

Similarly, 174,000 individuals, 18 percent of those unemployed in January, left the labour force between January and February 1981. However, this change was more than offset by the 215,000 individuals who entered the labour force and actively sought work.

In summary, even though the number of unemployed changed only marginally between January and February, many of the individuals unemployed in January were no longer unemployed in February, with 24 percent having obtained work and 18 percent no longer seeking work. The picture that emerges from these data is that of a highly dynamic labour force in which there is a great deal of movement among employment, unemployment and outside of the labour force each month.

Table 25-2 provides data on the significance of the various flows into unemployment. The picture of unemployment consisting almost entirely of individuals who lost their job (either temporarily or permanently) is clearly misleading; such job losers account for 40 to 60 percent of all unemployment. In recessions (such as during 1982-83) the absolute and relative importance of job losers increases, and the relative importance of job leavers declines. New entrants typically account for only 4 to 6 percent of unemployment; however, re-entrants (those moving from out of the labour force to unemployed *and* who previously were in the labour force) constitute a substantial proportion of the unemployed.

Incidence and Duration of Unemployment

Because of the dynamic nature of labour force movements, the understanding of unemployment requires information on the flows between various labour force states in addition to the stocks in each state at any point in time. Useful measures for this purpose are the incidence of unemployment — the proportion of individuals who become unemployed in any period — and the duration of unemployment — the length of time spent in the unemployed state before obtaining employment or leaving the labour force.[1] For any particular group of workers, incidence measures the probability of a member of the group becoming unemployed, while duration measures the length of time the individual can be expected to remain unemployed. Using the data in Figure 25-2, the incidence of unemployment for those employed in January 1981 was 1.5 percent (152,000 out of 10,462,000) while the incidence of unemployment among those out of the labour force in January 1981 was 3.2 percent (215,000 out of 6,758,000). The overall incidence among those either employed or not in the labour force in January 1981 was 2.1 percent.

The amount of unemployment at any point in time is affected by both

---

1 This is sometimes referred to as the duration of a "completed spell of unemployment" to distinguish it from the duration of an "interrupted spell" (i.e. a spell in progress). For further discussion of these duration concepts see Beach and Kaliski (1983).

TABLE 25.3
INCIDENCE AND DURATION OF UNEMPLOYMENT BY
AGE AND SEX, CANADA, 1980

Gender or Age Group		Unemployment Rate		Spells of Unemployment	Duration
		Actual	Calculated[1]	Incidence	(mos.)
Men	15-19	17.1	16.2	8.0	2.0
	20-24	11.5	11.0	4.2	2.6
	25-44	5.2	5.2	1.9	2.8
	45-64	4.2	4.4	1.7	2.6
	Average	6.9	6.8	2.7	2.5
Women	15-19	15.3	13.6	7.1	1.9
	20-24	10.7	9.6	4.2	2.3
	25-44	7.0	6.4	3.0	2.2
	45-64	5.8	5.8	2.5	2.3
	Average	8.4	7.7	3.6	2.2
Overall Average		7.5	7.1	3.1	2.3

Notes: [1] Calculated unemployment rate is the product of incidence and duration. Rounding may result in small differences.

Source: Economic Council of Canada, In Short Supply: Jobs and Skills in the 1980s, Ottawa: Supply and Services, Canada, 1982, Table 6.2.

the incidence and duration. Indeed, the unemployment rate (UR) can be expressed as the product of the incidence (I) and duration (D):[2]

$$UR = I \cdot D \qquad (25.1)$$

Table 25-3 shows the unemployment rate and the incidence and duration of unemployment for various age-sex groups in Canada in 1980. The most striking feature of the data in Table 25-3 is that the groups with the highest unemployment rates (males and females 15-19 years of age) have the lowest duration (2.0 and 1.9 months respectively). The very high youth unemployment rate is associated with a high probability of becoming unemployed rather than an unusually long time being required to find a job or to exit from the labour force. The data for individuals 20-24 years of age are less striking but tell a similar story. For these individuals, duration is about average but incidence is significantly above average, resulting in an unemployment rate well above that of most other groups. Older workers, on the other hand, have the lowest unemployment rates within each sex group. This reflects the fact that older workers are less likely to become unemployed; those that do become unemployed require a slightly longer than average period to find employment or leave the labour force. Females have a higher unemployment rate than males but suffer shorter spells of

2 When the labour force is in a steady state equilibrium (i.e. the fraction of the labour force in each state and the proportions flowing between states are constant) this relationship is exact. Otherwise the relationship is approximately correct. Equation (25-1) is an example of the steady-state identity that the stock at any point in time equals the flow times average duration.

unemployment. That is, the higher unemployment rate of females is associated with a higher probability of becoming unemployed rather than with longer spells of unemployment.

Changing Perspectives on Unemployment

The data summarized in Figure 25-2 and in Tables 25-2 and 25-3 suggest several conclusions:
(1) the labour force is highly dynamic, with large flows into and out of unemployment each period;
(2) about half the flow into unemployment is due to individuals losing their job; the remainder is associated with job leavers, new entrants and re-entrants;
(3) the average duration of unemployment is approximately 2 – 2 1/2 months;
(4) the age-sex groups with the highest unemployment rates have the shortest average unemployment durations, but the highest incidence of unemployment.

These conclusions are not peculiar to Canada in 1980-81, but have been reported in empirical studies carried out in various countries during the past two decades. (For Canada see Economic Council of Canada, 1976, 1982; Hasan and de Broucker, 1982; Beach and Kaliski, 1983. For the U.S. see Hall, 1970, 1972; Feldstein, 1973; Marston, 1976; and Clark and Summers, 1979.)

These general findings have important implications for the role of policies to deal with unemployment. The large amount of turnover in the labour force, the fact that job losers account for only about half the flow into unemployment, and the relatively short average duration of unemployment (especially among the groups with the highest unemployment rates) suggest that much unemployment may be caused not by a general shortage of jobs but by employment instability — brief spells of employment followed by periods of job search and/or exit from the labour force. In particular, the short observed duration of unemployment was regarded as evidence that most people could find an acceptable job fairly quickly. Feldstein (1973) used the term "the new unemployment" to describe this view of unemployment being primarily associated with rapid turnover and employment instability; this contrasted with the "old view" in which the unemployed were regarded as a stock of individuals without work for a lengthy period while waiting for a business upturn. The new view suggested that policies aimed at reducing turnover and employment instability may be more successful in achieving lower levels of unemployment than policies aimed at increasing the number of jobs.

Subsequent research, such as that of Clark and Summers (1979) and Akerlof and Main (1980) for the U.S., and Hasan and de Broucker (1982) and Beach and Kaliski (1983) for Canada, has indicated that the "new view" of unemployment contains important elements of truth but is an overly simplistic picture of unemployment. Three conclusions have emerged from this recent research; taking these into account results in a "modified new view." First, although the average duration of completed spells of un-employment is fairly short, much unemployment is accounted for by those suffering lengthy spells of unemployment. An example may help to illus-trate this point. Suppose that five individuals become unemployed, four for spells of one month each and the fifth for eight months. The average duration of unemployment for this group is 2.4 months, but two-thirds of all the unemployment (8 out of 12 months) is associated with the one long spell.

A second important consideration is that not all periods of un-employment end in employment. As Figure 25-2 suggests, a significant number of individuals end their search for work by withdrawing from the labour force. Some may leave the labour force to return to school, raise children or work in the home; however, as discussed previously, some may want paid work but have stopped searching for work because they believe no work is available or for other "economic reasons." By not clas-sifying as "unemployment" the period during which these individuals wanted work but were not searching for work, the duration of unemploy-ment may be considered to be understated. For example, consider an in-dividual who becomes unemployed, searches for work for two months, gives up and stops searching for three months, and then resumes the job search, finding work after a further two months. According to the official statistics, this person would have experienced two spells of unemployment, each lasting a brief two months. However, it could be argued that the individual experienced a single bout of unemployment lasting seven months. Even if this argument is rejected (i.e., the active job search requirement for being considered unemployed is retained), it is clear that, when many spells of unemployment end in withdrawal from the labour force, the fact that the average duration of unemployment is fairly short does not imply that most of the unemployed can find an acceptable job fairly quickly. In Canada in 1980, 44 percent of all bouts of unemployment ended in with-drawal from the labour force and 56 percent ended in employment (Eco-nomic Council of Canada, 1982, Table 6-9). A related observation is that spells of unemployment which end in employment are, on average, longer than those ending in withdrawal from the labour force. Thus the average length of time required to successfully find a job is understated by the duration statistics such as those reported in Table 25-3.

The third modification is related to the distribution of unemployment across the population. The implications of a specific unemployment rate differ acording to how widely the unemployment is distributed. For ex-ample, an unemployment rate of eight percent could mean that eight per-cent of the labour force is unemployed all year (i.e., the distribution of unemployment is highly concentrated) or that all of the labour force is unemployed for eight percent of the year (i.e., the distribution of un-employment is widely dispersed). The high rate of labour force turnover and the short average duration of unemployment led some analysts to believe that unemployment must be widely distributed among the labour force. In fact, this conclusion turns out not to be correct: unemployment is highly concentrated among a minority of the labour force. The reason for these apparently contradictory findings is that even though the average duration of unemployment is short, a minority of individuals suffer repeated spells of unemployment, sometimes interrupted by periods out of the labour force. For these individuals — the "chronically unemployed" — obtaining employment, especially durable employment, appears to be a difficult task.

UNEMPLOYMENT RATE AS A SUMMARY STATISTIC

Much of the previous discussion suggests that the unemployment rate may not be telling all that we think it tells us, or perhaps used to tell us, about such things as the aggregate state of the economy, the extent to which the labour market is in equilibrium, the tightness or looseness of the labour market, or the extent of hardship in the population. It is not that the unemployment rate is wrong; rather it may be asking too much of a single measure to indicate all these things, especially when dramatic demographic changes have occurred in the labour force, and institutional changes have occurred in such things as unemployment insurance, pensions and social assistance.

There are reasons to suggest that the unemployment rate may understate the degree of hardship and loss in the economy, and there are reasons to suggest that it may overstate the hardship and loss. For these reasons, complementary indicators have been suggested to supplement the aggregate unemployment rate.

Elements Understating Hardship and Loss

The reported unemployment rate may understate what could be labelled a true unemployment rate because it does not indicate the hidden unemployed. As previously discussed, the hidden unemployed include discouraged workers who gave up looking for work and who would therefore be counted as not in the labour force, as they engaged in such activities as household work, early retirement, or even school. The number of discouraged workers increases in periods or places of high unemployment. In addition, the hidden unemployed may even include people who drop out of the population that is being surveyed. For example, to the extent that crime increases during periods of high unemployment, these people may be engaging in (unreported) criminal activity, or if apprehended they may be in criminal institutions. In neither case would they be part of the labour force. Or, to the extent that vagrancy increases in times of high unemployment, these people usually would not be considered part of the population that is surveyed. Our unemployment figures do not reflect the loss or hardship of these hidden or disguised unemployed.

In addition, our aggregate unemployment figures by themselves do not indicate the extent to which some workers have added themselves to the labour market to maintain a declining family income associated with a high unemployment rate. In other words, they do not indicate the loss of household production or the loss of education on the part of these added workers who may be compelled by the high unemployment rate to leave the household or educational institutions or retirement.

Nor does the aggregate unemployment rate capture the fact that many employed people may be involuntarily employed only part-time. People are recorded as employed if they did any work during the survey reference period. The fact that some may want to do more work is not reflected. Underemployment can also take the form of individuals working temporarily in jobs that do not utilize their skills and abilities — such as the Ph.D chemist driving a taxi until a job as a chemist opens up.

In addition, a high unemployment rate by itself does not indicate the degree of hardship associated with the fact that most measures of income inequality are greater during periods of high unemployment. Hollister and Palmer (1972) and Maslove and Rowley (1975), for example, indicate that the poor, more than the non-poor, are adversely affected by high unemployment even if this means reduced inflation. On the labour market side this can occur for a variety of reasons: the poor are most likely to be unemployed; secondary workers from poor families are more likely to drop out of the labour force; the wages of the poor fall the most or rise the slowest; and their hours of work are reduced during periods of high unemployment. The unemployment rate by itself does not reflect the fact that poverty is exacerbated in periods of high unemployment.

Research in Canada, the U.K. and the U.S.A. has established a positive correlation between unemployment and a variety of social ills including mental and physical illness, suicide, mortality, crime, drug abuse, child abuse and social unrest. (See, for example, Brenner, 1973; Brenner and Mooney, 1983; Junankar, 1986; Kelvin and Jarrett, 1984; Platt, 1984; Stern, 1983.) Although the causal mechanisms remain a matter of debate (in particular, some of the causation may run from these social ills to unemployment in addition to causation in the opposite direction), these findings indicate that there are important social costs associated with unemployment in addition to the economic costs such as lost output and income. These social costs have significant implications for both the unemployed and for society as a whole through publicly funded institutions such as hospitals, police and social services.

These various factors suggest that the unemployment rate may understate the true loss and hardship in the economy. In addition, to the extent that these factors worsen in periods of high unemployment — hidden unemployment, the number of added workers, involuntary part-time employment, poverty and various social ills such as mental and physical illness, crime and suicide all increase — then this underestimate of the loss is most severe in periods of high unemployment, when conditions already are severe.

Elements Overstating Hardship and Loss

There are also reasons to believe, however, that the unemployment rate may be overstating the degree of hardship and loss in our economy, especially relative to the situation in the 1950s and early 1960s. Many of these reasons hinge on the fact that our unemployment increasingly has fallen on younger workers and married women, and for a variety of reasons there is a belief — held by some, but not all — that the hardship and loss associated with such unemployment is not as severe as that which is associated with the unemployment of males in families where only the male otherwise works.

Increasingly our unemployed consist of females and younger workers, as they have expanded their participation in labour force activities and increasingly are subject to a high incidence or likelihood of being unemployed. (See Chapter 5 for details of the changing patterns of labour force participation and Table 25-3 in this chapter for differences in the incidence of unemployment across age-sex groups.) To the extent that younger workers and women have alternative sources of income to rely upon, and to the extent that the economic well-being of the family is more dependent upon the employment of males, then there is the possibility that the economic hardship associated with a given unemployment rate is not as great now as when males dominated the labour market. This perspective, of course, can be challenged — and will be challenged increasingly — as the participation of women in labour market activities and their contribution to family income becomes regarded as permanent rather than secondary. As a more general proposition, with the growing proportion of families where both the husband and wife work, the unemployment of either may result in less hardship than when males tended to dominate the labour market and became unemployed. For example, since 1975, a period in which the aggregate unemployment rate generally exceeded seven percent, seventy to seventy-five percent of families with one family member unemployed had at least one family member employed. Even in 1983, when the unemployment rate reached 11.9 percent, 70 percent of families with one member unemployed had at least one member employed and 23 percent of families with one member unemployed had two or more members employed (Kaliski, 1985, Table 2-8).

This possibility of reduced hardship is buttressed by the fact that many of the unemployed may be looking for part-time jobs. This could be the case especially for married women who also maintain prime responsibility for household tasks. It may also be the case for students who go to school part-time. The unemployment rate counts all searchers equally, whether they are seeking part-time or full-time work.

The hardship associated with being unemployed may also be reduced, or at least cushioned, by the increased availability of more liberal unemployment insurance benefits. Although many changes have been made to Canada's unemployment insurance system during the past several decades, the most substantial changes were those made in 1971-72. These significantly increased the coverage of the UI program, reduced the number of weeks of previous work experience required to quality for UI benefits, increased the number of weeks for which benefits could be received, and raised the benefit rate. As a result of these and other changes to unemployment insurance and other social programs, Canadians are more protected from the loss of income due to unemployment than was the case in earlier periods.

These possibilities are not meant to play down the hardship associated with being unemployed. It is a serious loss to the economy and more importantly to the individuals and families involved. Nevertheless it is important to be aware that a six percent unemployment rate in the mid 1970s probably would not inflict the hardship that an identical rate would have inflicted on families in the 1950s. Whether an average unemployment rate of over six percent in the 1970s inflicts more hardship than an average rate of slightly over five percent in the 1960s, or four percent in the 1950s, remains an open question.

Complementary Measures

Because of these problems associated with a single aggregate unemployment estimate, some have suggested using complementary measures. In general, these measures are suggested to supplement rather than replace the information contained in the aggregate unemployment rate estimate. The measures include such things as disaggregate unemployment figures, supplementary information, hardship indices, and sub-employment indices. In addition, as discussed previously, statistics such as the labour force participation rate and employment rate can complement the unemployment rate as indicators of aggregate labour market activity.

Disaggregate unemployment figures simply involve reporting unemployment rates for various sub-groups, for example, prime work-age males, females, younger workers, or new entrants into the labour force. While such estimates are readily available from the Labour Force Survey, and they are published, they tend not to get much public attention nor to be portrayed by the media.

Supplementary information would also be useful on such factors as the degree of job search by the unemployed, the extent to which they are looking for part-time work, the duration of their unemployment, and the reasons they may have given up looking for work. Such information is increasingly available, especially from the Revised Labour Force Survey since 1976; nevertheless, it tends not to be widely publicized to the general public.

Hardship indices are also possible. To the extent that the unemployment of certain groups is regarded as not inflicting as much hardship as the unemployment of others, one way to construct such an index is to use weights that involve a lower emphasis for the group experiencing the least hardship. Weighing the unemployed by the average wage of their peer group, for example, would give more weight to married men since they tend to have higher wages. To the extent that wages are a proxy for the economic loss to the economy, the weighting would also reflect these differential losses.

While such a weighting scheme may reflect the differential hardship or loss, it is certainly not without its problems. It would imply, for example, that low-wage disadvantaged workers or females who are discriminated against would receive a lower weight in the hardship index. This may be perverse, for example, if one feels that hardship is minimized if it is shared. In such circumstances one would want to weight inversely to wages to reflect the compound hardship of a low-wage individual also being un-employed. Clearly the appropriate weight for hardship is not related to wages in a simple fashion. It is true that the family hardship may not be severe if a young worker with a low potential wage is unemployed; but it may be very severe if a mother in a single-headed family, also with a low potential wage, is unemployed.

Sub-employment indices of various kinds also have been proposed. Sub-employment indices reflect that portion of the labour force that is sub-employed, usually defined to include not only the unemployed, but also discouraged workers, involuntary part-time workers, and full-time workers who do not earn some minimal income. Variations on this theme are pos-sible. Levitan and Taggert (1974), for example, suggest an Employment and Earnings Inadequacy Index which excludes those in households of adequate family income, even though the earnings of one party may be low.

Computation of their index involves the following three steps: com-pute the sub-employed, defined as unemployed plus discouraged workers plus involuntary part-time workers plus employed family heads whose earnings are less than an officially defined poverty level; exclude those in households with adequate family income (perhaps because of assets or income from other family members); and divide by the sum of the labour force and discouraged workers. Their calculations, based on U.S. data for March, 1972, imply an Earnings Inadequacy Index of 11.5 percent, com-pared to an unemployment rate of 6 percent and a sub-employment rate of 15 percent.

These complementary measures are meant to be illustrative rather than exhaustive. Others are possible, and over time more will probably be proposed, implemented, and perhaps even utilized by the general public. The important point is that they are meant to supplement rather than to replace the aggregate unemployment rate as a measure of economic loss and hardship.

Labour Market Disequilibrium

The unemployment rate is also often used as a measure of the overall state of the economy and of the degree of disequilibrium in the labour market. A low unemployment rate is associated with a booming economy and with excess demand in the labour market while a high unemployment rate is associated with a recession and with excess supply in the labour market. However, this begs the question of what is meant by a "low" or "high" unemployment rate. Clearly some reference point is needed. However, as our discussion of the Canadian experience indicated, the level of unemployment that might be considered normal has changed substantially over time.

A useful reference point is the unemployment rate at which the economy-wide labour market is in equilibrium; that is, at which aggregate demand for labour equals aggregate supply of labour. This concept is referred to as the "natural" or equilibrium unemployment rate and is discussed in more detail in Chapter 27. There is aggregate excess demand in the labour market if the unemployment rate is below the natural rate, and excess supply if the unemployment rate exceeds the natural rate; indeed, that is what is meant by an equilibrium unemployment rate. However, because the natural rate is not directly observed, some care is required in interpreting increases or decreases in the unemployment rate as indicating increased slack or tightness in the labour market. A decrease in the unemployment rate could indicate either a tighter labour market or a decline in the natural rate; the former is associated with excess demand in the labour market while the latter is not. Relying solely on the unemployment rate as an indicator of the state of the economy could result in macroeconomic policy mistakes.

Perhaps the best example of a Canadian macroeconomic policy error caused in part by excessive reliance on the unemployment rate as a measure of the overall state of the economy occurred in the early 1970s. During the recession of 1970-71, unemployment climbed to over 6 percent, a level which was high by the experience of the 1950s and 1960s and which was considered indicative of substantial slack in the economy. When inflation fell somewhat, the authorities set out on an expansionary path. Although employment and output grew rapidly, the unemployment rate remained stubbornly above 6 percent during 1972 and 1973. The "high" level of unemployment was interpreted as indicating the need for further stimulus. The result was an overly expansionary policy during this period which, combined with the 1973 OPEC oil price shock, led to a substantial increase in inflation and ultimately to wage and price controls in 1975-78. In retrospect, the overly expansionary policy can be attributed in part to undue reliance on the unemployment rate as a measure of excess demand or supply and a concomitant failure to recognize that the natural unemployment rate had risen sharply during the early 1970s due mainly to the changing demographic structure of the labour force and the 1971-72 revisions to the unemployment insurance system.

Again, the lesson of this discussion is not that the unemployment rate is unsuitable as a measure of the state of the labour market, but rather that it should be used in conjunction with other indicators. In this case, although the unemployment rate remained approximately constant (at about

6.3 percent) between 1971 and 1973, employment grew very rapidly and the job vacancy rate more than doubled during this period, indicating an increasingly tight labour market.

QUESTIONS

1. (a) Discuss the various ways in which the number of unemployed typically are measured in Canada.
   (b) Which is the measure that receives the most publicity?
   (c) Discuss the strengths and weaknesses of the various measures.
2. Discuss the extent to which our aggregate unemployment rate measure may understate and overstate the degree of hardship associated with a given level of unemployment.
3. (a) Explain the meaning of the following measures of labour force utilization: (i) labour force participation rate, (ii) employment rate, and (iii) unemployment rate.
   (b) For each of these measures, describe circumstances under which that measure would be preferred to the other two.
   (c) Under what conditions will these three measures all move in the same direction? Under what conditions would they move in opposite directions?
4. Explain the concept of hidden unemployment. Discuss the pros and cons of including the hidden unemployed in our unemployment statistics.
5. Using the March issues of *The Labour Force* since 1979, construct an annual time series of the "discouraged worker" phenomenon for 1979 to the present. During which years were there relatively more discouraged workers? Why?
6. Explain the distinction between gross flows and net flows among various labour force states.
7. Discuss the differences between static and dynamic measures of unemployment.
8. In discussing the nature of unemployment, some analysts stress a shortage of jobs while others emphasize labour force turnover and employment instability.
   (a) Elaborate these competing perspectives on unemployment.
   (b) Describe research findings which attempt to distinguish between these competing perspectives. Which view is correct?
9. Why might we expect younger workers to have higher unemployment rates than older workers, and what does this imply about the changes in our aggregate unemployment rate over time?
10. Historically in Canada, female unemployment rates have been considerably lower than male unemployment rates; however, by the mid 1970s they began to exceed male rates.
    (a) Why might this be the case?
    (b) What does this imply about the time pattern of our aggregate unemployment rate?

11. Why is it that the groups with the highest unemployment rates also have the shortest average duration of unemployment?
12. (a) Indicate some of the uses for which our aggregate unemployment rates are often used.
    (b) Why might this single measure increasingly be inadequate for these purposes?
    (c) What are some of the alternatives and what are their strengths and weaknesses?

REFERENCES AND FURTHER READINGS

Akerlof, G. and B. Main. Unemployment spells and unemployment experience. *AER* 70 (December 1980) 885-893.

Akerlof, G. and B. Main. An experience-weighted measure of employment and unemployment durations. *AER* 71 (December 1981) 1003-1011.

Beach, C. and S. Kaliski. Measuring the duration of unemployment from gross flow data. *CJE* 16 (May 1983) 258-263.

Beach, C. and S. Kaliski. The impact of recession on the distribution of annual unemployment. *RI/IR* 41 (No. 2, 1986) 317-328.

Brenner, H. *Mental Illness and the Economy.* Cambridge: Harvard University Press, 1973.

Brenner, H. and A. Mooney. Unemployment and health in the context of economic change. *Social Science and Medicine* 17 (No. 16, 1983) 1125-1138.

Clark, K. and L. Summers. Labor market dynamics and unemployment: a reconsideration. *BPEA* (No. 1, 1979) 13-60.

Cook, P., G. Jump, C. Hodgins, and C. Szabo. *Economic Impact of Selected Government Programs Directed Toward the Labour Market.* Ottawa: Economic Council of Canada, 1976.

Disney, R. Recurrent spells and the concentration of unemployment in Great Britain. *EJ* 89 (March 1979) 109-119.

Economic Council of Canada. *People and Jobs: A Study of the Canadian Labour Market.* Ottawa: Information Canada, 1976.

Economic Council of Canada. *In Short Supply: Jobs and Skills in the 1980s.* Ottawa: Supply and Services Canada, 1982.

Feldstein, M. The economics of the new unemployment. *Public Interest* 33 (Fall 1973) 3-42.

Fellegi, J., G. Gray and R. Platek. The new design of the Canadian labour force survey. *Journal of American Statistical Association* (1967) 421-454.

Gilroy, C. Supplemental measures of labour force underutilization. *MLR* 98 (May 1975) 13-23.

Gramlich, E. The distributional effects of higher unemployment. *BPEA* (No. 2, 1974) 293-342.

Green, C. Labour market performance from an employment perspective. *CPP* 3 (September 1977) 315–323. Comment by S. Kaliski 3 (Autumn 1977) 515-517.

Hall, R. Why is the unemployment rate so high at full employment? *BPEA* (No. 3, 1970) 369-402.

Hall, R. Turnover in the labour force. *BPEA* 3 (1972) 709-756.

Hasan, A. and P. De Broucker. Duration and concentration of unemployment. *CJE* 15 (November 1982) 706-734.

Hollister, R. and J. Palmer. The implicit tax of inflation and unemployment. *Redistribution to the Rich and Poor*, K. Boulding and M. Pfaff (eds.). Belmont, Calif.: Woodsworth, 1972.

Hughes, J. The measurement of unemployment: an exercise in political economy. *IRJ* 7 (Winter 1976/77) 4-12.

Hurd, M. A compensation measure of the cost of unemployment to the unemployed. *QJE* 95 (September 1980) 225-244.

Jones, E. The elusive concept of underemployment. *JHR* 6 (Fall 1971) 519-564.

Junankar, P.N. Social Costs of Unemployment. Department of Economics, University of Essex, Discussion Paper No. 292, July 1986.

Kaitz, H. Analysing the lengths of spells of unemployment. *MLR* 93 (November 1970) 11-20.

Kaliski, S.F. Why must unemployment remain so high? *CPP* 10 (June 1984) 127-141.

Kaliski, S.F. Trends, changes and imbalances: a survey of the Canadian labour market. *Work and Pay: The Canadian Labour Market*. W.C. Riddell (ed.). Toronto: University of Toronto Press, 1985, 77-140.

Kelvin, P. and J. Jarrett. *Unemployment: Its Social Psychological Effects*. Cambridge: Cambridge University Press, 1984.

Levitan, S. and R. Taggart. *Employment and Earnings Inadequacy*. Balitmore: Johns Hopkins Press. 1974.

Marston, S. Employment instability and high unemployment rates. *BPEA* (No. 1, 1976) 169-210.

Maslove, A. and J. Rowley. Inflation and redistribution. *CJE* 8 (August 1975) 399-409.

Mincer, J. Determining the number of hidden unemployed. *MLR* 96 (March 1973) 27-30.

Monthly Labor Review. Measuring Unemployment. 102 (March 1979) 13–52.

Morgenstern, R. and N. Barrett. The retrospective bias in unemployment reporting by sex, race and age. *Journal of American Statistical Association* 69 (June 1974) 355-357.

Naemark, N. Comparing unemployment statistics with data from the Unemployment Insurance Commission. *Canadian Statistical Review* (March 1973).

Platt, S. Unemployment and suicidal behaviour: a review of the literature. *Social Science and Medicine* 19 (No. 2, 1984) 93-115.

Romer, C. Spurious volatility in historical unemployment data. *JPE* 94 (February 1986) 1-37.

Rosen, C. Bibliography: hidden unemployment and related issues. *MLR* 96 (March 1973) 31-37.

Siedule, T. and K. Newton. Cyclical, non-cyclical and hidden unemployment. *International Journal of Manpower* 1 (No. 4, 1980) 3-5.

Stern, J. The relationship between unemployment, morbidity and mortality in Britain. *Population Studies* 37 (1983) 61-74.

Vickery, C. The impact of turnover on group unemployment rates. *R.E. Stats.* 59 (November 1977) 415-426.

Vietorisz, T., R. Mier and J. Giblin. Subemployment: exclusion and inadequacy indexes. *MLR* 98 (May 1975) 3-12.

Werneke, D. Measuring economic hardship in the labor market. *AER* 69 (May 1979) 43-47.

CHAPTER 26
Unemployment: Causes and Consequences

The previous chapter discussed the meaning and measurement of un-employment and described the salient aspects of the Canadian experience. In this chapter we examine the causes and consequences of unemployment and the role of public policy in this area.

TYPES OF UNEMPLOYMENT

Economists usually distinguish among several types of unemployment. These differ according to their causes, their consequences, and the policies that are likely to be effective in dealing with them. The most common categories are frictional, structural, deficient demand, and seasonal un-employment. Each of these will be discussed in turn. As will become evident in the ensuing discussion, the distinctions are often not clear-cut, either conceptually or practically.

Frictional Unemployment

Frictional unemployment is associated with normal turnover in the labour force; it can thus be thought of as unemployment that would prevail even in a well-functioning labour market. Change is a pervasive feature of modern economies. As discussed previously, in each period some individuals enter the labour force to search for work while others leave to return to school, retire, or work in the home. Similarly, new jobs open up in some firms and disappear in others. As a consequence, unemployed workers and unfilled job vacancies will coexist at any point in time. This unemployment exists even if jobs and workers are potentially matched in the sense that the unemployed workers are qualified for the available jobs and are willing to fill these jobs; they simply have to be brought together and this process takes time. For this reason, frictional unemployment is often associated with job search activity within a given labour market. Because suitable unfilled vacancies exist for the frictionally unemployed, this type of unemployment will typically be of short duration; however, the optimal duration will depend on the benefits and costs of continued search, as discussed below.

Unfilled job vacancies and unemployed job seekers coexist because of imperfect information. Time and money are required for the unemployed to discover the available jobs, their rates of pay and their working conditions. Such is also the case for employers to identify applicants and determine their suitability. The process of matching job seekers with job vacancies yields benefits — both to the individual employers and employees involved and to society — but it also involves costs. By improving the flow of information, it may be possible to reduce the amount of frictional unemployment. However, it is unlikely that such unemployment could be eliminated, nor is it necessarily the case that reducing frictional unemployment would be desirable. In many circumstances the benefits of search and the acquisition of information by employers and job seekers will exceed the costs. In such cases it is both privately and socially optimal for the parties to engage in such activity. Furthermore, the additional benefits of reducing frictional unemployment — perhaps by reducing the time needed to locate job vacancies — may not exceed the additional costs associated with bringing about this change. In these circumstances it would not be desirable to implement policies intended to reduce frictional unemployment.

Frictional unemployment may also take the form of temporary layoffs. Even in the absence of fluctuations in aggregate economic activity, individual firms and industries are affected by changes in product demand due to changes in international economic conditions, consumer demand, weather, work stoppages, and so on. Employers may respond to reductions in demand in a variety of ways: inventory accumulation, wage and/or hours reductions affecting most or all of the work-force, or temporary layoffs affecting a portion of the work-force. The combination chosen will depend on a variety of factors discussed below. For some firms and industries temporary layoffs are a common form of adjustment to changing circumstances. As explained previously, individuals who have been awaiting recall to their former employer for six weeks or less are classified as unemployed even though they may not be searching for work. Temporary layoffs typically account for 7 to 12 percent of unemployment in Canada (Kaliski, 1985). About 20 percent of workers on temporary layoff search for work, perhaps because they are uncertain about being recalled or perhaps because they are using the opportunity to try to find a better job. Workers on temporary layoff are considered to be frictionally unemployed in the sense that the fluctuations in individual markets which give rise to layoffs are part of the normal "frictions" of a decentralized market economy. However, temporary layoffs are conceptually different from other forms of frictional unemployment in that job vacancies for these workers do not necessarily exist at the time of the survey; rather, the unemployed are waiting for their previous jobs to reappear.

Temporary layoffs in response to fluctuations in demand can be an efficient arrangement from the perspective of both employers and employees if other forms of adjustment (inventory accumulation, wage and/ or hours reductions) are costly, and if the costs to workers of brief periods of temporary unemployment (and reduced income) are not too high.

Structural Unemployment

Structural unemployment results when the skills or location of the unemployed are not matched with the characteristics of the job vacancies. Unemployed workers and job vacancies are considered to be in different labour markets, either by virtue of geography or because they do not coincide in terms of qualifications and characteristics. The analogy that is often used is that of matching square pegs to round holes. As is the case with frictional unemployment, structural unemployment is characterized by the coexistence of unemployed workers and job vacancies. However, in this case, successful matching of workers and jobs requires more than acquisition of information. In particular, employees or employers will either have to relocate — when there job vacancies in one region and unemployed workers in another — or alter their characteristics or requirements (in the case of mismatching along occupational and skill lines). Proposed solutions to structural unemployment usually involve improving the human capital characteristics of the workers by education or training programs or encouraging labour mobility and job search in other regions. They could also include adapting the characteristics of the jobs themselves by altering entrance requirements, rearranging the basic job components to adapt to available skills, and even job enrichment and job enlargement. Regional development policies which attempt to expand employment opportunities in areas with high levels of structural unemployment have also been used in Canada.

One of the most difficult issues relating to structural unemployment involves determining whether a particular situation is temporary or permanent. For example, suppose that there is an increase in demand in one industry, occupation or region, giving rise to job vacancies in that sector — and a decrease in demand in another industry, occupation or region, giving rise to unemployed workers in that sector. If these changes in demand are permanent in nature, the resulting unemployment is clearly structural and the best course of action will usually be to adjust to the structural change, perhaps via retraining or relocation. However, if the changes in demand are temporary in nature, the resulting unemployment is more frictional than structural and the best course of action may well be to simply wait for demand to return to normal levels in each sector. In these circumstances, costly activities such as relocation or retraining are inappropriate because they yield negligible (perhaps zero) benefits. Unfortunately it is not always evident in advance which situations are temporary and which are permanent. From the perspective of individuals adversely affected by economic change, this uncertainty implies that it may not be clear whether investments such as retraining or relocation are worthwhile. In these circumstances, some individuals may wait for the uncertainty to be resolved before taking action. Providing it is based on a careful assessment of the likelihood of demand returning to previous levels, and not on "wishful thinking," waiting for the resolution of uncertainty can be viewed as a productive activity analogous to the acquisition of information associated with job search. Waiting can result in the acquisition of information about future developments while job search can result in acquiring information about current job opportunities.

When the changes giving rise to structural unemployment are clearly permanent in nature, the best course of action — both from the perspective of the individuals involved and from that of society — usually will be to adjust to the altered circumstances. An exception occurs for people near the end of their working lives. For these individuals, the benefits of retraining or relocation may not justify the costs, and alternatives such as early retirement may be best, given the available options.

The distinction between frictional and structural unemployment can be blurred conceptually, and in practice it can be difficult to clearly delineate the two. Nevertheless, there are differences in degree if not in kind. Frictional unemployment is a result of the matching process; structural unemployment occurs when there is mismatching. Frictional unemployment is associated with job search in an individual labour market; structural unemployment involves more costly solutions, ranging from retraining for a job within the individual labour market to job search and relocation in other labour markets. Frictional unemployment is associated with a productive activity — the acquisition of information regarding job opportunities and applicants — and thus policies designed to reduce frictional unemployment are not necessarily desirable. Structural unemployment that is clearly permanent in nature is not associated with a productive activity and actions to reduce this type of unemployment should be taken. What the two have in common is that they are related to the characteristics of the workers and the job, not to the general state of aggregate demand in the economy. Even here, though, the distinction between demand-deficient unemployment and non-demand deficient unemployment (frictional, structural) may become blurred as the characteristics of the work-force and of jobs themselves may be related to the aggregate state of the economy.

Demand-Deficient Unemployment

Demand-deficient unemployment exists when there is insufficient aggregate demand in the economy to provide jobs. It is not a matter of workers engaging in normal job search or lacking the correct skills or being in the wrong labour market; rather it is a matter of insufficient aggregate demand to generate sufficient job vacancies. Therefore, job vacancies would fall short of the number of unemployed job seekers. That is, defining labour supply as employed plus unemployed, and labour demand as employed plus vacancies, then insufficient demand, defined as being less than supply, would imply vacancies being less than the number unemployed.

Demand-deficient unemployment is usually associated with adverse business cycle conditions; hence, the term cyclical unemployment is often used. However, it may also be associated with a chronic (as opposed to short-term cyclical) insufficiency of aggregate demand as occurred, for example, in the Great Depression of the 1930s. Since the cause of such unemployment is a deficiency of aggregate demand, its cures usually involve macroeconomic policies to increase consumption, investment, exports, or government spending, or to decrease imports and taxes. Monetary, fiscal, and exchange rate policies are the traditional macroeconomic instruments.

Seasonal Unemployment

Seasonal unemployment is often associated with insufficient demand in a particular season. In this sense it can be considered as demand-deficient unemployment; nevertheless, it is different in the sense that it is not a shortage of aggregate demand for the economy as a whole, but rather a shortage of demand in a particular season. The patterns are usually predictable over the year and specific to particular industries. For example, seasonal unemployment is usually prevalent in the winter months in construction, agriculture, and the tourist trade. Seasonal fluctuations in labour supply may also occur, the most significant example being the large number of college and university students who enter the labour force during the summer.

Seasonal unemployment is analogous in several respects to temporary layoffs, and is therefore often included under the rubric of frictional unemployment. Both seasonal unemployment and temporary layoffs involve the workers returning to their previous job or employer. To the extent that layoffs or seasonal unemployment are anticipated, employees generally will receive some compensation ex ante in the form of a wage premium to compensate them for the probability of being unemployed.

To a certain extent seasonal jobs could be adapted to employ more people over the slow season. Some construction jobs could be modified so as to be more continuous throughout the year. Tourist facilities can likewise adapt, for example, as winter ski areas become summer schools in other sports or crafts. In some industries like agriculture, migrant labour often moves to other labour markets, following the seasonal patterns of demand.

Clearly the fact that such adaptation of jobs and workers can and does go on illustrates that seasonal unemployment is not immutable. It is related to the costs and benefits of reducing such unemployment, and the private market will respond to changes in these costs and benefits. To the extent, for example, that the cost to employers and employees of seasonal unemployment is reduced by the availability of unemployment insurance benefits, then one may expect more seasonal unemployment.

Aggregate unemployment rates are often referred to as seasonally adjusted or unadjusted. The seasonally unadjusted figures simply show the unemployment rate as it is in a particular month, unadjusted for seasonal fluctuations. The seasonally adjusted figures show the unemployment rate that would have prevailed had the particular month not been associated with unusually high or low seasonal demand conditions. Those who are seasonally unemployed are not removed from the figures; they are simply averaged in over the year.

Involuntary Unemployment and Wage Rigidity

Another distinction often made is that between voluntary and involuntary unemployment. According to the most common definition of these terms, individuals are involuntarily unemployed if they are willing to work at the going wage rate for their skills or occupation but they are unable to find a job. Voluntary unemployment exists when a job is available but the worker is not willing to accept it at the existing wage rate. These definitions are based on the willingness to work at the prevailing wage, rather than on the reason for becoming unemployed, such as job loser or job leaver. Nonetheless, many job losers may be involuntarily unemployed and many job leavers voluntarily unemployed.

Cyclical unemployment is often viewed as being largely involuntary in nature because evidence suggests that many of those unemployed in economic downturns would accept work, even at wages below the prevailing wage. This phenomenon could be associated with a failure of the wage to adjust to a decline in aggregate demand, creating excess supply of labour at the existing wage rate. For this reason, involuntary unemployment and wage rigidity are often regarded as being closely linked. Explaining why wages may not adjust to "clear" the labour market is a puzzle that has challenged economists for many years. Leading responses to that challenge are examined in the next section.

EXPLANATIONS OF UNEMPLOYMENT

The economic theory of frictional, structural, and demand-deficient unemployment has received considerable attention, especially in the past two decades. To a considerable extent this interest has been motivated by the increase in unemployment that occurred in many countries during the 1970s and 1980s. In addition, many economists believed that the theory of unemployment suffered from a lack of clear microeconomic foundations similar to that which provides the basis for the theory of household or firm behaviour. Significant recent developments include search theory, implicit contracts, and efficiency wages. The relationship between unemployment insurance and unemployment has also been extensively investigated. This section discusses these and related developments and their contribution to understanding unemployment.

Search Unemployment

The job search and matching process is associated with imperfect information on both sides of the labour market. Unemployed workers are not aware of all available jobs, their rates of pay, location, and working conditions. Employers with job vacancies are not aware of all individual workers and their characteristics. If both sides were fully informed, the process of matching workers and jobs could take place in a few days, if not hours. However, because the acquisition of information about job opportunities and job applicants takes time, unemployment and unfilled vacancies coexist.

Following the important early contributions of Stigler (1962) and Phelps et al. (1970), the economics of job search has received considerable attention in the past two decades. To illustrate the main ideas we focus primarily on the job search process of employees. Employer search is discussed in Lippman and McCall (1976) and in the Canadian context in Maki (1971, Chapter 3).

Job search is an economic decision in that it involves both costs and benefits. There are two main aspects to the decision: (1) determining whether it is worthwhile *initiating* the job search process and (2) once begun, determining when to *discontinue* the process. For employees, initiating a job search or continuing to search rather than accepting the first job offer that comes along may yield benefits in the form of a superior job offer involving higher wages or better working conditions. Similarly, by continuing to search rather than filling the job with the first "warm body" that becomes available, the firm may obtain benefits in the form of more suitable or more qualified applicants. In both cases the magnitude of these benefits is uncertain; their size depends on the employee's expectations regarding the probability of receiving a superior job offer or on the firm's expectations regarding the quality of future applicants. Those engaged in search must make their decisions based on these expectations: i.e., on the information available ex ante. The realized or ex post benefits may turn out to be larger or smaller than the expected benefits.

The expected benefits have to be weighed against the costs of search. These include both the direct costs — such as the firm's costs of advertising positions and interviewing applicants and the employee's costs of sending applications and travelling to interviews — and the indirect or opportunity costs. For employees the opportunity costs are measured by the best alternative use of their time devoted to job search. For those who quit their previous job to search for a better one their opportunity cost would be their previous wage. For others the opportunity cost would be measured by the best job offer received so far or the wage that could be earned in some job that is known to be available. It could also be an individual's implicit home wage or the value of their time doing household work. For employers the opportunity cost of continuing to search is the difference between the value of the output that would be produced by the best known applicant and the wages that would be paid to that applicant.

Not all job seekers are unemployed; some individuals will search for a better job while employed. Employed search has the advantage of being less costly. However, it may also be less effective because of the difficulties associated with contacting potential employers and following up promising opportunities while working, especially if employed on a full-time basis.

In some circumstances individuals may choose to quit their current job in order to search for a better one, while in other circumstances employed search will be the preferred method.

The central assumption in the economic analysis of job search is that individuals will search in an optimal fashion: that is, will choose their search activities in order to maximize their expected utility. Note, however, that the assumption of optimal search behaviour does not imply that all unemployed job seekers have *chosen* to be unemployed or that all search unemployment is voluntary in nature. Individuals who quit their previous job in order to search for a new job — the "job leavers" in Table 25.2 — may have chosen unemployment. Rational employees would not do so unless the expected utility of searching for a new job exceeds the expected utility of remaining in the existing job. However, as Table 25.2 indicates, about half the unemployed are "job losers"; many of these individuals may have preferred to remain in their previous job. Nonetheless, given that they have lost their previous job, rational individuals will carry out their job search in an optimal fashion. In the case of a person who is risk-neutral, this assumption implies that the individual will choose the amount of search activity that maximizes the net expected benefit (expected benefits minus expected costs). Risk-averse employees will also take into account the costs and benefits of search, but will attach a greater weight to benefits and costs which are certain compared to those which are uncertain. The basic principles of optimal job search are most easily explained in the context of risk-neutral searchers. However, very similar principles and conclusions follow when individuals are risk-averse.

In order to maximize the net expected benefits of job search, employees should continue searching until the marginal expected benefit of search equals the marginal expected cost. This condition is simply another example of the rule that the net benefit of any activity is maximized by expanding the activity to the point at which its marginal benefit equals its marginal cost. Figure 26.1 shows the way in which the benefits and costs of search are likely to be related to the amount of time devoted to job search. The case in which search is worthwhile is illustrated (i.e. total expected benefits exceed total costs). For low levels of search, the marginal costs of search are fairly low because low-cost, usually informal, search processes can be used. For example, friends and relatives can be contacted, want ads examined, and perhaps a few telephone calls made. As the search continues, however, more costly processes are often necessary to acquire additional labour market information. For example, it may be necessary to apply directly to a company or to sign up with an employment service. In some cases it may even be necessary to change locations or to quit working if one already has a job. For these reasons the marginal cost of search probably rises with the amount of job search undertaken, as depicted in Figure 26.1.

The marginal benefits of search, on the other hand, probably are a declining function of the amount of search undertaken. One starts out the

Figure 26.1 Optimal Job Search

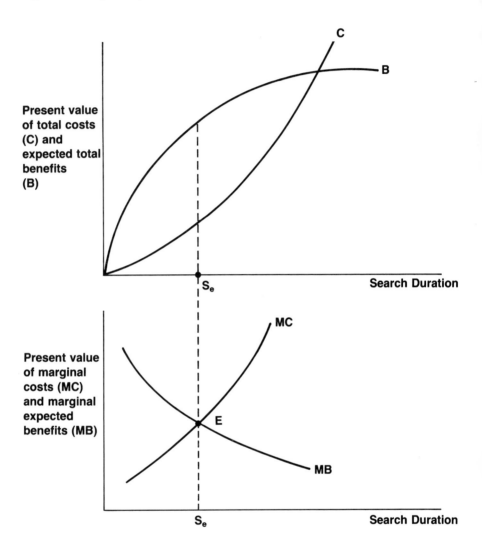

search process with an examination of the most promising alternatives and then continues examining further activities in the hope of finding an even better one. Obviously, a better alternative may occur; however, one may encounter diminishing returns with respect to the additional information. As search continues it becomes less likely — but still possible — that a better offer will be received simply because there are fewer options left to examine.

Given the costs and benefits of additional search, the rational individual will acquire labour market information and engage in search until the point E, where the marginal expected benefits equal the marginal cost.

To the left of E, the benefits of additional search exceed the cost and hence additional search is worthwhile; to the right of E, the benefits of additional search are not worth the costs. In this sense E will be an equilibrium with S_e being the optimal amount of expected search activity. Note, however, that S_e is the *expected* amount of search required to maximize net benefits. The actual amount of search undertaken in any particular situation may turn out to differ from S_e. For example, a lucky individual who receives an extremely good job offer during the first week will experience an actual search duration less than S_e because the best course of action will be to accept the job and discontinue the search.

The conditions for optimal search can alternatively be stated in terms of a "stopping rule": the individual should choose a minimum acceptable wage and search until a job paying this wage or better is found. The minimum acceptable wage is often referred to as a "reservation wage," although this concept is not identical to the reservation wage discussed in Chapter 5 on labour force participation. Choosing a minimum acceptable wage is equivalent to choosing an expected search duration. On average, given the distribution of wage offers in the market and the rate at which firms can be contacted, the individual will require the expected search duration to find an acceptable job. The minimum acceptable wage is therefore chosen to equate the marginal benefits and marginal costs of search.

Factors Determining Optimal Search

This framework is useful to illustrate how the optimal amount of search depends on the various factors underlying the cost and benefit schedules and how search activity will respond to shifts in these schedules. For example, factors affecting the expected benefits of job search are the dispersion of wage offers (for otherwise comparable jobs) and the expected duration of the job. If there is little variation in the attractiveness of different jobs in terms of wages and working conditions, there is little point in continuing to search once an offer has been received. In contrast, if some jobs are much more desirable than others, the optimal strategy may be to continue searching even after receiving an average job offer. Similarly, if some potential jobs are more desirable than others it will be rational to devote more time to search the longer is the anticipated duration of employment because of the longer period over which the benefits of a superior job can be enjoyed.

These two factors may help explain the observed differences in the average duration of unemployment across age and sex groups, as summarized in Table 25.3. Because of their limited work experience, youths typically face a less dispersed distribution of potential wages than older workers. In addition, many youths try out a variety of jobs before settling on a career; thus, on average, their expected duration of employment is much lower than is the case for adult workers. (See de Broucker and Hasan (1982) for some Canadian evidence.) For both these reasons, there is less incentive for youths than for adult workers to continue searching in the expectation of obtaining a better job. These considerations are consistent with the observation that the average duration of unemployment of youths is significantly lower than that of adults. Similarly, because adult women tend to exit from and re-enter the labour force more frequently than adult men, the expected duration of employment for women is lower than that for men, at least on average. This may help account for the fact that the average duration of search unemployment for adult women is lower than that for adult men, as shown in Table 25.3.

Shifts in the schedules may affect the number of searchers as well as the expected duration of search. For example, an increase in expected total benefits or a decrease in total costs will imply a larger number of people for whom search is worthwhile. As a consequence the following may be observed: more entry and re-entry into the labour force, an increase in the number of quits as more employed workers seek a new job, and more search by the employed.

Other factors affecting the benefits and costs of employee search are the institutional mechanisms for disseminating labour market information, the number of employers with job vacancies, the rate at which employers make job offers, the value of 'leisure' time (time spent not searching or working), the number of other searchers competing for the available jobs, and the occupational and regional segmentation of labour markets. Social and labour market policies can also alter the costs and benefits of search and hence its amount and duration. Unemployment insurance and portable pensions would reduce the total and marginal costs of search and hence increase the number of searchers and the optimal duration of search. Improving the arrangements for disseminating labour market information would increase the total benefits and, in most cases, the marginal benefits as well. Thus the number of job seekers would increase but the expected duration would fall. The total amount of search unemployment may either increase or decrease, depending on which effect is larger.

Aggregate economic conditions can also affect the schedules and hence the amount and duration of job search. In recessions the expected benefits of search decline because there are fewer unfilled vacancies and more job losers competing for the available jobs. The downward shift in the benefit schedule can be expected to result in fewer employed workers quitting their jobs to search for a new job, which explains why the quit rate varies pro-cyclically. The tendency for quits to decline in recessions is evident from Table 25-2 which shows that the proportion of job leavers fell sharply during the 1982–1983 recession and has subsequently gradually increased as the economy recovered. The decline in the benefits of search will also result in less entry into and more withdrawal from the labour force, as fewer of the unemployed find search worthwhile. This "discouraged worker" phenomenon was discussed previously in the context of hidden unemployment. Because of this phenomenon the labour force participation rate also varies pro-cyclically. As a further consequence, in a recession the rise in unemployment will be less than the decline in employment; the opposite occurs as the economy recovers from the recession.

The job search paradigm may also help explain why wages adjust slowly to excess supply or demand in the labour market. As noted above, the optimal search strategy involves choosing an acceptance wage and searching until a job offering this wage or better is found. Thus wages are not adjusted downward even if an acceptable job is not found quickly. Over time, unemployed searchers will revise downward their acceptance wages if they discover that their initial beliefs regarding the distribution of wage offers and the rate at which job offers are made were too optimistic, as would be the case if there were more labour supply or less demand than originally anticipated. However, because this learning process takes time, the adjustment of wages to excess demand or supply will occur less quickly than in the presence of complete information.

Empirical Evidence

A significant amount of job search takes place. In recent years about 10 to 15 percent of the labour force has been engaged in job search at any point in time (Statistics Canada, *The Labour Force*, various issues). About two-thirds of searchers are unemployed and one-third employed. On average, three to five percent of employed workers are searching for a new job. Groups that are more likely to engage in employed search are men, part-time workers, the highly educated and those in managerial, professional, and service occupations (Hasan and Gera, 1982).

TABLE 26.1
SEARCH ACTIVITY OF UNEMPLOYED, CANADA: APRIL, 1987

Search Activity	Number Using Activity (thousands)	Percent Using Activity[1]
Did not search	88	7
Searched	1183	93
Contacted employers directly	852	67
Looked at ads	578	45
Used public employment agency	484	38
Used other methods	370	29

Note: [1] The sum of the methods does not equal the total because an individual may use more than one method. The average number of methods used was 2.0.

Source: Statistics Canada, *The Labour Force*, April 1987. Reproduced with permission of the Minister of Supply and Services Canada.

Workers can engage in a variety of search activities ranging from informal discussions with friends and relatives to more formal activities such as contacting private or public employment agencies. In addition, varying degrees of success can be associated with each of these activities. Table 26.1 indicates the most common search activities used in Canada according to a recent Labour Force Survey. The most popular measure was to contact employers directly, followed by looking at ads and using a public employment agency. Most searchers used more than one method.

Using an activity, however, does not mean that it will be successful. In his study of the search activity of the unemployed in Canada, Maki (1971) found that informal search activities, such as contacting friends and relatives and local employers, were more successful than formal activities such as using a private or public employment agency. In their study based on U.S. data, Sheppard and Beltsky (1966) also rank the informal job-seeking technique of contacting friends and relatives to be most effective for all skill levels.

Hasan and Gera (1982) examine the search behaviour of both the employed and the unemployed in Canada. They conclude that, on average, employees who quit to search for a new job experience a wage increase while workers who are laid off experience a wage decrease. This finding is consistent with the theory of optimal search discussed above: job leavers would not quit to search unless they expected to be able to find a better job, whereas job losers need not anticipate being able to improve on their previous job even if they pursue an optimal search strategy.

In summary, labour market search is an important activity among the unemployed, some of the employed, and many employers. Most fundamentally, the economic analysis of job search helps explain the coexistence of unemployed workers and unfilled vacancies and the process through which these are matched. More specifically, search theory offers insights into several phenomena, including the duration of unemployment, the cyclical behaviour of quits and labour force participation, the sluggish adjustment of wages to changes in economic conditions, and the consequences of public policies such as unemployment insurance and the provision of labour market information.

Implicit Contracts

While search theory is concerned with unemployment that is associated with the process of matching job vacancies and unemployed workers, implicit contract theory deals with unemployment that may arise when firms and workers are already engaged in a continuing employment relationship. In particular, implicit contract theory seeks to explain phenomena such as rigid wages and the use of quantity adjustments (layoffs and rehires) rather than wage adjustments to respond to variations in product demand.

Implicit contract theory is based on the view that wage and employment behaviour reflects risk sharing between employers and employees. Risk sharing arises because of differences in attitudes toward risk between workers and the owners of firms. Specifically, workers are believed to be more risk-averse than the shareholders of firms. These differences in attitudes toward risk create potential gains from trade; that is, both parties can benefit from a risk-sharing arrangement. Because workers dislike fluctuations in their incomes, they prefer an arrangement whereby they receive a somewhat lower average or expected income provided their income is sufficiently less variable (more certain). The owners of firms also prefer this arrangement because average or expected profits are higher (due to lower labour costs), albeit more variable because of the stabilization of workers' incomes. In effect, the employment relation involves two transactions: (1) provision of labour services by employees in exchange for payment by employers, and (2) provision of insurance services by employers in exchange for payment of an insurance premium (acceptance of a lower wage) by employees. For reasons discussed below, workers are generally unable to purchase insurance against the risk of income fluctuations in regular insurance markets such as those that exist for accident, property, and life insurance. However, the continuing nature of the employment relationship makes feasible the implicit purchase of income insurance from the employer.

Seminal contributions to implicit contract theory were made by Azariadis (1975), Baily (1974) and Gordon (1974). A large literature, much of it highly technical in nature, has subsequently developed. Our purpose in this section is to present the basic elements of implicit contract theory in as non-technical a fashion as possible. Further details are available in surveys by Azariadis (1979), Azariadis and Stiglitz (1983), Hart (1983), and Rosen (1985).

Differences in attitudes toward risk between employers and employees provide the basis for both parties to benefit from a risk-sharing arrangement. Two reasons why workers may be more risk-averse than the owners of firms have been advanced. Perhaps the most significant factor is that for many workers their wealth consists largely of the value of their human capital, which cannot be diversified. In contrast, individuals whose wealth consists largely of financial capital can reduce the risk of a reduction in their wealth by holding a diversified portfolio; that is, by acquiring shares in (or income claims on) a variety of companies. It is not possible to diversify wealth holdings in the form of human capital because markets analogous to the stock market do not exist for buying and selling claims on the incomes of different individuals or groups of individuals. Such markets would constitute a form of slavery and would therefore be illegal, even if there were sufficient demand to make markets for trading in such claims viable. Workers, therefore, are in the awkward position of having most of their wealth in one risky asset — their human capital. As a consequence, they seek alternative ways of reducing the risk of fluctuations in the return on that asset, their employment income.

A second reason for differences in risk attitudes involves sorting according to innate risk preferences. Those who are venturesome — risk-neutral or perhaps even risk lovers — may be more likely to become entrepreneurs and thus the owners of firms. Cautious or risk-averse individuals may be more likely to become employees and wage earners.

If workers dislike the risk of fluctuations in their employment income, why don't they purchase income insurance from private insurance companies? Private markets for income insurance do not exist because of two phenomena — moral hazard and adverse selection — that result in the selling of such insurance being an unprofitable activity, despite the demand that exists for the product. Moral hazard exists when individuals can influence the risk against which they are insured. For example, suppose workers are insured against reductions in their income associated with becoming unemployed. If the fact that they are insured affects their behaviour such that they are then more likely to be unemployed and collecting insurance — perhaps because those who become unemployed search longer for a better job when they are insured or because they become more willing to accept a job with a high risk of layoff than they would if they were not insured — then the profitability of selling such insurance is reduced, perhaps to the point at which selling such insurance is unprofitable.

Adverse selection occurs when the insurer cannot observe the risk that a particular insuree represents. The insurer thus charges each customer the same rate. However, the high-risk individuals are more likely and the low-risk individuals less likely to purchase insurance. Thus the average risk among those who purchase insurance will be higher than the risk for the population as a whole. The insurer will therefore earn less — perhaps incurring a loss — than would be expected on the basis of population risk statistics. Furthermore, raising its insurance rates may not increase profitability because fewer individuals will purchase insurance at the higher rates *and* those who decide not to purchase insurance because of the higher rates will be the customers facing the lowest risk. Thus, with each increase in its rates, the insurance company ends up selling to a smaller number of customers with a higher average risk. In these circumstances, there may be no price that would enable insurance to be sold at a profit.

Moral hazard and adverse selection may exist in any insurance market. In some cases — such as automobile insurance for most individuals and life insurance for individuals under 65 — the reduction in profitability due to moral hazard and adverse selection is small enough that private insurance markets continue to exist. In other cases — such as life insurance for individuals over 65 and income insurance in the labour market — the reduction in profitability is evidently large enough that insurance against these risks can't be purchased in the usual fashion. The central hypothesis of implicit contract theory is that employees purchase income insurance indirectly from the employer. The continuing nature of the employment relationship enables the employer to deal with the moral hazard and adverse selection problems. The firm provides insurance only to its own employees, thus avoiding adverse selection. In addition, the firm controls the probability of income loss due to layoff or wage and/or hours reduction, thus avoiding the moral hazard problem.

Implicit contract theory applies to situations in which there is a long-term attachment between the firm and its workers. Many economists have suggested that in labour markets with these characteristics wages do not adjust each period to equate demand and supply. In contrast, many product and asset markets behave like "Walrasian auction markets" in which the price adjusts each period to clear the market. According to implicit contract theory this difference in behaviour reflects risk sharing in the labour market. The continuing nature of the employment relationship enables the firm to stabilize its employees' incomes over several periods by paying a wage above that which would exist with continuous market clearing when product demand conditions are weaker than normal and paying a wage below that which would exist with continuous market clearing when product demand conditions are stronger than normal.

The reasons for the importance of long-term attachments in the labour market have been discussed previously. Specific human capital is perhaps the most fundamental factor. As discussed in Chapter 18 on Human Capital, when employees acquire firm-specific human capital due to on-the-job training and experience, then both the employer and the employees subsequently earn rents. The worker receives a wage greater than the alternative wage and the firm earns a marginal revenue product greater than the worker's wage. The fact that both parties are earning rents provides the incentive for each to continue the employment relationship. A second reason for long-term attachments in the labour market is the cost of search and mobility discussed in the previous section. Because finding a new job is costly to employees and hiring new workers is costly to employers, both parties usually prefer to maintain the employment relationship.

Although employers and employees are assumed to be involved in a continuing employment relationship, the basic model of implicit contracts can be explained in a two-period setting. In the initial period, firms offer wage and employment contracts to workers and workers decide which firm's contract to accept. The wages and employment stipulated in these contracts may be contingent on the state of product demand realized in the second period. The contracts agreed to in the first period are then carried out in the second. Thus workers are mobile ex ante (in the initial period when they are choosing which firm's contract to accept) but immobile ex post (in the seond period when the uncertainty about product demand conditions is resolved and the terms of the contract are carried out). The assumption of ex post immobility is intended to reflect the continuing nature of the employment relationship and the cost of severing that relationship.

These contractual arrangements are not formal written agreements — hence the term "implicit contract" — but rather represent understandings that govern the behaviour of firms and workers. As stated colourfully by Okun (1981, p. 89), "Employers . . . rely heavily on the 'invisible handshake' as a substitute for the invisible hand that cannot operate effectively in the career labour market." The explicit contracts observed in the union sector may also reflect risk sharing to some degree, but the purpose of the analysis is to explain behaviour in the unorganized sector.

To keep the analysis simple, we will assume that the workers are homogeneous, each with utility function u(y) where y = w•h is income, w is the wage rate and h is hours worked. To focus on wages and employment, hours of work will be assumed to be constant at $\overline{h}$. A worker is thus either employed, working $\overline{h}$ hours, or unemployed, working zero hours. With hours of work fixed, an employed worker's utility can be written in terms of the wage rate alone, u(w). An unemployed worker receives utility u(k), where k is the value of leisure time and any unemployment benefit received from the unemployment insurance program. (Workers on layoff receive no income from the employer.) Because workers are homogeneous, which workers are laid off (should layoffs be required) is randomly determined.

Let N_o be the number of workers attached to the firm; this is the number of workers who agreed to join the firm's "labour pool" given the contract offered in the first period. The firm's labour supply curve in the second period is thus shown by S in Figure 26.2. At wage rates equal to or greater than the reservation wage k, the firm can employ up to N_o workers. The firm cannot employ any workers at wage rates below k.

We will discuss the case in which perfect competition prevails in the output market so that the price of output is not affected by the output produced and hence labour utilized. The analysis for other product market structures is similar. The firm's labour demand schedule is the locus of points for which wages are just equal to the value of the marginal product of labour, which in turn equals the marginal product of labour times the price at which the extra output is sold. That is, $D = VMP_N = MPP_N P$ where MPP_N is the marginal product of labour, and P is the price of output.

There is uncertainty about the state of the product market. When product market conditions are strong, the product price and the demand for labour will be high. The opposite holds in weak product market conditions. For ease of exposition we will assume that there are only two possible states of the product market — the "good state" in which the product price is high at P_a and the "poor state" in which the product price is low at P_b — and that these are equally likely to occur. The assumption of two equi-probable outcomes does not affect the analysis in any way except to make the results easier to present. An important assumption, however, is that both the employer and employees observe the state which is realized. When this *symmetric information* assumption holds the two parties can make the implicit wage-employment contract contingent on the observed state. When *asymmetric information* exists — for example, if the firm has better information about the state of the product market than the workers — this type of contingent contract may not be optimal because the firm will usually have an incentive to cheat. For example, if the wage rate depends on the state, the firm may want to claim that the poor state

Figure 26.2

(a) Wages and Employment with Market Clearing

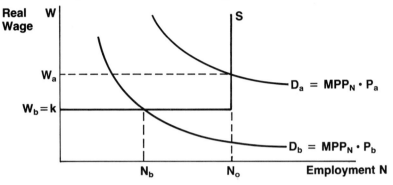

(b) Wages and Employment with Implicit Contracts

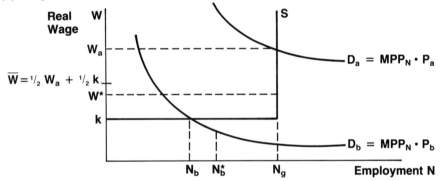

(c) Wages and Employment with Implicit Contracts and a Zero Reservation Wage

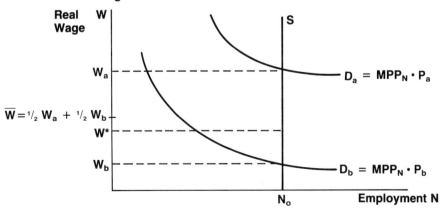

has been realized — whatever the actual state — in order to pay a lower wage. The nature of contracts under asymmetric information is discussed further below.

The behaviour of a continuously clearing labour market, as shown in Figure 26.2 (a), provides a useful benchmark for examining the influence of risk sharing on wages and employment. In the good state the wage rises to w_a and all the workers in the firm's labour pool are employed ($N = N_o$). In the poor state the wage falls to w_b (equal to the reservation wage k) and employment declines to N_b.

It is important to note that there is no involuntary unemployment with market clearing. In the poor state, the decline in demand produces excess labour supply and the wage rate declines. As the wage falls below k, some workers withdraw from employment. The result is an equilibrium at (w_b, N_b). Because the employed workers are paid the reservation wage k, unemployed workers do not envy the employed workers. Workers are indifferent between being employed and unemployed, given the equilibrium wage rate and their value of leisure time.

As is well known, in the absence of externalities and other sources of market failure, the competitive market-clearing outcome produces an efficient allocation of resources. In the case analysed here, the allocation of labour among firms was determined ex ante. However, there remains the question of how to best utilize each firm's labour pool. The allocation of workers shown in Figure 26.2 (a) — including the fact that $N_b N_o$ workers are not employed in the poor state — is efficient in the sense that it maximizes the value of output produced and income generated in each state. However, with market clearing, workers face an uncertain income stream. Income may fluctuate because both the wage rate and employment depend on the state which is realized. Because of this income uncertainty, the market-clearing outcome is not, in general, a pareto optimal arrangement — i.e., it is possible through risk sharing to make at least one of the parties better off without making the other party worse off — even though it does produce an efficient allocation of labour resources. An optimal arrangement takes into account both efficiency and risk-sharing considerations.

A Pareto optimal contract between a risk-neutral firm and risk-averse workers has the following features: (1) the real wage rate is independent of the state which is realized so that employed workers receive the same real wage whatever the level of product demand, and (2) layoffs may occur in weak states of demand; however, the number of workers laid off will be less than the number who would be voluntarily unemployed under market clearing. Figure 26.2 (b) shows an example of an optimal wage-employment contract. Employed workers receive the wage w^* in each state. Employment equals N_o in the good state and N_b^* in the poor state.

Several features of the optimal contract should be noted. First, the contract provides for a rigid real wage. Employed workers receive the same utility, whatever the state of product demand and the overall price level. The contract wage w^* is lower than the market-clearing wage in the good state and higher than with market clearing in the poor state. Second, there are layoffs in the poor state. However, the number of workers laid off $(N_b^* N_o)$ is less than the number that would voluntarily withdraw from employment with market clearing $(N_b N_o)$. Third, there is involuntary unemployment in the poor state, which is why layoffs are necessary. Employed workers receive utility $u(w^*)$ whereas unemployed workers receive utility $u(k)$; laid-off workers would prefer to be employed given that the wage does not decline in the poor state.

The way in which both parties may benefit from a risk-sharing arrangement can be seen in Figure 26.2. Even though the firm is paying a higher wage and employing more workers in the poor state than with market clearing, the savings in labour costs in the good state are sufficiently large — given a contract wage w^* less than the expected wage $\overline{w}$ — that expected profits are higher under the implicit contract. The risk-neutral firm will therefore be better off with risk sharing. Although their expected income is somewhat lower, risk-averse workers are also better off because their income is more certain. The reduction in the variability of workers' real income comes from two sources: real wage fluctuations are eliminated and more workers are employed in the poor state than with market clearing.

Workers' incomes are not fully stabilized, however. There remains some uncertainty due to the possibility of being laid off in weak demand conditions. In general, a contract that eliminates all income risk by stabilizing employment in addition to the wage is not optimal because in order for it to be in the firm's interest to emply all N_o workers in the poor state, the contract wage w^* would have to be lower than the reservation wage k. In these circumstances the workers would prefer not to be employed. Thus the optimal contract reduces, but doesn't necessarily eliminate, the income uncertainty that workers face.

The optimal contract represents a tradeoff between risk sharing and production efficiency. On the basis of risk sharing alone, the risk-neutral firm should absorb all the risk and the risk-averse workers should receive a fixed real income. For production efficiency alone, the real wage and employment should fluctuate as shown in Figure 26.2 (a). The optimal contract sacrifices some efficiency by employing more than N_b workers in the poor state. This inefficiency is reflected in the fact that the output produced by the additional $N_b N_b^*$ workers is less than the value of their leisure time. However, there is a benefit in terms of risk sharing because employing these additional $N_b N_b^*$ workers in the poor state reduces the probability of a worker being laid off and not receiving the contract wage w^*. However, completely eliminating income uncertainty would be too costly in terms of production efficiency. The optimal contract strikes a balance between these two competing considerations.

Layoffs are a feature of the implicit contract because of the interaction between risk sharing and the value placed by employees on time devoted to non-market activity. If the employees' reservation wage were zero — as would occur if there were no value placed on leisure time and no unemployment insurance benefits — the optimal contract would provide for a fixed real wage w* and fixed employment of N_o, as illustrated in Figure 26.2 (c). In this case there is no tradeoff between production efficiency and risk sharing, and employees' real income is completely stabilized. The higher the reservation wage k, the greater the tendency to employ layoffs in response to declines in demand, holding other influences constant, and the greater the tradeoff between production efficiency and risk sharing.

Several conclusions emerge from this discussion of risk sharing between the firm and its workers. Implicit contract theory can account for real wage rigidity, the use of layoffs to respond to reductions in demand, and the existence of involuntary unemployment. The optimal contract provides for a constant real wage and reduction in employment in the poor state. Because workers would prefer to be employed and earning the contract wage, the reduction in employment takes the form of layoffs. Those workers laid off are involuntarily unemployed in an ex post sense: given that the weak demand state occurs, that they are selected for layoff, and that the contract wage exceeds their reservation wage, they would prefer to be employed. However, the unemployment may be considered voluntary in an ex ante sense because the workers chose a wage-employment contract with some risk of layoff, and would make the same choice again in identical circumstances, given the Pareto optimal nature of the contractual arrangement. Thus the unemployment is involuntary in a rather limited sense.

Although implicit contract theory does provide a rigorous microeconomic explanation for wage rigidity, layoffs and involuntary unemployment (in a restricted sense), the theory has been criticized for its inability to explain unemployment in excess of the amount that would be observed if wages adjusted each period to equate labour supply and demand (Akerlof and Miyazaki, 1980). Indeed, according to the basic implicit contract model discussed in this section, the number of workers involuntarily laid off in weak demand conditions is less than the number that would voluntarily withdraw from employment with market clearing. However, this implication of the model is closely related to the assumption that both parties observe the state of demand. When this symmetric information assumption is relaxed, optimal contracts may imply unemployment in excess of the amount that would occur with market clearing.

In many circumstances employers have more information than their employees on the true nature of the demand conditions they are facing. Thus it is not possible for the two parties to have wages and employment contingent on the state of demand, as was the case under symmetric information, because workers cannot verify the outcome. Contracts need to be contingent on some variable which both parties observe. In these circumstances, implicit contracts will generally involve layoffs rather than wage reductions in weak demand conditions. Contracts which provide for wage reductions in poor demand conditions will not work because the firm has an incentive to claim demand is weak whatever the true state. This is so because paying a lower wage is not costly to the firm. However, layoffs do impose costs on the employer because output is lower with fewer employees and the firm runs the risk of losing employees and has to incur rehiring costs. Rigid wage contracts that involve layoffs in poor states and rehires in good states discourage the firm from bluffing about the true nature of its product market, forcing the firm to reveal the true state of demand by its choice of employment. Thus under asymmetric information there is an additional rationale for wage rigidity and layoff.

Efficiency Wages

Another explanation of wage rigidity and unemployment which has received considerable attention in recent years is the notion of "efficiency wages." While implicit contract theory emphasized the role of wages and employment in risk sharing, efficiency wage theory focuses on the effect of wages on incentives and worker productivity. The central hypothesis is that firms may choose to pay wages above the market-clearing level in order to enhance worker productivity. Because higher wages also reduce labour demand, the consequence of this policy may be excess labour supply and unemployment.

There are several reasons why firms may benefit from paying a wage above the level necessary to attract labour. In less-developed countries, higher wages may result in better-fed and thus healthier and more productive workers. In developed economies wages may affect productivity in a variety of ways. Higher wages may improve worker morale, discourage shirking and absenteeism by raising the cost to workers of being fired, and reduce turnover. Firms may also prefer to pay high wages in order to reduce the threat of unionization or to obtain a larger and higher quality pool of job applicants.

The incentive to pay high wages will generally differ across firms and industries. Efficiency wages are most likely to be observed when other methods of enhancing productivity — such as supervision and monitoring of employees or the use of piece-rate compensation systems — are costly or ineffective. The impact of employee work effort on the quality and quantity of output is also an important factor. Shirking by employees can have disastrous effects in some jobs (such as the operator in a nuclear power station or the driver of a bus) while in others the consequences are much less severe. Similarly, in some production processes the work is highly interdependent, so that poor work effort by one employee affects the output of the entire group; whereas in other situations only that employee's output is affected. Other determinants of efficiency wages may also differ from one firm or industry to another. For example, turnover is more costly to some employers than others because of differences in hiring and training costs. As discussed in Chapter 14 on Union Growth and Incidence, some firms are more likely to become unionized than others because of factors such as size and capital intensity. Thus the incentive to pay high wages in order to discourage unionization will be stronger in some organizations than in others.

If each firm sets its wage rate above the market-clearing level, labour demand will be less than labour supply, resulting in involuntary unemployment. Figure 26.3(a) illustrates the equilibrium when each firm's optimal or efficiency wage is w^*. The unemployed wish to work at the prevailing wage; indeed, they are willing to work at wage rates below the efficiency wage w^*. However, firms will not lower the wage rate because doing so would reduce the productivity of their existing work-force. The failure of wages to adjust to excess supply is a consequence of firm rather than worker behaviour.

Unemployment will result if wages are set above their market-clearing level in each sector. However, if there exist one or more sectors in which firms will pay the lowest wage necessary to attract labour, the consequence may be a dual labour market rather than unemployment. This point is illustrated in Figure 26.3(b) for the case in which there are two sectors in the economy, each employing the same type of homogeneous labour. Sector A consists of those firms which prefer to pay above-market wages in order to enhance productivity while sector B consists of employers who pay the market wage and who will lower the wage in the presence of excess supply. In the absence of efficiency wage effects, the equilibrium will be at (w_o, N_o) in each sector with the wage rate equalized across the two sectors ($w_o^A = w_o^B$). However, because sector A firms set their wage at w_1^A, employment declines to N_1^A. The resulting increased labour supply to sector B lowers wages and increases employment in that sector. In these circumstances, efficiency wages result in a dual labour market, with high- and low-wage sectors for homogeneous workers. Wages differ not because of differences in the human capital characteristics of the workers in each sector but because of differences in the incentives facing firms.

Efficiency wages may cause unemployment even when there are firms — such as those in sector B in Figure 26.3(b) — which have no incentive to pay above-market wages. Some workers may search or wait for jobs in the high-wage sector rather than accept employment at low wages. This outcome is more likely the larger is the wage gap between the sectors, the greater is the turnover (and thus the probability of a job opening up) in the high-wage sector, and the more productive is unemployed search compared to employed search. Minimum wage laws may prevent the downward wage adjustment needed to absorb the additional labour supply created by efficiency wages in the high-wage sectors. In this case unemployment results from the interaction between efficiency wages and minimum-wage legislation.

The above analysis suggests that, in addition to being a source of wage rigidity and unemployment, efficiency wages may influence the occupational and industrial wage structure. Wages may differ not only because of differences in education, training, and other human capital characteristics of workers; not only because of job characteristics such as

Figure 26.3

(a) Labour Market Equilibrium with Efficiency Wages

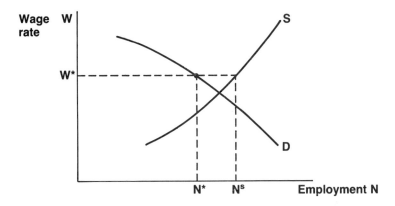

(b) Efficiency Wages and Dual Labour Markets

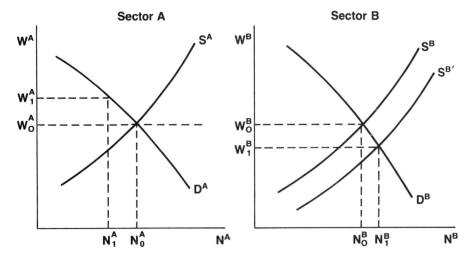

health and safety; but also because of such factors as the costs of monitoring and supervising employees, the importance of work effort to product quality and quantity, turnover costs, and the probability of union organization.

Efficiency wage theory also implies that unemployment may act as a "worker discipline device" (Shapiro and Stiglitz, 1984). Employees are assumed to be motivated to work hard when they fear losing their job. Their work effort will thus be greatest when their wage is high relative to the next best alternative, as discussed above, and/or when unemployment is high. The greater the unemployment rate, the longer the expected search period facing a worker laid off and therefore the greater the cost of shirking on the present job.

UNEMPLOYMENT INSURANCE AND UNEMPLOYMENT

The relationship between unemployment insurance and unemployment has been the subject of considerable recent theoretical and empirical research. Unemployment insurance is intended to provide workers with protection against the risk of income loss due to unemployment. However, the unemployment insurance program may also affect the incidence and duration of unemployment by altering the incentives facing workers and firms. In this section we examine the influence of unemployment insurance on job search, layoffs, seasonal unemployment, and inter-regional mobility. A brief description of the main features of Canada's unemployment insurance system is also provided.

Because economic circumstances continually change, risk and uncertainty are often present. As discussed previously in the context of implicit contract theory, labour market risks are especially significant because workers are generally unable to diversify their human capital wealth. In addition, comprehensive private insurance markets which would enable most workers to purchase insurance against the risk of unemployment (and possibly other sources of loss of labour market income) have generally failed to emerge despite the demand that evidently exists for such insurance. According to the economic theory of risk and insurance, this absence of private insurance markets is probably due to moral hazard and adverse selection. In the context of unemployment insurance, moral hazard implies that individuals with insurance are more likely to become or remain unemployed. Adverse selection in this context implies that the purchasers of insurance will be those who are most likely to become unemployed. Relative to a situation without moral hazard and adverse selection, these two effects reduce the profitability of selling insurance, and may result in a situation in which the sale of insurance is not profitable at any price.

The experience with Career Guard, an insurance plan to protect executives who might be fired, illustrates these effects. (See "Insurance Against Being Fired: A Plan that Just Didn't Fly" *Financial Post*, May 29, 1983, p. 1). Although this insurance policy didn't cover executives fired within six months of purchasing insurance, the entrepreneurs who started Career Guard nonetheless discovered that a very high proportion of those who purchased insurance were dismissed by their employers subsequent to the six-month qualifying period. It appears that Career Guard failed primarily because of adverse selection — those executives who knew they were likely to be dismissed were the main purchasers of insurance, and the insurer couldn't distinguish high-risk from low-risk customers. Moral hazard may also have played a role.

Moral hazard and adverse selection are generally present in any insurance situation. Whether they prevent the emergence of private insurance markets depends on their magnitudes. For example, in life insurance, moral hazard is not a serious problem because few individuals will take their own lives in order to collect insurance. Insurance companies often reduce the already small amount of moral hazard by not paying insurance in the event of suicides or murder by a beneficiary. Adverse selection is minimized by such means as not selling insurance to some high-risk groups (e.g. sky divers), charging differential fees to others (e.g. smokers), and requiring medical examinations for certain individuals seeking insurance.

In the absence of private sector provision, governments in many countries have introduced unemployment insurance (UI) as part of social policy. Canada's unemployment insurance system was established in 1940, following the recommendations of the Royal Commission on Dominion-Provincial Relations and the resolution, through a constitutional amendment, of the difficulties which had resulted in an earlier attempt to introduce UI being declared outside the legislative authority of the federal government. The UI fund is financed mainly by premiums collected from employers and employees. Coverage is compulsory for those groups that come under the Act, a feature which significantly reduces the effects of adverse selection. However, as the empirical evidence reviewed below indicates, moral hazard effects do occur.

Canada's unemployment insurance system has evolved significantly over time. Between 1940 and 1971 there were gradual and modest changes in the eligibility, coverage, and benefit and financing provisions of the UI Act. Dramatic changes to these key features of the act were made in 1971/72, including a substantial expansion in coverage, an increase in the benefit rate (benefits as a proportion of previous earnings), a reduction in the minimum period of employment required to qualify for benefits, an increase in the maximum benefit period, and introduction of extended benefits in regions with high unemployment. With these changes, UI covered a much larger proportion of the labour force (about 90 percent) and became considerably more "generous." Making UI benefits taxable offset this increased generosity to some degree. The 1971/72 changes were also partially reversed by revisions made in 1979. Nonetheless, the UI system of today contrasts sharply with that of pre-1971 in terms of coverage and the generosity of its provisions. These dramatic changes have provided a rather unique "social experiment" for studying the impact of unemployment insurance on labour market behaviour. Accordingly, many of the empirical studies contrast pre- and post-1971/72 behaviour (and, in some cases, pre- and post-1979 behaviour also). Of course, the 1971/72 and 1979 changes did not constitute a controlled experiment. As is so frequently the case in empirical research, controlling for other factors which may have affected behaviour represents a major challenge.

On the basis of economic theory, changes in the provisions of the unemployment insurance system can be expected to affect labour force behaviour in several ways. Indeed, examining the impact of such changes provides a useful test of the theories of unemployment discussed previously in this chapter and of the analysis of the incentive effects of alternative income maintenance schemes discussed in Chapter 4. The following effects are discussed in turn: incidence and duration of search unemployment, temporary layoffs, employment instability and seasonal unemployment, labour force participation, and inter-regional labour market mobility.

Analysis of the relationship between unemployment and unemployment insurance is complicated by the fact that the UI program has several key parameters, including the benefit rate, the minimum employment period to qualify for benefits, the maximum duration of benefits, and the coverage of the labour force. For concreteness the discussion below will focus on the consequences of an increase in the benefit rate. In most circumstances, changes in other program parameters which also increase the generosity of the UI system will have the same effect as an increase in benefit rate, and vice versa.

Unemployment insurance can affect the incidence and duration of search unemployment by altering the costs and benefits of job search. Several cases need to be considered, depending on whether the individual is (1) employed, (2) unemployed and eligible for UI benefits, and (3) not eligible for benefits. For the employed, an increase in the benefit rate makes unemployed search more attractive relative to employed search; as a consequence, the incidence of unemployment is predicted to rise. Evidence appears to support this prediction. Kaliski (1985) notes that the ratio of employed to unemployed search rose sharply following the introduction in 1979 of a reduced benefit rate and tighter qualification requirements.

For the unemployed who are eligible for benefits (because of a previous spell of employment), an increase in the benefit rate lowers the marginal cost of search. According to the theory of optimal search, the expected or average duration of job search will increase. This prediction has been extensively tested. Cousineau (1985) summarizes various Canadian and U.S. studies. Early Canadian studies using aggregate data concluded that the 1971/72 changes to the UI Act — which increased the benefit rate from 43 to 67 percent, among other changes — raised the average duration of unemployment by 1-1/2 to 2 weeks (Green and Cousineau, 1976; Rea, 1977; Maki, 1977; Lazar, 1978). This increase of approximately 20 percent in duration corresponds to an increase in the unemployment rate of one to one and one-half percentage points. More recent studies in Canada and the U.S. employ micro data which allow for more careful testing of UI effects. Using gross flow data, Beach and Kaliski (1983) find that the 1979 revisions — which lowered the benefit rate from 67 to 60 percent and tightened qualification requirements — resulted in an increase in the flow from unemployment to employment and a reduced duration of unemployment for all age-sex groups. Studies by Glenday and Alam (1982) and Ham and Rea (1987), using micro data on the employment and unemployment experience of individuals, confirm significant effects of UI entitlements on the duration of job search.

Changes in the benefit rate may also affect the search behaviour of those who are not eligible for UI. Such individuals may be entering the labour force for the first time, be re-entering after an extended absence from the labour force, or have exhausted their benefits. In these circumstances it may be rational to accept employment quickly, even temporary work, in order to subsequently qualify for UI benefits. In effect, a job has two components: the income received directly and a "ticket" entitling the worker to benefits in the event of unemployment. Consequently, for individuals ineligible for benefits, an increase in the benefit rate does not affect the costs of search but lowers the marginal benefit of search, thus reducing optimal search duration.

There is no direct evidence on this effect in Canada, but it is likely to be small. Consider for example, a 10 percent increase in the benefit rate. For individuals who qualify for UI benefits, this change has a significant effect on the costs of job search. However, for those not eligible for benefits, the *additional* incentive to accept a job quickly is not large. Furthermore, this response, to the extent that it occurs, is confined to new entrants, some re-entrants, and UI exhaustees, a small fraction of the unemployed.

In summary, unemployment insurance affects job search behaviour in several ways. For workers who qualify for UI, a more generous benefit structure lowers the cost of job search, thus raising average search duration, and makes unemployed search more attractive relative to employed search, thus increasing the incidence of unemployment. Empirical evidence supports these predictions of the theory of optimal search behaviour. The strongest evidence relates to the impact on search duration. Possibly offsetting these effects to some extent, a more generous benefit structure may reduce search duration for those currently ineligible for UI. This latter effect is likely to be small, in which case the overall impact of a more generous benefit structure will be to increase search duration. Empirical studies of the 1971/72 UI changes conclude that the overall duration of unemployment did increase significantly.

The impact of UI on layoffs can be analysed using implicit contract theory. As discussed previously, optimal risk-sharing arrangements may provide for layoffs in adverse product market conditions when the value of the marginal product of labour falls below the workers' reservation wage. An increase in the benefit rate raises the reservation wage, thus increasing the number of states in which layoffs will occur and increasing the number of workers laid off in each adverse state. These predictions can be illustrated by shifting up the labour supply curve S in Figure 26.2(b).

The theory of compensating wage differentials discussed in Chapter 17 is also relevant to the analysis of layoffs. Although all firms and industries experience fluctuations in demand due to cyclical, seasonal, and other factors, these variations are much larger for some employers than others. Firms can adjust to these disturbances in various ways: through inventories, by altering the time lag between orders and shipments, by diversifying product lines, by saving work for slack periods, by adjusting wages and/ or hours of work, and by layoffs and rehires. Firms will choose the least-cost method of adjustment. Unemployment insurance lowers the cost of adjusting through layoffs relative to other methods because, in the absence of UI, employers who rely extensively on layoffs will have to pay a compensating wage to attract employees. In this way a higher benefit rate may contribute to larger variations in employment in response to cyclical and seasonal fluctuations in demand.

The financing of the UI program is also relevant. Under "experience rating," employers' UI premiums are related to the amount of benefit payments to their employees. Firms which rely heavily on layoffs will pay a penalty in the form of higher UI premiums, thus providing an incentive to utilize other forms of adjustment. Canada's unemployment insurance system is not experience-rated, a feature which has been the subject of considerable policy discussion (Kesselman, 1983; Riddell, 1985). As a consequence, industries with stable employment patterns cross-subsidize those with unstable employment. In the United States, various states have experience rating in their unemployment insurance programs.

The relationship between UI and employment instability has been investigated in a number of empirical studies. Much of this research has been carried out in the United States, utilizing differences that exist across states in the degree to which UI is experience-rated. Studies by Feldstein (1978), Topel (1983) and Saffer (1982, 1983) indicate that incomplete experience rating has a significant impact on the incidence of layoffs; i.e., the lower the degree of experience rating the greater the use of layoffs, ceteris paribus. In Canada, Kaliski (1976) found that for the majority of industries and provinces, the trend toward reduced seasonality in employment moderated, or even reversed, after 1971. The increase in seasonal fluctuations in employment was particularly large in construction, one of the industries most heavily subsidized by UI. Glenday and Alam (1982) conclude that the regional extended benefits (longer entitlement periods in regions with high unemployment) contribute to the amount of seasonal unemployment and short-term employment instability in high unemployment regions.

The choice between hours reductions and layoffs has received special policy attention. As discussed in Reid (1985) and Riddell (1985), UI may bias employers and employees toward the use of layoffs as opposed to reductions in hours of work. This is so because workers on layoff qualify for UI benefits while those whose "unemployment" takes the form of reduced hours do not. This bias can be offset in one of two ways: (1) have UI premiums experience-rated so that firms pay a penalty for adjustments in the form of layoffs or (2) introduce a UI-assisted worksharing program. Canada has followed the latter route. As described in Chapter 5 and Reid (1985) the Canadian program basically provides UI benefits of two-thirds of each employee's lost wages for voluntarily giving up an average of one day of work per week so that other workers in the firm would not have to be laid off.

Unemployment insurance also affects employment and unemployment through its impact on labour force participation. This aspect was analysed in Chapter 5 using the income-leisure choice model, and the reader may wish to review that discussion at this time. The analysis applies to situations in which employees can adjust their weeks of employment and non-employment in response to the incentives inherent in the UI system. The many individuals for whom a job entails being employed throughout the year do not fit in this category. The relevant group consists of those who work less than a full year either because the worker quits after a certain period of employment or because the job itself is short-term in nature, as is the case in much seasonal work.

Our earlier analysis showed that more generous UI will decrease weeks worked by those who, prior to the change, worked more than the minimum number of weeks required to qualify for benefits, whereas more generous UI will increase weeks of employment for those who previously did not qualify. Most of the latter group would have been out of the labour force prior to the change; for these individuals, higher UI benefits make labour force participation sufficiently attractive to obtain at least enough employment to qualify for benefits. (In Chapter 5 we compared equilibria with and without unemployment insurance. The analysis of equilibria with different UI benefit levels is very similar.)

These two responses have offsetting effects on employment, reducing weeks worked by those with relatively strong labour force attachment and increasing weeks worked by those with little or no labour force attachment. Total employment may therefore increase or decrease. However, the impact on labour force participation and unemployment is unambiguous. Labour force participation is predicted to rise because of the entry by those who now wish to obtain enough work to qualify for UI. Those who previously qualified for benefits do not exit from the labour force, although they do work fewer weeks. Measured unemployment increases for both groups: those who previously qualified for UI because they now spend less time employed and more time unemployed, while those previously not eligible spend more time employed and unemployed and less "not in the labour force."

These predictions of the income-leisure choice model refer to desired combinations of employment and non-employment given the individual's preferences and constraints. Of course, not all workers can achieve their desired allocation of time to work and non-market activity, especially in the short run. However, as discussed in Chapter 17, firms have an incentive to offer jobs with more desirable and fewer undesirable characteristics because doing so reduces the compensating wage that must be paid in equilibrium. Thus if short-term employment is desirable for some workers, jobs with these features can be expected to emerge. In this way, changes in the UI system may affect not only employee behaviour but also the structure of labour demand.

Canadian evidence on these effects is limited. Most studies use aggregate data and are therefore not able to distinguish changes in annual patterns of employment from unemployment associated with longer-search duration or greater use of layoffs. One exception is Glenday and Alam

(1982) who study the behaviour of a 10 percent sample of all those who filed a UI claim during 1975-1979. They find evidence that some users of UI display consistent patterns of employment and non-employment; 35 percent of their sample had average periods of employment of less than 6 months, an additional 25 percent had average periods of employment between 6 and 12 months, and 65 percent of the sample had average periods of unemployment less than 6 months. Glenday and Alam use the income-leisure choice model to analyse the differences in these patterns among different regions. They conclude that UI benefits contribute to the amount of employment instability; in particular, the regional differentiation of benefits reinforces the short-term and seasonal nature of much of the employment in high unemployment regions.

Unemployment insurance may also affect the inter-regional mobility of the labour force. The regional extended benefits, in particular, appear to retard inter-regional mobility by providing benefits for longer periods in regions with high unemployment (Winer and Gauthier, 1982; Vanderkamp, 1986).

In summary, the unemployment insurance system has numerous effects on labour force behaviour, including the incidence and duration of search unemployment, layoffs, annual patterns of employment and unemployment, labour force participation, and inter-regional mobility. A substantial amount of empirical research has been devoted to estimating the size of these effects. Although there are some offsetting influences, the overall impact of a more generous UI benefit structure is to increase unemployment. Numerous studies have estimated that the 1971/72 revisions added between 0.5 and 2 percentage points to the unemployment rate, while the 1979 revisions reduced unemployment by up to 0.5 percentage points (Kaliski, 1985). This does not imply that the 1971-72 changes were undesirable or that those in 1979 were desirable; it simply points out that the changes affected our aggregate unemployment rate and that this should be considered in interpreting this statistic. More generally, the tradeoffs inherent in the unemployment insurance system need to be recognized in the design of UI financing and benefits. The more generous the benefit structure, the greater the insurance value of the program but also the larger the adverse incentive effects and the amount of induced unemployment. Optimal UI design must strike a balance between these social costs and benefits.

QUESTIONS

1. Indicate the main types of unemployment, their causes, and the usual policies discussed to curb each type of unemployment.
2. Frictional unemployment is optimal. Discuss.
3. In the late 1950s and early 1960s there was considerable debate over the relative importance of structural versus demand deficient unemployment. Much of the debate waned during the relatively full em-

ployment period of the mid and late 1960s. What does this imply about the existence of structural unemployment?

4. There is some renewed interest in the issue of structural unemployment, associated with the demographic changes in the labour force, and with the high unemployment that has occurred even during periods of inflation. Discuss why this may be the case.

5. Why might the so-called *natural* or *full-employment* unemployment rate have increased over time?

6. Indicate some basic differences between frictional and structural unemployment. If possible, provide examples of when it may be unclear as to whether to categorize a worker as frictionally or structurally unemployed.

7. All unemployment can be categorized as frictional, structural, or demand deficient. Discuss.

8. Discuss the various components of the cost and benefits of job search for employees. How might the availability of unemployment insurance alter those components? Discuss other factors that may have had important effects on the costs and benefits, and hence duration, of job search.

9. Discuss the costs and benefits of job search for younger workers and females. Relate these factors to their unemployment duration.

10. In recent years, private employment agencies have taken over much of the placement function of the public employment agency. Discuss the pros and cons of this phenomenon.

11. Discuss the implications of job search theory for the following phenomena: unemployment duration, the cyclical behaviour of quits, and the phenomenon of wage rigidity over the business cycle.

12. Discuss the implications of implicit contract theory for the following phenomena: wage rigidity over the business cycle, labour hoarding, and layoffs as opposed to wage reductions.

13. If workers are risk averse, why might they enter into contractual arrangements that could involve the risk of layoffs as opposed to minor wage adjustments?

14. Why don't we observe private insurance companies selling unemployment insurance? How could employers provide such insurance?

15. Discuss the distinction between voluntary and involuntary unemployment.

16. Discuss the importance of asymmetric information in implicit contract theory.

17. What is meant by efficiency wages and why do they arise? What are their implications for labour market behaviour?

18. Discuss the various design features (policy parameters) of unemployment insurance that can affect the benefits from such insurance and hence the behaviour of recipients.

19. Discuss the various elements of labour market behaviour that can be affected by unemployment insurance.

20. Discuss the relationship between compensating wages for the risk of unemployment and unemployment insurance.
21. Discuss the pros and cons of experience rating in unemployment insurance.

REFERENCES AND FURTHER READINGS

Abraham, K.G. Structural/frictional vs. deficient demand unemployment: some new evidence. *AER* 73 (September 1983) 708-724.

Akerlof, G. and H. Miyazaki. The implicit contract theory of unemployment meets the wage bill argument. *R.E. Studies* 47 (January 1980) 321-338.

Akerlof, G.A. and J.L. Yellen (eds.). *Efficiency Wage Models of the Labour Market*. Cambridge: Cambridge University Press, 1986.

Annable, J. A theory of downward rigid wages and cyclical unemployment. *EI* 15 (July 1977) 326-349.

Ashenfelter, O. and J. Ham. Education, unemployment, and earnings. *JPE* 87 (October 1979) S99-S116.

Atkinson, A., J. Gomulka, J. Micklewright and N. Rau. Unemployment benefit, duration and incentives in Britain: how robust is the evidence? *JPubEc* 23 (February/March 1984) 3-26.

Azariadis, C. Implicit contracts and underemployment equilibria. *JPE* 83 (December 1975) 1183-1202.

Azariadis, C. On the incidence of unemployment. *R.E. Studies* 43 (February 1976) 115-126.

Azariadis, C. Implicit contracts and related topics: a survey. *The Economics of the Labour Market*, Z. Hornstein et al. (eds.). London: HMSO, 1979, 221-248.

Azariadis, C. and J.E. Stiglitz. Implicit contracts and fixed price equilibria. *QJE* 98 (Supplement 1983) 1-22.

Baily, M.N. Wages and employment under uncertain demand. *R.E. Studies* 41 (January 1974) 37-50.

Barnes, W. Job search models, the duration of unemployment and the asking wage: some empirical evidence. *JHR* 10 (Spring 1975) 230-240.

Barrett, N. and R. Morgenstern. Why do blacks and women have high unemployment rates? *JHR* 9 (Fall 1974) 452-464.

Barron, J., R. McAfee and P. Speaker. Unemployment insurance and the entitlement effect: a tax incidence approach. *IER* 27 (February 1986) 175-186.

Barron, J. and S. McCafferty. Job search, labour supply and the quit decision. *AER* 67 (September 1977) 683-691.

Barron, J. and W. Mellow. Unemployment insurance: the recipients and its impact. *SEJ* 47 (January 1981) 606-616.

Beach, C.M. and S.F. Kaliski. On the design of unemployment insurance: the impact of the 1979 amendments. *CPP* 9 (June 1983) 164-173.

Beach, C.M. and S.F. Kaliski. Structural unemployment: demographic change or industrial structure? *CPP* 12 (June 1986) 356-367.

Becker, J. *Experience Rating in Unemployment Insurance*. Baltimore: Johns Hopkins University Press, 1972.

Benjamin, D. and L. Kochin. Searching for an explanation of unemployment in interwar Britain. *JPE* 87 (June 1979) 441-478. Also comments 90 (April 1982) 369-436.

Berman, B. Alternative measures of structural unemployment. *Employment Policy and the Labour Market*, A. Ross (ed.). Berkeley: University of California Press, 1965.

Bjorklund, A. and B. Holmlund. The duration of unemployment and unexpected inflation: an empirical analysis. *AER* 71 (March 1981) 121-131.

Blau, D. and P. Robins. Job search, wage offers, and unemployment insurance. *JPubEc* 29 (March 1986) 173-198.

Boadway, R. and A. Oswald. Unemployment insurance and redistributive taxation. *JPubEc* 20 (March 1983) 193-210.

Brechling, F. The incentive effects of the U.S. unemployment insurance tax. *Research in Labor Economics*, R. Ehrenberg (ed.). Greenwich, Conn.: JAI Press, 1977.

Bruce, C. and J. Marshall. Job search and frictional unemployment. *RI/IR* 31 (No. 3, 1976) 402-414.

Burdett, K. A theory of employee job search and quit rates. *AER* 68 (March 1978) 212-220.

Burdett, K. and B. Hool. Layoffs, wages and unemployment insurance. *JPubEc* 21 (August 1983) 325-358.

Burgess, P. and J. Kingston. The impact of unemployment insurance benefits on reemployment success. *ILRR* 30 (October 1976) 25-31.

Calvo, G. Quasi-Walrasian theories of unemployment. *AER* 69 (May 1979) 102-107.

Chapin, G. Unemployment insurance, job search, and the demand for leisure. *WEJ* 9 (March 1971) 102-107. Comment by Kingston and Burgess 9 (December 1971) 447-452.

Chesher, A. and T. Lancaster. The estimation of models of labour market behaviour. *R.E. Studies* 50 (October 1983) 609-624.

Chiswick, B. The effect of unemployment compensation on a seasonal industry: agriculture. *JPE* 84 (June 1976) 591-602.

Cousineau, J.M. Unemployment insurance and labour market adjustments. *Income Distribution and Economic Security in Canada*, F. Vaillancourt (ed.). Toronto: University of Toronto Press, 1985, 187-214.

Cousineau, J. and C. Green. Structural unemployment in Canada: 1971-1974. Did it worsen? *RI/IR* 33 (No. 2, 1978) 175-192.

Cripps, T. and R. Tarling. An analysis of the duration of male unemployment in Great Britain: 1932-1973. *EJ* 84 (June 1974) 289-316.

de Broucker, P. and A. Hasan. An assessment of the turnover view of labour markets: some Canadian evidence. Paper presented at the Eastern Economics Association annual meeting, 1982.

Della Valle, P. and B. Meyer. Changes in relative female-male unemployment: a Canadian-United States comparison. *RI/IR* 31 (No. 3, 1976) 417-430.

Demsetz, H. Structural unemployment: a reconsideration of the evidence and the theory. *Journal of Law and Economics* 4 (October 1961) 80-92.

Denton, F. and S. Ostry. *An Analysis of Post-War Unemployment*. Staff Study No. 3, Economic Council of Canada. Ottawa: Queen's Printer, 1964.

Diamond, P. Mobility costs, frictional unemployment and efficiency. *JPE* 89 (August 1981) 798-812.

Disney, R. Recurrent spells and the concentration of unemployment in Great Britain. *EJ* 89 (March 1979) 109-119.

Doherty, N. National insurance and absence from work. *EJ* 89 (March 1979) 50-65.

Donner, A. Regional unemployment rates and total economic growth in Canada, 1953-1968. *RI/IR* 26 (August 1971) 721-725.

Donner, A. and F. Lazar. An econometric study of segmented labour markets and the structure of unemployment: the Canadian experience. *IER* 14 (June 1973) 312-327.

Eaton, C. and P. Neher. Unemployment, underemployment and optimal job search. *JPE* 83 (April 1975) 355-376.

Eaton, C. and W. White. The economy of high wages. *Economica* 50 (May 1983) 175-182.

Edgell, L. and S. Wander. Unemployment insurance: its economic performance. *MLR* 97 (April 1974) 33-40.

Ehrenberg, R. and R. Oaxaca. Unemployment insurance, duration of unemployment and subsequent wage gain. *AER* 66 (December 1976) 754-766.

Englander, F. and S. Director. Benefit levels, enforcement stringency, and the level of initial claims for unemployment insurance. *SEJ* 52 (April 1986) 1140-1144.

Feinberg, R. Risk aversion, risk and the duration of unemployment. *R.E. Stats.* 59 (August 1977) 264-271.

Feldstein, M. The economics of the new unemployment. *Public Interest* 33 (Fall 1973) 3-42.

Feldstein, M. *Lowering the Permanent Rate of Unemployment.* Study for the Joint Economic Committee, 93rd Congress, 1973.

Feldstein, M. Unemployment compensation: adverse incentives and distributional anomalies. *National Tax Journal* 37 (June 1974) 231-244.

Feldstein, M. The importance of temporary layoffs. *BPEA* (No. 3, 1975) 725-745.

Feldstein, M. Temporary layoffs in the theory of unemployment. *JPE* 84 (October 1976) 937-958.

Feldstein, M. The effect of unemployment insurance on temporary layoff unemployment. *AER* 68 (December 1978) 834-846.

Feldstein, M. and J. Poterba. Unemployment insurance and reservation wages. *JPubEc* 23 (February/March 1984) 141-168.

Fields, G. Direct labor market effects of unemployment insurance. *IR* 16 (February 1971) 1-14.

Furstenberg, G. von. Stabilization characteristics of unemployment insurance. *ILRR* 29 (April 1976) 363-376.

Gallaway, L. Labour mobility, resource allocation and structural unemployment. *AER* 52 (September 1963) 694-716.

Glenday, G. and J. Alam. The labour market experience of individuals: unemployment insurance and regional effects. Mimeo. Toronto: York University, 1982.

Gordon, D. A neoclassical theory of Keynesian unemployment. *EI* 12 (December 1974) 431-459.

Gramlich, E. The distributional effects of higher unemployment. *BPEA* (No. 2, 1974) 293-342.

Green, C. Labour market performance from an employment perspective. *CPP* 3 (September 1977) 315-323. Comment by S. Kaliski 3 (Autumn 1977) 515-517.

Green, C. and J.-M. Cousineau. *Unemployment in Canada: The Impact of Unemployment Insurance.* Ottawa: Economic Council of Canada, 1976.

Gronau, R. Information and frictional unemployment. *AER* 61 (June 1971) 290-301.

Grossman, S. and O. Hart. Implicit contracts, moral hazard, and unemployment. *AER* 71 (May 1981) 301-307.

Grubel, H., D. Maki and S. Sax. Real and insurance induced unemployment in Canada. *CJE* 8 (May 1975) 174-191. Comments by S. Kaliski and reply 8 (November 1975) 600-605.

Gujarati, D. The behaviour of unemployment and unfilled vacancies. *EJ* 82 (March 1972) 195-204. Comment by J. Foster and reply 83 (March 1973) 192-202.

Hall, R. The rigidity of wages and the persistence of unemployment. *BPEA* (No. 2, 1975) 301-350.

Hall, R. Why is the employment rate so high at full unemployment? *BPEA* (No. 3, 1970) 369-402.

Halpin, T. The effect of unemployment insurance on seasonal fluctuations in employment. *ILRR* 32 (April 1979) 353-362.

Ham, J.C. and S.A. Rea, Jr. Unemployment insurance and male unemployment duration in Canada. *JOLE* 5 (July, 1987) 325-353.

Hamermesh, D. *Jobless Pay and the Economy*. Baltimore: Johns Hopkins University Press, 1977.

Hamermesh, D. Unemployment insurance and labor supply. *IER* 21 (October 1980) 517-546.

Hansen, B. Excess demand, unemployment, vacancies and wages. *QJE* 84 (February 1970) 1-23.

Hart, O.D. Optimal labour contracts under asymmetric information: an introduction. *R.E.Studies* 50 (January 1983) 3-35.

Hasan, A. and S. Gera. *Job Search Behaviour, Unemployment and Wage Gains in Canadian Labour Markets*. Ottawa: Economic Council of Canada, 1982.

Heckman, J. and G. Borjas. Does unemployment cause future unemployment? *Economica* 47 (August 1980) 247-284.

Hey, J. and K. Mavronmaras. The effect of unemployment insurance on the riskiness of occupational choice. *JPubEc* 16 (December 1981) 317-342.

Holen, A. and S. Horowitz. The effect of unemployment insurance and eligibility enforcement on unemployment. *Journal of Law and Economics* 17 (October 1974) 403-432.

Johnson, W. A theory of job shopping. *QJE* 92 (May 1978) 261-278.

Kaitz, H. Analysing the lengths of spells of unemployment. *MLR* 93 (November 1970) 11-20.

Kaliski, S. Structural unemployment: a new stage in the debate. *Canadian Banker* (Autumn 1967) 72-77.

Kaliski, S. Structural unemployment in Canada: towards a definition of the geographic dimension. *CJE* (August 1968) 551-565.

Kaliski, S. Structural unemployment in Canada: the occupational dimension. *CJE* 2 (May 1969) 250-267.

Kaliski, S. Unemployment and unemployment insurance: testing some corollaries. *CJE* 9 (November 1976) 705-712.

Kaliski, S. Trends, changes and imbalances: a survey of the Canadian labour market. *Work and Pay: The Canadian Labour Market*, W.C. Riddell (ed.). Toronto: University of Toronto Press, 1985, 77-140.

Katz, A. Schooling, age and length of unemployment. *ILRR* 27 (July 1974) 597-605.

Katz, A. (ed.). The economics of unemployment insurance: a symposium. *ILRR* 30 (July 1977) 431-526.

Keiffer, N. and G. Neumann. An empirical job search model, with a test of a constant reservation-wage hypothesis. *JPE* 87 (February 1979) 89-108.

Kesselman, J.R. *Financing Canadian Unemployment Insurance*. Toronto: Canadian Tax Foundation, 1983.

Killingsworth, C. The bottleneck in labour skills. *The Battle Against Unemployment*, A. Okun (ed.). New York: Norton and Co., 1965.

Lancaster, T. Econometric methods for the duration of unemployment. *Econometrica* 47 (July 1979) 939-956.

Lazar, F. Regional unemployment rate disparities in Canada. *CJE* 10 (February 1977) 112-129.

Lazar, F. The impact of the 1971 unemployment insurance revisions on unemployment rates: another look. *CJE* 11 (August 1978) 559-569.

Lazar, F. and A. Donner. The dimension of Canadian youth unemployment: a theoretical explanation. *RI/IR* 28 (No. 2, 1973) 295-324.

Lilien, D. The cyclical pattern of temporary layoffs in United States manufacturing. *R.E. Stats* 62 (February 1980) 24-31.

Lilien, D. Sectoral shifts and cyclical unemployment. *JPE* 90 (August 1982) 777-793.

Lippman, S. and J. McCall. The economics of job search: a survey. *EI* 14 (June 1976) 155-189 and (September 1976) 347-368. Comment by G. Borjas and M. Goldberg 16 (January 1978) 119-125.

Lippman, S. and J. McCall (eds.). *Studies in the Economics of Search*. Amsterdam: North Holland, 1979.

Lipsey, R. Structural and deficient demand unemployment reconsidered. *Employment Policy and the Labour Market*, A. Ross (ed.). Berkeley: University of California Press, 1965, 210-255.

Mackay, D. and G. Reid. Redundancy, unemployment and manpower policy. *EJ* (December 1972). Comment by T. Lancaster 86 (June 1976) 335-338.

Main, B. The length of a job in Great Britain. *Economica* 49 (August 1982) 325-334.

Maki, D. *Search Behaviour in Canadian Job Markets*. Special Study No. 15. Ottawa: Economic Council of Canada, 1971.

Maki, D. Regional differences in insurance-induced unemployment in Canada. *EI* 13 (September 1975) 389-400.

Maki, D. Unemployment insurance, unemployment duration, and excess supply of labour. *RI/IR* 31 (No. 3, 1976) 368-376.

Maki, D. Unemployment benefits and the duration of claims in Canada. *Applied Economics* 9 (1977) 227-236.

Malcomson, J. Unemployment and efficiency wage hypothesis. *EJ* 91 (December 1981) 848-866.

Marston, S. The impact of unemployment insurance on job search. *BPEA* (No. 1, 1975) 13-60.

Marston, S. Employment instability and high unemployment rates. *BPEA* (No. 1, 1976) 169-210.

Marston, S. Two views of the geographic distribution of unemployment. *QJE* 100 (February 1985) 57-79.

Mattila, J. Job quitting and frictional unemployment. *AER* 64 (March 1974) 235-239.

McCall, J. Economics of information and job search. *QJE* (February 1970) 113-126. Comment by Peterson and reply (February 1972) 127-134.

McGregor, A. Unemployment duration and the reemployment probability. *EJ* 88 (December 1978) 693-706.

Medoff, J.L. Layoffs and alternatives under trade unions in U.S. manufacturing. *AER* 69 (June 1979) 380-395.

Mellow, W. Search costs and the duration of unemployment. *EI* 16 (July 1978) 423-430.

Melvyn, P. Youth unemployment in industrialized market economics. *ILR* 116 (July-August 1977) 23-38.

Metcalf, D. Urban unemployment in England. *EJ* 85 (September 1975) 578-589.

Mortensen, D.T. Job search and labor market analysis. *Handbook of Labor Economics*, O. Ashenfelter and R. Layard (eds.). Amsterdam: North Holland, 1986.

Moy, J. and Sorrentino, C. Unemployment in nine industrialized nations. *MLR* 98 (June 1975) 9-18.

Munts, R. and I. Garfinkel. *The Work Disincentive Effects of Unemployment Insurance*. Kalamazoo, Mich.: W.E. Upjohn Institute, 1974.

Nickell, S. The effect of unemployment and related benefits on the duration of unemployment. *EJ* 89 (March 1979) 34-49.

Nickell, S. Estimating the probability of leaving unemployment. *Econometrica* 47 (September 1979) 1249-1266.

Nickell, S. Education and lifetime patterns of unemployment. *JPE* 87 (October 1979) S117-S132.

Nickell, S. A picture of male unemployment in Britain. *EJ* 90 (December 1980) 776-794.

Nickell, S. The determinants of equilibrium unemployment in Britain. *EJ* 92 (September 1982) 555-575.

Niemi, B. The male-female differential in unemployment rates. *ILRR* 27 (April 1974) 331-350.

Okun, A.M. *Prices and Quantities*. Washington: The Brookings Institution, 1981.

Osberg, L. Unemployment insurance in Canada: a review of the recent amendments. *CPP* 5 (Spring 1979) 223-235.

Ostry, S. *Unemployment in Canada*. 1961 census monograph. Ottawa: Dominion Bureau of Statistics, 1968.

Parsons, D. Quit rates over time: a search and information approach. *AER* 63 (June 1973) 390-401.

Parsons, D. Unemployment, the allocation of labour, and optimal government intervention. *AER* 70 (September 1980) 626-635.

Phelps, E.S. et al. *Microeconomic Foundations of Employment and Inflation Theory*. New York: Norton, 1970.

Pissarides, C. Risk, job search and income distribution. *JPE* 82 (November/ December 1974) 1255-1269.

Polemarchakis, H. and L. Weiss. Fixed wages, layoffs, unemployment compensation and welfare. *AER* 68 (December 1978) 909-917.

Ragan, J. The voluntary leaver provisions of unemployment insurance and their effect on quit and unemployment rates. *SEJ* 51 (July 1984) 135-146.

Rea, S. Unemployment insurance and labour supply: a simulation of the 1971 Unemployment Insurance Act. *CJE* 10 (May 1977) 263-278.

Reder, M. Wage structure and structural unemployment. *R.E. Studies* 31 (October 1964) 309-322.

Reder, M. The theory of frictional unemployment. *Economica* 36 (February 1969) 1-28.

Reid, F. Reductions in work time: an assessment of employment sharing to reduce unemployment. *Work and Pay: The Canadian Labour Market*, W.C. Riddell (ed.). Toronto: University of Toronto Press, 1985, 141-170.

Reid, F. Combatting unemployment through work time reductions. *CPP* 12 (June 1986) 275-285.

Riddell, W.C. (ed.). *Work and Pay: The Canadian Labour Market*. Toronto: University of Toronto Press, 1985.

Rosen, S. Implicit contracts: a survey. *JEL* 23 (September 1985) 1144-1175.

Saffer, H. Layoffs and unemployment insurance. *JPubEc* 19 (October 1982) 121-130.

Saffer, H. The effects of unemployment insurance on permanent and temporary layoffs. *R.E. Stats.* (1983) 647-652.

Salop, S. A model of the natural rate of unemployment. *AER* 69 (March 1979) 117-125.

Samson, L. A study of the impact of sectoral shifts on aggregate unemployment in Canada. *CJE* 18 (August 1985) 518-530.

Schofield, J. Urban size and unemployment. *CJE* 13 (August 1980) 490-499.

Shapiro, C. and J.E. Stiglitz. Equilibrium unemployment as a worker discipline device. *AER* 74 (June 1984) 433-444.

Sheppard, H. and A. Beltsky. *The Job Hunt*. Baltimore: Johns Hopkins Press, 1966.

Siedule, T., N. Skoulas, and K. Newton. *The Impact of Economy-Wide Changes in the Labour Force*. Ottawa: Economic Council of Canada, 1976.

Skolnik, M. and F. Siddiqui. The paradox of unemployment and job vacancies. *RI/IR* 31 (No. 1, 1976) 32-54. Comment by F. Reid, and reply 32 (No. 1, 1977) 133-138.

Smith, D.C. Seasonal unemployment and economic conditions. *Employment Policy and the Labour Market*, A. Ross (ed.). Berkeley: University of California Press, 1965.

Solon, G. Labour supply effects of extended unemployment benefits. *JHR* 14 (Spring 1979) 247-55.

Solow, R. On theories of unemployment. *AER* 70 (March 1980) 1-11.

Stephenson, S. The economics of youth job search behaviour. *R.E. Stats.* 58 (February 1976) 104-111.

Stigler, G.J. Information in the labour market. *JPE* 70 (October 1962) 94-105.

Swan, N. Unemployment insurance and labour force participation with application to Canada and its Maritime provinces. *Labour Law Journal* (August 1975) 511-518.

Tandan, N. A comparison of unemployment in selected industrial countries. *Notes on Labour Statistics*. Ottawa: Statistics Canada, 1972, 55-64.

Tandan, N. The decline in the female-male unemployment rate differential in Canada, 1961-1972. *Notes on Labour Statistics*, Ottawa: Statistics Canada, 1973, 5-12.

Thurow, L. The changing structure of unemployment: an econometric study. *R.E. Stats.* 47 (February 1965) 137-149.

Topel, R.H. On layoffs and unemployment insurance. *AER* 73 (September 1983) 541-559.

Turvey, R. Structural change and structural unemployment. *ILR* 116 (September-October 1977) 209-215.

Vanderkamp, J. An application of Lipsey's concept of structural unemployment. *R.E. Studies* 33 (July 1966) 221-225.

Vanderkamp, J. The effect of out-migration on regional employment. *CJE* 3 (November 1970) 541-549.

Vanderkamp, J. The efficiency of the interregional adjustment process. *Disparities and Interregional Adjustment.*, K. Norrie (ed.). Toronto: University of Toronto Press, 1986, 53-108.

Vickery, C. The impact of turnover on group unemployment rates. *R.E. Stats.* 59 (November 1977) 415-426.

Vickery, C. Unemployment insurance: a positive reappraisal. *IR* 18 (Winter 1979) 1-17.

Warner, J., C. Poindexter and R. Fearn. Employer-employee interaction and the duration of unemployment. *QJE* 94 (March 1980) 211-234.

Whipple, D. A generalized theory of job search. *JPE* 81 (November/December 1973) 1170-1189.

Winder, J. Structural unemployment. *The Canadian Labour Market*, A. Kruger and N. Meltz (eds.). Toronto: Centre for Industrial Relations, University of Toronto, 1968.

Winer, S.L. and D. Gauthier. *Internal Migration and Fiscal Structure.* Ottawa: Economic Council of Canada, 1982.

Wolcowitz, J. Dynamic effects of the unemployment insurance tax on temporary layoffs. *JPubEc* 25 (November 1984) 35-52.

Yaniv, G. Unemployment insurance benefits and the supply of labor of an employed worker. *JPubEc* 17 (February 1982) 71-88.

Yellen, J. Efficiency wage models of unemployment. *AER* 74 (May 1984) 200-205.

Zaidi, M. Structural unemployment, labour market efficiency and the intrafactor allocation mechanism in the United States and Canada. *SEJ* 35 (January 1969) 205-213. Comment by B. Mabry and reply 39 (October 1972) 307-310.

27 Wage Changes, Price Inflation and Unemployment

Previous chapters dealt with a variety of wage *structures*, such as the occupational, industrial, and regional wage structures. In this chapter, we deal with the aggregate wage *level* and its determinants, in particular how it is affected by other aggregate variables such as the price level and unemployment. Often this topic is analysed at the macroeconomic level of aggregation of the economy as a whole; however, increasing attention is being paid to its microeconomic foundations — that is, how aggregate wage changes and movements in aggregate employment and unemployment are the results of decisions made by many individual workers, unions and firms. In addition, empirical analysis of the determinants of wage changes is often made at the more disaggregate level of the industry, or for individual wage contracts, as well as the economy as a whole.

The focus of our analysis is on the labour market dimensions of the issue. Since this is essentially a topic of macroeconomics, a more complete treatment is left to texts and courses in macroeconomics.

CANADIAN EXPERIENCE

Table 27.1 summarizes Canada's long-term experience with respect to inflation, unemployment, and related economic aggregates. (See also Figure 25.1). In order to abstract from the effects of business cycles, the table shows average performance between the postwar cyclical peak years of 1956, 1966, 1973 and 1981. Average data for the period prior to 1947 are also included for historical perspective. However, because this period includes both the Great Depression and World War II, the averages mask considerable variability.

Overall economic performance was excellent during the first two decades of the postwar period. Two bursts of inflation occurred during this period, one immediately after the war and the second during the Korean War (1950–53). Otherwise, inflation rates were low by the standards of both previous and subsequent experience and displayed no obvious trend until they began to creep upward in the mid 1960s. Unemployment rates were also low by the standards of other periods, although they did rise significantly during the 1957–58 recession and remained above normal levels until the early 1960s. Productivity and real income per capita grew at rapid rates from 1947 to 1973 compared to rates attained earlier and subsequently. Employment also grew rapidly.

A marked deterioration in economic performance is evident after 1973.

The coexistence of high inflation and high unemployment — a phenomenon often referred to as 'stagflation' — during the 1974–81 period was the most dramatic departure from the past. Prior to the 1970s, increases in unemployment were generally accompanied by decreases in the rate of inflation and vice versa. A sharp decline in productivity growth also occurred and real income growth slowed considerably. Only employment growth remained healthy.

The final period is dominated by the onset of and recovery from the severe recession of 1982–83. Unemployment rose dramatically and the rate of inflation fell substantially. Productivity growth recovered somewhat and real income growth increased. Employment growth remained healthy by historical standards, but lower than the very rapid pace set in the 1960s and 1970s.

TABLE 27.1
AGGREGATE ECONOMIC TRENDS, CANADA, 1927-86

| | Growth Rate[1] of | | | Annual Average | |
Period	Real Income Per Capita[2]	Productivity[3]	Employment[4]	Inflation Rate[5]	Unemployment Rate[6]
1927-46	2.2	2.1	1.4	0.1	8.1
1947-56	2.6	3.5	1.8	4.3	3.2
1957-66	2.4	2.1	2.5	2.0	5.5
1967-73	3.9	2.5	3.0	4.4	5.2
1974-81	1.7	0.1	2.9	9.7	7.3
1982-86	2.9	1.7	2.2	4.6	10.9

Notes: [1]Growth rates are averages of compound increases from the level in the year before the period specified to the level in the final year of the period specified.
[2]Real GNE divided by population.
[3]Real GNE per person employed.
[4]Civilian employment; minor non-comparabilities in series occur in 1946 and 1966.
[5]As measured by the Consumer Price Index.
[6]Minor non-comparabilities occur in 1946 and 1966.
Sources: M.C. Urquhart (ed.) *Historical Statistics of Canada,* Toronto: Macmillan, 1965; Bank of Canada, *Bank of Canada Review,* various issues; Statistics Canada, *National Income and Expenditure Accounts,* various issues.

Inflation and unemployment vary with the state of the business cycle, unemployment rising in recessions and declining in booms and inflation generally falling in recessions and rising in booms. However, as the data in Table 27.1 indicate, there are also large variations in the average levels of inflation and unemployment from one business cycle to another. The rate of inflation averaged only two percent during the decade 1957–66 but almost ten percent during 1974–81. Similarly, the unemployment rate averaged 3.2 percent during the first decade of the postwar period (1947–56) but 10.9 percent during 1982–86. Explaining these variations has been the subject of a great deal of economic research.

A more detailed summary of recent experience is provided in Table 27.2. Two measures of wage inflation, both based on large unionized employers, and one measure of price inflation are shown. All major collective agreements in force includes deferred increases and cost-of-living-allowance (COLA) increases negotiated in previous periods but occurring in the year noted; new non-COLA settlements includes only settlements reached during the period noted (some of which may take effect in subsequent periods). Other measures of wage and price change tell a very similar story of events during these two decades.

Several aspects of the 1967–86 experience should be noted. Inflation crept upward during the late 1960s, with the rate of price increase falling below 4 percent only during the brief 1970/71 recession (brought on by the restrictive monetary policy introduced in 1970 — see the drop in money supply growth in column one of Table 27.2). Real wage growth (the rate of wage change less the rate of change of prices) was very high during this period. Despite rapid employment growth (except during the 1970/71 recession), the unemployment rate also moved upward and by 1971/72 exceeded 6 percent, a high level by the standards of the previous postwar period. After 1970/71 Canada, together with most other Western economies, embarked on an expansionary path, as is evident from the high rates of money supply growth during 1971–73. Employment grew extremely rapidly during 1972–74 but only a modest decline in unemployment took place. Wage and price inflation climbed sharply; by 1975 wage increases exceeded 19 percent and price inflation had reached almost 11 percent. The 1973 OPEC oil price increase contributed to the higher rates of inflation while at the same time causing a recession in many Western countries in 1974/75. In part because Canada is a producer as well as consumer of oil, this recession was milder here than in many countries; nonetheless, employment growth declined noticeably and unemployment rose. The 1974/75 experience provided a clear example of stagflation — increased inflation and unemployment.

Faced with the continuing escalation in wage and price increases and the deteriorating demand conditions associated with the world recession, the federal government introduced the Anti-Inflation Program (AIP) in October 1975. The key ingredients in the program were mandatory wage and price (or profit) controls and gradual reduction in the growth in aggregate demand through fiscal and monetary restraint.

During the 1975–78 AIP, wage settlements declined substantially; price increases also fell, although by a smaller amount. As discussed later in this chapter, most empirical studies attribute some of this decline in inflation to the controls program. The reduction in demand due to fiscal and monetary restraint also played a role. Because of the slack economic conditions, unemployment rose to over 7 percent in 1976 and over 8 percent in 1977 and 1978.

TABLE 27.2
INFLATION, UNEMPLOYMENT AND RELATED ECONOMIC AGGREGATES, CANADA, 1967-86

| | Rate of Change[1] of | | | New Non-COLA Settlements in Major Collective Agreements[3] | | |
| | Money Supply (M1) | Consumer Price Index | Wage Rates in Major Collective Agreements[2] | Employment | | Real Wage Settlements in Major Collective Agreements[4] | Unemployment Rate |
Year	(1)	(2)	(3)	(4)	(5)	(6)	(7)
1967	9.8	3.6	—	2.9	8.4	4.8	3.8
1968	4.4	4.0	8.0	1.9	7.5	3.5	4.5
1969	7.1	4.6	9.1	3.1	7.6	3.0	4.4
1970	2.4	3.3	8.5	1.1	8.7	5.4	5.7
1971	13.0	2.9	7.8	2.3	7.9	5.0	6.2
1972	14.4	4.8	7.4	3.0	8.8	4.0	6.2
1973	14.5	7.5	8.3	5.0	11.0	3.5	5.5
1974	9.3	10.9	12.3	4.2	14.7	3.8	5.3
1975	14.0	10.8	14.2	1.7	19.2	8.4	6.9
1976	8.0	7.5	14.3	2.1	10.9	3.4	7.1
1977	8.5	8.0	11.2	1.8	7.9	−0.1	8.1
1978	10.1	9.0	6.8	3.5	7.1	−1.9	8.3
1979	6.9	9.1	7.8	4.1	8.8	−0.3	7.4
1980	6.2	10.1	9.7	3.0	11.1	1.0	7.5
1981	3.3	12.5	11.5	2.8	13.4	0.9	7.5
1982	− 0.1	10.8	10.3	−3.3	10.1	−0.7	11.0
1983	10.1	5.8	4.7	0.8	5.6	−0.2	11.9
1984	3.3	4.4	3.6	2.5	3.5	−0.9	11.3
1985	4.3	4.0	3.5	2.8	3.7	−0.3	10.5
1986	4.9	4.1	3.4	2.9	3.5	−0.6	9.6

Notes: [1]Year-to-year percentage change.
[2]All major collective agreements in force.
[3]Compound annual average percentage increase in base wage rates over the duration of the contract, new non-COLA settlements only. Contracts containing COLA clauses are excluded because the value of these increases is not known at the time the contract is signed.
[4]Column (5) minus column (2).
Sources: Bank of Canada, *Bank of Canada Review*, various issues; Labour Canada, *Major Wage Settlements*, various issues; Statistics Canada, *The Labour Force*, various issues.

The combination of the 1974/75 world recession and the 1975–78 AIP resulted in some moderation of inflationary pressures. Nonetheless, in the late 1970s inflation began to move upward again in Canada and elsewhere. In 1979 the second major OPEC oil price increase occurred. By the end of the decade rates of price inflation exceeded 10 percent in both the United States and Canada. A variety of aspects of economic behaviour suggested that expectations of continuing inflation were deeply entrenched.

The consequence of these developments was the adoption of a much more determined anti-inflationary stance by the monetary authorities in the United States and subsequently in Canada, as is indicated by the sharp drop in money supply growth in 1981 and 1982. The general results of this policy change are evident from Table 27.2. Initially, the impact of the reduced growth in aggregate demand fell primarily on output and employment: employment declined by over 3 percent in 1982 and unemployment soared to 11 percent. Wage and price inflation moderated only slightly during the first year of the recession. However, as the impact of the severe recession became more widely felt, inflation began to decline dramatically. The adoption of the federal "6 and 5" wage restraint program and related provincial programs which limited the wage increases of public sector employees may also have played a role in the decline in wage increases. By 1984 the rates of wage and price inflation were the lowest since the 1960s. The restrictive monetary policy, possibly with some additional contribution from the public sector wage control programs, had clearly achieved its objective of ending a deeply entrenched inflation. Equally clear was the enormous cost of such a policy — high unemployment, business failures, mortgage foreclosures, and reduced output.

As this brief review of the Canadian experience indicates, inflation and unemployment have been dominant policy concerns for the past two decades. They remain major challenges facing policy makers today. We begin our discussion of the labour market dimensions of inflation and unemployment with an examination of the determinants of wage changes.

DETERMINANTS OF WAGE CHANGES

Wage changes play a significant role in the inflationary process. Labour costs are an important component of total cost and reductions in the rate of price increase are unlikely to occur, other than temporarily, without accompanying reductions in the rate of wage increase. For this reason, policies to control inflation are typically directed to achieving reductions in wage as well as price increases. The first step in the design of such policies is to understand the factors which influence wage determination.

Unemployment Rate

In his classic article based on data from the United Kingdom for the period 1861–1957, Phillips (1958) estimated a negative relationship between aggregate money wage changes and unemployment in the economy as a whole — a relationship now generally referred to as the Phillips curve, as depicted in Figure 27.1(e). Much subsequent research has been devoted to the theoretical underpinnings of this relationship as well as to empirical investigations of other determinants of aggregate wage changes.

Figure 27.1 Wage Changes, Excess Demand and Unemployment

(a) Disequilibrium in Individual Labour Markets

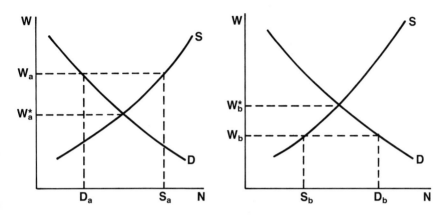

(b) The Relationship between Wage Changes and Excess Demand

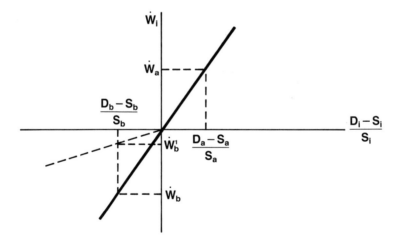

Lipsey (1960) explained the negative relationship on the basis that (1) the unemployment rate is a measure of the overall excess demand or supply in the aggregate labour market and (2) the rate of wage change is a function of the amount of excess labour demand or supply. Aggregation over individual labour markets, each with possibly different amounts of excess demand or supply, is a key aspect of this explanation.

Figure 27.1 illustrates the main elements of Lipsey's theory. At any point in time some labour markets are characterized by excess demand for labour and others by excess supply, as shown in panel (a) of Figure 27.1. Basic economic theory predicts that wages will be rising in those markets characterized by positive excess demand and falling in markets with negative excess demand (excess supply). The rate at which wages adjust is

Figure 27.1

(c) The Relationship between Unemployment and Job Vacancies

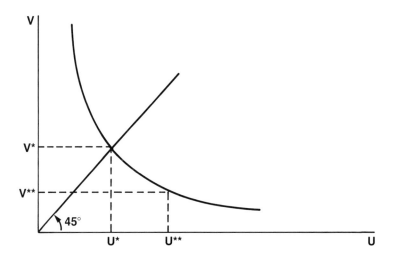

(d) The Relationship between Aggregate Excess Demand and Unemployment

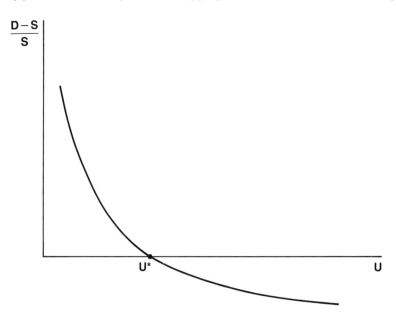

(e) The Relationship between Wage Changes and Unemployment

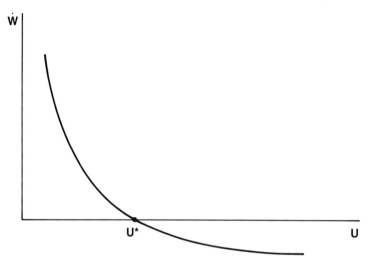

assumed to be related to the amount of excess demand. This relationship may take various forms; for purpose of illustration it is shown in Figure 27.1(b) as being linear throughout (heavy line). Alternatively (shown by the dashed line), it could be linear with a kink at the origin, if wages rise more quickly in response to positive excess demand than they fall in response to negative excess demand, or even non-linear (not shown). Note that the amount of excess demand in market i, D_i-S_i, is expressed relative to the size of the market, $\dfrac{D_i\text{-}S_i}{S_i}$, because excess demand of 25 workers has a different impact in a market with 50 workers than in a market with 500 workers.

The aggregate rate of wage change $\dot{W}$ is simply the weighted sum of the wage changes in each individual market, the weights α_i being employment in market i:

$$\dot{W} = \Sigma \, \alpha_i \, \dot{W}_i \tag{27.1}$$

Because the rate of wage change in market i is related to the amount of excess demand in that market, the aggregate rate of change of wages is a function of aggregate excess labour demand:

$$\dot{W} = f\left(\frac{D\text{-}S}{S}\right) \tag{27.2}$$

The next step is to relate aggregate excess labour demand to observable counterparts, the unemployment rate (U) and the job vacancy rate (V):

$$\frac{D\text{-}S}{S} = V\text{-}U \tag{27.3}$$

This implies a relationship between the rate of wage change and the excess of job vacancies over unemployment:

$$\dot{W} = f(V - U) \tag{27.4}$$

If there is a stable relationship between the unemployment rate and the job vacancy rate, as depicted in Figure 27.1(c), then U alone can be used to measure aggregate excess demand. Substituting the relationship

$$V = g(U) \tag{27.5}$$

into equations (27.3) and (27.4) gives:

$$\frac{D\text{-}S}{S} = g(U) - U = h(U) \tag{27.5}$$

which is shown in Figure 27.1(d) and

$$\dot{W} = f(g(U) - U) = F(U) \tag{27.6}$$

which is the Phillips curve shown in panel (e) (F' (U) < o).

From equation (27.3) there will exist values of the job vacancy rate and unemployment rate which imply aggregate excess labour demand equals zero. These are shown as V* and U* in panels (c), (d), and (e) of Figure 27.1. At U* the aggregate labour market is in equilibrium in the sense that aggregate demand for labour equals aggregate supply and the aggregate rate of wage change equals zero (i.e. F(U*) = 0). For this reason, U* is called the *equilibrium* or *natural unemployment rate*. Note, however, that individual labour markets need not be in equilibrium. As discussed in Chapters 25 and 26 on unemployment, because of imperfect information, the process of matching workers and jobs takes time. Thus unfilled job vacancies and unemployed workers will coexist at any point in time. This disequilibrium at the micro level is nonetheless consistent with aggregate labour market equilibrium in that the excess demand (unfilled job vacancies) in some markets is offset by an equal amount of excess supply (unemployed job seekers) in other markets. The aggregate rate of wage change equals zero because markets in which wages are rising due to excess demand are offset by markets in which wages are declining.

Under the assumptions illustrated in Figure 27.1, the aggregate labour market is in equilibrium when the unemployment rate equals the job vacancy rate, as depicted in panel (c). However, this outcome need not occur in general. In particular, if the relationship between wage changes and excess demand is kinked at the origin as depicted by the dashed line in panel (b), aggregate labour market equilibrium will require an unemployment rate in excess of the job vacancy rate, such as is illustrated by U** and V** in Figure 27.1(c). In these circumstances, because wages fall less rapidly in response to excess supply than they rise in response to excess demand, the aggregate amount of excess supply must exceed the amount of excess demand in order for the aggregate rate of wage change to equal zero. Thus downward wage rigidity — or, more generally, asymmetry in the response of wages to excess demand versus excess supply — results in a higher equilibrium unemployment rate.

The natural unemployment rate depends on numerous factors discussed in Chapters 25 and 26 such as the magnitude and frequency of seasonal, cyclical and other economic disturbances, the job search behaviour of employers and workers and the efficiency of the matching process, the use of layoffs to respond to changes in demand, the amount of labour force turnover, the age-sex composition of the labour force, and labour market policies such as minimum wages and unemployment insurance. Although some of these factors remain approximately constant over time, others change and therefore alter the equilibrium level of unemployment. In these circumstances, the appropriate measure of aggregate excess demand for labour is the difference between the observed and natural unemployment rates, U-U*, with $U > U^*$ implying excess supply of labour and $U < U^*$ implying excess demand. That is, when the equilibrium unemployment rate itself may be changing, the unemployment rate is not a reliable measure of aggregate excess demand and U-U* should be employed in the wage equation in lieu of U. This requires a modification of equation (27.6):

$$\dot{W} = F(U\text{-}U^*), \quad F'\ (\cdot) < 0, \quad F(0) = 0 \tag{27.7}$$

This clearly presents a challenge for empirical research on wage determination in that the natural unemployment rate is not directly observed. We discuss the way empirical studies have dealt with this issue in a subsequent section.

An increase in the natural unemployment rate will shift the Phillips curve upward, resulting in larger wage increases at each unemployment rate, because there will be increased excess demand (or reduced excess supply) at each measured unemployment rate. The unemployment-vacancies relationship will also generally shift to the right because increased excess demand for labour at each unemployment rate is usually associated with more job vacancies at each level of measured unemployment. However, in some circumstances an increase in the natural rate is associated with a movement along, rather than a shift in, the U-V relationship. An example is the movement from U* to U** in Figure 27.1(c), which could have been caused by an increase in the degree of downward wage rigidity in the economy, as illustrated by the shift from the linear to the kinked relationship between wage changes and excess demand in Figure 27.1(b).

In summary, Lipsey's (1960) explanation of the Phillips curve is based on two stable relationships: a positive relation between wage changes and excess demand for labour and an inverse relation between excess demand for labour and the unemployment rate. The latter can be derived by expressing excess labour demand as the difference between the number of unfilled job vacancies and the number of unemployed workers, and assuming a stable (inverse) relation between unemployment and vacancies. The assumption of a stable relationship between the vacancy rate V and the unemployment rate U implies that there is a one-to-one relationship between excess demand and the unemployment rate.

Phillips' original paper indicated that the relationship between wage changes and unemployment in the U.K. had remained stable for almost one hundred years. However, in many countries, including Canada, the temporal stability of this relationship began to be questioned in the late 1960s and early 1970s; the upward drift in wage and price inflation beginning in the mid 1960s resulted in rates of wage increase well above those predicted by estimated Phillips curves. One explanation for this development was that the relationship between the unemployment rate and excess demand for labour had changed; as noted above, such a change could be due to an increase in the natural unemployment rate, perhaps associated with the changing composition of the labour force and revisions to the unemployment insurance system. Evidence relating to this explanation is discussed subsequently. Another leading explanation involved inflationary expectations.

Expected Inflation

Seminal contributions by Friedman (1968) and Phelps (1967, 1968) attacked the theoretical basis for a stable or permanent relationship between wage inflation and unemployment. Friedman and Phelps emphasized the role of inflationary expectations in the wage determination process. If both employers and employees expect prices to increase, they will adjust wage changes upward by the amount of expected inflation in order to achieve the desired change in real wages.

Expected inflation is a general term which includes several components: changes in the firm's product prices, in wages in similar firms and industries, and in the cost of living. These reflect the fact that what matters to employers and employees are *relative wages* and *real wages*. To workers, what is important are wages relative to those received by comparable workers in other firms and industries (relative wages) and relative to the cost of living (real wages). Thus, expectations about wage changes elsewhere and about changes in the cost of living will influence wage determination, especially when wages are not set or negotiated frequently. To firms, what is important are wages relative to wages elsewhere (which affects the firm's ability to attract and keep workers) and relative to the prices that the firm can charge for its products (which affects the firm's ability to pay). Thus expectations about product price increases should also be a factor in wage determination. In the analysis that follows we will focus on price expectations and thus on issues relating to real wages. The analysis of wage expectations and issues relating to relative wages results in similar conclusions (Phelps, 1968).

The role of expected inflation is illustrated in Figure 27.2. Two individual labour markets, market a with excess supply for labour at the current price level (p_0) and market b with excess demand at p_0, are used for pur-

Figure 27.2 Wage Changes and Expected Inflation

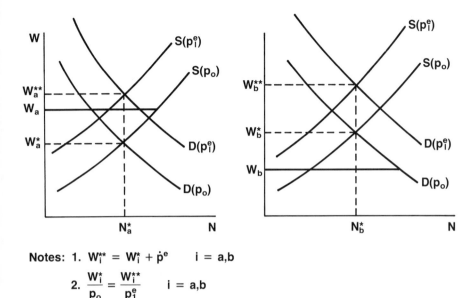

Notes: 1. $W_i^{**} = W_i^* + \dot{p}^e$ $i = a,b$

2. $\dfrac{W_i^*}{p_o} = \dfrac{W_i^{**}}{p_i^e}$ $i = a,b$

poses of illustration. During the period for which the wage rate is being determined, the price level is expected to rise from p_o to p_i^e, equivalent to an expected inflation rate of $\dot{p}^e$. Thus both the labour demand and labour supply curves shift up by the expected increase in the price level. Labour demand is a function of the price level because, as indicated in Chapter 9, the firm's labour demand schedule is the marginal revenue product of labour, defined as the marginal physical product times the price at which the product is sold. Hence, an increase in the price of output, other things being equal, will shift up the demand for labour by the amount of the price increase. The labour supply schedule is also a function of the price level, as discussed in Part I on Labour Supply, because the worker's desired supply of labour depends on the real wage — the money wage divided by the price level for consumption goods and services. An increase in these prices will thus increase the asking wage for any specific quantity of labour by exactly the increase in the price level. The labour supply curve thus shifts vertically upward by the amount of expected inflation.[1] Even though the current equilibrium wages in markets a and b are W_a^* and W_b^* respectively, the equilibrium wages for the period for which the wage rate is being determined are W_a^{**} and W_b^{**}. Thus the observed wage change will be from W_i to W_i^{**} in market i (i=a,b). This wage change can be expressed

---

1 The relevant price level in the labour supply function is the price level of consumption goods (e.g. the Consumer Price Index) while the relevant price in the labour demand function is the firm's product price. For expositional purposes, these are assumed to increase at the same rate. The analysis can easily be generalized to deal with differential rates of price increase.

as the sum of two components: (1) from W_i to W_i^*, reflecting the current amount of excess demand or supply in market i, and (2) from W_i^* to W_i^{**}, reflecting the expected increase in the price level. Following the previous derivation of the relationship between wage changes and the current amount of aggregate excess demand for labour as measured by the unemployment rate, the Phillips curve becomes:

$$\dot{W} = F(U\text{-}U^*) + \dot{p}^e \qquad (27.8)$$

This relationship — often referred to as the "expectations-augmented Phillips curve," reflecting the addition of the expected inflation term $\dot{p}^e$ — is illustrated in Figure 27.3. There are a family of Phillips curves, each based on a particular expected inflation rate. Increases in expected inflation shift the Phillips curve vertically upward by the amount of the increase in $\dot{p}^e$; decreases in inflationary expectations shift the relationship downward.

As before, the natural unemployment rate U^* is defined as the level at which aggregate demand for labour equals aggregate supply. Because the aggregate labour market is in equilibrium, real wages are constant at U^*.[2] However, changes in nominal wages may be taking place due to expected inflation, as illustrated by points a, c, and d in Figure 27.3. At each of these points money wages are increasing at the expected inflation rate, with the result that expected real wages are constant. At unemploy-

Figure 27.3 Wage Changes, Unemployment and Expected Inflation

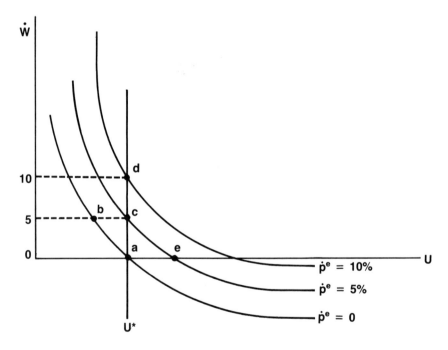

2 The possibility of real wage growth due to productivity growth is discussed below. For the moment, aggregate productivity growth is assumed to be zero.

ment rates below U*, such as the point b in Figure 27.3, aggregate labour demand exceeds aggregate supply and expected real wages are increasing. At unemployment rates above U*, such as point e, expected real wages are declining, reflecting aggregate excess supply of labour.

An important aspect of the Friedman-Phelps theory of inflationary expectations is the prediction that both the labour demand and labour supply functions will shift upward by the anticipated increase in the price level. This prediction arises because firms' profits and workers' utility depend on the real wage; increases in the price level thus require an equal increase in the nominal wage at each level of employment to maintain the real wage. As a consequence, the equilibrium level of employment in each individual labour market is not altered by a change in the price level, once nominal wages have adjusted to the higher (expected) price level. This property can be seen in Figure 27.2. In both markets, the labour demand and labour supply functions shift up by the same amount, resulting in the same equilibrium level of employment N_i^* and equilibrium real wage as prevailed before the expected increase in the price level. Because the equilibrium in each market is unchanged, the unemployment rate at which aggregate demand for labour equals aggregate supply is also not altered by changes in the price level, once these changes are anticipated and taken into account by both employers and employees in wage determination. The Phillips curve thus shifts vertically upward by the anticipated increase in the price level, as depicted in Figure 27.3.

In contrast, if workers display "money illusion" by not raising their asking wage for a given quantity of labour by the same proportion as the anticipated increase in prices, then a change in the price level may alter the equilibrium level of employment in each market and the equilibrium unemployment rate for the economy as a whole. In these circumstances, wage changes do not adjust fully by the expected rate of inflation so the expectations-augmented Phillips curve becomes

$$\dot{W} = F(U-U^*) + \lambda \, \dot{p}^e \tag{27.9}$$

where $\lambda < 1$ is a parameter reflecting the degree of money illusion, $\lambda = 1$ implying no money illusion. A number of empirical studies (discussed below) have tested the Friedman-Phelps prediction of a unit coefficient ($\lambda = 1$) in the wage equation.

In summary, Friedman (1968) and Phelps (1967, 1968) emphasized the role of inflationary expectations in the wage determination process. If wages are adjusted simply to eliminate the *current* amount of excess labour demand or supply, then the unemployment rate (or some other measure of excess demand) may be the sole determinant of wage changes. However, because wages are set or negotiated periodically, employers and employees look not only at current conditions but at the conditions *expected to prevail* during the remainder of the wage contract (or period for which the wage is set). This "forward-looking" aspect provides the rationale for including the expected inflation variable.

The role of inflationary expectations in wage determination is widely accepted. It is well grounded in the microeconomic theory of the behaviour of workers and firms; it is capable of explaining much of the upward drift in wage settlements since the 1960s; and it is evident to even the most casual observer of the wage determination process.

The relationship between wage changes, unemployment, and expected inflation summarized by equation (27.8) has profound implications for macroeconomic policy. In particular, it implies that there is no long-run tradeoff between inflation and unemployment even though these two variables may be inversely related in the short run. This important implication is discussed more fully subsequently in this chapter. At this point we continue to examine the main factors that influence wage changes.

Catch-up for Unanticipated Inflation

Wages are typically determined periodically, with the duration of the wage contract usually explicit in the union sector and implicit in the nonunion sector. No matter how much effort employers, employees and their representatives devote to forecasting inflation and wage increases in other firms and industries, the actual changes in the price level and in wages elsewhere during the contract period may differ from the expected change. Consequently, the real or relative wage at the end of the contract will generally not equal the real or relative wage that was expected to prevail at the time the wage was originally determined. If inflation is greater than anticipated, workers will desire an additional "catch-up" wage increase because of the unanticipated decline in their purchasing power. Similarly, if the increase in wages in related industries and occupations is greater than expected, workers will desire an additional increase to restore wage relativities. In contrast, if prices or other firms' wages increase less rapidly than anticipated, there will be pressure from the firm to adjust wages downward, or to have them increase less quickly in the future.

The effect of unanticipated inflation is illustrated in Figure 27.4. For purposes of illustration, it is assumed that wages are set to yield labour market equilibrium at the end of the contract. At the beginning of the current contract period (end of previous contract), the wage is W_o. Given the anticipated rise in the price level to p_1^e, the appropriate wage increase is from W_o to W_1^*. However, because the actual rise in the price level (to p_1^a) exceeds the expected rise, the actual equilibrium wage is W_1^a. An additional "catch-up" wage increase from W_1^* to W_1^a is therefore needed to restore equilibrium.

To account for the influence of this catch-up factor, a number of empirical studies have included as an explanatory variable in the wage equation a measure of the difference between the actual rate of inflation over the previous wage contract and the expected rate of inflation at the time the previous contract began (e.g. Turnovsky, 1972; Riddell, 1979; Christofides, Swidinsky and Wilton, 1980a). Note that this variable measures the amount of excess demand or supply due to unanticipated inflation,

Figure 27.4 Wage Changes and Unanticipated Inflation

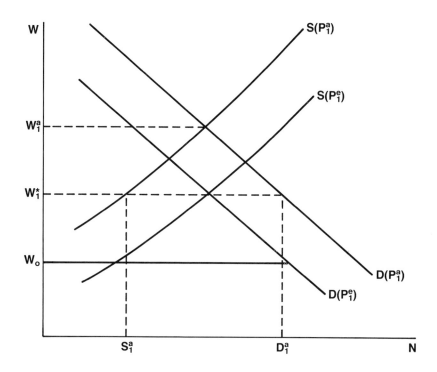

given by $D_1^a - S_1^a$ in Figure 27.4. Thus this catch-up variable would not be needed (and would not have any explanatory power) if the unemployment rate (or other measures of excess demand) were perfect measures of the excess demand or supply of labour. That is, unanticipated inflation should be reflected in the observed levels of job vacancies and unemployed job seekers. The catch-up variable should therefore be interpreted as a supplementary measure of excess demand or supply in the labour market; it is useful to the extent that movements in the unemployment rate do not fully capture all variations in excess demand for labour.

If inflation or other economic circumstances deviate substantially from the expectations upon which wages were determined, the parties may not wait until the end of the contract period to make an upward or downward adjustment. Such adjustments are more likely to occur in the nonunion sector where the wage rate and the length of the period for which it is in force are not part of a formal contract but rather are implicit understandings about normal behaviour. Nonetheless, even in the union sector, where wage agreements are legal contracts with a fixed duration, a significant change in economic conditions (relative to what was expected) may cause one side to request and the other to agree to renegotiate the terms of the contract. (Indeed, some contracts contain "reopener provisions" which stipulate the circumstances under which such renegotiation may be necessary.) Examples of such adjustments took place in Canada in the 1970s because of unanticipated increases in inflation and in the 1980s because of an unanticipated decline in inflation and in product market conditions due to the 1982/83 recession.

Productivity Growth

In wage determination, the direct concern of employers and employees may be the nominal or money wage, but their ultimate concern is with the real wage. Thus any factors that influence real wage growth should also be included as explanatory variables in the wage equation. This can be seen by subtracting $\dot{p}^e$ from both sides of equation (27.8):

$$\dot{W} - \dot{p}^e = F(U - U^*) \tag{27.10}$$

The dependent variable is the (expected) growth in real wages; thus any additional determinants of real wage growth should be included on the right hand side of equation (27.10).

The primary determinant of real wage growth is the trend rate of productivity growth. Over the long term, real wages have tended to increase at the rate of growth of productivity (Allen, 1986). This tendency is also evident in the postwar Canadian experience: the sharp decline in productivity growth after 1973 was accompanied by a decline in the rate of growth of real income per capita (Table 27.1) and in the rate of increase in real wages (Table 27.2).

The relationship between productivity and real wage growth can be understood most easily at the level of the economy as a whole. Higher productivity implies that it is possible to produce more output with the same inputs. Thus, other factors being constant (including employment of inputs), an increase in productivity will increase the economy's total output or national income and therefore real income per capita. Wages and salaries make up over 75 percent of national income. Unless there is a massive shift towards profits in the functional distribution of income, an increase in real per capita income will be associated with higher real wages and salaries. The relationship between aggregate output, labour's share of total output or income, productivity and real wages is explained more formally below.

At the level of an individual labour market, the relationship between productivity and real wages is more complex (Allen, 1986). Higher productivity may either increase or decrease labour demand, depending on the magnitude of several offsetting factors. These include a displacement effect — less labour is required per unit of output — and a product demand effect — higher productivity lowers costs and therefore product prices, resulting in an increase in product demand and thus labour demand. As a consequence, productivity gains may result in lower real wages and/or employment in some labour markets.

Technical changes introduced in individual labour markets also have effects throughout the economy. These general equilibrium effects often provide the mechanism through which productivity gains result in real wage increases for the average worker. Increased efficiency in the production of one commodity lowers its price, resulting in higher real incomes for all consumers of that commodity. As a consequence, the demand for all normal goods increases, raising labour demand and therefore real wages throughout much of the economy. Average real wages rise, although there may be lower real wages in some individual labour markets. Productivity improvements tend to reduce costs of production, whereas wage increases raise costs. Thus productivity growth affects the relationship between wage changes and price changes. These aspects are discussed more fully below.

Other Determinants of Money Wage Changes

In addition to productivity growth, expected inflation, catch-up for unanticipated inflation and unemployment, a number of other variables have been suggested as determinants of money wage changes. In many cases, these variables are included (a) to control for certain factors, given the particular nature of the data set employed in the empirical work, or (b) to act as a proxy for other variables for which data was not available. In other cases, they are included in a more or less *ad hoc* fashion, often without a careful theoretical rationale, simply to reflect institutional features that are believed to affect money wage changes. While these factors may truly have an exogenous effect, they may also simply reflect a common set of underlying forces. Hence, the importance of an appropriate theoretical foundation to sort out cause and effect — the crucial linkage for most policy purposes.

The rate of increase of wages in the United States, for example, may be regarded as a determinant of wage changes in Canada. This could occur through wage spillovers from key groups in the United States, through international unions, multinational corporations, or pressures for wage parity. Again, the extent to which U.S. wages would exert an independent influence, as opposed to Canadian and U.S. wages moving together in response to a common set of forces, would be a difficult issue to disentangle.

Profits have been regarded as a determinant of wage changes largely on the belief that high profits reflect a greater ability to pay or a higher opportunity cost of resisting wage demands and engaging in a strike. They could also reflect short-run demand changes over a business cycle, as well as reverse causation in that wage increases may affect profitability. Again, cause and effect becomes difficult to disentangle without a well-specified theoretical rationale.

Changes in unionization also have been regarded as an independent determinant of money wages. While unions can undoubtedly have an impact on the wages of their members, their impact on the rate of *change* of the *aggregate* wage level is a much more complicated matter. As discussed in Chapter 16, unions affect the wages and employment of both union and nonunion workers, the union-nonunion wage differential reflecting both higher wages for union members and a lower average wage in the nonunion sector (although some nonunion workers receive higher wages due to threat effects). The change in the aggregate wage level depends on the magnitude of these two offsetting effects. The empirical evidence indicates that, although unionization does lower the average wage in the nonunion sector, most of the differential is associated with higher wages in the union sector. Thus unionization does tend to raise the aggregate wage level. However, this constitutes a "one time" increase associated with the creation of a union-nonunion wage differential. In order to have a continuing effect on the aggregate rate of wage change, either an increase in the union-nonunion wage differential or an increase in the extent of unionization must occur. Calculations indicate that these contribute relatively little to the aggregate rate of wage change. For example, the aggregate wage level increased by 44 percent in the U.S. between 1967 and 1973; Ashenfelter (1978) concluded that the combined effect of increases in union density and in the union-nonunion wage differential accounted for only one to two percentage points of this increase. Similar conclusions have been reached in other empirical studies.

Market imperfections also have been discussed, especially in the context of insulating wages from competitive pressures. In the context of dual labour market analysis, for example, aggregate money wage changes could emanate from institutional changes, and from changes in administrative practices, or segmentation of the labour market. This would be facilitated by the ability to pass wage cost increases on to consumers via administrative pricing in non-competitive product markets. To a certain extent the belief in these market imperfections and non-competitive forces — most notably monopoly power in the product market and union power in the labour market — were part of the rationale for wage-price controls and guidelines. The exact manner in which these imperfections would affect the wage and inflation process, however, was seldom spelled out clearly. In particular, while imperfections could explain why the price and wage *levels* are higher than they would be in the absence of the imperfections, they do not explain the *changes* in prices and wages, unless one believes that the imperfections themselves change rapidly.

Unusual events — in particular, large wage settlements in specific sectors of the economy — often have been discussed as important determinants of aggregate money wage changes in the economy as a whole. The belief is that unusually high settlements in specific sectors have set off a chain reaction, spilling over into other sectors. In Canada, such key settlements allegedly have included Seaway workers in the late 1960s, construction trades in the 1960s and early 1970s, and the public sector in the 1970s.

While it can be tempting to regard these settlements as setting off inflationary wage settlements elsewhere, there is a danger in such *ad hoc* theorizing about the impact of peculiar events. Certainly they can affect the magnitude of wages in a particular sector, and hence they can affect the wages of that sector relative to other sectors, at least in the short run. Nevertheless, the mechanism whereby this affects aggregate wages in the economy as a whole is not clear. What appears to be a spillover effect may simply be a variety of sectors responding to the same set of economic forces. And even if there are purely institutional spillover effects, it is not clear that they will persist in the long run. There will always be a group that stands out as receiving unusually large settlements in a given short period of time. Some of the gain may reflect a catch-up, some may reflect a short-run demand increase, and some may be a purely transitory gain that will be dissipated over time. Unusually high wage settlements in a particular sector may be a *symptom* of any of a variety of factors; it is another matter, however, to argue that they are the *cause* of general increases in aggregate money wages.

A variety of public policies may also affect aggregate wage changes. In some cases these effects are intended, while in others they are incidental consequences. Incomes policies are designed to restrain wage and price increases. In Canada these have generally taken the form of guidelines or direct controls on wage and price increases. The economic rationale for such policies and Canada's experience with them are discussed subsequently in this chapter. Changes in taxation may affect wage changes, although such effects are usually unintended consequences. Payroll taxes affect labour demand and income taxes affect labour supply. Thus if tax changes are large enough and apply throughout much of the economy, they may affect the aggregate wage level. As was the case with several other factors discussed in this section, such changes have a one-time impact on the aggregate wage level. However, if income tax rates are not indexed to changes in the price level — as was the case in Canada prior to 1973 and as remains the case in many countries — their taxation may affect wage changes on a continuing basis in an inflationary period, as individuals are pushed into higher tax brackets due to increases in their nominal incomes associated with inflation.

In summary, in addition to the main determinants of wage changes, a number of other factors may affect labour demand or labour supply and therefore the wage level. In many cases these exert a one-time impact; however, some may exert a continuing influence on aggregate wage changes.

EMPIRICAL EVIDENCE

A large number of studies of the determinants of wage changes have been carried out in Canada. Early studies such as Kaliski (1964), Bodkin, Bond, Reuber and Robinson (1966), Vanderkamp (1966, 1972), Zaidi (1969), Reuber (1970), Swidinsky (1972), Turnovsky (1972) and Beare (1973) used as the dependent variable the annual or quarterly rate of change in an aggregate earnings index (such as average hourly earnings). Aggregate earnings indexes cover a substantial proportion of the labour force; however, there are several problems associated with their use in this context. Earnings depend not only on the hourly wage rate but also on factors such as overtime pay and bonuses. Average wage or earnings indexes may also be affected by changes in the composition of employment; for example, if firms lay off mainly junior, low-wage employees in a cyclical downturn and rehire these employees in the upturn, the average wage or earnings index will vary countercyclically even if wage rates and earnings for each type of employee do not. For this reason, it would be preferable to use indexes based on fixed employment weights. Unfortunately, the average earnings indexes available in Canada do not have this feature.

Another important measurement issue relates to the distinction between current and deferred wage changes. In the postwar period there has been a marked trend toward the use of multi-year contracts in the unionized sector. Multi-year contracts often contain deferred increases. The magnitude of these may be predetermined (i.e., fixed at the time the contract is signed) or indexed to changes in the Consumer Price Index via a cost-of-living-allowance or COLA clause. The observed change in average wages or earnings at any point in time is thus a mixture of current and deferred changes. Yet the determinants of these two types of wage change clearly differ.

Table 27.2 shows that the differences can be large. Column (3) shows the percentage change in base wage rates which occurred during the year; that is, contains both current and deferred increases in all major collective agreements. Column (5) shows the percentage change in base wage rates in new non-COLA settlements reached during the period. These are calculated on a life-of-the-contract basis; that is, show the compound annual average increase in wages (both current and deferred) to take place over the duration of the agreement. Contracts containing COLA clauses are excluded because the value of these increases is not known at the time the contract is signed. The difference between the two series is at times as much as 5 percent; at other times the difference is negligible.

Another implication of multi-year contracts is that the fraction of the labour force negotiating a new agreement varies from year to year. In some years as few as 30 percent of major collective agreements are renegotiated while in other years more than 60 percent are renegotiated. Thus, some of the variation in aggregate earnings (or wage) indexes is simply due to the timing of the "bargaining calendar."

In view of these difficulties associated with aggregate index data, researchers have increasingly turned to data on individual contracts. This approach treats each negotiated settlement as an observation and to a considerable extent circumvents the two problems discussed above. In particular, deferred increases are not so problematic in that all the increases to take effect during the contract are included in calculating the percentage change in wages, which is then explained in terms of economic conditions prevailing at the time the contract was signed. Similarly, variations in the proportion of the labour force bargaining in each period are evidently less of a problem in that one observes the underlying rate of change of wages. In addition to lessening the measurement difficulties associated with analyzing the determinants of wage changes, the use of contract data also provides considerably more micro detail and therefore permits the testing of some hypotheses which would simply not be feasible with more aggregative data. Canadian studies based on individual wage contracts include Sparks and Wilton (1971), Cousineau and Lacroix (1977), Riddell (1979), Christofides, Swidinsky and Wilton (1980a, 1980b) and Christofides and Wilton (1985).

Not all of the recent studies treat each individual contract as an observation. Reid (1979) and Riddell and Smith (1982) use more aggregative measures by employing as the dependent variable a weighted (by number of employees) average of the individual wage changes negotiated during the period; that is, a series such as that shown in Column (5) of Table 27.2. The use of these aggregate measures of the rate of change of wages does not raise the problems associated with aggregate measures obtained from wage index data. In addition, some researchers — such as Fortin and Newton (1982) — continue to use aggregate earnings indexes because these cover more of the labour force, including the nonunion sector.

Each of the empirical studies of Canadian wage changes employs the basic expectations-augmented Phillips curve specification discussed above. However, they differ in several ways, including the measurement of excess demand for labour, the measurement of inflationary expectations and in the role of catch-up for unanticipated inflation.

Each of the studies includes a measure of excess demand for labour. Generally this variable is found to be a significant determinant of wage changes; however, in contrast to Phillips' original study, recent analyses find that the aggregate unemployment rate is often insignificant or even perversely signed (e.g. Christofides, Swidinsky and Wilton, 1980a). This outcome is not unexpected. As discussed in Chapters 25 and 26 on unemployment, because of substantial changes in the age-sex composition of the labour force and in social programs such as unemployment insurance, the meaning of (say) a 6 percent unemployment rate in the 1970s differed considerably from that in the 1950s. In other words, the demographic trends and changes in social policies have raised the equilibrium unemployment rate, and consequently the aggregate unemployment rate has not remained a consistent measure of the "tightness" of the labour market.

There are several ways to deal with this situation. A number of authors have constructed adjusted unemployment-rate series which are intended to provide a consistent measure of excess demand and thus can be used in lieu of the measured unemployment rate to explain wage changes. Fortin and Newton (1982) is an example of this approach in the Canadian setting. These adjusted measures are typically weighted averages of the unemployment rates of different age-sex groups, with groups such as males aged 25-44 being assumed to contribute more to excess labour demand than females and youths. Alternatively, some authors use the job vacancy rate on the assumption that the developments that raised U* did not significantly alter the equilibrium job vacancy rate V* (Reid, 1979; Christofides, Swidinsky and Wilton, 1980a, 1980b).

An alternative procedure, used for example by Riddell and Smith (1982), is to measure aggregate excess demand for labour as the difference between the actual and natural unemployment rates, U − U* as in equation (27.8). A second equation is added to account for changes in U* in terms of the demographic, legislative and other changes. When this is done, the coefficient on the excess demand variable has the predicted sign and is statistically significant.

The conclusion that excess demand for labour exerts a significant influence on wage changes implies that there is a relationship between wage inflation and unemployment in the short run, holding constant inflationary expectations and the natural unemployment rate. Changes in the natural rate have shifted this short-run Phillips curve upward, resulting in higher wage inflation at each measured unemployment rate. Another important conclusion is that the short-run Phillips curve is fairly flat. Because the relationship is generally found to be nonlinear as depicted in Figure 27.3, the slope depends on the unemployment rate. Evaluated at the average unemployment rate during the sample period, a slope of 0.5 is a typical estimate, implying that a one percentage point increase in the unemployment rate reduces the rate of wage inflation by one-half of one percent. As discussed below, such estimates indicate that the costs of reducing inflation by monetary and fiscal restraint (thereby reducing excess demand in labour and product markets) may be extremely high.

Both expected inflation and catch-up for unanticipated inflation appear to play significant roles in wage determination. Empirical studies indicate that much of the upward shift in the Phillips curve during the 1960s and 1970s was associated with the rise in inflationary expectations. Catch-up forces also contributed to the upward shift in the late 1960s and early 1970s. This factor can work in either direction; more recently, with the decline in inflation in the early 1980s, lower than anticipated inflation has exerted additional downward pressure on wage increases.

A fundamental difficulty is that inflationary expectations are not generally observed. Empirical analysis thus requires constructing a proxy for expected inflation; as a consequence, the results represent a joint test of the theory of the determinants of aggregate wage changes and the theory of expectations formation. This joint hypothesis testing problem is exacerbated by the fact that any errors in measuring expected inflation will also cause errors in the measurement of unanticipated inflation.

Early research was often based on the hypothesis of adaptive expectations, according to which the expected rate of inflation could be expressed as a distributed lag of previous inflation rates. This approach was criticized on the basis that these expectations need not be consistent with the actual process generating inflation. In other words, the adaptive expectations hypothesis implies that those involved in forming expectations may repeatedly over- or under-predict inflation without revising their forecasting behaviour. For this reason, economists have increasingly adopted the hypothesis of rational expectations, according to which individuals' expectations represent an optimal forecast given the available information regarding the process that actually generates inflation. The most controversial aspect of rational expectations is the information set that market participants are assumed to possess and use in forming their expectations. In much theoretical work in macroeconomics, market participants are assumed to understand the structure of the economy, including knowing the parameters of the various relationships among variables. In empirical work on wage determination, much weaker versions of rational expectations are generally assumed. A common assumption is that in forecasting inflation individuals use only the previous inflationary experience as their information set. Rational expectations of inflation can generally be written as a distributed lag of previous inflation rates; however, the distributed lag weights must reflect the actual relationship between current and past inflation rather than being arbitrary as is the case under adaptive expectations.

A central empirical issue is the prediction of Friedman (1968) and Phelps (1967, 1968) that wage changes will adjust fully to reflect changes in expected inflation. In these circumstances there is no long-run relationship between wage inflation and unemployment; the long-run Phillips curve is vertical at the natural unemployment rate as depicted in Figure 27.3. As noted previously, this prediction implies $\lambda = 1$ in equation (27.9). Tests of this "natural rate hypothesis" have generally confirmed the $\lambda = 1$ prediction. Some apparent exceptions are discussed below.

However expectations of future inflation are formed, they will often turn out to be incorrect. The catch-up variable is intended to capture the effects of over- or under-prediction of changes in the price level. When wage increases fully reflect expected inflation, the catch-up variable can be measured as the difference between the actual rate of inflation since the wage was last determined and the expected rate of inflation at that time, $\dot{p}_{t-1} - \dot{p}^e_{t-1}$. This catch-up specification was originally used by Turnovsky (1972) with aggregate data and subsequently employed by Riddell (1979) with individual contract data. Because the length of wage contracts varies considerably across bargaining units, it is difficult to incorporate the influence of unanticipated inflation adequately with aggregate data. With individual contract data, both expected inflation and catch-up can be precisely related to the actual timing of wage settlements.

If for some reason wage changes do not fully incorporate expected inflation, then the specification $\dot{p}_{t-1} - \dot{p}^e_{t-1}$ will not be appropriate. In this context, Christofides, Swidinsky and Wilton (1980a) have introduced the distinction between unanticipated and uncompensated inflation. The latter is the difference between the actual rate of inflation since the wage was last determined and the amount of expected inflation incorporated in the previous wage change, $\dot{p}_{t-1} - \lambda \dot{p}^e_{t-1}$. When $\lambda = 1$ unanticipated and uncompensated inflation are equal. However, Christofides, Swidinsky and

Wilton argue that, because of uncertainty about future inflation, employers and employees may prefer wage settlements that do not fully incorporate expected inflation ex ante, leaving the remainder to be adjusted ex post. Thus they predict $\lambda < 1$ so that ex ante expectations contribute less to the current wage change and ex post adjustments for realized inflation contribute more. Although the theoretical support for this argument is weak, Christofides, Swidinsky and Wilton (1980a) do find empirical support for this hypothesis. However, although they estimate $\lambda < 1$, the combined ex ante and ex post adjustment for inflation is equal to unity. Thus these empirical results also support the conclusion that there is no long-run relationship between wage inflation and unemployment.

Although the Christofides et al. (1980a) conclusion that λ is systematically less than unity is consistent with the proposition that there is no long-run trade-off between inflation and unemployment, the extent to which wages adjust to expected inflation on an ex ante versus ex post basis is clearly important for the short-run dynamics of unemployment and inflation. Even with full ex ante compensation for expected inflation, the existence of a catch-up adjustment for forecast errors implies that unanticipated disturbances will have effects that will persist for several years. The smaller the ex ante compensation and thus the larger the ex post compensation, the more significant are the delayed responses to economic shocks. Even if expectations are forward-looking, there is therefore an important backward-looking aspect to wage determination. Several Canadian studies suggest that this aspect is quantitatively significant.

The impact of the 1975-78 Anti-Inflation Program on wage and price inflation has been extensively investigated. Studies include Auld, Christofides, Swidinsky and Wilton (1979), Cousineau and Lacroix (1978), Christofides and Wilton (1985), Fortin and Newton (1982), Reid (1979), and Riddell and Smith (1982). As can be seen in Table 27.2, wage increases fell substantially during the 1975-78 period, with new non-COLA settlements declining from over 19 percent prior to the introduction of controls in October 1975 to under 11 percent in the first year of the program (1976) and under 8 percent in the last two years of the program (1977 and 1978). The main objective of the empirical research has been to determine how much of this decline (if any) can be attributed to the wage-price controls program and how much is associated with other factors such as the higher unemployment and slack economic conditions which prevailed during this period.

Empirical studies are unanimous in concluding that the controls program had a significant effect on the rate of wage increase. Most estimates of the impact on new wage settlements are in the range of 3 to 4 percent per year. This is a very large impact. Assuming the slope of the short-run Phillips curve to be approximately 0.5, the same direct effect on wage inflation would have required unemployment rates of 13 to 14 percent throughout the three-year period rather than the 7 to 8 percent unemployment rates actually experienced. Studies by Riddell and Smith (1982) and Christofides and Wilton (1985), which include data from the post-controls period, also conclude that the AIP was not followed by a wage explosion or "post-controls bubble," as has been the case in many other attempts at achieving wage restraint. The policy implications of these findings are discussed below.

PRICE INFLATION AND UNEMPLOYMENT

We have seen how actual and expected changes in the price level affect wages. However, because of their effect on labour costs, wage changes also influence prices. Thus any factor such as unemployment or expected inflation which affects the rate of change of wages will also affect the rate of change in prices as changes in labour costs associated with wage changes feed through into prices. This implies that there will exist a relationship between price inflation and unemployment, holding constant other factors, as well as between actual and expected price inflation. These relationships and their implications are briefly examined in this section. Further discussion is provided in textbooks on macroeconomics.

Because labour costs are a substantial proportion of total costs, a common assumption in empirical work on price determination is that the output price p can be written as a mark-up m times the labour cost per unit of output, or unit labour cost. The mark-up reflects both other costs such as raw materials and a normal rate of profit. Unit labour cost is simply the wage rate (dollars per employee-hour) divided by output Q per employee-hour N or average labour productivity. Thus

$$p = m \cdot \frac{W}{A} \tag{27.11}$$

where A is average labour productivity (Q/N). Totally differentiating (27.11), assuming the mark-up is approximately constant over time (dm = 0), and dividing the left-hand side by p and the right-hand by $m \cdot \dfrac{W}{A}$ gives:

$$\dot{p} = \dot{W} - \dot{A} \tag{27.12}$$

where $\dot{p} = dp/p$ and similarly for $\dot{W}$ and $\dot{A}$. This relationship between price inflation, wage inflation and labour productivity growth is derived more formally below under competitive rather than mark-up pricing. Note that equation (27.12) can be rewritten as

$$\dot{W} - \dot{p} = \dot{A} \tag{27.13}$$

which states that, with a constant mark-up on unit labour costs, real wages will grow at the rate of productivity growth. The historical tendency for real wages to increase at the rate of productivity growth was discussed previously. This analysis provides an explanation for this phenomenon; namely, that mark-ups on unit labour cost are approximately constant.

Combining equations (27.12) and (27.9) gives the relationship between price inflation and unemployment:

$$\dot{p} = F(U - U^*) - \dot{A} + \lambda \dot{p}^e \qquad (27.14)$$

Holding constant productivity growth and expected inflation, price inflation and unemployment are inversely related in the same way as wage inflation and unemployment. Changes in productivity growth or expected inflation shift this relationship upward or downward. Figure 27.5 illustrates this "price Phillips curve" relationship for the case in which the Friedman-Phelps prediction that $\lambda = 1$ holds. As before, there is a family of price Phillips curves, each for a different expected inflation rate. These are referred to as short-run Phillips curves because they depict the relationship between inflation and unemployment during the period in which inflationary expectations do not adjust to changes in the actual rate of inflation. For example, by employing expansionary monetary and fiscal policy, it may be possible to move the economy from point a in Figure 27.5 to point b. However, the latter outcome is not sustainable in the long run because actual inflation exceeds expected inflation. The set of outcomes that can be maintained on a permanent basis are those points such as a, c, and d in Figure 27.5 at which actual and expected inflation are equal. At any other points, actual and expected inflation will diverge, causing employers and employees to adjust their expectations and consequently their behaviour.

This analysis implies that there is a temporary or short-run tradeoff

Figure 27.5 The Relationship Between Inflation and Unemployment

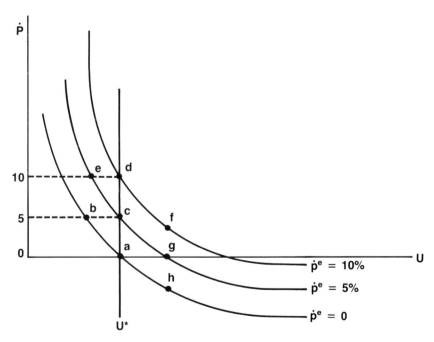

between inflation and unemployment, other things being equal. However, there is no permanent or long-run tradeoff between these two variables.[3] The long-run relationship between inflation and unemployment is vertical at the natural or equilibrium unemployment rate U*, as depicted in Figure 27.5. Formally, macroeconomic equilibrium requires that

$$\dot{p}^e = \dot{p} \tag{27.15}$$

Substituting equation (27.15) into equation (27.14) gives the long-run or equilibrium relationship between inflation and unemployment:

$$F(U - U^*) - \dot{A} = 0 \tag{27.16}$$

Because the rate of inflation does not appear in (27.16), equation (27.15) and (27.16) are consistent with any steady rate of inflation.

The absence of a permanent tradeoff can be illustrated by examining the implications of attempting to maintain unemployment below the natural unemployment rate U* on a continuing basis. For example, beginning in long-run equilibrium at point a in Figure 27.5, the authorities may be able to move the economy to point b via expansionary monetary or fiscal policy. However, once workers and firms adjust to the higher rate of inflation, the short-run Phillips curve will shift up and the economy will return to U* at c (given the higher level of inflationary expectations). Attempting to maintain the lower level of unemployment will require further stimulus to the economy, resulting in higher inflation such as at point e. Thus a policy of maintaining U < U* will be associated with steadily increasing inflation. For this reason, U* is sometimes referred to as the "Non-Accelerating Inflation Rate of Unemployment" or NAIRU. As the NAIRU designation emphasizes, at U = U* the rate of inflation will tend to remain constant, whereas inflation will tend to accelerate if U < U* is maintained over an extended period.

This discussion illustrates how overly expansionary aggregate demand policies may have contributed to the upward drift in inflation during the 1960s and early 1970s, as described previously in this chapter. Such policies may have been adopted for several reasons: (1) because of a belief that there existed a permanent tradeoff between inflation and unemployment (a view that was prevalent during that period) and that it was preferable to accept a bit more inflation in exchange for lower unemployment; (2) because of a belief that the unemployment rate consistent with steady inflation was in fact lower than the true value of U*; or (3) possibly with full recognition that the consequences would be increased inflation in the longer term, albeit lower unemployment and a more buoyant economy in the short run.

The reduction of inflation by a policy of demand restraint can also be

---

3 If workers display permanent money illusion ($\lambda < 1$ in equation (27.14)), there will be a tradeoff between inflation and unemployment even in the long run. This tradeoff will be steeper than the short-run counterpart. See question 8 at the end of this chapter.

illustrated with reference to Figure 27.5. Beginning at a point like d with an ongoing inflationary spiral — in which wages are rising because workers and firms expect prices to rise and prices are rising due to higher wages — a sharp reduction in aggregate demand such as occurred in 1981/82 will cause unemployment to rise and inflation to fall, moving the economy to a point such as f in the short run. As expectations adjust to the lower rate of inflation, the Phillips curve shifts down, enabling the authorities to achieve a permanently lower rate of inflation such as at point c. Alternatively, continued restraint would move the economy from f to g to h, eventually resulting in a return to price stability at point a.

THE WAGE-PRICE-PRODUCTIVITY NEXUS: MATHEMATICAL EXPOSITION*

The relationship between wage changes, price changes, and productivity growth was derived above under the assumption that prices are set according to a constant mark-up on unit labour costs. This relationship can also be derived under competitive pricing behaviour. To illustrate this we assume output Q is related to the inputs of labour N and capital K according to a Cobb-Douglas production function:

$$Q = \alpha N^\beta K^\gamma \tag{27.17}$$

The marginal product of labour can be derived as

$$\partial Q/\partial N = \beta \alpha N^{\beta-1} K^\gamma = \beta(Q/N) = \beta A \tag{27.18}$$

where A is the average product of labour. As indicated in our earlier discussion of the demand for labour, a firm which is competitive in the product and labour markets will employ labour to the point at which the value of the marginal product of labour equals the wage rate. Therefore

$$W = p\beta A \tag{27.19}$$

Totally differentiating (27.19) and dividing the left-hand side by W and the right-hand side by pβA yields:

$$\dot{p} = \dot{W} - \dot{A} - \dot{\beta} \tag{27.20}$$

Interpretation of this equation is aided by noting that β is labour's share of the value of output. This can be seen by multiplying both sides of equation (27.19) by N and dividing by pQ to obtain:

$$\beta = \frac{WN}{pQ} \tag{27.21}$$

Thus equation (27.20) states that under competitive pricing, the rate of change of prices will equal the rate of change of wages minus the rate of productivity growth when labour's share is constant. This result is similar to that derived earlier under mark-up pricing except that the assumption of a constant mark-up is replaced by constancy of labour's share.

Equation (27.20) also indicates that if real wages increase at the rate of growth of labour productivity then labour's share will be constant. That is, if $\dot{W} = \dot{p} + A$ then $\dot{\beta} = 0$ (labour's share would not increase). This is important because one could easily make the mistake of thinking that if wage increases exceeded inflation by the amount of the productivity increase, then labour is receiving *all* of the gains of the productivity increase. This is not so: labour's share would not increase under such circumstances. In fact all factors of production can have an increase in their real return equal to the productivity increase and there would be no change in factor shares.

ANTI-INFLATION POLICY

The problems of inflation and unemployment have been at the forefront of the policy agenda throughout the past several decades. They remain major challenges today. This section briefly examines the main policies that have been advocated and/or adopted in order to achieve price stability and low levels of unemployment. These policies are discussed in terms of the two major challenges that policy makers face in dealing with inflation and unemployment:

(1) how to maintain desirable levels of employment without steadily increasing inflation; and

(2) how to stop or reduce in severity an inflationary wage-price spiral should one develop.

Full Employment and Price Stability

The economic theory and empirical evidence examined in this chapter indicate that there is a tradeoff between inflation and unemployment in the short run but not in the long run. This conclusion has significant implications for economic policy. In particular, attempting to achieve lower levels of unemployment in exchange for higher rates of inflation is not a feasible option on a continuing basis. Using monetary and fiscal policies to maintain the economy at an unemployment rate below the natural unemployment rate or NAIRU will lead to a continually increasing inflation rate. Thus when the objectives of price stability and high levels of employment are considered together, the natural unemployment rate emerges as an appropriate definition of full employment: it is the unemployment rate that is feasible on a sustained basis and is compatible with price stability.

At the same time, the objectives of full employment and price stability are compatible with each other, providing that full employment is defined as the level of employment at which $U = U^*$. If an inflationary wage-price spiral develops, it may be necessary to accept higher unemployment and reduced output *temporarily* in order to restrain inflationary pressures, but it is not necessary to accept unemployment in excess of the natural rate on a *permanent* basis.

The natural unemployment rate or NAIRU is an appropriate definition of full employment in the sense that it is compatible with price stability (or any steady rate of inflation) whereas lower unemployment rates are not. However, U* may be considered too high in terms of other social objectives such as minimizing the hardship, poverty, and lost output associated with unemployment and providing ample employment opportunities. In these circumstances, policy makers should attempt to lower U* directly using structural and labour market policies rather than attempting to lower U below U* using monetary and fiscal policies. Policies to reduce frictional, structural, and seasonal unemployment include mobility and adjustment assistance, provision of labour market information to improve the search and matching process, and training and retraining. Labour market policies that contribute to a higher NAIRU, such as minimum wages and unemployment insurance, could also be examined. In designing these programs, policy makers need to recognize the tradeoff that exists between the immediate objectives of the program (such as providing insurance against the risk of unemployment in the case of UI) and the consequences of the program for the amount of frictional, structural, and seasonal unemployment in the economy.

Pursuing a full employment goal that is consistent with price stability (or a low stable rate of inflation) may succeed in preventing a wage-price spiral from developing, as occurred during the 1960s and 1970s. However, should wage and price inflation again climb to unacceptable levels several alternative polices are available for halting an inflationary spiral — ranging from pure reliance on demand restraint to various forms of incomes policies. The theoretical and empirical analysis discussed in this chapter sheds some light on the costs and benefits of these alternative anti-inflationary strategies.

Demand Restraint

There is general agreement among economists that restraint in aggregate demand — in particular in the rate of increase of the money supply — must play a role in halting an inflationary wage-price spiral. There are, however, differences in opinion regarding how costly such a policy will be in terms of high unemployment and reduced output. Those who believe that the costs of reducing inflation are extremely high often advocate additional policies such as wage and price controls.

In the context of the framework developed in this chapter, demand restraint reduces the amount of excess demand for labour (lowers U relative to U*), thus reducing the rate of wage and price increases. As actual inflation falls, expectations of future inflation decline and the short-run Phillips curve shifts down. Demand restraint may also impact directly on expectations. If those involved in wage and price determination form expectations rationally, they will realize that a policy of demand restraint will reduce wage and price inflation. Thus, if they believe the authorities are determined to follow this policy, they will lower their expectations, thus directly reducing wage and price increases.

The problem with this approach is that it may require a prolonged period of high unemployment and weak economic conditions in order to achieve a significant reduction in the rate of inflation. This will especially be the case if the restraint policy has little direct impact on expectations — either because those involved in wage and price determination do not form their expectations in a rational, forward-looking manner or because they do not believe that the announced policy will be followed. In these circumstances, the initial impact of the reduction in aggregate demand (or its rate of increase) will be on output and employment. The inflationary spiral can be broken, but only at a very high cost. The approximate magnitude of these costs can be calculated from the empirical studies of the determinants of wage and price changes discussed previously in this chapter. If the slope of the short-run Phillips curve is approximately 0.5, each one percent reduction in the rate of wage and price inflation requires an increase in the unemployment rate of two percentage points. This estimate is an upper bound on the approximate cost because it does not allow for any direct impact of demand restraint on expectations. Nonetheless, inspection of Table 27.2 indicates that this rough estimate predicts the experience of the demand restraint policy implemented in 1982/83 reasonably well. Between 1981 and 1985, price inflation declined from 12.5 to 4.0 percent, a drop of 8.5 percentage points. The decline in wage inflation was similar in magnitude. This reduction in wage and price inflation was accompanied by an increase in unemployment of 3.5 percentage points in 1982 (11.0 − 7.5), followed by increases of 4.4 in 1983 (11.9 − 7.5), 3.8 in 1984 and 3.0 in 1985. During this four year period, the cumulative increase in unemployment above its previous level was 14.7 percentage points. The reduction in the rate of inflation was 8 percent, just slightly more than would be predicted by assuming a slope of 0.5 for the short-run Phillips curve and no direct impact on expectations.

The experience of the 1982–83 recession and its aftermath provides a vivid illustration of both the effectiveness of a determined policy of demand restraint in bringing about a substantial reduction in inflation and the extraordinarily high costs associated with this approach. As a consequence of the latter, economists and policy makers have searched for — and in some cases implemented — alternative ways of making the transition to a lower inflation rate with less severe adverse consequences. The following are discussed in turn: enhancing credibility, incomes policies, and increased wage and price flexibility.

Enhancing Credibility

If those involved in wage and price determination form their expectations in a rational, forward-looking manner, they will take into account the policy stance of the monetary and fiscal authorities in predicting future inflation. In these circumstances, if the authorities can make believable their commitment to a policy of demand restraint, the transition to a lower rate of inflation can be made more easily due to the policy's direct impact on expectations. As a consequence, more of the reduction in aggregate demand falls on wages and prices and less on employment and output.

Establishing or enhancing credibility is not a simple matter. Simply announcing that a restraint policy will be followed is unlikely to be effective. The citizenry may be skeptical about the ability or willingness of the authorities to continue with such a potentially costly policy. Over time, credibility can be enhanced by adopting and maintaining a policy stance — such as non-accommodation of inflation — which can be learned by firms, unions and workers and taken into account in wage and price determination. For this reason, macroeconomists have increasingly focused on the question of the appropriate policy rules to be followed by the monetary and fiscal authorities (Taylor, 1982).

However, recent experience indicates that enhanced credibility is not easily achieved in the short run. A dramatic shift to a disinflationary stance was made by the monetary authorities in the United States and the United Kingdom in 1979. Canada followed in 1981. The determination to persist with this policy was clearly and repeatedly stated by the relevant authorities. This experience, particularly that of the United States and the United Kingdom, provides a test of the hypothesis that inflation can be reduced at low cost in terms of lost output and employment by committing to and carrying out a determined policy of demand restraint. A large number of studies of these policy experiments, reviewed in Riddell (1986, Ch. 3), have been carried out. The results do not support the hypothesis. The costs of reducing inflation by this determined policy of demand restraint were extremely high and do not appear to have been significantly reduced by the attempt to make a clear commitment to a disinflationary stance.

Incomes Policies

The term "incomes policy" refers to a wide range of programs that intervene in wage and price setting in order to influence the rate of inflation. These include voluntary mechanisms such as the setting of guidelines or attempting to reach agreement on norms for wage and price increases, mandatory controls on wages, prices or profits, and incentive-based incomes policies that employ taxes, subsidies, or other incentives to restrain wage and price increases.

In the postwar period governments have experimented with a variety of incomes policies. In Canada, these experiments included a number of attempts at voluntary restraint such as that involving the Prices and Incomes Commission during the late 1960s and early 1970s. In addition, mandatory wage and profit controls were a central part of the Anti-Inflation Program of 1975–78. Wage controls were also applied to public sector employees in the federal "6-and-5" program and associated provincial programs introduced in 1982 to complement the demand restraint policy in effect at that time. Similarly, in the United States, incomes policies were employed during the Korean War period (the Wage Stabilization

Board of 1950–53), during the Kennedy and Johnson administrations (the guideposts of 1962–66), during the Nixon administration (the wage-price controls of 1971–74), and during the Carter administration (1977–81). In many European countries, periods without incomes policies of some form were less common than periods with such policies. There is thus a rich history of experience with incomes policies from which we may be able to infer their advantages and disadvantages.

In principle, temporary wage and price controls can achieve a lasting reduction in inflation provided they are carefully coordinated with a program of demand restraint. In effect, the direct controls ensure that the reduction in aggregate demand (or in its rate of growth) falls primarily on wages and prices rather than on employment and output. Expectations of future inflation will also decline if the citizenry observes both lower actual inflation and monetary and fiscal policy that is appropriate for maintaining the lower rate of wage and price increase. This rationale for a temporary incomes policy combined with demand restraint is very similar to that for enhancing credibility. Both indicate the possibility of breaking an inflationary wage-price spiral without incurring severe adverse consequences in the form of high unemployment and reduced output.

Experience with wage and price control programs in the United Kingdom and the United States, reviewed in more detail in Riddell (1986, Chapter 4), has been mixed. In several cases the programs appear to have had little impact other than of a temporary nature. In other cases the policy appears to have achieved some moderation in inflation. A common characteristic of the unsuccessful programs is the failure of the authorities to combine the incomes policy with the appropriate demand restraint. In these circumstances the controls program and monetary and fiscal policy are working at cross purposes. Thus even if controls are successful in restraining inflation in the short run, their long-run impact is minimal as wage and price increases move sharply upward in the post-controls period. In some cases the overly expansionary monetary and fiscal policy and the concomitant excess demand in product and labour markets led to the demise of the incomes policy.

The Canadian experience, in particular the Anti-Inflation Program of 1975–78, has been more favourable. As discussed previously, econometric studies generally conclude that the wage and price controls reduced new wage settlements by 3–4 percent in each of the three years of the program, and price inflation by 1–3 percent per year, with the reduction in price inflation concentrated in the second half of the program and continuing well beyond the end of the AIP. The somewhat greater success of Canada's 1975–78 controls program relative to the experience of the United States and the United Kingdom can probably be attributed to two key design features: the coordination of the wage and price controls with monetary and fiscal restraint, and the use of gradually declining norms for wage and price increases. The latter are important in Canada (and in the United States) because wage contracts in the union sector are often two to three years in length. Attempting to achieve an extremely rapid reduction in the rate of wage change will cause large inequities in the relative wage structure as groups whose contracts come up for renewal early in the controls program are treated substantially differently than those who renegotiated wages prior to the imposition of controls. Gradually declining norms for wage increases facilitate winding down the wage-price spiral without causing severe inequities that may undermine support for the program and impose high penalties on certain groups.

Although both economic theory and empirical evidence indicate that the combination of wage and price guidelines and appropriate restraint in aggregate demand represent an attractive alternative to reliance on demand restraint alone to reduce inflation, it would be a mistake to resort to controls on a regular basis. The interference with individual freedom and the inevitable inequities associated with mandatory limits on wage and price increases result in a loss in goodwill between different groups in society and alter the relationship between the citizens and the state. For this reason and others, controls should be limited to situations in which there is widespread agreement on the need to reduce inflation to more acceptable levels.

Because direct controls are a tool that should be used infrequently, and because the experience of some countries with their use has been disappointing, there has also been considerable interest in alternative policies for restraining inflation. Incentive-based incomes policies are schemes that create incentives for moderating wage and price increases without otherwise interfering with market forces. Tax-based incomes policies have received the most attention (Seidman, 1978, 1981; Layard, 1982). These utilize taxes or subsidies to provide incentives for wage and price restraint. There is little experience with these policies, but they continue to receive attention as an alternative to direct wage and price controls.

Some economists (Lerner, 1978; Lerner and Colander, 1980) have advocated elaborate schemes in which firms would require permits to increase prices (or wages) by a certain amount. The number of permits issued to firms would be restricted in order to achieve the desired overall rate of inflation. Permits would trade in an open market so that firms that wish to raise their prices more than average could purchase additional permits from firms wishing to raise prices less than average. In this way, relative prices can change despite the restraints on the overall rate of price increase.

Encouraging Wage and Price Flexibility

Disinflation via demand restraint is a costly policy to pursue because of the persistence or momentum in the inflationary process. Because of this inertia, most of the initial impact of the reduction in aggregate demand falls on output and employment. Only subsequently, as weak product and labour market conditions take their toll, do wage and price increases moderate. If wages and prices were more responsive to changes in economic conditions, inflation could be reduced without massive increases in unemployment. Enhanced credibility may be an effective means of increasing wage and price responsiveness if the main source of persistence is slowly adjusting expectations. However, if inertia is due to other factors, alternative approaches may be more successful. An approach that has received considerable attention involves the institutional features of wage determination.

Countries differ considerably in their wage-setting arrangements (Sachs, 1979; Gordon, 1982; Riddell, 1983). A distinguishing feature of the Japanese economy is the extensive use of bonus payments. These semi-annual bonuses represent a substantial proportion of Japanese employees' total income (about 25 percent on average); their magnitude in any year depends in part on the economic performance of the firm and industry. Japan is also characterized by short-wage contracts (one year) and synchronized bargaining (wage negotiations take place at approximately the same time) in the form of the "spring wage offensive." Canada and the United States are unique in the degree to which long-term (often two or three years) overlapping (rather than synchronized) wage contracts are common in the union sector. The extent of wage indexation in the form of cost-of-living-allowance clauses is low; thus real wages are not rigid but nominal wages display considerable inertia. European countries vary. Some (e.g. Italy) employ long-term contracts but these do not overlap. Several (e.g., Sweden, Norway, Austria, Germany) have short contracts and synchronized, usually centralized bargaining. The United Kingdom is characterized by one-year contracts (although these do not have a predetermined expiry date as in North America) and non-synchronized negotiations. Many European countries have wages either explicitly or implicitly indexed to changes in the price level; wages thus display "real wage rigidity."

These countries also differ substantially in their macroeconomic performance during the past two decades. Japan weathered the contractions of the postwar period, including the 1973 and 1979 OPEC oil price shocks, with relatively little increase in unemployment. Some of this is undoubtedly due to other factors, but their wage-setting institutions (synchronized bargaining, annual contracts, substantial bonus payments) probably contributed to this remarkable performance. Canada and the U.S. found it difficult to restrain inflation at low cost, and suffered significant increases in unemployment in response to the two oil price shocks. In both countries, however, unemployment subsequently began to decline. Although there are important differences among the European countries, as a group they suffered the largest increases in unemployment in response to the 1973 and 1979 OPEC oil price shocks. Furthermore, in many of these countries unemployment has not substantially declined.

Research by Taylor (1980, 1983) and others has indicated that the long-term overlapping contracts used in the union sector in the United States are an important source of persistence in wage and price inflation. Even with rational expectations and a fully credible disinflationary policy, wage and price changes respond only slowly to a reduction in aggregate demand. In Canada, the use of long-term overlapping contracts and the extent of observed persistence in wage settlements is broadly similar to that in the U.S. (Riddell, 1983).

Although some economists have proposed imposing shorter wage contracts as a means of increasing wage and price responsiveness and thus reducing the costs of following a disinflationary policy, the proposed reform that has received the most attention is Weitzman's (1984) suggestion that profit-sharing be adopted on a widespread basis. The bonus payments used in Japan can be reviewed as a form of profit-sharing (although bonuses are not explicitly tied to profits), and Weitzman has attributed Japan's remarkable economic performance with respect to inflation and unemployment to the widespread use of these bonuses.

Weitzman (1984) argues that there is a fundamental difference between an economy in which workers are paid a fixed hourly wage and one in which workers are paid a share of revenue or profit. In the wage economy, the labour market is in equilibrium when the demand for labour equals the supply of labour. In the share economy, however, in equilibrium there is unsatisfied demand or unfilled job vacancies at the prevailing negotiated shares. This excess demand for labour will act as a cushion, protecting the economy from significant deviations from full employment. Any reduction in labour demand will be offset by the existence of unfilled vacancies.

The reason for this important difference is that with the share-compensation system the firm can increase profits by expanding employment and output because, with profit-sharing, the marginal cost of labour is a declining function of employment. Thus as the firm expands employment the average cost of labour (and compensation per employee) declines. With the wage system the firm will expand employment only to the point at which the additional revenue generated by the extra employment equals the additional cost which is the hourly wage.

Flexible compensation arrangements such as profit-sharing and gain-sharing, which relate employee remuneration to the economic performance of the firm or industry, are often recommended for their *micro* benefits at the level of the individual enterprise. By giving employees a greater financial stake in the enterprise and an opportunity for benefiting directly from its performance, the adversarial nature of labour-management relations may be replaced by a more cooperative, problem-solving approach. Additional potential benefits include increased levels of employee motivation, leading to higher productivity and organizational effectiveness and thus greater income to be shared by employers and employees. However, it may be the case that the most significant effects of these compensation arrangements are *macro* rather than micro benefits. Indeed, as Weitzman (1984) argues, there may be a rationale for public policy to encourage these compensation arrangements (for example by taxing income in the form of profit shares at a lower rate than income from a fixed wage) because of a "macroeconomic externality." In particular, benefits in the form of greater stability in employment and output accrue to society as a whole and not just to the parties choosing a compensation system.

In summary, the high degree of real wage rigidity displayed by many European countries is believed by many analysts to be a dominant factor accounting for the sharp rise and severe persistence of unemployment in those societies. Canada and the U.S., characterized by nominal wage inertia but more flexible real wages, have suffered large increases in unemployment but the higher levels of unemployment have not persisted as in Europe. Nonetheless, the process of reducing inflation in North America has been very costly and alternative approaches warrant attention. Japan, with the most flexible wages, has not even suffered significant increases in unemployment and has been able to reduce inflation at relatively low cost. The thesis that institutional changes to compensation arrangements should be made in order to increase wage and price flexibility is likely to continue to receive attention in research and policy debates.

QUESTIONS

1. Discuss the theoretical rationale, if any, for the use of the unemployment rate as a determinant of the rate of increase in aggregate money wages.
2. Distinguish between the wage inflation-unemployment trade-off curve and the price inflation-unemployment trade-off curve.
3. In the econometric estimation of aggregate money wage equations, the unemployment rate is often entered in reciprocal form (i.e., $1/U$), with an expected positive sign, to capture the non-linear relationship whereby the Phillips curve is convex to the origin. Illustrate why this is the case, and why a positive sign would reflect a negative relationship between $\dot{w}$ and U.
4. The original Phillips curve literature was often criticized for simply reflecting an unstable empirical relationship without any theoretical rationale for the relationship. Consequently, the policy implications were often wrong, and when the underlying causal determinants changed, the old empirical relationship no longer predicted well. This illustrates the importance of theory for accurate prediction and for policy prescriptions. Discuss.
5. Trace out the wage and price inflation-unemployment curves, both in the short-run and the long-run, from the adjustment process portrayed in Figure 27.2. What if the asking wage of labour increased by more than the inflation rate of a given year, perhaps because of a catch-up process or because of an anticipation of even higher inflation in the future? Illustrate this in Figure 27.2, and illustrate the new point in the inflation-unemployment trade-offs. What if this were prevented by a wage-price control program that restricted wage increases to the price inflation of that year? (Illustrate on the diagram and on the trade-off

curves). Could this provide a rationale for a controls program to move the economy towards its long-run equilibrium without experiencing a phase of high unemployment necessary to moderate wage demands? Does it matter if the original wage demands in excess of actual inflation were based on a catch-up for past inflation, or an expectation of future inflation? What if the controls were not accompanied by the appropriate monetary and fiscal policies to curb inflationary pressures? What if inflation continued in spite of the wage controls, perhaps because the price-markup over labour costs were increased?

6. Illustrate how the adjustment process of Figure 27.2 could arise from a job search process whereby job seekers face a distribution of money wage offers and have an acceptance or reservation wage in money terms. That is, they will continue to remain unemployed and search (sample the distribution of money wage offers) until they receive their reservation wage. Indicate how an increase in aggregate demand and its accompanying increase in the aggregate price level may reduce search unemployment in the short-run, but may not reduce it in the long run when the reservation wage adjusts to the inflation.

7. "Any microeconomic theory of behaviour that requires wage rigidities due to such things as unanticipated inflation, wage lags or money illusion in the collective bargaining or job search process, could only explain phenomena in the short run, not in the long run." Discuss.

8. Illustrate the long-run relationship between price inflation and unemployment for different values of λ in equation 27.9; for example, $\lambda = 0.5, \lambda = 0.8, \lambda = 0.95$. What happens as λ approaches unity?

9. "If price inflation is 6 percent and productivity growth 2 percent, and if money wages increase by 8 percent, then labour receives *all* of the productivity increase and nothing is left over for other factors of production." Discuss.

10. Discuss the extent to which non-competitive forces such as monopolies and powerful unions could lead to wage and price inflation.

11. Assume that the following short-run *hypothetical* Phillips curve is estimated econometrically:

$$\dot{W} = 2.5 + .9\,\dot{p}^e - .25U$$

where $\dot{W}$ is the annual rate of change in money wages, $\dot{p}^e$ is the annual expected inflation rate, and U is the unemployment rate. All variables are expressed in percentage terms and their averages over the sample period are 10 for $\dot{W}$, 10 for $\dot{p}^e$, and 6 for U. The estimated coefficients are all significantly different from zero, and the coefficient of $\dot{p}^e$ is not significantly different from one, according to conventional significance tests.

(a) What is the expected rate of change of money wages that would result if expected inflation were 10 percent and the unemployment rate 6 percent?

(b) What would happen if the unemployment rate were raised to 10 percent?

(c) What would happen if expected inflation were moderated to 5 percent?

(d) What does the coefficient for the inflation-expectations variable imply about the formation of expectations?

(e) What does the coefficient of the unemployment rate variable imply about the shape of the Phillips curve?

(f) Plot a Phillips curve assuming expectations of inflation of 5 percent. Plot a Phillips curve assuming expectations of inflation of 10 percent. What happens to the Phillips curve if expectations of inflation increase from 5 to 10 percent?

(g) Assume that the short-run aggregate price equation was estimated as $\dot{p} = 2 - .25U + 1.1W$ and that, in the long run, actual inflation equals expected inflation: that is, $\dot{p} = \dot{p}^e$. Utilize the short-run Phillips curve and aggregate price equations, and the long-run equilibrium condition to solve for the long-run Phillips curve. Compare the shape of the long-run and short-run Phillips curves. Solve for the long-run or natural rate of unemployment as a function of money wages.

REFERENCES AND FURTHER READINGS

A. Phillips Curve and the Wage-Price-Unemployment Relationship

Alkerlof, G. Relative wages and the rate of inflation. *QJE* 83 (August 1969) 353-374.

Allen, R.C. The impact of technical change on employment, wages and the distribution of skills: a historical perspective. *Adapting to Change: Labour Market Adjustment in Canada*, W.C. Riddell (ed.). Toronto: University of Toronto Press, 1986, 71-110.

Archibald, G.C. The Phillips curve and the distribution of unemployment. *AER* 59 (May 1969) 124-134.

Ashenfelter, O. Union relative wage effects: new evidence and a survey of their implications for wage inflation. *Econometric Contributions to Public Policy*, R. Stone and W. Peterson (eds.). New York: St. Martin's Press, 1978, 31-60.

Ashenfelter, O., G. Johnson and J. Pencavel. Trade unions and the rate of change of money wages in United States manufacturing industry. *R.E. Studies* 39 (January, 1972) 27-54.

Ashenfelter, O., and J. Pencavel. Wage changes and the frequency of wage settlements. *Economica* 42 (May 1975).

Beare, J. Wage and price change relationships in post-war Canada. *CJE* 6 (May 1973) 260-266.

Behman, S. Wage determination process in U.S. manufacturing. *QJE* 82 (February 1968) 117-142.

Bhatia, R. Unemployment and the rate of change of money earnings in the United States, 1900-1958. *Economica* 28 (August 1961) 286-96.

Black, S. and H. Kelejian. The formulation of the dependent variable in the wage equation. *R.E. Studies* 39 (January 1972) 55-59.

Bodkin, R., E. Bond, G. Reuber, and T. Robinson. *Price Stability and High Employment*. Special Study No. 5. Ottawa: Economic Council of Canada, 1966.

Brechling, F. The trade-off between inflation and unemployment. *JPE* 76 (July/August 1968) 712-737.

Brenner, R. The death of the Phillips curve reconsidered. *QJE* 91 (August 1977) 389-418.

Bruce, C. The wage spiral: Canada 1953-1970. *EJ* 95 (June 1975) 372-376.

Christofides, L., R. Swidinsky and D. Wilton. A microeconometric analysis of the Canadian wage determination process. *Economica* 47 (May 1980a) 165-178.

Christofides, L., R. Swidinsky and D. Wilton. A microeconometric analysis of spillovers within the Canadian wage determination process. *R.E. Stats.* 62 (May 1980b) 213-221.

Christofides, L. and D. Wilton. Wage determination in the aftermath of controls. *Economica* 52 (February 1985) 51-64.

Cousineau, J.M. and R. Lacroix. *Wage Determination in Major Collective Agreements in the Private and Public Sectors*. Ottawa: Economic Council of Canada, 1977.

Corry, B. and D. Laidler. The Phillips relation: a theoretical explanation. *Economica* 34 (May 1967) 189-197.

Dicks-Mireaux, L. and J. Dow. The determinants of wage inflation: the United Kingdom, 1946-1956. *The Journal of the Royal Statistical Society* Series A, 22 (1959).

Donner, A. Labour turnover, expectations and the determination of money wage changes in U.S. manufacturing. *CJE* 5 (February 1972) 16-34.

Dow, J.C. and L. Dicks-Mireaux. Excess demand for labour. *Oxford Economic Papers* N.S. 10 (February 1959).

Eatwell, J., J. Llewellyn and R. Tarling. Money wage inflation in industrial countries. *R.E. Studies* 41 (October 1974) 515-523, and comment by R. Thomas 43 (October 1976) 551-552.

Eckstein, O. Money wage determination revisited. *R.E. Studies* 35 (April 1968) 133-143.

Eckstein, O. and T. Wilson. The determination of money wages in American industry. *QJE* 76 (August 1962) 379-414.

Flanagan, R. Wage interdependence in unionized labour markets. *BPEA* (No. 3, 1976) 635-682.

Flanagan, R. The U.S. Phillips curve and international unemployment rate differentials. *AER* 63 (March 1973) 114-131. Comments by M. Barrett and reply 65 (March 1975) 225-231, comments by R. Avelsson et al. 67 (March 1977) 218-224.

Fortin, P. and K. Newton. Labour market tightness and wage inflation in Canada. *Workers, Jobs and Inflation*, N.M. Baily (ed.). Washington: Brookings Institution, 1982, 243-278.

Fried, J. Inflation-unemployment trade-offs under fixed and floating exchange rates. *CJE* 6 (February 1973) 43-52.

Friedman, M. The role of monetary policy. *AER* 58 (March 1968) 1-17.

Friedman, M. Nobel lecture: Inflation and unemployment. *JPE* 85 (June 1977) 451-472.

Gordon, R. Wage-price controls and the shifting Phillips curve. *BPEA* (No. 2, 1971) 385-421.

Green, C. The employment ratio as sign of aggregate demand pressure. *MLR* 100 (April 1977) 25-32.

Grossman, H. The cyclical pattern of unemployment and wage inflation. *Economica* 41 (November 1974) 403-13.

Hall, R. The process of inflation in the labour market. *BPEA* (No. 2, 1974) 343-410.

Hall, R. Prospects for shifting the Phillips curve through manpower policy. *BPEA* (No. 3, 1971) 659-702.

Hamermesh, D. Wage bargains, threshold effects and the Phillips curve. *QJE* 84 (August 1970) 501-517. Comment by A. Gustman and reply, 86 (May 1972) 332-341.

Hamermesh, D. Market power and wage inflation. *SEJ* 39 (October 1972) 204-212.

Hansen, B. Excess demand, unemployment, vacancies and wages. *QJE* 84 (February 1970) 1-24.

Hines, A. Trade unions and wage inflation in the United Kingdom, 1893-1961. *R.E. Studies* 31 (October 1964) 221-242.

Holmes, J. and D.J. Smyth. The relation between unemployment and excess demand for labour. *Economica* 37 (August 1970) 311-315.

Holt, C., C. MacRae, S. Schweitzer and R. Smith. *The Unemployment Inflation Dilemma: A Manpower Solution*. Washington: Urban Institute, 1971.

Kaliski, S.F. The relation between unemployment and the rate of change of money wages in Canada. *IER* 5 (January 1964) 1-33.

Kaliski, S.F. and D.C. Smith. Inflation, unemployment and incomes policy. *CJE* 6 (November 1973) 574-591.

Kotowitz, J. *The Effect of Direct Taxes on Wages*. Anti-Inflation Board Report. Ottawa: Supply and Services, 1979.

Kuh, E. A productivity theory of wage levels — an alternative to the Phillips curve. *R.E. Studies* 34 (October 1967) 333-360.

Laidler, D. and D. Purdy. *Inflation and Labour Markets*. Toronto: University of Toronto Press, 1974.

Levi, M. and J. Makin. Inflation uncertainty and the Phillips curve: some empirical evidence. *AER* 70 (December 1980) 1022-1027.

Lipsey, R. The relationship between unemployment and the rate of change of money wage rates in the United Kingdom, 1862-1957: a further analysis. *Economica* 27 (February 1960) 1-31.

Lipsey, R. and P. Steiner. The relationship between profits and wage rates. *Economica* 28 (May 1961) 137-159.

Lucas, R. and L. Rapping. Price expectations and the Phillips curve. *AER* 59 (June 1969) 342-350.

Lucas, R. and L. Rapping. Real wages, employment and inflation. *JPE* 77 (September/October 1969) 721-754.

Matsukawa, S. The equilibrium distribution of wage settlements and economic stability. *IER* 27 (June 1986) 415-438.

McCallum, B. Wage rate changes and the excess demand for labour. *Economica* 41 (August 1974) 269-277.

McGuire, R. and L. Rapping. The role of market variables and key bargains in the manufacturing wage determination process. *JPE* 76 (October 1968) 1015-1036.

Mehra, Y. Spillover in wage determination in U.S. manufacturing industries. *R.E. Stats.* 68 (August 1976) 300-312.

Meyer, B. A comparison of the U.S. and Canadian wage adjustment mechanisms: 1948-1967. *RI/IR* 29 (December 1974) 846-856.

Mitchell, D. Union wage determination. *BPEA* (No. 3, 1978) 537-592.

Mortensen, D. Job search, the duration of unemployment and the Phillips curve. *AER* 60 (December 1970) 847-862. Comment by P. Gayer and R. Goldfarb and reply 62 (September 1972) 714-719.

Packer, A. and S. Park. Distortions in relative wages and shifts in the Phillips curve. *R.E. Stats.* 55 (February 1973) 16-22.

Parkin, M. Incomes policy: some further results on the determination of the rate of change of money wages. *Economica* 37 (November 1970) 384-401.

Perry, G. *Unemployment, Money Wage Rates and Inflation*. Cambridge, Mass.: M.I.T. Press, 1966.

Perry, G. Determinants of wage inflation around the world. *BPEA* (No. 2, 1975) 403-448.

Phelps, E. Phillips curves, expectations of inflation and optimal unemployment over time. *Economica* 34 (August 1967) 254-281.

Phelps, E. Money-wage dynamics and the labor-market equilibrium. *JPE* 76 (July/August 1968) 678-711.

Phillips, A. The relation between unemployment and the rate of change of money wage rates in the United Kingdom, 1861-1957. *Economica* 25 (November 1958) 283-299. Comment by G. Routh 36 (1959) 299-315.

Pierson, G. The effect of union strength and the U.S. Phillips curve. *AER* 58 (June 1968) 456-467.

Reid, F. Unemployment and inflation: an assessment of Canadian macroeconomic policy. *CPP* 6 (Spring 1980) 283-299.

Reid, F. and N. Meltz. Causes of shifts in the unemployment-vacancy relationship. *R.E. Stats.* 61 (August 1979) 470-475.

Rees, A. The Phillips curve as a menu for policy choice. *Economica* 37 (August 1970) 227-238.

Rees, A. and M. Hamilton. The wage-price-productivity perplex. *JPE* 75 (February 1967) 63-70.

Reuber, G. Wage adjustments in Canadian industry. *R.E. Studies* 37 (October 1970) 449-468.

Riddell, W.C. The empirical foundations of the Phillips curve: evidence from Canadian wage contract data. *Econometrica* 47 (January 1979) 1-24.

Riddell, W.C. and P.M. Smith. Expected inflation and wage changes in Canada, 1967-1981. *CJE* 15 (August 1982) 377-394.

Ross, S. and M. Wachter. Wage determination, inflation and the industrial structure. *AER* 63 (September 1973) 675-692.

Rowley, J. and D. Wilton. Quarterly models of wage determination: some new efficient estimates. *AER* 63 (June 1973) 380-389.

Rowley, J. and D. Wilton. Wage determination: the use of instrumental assumptions. *IER* 14 (June 1973) 525-529.

Rowley, J. and D. Wilton. Quarterly models of wage determinants. *QJE* 88 (November 1974) 671-680.

Rowley, J. and D. Wilton. Empirical foundations for the Canadian Phillips curve. *CJE* 7 (May 1974) 240-259.

Rowley, J. and D. Wilton. *The Determination of Wage Change Relationships*. Ottawa: Economic Council of Canada, 1977.

Sellakaerts, W. and M. Chossudovsky. A comparison of optional and actual policies for high employment and price stability under external inflational conditions: the Canadian experience. *SEJ* 41 (October 1974) 206-214.

Siebert, C. and M. Zaidi. The short-run wage-price mechanism in U.S. manufacturing. *WEJ* 9 (September 1971) 278-88.

Smith, Douglas. Wage linkages between Canada and the United States. *ILRR* 29 (January 1976) 258-268.

Smyth, D. Unemployment and inflation: a cross-country analysis of the Phillips curve. *AER* 61 (June 1971) 426-429.

Sparks, G. and D. Wilton. Determinants of negotiated wage increases. *Econometrica* 39 (September 1971) 739-750.

Swan, N. and D. Wilton (eds.). *Inflation and the Canadian Experience*. Kingston: Industrial Relations Centre, Queen's University, 1971.

Swidinsky, R. Trade unions and the rate of change of money wages in Canada, 1953-1970. *ILRR* 25 (April 1972) 363-375.

Taylor, J. Staggered wage setting in a macro model. *AER Proceedings* 69 (May 1979) 108-113.

Turner, H.A. and D. Jackson. On the determination of the general wage level – a world analysis. *EJ* 80 (December 1970) 827-849. Comment by J. Knight and R. Mabro and reply 82 (June 1972) 677-693, and an interchange 83 (June 1973) 520-526.

Turnovsky, S. The expectations hypothesis and aggregate wage equation: empirical evidence for Canada. *Economica* 39 (February 1972) 1-17.

Vanderkamp, J. Wage and price level determination: an empirical model for Canada. *Economica* 33 (May 1966) 194-218.

Vanderkamp, J. Wage adjustment, productivity and price change expectations. *R.E. Studies* 39 (January 1972) 61-72.

Vrooman, W. Manufacturing wage behavior with special reference to the period 1962-1970. *R.E. Stats.* 52 (May 1970) 160-167.

Wachter, M. The changing cyclical responsiveness of wage inflation. *BJIR* (No. 1, 1976) 115-168.

Watanabe, T. Price changes and the rate of changes of money wage earnings in Japan, 1955-1962. *QJE* 80 (February 1966) 31-47.

Waud, R. Inflation, unemployment, and economic welfare. *AER* 60 (September 1970) 631-644. Comment by G. Tullock and reply 62 (December 1972) 1004-1006.

Weitzman, M.L. *The Share Economy: Conquering Stagflation*. Cambridge, Mass: Harvard University Press, 1984.

Wiles, P. Cost inflation and the state of economic theory. *EJ* (June 1973) 377-398.

Zaidi, M. The determination of money wage rate changes and unemployment-inflation "trade-offs" in Canada. *IER* 10 (June 1969) 207-219.

Zaidi, M. Unemployment, vacancies and conditions of excess demand for labour in Canada. *Applied Economics* 2 (1970) 101-112.

B. Anti-inflation Policy

Ashenfelter, O. The withering away of a full employment goal. *CPP* 9 (March 1983) 114-125.

Ashenfelter, O. and R. Layard. Incomes policy and wage differentials. *Economica* 50 (May 1983) 127-144.

Auld, D., L. Christofides, R. Swidinsky and D. Wilton. The impact of the Anti-Inflation Board on negotiated wage settlements. *CJE* 12 (May 1979) 195-213.

Bailey, M. Contract theory and the moderation of inflation by recession and by controls. *BPEA* (No. 3, 1976) 585-634.

Barber, C.L. and J.C.P. McCallum. *Controlling Inflation: Learning from Experience in Canada, Europe and Japan.* Toronto: James Lorimer, 1982.

Brunner, K. and A. Meltzer (eds.). *The Economics of Price and Wage Controls.* New York: North Holland, 1976.

Bruno, M. and J. Sachs. *The Economics of Worldwide Stagflation.* Cambridge, Mass: Harvard University Press, 1984.

Cousineau, J.M. and R. Lacroix. L'impact de la politique Canadienne de contrôle des prix et des revenues sur les ententes salariales. *CPP* 4 (Winter 1978) 88-100.

Feige, E. and D. Pearce. The wage-price control experiment — Did it work? *Challenge* (July/August 1973) 40-44.

Flanagan, R.J., D.W. Soskice and L. Ulman. *Unionism, Economic Stabilization and Incomes Policies: The European Experience.* Washington: Brookings Institution, 1983.

Foot, D.K. and D.J. Poirier. Public decision making in Canada: the case of the anti-inflation board. *IER* 21 (June 1980) 489-504.

Goodwin, C. (ed.). *Exhortion and Controls: The Search for a Wage-Price Policy, 1945-1971.* Washington: Brookings Institution, 1975.

Gordon, R.J. The response of wages and prices to the first two years of controls. *BPEA* (No. 3, 1973) 765-779.

Gordon, R.J. Wage-price controls and the shifting Phillips curve. *BPEA* (No. 2, 1972) 385-421.

Gordon, R.J. Why U.S. wage and employment behaviour differs from that in Britain and Japan. *EJ* 92 (March 1982) 13-44.

Hagens, J.B. and R.R. Russell. Testing for the effectiveness of wage-price controls: an application to the Carter program. *AER* 75 (March 1985) 191-207.

Haythorne, G. Prices and incomes policy: the Canadian experience. *ILR* 108 (December 1973) 485-503.

Howitt, P. Indexation and the adjustment to inflation in Canada. *Postwar Macroeconomic Developments,* J. Sargent (ed.). Toronto: University of Toronto Press, 1986, 175-224.

Kahn, G.A. International differences in wage behavior: real, nominal, or exaggerated? *AER* 74 (May 1984) 155-159.

Kaliski, S. and D. Smith. Inflation, unemployment and incomes policy. *CJE* 6 (November 1973) 574-591.

Layard, R. Is incomes policy the answer to unemployment? *Economica* 49 (August 1982) 219-239.

Lerner, A.P. A wage increase permit plan to stop inflation. *BPEA* 2 (1978) 491-505.

Lerner, A.P. and D. Colander. *MAP: A Market Anti-Inflation Plan.* New York: Harcourt Brace Jovanovich, 1980.

Lipsey, R. and J. Parkin. Incomes policy: a reappraisal. *Economica* 37 (May 1970) 115-138.

Lipsey, R.G. The understanding and control of inflation: is there a crisis in macroeconomics? *CJE* 14 (November 1981) 545-576.

Maslove, A.M. and G. Swimmer. *Wage Controls in Canada 1975-1978*. Montreal: Institute for Research on Public Policy, 1980.

Pencavel, J. The effects of income policies on the frequency and size of wage changes. *Economica* 45 (May 1982) 147-160.

Perry, G. Wages and the guideposts. *AER* 57 (September 1967) 897-904. Comments by P. Anderson, M. Wachter and A. Throop and reply 59 (June 1969) 351-369.

Reid, F. Canadian wage and price controls. *CPP* 2 (Winter 1976) 104-113.

Reid, F. The response of wages to the removal of controls: the American experience. *RI/IR* 32 (No. 4, 1977) 621-628.

Reid, F. *An Analysis of U.S. Wage Controls and Implications for Canada*. Anti-Inflation Board Report. Ottawa: Supply and Services, 1978.

Reid, F. The effect of controls on the rate of wage change in Canada. *CJE* 12 (May 1979) 214-227.

Reid, F. Control and decontrol of wages in the United States: an empirical analysis. *AER* 71 (March 1981) 108-120.

R.E. Stats. Symposium: the future of U.S. wage-price policy. 54 (August 1972) 213-231.

Riddell, W.C. The responsiveness of wage settlements in Canada and economic policy. *CPP* 9 (March 1983) 9-23.

Riddell, W.C. *Dealing with Inflation and Unemployment in Canada*. Toronto: University of Toronto Press, 1986.

Sachs, J.D. Wages, profits and macroeconomic adjustment: a comparative study. *BPEA* (No. 2, 1979) 269-319.

Sachs, J.D. Real wages and unemployment in OECD countries. *BPEA* (No. 1, 1983) 255-289.

Schelling, T.C. Establishing credibility: strategic considerations. *AER* 72 (May 1982) 77-80.

Seidman, L.S. Tax-based incomes policies. *BPEA* 2 (1978) 301-348.

Seidman, L.S. Equity and tradeoffs in a tax-based incomes policy. *AER* (May 1981) 295-300.

Smith, D. *Incomes Policies: Some Foreign Experiences and their Relevance for Canada*. Special Study No. 4. Ottawa: Economic Council of Canada, 1966.

Taylor, J.B. Aggregate dynamics and staggered contracts. *JPE* 88 (February 1980) 1-23.

Taylor, J.B. Establishing credibility: a rational expectations viewpoint. *AER* 72 (May 1982) 81-85.

Taylor, J.B. Union wage settlements during a disinflation. *AER* 73 (December 1983) 981-993.

Ulman, L. and R. Flanagan. *Wage Restraint: a Study of Incomes Policies in Western Europe*. Berkeley: University of California Press, 1971.

Wallis, K. Wages, prices and incomes policy: some comments. *Economica* 38 (August 1971) 304-310.

Weitzman, M.L. *The Share Economy: Conquering Stagflation*. Cambridge, Mass.: Harvard University Press, 1984.

Index